PR
4470
.F69
v. 7
pt. 1

Coleridge, Samuel Taylor

Biographia literaria,
or Biographical sketches
of my literary life and
opinions.

DATE DUE

THE COLLECTED WORKS OF
SAMUEL TAYLOR COLERIDGE · 7
BIOGRAPHIA LITERARIA

General Editor: KATHLEEN COBURN

Associate Editor: BART WINER

THE COLLECTED WORKS

SAMUEL TAYLOR COLERIDGE

1. From a crayon drawing by George Dawe, December 1811
Collection Lord Coleridge, Ottery St Mary
reproduced by kind permission

THE COLLECTED WORKS OF

Samuel Taylor Coleridge

Biographia Literaria

OR

Biographical Sketches of My Literary Life and Opinions

I

EDITED BY

James Engell and W. Jackson Bate

ROUTLEDGE & KEGAN PAUL

✤ BOLLINGEN SERIES LXXV
PRINCETON UNIVERSITY PRESS

The Collected Works, sponsored by Bollingen Foundation,
is published in Great Britain
by Routledge & Kegan Paul Ltd
39 Store Street, London WC1
ISBN 0-7100-0896-1
and in the United States of America
by Princeton University Press, 41 William Street
Princeton, New Jersey
ISBN 0-691-09874-3
LCC 68–10201
The Collected Works constitutes
the seventy-fifth publication in Bollingen Series

The present work, number 7 of the Collected Works,
is in 2 volumes, this being 7: I

Printed in the United States of America
by Princeton University Press

THIS EDITION
OF THE WORKS OF
SAMUEL TAYLOR COLERIDGE
IS DEDICATED
IN GRATITUDE TO
THE FAMILY EDITORS
IN EACH GENERATION

CONTENTS

──────I──────

Biographia Literaria Volume I

II

Biographia Literaria Volume II

LIST OF ILLUSTRATIONS

I

II

EDITORS' PREFACE:
PLAN OF THIS EDITION;
ACKNOWLEDGEMENTS

IN preparing this edition of the *Biographia Literaria*, James Engell is responsible for the annotation of Volume I (chs 1–13) and W. J. Bate for that of Volume II (chs 14–24).

The editors have viewed the annotation as by far their most challenging task. However widely the *Biographia* has been acknowledged as a classic and however well known it is in parts, it still remains a difficult work, highly allusive in places and even fragmentary, especially in the so-called "philosophical chapters" of Volume I (particularly chs 5–9 and 12). Moreover, these chapters are complicated, to a degree hardly true of any other classic, by the vexed problem of plagiarism, or the unacknowledged use of sources. Since the 1830s, and especially during the last generation, this has been the subject of accusation (varying from gentle to severe), defensive disregard, and above all, for many readers, confusion. A special effort has been made in this edition, therefore, to pursue this subject as exhaustively as possible and to present the actual facts. We at first thought of presenting the results largely in the Introduction, with comparatively brief references in the annotation. But we became increasingly convinced that the only method of clarifying this subject was to present the detail with completeness in the annotation itself, where, on each page, immediate comparison with Coleridge's own text can be made. Our procedure is to print the German texts when Coleridge translates so closely that any translation of our own would do nothing more than duplicate his. When Coleridge merely paraphrases, or translates very loosely, we add a literal translation, after the German text, so that the reader can make comparisons. The facts are often more complex than is generally recognised. In pursuing Coleridge's "borrowings" we must frequently leap from one page to another some distance away, or to another work, and then back again.

Hence the disparity in bulk of annotation between the latter half of Volume I, containing the "philosophical chapters", and the rest of the edition. Considering how central these chapters are to our understanding of Coleridge's thought as a whole, how crammed they are with allusions of every kind, and weighted by the problem of sources we have mentioned, the increase in annotation has been inevitable. The essential problem, for these chapters, has been to condense the presentation of the materials without becoming cryptic.

In contrast to the annotation, an Introduction to the *Biographia* presents an almost directly opposite, as well as a simpler, problem. The real commentary on the intellectual content of the *Biographia* is to be found in the large number of books and articles, particularly since World War II, devoted to Coleridge as a critic and a thinker generally. For the *Biographia* is so much at the centre of most of Coleridge's greater prose writings, particularly his literary criticism, that one can hardly discuss a single significant topic raised in the *Biographia* unless one also moves to his other writings for nuance or even for clarification. To provide an Introduction to the intellectual content of the *Biographia* would therefore be to provide an introduction to Coleridge generally as a mind and a critic.

Rather than trying to give one more distillation of the well known, we have used the limited space of the Introduction for two purposes. In the first part of the Introduction, written by W. J. Bate, we have discussed the peculiar circumstances in which the book was written (or largely dictated), and the problem of chronology and order of composition. The questions of circumstances and chronology are by no means of merely pedantic or even of psychological interest, though the psychological interest is especially strong. The second part of the Introduction, written by James Engell, concentrates on problems in the intellectual content of the *Biographia*.

As a frontispiece we print a reproduction of the crayon drawing made by George Dawe in 1811. John Morgan had suggested as an illustration for the first edition of the *Biographia* an engraving from a drawing to be made from Dawe's bust of Coleridge. See the letters of Morgan to William Hood of 10, 14, and 17 Aug 1815 in Appendix C, below.

Our acknowledgements begin with thanks to Professor Kathleen Coburn, the General Editor of the *Collected Works*, both for her personal help and for her great edition of the *Notebooks*, to which, as our own notes show, we have constantly resorted; and with thanks to Mr Bart Winer, the Associate Editor of the *Collected Works*, who has given us invaluable aid in preparing the edition for the press. Our indebtedness to the editions of H. N. and Sara Coleridge (1847), John Shawcross (1907), and George Watson (rev ed 1975) is obvious, though it has been impossible, without overburdening the notes, to record every instance in which our notes are similar, though we have, we believe, cited our indebtedness to them and to other scholars for their original contributions. Our debt to the work of Sara Coleridge, in the 1847 edition, is particularly heavy. ✓

For aid in tracking Coleridge's quotations and allusions, we thank Professors Douglas Bush, Mason Hammond, John Finley, John Murdoch, David Perkins, Larry Benson, Glen Bowersock, James Mays, Trevor Levere, and the Rev John Boyd, S.J. Professor Emerson Marks, who has studied exhaustively the theory of poetic diction in the eighteenth century and the Romantic period, generously placed at our disposal the manuscript of *Coleridge on the Language of Verse*. In addition he carefully went over, and made many helpful suggestions for, our own necessarily brief treatment of the subject as it relates to the *Biographia*. Professor George Whalley kindly sent us material relevant to the *Marginalia* cited in our edition, and also copies of the correspondence he had assembled relating to the writing and publication of the *Biographia*. Professor Daniel Fogel sent us in advance of publication his study of the chronology of Coleridge's writing of the book; and Mrs Lorna Arnold and Professor Douglas Bush gave us invaluable aid in facing problems with Coleridge's Greek in the 1817 edition. For other help we are indebted to Mrs Prudence Steiner, Dr William A. Bond, Mr Edward Doctoroff, Miss Linda Segal, Miss Anne Macaulay, and Dr James E. Walsh, as well as to the authorities generally of the British Library (especially for the use of the books annotated by Coleridge), the Harvard College Library, the Boston Athenaeum, the New York Public Library, the Bodleian, and the Victoria College Library. We are grateful to Mrs N. F. D. Coleridge for her kindness in letting us photograph and reproduce an annotation in a copy of the *Biographia* that originally belonged to Derwent Coleridge.

Among the scholars to whose writings we owe an especially

heavy debt are Professors René Wellek, Thomas McFarland, the late E. L. Griggs, I. A. Richards, David Erdman, the late Barbara E. Rooke, G. N. G. Orsini, L. C. Knights, Reginald Foakes, Richard Fogle, J. R. de J. Jackson, Harry Levin, Carl Woodring, the Rev Joseph Appleyard, S.J., the Rev J. R. Barth, S.J., as well as all of the editors of volumes already published in the *Collected Works*.

For financial help in defraying expenses involved in research we express our gratitude to the Ford Foundation and Bollingen Foundation.

                                                        J. E.
                                                        W. J. B.

Cambridge, Massachusetts

EDITORIAL PRACTICE,
SYMBOLS, AND ABBREVIATIONS

THE TEXT is that of the 1817 edition. This is the only authoritative text as it was the only English edition published during Coleridge's lifetime. Nor has any manuscript copy ever been discovered. The peculiar circumstances of the book's composition, the fact that the greater part of it was dictated, the long delays and difficulties with the printers at Bristol, the change of publishers to a minor firm that soon afterwards went out of business, amply explain why no manuscript survived either in the Coleridge family or elsewhere.

In following the 1817 text, obvious misprints are silently corrected. It is usually possible to tell the difference between a printer's error and a mistake of Coleridge, or of John Morgan, to whom the larger part of the *Biographia* was dictated. But if there is doubt, any correction in the present text is mentioned in a textual note. Punctuation, capitalisation, and italics, in both the text and quotations within the text, have been reproduced without change unless, as happens in a very few cases, the punctuation interferes with the obvious sense of the sentence. In such instances the change is recorded in the textual notes. On the other hand, accents in Greek, French, and Italian have been normalised in accordance with the practice of the *Collected Works* generally. A special if minor problem arises in the case of proper names (e.g. "Spencer" for "Spenser", "Hobbs" for "Hobbes", "Shakspeare" for "Shakespeare"). Coleridge sometimes spells these names in the conventional way. The text adjusts the spelling of such names according to Coleridge's usual practice, but such changes are recorded in the textual notes. On the rare occasions when Coleridge habitually misspells a name (e.g. "Condilliac" for "Condillac") the idiosyncracy in spelling is preserved.

Coleridge's footnotes are indicated by symbols (*, †, etc) and are printed full measure. The editors' footnotes are numbered and (when not too brief) are printed in double columns. The order of the editors' footnotes follows (perhaps Coleridgian) logic; i.e. it is assumed that when the text contains an asterisk or a dagger the reader then turns from text to note and then goes back again. The editors' footnotes, which are sometimes notes on Coleridge's footnotes, follow that order. Thus the footnote indicators within the text may leap from 1 to 5, notes 2–4 being notes on Coleridge's footnotes. Textual notes at the foot of the page, preceding the editors' footnotes, are designated by superior letters ($^{a-b}$, etc).

The editions referred to in the editors' footnotes are, when they are known, those that Coleridge used. Exceptions are made in the case of writers, particularly German philosophers, for whom such editions, found only in a few libraries, are unavailable to most readers, but for whom the standard modern editions may be readily available. In such instances, we have cited both Coleridge's edition and the standard modern edition, provided its text in the relevant passage is the same as that used or probably used by Coleridge.

Coleridge manuscripts, where quoted, are printed literatim, including cancellations, except that "it's", "its' ", "your's", and "yours' " have been standardised to "its" and "yours". The following symbols are also used in quoting from mss (with "wild" as an example):

[wild]	A reading supplied by the editor.
[?wild]	An uncertain reading.
[?wild/world]	Possible alternative readings.
⌐wild¬	A tentative reading (owing to obliterations, torn paper, etc).
[. . .]	An illegible word or phrase.
⟨wild⟩	A later insertion by Coleridge.

Strokes, dashes, and other symbols are Coleridge's.

A final note should be added about the parallel passages quoted from German philosophers in the "philosophical chapters" (5–9, 12–13). Wherever possible, the quotation is taken from the particular edition Coleridge used, and employs the wording, spelling, and punctuation of that edition. For the convenience of the reader, reference is also given to the standard editions of these writers, which are, again, in the relevant passages identical except, in some cases, for minor differences, principally in spelling and punctuation. On the other hand, mere references of a general sort, not involving parallel passages, are sometimes only to the standard editions.

ABBREVIATIONS

(In the works listed, place of publication is London,
unless otherwise noted)

A-J	The Anti-Jacobin (1797–8); The Anti-Jacobin Review (1798–1821).
Allsop	[Thomas Allsop] *Letters, Conversations and Recollections of S. T. Coleridge* (2 vols 1836).
AM	S. T. Coleridge *The Rime of the Ancient Mariner.*
AR (1825)	S. T. Coleridge *Aids to Reflection in the Formation of a Manly Character* (1825).
A Reg	The Annual Register (1758–).
A Rev	The Annual Review (1802–8).
Barfield	Owen Barfield *What Coleridge Thought* (Middletown, Conn 1971).
Bate *BP*	W. J. Bate *The Burden of the Past and the English Poet* (Cambridge, Mass 1970).
B Critic	The British Critic (1793–1826).
BL (1817)	S. T. Coleridge *Biographia Literaria* (2 vols 1817).
BL (1847)	S. T. Coleridge *Biographia Literaria* ed H. N. and Sara Coleridge (2 vols 1847).
BL (1907)	S. T. Coleridge *Biographia Literaria* ed John Shawcross (2 vols Oxford 1907).
BL (1920)	S. T. Coleridge *Biographia Literaria* ed George Sampson (Cambridge 1920).
BL (1975)	S. T. Coleridge *Biographia Literaria* ed George Watson (1956; rev 1965, 1975).
Bl Mag	Blackwood's Magazine (1817–).
BM	British Library, formerly Library of the British Museum
B Poets	The Works of the British Poets ed Robert Anderson (13 vols Edinburgh 1792–5; vol xiv 1807).
Bristol LB	George Whalley "The Bristol Library Borrowings of Southey and Coleridge" *Library* IV (Sept 1949) 114–31.
B Works	George Berkeley *Works* ed A. A. Luce and T. E. Jessop (9 vols 1948–57).
C	Samuel Taylor Coleridge
C&S (*CC*)	S. T. Coleridge *On the Constitution of the Church and State* ed John Colmer (London & Princeton, N.J. 1976). *The Collected Works of Samuel Taylor Coleridge* x.
Carlyon	Clement Carlyon *Early Years and Late Reflections* (1836).

C Bibl (Haney 1903)	John L. Haney *A Bibliography of S. T. Coleridge* (Philadelphia 1903).
C Bibl (Haven & Adams)	R. and J. Haven and M. Adams *Samuel Taylor Coleridge: An Annotated Bibliography* . . . Vol I: 1793–1799 (Boston, Mass 1976).
CC	*The Collected Works of Samuel Taylor Coleridge* (London & Princeton, N.J. 1969–).
CL	*Collected Letters of Samuel Taylor Coleridge* ed E. L. Griggs (6 vols Oxford & New York 1956–71).
C Life (B)	W. J. Bate *Coleridge* (New York 1968).
C Life (C)	E. K. Chambers *Samuel Taylor Coleridge* (1938).
C Life (G)	James Gillman *Life of Samuel Taylor Coleridge* (1838).
C Life (H)	Lawrence Hanson *The Life of Samuel Taylor Coleridge, the Early Years* (1938).
CM (*CC*)	S. T. Coleridge *Marginalia* ed George Whalley (5 vols London & Princeton, N.J. 1980–). *The Collected Works of Samuel Taylor Coleridge* XII.
CN	*The Notebooks of Samuel Taylor Coleridge* ed Kathleen Coburn (New York, Princeton, N.J. & London 1957–).
Conciones	S. T. Coleridge *Conciones ad Populum. Or Addresses to the People* (Bristol 1795).
C on Sh	*Coleridge on Shakespeare: the Text of the Lectures of 1811–12* ed R. A. Foakes (1971).
Cottle *E Rec*	Joseph Cottle *Early Recollections; Chiefly Relating to the Late Samuel Taylor Coleridge* . . . (2 vols 1837).
Cottle *Rem*	Joseph Cottle *Reminiscences of Samuel Taylor Coleridge and Robert Southey* (1847).
CRB	Henry Crabb Robinson *on Books and Their Writers* ed Edith J. Morley (3 vols 1938).
CRD	*Diary, Reminiscences, and Correspondence of Henry Crabb Robinson* ed Thomas Sadler (3 vols 1869).
C Rev	*The Critical Review* (1756–1817).
C 17th C	*Coleridge on the Seventeenth Century* ed R. F. Brinkley (Durham, N.C. 1955).
CW	*Complete Works of Samuel Taylor Coleridge* ed W. G. T. Shedd (7 vols New York 1853).
DC	Derwent Coleridge
De Q	Thomas De Quincey

De Q Works	*The Collected Writings of Thomas De Quincey* ed David Masson (14 vols Edinburgh 1889–90).
DNB	*Dictionary of National Biography* (1885–).
DW	Dorothy Wordsworth
DWJ	*Journals of Dorothy Wordsworth* ed E. de Selincourt (2 vols 1959).
E&S	*Essays and Studies* (Oxford 1910–).
Ed Rev	*The Edinburgh Review* (Edinburgh & London 1802–1929)
EHC	Ernest Hartley Coleridge
EIC	*Essays in Criticism*
ELH	*Journal of English Literary History*
E Mag	*The European Magazine* (1782–1826)
Engell *CI*	James Engell *The Creative Imagination: Enlightenment to Romanticism* (Cambridge, Mass 1981).
EOT (CC)	S. T. Coleridge *Essays on His Times* ed David V. Erdman (3 vols London & Princeton, N.J. 1978). *The Collected Works of Samuel Taylor Coleridge* III.
Fichte *GA*	J. G. Fichte *Gesamtausgabe: Der Bayerischen Akademie der Wissenschaften* ed R. Lauth and H. Jacob (in process, Stuttgart–Bad Cannstatt 1965–).
Fichte *Grundlage*	*Grundlage der gesammten Wissenschaftslehre* (Jena & Leipzig 1794). The ed C used.
Fichte *SW*	J. G. Fichte *Sämmtliche Werke* ed I. H. Fichte (8 vols Berlin 1845–6).
Fichte *Ueber*	*Ueber den Begriff der Wissenschaftslehre* (Jena & Leipzig 1798). The ed C used.
Fichte *Versuch*	*Versuch einer Kritik aller Offenbarung* (Königsberg 1793). The ed C used.
Friend (CC)	S. T. Coleridge *The Friend* ed Barbara E. Rooke (2 vols London & Princeton, N.J. 1969). *The Collected Works of Samuel Taylor Coleridge* IV.
Fruman	Norman Fruman *Coleridge, the Damaged Archangel* (New York 1971).
G Mag	*The Gentleman's Magazine* (1731–1907).
H Works	*Complete Works of William Hazlitt* ed P. P. Howe (21 vols 1930–4).
HC	Hartley Coleridge
HCR	Henry Crabb Robinson
HEHL	The Henry E. Huntington Library and Art Gallery, San Marino, California

HNC	Henry Nelson Coleridge
IF	Isabella Fenwick
IS	*Inquiring Spirit, a New Presentation of Coleridge from His Published and Unpublished Prose Writings* ed Kathleen Coburn (2nd ed Toronto 1979).
Jacobi *ULS*	F. H. Jacobi *Über die Lehre des Spinoza* (enlarged ed Breslau 1789). The ed C used.
JHI	*Journal of the History of Ideas* (Philadelphia 1940–).
Johnson *Lives*	Samuel Johnson *Lives of the English Poets* ed G. B. Hill (3 vols Oxford 1905).
Johnson *Works*	*Yale Edition of the Works of Samuel Johnson* (New Haven 1958–).
Kant *KRV*	Immanuel Kant *Kritik der reinen Vernunft* (Riga 1781; rev 1787). C's copy (1799) is a reprint of the rev ed 1787, with the same pagination.
L&L	*Coleridge on Logic and Learning* ed A. D. Snyder (New Haven 1929).
LB (1798)	[William Wordsworth and S. T. Coleridge] *Lyrical Ballads* . . . (1798).
LB (1800)	[William Wordsworth and S. T. Coleridge] *Lyrical Ballads* . . . (1800).
LCL	Loeb Classical Library
Lects 1795 (*CC*)	S. T. Coleridge *Lectures 1795: on Politics and Religion* ed Lewis Patton and Peter Mann (London & Princeton, N.J. 1971). *The Collected Works of Samuel Taylor Coleridge* I.
Lects 1808–19	S. T. Coleridge *Lectures 1808–19: On Literature* ed R. A. Foakes (in ms). *The Collected Works of Samuel Taylor Coleridge* V.
LL	*The Letters of Charles and Mary Lamb* ed Edwin W. Marrs, Jr (3 vols Ithaca, N.Y. 1975–).
Logic (*CC*)	S. T. Coleridge *Logic* ed J. R. de J. Jackson (London & Princeton, N.J. 1981). *The Collected Works of S. T. Coleridge* XIII.
LR	*The Literary Remains of Samuel Taylor Coleridge* ed H. N. Coleridge (4 vols 1836–9).
LS (*CC*)	S. T. Coleridge *A Lay Sermon* ed R. J. White (London & Princeton, N.J. 1972). In S. T. Coleridge *Lay Sermons. The Collected Works of Samuel Taylor Coleridge* VI.
L Works	*The Works of Charles and Mary Lamb* ed E. V. Lucas (7 vols 1903–5).

Maass	J. G. E. Maass *Versuch über die Einbildungskraft* (1792; 2nd ed Halle & Leipzig 1797). C's was the 2nd ed.
McFarland	Thomas McFarland *Coleridge and the Pantheist Tradition* (Oxford 1969).
McFarland "SI"	Thomas McFarland "The Origin and Significance of Coleridge's Theory of Secondary Imagination" *New Perspectives on Coleridge and Wordsworth* ed Geoffrey Hartman (New York & London 1972) 195–246.
M Chron	*The Morning Chronicle* (1769–1862).
Misc C	*Coleridge's Miscellaneous Criticism* ed T. M. Raysor (Cambridge, Mass 1936).
MLN	*Modern Language Notes* (Baltimore 1886–).
MLR	*Modern Language Review* (Cambridge 1905–).
M Mag	*The Monthly Magazine* (1796–1843).
MPL	S. T. Coleridge *A Moral and Political Lecture* (Bristol [1795]).
M Post	*The Morning Post* (1772–1937).
M Rev	*The Monthly Review* (1749–1845).
Mrs C	Sara (Fricker) Coleridge
N&Q	*Notes and Queries* (1849–).
NED	S. T. Coleridge *Notes on English Divines* ed D. Coleridge (1853).
NYPL	The New York Public Library
NYUL	New York University Library
OED	*The Oxford English Dictionary* (13 vols Oxford 1933).
Omniana	*Omniana* ed R. Southey with articles by S. T. Coleridge (2 vols 1812).
Orsini	G. N. G. Orsini *Coleridge and German Idealism* (Carbondale and Edwardsville, Ill 1969).
PA	"On Poesy or Art" in *Biographia Literaria* ed John Shawcross (Oxford 1907) ii 253–63.
PGC	"On the Principles of Genial Criticism" in *Biographia Literaria* ed John Shawcross (Oxford 1907) ii 219–52.
P Lects (1949)	*The Philosophical Lectures of Samuel Taylor Coleridge* ed Kathleen Coburn (London & New York 1949).
PMLA	*Publications of the Modern Language Association* (Baltimore 1886–).
Poems (1796)	S. T. Coleridge *Poems on Various Subjects* (1796).

Poems (1797)	S. T. Coleridge *Poems* (2nd ed 1797).
Poems (1803)	S. T. Coleridge *Poems* (1803).
PQ	*Philological Quarterly* (Iowa City 1922–).
Prelude (1959)	William Wordsworth *The Prelude* ed E. de Selincourt, rev H. Darbishire (Oxford 1959).
PW	S. T. Coleridge *Poetical Works* (various).
PW (EHC)	S. T. Coleridge *Complete Poetical Works* ed E. H. Coleridge (2 vols Oxford 1912).
PW (JDC)	S. T. Coleridge *Poetical Works* ed J. D. Campbell (1893).
QR	*The Quarterly Review* (1809–1952).
Reed	Mark Reed *Wordsworth: the Chronology of the Early Years, 1770–1799* (Cambridge, Mass 1967).
RS	Robert Southey
RSL	Royal Society of Literature
RX	John Livingston Lowes *The Road to Xanadu* (Boston 1927; rev 1930).
SC	Sara (Coleridge) Coleridge
Schelling *Abhandlungen*	F. W. Schelling *Abhandlungen zur Erläuterung des Idealismus* . . . (included in *Philosophische Schriften*, below).
Schelling *Darlegung*	F. W. Schelling *Darlegung des wahren Verhältnisses der Naturphilosophie* (Tübingen 1806). C's ed.
Schelling *Einleitung*	F. W. Schelling *Einleitung zu seinem Entwurf eines Systems der Naturphilosophie.* (Jena & Leipzig 1799). C's ed.
Schelling *Ideen*	F. W. Schelling *Ideen zu einer Philosophie der Natur.* (Landshut 1803). C's ed.
Schelling *Phil Briefe*	F. W. Schelling *Philosophische Briefe über Dogmatismus und Kriticismus* (included in *Philosophische Schriften*, below).
Schelling *Phil Schrift*	F. W. Schelling *Philosophische Schriften* (Landshut 1809). C's ed.
Schelling *Phil und Rel*	F. W. Schelling *Philosophie und Religion* (Tübingen 1804). C's ed.
Schelling *STI*	F. W. Schelling *System des transscendentalen Idealismus* (Tübingen 1800). C's ed.
Schelling *SW*	F. W. Schelling *Sämmtliche Werke* ed K. F. A. Schelling (14 vols Stuttgart & Augsburg 1856–61).
Schelling *Über das Wesen*	F. W. Schelling *Philosophische Untersuchungen über das Wesen der menschlichen Freyheit* . . . (included in *Philosophische Schriften*, above).

Schelling *Vom Ich*	F. W. Schelling *Vom Ich als Prinzip der Philosophie* (included in *Philosophische Schriften*, above).
Schelling *Vorlesungen*	F. W. Schelling *Vorlesungen über die Methode des akademischen Studiums* (Tübingen 1803).
Schiller *AE*	Friedrich Schiller *On the Aesthetic Education of Man* ed and tr Elizabeth M. Wilkinson and L. A. Willoughby (Oxford 1967).
SH	Sara Hutchinson
Sh C	*Coleridge's Shakespearean Criticism* ed T. M. Raysor (2 vols Cambridge, Mass 1930).
SIR	*Studies in Romanticism* (Boston 1961–).
SL	S. T. Coleridge *Sibylline Leaves* (1817).
SM (CC)	S. T. Coleridge *The Statesman's Manual* ed R. J. White (London & Princeton, N.J. 1972). In S. T. Coleridge *Lay Sermons. The Collected Works of Samuel Taylor Coleridge* VI.
Studies	*Coleridge: Studies by Several Hands . . .* ed Edmund Blunden and E. L. Griggs (1934).
TL (1848)	S. T. Coleridge *Hints Towards the Formation of a More Comprehensive Theory of Life* ed Seth B. Watson (1848).
TLS	*The Times Literary Supplement* (1902–).
TT	*Specimens of the Table Talk of the Late Samuel Taylor Coleridge* ed H. N. Coleridge (2 vols 1835). References to *TT* are by date of remark quoted.
TWC	*The Wordsworth Circle* (Philadelphia 1970–).
V & A	Victoria and Albert Museum, London
VCL	Victoria College Library, University of Toronto
Watchman (CC)	S. T. Coleridge *The Watchman* ed Lewis Patton (London & Princeton, N.J. 1970). *The Collected Works of Samuel Taylor Coleridge* II.
Wellek	René Wellek *Immanuel Kant in England* (1931).
WL (E)	*The Letters of William and Dorothy Wordsworth: the Early Years 1787–1805* ed E. de Selincourt rev Chester L. Shaver (Oxford 1967).
W Life (M)	Mary Moorman *William Wordsworth* (2 vols Oxford 1965).
W Prose	*The Prose Works of William Wordsworth* ed W. J. B. Owen and J. Worthington Smyser (3 vols Oxford 1974).
WPW	*Wordsworth's Poetical Works* ed E. de Selincourt and Helen Darbishire (5 vols Oxford 1940–9).
WW	William Wordsworth

CHRONOLOGICAL TABLE
1772–1834

(public events to the end of 1817, the year that
Biographia Literaria was published)

1772	(21 Oct) C b at Ottery St Mary, Devonshire, to the Rev John and Ann (Bowdon) Coleridge, youngest of their 10 children	George III king (1760–1820) Wordsworth 2 years old Scott 1 year old *M Post* began
1774		Southey b
1775		American War of Independence C. Lamb b
1776		Adam Smith *Wealth of Nations* Gibbon *Decline and Fall*
1778		Hazlitt b Rousseau and Voltaire d
1781	(4 Oct) Death of C's father	Kant *Kritik der reinen Vernunft* Schiller *Die Räuber*
1782	(Jul) Enrolled at Christ's Hospital, Hertford (Sept) Christ's Hospital School, London, with C. Lamb, G. Dyer, T. F. Middleton, Robert Allen, J. M. Gutch, Le Grice brothers; met Evans family	Priestley *Corruptions of Christianity* Rousseau *Confessions*
1783		Pitt's first ministry (–1801)
1784		Samuel Johnson d
1785		De Quincey b Paley *Principles of Moral and Political Philosophy*
1789		(14 Jul) French Revolution Blake *Songs of Innocence* Bowles *Sonnets*
1790		Burke *Reflections on the Revolution in France*
1791	(Sept) Jesus College, Cambridge, Exhibitioner, Sizar, Rustat Scholar; met S. Butler, Frend, Porson, C. Wordsworth, Wrangham	(Mar) John Wesley d Paine *Rights of Man* pt I (pt II 1792) Boswell *Life of Johnson* Anti-Jacobin riots at Birmingham
1792	(3 Jul) *Encaenia*, C's prize-winning Greek Sapphic *Ode on the Slave-Trade*	Pitt's attack on the slave-trade Fox's Libel Bill

1793   (May) Attended Cambridge trial of Frend
      (15 Jul) First poem in *Morning Chronicle*
      (2 Dec) Enlisted in 15th Light Dragoons as Silas Tomkyn Comberbache

(21 Jan) Louis XVI executed
(1 Feb) France declared war on England and Holland
(Mar–Dec) Revolt of La Vendée
(16 Oct) Marie Antoinette executed
(16 Oct) John Hunter d
Godwin *Political Justice*
Wordsworth *An Evening Walk* and *Descriptive Sketches*

1794   (7–10 Apr) Back at Cambridge
      (Jun) Poems in *Cambridge Intelligencer*; set out with Joseph Hucks to Oxford (met Southey), pantisocracy hatched; Welsh tour
      (Aug–Sept) Met Thomas Poole, engaged to Sara Fricker
      (Sept) With RS published *The Fall of Robespierre* (Cambridge); *Monody on Chatterton* published with *Rowley Poems* (Cambridge)
      (Dec) Left Cambridge; sonnets in *M Chron*
      (24 Dec) Began *Religious Musings*

(17 May) Suspension of Habeas Corpus
Robespierre executed; end of the Terror
(Oct–Dec) State Trials: Tooke and Thelwall acquitted of charge of treason
(–1795) Paine *Age of Reason*
Paley *Evidences of Christianity*

1795   (Jan) Bristol lodgings with George Burnett, RS
      (Feb) Political lectures
      (May–Jun) Lectures on Revealed Religion
      (16 Jun) Lecture on the Slave-Trade
      (Aug–Sept) Quarrel with RS, pantisocracy abandoned
      (Aug) Met WW
      (4 Oct) Married Sara Fricker
      (26 Nov) Lecture on the Two Bills
      (3 Dec) *Conciones ad Populum* published
      (Dec) *An Answer to "A Letter to Edward Long Fox"* and *Plot Discovered* published; *Watchman* planned

(Jun–Jul) Quiberon expedition
(26 Sept) WW and DW at Racedown
(Oct) Keats b
(Nov) Directory begins
(6 Nov) Treason and Convention Bills introduced
(18 Dec) Two Acts put into effect
Lewis *Ambrosio, or the Monk*

1796   (9 Jan–13 Feb) Tour to Midlands to sell *The Watchman*; met Erasmus Darwin, Joseph Wright (painter)
      (1 Mar–13 May) *The Watchman* in ten numbers
      (16 Apr) *Poems on Various Subjects*

(Jul) Robert Burns d
(Sept) Mary Lamb's violent illness
(Nov) Catherine of Russia d
England treating for peace with France
Threats of invasion of England
Jenner performs first smallpox vaccination

(19 Sept) Hartley b; reconciliation with RS
(31 Dec) *Ode on the Departing Year* in *Cambridge Intelligencer*; move to Nether Stowey

Burke *Letters on a Regicide Peace*
Dr Thomas Beddoes *Essay on the Public Merits of Mr Pitt*

1797   (Mar) WW at Stowey
(5 Jun) At Racedown
(Jul) DW, WW, and Lamb at Stowey; DW and WW in Alfoxden House
(16 Oct) *Osorio* finished; *Poems, to Which Are Now Added, Poems by Charles Lamb and Charles Lloyd*
(Nov) C is engaged by *M Post*
(13–16 Nov) C's and WW's walk to Lynton and *Ancient Mariner* begun
(12 Dec) C's *Melancholy. A Fragment* in *M Post*
(26 Dec) C's *The Visions of the Maid of Orleans, a Fragment* in *M Post*
(30 Dec) C's stanzas *To Sir John Sinclair, Alderman Lushington, and the whole Troop of Parliamentary Oscillators* in *M Post*

Pitt, as Chancellor of the Exchequer, proposes to finance the renewed war against France by increasing taxes
(Feb) Bank of England suspends cash payments
(Apr–Jun) Mutinies in the British Navy
(26 May) Grey's motion for Parliamentary Reform defeated; Fox and Grey lead a Whig secession from attendance in Parliament
(9 Jul) Burke d
(17 Oct) France and Austria sign peace treaty
(Nov) Frederick William II of Prussia d; Frederick William III begins rule
(20 Nov) *Anti-Jacobin, or Weekly Examiner* begins

1798   (2 Jan) First prose that is definitely C's appears in *M Post*
(Jan) C's Unitarian sermons at Shrewsbury; Wedgwood annuity £150 accepted; C's *Fire, Famine, and Slaughter* in *M Post*
(Mar) *Ancient Mariner* completed
(5 Mar) Wordsworths receive notice that their lease of Alfoxden will not be renewed
(11 Mar) C and Wordsworths decide to go to Germany
(18 Sept) *Lyrical Ballads* published; WW, DW, Chester, and C to Hamburg
(Oct) C to Ratzeburg

(Feb–Oct) Irish rebellion
(Apr) Helvetic Republic
(12 Jun) Malta taken by French
(Jul) Bonaparte invades Egypt
(9 Jul) *Anti-Jacobin* last number
(1–2 Aug) Nelson's victory in the Battle of the Nile
Lloyd *Edmund Oliver*
Bell introduces Madras system of education in England

1799   Stuart buys *Courier*
(Apr) C had news of death of Berkeley; C at University of Göttingen
(May) Ascent of Brocken
(29 Jul) In Stowey again
(Sept–Oct) Devon walking tour with RS; met Humphry Davy in Bristol; experiments with nitrous oxide

(Jan) First attempt at a vote for Union defeated in the Irish Parliament
(Apr) Newspaper Act
(25 Jul) Bonaparte drives Turks from Aboukir
(29 Aug) Pope Pius VI d as a prisoner at Valence, France
(8 Oct) Bonaparte suddenly appears in France

(Oct–Nov) First Lakes tour, with WW

(26 Oct) Met Sara Hutchinson

(10 Nov) C receives Stuart's offer to come to London on full salary

(27 Nov) Arrives in London to accept *M Post* offer

(Dec) DW and WW at Town End (later Dove Cottage)

(4 Dec) C and Davy visit Godwin

(7 Dec) Series on the French Constitution begun in *M Post*

(9 Nov) Bonaparte first consul under new constitution

Schiller *Die Piccolomini* and *Wallensteins Tod* published

Royal Institution founded

1800 (Jan–16 Apr) *M Post* reporter and leader-writer; translating *Wallenstein* at Lamb's

(27 Jan) C's obituary of George Washington in *M Post*

(4–18 Feb) Parliamentary reporting

(2 Mar) Mrs C leaves London

(Mar) C at Pentonville with Lamb; offered proprietary share in *M Post*, declines offer

(Apr) To Grasmere and WW

(May–Jun) In Stowey and Bristol

(24 Jul) Move to Greta Hall, Keswick

(Sept–Oct) Superintends printing of *Lyrical Ballads* (2nd ed)

(Oct) C and Poole defend Monopolists

(Oct) Thinks of writing "an Essay on the Elements of Poetry", which "would in reality be a *disguised* System of Morals & Politics" (*CL* I 632).

(18 Jan) Debate over Union in Dublin

(3 Feb) Fox returns to Parliament

(Feb) Bill for Union passed

(Mar–Apr) Pius VII Pope

(Apr) Commons approves bill for Union

(25 Apr) Cowper d

(14 Jun) Battle of Marengo

Burns *Works* ed Currie

Union of Great Britain and Ireland

(5 Sept) Malta after long siege falls to English

1801 (Jan) *Lyrical Ballads* (1800) published; prolonged illnesses

(21 Jan) C returns to London

(Jul–Aug) With SH at Stockton; writes *Tranquillity* ode

(15 Nov) In London

(27 Nov) Series on cabinet changes begun in *M Post*

Christmas at Stowey

Davy lecturer at Royal Institution

(Jan) Evangelicals begin monthly *Christian Observer*

(Feb) Pitt, Grenville, and Windham resign

(Mar) Addington ministry (–1804)

Southey *Thalaba*

1802 (25 Jan) Returns to London with Poole; under care of Stuart and the Howells

(Mar–Nov) In Lakes, severe domestic discord

(4 Apr) *A Letter to* —— [Sara Hutchinson] . . .

(25 Mar) Peace of Amiens

(18 Apr) Erasmus Darwin d

(8 May) Bonaparte life consul

(2 Oct) WW marries Mary Hutchinson

(Oct) French army enters Switzerland

(Jul) Translates part of Gessner's *Erste Schiffer*

---- (Jul) Tells RS of WW and himself "there is a radical difference in our theoretical opinions respecting Poetry—this I shall endeavour to get to the bottom of" (*CL* II 830)

(Aug) Scafell climb; visit of the Lambs

(Sept–Nov) Writing for *M Post*

(4 Oct) *Dejection* ode in *M Post*

(11 Oct–31 Dec) Articles in *M Post* on the impostor Hatfield and Mary of Buttermere

(14 Oct) *France. An Ode* in *M Post*, revision of *Recantation*

(Nov) Three-day visit to London; tour of South Wales with Tom and Sally Wedgwood

(23 Dec) Sara C b

Fox encounters Bonaparte at his levée in Paris

Edinburgh Review founded

Cobbett's *Weekly Political Register* founded

Malcolm Laing *History of Scotland*

Paley *Natural Theology*

Spinoza *Opera* ed Paulus (1802–3)

1803 (Jan–Feb) In Somerset with Wedgwoods, Poole; with Lamb in London; makes his will

(Jun) *Poems* (1803)

(summer) Visits by Hazlitt, Beaumonts, and S. Rogers to Lakes; Hazlitt's portrait of C

(Jul–Aug) "The Men and the Times" in *M Post*

(15–29 Aug) Scottish tour with DW and WW

(30 Aug–15 Sept) Scottish tour alone

(15 Sept) Return to Keswick

(Sept–Oct) Plans "to write my metaphysical works, as *my Life, & in* my Life—intermixed with all the other events/ or history of the mind & fortunes of S. T. Coleridge" (*CN* I 1515).

(Jan) Charles Erskine elected cardinal

(Feb) Act of Mediation in Switzerland; Col Despard, one of the United Englishmen, hanged as an organiser of sedition

(8 Mar) Royal message on the war

(30 Apr) Louisiana bought by U. S. from France

(18 May) Official declaration of the war with France

(25 May) Emerson b

(Sept) Emmet's execution in Ireland

Cobbett *Parliamentary Debates* (later Hansard)

Chatterton *Works* ed RS and Cottle

Malthus *Principles of Population* (2nd ed)

1804 (Jan) Ill at Grasmere; portrait by Northcote

(24 Jan) To London

(Feb–Mar) C writes for *Courier* on Sheridan and Addington and the Volunteers

(9 Apr) In convoy to Malta

(Jul) As private secretary to Alexander Ball, British High Commissioner at Malta, C drafts "Observations on Egypt" and

(12 Feb) Kant d

(14 Feb) King George becomes "ill"

(Mar) Code Napoléon

(Apr) Collapse of Addington's administration; 2nd Pitt ministry (–1806)

(18 May) Napoleon made emperor

(12 Dec) Spain declares war on Britain

other papers, some versions intended for *Courier*
(Aug–Nov) Sicily, two ascents of Etna; stays with G. F. Leckie

1805 (Jan) Appointed Acting Public Secretary in Malta; news of loss of John Wordsworth on *Abergavenny*
(Sept–Dec) In Sicily
(Dec) To Naples and Rome

Henry Addington becomes Viscount Sidmouth
(Apr) Third Coalition against France
(9 May) Schiller d
(21 Oct) Nelson's victory at Trafalgar
Hazlitt *Principles of Human Action*

1806 (Jan) In Rome, meets Washington Allston, the Humboldts, L. Tieck, and Schlegel; to Florence, Pisa
(Mar) Meets Angelica Catalani
(23 Jun) Sails from Leghorn
(17 Aug) Lands in England; London, job-hunting.
(26 Oct) In Kendal
(Nov) Keswick, determined on separation from Mrs C
(Dec) At Coleorton with WW and SH, crisis of jealous disillusionment with them

(Jan) Pitt d, "Ministry of All the Talents"
(6 Aug) Holy Roman Empire ends
(13 Sept) Fox d
British blockade
(Oct) Austerlitz (Prussians defeated)
(14 Oct) Jena
(Nov) Berlin Decree and Continental System
Arndt *Geist der Zeit*

1807 Coleorton; hears WW read *Prelude* and writes *Lines to William Wordsworth*
(Jun) With C family at Stowey
(Aug) Meets De Quincey; in Bristol
(Nov) In London

(Feb) Napoleon fights Russia
(Mar) Portland ministry (–1809)
(25 Mar) Abolition of slave-trade
(Jul) Peace of Tilsit
(Aug) Truce between Russia and Turkey
(Dec) Peninsular War begins
WW *Poems in Two Volumes*
RS *Letters from England by Don Espriella; Specimens of the Later English Poets*
C. and M. Lamb *Tales from Shakespeare*

1808 C translates and revises *Geist der Zeit*
(15 Jan–Jun) In rooms at *Courier* office, Strand; lectures at Royal Institution on Poetry and Principles of Taste; illnesses, Bury St Edmunds
(Jun–Aug) Bristol, Leeds, Keswick
(Jul) Review of Clarkson's *History of the Abolition of the Slave-Trade* in *Ed Rev*

Bell–Lancaster controversy
Joseph Bonaparte made king in Spain
(1 May) Hazlitt marries Sarah Stoddart
(14 Nov) Arrival of British troops under Moore in Salamanca
(23 Nov) All of the Spanish armies routed
(Dec) Palafox and Saragossa townspeople again fight off French; Dr T. Beddoes d

(1 Sept) Arrives Allan Bank, Grasmere

(Nov) First Prospectus of *The Friend*, Kendal

(4 Dec) Madrid reoccupied by French

Dalton *New System of Chemical Philosophy* and publication of atomic theory

Lamb *Specimens of English Dramatic Poets*

Scott *Marmion*

John and Leigh Hunt's *Examiner* begins

Goethe *Faust* pt I

1809

(1 Jun) *The Friend* No 1 published

(8 Jun) *Friend* No 2

(10 Aug) *Friend* No 3

(7 Sept) *Friend* No 4

(14 Sept) *Friend* No 5

(21 Sept) *Friend* No 6

(28 Sept) *Friend* No 7

(5 Oct) *Friend* No 8

(12 Oct) *Friend* No 9

(19 Oct) *Friend* No 10

(26 Oct) *Friend* No 11

(4 Nov) C's mother d

(9 Nov) *Friend* No 12

(16 Nov) *Friend* No 13

(23 Nov) *Friend* No 14

(30 Nov) *Friend* No 15

(1 Dec) News of Cortes' proclamation in *Courier*

(7 Dec) *Friend* No 16

(7 Dec–20 Jan 1810) "Letters on the Spaniards" in *Courier*

(14 Dec) *Friend* No 17

(21 Dec) *Friend* No 18

(28 Dec) *Friend* No 19

Tirolean patriot Andreas Hofer drives out Bavarians twice and Austrians twice

(Jan) Sir John Moore d; victories in the Peninsula.

(Feb) *Quarterly Review* founded

(9 Mar) Byron *English Bards and Scotch Reviewers*

(May) Napoleon's capture of Vienna and his excommunication; Pius VII imprisoned

WW *Convention of Cintra* pamphlet

(Jul–Nov) Walcheren expedition

(Aug) Attack on Flushing

(Sept) Wellington defeats French under Masséna at Busaco

(21 Sept) Canning–Castlereagh duel

(Oct) Perceval ministry (–1812)

(14 Oct) Peace of Schönbrunn

(20 Oct) Alexander Ball d in Malta

Schlegel *Über dramatische Kunst und Litteratur*

1810

(4 Jan) *Friend* No 20

(11 Jan) *Friend* supernumerary

(25 Jan) *Friend* No 21

(31 Jan) *Friend* No 22

(8 Feb) *Friend* No 23

(15 Feb) *Friend* No 24

(22 Feb) *Friend* No 25

(1 Mar) *Friend* No 26

(Mar) SH leaves for Wales

(15 Mar) *The Friend* No 27, last number

(3 Apr) Writes on "Parties" in *Courier*

(Oct) To London; Montagu precipitates WW–C quarrel; with Morgans in Hammersmith

Louis Bonaparte deposed as King of Holland; Bernadotte elected as successor to Swedish throne; French driven from Portugal

(Mar) Battle over admission of press to House of Commons

(May) First reform bill since 1797 introduced

(21 Jun) Burdett released from Tower

(Jul) Napoleon annexes Holland

(Dec) King George's insanity generally conceded

WW *Guide to the Lakes*

Mme de Staël *De l'Allemagne*

Scott *Lady of the Lake*

(Nov) Personal association with HCR begins

RS *Curse of Kehama*

1811 (Mar–Apr) Miniature painted by M. Betham; meets Grattan
(20 Apr) First *Table Talk* recorded by John Taylor Coleridge
(May–Sept) Regular contributions to *Courier*
(4 Sept) C publishes attack on *Hibern-Anglus* in *Courier*
(18 Nov–27 Jan 1812) Lectures on Shakespeare and Milton at Scot's Corporation Hall, Collier, Byron, Rogers, Robinson attending
(Dec) George Dawe bust of C

(5 Feb) Prince of Wales made Regent
(1 Jun) Papers admit an "alarming increase" in the King's "illness"
(18 Jun) Debate on Catholic Emancipation ("Catholic claims")
(27 Jun) Lord Stanhope introduces a bill to make banknotes legal tender
(Nov) Bread riots in Nottingham
(Nov to 1815) Luddite uprisings
(25 Nov) Dr Marsh delivers address to University of Cambridge, concerning the Bible Society
Shelley *Necessity of Atheism*
Sir John Joseph Dillon *The Letters of Hibern-Anglus*

1812 (Jan–May) Essays in *Courier*
(Feb–Mar) Last journey to the Lakes to collect copies of *Friend*
(Apr) With the Morgans, Berners Street, Soho
(May–Aug) Lectures on drama in Willis's Rooms; portrait by Dawe
(May) Lamb and HCR patch WW quarrel
(14 May) C writes obituary on Perceval for *Courier*
(Jun) Catherine Wordsworth d; *The Friend* reissued
(3 Nov–26 Jan 1813) Shakespeare lectures in Surrey Institution
(Nov) Half Wedgwood annuity withdrawn; RS and C *Omniana*
(Dec) Thomas Wordsworth d

(Mar) Wellington captures Badajoz
(11 May) Spencer Perceval assassinated in the House of Commons by John Bellingham
(Jun) Lord Liverpool forms a cabinet with his former colleagues in the last Perceval administration
(18 Jun) U. S. declares war on Great Britain
(22 Jun) Napoleon opens war on Russia
(Oct–Dec) The retreat from Moscow
(18 Dec) Napoleon reaches Paris and issues the 29th Bulletin of the Grand Army

1813 (23 Jan) *Remorse* opened at Drury Lane and runs 20 nights
(2 Sept) Meets Mme de Staël
(Oct–Nov) Bristol lectures on Shakespeare and education; with Morgans at Ashley
(2 Oct) C's last article in *Courier* until 4 Jan 1814
(Dec) Illness

(Jul–Aug) Peace Congress at Prague a failure
(10 Aug) Austria declares war on Napoleon
(Sept) Sir Walter Scott declines laureateship; RS becomes poet laureate
(Autumn) Wellington successful in Peninsula; Switzerland, Holland, Italy, Rhineland, Spain, Trieste, Dalmatia freed of French rule

(Dec) Austria's accession to Allies'
force
RS *Life of Nelson*
Northcote *Memoirs of Reynolds*
Leigh Hunt imprisoned for libel
(1813–15)

1814 (Jan) Illness
(Apr) Lectures at Bristol on Milton, Cervantes, Taste; lecture on French Revolution and Napoleon; under medical care of Dr Daniel for addiction and suicidal depression
(3 May) Charles Danvers d
(1 Aug) *Remorse* performed in Bristol
(Aug–Sept) Allston portrait of C; Allston's exhibition of paintings; essays "On the Principles of Genial Criticism" published in *Felix Farley's Bristol Journal*
(Sept) At Ashley with the Morgans
(20 Sept–10 Dec) Letters "To Mr. Justice Fletcher" in *Courier*

(1 Jan) Invasion of France by Allies
(Mar) Allied forces reach Paris
(9 Mar) Castlereagh obtains four-power pact against separate negotiations
(22 Mar) Ministers decide against further negotiation with Bonaparte
(31 Mar) Inhabitants of Paris invited to choose what kind of government France should have
(2 Apr) Senate declares the Emperor deposed
(6 Apr) Napoleon's abdication
(May) First Treaty of Paris; Napoleon exiled to Elba; restoration of the Bourbons
(Sept–Jun 1815) Congress of Vienna
(24 Dec) Peace of Ghent signed by Britain and U. S.
Inquisition re-established in Spain
WW *Excursion*
Scott *Waverley*
Cary's *Dante* completed

1815 (Mar) At Calne with the Morgans
(Apr–May) C to collect his poems with a new "preface". Receives 1815 ed of WW's *Poems*. Tells WW he plans to finish his own Preface "in two or at farthest three days" (*CL* IV 576)
(Jun) *Remorse* performed at Calne
(Jul–Sept) Extends preface to "an Autobiographia literaria, or Sketches of my literary Life & opinions, as far as Poetry and poetical Criticism is concerned" (*CL* IV 578–9). By 29 Jul has written chs 1–4 and 14–22 (part). In Aug and Sept writes chs 5–13. On 19 Sept sends ms to printer.
(Oct) Printing of *BL* begins, together with *Sibylline Leaves*

(Mar–Jun) The Hundred Days: Napoleon escapes from Elba, returns to France
(6 Apr) Allies mobilise vs Napoleon
(18 Jun) Waterloo
Restoration of Louis XVIII
Napoleon from Plymouth to St Helena
(20 Nov) Second Treaty of Paris
WW *Poems* of 1815; *The White Doe of Rylstone*
Scott *Guy Mannering*

1816 (Feb) Grant from Literary Fund, also from Byron
(Mar) London: illness
(10 Apr) Sent *Zapolya* to Byron
(Apr–May) Gutch discovers *BL* and *SL* will be of unequal size. C advised to split *BL* into 2 vols, making 3 vols proportionate
(15 Apr) Accepted as patient and house-mate by Dr Gillman, Moreton House, Highgate
(May–Jun) *Christabel* published (three editions); renews acquaintance with Hookham Frere
(Jul) C contracts with Gale and Fenner to publish *BL* and any future works. Gutch tells C that Vol II of *BL* will be considerably smaller than Vol I and asks for more material. Meanwhile Gutch stops printing *BL*
(Dec) *Statesman's Manual* published; Hazlitt's antagonistic reviews in *Examiner* (Jun, Sept, Dec) and *Edinburgh Review* (Dec)

(Feb) Byron *Siege of Corinth*
(24 Apr) Byron's departure from England
(21 Jun) Motion for relief of Roman Catholics rejected in the Lords
(7 Jul) Sheridan d
Parliamentary Committee on Education of the Poor
(2 Dec) Spa Fields Riot
Shelley *Alastor and Other Poems*
Peacock *Headlong Hall*
Maturin *Bertram*
J. H. Frere ms tr of Aristophanes

1817 (Jan–Jun) Gale and Fenner negotiate with Gutch to get printed sheets of *BL*. C considers ways of padding out Vol II, considers inserting *Zapolya* but decides to insert "Satyrane's Letters" and critique of *Bertram* and also to extend ch 22
(Apr) Second *Lay Sermon* published
(14 Apr) *Remorse* revived
(Jul) *Biographia Literaria, Sibylline Leaves* published
(summer) Met J. H. Green
(Sept) Met Henry Cary
(Nov) *Zapolya* published; C's tr of Hurwitz's *Hebrew Dirge* for Princess Charlotte; Tieck visited C

(13 Feb) RS *Wat Tyler*
(4 Mar) Habeas Corpus suspended
(4 Mar) *Cobbett's Political Register* reduced price to 2d
(27 Mar) Sidmouth Circular on libels
(Apr) *Blackwood's Magazine* founded as *Edinburgh Monthly Magazine*
(6 Nov) Death of Princess Charlotte
Elgin Marbles purchased and put in BM
Hazlitt *Characters of Shakespeare's Plays*
Ricardo *Principles of Political Economy*
1st American ed of *BL*

1818 (Jan) "Treatise on Method" in *Encyclopaedia Metropolitana* published
(Jan–Mar) Lectures on poetry and drama
(Jan) Met T. Allsop
(Apr) Pamphlets supporting Peel's Bill against exploitation of child-labour
(Nov) *The Friend* (3-vol edition)

(Dec) Lectures on the History of Philosophy (Dec–Mar 1819); literary lectures (Dec–Mar 1819)

1819 (Mar) Financial losses in bankruptcy of Rest Fenner
       (29 Mar) Lectures end

— (11 Apr) Met Keats in Millfield Lane; HC elected Fellow of Oriel; revived interest in chemistry; occasional contributions to *Blackwood's* to 1822

1820 (May) HC deprived of his Oriel Fellowship
       (Oct) DC to St John's, Cambridge

1821 (Jul) Visited brother Rev George C
       (Autumn) Invitation to lecture in Dublin refused

1822 (Spring) C's "Thursday-evening class" began; SC's tr of Martin Dobrizhoffer *An Account of the Abipones, an Equestrian People of Paraguay*
       (Nov–Feb 1823) Wife and daughter visit C, Highgate
       (29 Dec) HNC began recording his *Table Talk*
       Edward Irving's first visit
       DC left Cambridge prematurely

1823 (Sept) *Youth and Age* begun
       (Dec) Gillmans and C move to 3, The Grove

1824 (Mar) Elected FRSL, annuity of £100
       (Jun) Carlyle and Gabriele Rossetti called at Highgate
       DC B.A. Cambridge

1825 (May) *Aids to Reflection* published
       (18 May) RSL lecture "On the *Prometheus* of Aeschylus"
       Proposed three lectures on projected London University

1827 (10 May) Thomas Chalmers called at Highgate; C's serious illness; receives Eucharist for first time since Cambridge; visit from Poole
       DC married Mary Pridham
       Sir George Beaumont d, leaving £100 to Mrs C

1828 (22 Apr) Fenimore Cooper met C
       (21 Jun–7 Aug) Netherlands and Rhine tour with Dora and WW
       (Aug) *Poetical Works* (3 vols); John Sterling called at Highgate

1829 *Poetical Works* (2nd ed)
       Poetical Works of Coleridge, Shelley, and Keats (Galignani, Paris)
       (Sept) SC married cousin HCN; Lady Beaumont left C £50; Poole visited Highgate
       (Dec) *On the Constitution of the Church and State*

1830 *On the Constitution of the Church and State* (2nd ed)
       (Jun) HNC and SC settled in Hampstead
       (Jul) C makes his will

1831 Last meetings with WW
       Aids to Reflection (2nd ed)

1832 Legacy of £300 from Steinmetz

1833 HC's *Poems* dedicated to C
       (24 May–9 Jun) To Cambridge for meetings of British Association
       (5 Aug) Emerson called at Highgate
       HC's *Biographia Borealis*

1834 (Jul) Proofs of *Poetical Works* (3rd ed)
       (25 Jul) Death at Highgate

EDITORS' INTRODUCTION

PART I

> Seem to have made up my mind to write my metaphysical works, as
> *my Life*, & *in* my Life—intermixed with all the other events/ or
> history of the mind & fortunes of S. T. Coleridge.
>
> SEPTEMBER–OCTOBER 1803: *CN* I 1515

COLERIDGE'S *Biographia Literaria*, written in desperation of
spirit when he was approaching forty-three (1815), has
emerged over the last century—after a generation of comparative
neglect—as one of the classics of English literature. It has also
become established as one of the supreme works in the history of
literary criticism, perennially germinal in providing premises,
values, and aims to other writers and critics from the later nineteenth century until the present.

By the beginning of our own century the prestige of the work, at
least in the English-speaking world, had risen to a level that could
be expressed by two quotations. The more moderate (1906) is a
remark of Arthur Symons:

The *Biographia Literaria* is the greatest book of criticism in English,
and one of the most annoying books in any language. The thought of
Coleridge has to be pursued across stones, ditches, and morasses; with
haste, lingering, and disappointment; it turns back, loses itself, fetches
wide circuits, and comes to no visible end. But you must follow it step
by step; and, if you are ceaselessly attentive, will be ceaselessly
rewarded.[1]

But a surprising number of people felt even this tribute to be
needlessly grudging and were inclined to sympathise with the
eulogy of George Saintsbury in his influential—and, for decades,
standard—*History of Criticism* (1902–4): "So, then, there abide
these three, Aristotle, Longinus, and Coleridge." He adds that, if
all professors of literature were disestablished, and the proceeds
of their chairs were used to furnish "every one who goes up to the

---

[1] *BL* Introduction (1906) x–xi.

xli

University with a copy of the *Biographia Literaria*, I should decline to be the person chosen to be heard against this revolution, though I should plead for the addition of [Aristotle's] the *Poetics* and of Longinus".[1]

It is remarkable that a work of literary criticism (at least a relatively modern one) that so attracted Saintsbury and his generation should survive the radical change from conventional nineteenth-century modes of taste to those of "High Modernism" (the 1920s to the end of 1950s). The *Biographia* not only survived but continued to incite a deep respect, though often for different reasons. And it has lost none of its interest (though the interest now is almost as much human as intellectual) in the transition still taking place from the age of Yeats, Pound, Joyce, and Eliot to the "post-modern".

A more formidable test of the vitality of the book is the fascination it has continued to hold for professional critics since the 1930s, despite the extraordinary growth in differing critical approaches apart from the larger shifts in literary taste or sensibility mentioned above. Since the 1930s we have passed from old-fashioned "positivistic" literary history, accompanied by general "appreciationism", through the "history of ideas", the "New Criticism" with its emphasis on image and metaphor, and the larger formalisms that have concentrated on *genre*, to more specialised approaches: stylistic, from semantic to structuralist; psychological, of which there are many forms varying from the psychoanalytic to "psycho-history" and "psycho-biography"; the revived interest in the "theory of literature", which turns for suggestions—as Coleridge himself did—to the Continent, especially to the fertile genius of intellectual Germany in the period from about 1760 to 1830. In all of these approaches, no one has ever been displeased to discover that, for whatever he is discussing or urging, he can find a precedent in Coleridge: a general insight or a quotation that might give both vividness of expression and intellectual lineage.

This is a strong compliment that we pay to few critics aside from Aristotle, Johnson, and Goethe, and it illustrates the hold that Coleridge has on the literary conscience. Our knowledge of Coleridge's life and character brings him even closer to ourselves. We do not assume we are consulting the Delphic Oracle. Instead we

[1] III 230–1.

repeatedly experience the surprise that someone so near us in time, someone as flawed as the rest of us, should prove so clairvoyant and put so memorably the insights that seem to tumble from him. Nor can we forget in reading the *Biographia* that it was written by a poet, one of the greatest poets of the last three centuries.

Yet no work of even remotely comparable importance is admittedly so uneven, or—to use a word I. A. Richards applied to Coleridge as a poet—so "vulnerable". Coleridge's *Biographia* is in many respects a very naked work, written after fourteen years of profound unhappiness and lack of self-confidence. This is a long period in the life of any human being, but especially in the critical period from twenty-nine to forty-three. Moreover, the last seven of these years had been an especially painful time. As he now tried to pull himself above the surface, his brilliance is usually present. Although the genius of the work may be occasionally deflected by the commonplace, even at moments by the bathetic, there are entire chapters in which Coleridge can lose himself in his subject, and in doing so lifts us to a plane that leaves us astonished, thoughtful, and refreshed, and with the conviction that there is really no one like him. Yet there are also parts of the work in which he will fall into a defensive attitude; and since defensiveness was never Coleridge's *forte*, he becomes indirect and often vulnerable. Moreover, at crucial moments, given his distressing situation at the time, he will also snatch at other writing—sometimes by himself, sometimes by others—to fill out the requisite number of pages. There is some justice to Leslie Stephen's remark that the book seems to have been "put together with a pitchfork".[1]

As a result the *Biographia* has been periodically attacked from the time it appeared, and almost always for the same reasons. This again is a tribute to the importance of the *Biographia*. For it shows that people cannot simply let it alone. The true expression of disdain, as Samuel Johnson was fond of saying, is neglect. Within the first thirty years after the book was published, most of the charges that could be made against it had already been made. These essentially come under two headings:

(1) The structure, or lack of structure, of the book.

(2) The tangled but always fascinating problem of plagiarism, especially in the so-called "philosophical chapters" (5–9, 12–13).

---

[1] "Coleridge" *Hours in a Library* (1892) III 355.

GENERAL BACKGROUND

By July 1800, when Coleridge, still only twenty-seven, moved
north with his family to Keswick in order to be near Wordsworth,
the brilliant first period of his career was coming to a close. Very
quickly psychological problems were complicated by his addiction
to laudanum and the withdrawal symptoms that immediately con-
fronted him whenever he tried to free himself from it.

Difficulties in his marriage, long stirring beneath the surface,
grew acute; and within another year (1802) the waiflike existence
we associate with Coleridge, in his youth and again in his middle
years, had begun. Then followed his trip to Malta (9 April 1804),
where he served as secretary to Alexander Ball, his return (17
August 1806), his separation from his wife, the Royal Institution
lectures of 1808, the writing of the brilliant, if difficult, periodical
The Friend (1809–10), and his devastating estrangement from
Wordsworth because of his feeling (as he told Charles Lamb) that
"Wordsworth has given me up". Their personal relationship was
virtually wrecked. His friend John Morgan took him into his rooms
in Hammersmith and tried to help him cut down his use of opium.
All this time and afterwards he continued to write, though in no
way that really satisfied his self-expectation or the hopes of his
friends. There were also the famous lectures on Shakespeare and
Milton at Scot's Corporation Hall off Fetter Lane (18 November
1811 to 27 January 1812), which not only are one of the classics
of English criticism but aroused popular interest at the time (Coleridge, said Byron, who attended some of the lectures, is "a kind of
rage at present"). In fact, on the production of his tragedy *Remorse*
in January 1813 (it ran for twenty nights at Drury Lane) he became
overnight a celebrity. Various courses of lectures in London and
Bristol followed. During all these years, Coleridge continued to
write the remarkable collection of insights and meditations—
psychological, philosophical, literary—in his notebooks.

In a few sentences, even the shallowest summary of Coleridge's
life, above all the complexities of his inner life for these fifteen
years from 1800 until 1815, can scarcely be given, but the general
situation should be kept in mind as 1815 is approached, the year
the *Biographia* was written. On 19 December 1813, following the
first course of lectures at Bristol, he wrote:

The Terrors of the Almighty have been around & against me—and tho'
driven up and down for seven dreadful Days by restless Pain, like a
Leopard in a Den, yet the anguish & remorse of Mind was worse than
the pain of the whole Body.—O I have had a new world opened to me,
in the infinity of my own Spirit!—Woe be to me, if this last Warning
be not taken.[1]

By April 1814, he was ready, as he told his old friend Joseph
Cottle, "to place myself in a private madhouse, where I could
procure nothing but what a Physician thought proper".[2] Yet in
the summer of 1814 he managed to compose the three brilliant
essays, "On the Principles of Genial Criticism Concerning the Fine
Arts", which he began as an attempt to call attention to the work
of his friend the American painter Washington Allston, then
exhibiting in Bristol.

From Bristol, where he was staying much of the time, he moved
to Ashley September 1814 to stay with his friends the Morgans,
then in March 1815 moved with them to Calne, Wiltshire, where
they stayed in rooms rented in the house of a surgeon, Mr Page.
Here the Morgans again tried to help him confine his use of opium.
In addition to everything else he did for Coleridge, John Morgan
also served as his amanuensis, encouraging him to go ahead with
his writing. This was to prove of the greatest value for Coleridge,
who, like Johnson, always suffered from the struggles in that triple-
split act of writing in which one part of the self serves as bailiff,
dragging a second part to the bar of judgement represented by a
third part of the self. Speech, as distinct from writing, offered a way
out of this. It is important for us to realise this fact. For most of
the *Biographia* was dictated to John Morgan, without whose help
we might never have had it. To remember this will help to explain
many characteristics of the book.

THE IMMEDIATE BACKGROUND (1815): ORIGINAL INTENTION OF THE WORK

By March 1815 Coleridge was making an enormous effort to
redeem himself. From this date until his death in 1834, however
much he condemned himself, he was prolific in writing, if not

[1] To Mrs. J. J. Morgan: *CL* III 463–4. [2] *CL* III 477.

always in publishing, unless we use a standard that few of us would care to have applied to ourselves. As with Johnson, most of the legendry about Coleridge's indolence was created by his own talk about himself.

One of his first thoughts in 1815 was, quite naturally, to draw on capital and pull together what he had already written. Hence his intention to bring out a volume of poems hitherto uncollected in book form, and to introduce it with a "Preface" in which he hoped to discuss his general principles of poetry. From the start he was thinking, as a prototype, of Wordsworth's controversial and important Preface to the second edition of *Lyrical Ballads* (1800). He could himself feel partly responsible for that Preface. In fact "it was at first intended", as he told William Sotheby (1802), "that the Preface should be written by me".[1] But as most of the poems were by Wordsworth, it was more appropriate that the Preface come from him. Hence Coleridge continued to urge it on Wordsworth, who finally agreed to do it and who later (with some self-defensiveness that overstated the situation) said that he was wearied with references to "what is called Mr. Wordsworth's theory and his Preface":

I never cared a straw about the theory—& the Preface was written at the request of Coleridge out of sheer good nature—I recollect the very spot, a deserted Quarry in the Vale of Grasmere where he pressed the thing upon me, & but for that it would never have been thought of.[2]

But it was naturally not the Preface that Coleridge himself would have written. Strong private disagreement seems to have existed even before the Preface was published, despite Coleridge's attempt early to assure himself as well as others (e.g. in his letter to Daniel Stuart c 30 September 1800) that "The Preface contains our joint opinions on Poetry".[3] The truth is that Wordsworth, once embarked (however unwillingly) on the 1800 Preface, concentrated entirely on what applied to his own poetry or on aspects of it that he felt needed a defence. No room at all was made for the kind of poetry that Coleridge was originally going to contribute when the *Lyrical Ballads* was first planned (that in which "the incidents and agents were to be, in part at least, supernatural"). Immediately on completing the Preface, Wordsworth had second thoughts about

[1] *CL* ii 811.
[2] Ms note to Barron Field's memoir. *W Prose* i 167.
[3] *CL* i 627.

Coleridge's *Christabel*, which was expected to appear in the second edition of the *Lyrical Ballads* (1800). How could such a poem possibly fit into a volume with a Preface justifying the poetry of ordinary events and common life? A controversy of sorts appears to have risen briefly. It ended with Wordsworth asking the printer to omit the poem and to cancel a crucial passage of the Preface that spoke of the essential agreement of the two men and turn it into a mere list of the poems included from Coleridge.[1] Although the printer did not cancel the passage, Coleridge, obviously hurt, tended to be more reticent about the matter than we might expect. Even so, two years later he wrote to Southey (29 July 1802):

. . . altho' Wordsworth's Preface is half a child of my own Brain/ & so arose out of Conversations, so frequent, that with few exceptions we could scarcely either of us perhaps positively say, which first started any particular Thought . . . yet I am far from going all lengths with Wordsworth. . . . I rather suspect that some where or other there is a radical Difference in our theoretical opinions respecting Poetry—/ this I shall endeavor to go to the Bottom of . . .[2]

Meanwhile Coleridge had himself thought, and continued in the following years to think, of writing a formal discussion of his views on poetry. This was something that naturally engaged him deeply. He had been reared on the classics, knew them intimately, had been brought up in the later eighteenth-century admiration of the "greater *genres*", dramatic tragedy and the epic. In one of those comparisons of which he was so fond, likening himself to awkward birds who can neither fly nor sing well, he had said: "I have too clearly before me the idea of a poet's genius to deem myself other than a very humble poet; but in the very possession of the idea, I know myself so far a poet as to feel assured that I can understand and interpret a poem in the spirit of poetry. . . . Like the ostrich, I cannot fly, yet I have wings that give me the feeling of flight. . .".[3] It is perhaps sufficient to refer to Coleridge's letter of 9 April 1814 (to Thomas Curnick): the difficulties of the modern poet, facing the problem of what was left to do in poetry, were such that "I myself have for many years past given it up in despair".[4]

[1] *WL* (*E*) 304–5. See Marilyn Katz *TWC* ix (1978) 50–6. Cf esp Stephen Maxfield Parrish *PMLA* 73 (1958) 367–74 and Nathaniel Teich *TWC* iii (1972) 61–70.
[2] *CL* ii 830.

[3] Annotation on a flyleaf of J. H. Heinrichs *Apocalypsis graece* (Göttingen 1821). *CM* (*CC*) i 482.
[4] *CL* iii 469–70. Cf. Bate *BP* 90–1, 109–10.

Yet the admired Wordsworth, far less troubled by such thoughts, had gone ahead. He was at once establishing a new path for poetry (encouraged constantly by Coleridge)—a "philosophical" exploration of the "inner life"—and, at the same time, he was prolific. Wordsworth could do this, as Coleridge thought, only by concentrating on specific matters, which by definition meant excluding other aims and ideals. Coleridge admired this immensely: admired ambivalently what he called "rectilinear" virtue as he had encountered it in Southey and Wordsworth; and this ability of Wordsworth to forge ahead was a reflection of that quality. Inevitably, at least for poetry, Coleridge could see what he felt to be limitations in Wordsworth's approach (both in Wordsworth's Prefaces and, in a different way, in the poetry itself) and wanted to express them. Hence there is a long history of protests, qualifications, and definitions of purpose that led up to the "Preface" he was himself to write—the Preface that turned into the *Biographia*. He thought in 1811 of such a preface while he was negotiating with Thomas Longman about a proposed volume of poems (the project was later dropped). He would not add notes to the poems, but "a Preface of 30 pages, relative to the principles of Poetry, which I have ever held, and in reference to myself, Mr Southey, and Mr Wordsworth, I should think it necessary to add".[1]

Coleridge needed financial help, partly to pay the destitute Morgan for his own share of the expenses and partly to help pay for his son Hartley to go to Oxford. He sounded out his friend Joseph Cottle at Bristol (7 March 1815) about a possible advance of £30 to £40 for whatever manuscripts he could gather or write freshly. Without waiting for the refusal he was rightly afraid he would get, he also wrote another friend, William Hood, asking whether Hood might be able to find four or five people whom "I . . . believe interested in my welfare", and have them serve

---

[1] *CL* III 324. As time passed he also had a personal incentive to dissociate himself from the Preface to *LB* (1800). This was his belief that others, assuming Coleridge himself subscribed to its central arguments, were applying them, in a routine and mechanical way, to his own work. Cf his remark to RS (9 Feb 1813), speaking about reviews of his play *Remorse,* attacking him for "sentimentalities, puerilities, whinings, and meannesses (both of style & thought)": "if it had not been for *the Preface* to W's Lyrical Ballads [such critics] would themselves have never dreamt of affected Simplicity & Meanness of Thought & Diction—. This Slang has gone on for 14 or 15 years, against us—& really deserves to be exposed". *CL* III 433. Cf *CN* I 1673 and n.

as sponsor for the poems he would send. Otherwise "I must instantly dispose of all my Poems, fragments and all, for whatever I can get, from the first rapacious Bookseller that will give *any* thing—and then try to get my Livelihood where I can by receiving or waiting on Day-pupils, Children or Adults. . . ." Hood, a generous man, tried to line up contributors, and in April they advanced Coleridge £72.5.6 and, during the remainder of the year, another £35.[1] One of the contributors was John Mathew Gutch (1776–1861), who had been a schoolfellow of Coleridge at Christ's Hospital, and was now a journalist who published books in Bristol and was also proprietor and printer of *Felix Farley's Bristol Journal* (in which Coleridge's essays "On the Principles of Genial Criticism" had appeared the previous year). It was also arranged that Gutch take responsibility for the printing of both the poems and what turned into the *Biographia*, the actual printing being done by the firm of John Evans and Co of Bristol. Meanwhile Coleridge hoped to find a London publisher. Leaving no stone unturned, he overcame his inhibitions and wrote a rather awkward letter of self-introduction to Lord Byron asking him to look at his poems and, if Byron thought them worth it, recommend them "to some respectable Publisher":

A general Preface will be pre-fixed, on the principles of philosophic and genial criticism relatively to the Fine Arts in general; but especially to Poetry: and a Particular Preface to the Ancient Mariner and the Ballads, on the employment of the Supernatural in Poetry and the Laws which regulate it—in answer to a note of Sir W. Scott's in the Lady of the Lake. Both volumes will be ready for the Press by the first week in June.[2]

Byron agreed to help, and also suggested Coleridge write another dramatic tragedy like his *Remorse* (1813). Since Byron was a member of the committee that managed Drury Lane, Coleridge took the suggestion seriously and by the following autumn started to write *Zapolya*.

Then, in late April (probably 27 April), the now famous 1815 edition of Wordsworth's *Poems* was published, with a new Preface. Coleridge, as we have noted, had been thinking of Wordsworth all along. The rupture in their relations in 1810 had led to no coolness

[1] To Cottle [11] Mar 1815: *CL* IV 551, and, for Hood's account, 551n.   [2] [30 Mar 1815]: *CL* IV 561.

in Coleridge's respect for Wordsworth as a poet, but only hurt, indignation, and perhaps an emotion—naturally repressed—as close to anger as his inner censor could allow him to feel toward a friend. Now, in this new edition of his *Poems*, with its new Preface, Wordsworth had suddenly done exactly what Coleridge himself had been planning to do. At the same time Wordsworth had relegated to the past much of what Coleridge would have taken issue with in the famous Preface to the *Lyrical Ballads*, fifteen years before (1800). Wordsworth had done this by having that original Preface printed at the end, as a sort of curiosity. Worst of all, in the new Preface he devoted a good deal of discussion to the distinction between "fancy" and "imagination", which Coleridge considered to be far less Wordsworth's property than his own. Wordsworth, he could fairly argue, would never have heard of this important "distinction"—certainly would never have been able to make a large issue of it—had it not been for Coleridge.

Wordsworth's new edition of the *Poems* and its Preface continued to haunt Coleridge all through the writing of the *Biographia*: to such an extent that, as late as mid-August, when he had completed over half of his own manuscript, he was still thinking of his work—both Preface and the poems—as a rival twin to Wordsworth's edition. He could hardly have been unaware of the radical difference between the works in one way at least: the disproportion of the size of the "preface" in relation to the poems. Yet such was the hold Wordsworth's edition had on his mind that on 10 August he had Morgan write William Hood that Coleridge wished his work ("Preface" as well as poems) "printed in the size of Wordsworth's last edition. of Poems &c. the prefatory remarks same sized type ⟨as Wordsworth's *last* preface, not his old preface⟩".[1] The rival to be matched, in other words, was not the old Preface to the *Lyrical Ballads* (1800). Hood had probably not seen the new edition of Wordsworth. In any case it was not clear to him what Coleridge was requesting. For Morgan on 14 August wrote back with a painstaking detail that reflects Coleridge's near obsession with Wordsworth's new Preface:

My dear Hood—
    Just received your's—and was about to write to in order to explain, what I believe needed explanation, the directions for the size of the type

[1] VCL mss; see below, App C, II 283.

for C's preface. Col: means it to be printed like, in all respects, Mʳ Wordsworth['s] last edition ~~of Poems~~ entitled *"Poems by Wᵐ Wordsworth including Lyrical Ballads and~~-~~ the miscellaneous pieces of the author with additional ~~notes~~ poems a new preface and a supplementary essay"*. The preface to these 2 volumes: that preface which ~~goes~~ precedes the poem, is the one which he has fixed on as a prototype for his preface. You know there is at the end of the first volume *"the supplementary essay"* in small type—'tis not that which he means—there is likewise at the end of Vol: 2ⁿᵈ the preface to the former edition of Lyrical Ballads, now reprinted, also in small type—tis not that either, but tis the preface entitled preface prefixed to the poems in the 1ˢᵗ Vol: Excuse my ~~p~~ circumstantiallity about this. . . .[1]

Coleridge's "Preface" had become far more than a preface and was fast turning into a book. Wordsworth's Preface had so crystallised Coleridge's own intentions at the end of May that it was still serving, in Morgan's word, as a "prototype". Meanwhile—to return to the early stages of the work—Coleridge had written Wordsworth (30 May) that, for the poems he was himself collecting for publication, "I have only to finish a Preface which I shall have done in two or at farthest three days".[2] He may, as a Preface, have written something of what we now call the *Biographia*: possibly a few pages, possibly as much as would fill a chapter or two. (Mary Lamb said he had originally been thinking of "five or six pages".) But the probabilities are very strong that he only now, at the beginning of June 1815, began seriously to work on this "Preface" that became the *Biographia*, although, as we have seen, he had been long meditating a statement of poetic principles and theory.

THE WRITING AND EMERGING FORM OF THE *BIOGRAPHIA*

With few works of comparable importance is it so helpful to know the actual process and circumstances of the writing. The problem of what sections were written first and what last is peculiarly vexed and at the same time significant.[3] These considerations have

---

[1] VCL mss; see below, App C, II 284.

[2] *CL* IV 576.

[3] Cf Griggs's Introduction to *CL* III xlvii–liii and his notes to *CL* IV 579, 584–5, 619, 657–60, 664, 703–4.

See also Daniel Fogel "Compositional History of the *Biographia Literaria*" *Studies in Bibliography* (University of Virginia) III (1977) 219–34.

a vital bearing on the character of the book—its flow, its varying textures (for we must use the plural in speaking of this book), and, above all, its structure. The last consideration—the order in which the book was written—is of special interest in approaching the "philosophical chapters" (5–13), which, though inserted in the early-middle of the book, were, it seems, partly written last, with the hope of enlarging its scope.

We should start by noting the speed with which the book was written. Begun probably in late May or early June 1815, it was finished—as far as Coleridge was concerned—by 19 September.[1] In other words, the actual writing was done in about three and a half months. Secondly, the book was largely if not wholly dictated, and dictated, moreover, in exceptionally trying circumstances. For in beginning this large general effort to redirect the course of what remained of his life, he was simultaneously trying to cut down on his use of laudanum. We can especially appreciate the double demand Coleridge was making on himself. Obligation, as he said, tended to "stun" rather than arouse him; and self-demand was always the principal burden from which he sought escape. Yet now, as he began this effort to finish the book, he was resolved not to fail. Day after day, throughout the summer of 1815, he continued assembling materials and dictating from 11 to 4 P M and again from 6 to 10 in the evening. "I have given a full account (raisonné) of the Controversy", he writes R. H. Brabant (29 July), "concerning Wordsworth's Poems & Theory, in which my name has been so constantly included".[2] We can easily picture the situation: the repeated attempt to contain or suppress anxiety, as he dictated, arguing against Wordsworth, often snatching at one of his notebooks in order to capitalise on material assembled over the years (observations, quotations from other writers, outlines of earlier or projected lectures and essays), or occasionally incorporating sentences from *The Friend*.

[1] *CL* iv 584n, 588.
[2] *CL* iv 579. Dictation was an old habit of C's. Large parts of *The Friend* had been dictated to SH. See *Friend (CC)* i lv, lxxxvii. Instances that indicate C was dictating *BL* are occasionally mentioned in the notes. Three examples may be cited here in which Morgan misheard (also sug- gesting C may not have read either the ms or the proof very carefully): the reference to Elijah rather than Elisha (ch 7, i 120); and, in ch 9, the references to Gemistius (for Gemistus) Pletho and "De Thoyras" for Thaulerus or Taulerus (i 144, 149).

Naturally, as the work grew, it began to change its character from the mere "Preface" he had first planned for his poems. By the end of July 1815 it had already become, in length alone, a book in its own right. Of greater interest, by far, is the kind of book it had become (or had almost become). No form of writing came more easily and habitually to Coleridge than the *apologia*, however brilliantly he could transcend the form. Here the situation, as never before, was such as to tempt him to it: the accumulated distress and self-doubt of ten to fifteen years; the need to put the past into perspective, and to prove to others as well as himself that it was not wasted, as he prepared to salvage the years remaining to him. Understandably, the "Preface" quickly turned into a form of autobiography. But almost as quickly one of the most distinctive qualities of Coleridge began to emerge—the wrestle between his deep need, on the one hand, to apologise, to explain, and, on the other hand, his strong inner taboo against dwelling on self, and his natural instinct to empathise or identify with others. Hence his *apologia*, as it discussed the perils of the literary profession, soon turned vicariously to a defence of his friend Robert Southey and to a consideration of the reviews that had attacked him. Then, starting with what became Chapter 4, he turned to Wordsworth, that other and greater model of "rectilinear virtue" who had been so important in Coleridge's life. At the same time he began discussing his distinction between "fancy" and "imagination" with an eye to Wordsworth's own new Preface, to conversations in happier days with Wordsworth, and with a desire to correct him gently. Then, after a few pages on the history of the association psychology—possibly dictated with a thought of inserting it later, at some crucial point—he probably went on with what are now Chapters 14 to 16, moving into the famous critique of Wordsworth that begins in Chapter 17.

By the end of July, then, he had written, as one large unit, what was later broken down into Chapters 1–4 (possibly some of 5) and Chapters 14 up to part of 22, to a point where he considered his criticism of Wordsworth completed; and he had also probably written, as a conclusion, some of what later became Chapter 24. The first news of the immediate project so absorbing him is the letter (29 July) to Brabant:

The necessity of extending, what I first intended as a preface, to an Autobiographia literaria, or Sketches of my literary Life & opinions, as far as Poetry and *poetical* Criticism is [are] concerned, has confined me to my Study from 11 to 4, and from 6 to 10, since I last left you.— I have just finished it, having only the correction of the *Mss.* to go thro'.—I have given a full account (raisonné) of the Controversy concerning Wordsworth's Poems & Theory, in which my name has been so constantly included—I have no doubt, that Wordsworth will be displeased—but I have done my Duty to myself and to the Public, in (as I believe) compleatly subverting the Theory & in proving that the Poet himself has never acted on it except in particular Stanzas which are the Blots of his Compositions.—One long passage—a disquisition on the powers of association, with the History of the Opinions on this subject from Aristotle to Hartley, and on the generic difference between the faculties of Fancy and Imagination—I did not indeed altogether insert, but I certainly extended and elaborated, with a view to your perusal—as laying the foundation Stones of the Constructive or Dynamic Philosophy in opposition to the merely mechanic—.[1]

The latter part of what Coleridge says could imply that he had also made at least a fair start on the so-called "philosophical chapters" (5 to 13). But he had probably by this time dictated only five or six pages of that large section. For the faithful Morgan, eager for Coleridge to keep good relations with his new sponsors, Hood and Gutch, wrote to Hood (August 10):

At length I am enabled to send you 57 sides of C.'s work—the rest (full 100 sides) is finished, and not finished—that is, there is a metaphysical part of about 5 or 6 sheets which must be revised or rather re-written—this I trust will be done in a few days, and the next parcel (coming I think certainly next week) will contain the whole of prefacing work (for you will see how ridiculous it woᵈ be to call it ~~preface~~ preface) and those poems which he means to publish besides those you already have, and their proper order.[2]

By "sides" Morgan refers to pages; and the phrase "5 or 6 sheets"—as Daniel Fogel cogently argues—refers not to printer's "sheets" in the technical sense, of which Morgan was probably ignorant, but to manuscript sheets of paper, that is, about twenty to

---

[1] *CL* IV 578–9.

[2] See below, App C, II 283. That so much of the book was written by early or mid-August is confirmed by Mary Lamb's letter to Sara Hutchinson (20 Aug), in which she says that Coleridge "is very hard at work at the preface to a new Edition which he is just going to publish in the same form as Mr Words-worth's—at first the preface was not to exceed five or six pages it has however grown into a work of great importance. I believe Morgan has already written nearly two hundred pages, the title of it is 'Auto biographia Literaria': to which are added 'Sybilline Leaves,' a collection of Poems by the same Author." *LL* III 192.

twenty-four pages. The section Morgan sent is plainly what afterwards became Chapters 1 to 3. For Coleridge later (17 September)
sent tentative chapter headings for this section when he wrote to
tell Gutch that he had completed the work and to explain what had
happened to the original plan of a combination "of Poems *and* a
Preface". He had been encouraged to think that "a detailed publication of my opinions concerning Poetry & Poets, would excite
more curiosity and a more immediate Interest than even my
Poems". Hence a new and different work:

Biographical Sketches of my LITERARY LIFE, Principles, and Opinions, chiefly on the Subjects of Poetry and Philosophy, and the Differences at present prevailing concerning both: by S. T. COLERIDGE.
To which are *added*, SIBYLLINE LEAVES, or a Collection of Poems,
by the same Author.

He regarded the "Literary Life", in comparison with the "Collection of Poems", to be "the *main* work", and, because of its length,
he thought it should be broken up into "*Chapters*". The "first part
of the Work", sent to Gutch in early August because of "Morgan's
extreme anxiety", he wished to divide "into two or three Chapters,
the first headed—Occasion of the Work. Volume of Juvenile
Poems. The discipline of my Understanding at School.—Chapter
II. Are Authors an especially irritable Race? and what Authors?
Of Reviewers and Reviews—. Chapter III. Neither the Writer's,
nor Mr Southey's Publications the true cause or occasion of the
charge, that there has risen a new School of Poets". Of special
interest is the remark that, by the time Morgan had sent this
section (10 August), the whole of the book had been written

excepting only the philosophical Part which I at that time meant to
comprize in a few Pages.—This has now become not only a sizeable
Proportion of the whole, not only the most interesting portion to a
certain class, but with the exception of four or five Pages of which
due warning is given, the most *entertaining* to the general Reader,
from the variety both of information and of personal Anecdotes—.[1]

In short, whatever he may have written of "the philosophical
Part" (Chapters 5–13) was of minor significance by 10 August, and
it is the expansion of this part to which he then turned. By the time
he finished, about six weeks later, these additional chapters made
up about forty-five per cent of the entire manuscript. His remark

[1] *CL* IV 584–6.

that this new section could be "the most interesting portion to a certain class" was doubtless an attempt to reassure Gutch and Hood, who might have found it formidable reading and without popular appeal. And the additional assurance that it could even be "the most *entertaining* to the general Reader" unquestionably refers to the long Chapter 10, which becomes frankly autobiographical, discursive, and anecdotal. It was an attempt to entertain, yet possibly underlying it was the need to defer facing the challenge of Chapters 12 and 13, and possibly as well to relieve the otherwise heavily metaphysical character of this whole section. He had every reason to prompt him to expand this section. (1) The book was, after all, to be his own Preface-expanded-into-autobiography. Yet it had turned out that there was relatively little about himself and his own fundamental "opinions". (2) Present always in his mind was the *magnum opus*, the "Logosophia". Now, in dictating the *Biographia*, the opportunity came to say something about his own fundamental opinions—his reaction from the "mechanical" philosophy of the seventeenth and eighteenth centuries, and his love—hard-earned—of the "idealistic" philosophies from Plato and the Neoplatonists down through those of eighteenth-century Germany. This was the opportunity to insert some pages, even a few chapters, on this subject, if only as a threshold-shuffle before his own "Logosophia"—the *magnum opus* that had for long filled his mind. Hence, as he was finishing this "philosophical" section and preparing to send the finished manuscript to Gutch, he told him (17 September) that he thinks this new book "will be an important Pioneer to the great Work on the *Logos*, Divine and Human, on which I have set my Heart and hope to ground my ultimate reputation". By now, with these further chapters added, the new Wordsworth Preface had finally ceased to be the "prototype" it still had been in August. For Coleridge added—thinking back to his anxiety about matching the format of Wordsworth's edition, "As to the Size and Type I care nothing, provided only the Volumes be a handsome Octavo, in clear Type. . . ."[1]

The fatigue of these hurried final weeks, as he tried to insert a philosophical vestibule for the "Logosophia", had a catalytic effect on his own lack of confidence, his own self-condemnation of his habit of over-promising, and of over-assuring others (though it

[1] *CL* iv 585.

was really himself he was assuring) of what he would do. It is now that he turned to J. G. E. Maass and other German sources, particularly in Chapter 12, to Schelling and his own notebooks (especially N 61). The culmination of this "philosophical" section was to be the discussion of "the imagination, or esemplastic power", but there was no time left. Morgan had told Gutch in August that the work would be ready almost immediately. Coleridge was still in the midst of Chapter 12 on 16 September, to judge from the date of a footnote (though the footnote could have been added later); and this was three days before the completed book was sent to Gutch. Facing a deadline already postponed, and thinking ahead to all the other work (including the "dramatic tragedy" he would send to Byron and to Drury Lane), he finessed the long-promised discussion of the imagination, and in its place (Chapter 13) wrote that long letter to himself (from a friend whose "practical judgement" he respected) advising him to "withdraw" that discussion and reserve it for "your announced treatises on the Logos or communicative intellect in Man and Deity". Even the informed "friend" found it difficult to follow. The general public would have all the more reason to complain. The chapter, when printed, would amount to at least a hundred pages. This would greatly increase the expense of the book. In view of the title of the book—"My Literary Life and Opinions"—the reader could "accuse you of a sort of imposition on him". There may be already too much "metaphysical disquisition" for a work of this kind:

In that greater work to which you have devoted so many years, and study so intense and various, it will be in its proper place. Your prospectus will have described and announced both its contents and their nature; and if any persons purchase it, who feel no interest in the subjects of which it treats, they will have themselves only to blame.[1]

In response to this "very judicious letter" Coleridge decided to print only two short paragraphs "stating the main result of the Chapter". With Morgan hastening to bundle off the manuscript to Gutch, this "letter addressed to myself as from a friend", as Coleridge later told Thomas Curtis (29 April 1817), was written in a burst of speed "without taking my pen off the paper except to dip it in the inkstand".[2]

[1] See ch 13, below, i 303–4.   [2] *CL* iv 728.

The "philosophical" chapters, then, were finished in about a
month, at the end of what for Coleridge—what for anyone—was
a long stretch of energy. The fact has a direct bearing not only on
the "structure" of the *Biographia* but, above all, on the famous
"plagiarisms". This is not to excuse the plagiarisms. But a distinction can be kept in mind between "excuse" and a mere explanation
of circumstances that could seduce or frighten Coleridge into acts
against which the cushions of leisure, financial security, calmer (or
firmer) temperaments, or even sheer moralism would preserve
others. In connection with the "plagiarisms" the reader should bear
in mind the chronology of the work, the circumstances, the pressures to get it done rapidly, the self-doubts, the exhaustion.

LATER PROBLEMS AND ADDITIONS; PUBLICATION; RECEPTION

The *Biographia*, when Morgan dispatched it on 19 September
1815, was approximately three-fourths of the work as we know it.
Coleridge hoped to turn at once to other writing. Reopening correspondence with Byron, and promising him a tragedy for Drury
Lane within two months, he also began thinking of several dramatic projects, one of them being *Zapolya: A Christmas Tale*,
which he viewed as "a tragic Romance on the plan of the Winter's
Tale".[1]

Then he became seriously ill for six weeks (November and early
December), partly from sheer exhaustion, partly from the growing
congestive heart disease that was to trouble him henceforth, and
partly because, in his anxiety, he began to use more laudanum
while also struggling against it—the attempts to cut down on it
invariably producing the withdrawal symptoms that he could half
consider to be explained by other causes (for genuine knowledge of
withdrawal symptoms was lacking). Ill as he was, he clung to his
resolution: "I have a great, a gigantic effort to make & I will go
thro' with it or die".[2] When he was not working, as he told
Morgan, he was "Thinking, Planning, and Resolving to resolve—&
praying to be able to execute".[3] Inevitably he began to take refuge
in increased doses of laudanum. Ill again at the start of 1816, he

[1] 10 Apr 1816: *CL* IV 627.
[2] To William Money [8 Nov 1815]: *CL* IV 609.
[3] [? Nov 1815]:*CL* IV 611.

managed to finish *Zapolya*, and in late March took it to London to submit it to Covent Garden. He was probably too embarrassed to submit it to Byron for Drury Lane. It was by no means the tragedy he had promised. He could also have been embarrassed because he had assured Byron that the "tragedy" would be ready back in December. Neither Byron nor the others on the Drury Lane Committee cared, needless to say, about the frantic timetable Coleridge had inflicted on himself. As so often, the taskmaster that he dreaded and tried, by over-promising, to assure or evade was lodged within himself. Within a few days, Covent Garden refused the play, and Coleridge with desperation and apology sent it to Byron (10 April). Meanwhile he had taken unpropitious lodgings above an apothecary's shop, 43 Norfolk Street, the Strand. By the time he sent *Zapolya* to Byron he was fast collapsing into the state from which he was rescued when James Gillman of Highgate (15 April) took him in as a house patient.

The story, familiar as it is, has rapidly been summarised in order to remind the reader of the situation in which the rest of the *Biographia* was composed. Printing of the work had begun the previous October. Now, in April, the Bristol printers discovered that the *Biographia*, already about two-thirds printed, was proving to be considerably longer than its "companion" volume of poems, *Sibylline Leaves*, which was to have been a book of the same size. Probably the printers had misestimated because Coleridge had been able to provide fewer poems for the second volume than he had led Gutch to expect; for he was quite aware of the length of the *Biographia*, estimating it as a book of "500 pages Octavo", an estimate that proved fairly close. In any case, Gutch mentioned to Morgan, then on a visit to Bristol, that the two works—the *Biographia* and the poems—would be quite disparate in size, and made the poor suggestion that the *Biographia* itself be split into two volumes, "in order to prevent *disproportion*". There was enough material, said Gutch, to make up two volumes of the *Biographia*.[1] Morgan immediately passed on the information to Coleridge, and discussed the problem with John Murray, who also thought this a sensible procedure: three volumes, relatively uniform in size, the first two consisting of the *Biographia* and the third

[1] *CL* III xlix–l.

of the poems. Hence Morgan (6 May), writing on behalf of Coleridge, told Gutch to go ahead with the plan.[1]

Then Coleridge, in agreeing to this recommendation, made an unfortunate decision. Or if it was not unfortunate (considering the alternatives) it was at least a decision that was to complicate his life for another year and also to affect the character of the future Volume ɪɪ. To divide the *Biographia* evenly would involve breaking it after Chapter 10 or at least after 11 (for 11 was too slight a thing to serve as an opening chapter to Volume ɪɪ; it was a sort of appendix to the long Chapter 10). But this would involve breaking the work in the midst of those "philosophical chapters" (5–13) that he had probably written last and had then placed in the centre of the manuscript. In that case Chapter 12 (entitled "A Chapter of requests and premonitions concerning the perusal or omission of the chapter that follows"), which drew so heavily on Schelling, would be serving as the very start of Volume ɪɪ, followed by Chapter 13, in which Coleridge had evaded his long-promised discussion "On the imagination, or esemplastic power".

To single out these two chapters for prominence, by beginning his second volume with them, was naturally an upsetting idea for Coleridge. There was also the problem of continuity. Chapters 5 to 13 were a unit. Chapters 10 and 11, in the centre of this larger unit, had admittedly become a sort of interlude, which could help to lighten the otherwise unrelieved "metaphysical" character of the entire section. But aside from this "interlude", the chapters in this section (5–12) built progressively on each other, supported each other, and in the process could help to excuse any faults they might have or any omissions from his announced intention. Finally, Chapter 12, as an opening chapter, would be formidable reading.

Better by far to begin the second volume with Chapter 14, which introduced his general discussion of poetry in an accessibly readable way, followed by the two chapters (on Shakespeare and poetry of the fifteenth and sixteenth centuries) that led up to the sustained critique of Wordsworth in Chapters 17 to 22. Hence, in telling Gutch to proceed with the division of the book, Morgan (6 May) also told him, at Coleridge's request, possibly at Coleridge's dictation, to end the first volume with "the last Copy I sent (I mean the distinction between Fancy & the Imagination)". By "last Copy" he

[1] VCL mss; see below, App C, ɪɪ 286–7.

refers to the "philosophical" chapters, ending with Chapter 13, sent the previous September. Meanwhile Morgan also sent along whatever further poems that they thought could help to swell out *Sibylline Leaves*: "I send you *all* the Poetry we are able to collect". *Christabel*, since it was sold to John Murray, "must not be inserted". Other pieces Coleridge and Morgan had hoped to locate "are lost I fear for ever—the Volume must end there. Col: will prefix to it & send this week an essay on the imaginative in Poetry making the whole Volume about 350 pages quite large enough".[1] The "essay" was never written.

Then, in July (1816), while the final chapter was being printed (the first part of the present Chapter 22), Coleridge learned from Gutch that the new Volume II had proved far too short. Still another 150 pages would be needed in order to make it uniform with Volume I. Coleridge, for a while, was stunned. He had assumed that the *Biographia* was safely behind him, and would be published before the end of the year. Meanwhile, his life now, in accordance with the resolution of which the *Biographia* had marked the first stage, had changed and he was embarked on other projects, including the "Lay Sermons", and was hoping to start a new edition of *The Friend*.

At the time he heard the news, Coleridge had just received proofs of the first fourteen pages of the "final" chapter (22). Completely at a loss, he held the proof-sheets, wondering what next to do. One alternative—perhaps the obvious course from the point of view of the publisher—would be to start expanding this chapter and then continue on with some more. He had not yet submitted to the publisher a descriptive title for this final chapter, doubtless having expected to think up an appropriate one by the time he returned the proof. As he continued to hesitate for several days, the exasperated Gutch, by-passing Coleridge, wrote to Gillman— probably assuming Gillman was now Coleridge's official "keeper" —what Coleridge considered a "threatening" letter. Coleridge wrote back with hurt indignation (6 August) at Gutch having written to Gillman rather than to him personally. He reminded Gutch that it was on his and John Murray's advice that the book was to be divided into two volumes. Now

[1] Ibid.

(it being too late to recur to the original plan) I have no way to remedy it, but by writing *a hundred and fifty pages* additional—on *what, I* am left to discover—And the perplexity of planning, and the labor of executing this, are the true and only causes of the Delay, of which not You, but I, have the *right* to complain, tho' both of us have sufficient Cause to regret it.[1]

He returned the corrected proofs, though omitting (understandably) to send a title or heading—for he still had to think of what next to add—and asked for a bill for the printing costs, the whole of which, if reasonable, his London publishers would pay. This was the firm of Gale and Fenner, a minor house noted chiefly for its religious publications. Coleridge, moved by the high principles of the firm and by the thought of forming "a connection with a religious house", in a hasty moment promised them all his present and future publications. (The firm was to become bankrupt in early 1819.) Finally, on 18 December (1816) Gutch sent a sizable bill (£284.18.4), and also demanded the £107.5.6 advanced to Coleridge personally in 1815. There is no need to recount in detail the negotiations between Gutch and Gale and Fenner, who finally agreed to pay £265.0.4, except to say that, when the printed sheets arrived in April, they were in such disorder that almost another month was lost in arranging them.[2] The immediate concern is with what Coleridge, in the midst of other work and other anxieties, did to fill the gap left by Gutch's miscalculation.

I. About a fourth of the space was taken care of by extending Chapter 22, the concluding chapter in his critique of Wordsworth. The discussion shows signs of "padding", especially in the liberal use of quotation.

II. For about half of the space to be filled he reached back to the series of "Satyrane's Letters" that had appeared in three issues of *The Friend*: 23 November (No 14), 7 December (No 16), and 21 December 1809 (No 18). These had been in turn assembled largely from letters he had earlier written to his wife and to Tom Poole, relating some of his experiences on his trip to Germany.

[1] *CL* iv 661.
[2] *CL* iii li; iv 659–60, 700–2, 707–8. VCL mss; below, ii 292, 295–6. The Bristol printing stopped at Vol ii p 144 (ii 130 in this ed), and Gale and Fenner printed the last 165 pages of Vol ii. Because of the condition of the printed sheets, the expense of shipping, and allowance for damaged and missing copies, Gale and Fenner deducted £41.5.6 from the sum they had agreed to pay, and the account was finally settled at £223.14.10.

For a short while, before deciding to use these letters, Coleridge had toyed with the idea of shoving *Zapolya* into the breach. This would have added to his already "immethodical miscellany" (as he himself called it in Chapter 4). But fortunately, at a consultation Coleridge and Gillman held at Highgate with the publishers the idea was dropped and "Satyrane's Letters" were selected "as in every respect more appropriate".[1] The "Letters" were by no means an unfortunate choice. They certainly fitted in with the autobiographical character of the book, especially the first few chapters. Though their intellectual significance is limited, they are attractive in an anecdotal way, especially to the modern reader, who takes Coleridge's greatness for granted and who is naturally interested in the experiences of such a man on a trip that proved an important turning-point in his life.

III. Finally, for the remaining quarter of empty space, he appropriated and somewhat condensed a long criticism he had recently dictated to Morgan on the quasi-Gothic tragedy *Bertram* (1816) by the Irish novelist and playwright Charles Robert Maturin (1782–1824), who is now remembered, if at all, only for his novel *Melmoth the Wanderer* (1820) and because his play was discussed by Coleridge. *Bertram* had been produced at Drury Lane on 9 May and ran for twenty-two nights, with Edmund Kean in the main rôle. For this Maturin received £1000, and meanwhile, in printed form, the play was selling widely (it went through seven editions in 1816). Coleridge, who learned in July that *Zapolya* was rejected by Drury Lane, could possibly feel that *Bertram* had been selected in its place, though *Bertram* actually had been accepted the previous December (1815), well before *Zapolya* was submitted. In any case an understandable sense of indignation at the success of such an inferior work stung him into dictating the extended criticism of it that was published as a series of five "letters" to *The Courier* (29 August and 7, 9, 10, and 11 September 1816).

There are several things in this critique of *Bertram* of which we

---

[1] *Zapolya* was already committed to John Murray. But this was not the reason it was dropped. Murray gave Coleridge permission to use it for this purpose. Trouble later arose with Murray because Gale and Fenner, after it was decided not to use *Zapolya* for the *Biographia*, thought of bringing it out as a separate publication. Murray then wrongly suspected that this may have been Coleridge's intention and naturally demanded return of the advance he had given Coleridge. *CL* IV 703–6, 709.

could justly complain, especially when we are considering it as a part of what we regard as one of the master-works of literary criticism. Coleridge, after attacking "anonymous" reviews in the *Biographia,* had himself written this critique of *Bertram* as an anonymous group of "Letters to the Editor". There were perhaps excuses, considering the critique only as a contribution to the *Courier.* His resentment at the popularity of the play is understandable, if not commendable. Having always borne in mind how inadequate he himself felt in comparison with what the "drama" (i.e. Shakespeare) should be and do, why should he not have treated this hollow, booming work as he did when he thought it was being given such welcome by the managers of Drury Lane? He could even have encouraged himself to include the critique now because of a guilty conscience: by openly acknowledging the critique as his own (though tactfully omitting some of the sarcastic portions at the start), the act might atone for its anonymous character.[1] But the reader feels little or no interest in the object of attack. As Johnson said of Mark Akenside's odes: "To what use can the work be criticised that will not be read?"[2] The discussion seems especially out of place in a book of such magnitude of mind. Yet even in this chapter (23) there are often perceptive, even profound insights; for Coleridge naturally draws on reflections about poetry and the drama that had been in his mind for years.

After these insertions, Coleridge took what he had already written as a conclusion to the work (in the manuscript he had sent to John Gutch in September 1815), and revised it. He made a special effort to defend briefly three works of his own that had appeared since he had finished the original manuscript. One was his poem *Christabel* in the volume published by John Murray (*Christabel; Kubla Khan, a Vision; The Pains of Sleep* [1816]), which had been disparaged in the *Anti-Jacobin Review,* the *Champion,* the *Examiner,* the *Edinburgh Review,* and the *British Review.* A second was *Zapolya,* rejected by Covent Garden and Drury Lane, and about to be published by Rest Fenner (1817), as the firm formerly called Gale and Fenner was now known. The third was *The Statesman's Manual* (1816), to which Hazlitt devoted two strangely cruel and indiscriminate attacks in the *Examiner* (the

[1] Maturin wrote a polemical reply to C's criticism, but Walter Scott dissuaded him from publishing it. [2] "Akenside" *Lives* III 419–20.

first of which was written three months before the book was
published and before Hazlitt had seen the work), followed by a
third attack in the *Edinburgh Review*.

Finally, in July 1817, *Biographia* was published. An American
edition was published later in the year by Kirk and Mercein of
New York, presumably based on a transcript made by Launcelot
Wade, the son of Coleridge's friend Josiah Wade.[1]

Reviews were generally unfavourable, tending to concentrate—
when not speaking of Coleridge's character or his career as a
whole—on three things in particular: the lack of organisation;
Coleridge's own disparaging comments on reviewing, which naturally aroused a desire to retaliate; and finally his fondness for
metaphysics.[2] The last of these charges is almost invariably the
result not of a more sophisticated knowledge correcting Coleridge
but simply an anti-intellectual aversion to metaphysics: e.g.
". . . intermingled with such a cloudiness of metaphysical jargon
in the mystical language of the Platonists and schoolmen, of Kant
and Jacob Behmen" (*New Monthly Magazine*); "German metaphysics, or metaphysics, if possible, still more obscure . . . other
parts as unintelligible as the metaphysics" (*New Annual Register*);
and (the misspellings of the names Fichte and Schelling may be
noted) ". . . incidental criticisms upon Behmen, and Schilling, and
Fichti, and Kant, and other inscrutable thinkers" (*British Critic*).

The two most important reviews were those by John Wilson in
Blackwood's and by Hazlitt in the *Edinburgh Review* (probably
somewhat touched up by its editor, Francis Jeffrey). Both are well
known—Wilson's for its indiscriminate (and, surprising in so
intelligent a man, stupid) savagery; and Hazlitt's, however headily
perverse in places, for its verve and gusto. This latter review, by

[1] *CN* III 4179, *CL* IV 596. A 2nd
American ed was published in New
York by Leavitt, Lord, & Co (1834),
which also exists with a Boston im-
print (Crocker and Brewster) of the
same year. *C Bibl* (Haney 1903) 17
lists a third (New York 1843; no
publisher mentioned); but it has not
been located.

[2] *B Critic* NS VIII (1817) 460–81;
Literary Gazette No 29 (1817) 83–5;
M Mag XLIV (1817) 153–60; *New
Annual Register* XXXVIII (1817) 145;

New Monthly Mag VIII (1817) 50;
Portico [Baltimore] IV (1817) 417–
27; *Athenaeum* [Boston] II (1817)
65; *American Monthly Magazine
and Critical Review* II (1817) 105–
14; *Ed Rev* XXVIII (1817) 488–515;
Bl Mag II (1817) 3–18, 285–7; *M
Rev* LXXXVIII (1817) 124–38. *C Bibl*
(Haven & Adams) 30–41. Most of
the above are reprinted in *Coleridge:
the Critical Heritage* ed J. R. de J.
Jackson (1970) 294–387.

the greatest English critic of the period except for Coleridge himself, not only typifies what many of the reviewers seem to have felt and lacked the confidence and talent to say, but it is also a prototype of most of the adverse criticism of the *Biographia* from Coleridge's time to our own. Moreover, there is just enough truth in it, however reductively put, to make even the modern admirer of Coleridge smile. Hazlitt has been speaking of Coleridge's early poetic interests:

. . . Mr. Coleridge has ever since, from the combined forces of poetic levity and metaphysic bathos, been trying to fly, not in the air, but under ground—playing at hawk and buzzard between sense and nonsense,—floating or sinking in fine Kantean categories, in a state of suspended animation 'twixt dreaming and awake,—quitting the plain ground of "history and particular facts" for the first butterfly theory, fancy-bred from the maggots of his brain,—going up in an air-balloon filled with fetid gas from the writings of Jacob Behmen and the mystics, and coming down in a parachute made of the soiled and fashionable leaves of the Morning Post,—promising us an account of the Intellectual System of the Universe, and putting us off with a reference to a promised dissertation on the Logos, introductory to an intended commentary on the entire Gospel of St. John.

Finally, Hazlitt also illustrates the anti-metaphysical prejudices Coleridge had to face. For he was far more philosophically informed than any other reviewer of the book (though his reading was mainly in British philosophy from Hobbes and Locke to the close of the eighteenth century). Yet, after justly rapping Coleridge's knuckles for emphasising the priority of Descartes over Hobbes in the history of the associationist psychology, he is able to add: "As for the great German oracle Kant, we must take the liberty to say, that his system appears to us the most wilful and monstrous absurdity that ever was invented."[1] In fairness to both Hazlitt and Coleridge, however, one should remember that the personal feelings between the two men were complex, and that, within a few months after his review, Hazlitt was able to state of Coleridge, at the close of his *Lectures on the English Poets*—admittedly referring to an earlier period of Coleridge's life:

. . . he is the only person I ever knew who answered to the idea of a man of genius. . . . His mind was clothed with wings; and raised on them, he lifted philosophy to heaven. . . . That spell is broke; that time is gone for ever . . . but still the recollection comes rushing by

[1] *Ed Rev* XXVIII (1817) 491, 497.

with thoughts of long-past years, and rings in my ears with never-dying sound.[1]

After 1817 there was no further English edition of the *Bio-graphia* until thirty years later, when Sara Coleridge published the 1847 edition with which she and her late husband had hoped to rescue and justify the book. During the intervening years the charge of plagiarism had risen, and a special effort was made by Sara Coleridge to recognise Coleridge's borrowings from the German.[2] During the next fifty years after 1847, the book continued to be available through frequent reprints of this edition, in both England and America, and also through various reprintings of the Bohn Standard Library edition (1865); and it was naturally included in the *Complete Works* edited by W. G. T. Shedd (1853; reprinted 1884). At the end of this period Everyman's Library brought out an edition (1906) with an Introduction by Arthur Symons, and, far more important, the Clarendon Press issued the still memorable edition by John Shawcross (1907). The latter was the second annotated edition (the first being 1847). The third annotated edition (though it omits large sections of the book, and is essentially a selection) was prepared by George Sampson (Cambridge University Press 1920). The fourth is the revised Everyman's Library edition by George Watson (1956; further revised 1965, 1975). The present is accordingly the fifth annotated edition.

PART II

GENERAL CHARACTER AND STRUCTURE

As with most major works, the *Biographia* combines several levels of intellectual interest. In particular it is rivalled only by the Shakespeare lectures as the central work of criticism by a writer who is also one of the greatest of literary critics. Coleridge is without question the most philosophically oriented and informed critic in the English-speaking world who also (the qualification should be emphasised) possesses the close empirical sense of style for which English "poet-critics" have always been famous (from Sidney and Ben Jonson to Dryden, Johnson, Wordsworth, Arnold, and Eliot). Into the *Biographia* he funneled at least twenty years

[1] *H Works* v 167.   [2] See below, I cxv.

of speculation about the criticism and uses of poetry and about the psychology of art, enriched by his wide reading in the history of criticism from Aristotle to the end of the eighteenth century.

Because of his experience as a poet he had long believed that critical observations must rest squarely on "philosophical principles". In fact, his own judgement of the purpose and value of the *Biographia* is that it is mainly "an application of the rules, deduced from philosophical principles, to poetry and criticism". Writing this statement after the book was substantially completed, he decided to place the remark at the beginning; perhaps he was hinting gently how the *Biographia* should be approached and read. Time and again he returns to philosophy as the foundation of criticism. This hopeful return is the essence of the *Biographia*. We can remember at what an extraordinarily young age he combined philosophy and poetry, in Lamb's statement that Coleridge at Christ's Hospital was "Logician, Metaphysician, Bard!". The order of the words is significant, especially when we realise that a precocious philosopher is rarer than a precocious poet. The terse and elegant formula of Chapter 15, "No man was ever yet a great poet, without being at the same time a profound philosopher", comes appropriately just a few pages after the "philosophical chapters" are behind the reader, a groundwork hopefully laid, and the practical criticism begun.[1] Perhaps to Coleridge's own mind his highest praise of Wordsworth was that he alone seemed capable of writing "the First Genuine Philosophic Poem".[2] And when Coleridge makes his last negative comment on Wordsworth in the *Biographia* (Chapter 22), he directs it not against Wordsworth's poetry but against his critical theories, and requires a "substitution of more philosophical principles" for Wordsworth's critical "sentiments" and loose observations.[3] Aside from personal circumstances and the need to do something to escape the rut of unproductivity, this "substitution of more philosophical principles" was one of the powerful motives behind the *Biographia* in the first place. The audacity of this plan explains at once, more than anything else, the marked virtues, the profundity, and the weak spots of the book.

In contrast to the vague "spiritual Light" that Coleridge felt abiding in his own "brain marrow as visible Light appears to do in

[1] Ch 15, below, II 25–6.   [3] Ch 22, below, II 119.
[2] Ch 22, below, II 156.

sundry rotten mackerel & other *smashy* matters",[1] the idea of philosophic principles, if not the principles themselves, could act like a lens to focus and direct this higher, more diffuse "spiritual Light" that possessed "an affinity with all things".[2] In literature "the organic Whole"[3] of any work, of a Shakespearian play or a short lyric, would reveal itself to those who could fathom its secret fluid organisation and could separate—or hold in suspension long enough for examination—"the omnipresence of all in each, platonically speaking".[4] It was just this interpenetration and union of the one with the many that the "poetic imagination", the highest critical value, was to enlarge upon. It would intensify, in degree, the most pivotal and synthetic principle of philosophy, the "philosophic imagination". As Coleridge approaches the thirteenth chapter he promises that his results in the philosophical chapters so far, substantiated by the theses of Chapter 12, "will be applied to the deduction of the Imagination, and with it the principles of production and of genial criticism in the fine arts".[5] And if Coleridge, turning to a combination of empirical thought and German transcendentalism, was tacitly attempting, as he phrased it, "to complete the critical system"[6] that Kant himself admitted only to have begun, we should not disregard the Platonic element Coleridge stresses continually. The esemplastic power unifies "all in each" and arranges all ideas and expressions in one scale. Of course the hope was grandiose—to do all this and in such a short time. The *Biographia* falls short of its own projection, and Coleridge himself, later uneasy, admitted it. But to a high degree the strength of the book is due to his realisation that each step in his career stemmed from "a more thorough revolution in my philosophic principles".[7] An impartial and solid "philosophic reason, independent of all foreseen application to particular works and authors",[8] was making his *actual* applications of the greatest possible worth when finally they came, as they do come profusely in the second volume.

For help, Coleridge turned not only to the history of criticism but to the brilliant theorising about art that is one of the glories of German thought from the 1760s to the early 1800s. It attracted him profoundly. For one thing, this theorising often went hand in

[1] *CN* II 2372.
[2] Ibid.
[3] Ch 12, below, I 234.
[4] *CN* II 2372.
[5] Ch 12, below, I 264.
[6] Ch 9, headnote, below, I 140.
[7] Ch 10, below, I 205.
[8] Ch 21, below, II 110–11.

hand with the new critical philosophy. Coleridge's use of the German thinkers unfolds and multiplies insights. His curiosity and range permit us to use him for suggestions whatever our critical approach.

His admiration for the Germans was unabashed. In 1817, eighteen years after his only visit there, he still referred to Germany as "the only Country in which a man dare exercise his *reason* without being thought to have lost his Wits, & be out *of his Senses*".[1] The *Biographia* presented an opportunity to recapture and relate his own philosophic odyssey of more than twenty years, to repent for early misdirection and for "errors" nagging at his conscience, even while trying to find himself in a unique conflux of Neoplatonism, British empiricism (as he viewed it), and the new German development, so staggering in range from 1780 to 1810. All this was to be done in about eighty pages, the last thirty-five of which seem to have been dictated in three days, and directed to a general reading public. As a result he often digresses, indulges in thin humour, and apologises too much (this last had been one sharp criticism of his lectures, which only made him more nervous and apprehensive—and hence more apologetic—about the reception of anything he said). But if others had more capacity for system and planning, no one else at that time had the imaginative insight and knowledge—and if they had these also had the courage—to tackle such large philosophic subjects, especially those imported from Germany and facing an intellectual tariff barrier.

The *Biographia* was the second of Coleridge's works, after *The Friend* (1809–10), that, as John Stuart Mill later implied, opened the intellectual sights and deepened the perspective of the nineteenth-century English-speaking world. With the development of the Empire since the later seventeenth century, Britain had been hurtled into an international prominence that was inevitably mercantile, positivistic, practical. Naturally the pressures coalesced with traditional British empiricism, stretching back to William of Occam and given a stronger basis with Bacon (at least one side of Bacon), Newton, and the school of British philosophy that followed Hobbes and Locke. By Coleridge's time this quasi-mercantile, utilitarian philosophy seemed to him to be established as the prevailing, even the "official" British philosophy: associa-

1 To C. A. Tulk Sept 1817: *CL* iv 775; cf 761.

tionist in psychology (Hartley, Priestley); sceptical of the transcendental (whether Platonic or German); often naïvely materialistic, even reductionistic. He could not help thinking, too, that if one
carried it far enough, as one was obliged to carry any philosophy
to its limits, the prevailing English one would end in atheism.[1] He
felt that his native country, however sound its instincts, had developed an intellectual aversion to metaphysics and was in need of a
rescuer. He refers to his opposition as "the earth-clod philosophers". "The histories and political economy of the present and
preceding century partake in the general contagion of its mechanic
philosophy."[2] Could he not counteract this by articulating a
philosophy less materialistic and larger-minded? He could feel
qualified in his sympathies with, and had grown up in, the British
tradition. (His first son, after all, was named after David Hartley.)

If as a schoolboy he had been drawn to Plato, Plotinus, and the
Neoplatonists generally, sensing and searching after a "spiritual
Light", he could, more than anyone else, later pull together a
large part of the critical legacy of eighteenth-century English and
Scottish criticism (mainly in his approach to the imagination)
and unite it with the values and interests of German criticism and
philosophy. When we think of his relation to the eighteenth century in which he was born and grew up, we should not be misled
by his own tendency to distort and take issue with Johnson, with
whom he shared much, in the way T. S. Eliot shared much with
Matthew Arnold; or by his militant attacks on Pope and the "high
neo-classic mode", which Coleridge hastily associated with
"French" (i.e. genuinely "foreign") elitism, formalism, polish, and
lack of sincerity, all typified by his remark about the "wit-hardened
heart of Voltaire". The eighteenth century, after all, was richly
varied. Well before it produced Coleridge himself (1772), it had
already created the "romantic" interests in imagination, genius,
"passion", "natural language", suggestiveness, originality, and
sincerity that were to dominate British (and much German) thinking by the 1780s and then to continue, in an accumulative wave,
across the century line.

Whereas the late Victorians and Edwardians felt close kinship
with him ("So, then, there abide these three, Aristotle, Longinus,
and Coleridge"), it is typical of reactions to Coleridge that the

---

[1] E.g. *CL* IV 758–62 (to Lord Liverpool 28 Jul 1817).   [2] *SM* (*CC*) 28.

"New Criticism", which flourished from the 1930s to the 1960s, regarded him as one of its presiding deities. The interest of "New Criticism" in metaphor, symbol, and semantics found in Coleridge a prototype for what he was the first to call "practical criticism"— a phrase appropriated by I. A. Richards for his *Practical Criticism* (1929), which initiated the kind of close analysis of texts that we associate with both the "New Criticism" and the varieties of analytic criticism developing from it. On the other hand, the interest in the theoretical foundations of art is also in part derived from Coleridge, though we are increasingly going back to his own mentors in the Germany of 1750 to 1820, where art theory was carried further than it has ever been until very recently.

In his thirties Coleridge began to combine modern science, psychology, and insights into the human *psyche* with the classical values, exemplified above all by Plato, of permanence and ultimate significance. What gave him the immediate confidence that this was possible was his discovery of the German exploration of these subjects and interests during the later eighteenth century. Here he felt that he had at last found the key, or at least a key of sorts. The Germans, owing especially to the influence of Leibniz, had taken the developments of modern science in their stride, without losing hold either of "classical" values or (though this varied) "religious" or at least potentially religious values. In particular, the German rediscovery of Spinoza and the development of German romantic pantheism attracted him deeply.[1] German thought seemed to be doing many things at once without losing its centripetal hold on the ideals of unity to which the true philosopher, as Coleridge felt, is forever dedicated. It welcomed every discovery and nuance of science and of psychology. Above all it had evolved a new philosophy of "organicism", in which the "many" (individuality, diversity, particularity) were seen as *in process*, stemming from or evolving towards unities that themselves were in process from (or to) a higher unity. Kant especially had started to fill in an epistemology that could, as Coleridge began to view him, take much of this for granted, though he felt that Kant's "pure analysis" of "the speculative intellect alone", and not of ultimate being, was reserved and should be supplemented.

The *Biographia* is, in one of its aspects (especially in the

---

[1] This is one of the themes of Thomas McFarland's authoritative *Coleridge and the Pantheist Tradition* (1969).

"philosophical chapters"), a sort of foreshadowing of Coleridge's promised "Logosophia", the work that was to pull everything together in a consideration (ultimately religious) of the "communicative intelligence". This is one of the reasons why the *Biographia*, before he finished it, took the form that it did. It could be a testing-ground where, if mistakes were made, they would not be marring any presentation of a philosophic system or series of connected treatises. Yet there is an over-all unity to the *Biographia* to which the philosophical chapters contribute.[1]

"A TOTAL AND UNDIVIDED PHILOSOPHY"

Of the long strands of metaphysics and criticism that stretch through the *Biographia*, a crucial one is Coleridge's announcement of "a total and undivided philosophy", in which "philosophy would pass into religion, and religion become inclusive of philosophy".[2] The announcement is a climactic and, at least at first, an enigmatic one. Coming at the end of Thesis IX in Chapter 12 (and looking back to the crucial scholium for Thesis VI), Coleridge thus arrives at the "spiritual Light" shining through his system and in the last third of Chapter 12 introduces religion and God as the high-water mark of the philosophical chapters. And with the Theses originally intended to form part of the "Logosophia", Coleridge hoped the "total and undivided philosophy" would also characterise that great work, which would explain and unify, once and for all, the important elements of his thought.

The development of the philosophical chapters, from materialism and associationism to transcendentalism, ends—as Coleridge thought it should—with God. No matter in what order he wrote the *Biographia*, he arranged that the philosophy of its first volume concludes with divinity, just as the second volume builds to a crescendo in Chapter 24, with the proclamation of Christ and of God the Father, the same "great I AM" of Theses VI and IX. When some contemporaries unfairly charged Coleridge with being nothing but a religious "fanatic", they at least had identified the beginning and end of much of his endeavour. He tried to find an anchorage for his philosophy in the bottomless sea of faith. We might remember his remark in the last chapter: "Poor unlucky

---

[1] See below, I cxxxii.   [2] Ch 12, below, I 282–3.

Metaphysics! . . . A single sentence expresses the object and thereby the contents of this science . . . Know thyself: and so shalt thou know God, as far as is permitted to a creature, and in God all things".[1] There is no sense of blitheness or of avoiding an issue when he defends the proposition "that true metaphysics are nothing else but true divinity".[2] "Religion", he says in a letter of 28 July 1817, "is at all times the centre of Gravity in the machine, and with and through which Philosophy acts on the community in general".[3]

When Coleridge faces the major question in Western philosophy, crucial from Descartes to Kant and his followers—the relation between thinking (or knowing) and being—he does not view it as an easy escape to say that, "Jehovah . . . revealed the fundamental truth of all philosophy", the scripture that Coleridge insists should be read "I am in that I am".[4] Such an assumption (and all philosophers must have a first assumption) was in Coleridge's very nature. Philosophy was to go beyond "the mere reflective faculty"; it needed "to keep alive the *heart* in the *head*", just as—Coleridge confessed—the writings of Jakob Böhme and other mystics "acted in no slight degree to prevent my mind from being imprisoned within the outline of any single dogmatic system".[5]

One great hope then—and no one knew better than Coleridge how tenuous it could sound—was to provide a basic view of man, of God, and of the act of creating in general, a view, bolstered by recent discoveries in psychology and science, that could be turned directly to art and critical writing. For what, after all, was art and its criticism but the imitation and reflection of the life between man and nature, the story of the subjective mind or being as it meets and experiences the objective, created world, a universal story, yet one that each work of art transforms into a miracle of mediation by shaping and by creating anew the particulars of mind and nature themselves? Art becomes the *living* image rather than the abstract explanation of higher truths. The Scriptures contain

the living *educts* of the Imagination; of that reconciling and mediatory power, which incorporating the Reason in Images of the Sense, and

---

[1] Ch 24, below, II 240, C's n.   [4] Ch 12, below, I 275, C's n.
[2] Ch 12, below, I 291.   [5] Ch 9, below, I 152.
[3] To Lord Liverpool: *CL* IV 759–60.

organizing (as it were) the flux of the Senses by the permanence and self-circling energies of the Reason, gives birth to a system of symbols, harmonious in themselves, and consubstantial with the truths, of which they are the *conductors*.[1]

Art and metaphysics share different levels of the same framework. The "total and undivided philosophy" results from that "equatorial point" where the study of the self, of the subjective being and its reason, meets the study of nature cultivated through the senses. Art makes that "equatorial point" something concrete. It provides the physical answer, man's necessarily *creative* answer, to the metaphysical question how man and nature can be one and can be directed together, in their wild multiplicity, to a "harmonized Chaos", a meaningful universe that is the "choral Echo" or artistry of the supreme creator. Art is the "Mediatress, the reconciliator of Man and Nature".[2] Such a connection between art and philosophy at least explains why Coleridge gave the purpose of the *Biographia* as "an application of the rules, deduced from philosophical principles, to poetry and criticism". He repeats the same idea immediately before launching into the theses of Chapter 12, results of which, he says, will be applied to "the principles of production and of genial criticism in the fine arts". The "total and undivided philosophy" is a pervasive theme; for him art and aesthetic criticism become its human inspiration and finer breath.

Coleridge did not want the integrity of the total and undivided philosophy to depend wholly on a mystical bond between philosophy and religion. One had, after all, to attempt to explain why there was a creation and what was responsible for it. The whole system—with the universe it explained, including man and his art—would, in all its manifestations, be connected to the beginning, to this first spirit of creation. Since an upward tension animated the whole and irradiated from the highest good, each level of creation, each matter or life-form in nature, each faculty or power of the mind, would share this tension through all levels above it, even while serving itself as a filter through which the higher organisation illuminated the simpler minutiae of "the organic Whole". The philosophy that could affirm this schema would be one that championed "the principle of subsumption". It was one way to tackle some of the same problems Spinoza and Leibniz had faced. Subsumption, too, implied that the one (the original creator)

---

[1] *SM (CC)* 29.

[2] *CN* III 4397 f 53ᵛ; ch 24, below; *CN* III 4397 f 47ᵛ.

and the many (its creations) existed in close relation as "multëity in unity". In fact, if the system really were "total" and connected, then pantheism of some sort would be a natural, seemingly an inevitable, conclusion. At any rate, Coleridge's concern for the principle in general might best and most briefly be seen in his use of a favourite quotation from *Paradise Lost* at the beginning of Chapter 13, the opening of which gives the essence:

> O Adam, One Almighty is, from whom
> All things proceed, and up to him return,
> If not depraved from good . . .

As a principle applying to the whole cosmos and everything in it, "multëity in unity" extended to aesthetics also. Art and taste could reflect the harmony of the larger world, and this refined reflection or imitation might then be considered "the beautiful".

Coleridge took for granted the opposition of the self ("spirit" or "self-consciousness") and of nature (the objective world). The self *could* be an object, but only to itself in the original proposition, "I am". This, in fact, was why the I am—ultimately God—was the starting-point of the system. "The pith of my system", said Coleridge two years before he died, "is to make the senses out of the mind—not the mind out of the senses, as Locke did." [1]

The dialectic of matter and spirit, the "polar logic" of nature and mind, objective and subjective, gave the system great flexibility. We can think of this dialectic, with its initial stress on an *act* of intelligence that creates matter or nature, as the "dynamic" in the concept of the "dynamic philosophy". It requires a "force" or creative act to transform and to reconcile the two "halves" of the whole. The idea would bring into play Leibniz, Kant, Schelling, and others, all of whom tried to find harmony between the opposites, either by claiming it simply was pre-established, as in the case of Leibniz, or, like Schelling, by using the imagination as the unique power sharing in and building the opposites. Coleridge's aphoristic definition of the imagination is thus: "the Laboratory, in which Thought elaborates Essence into Existence".[2] Near the beginning of the *Philosophical Lectures*, Coleridge wrote:

> One cannot help thinking, provided the mind is beforehand impressed with a belief of a providence guiding this great drama of the world to its conclusion . . . that a certain unity is to be expected from the very circumstances of opposition, and that these are . . . imperfect halves, which, after a series of ages, each maturing and perfecting, are

[1] *TT* 25 Jul 1832.   [2] *CN* II 3158, III 4398.

at length to meet in some one point comprising the excellencies of both.[1]

Seen in its grander perspective, the dialectic did away with itself. It generated a synthesis and extinguished dualism. Ever since Descartes the spectre of an irreconcilable dualism had flitted in and about the halls of European philosophy, a sightless bat impossible to catch and exterminate. Kant could not even claim a clear victory. Leibniz's pre-established harmony might work, but, if so, only by *fiat*, by a sort of incantation or spell that was supposed to banish the thing. For Coleridge dualism implied a universe that was "lifeless and godless". He faults Descartes' "I think therefore I am" in Chapters 9 and 12 because it is illogical and ultimately compatible only with dualism. The dynamic nature of the total and undivided philosophy (for which Coleridge understandably gives some credit to Kant and Schelling) might at last rid the philosophic house of what Coleridge, and many others, considered a sinister pest.[2]

The dialectic surfaced as a central issue of mediaeval philosophy and engaged the "elder divines" (Donne, Jeremy Taylor, Henry More) whom Coleridge refers to with affection. The Nominalists and the Realists had debated about things and words, the material and the intellectual. They were on the track, and this explains why Coleridge occasionally stresses them. He decides himself to side with the ideal camp—or so it seems at first. At the beginning of the *Biographia* he declares that "the mind is affected by thoughts, rather than by things" and it thinks things important only "when by means of meditation they have passed into *thoughts*".[3] But in the final analysis things and thoughts join as one. That was the miracle of poetry, after all. In an important notebook entry of 1806 Coleridge speculates "Reo=reor . . . and res the second person singular of the Present Indicative" of a verb meaning "to think". The conscious self becomes an intermediary for things and thoughts, and in the self they become one. If things and thoughts had a true interpenetration, then Coleridge muses, that would be "the Iliad of Spinozo-Kantian, Kanto-Fichtian, Fichto-Schellingian Revival of Plato-Plotino-Proclian Idealism".[4] He is having some fun, but making a profound connection.

German transcendentalism promised a higher synthesis. Cole-

---

[1] *P Lects* Lect 2 (1949) 87; cf. 106–8, 116.
[2] Ch 9, below, I 145, ch 12, I 275–7, C's n.
[3] Ch 2, below, I 31; cf ch 5, I 90, ch 18, II 62.
[4] *CN* II 2784 and n.

ridge felt sure that Kant had envisioned such a major step, but one that he "either did not think it prudent to avow, or which he considered as consistently *left behind* in a pure analysis, not of human nature in toto, but of the speculative intellect alone".[1] Kant himself had said that the *Kritik der reinen Vernunft* stood only as a "*Propaideutik*", an entry-way for a larger philosophy that went beyond the theoretical and the epistemological. The second and third critiques, significantly about morality and aesthetics, provided further landing-places to a higher totality. Kant's statements about the existence of free will, immortality, and the necessity of assuming the existence of a Supreme Being—these, Coleridge felt, were of central importance. Kant's interpreters were mistakenly creating narrow and theoretical systems, dogmatic ones (as both Fichte and Schelling pointed out), quarrelling over the first critique instead of viewing it as the groundwork for a greater whole embracing morality, art and aesthetics, science, even cosmology and religion.

It was necessary, then, Coleridge said, "to complete the critical system", "to add the key-stone of the arch".[2] Fichte began to do this but had become bogged down in the idea of the Ego and saw it too much as the centre rather than as the means to a higher scheme. Kant even branded Fichte's work as "mere logic", and this was probably enough to lower Fichte in Coleridge's esteem. It is "to Schelling", says Coleridge, "we owe the completion, and the most important victories, of this revolution in philosophy".[3] Coleridge was not referring to the early Schelling of the 1790s and to the Schelling of the *System des transscendentalen Idealismus* (1800) alone. It is commonly assumed that Coleridge combines "traditional" theology with the dynamic philosophy of Schelling. This is true only if we restrict ourselves primarily to Schelling's *System* and to works of the 1790s like the *Abhandlungen*. For in Schelling's later works the ultimate ideal becomes God, is named as God. From 1802 or 1803 Schelling was moving directly in the area of that total and undivided philosophy where religion and philosophy merge. So, later in life, when Coleridge says that he must be content to remain "a high German transcendentalist", the word "high" carries significance; it implies a transcendentalism that has been carried to the extremes of development—not in narrowing its scope by quibbling over a theoretical foundation, but

---

[1] Ch 9, below, I 154.
[2] Ch 9, below, I 140, 158.
[3] Ch 9, below, I 163.

in expanding its scope to include natural science, psychology, art, and religion.

The attraction of the total and undivided philosophy was, as its name implied, that it could fulfil many ideals at once. The Platonic and Neoplatonic could find a home in the hierarchical structure, in their emphasis on the interpenetration of divinity and the good in the whole dynamic universe. The ancient dichotomy between the spiritual and the material would be transcended. The mediaeval hope of unity and the Renaissance ideal of the whole man would work hand in hand with the new discovery of the organic, and even with the most recent discussions of associationism and psychology. On another plane, the new critical philosophy from Germany realigned everything to an altered and truer bearing, correcting, so to speak, the difference between the magnetic and true north. Reason, aesthetics, even religion gained by it. The Bible, specifically the Christian faith with Christ as God's concrete and human form remaining divine even as He lived in this world, was in its own way a mythic and holy book written in symbols that explained creation, nature, God, and man in a poetic language; so it too would be included. The list becomes longer, seeming at times to hold the seeds of contradiction and even self-destruction.

Armed with the concept of the imagination, that creative and communicative power in both God and man, Coleridge hoped not so much for a facile return to God (the original and persisting union of the subjective and objective) as he did for art that reconciled the productive self with the nature it experienced and, by doing this, opened up the "organs of spirit" by providing them with symbols in concrete form. Coleridge had been developing the idea, in one guise or another, for fifteen years. The *Biographia* was partially a defence of the conduct and opinions such a life produced. On the track of the highest causes of things and of ideas, Coleridge concluded that their causes were, metaphysically speaking, identical. He was frankly trying to explain what Einstein later called the most incomprehensible property of the universe, the fact that it is so comprehensible.

Any pattern or diagram falsifies to some degree. But with the aid of a general scheme we can, at a glance, see the position of the elements of Coleridge's thought at the time he wrote the *Biographia*. Not all the relationships are, or can be, indicated. Ideally the system is organic, holistic. The lines of connection are intended to serve only as initial guides.

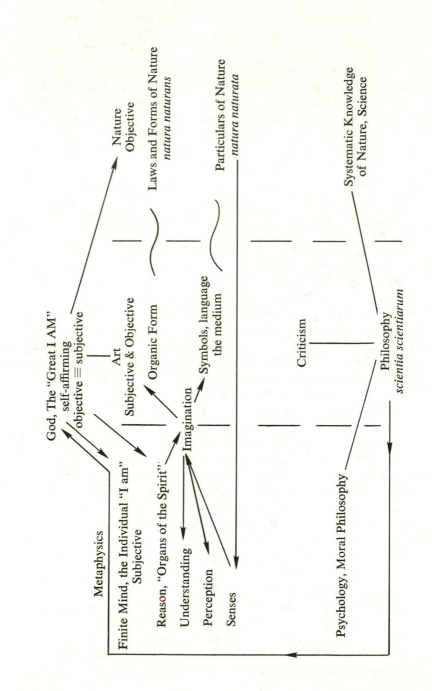

Nature
Objective

Laws and Forms of Nature
natura naturans

Particulars of Nature
natura naturata

Systematic Knowledge
of Nature, Science

God, The "Great I AM"
self-affirming
objective ≡ subjective

Art
Subjective & Objective

Organic Form

Symbols, language
the medium

Criticism

Philosophy
scientia scientiarum

Metaphysics

Finite Mind, the Individual "I am"
Subjective

Reason, "Organs of the Spirit"

Understanding

Imagination

Perception

Senses

Psychology, Moral Philosophy

The system was clearly optimistic. If nothing else, it gave mankind an important and understandable place in the cosmos. This seemed inevitable to Coleridge; the other possibility, that of being isolated, ignorant of what our knowledge meant and therefore ignorant and lost forever, was hideous and unacceptable. Such alienation and paralysis reflected, for one thing, the dejection and personal hopelessness he was trying gallantly to escape by working and producing again. That activity itself, that imagination, *was* the main reason for the bright view—man possessed a productive and creative power that could join him to the world. There was a natural correspondence between the mind and nature, symbolised in art; both mind and nature (the mind itself viewed, in fact, as part of nature) ultimately came from a primal creation. All things were seen in God, " 'in whom we live, and move, and have our being' ".[1] As imaginative acts of the mind lead us out into nature,

. . . the mind . . . then looking abroad into nature finds that in its own nature it has been fathoming nature, and that nature itself is but the greater mirror in which he beholds his own present and his own past being . . . while he feels the necessity of that one great Being whose eternal reason is the ground and absolute condition of the ideas in the mind, and no less the ground and the absolute cause of all the correspondent realities in nature. . . .[2]

THE IMAGINATION

A "synthetic and magical power"; its triple function

The total and undivided philosophy assumed, even demanded, a power to resolve the dialectic between mind and nature. This "synthetic and magical power" is inevitably the imagination, the highest degree of which is "poetic".[3] Imagination belongs neither to the purely subjective nor to the purely objective, neither to the ideal nor to the real, to the spiritual or the concrete. Reconciling and harmonising these opposites, it partakes of both. Coleridge designates it as a force or power, an energy that transforms and blends idea and image, thought and thing. It connects external nature to the acts of reflection performed by the inner life of the self-conscious mind.[4]

---

[1] Ch 12, below, i 277, C's n.
[2] *P Lects* Lect 11 (1949) 333–4; cf *CN* ii 2546.

[3] Ch 14, below, ii 16.
[4] Ch 13, below, i 299–300.

Polarities (or) opposites, whether in a magnet, a battery, or in clashing personalities, create a tension or energy between themselves. This energy itself connects the polarities and flows back and forth between them and mixes their elements.[1] The polarity of the earth as a giant magnet has itself "flipped" or reversed itself in the past because of the connecting field of energy; batteries store power and eventually run dead because of it; and individuals, as we are fond of saying, are attracted to their opposites. This fundamental principle of power joining opposites underlies the concept of the imagination as a reconciling "power". Coleridge places two quotations from Leibniz together at the beginning of Chapter 13 ("On the imagination") to draw attention to this principle. Leibniz contends that things in nature cannot account for their own being or flux. Even the "metaphysical principles" of cause and effect, action and reaction, cannot account for the full truth of corporeal things. "Some principle", says Leibniz, "superior to material mass, must so to speak be formally added. . . . This principle of things . . . is not, we should remember, to be explained only by the *idea* of powers." No. Of course not! Coleridge calls "this principle" the imagination. It connects, by an *act*, the existence of matter with the essence of ideal forms. In fact, it shapes the matter in the process of evolving an ideal or intellectual form. Therefore, "The *rules* of the IMAGINATION are themselves the very powers of growth and production."[2]

In the *Biographia* (and as a discernible tendency in his thought since shortly after returning from Germany), Coleridge sees the imagination unifying or reconciling the self and nature on three different but analogous levels. These three reconciliations are represented by perception, art, and philosophy. Each involves a mingling or union of "the individual I am" with the created universe, the work of "the infinite I AM".[3] The imagination thus performs three syntheses that are the same in *kind* but that differ in *degree*. Coleridge introduces "potence" in Chapter 12 with the hope of explaining this difference in degree within the one general activity. "First" or "second" potence, for example, would indicate the degree or level of the power. Schelling proceeded this way at times and used "*Potenz*", a term probably borrowed from Bruno through Friedrich Jacobi's *Ueber die Lehre des Spinoza*.[4]

---

[1] Ch 14, below, II 16–17.
[2] Ch 18, below, II 84.

[3] Ch 13, below, I 304.
[4] Ch 12, below, I 287; see McFarland xxxii–xxxv.

Yet Coleridge stresses that the imagination, "in all its degrees and determinations", always has certain qualities and remains one *kind* of power. It creates and communicates through symbols. Its medium, whether in perception, art, or philosophy, is symbolic in the widest sense of the word, for a symbol embodies an objective externality, a definite shape or sign of recognition that becomes identified with the internal processes of mind and feeling that it represents. These processes spring to life, they are called upon and led out into the world and become the "living *educts*" of the imagination. A symbol is also "connatural" or "consubstantial": it fuses the nature of mind with the reality of nature. Symbols are thus esemplastic, shaping into one. The symbols of perception grow so habitual that frequently we fail to regard them as symbols. But language, numbers, and mental images are all symbolic reflections of what we originally perceive. (Coleridge came to believe that our symbols of perception are constitutive with nature; they truly represent the ideal form and divine power responsible for creating nature and nature's laws.) Art is symbolic on a higher level. Its symbols represent the mind perceiving its own self in relation to nature. Finally, philosophy complements art and gives us an intellectual language or symbolism for what in art is an imagistic or material system. Coleridge might say that it is his own philosophic imagination that produced a theory and explanation of the imagination on all its levels. This is why he says, "In philosophical language, we must denominate this intermediate faculty in all its degrees and determinations, the IMAGINATION."[1]

Coleridge talks about symbols frequently. But one notebook entry may help summarise his intrinsic connection between imagination and symbol:

All minds must think by some *symbols*—the strongest minds possess the most vivid Symbols in the Imagination—yet this a *want*, ποθον, *desiderium*, for vividness of *symbol*: which has something that is *without*, that has the property of *Outness* (a word which Berkeley preferred to "Externality") can alone fully gratify even that not fully— for the utmost is only an approximation to that absolute *Union*, which the soul sensible of its imperfection in itself, of its *Halfness*, yearns after. . . .[2]

A symbol, an image, is the elemental handiwork of the imagination. A symbol is that "local habitation and a name" that gives a hint—the more vivid the better—of the higher unity between the

---

[1] Ch 7, below, I 124–5.   [2] *CN* III 3325.

self and the world. "An IDEA, in the *highest* sense of that word, cannot be conveyed but by a *symbol*".[1]

The imagination also "is at once both active and passive" on all its levels. It must receive something from nature and something from the mind's own self-reflection as well before it can produce a symbolic bond between the two. It is typical of Coleridge that to communicate this idea of the active and passive nature of the imagination he employs an image, a symbol or "emblem". His emblem is an example of his own theory that perception, art, and philosophy can aid each other to one end. "Most of my readers", he says in Chapter 7, will have perceived

a small water-insect on the surface of rivulets . . . and will have noticed, how the little animal *wins* its way up against the stream, by alternative pulses of active and passive motion, now resisting the current, and now yielding to it in order to gather strength and a momentary *fulcrum* for a further propulsion. This is no unapt emblem of the mind's self-experience in the act of thinking. There are evidently two powers at work, which relatively to each other are active and passive; and this is not possible without an intermediate faculty, which is at once both active and passive. (In philosophical language, we must denominate this intermediate faculty in all its degrees and determinations, the IMAGINATION. . . .)[2]

The two powers must be active and passive, giving and taking, relative to each other. Only in that way can the dialectic continue to work without winding down. If the power or energy flows solely in one direction—for instance, if the mind is full only of a consciousness of itself, an active tyranny of self-consideration—it will become self-enclosed and solipsistic or, if the power flows all in the other direction, the mind will become a passive automaton responding only to the stimuli of nature and circumstance. There is a mediating balance of active and passive that keeps the mind healthy because it keeps the imagination healthy. This is the key to what for centuries were referred to as the "diseases of the imagination", a gross imbalance in the mediation of self and nature, ending, as its two extremes, in either a sharp self-concentration, self-delusion, and paralysis or in an equally self-destructive disregard for one's own person. Coleridge, who himself could feel both extremes and wanted desperately—by any means available—to

[1] Ch 9, below, i 156.   [2] Ch 7, below, i 124–5.

escape their psychological rack, might have chosen Hamlet and Ophelia as examples.

When Coleridge speaks of the imagination "in all its degrees and determinations" and of "a superior degree of the faculty, joined to a superior voluntary controul over it", which is used "especially on the subject of poetry"; when he holds the "primary IMAGINATION to be the . . . prime Agent of all human Perception" and the "secondary", "differing only in *degree*", to be "an echo of the former" but now "co-existing with the conscious will" in a struggle to "idealize and to unify"; when he speaks specifically of the poet as one who puts his creative imagination "in action by the will and understanding"; when he distinguishes the "*creative words* in the world of imagination" from those that are not; and when he explains that there is a "philosophic imagination" and "a philosophic, no less than a poetic genius", he is bringing to a culmination and putting into short form scores of similar and overlapping functions of the imagination made by earlier thinkers.[1] His concepts are not original in their basic scheme (although no one made exactly the same distinctions or brought together the same terms in doing so), but they are perennially significant because they suggest so much about the relationship between perception, art, and philosophy, and unify these through the idea of the imagination as one kind of power.

We can think of Kant's reproductive, productive, and aesthetic imaginations as an immediate forerunner.[2] Schelling also divides imagination into three levels (*erste, zweite, dritte Potenz*, after the mathematical use of "power"), expressed in the *System des transscendentalen Idealismus* as roughly corresponding to perception, philosophy, and artistic creativity. Coleridge has this in mind, too. However, Kant and Schelling were indebted for their divisions of the imagination to Johann Nicolaus Tetens, the brilliant psychologist whose *Philosophische Versuche über die menschliche Natur und ihre Entwicklung* (1775–6) apportions the imagination into *Perceptionsvermögen, Phantasie,* and *Dichtungskraft.* (Kant also

---

[1] Ch 7, below, I 125; 13, I 304; 14, II 16; 22, II 129; 12, I 241; 13, I 299. These quotations contain basically all that C says in *BL* about dividing the imagination into levels or degrees.

[2] For C on the imagination and his reading in German thinkers on this subject generally see Engell *CI.*

employs some of these.) Coleridge read and annotated Tetens's *Versuche* and in a notebook remarks,

In the Preface of my Metaphys. Works I should say—Once & all read Tetens, Kant, Fichte, &c—& there you will trace or if you are on the hunt, track me.[1]

But Tetens himself relied directly, too, on someone else. As he states in a note full of praise, this is the Scot Alexander Gerard and his *Essay on Genius* (1774), widely popular in Germany. From Gerard (also a source for Kant) Tetens took the idea that genius reveals the *highest* form of imagination. Kant's "reproductive" and "productive" imaginations could be said to have their roots in Gerard's contention that genius is an especially productive and creative form of imagination. Tetens was also going back to Christian Wolff for ideas about the imagination as a power with more than one level. Wolff's *Psychologia empirica* (1732) and *Psychologia rationalis* (1734) divide the imaging power into *imaginatio*, which reproduces images, and into a separate *facultas fingendi*, which blends and joins images into new and simple wholes.

What was happening was that philosophers were expanding the rôle of the imagination to include more than its old task of the perception and retention of sense images for re-presentation. The more general *Vorstellungskraft*—as used by Tetens and others—carried this broad but not very suggestive meaning. As the eighteenth century progressed, the imagination was keeping its elementary slot in faculty psychology between the senses and the understanding, but was also being credited with artistic creativity. And when, in the 1780s and 1790s, philosophy became conscious of itself in a new way, it was inevitable that the imagination would then be credited (by Kant, but especially by Fichte and Schelling) with the productive steps necessary to create philosophy itself.

But the double or triple quality of the imagination, while strongest in Germany, where it was reinforced by the use of many varied terms—all under the umbrella of a general meaning of either *Einbildungskraft* or *Vorstellungskraft*—this double or triple quality had also permeated British thought by the end of the century. So that Thomas Reid says in 1785 that a "constant ebullition of thought" and constant motion of "sentiments, passions and affec-

[1] *CN* ii 2375.

tions . . . has, by modern philosophers, been called the *imagination*. I think it was formerly called the *fancy*, or the *phantasy*. If the old name be laid aside, it were to be wished that it had got a name less ambiguous than that of imagination, a name which has two or three meanings besides".[1] Actually, the tradition of a troikalike or at least a double-natured imagination had been in England and Scotland over a century. Hobbes, consciously using fancy and imagination as synonyms, gave fancy two rôles, one as the involuntary and immediate organiser and perceiver of separate sensory data, the other as "creator of civilization and the arts". And if Locke did not venture to discuss the arts or genius in the way Hobbes did (and as others, like Addison and Akenside, soon would), at least Locke spoke of imagination as a perceiving power that operates spontaneously but also of a "power" that "acts voluntarily" and joins simple ideas and images into larger and more complex wholes. Very likely Locke served as one source for Wolff's discussions.[2]

While Locke's followers and Berkeley continued the empirical tradition of the imagination as the "perceiver", Addison and Akenside, with more aesthetic and artistic interests, carried the imagination further into the realm of art. Addison speaks of primary and secondary pleasures of the imagination; the "primary" are essentially perceptive, the "secondary" are aesthetic with an implied creativity. Akenside's *The Pleasures of Imagination* (1744) put the imagination on a cosmic scale and gave it powers ranging from simple visual appreciation to an almost mystical communication with the creative secret of the universe. Wordsworth, in *The Prelude*, traces how the imagination grows from its earliest powers of engaging nature to the advanced stages of creating poetry and philosophy that illuminate that engagement, a topic that was a favourite one between Coleridge and him. In France, there is even a parallel to the division of the imagination into levels. Condillac, in his *Essai sur l'origine des connaissances humaines*, again sees this power really as two different functions.

If one wanted to dig back even more, as Coleridge was so fond of doing, Bacon's *Advancement of Learning* offered a clear analysis of imagination in its poetic and philosophical sides. It is here, too,

---

[1] *Essays on the Intellectual Powers of Man* IV ch 4: *Works* ed D. Stewart (1814) II 436–7.

[2] For this and the following paragraph, see Engell *CI* 17–21, 33–47.

that Matthew Arnold may have gleaned his phrase "imaginative reason".

> Neither is the imagination simply and only a messenger; but is invested with, or at least wise usurpeth no small authority in itself. . . . For we see that, in matters of faith and religion, we raise our imagination above our reason; which is the cause why religion sought ever access to the mind by similitudes, types, parables, visions, dreams. . . . Nevertheless, because I find not any science that doth properly or fitly pertain to the imagination, I see no cause to alter the former division [of man's faculties into reason and will]. For as for poesy, it is rather a pleasure or play of imagination, than a work or duty thereof. . . . As for the power of the imagination in nature . . . we have mentioned it in the doctrine *De Anima*. . . . And lastly, for imaginative or insinuative reason, which is the subject of rhetoric, we think it best to refer it to the arts of reason.[1]

Although Coleridge seems not to have been aware of the analysis of the imaginative or associative power made by Germans like Hissmann in his early history of associationism and Johann Georg Sulzer in his *Allgemeine Theorie der schönen Künste* (1771–4; 1792–9), he was familiar with all the others just mentioned. And all of them were interrelated, almost tangled, in their common sources, cross-currents, and influences. Coleridge thought of himself, in short, as one trying to bring order out of what—especially in England—seemed a long and vexed attempt to establish specific concepts and terms for what had been floating in the intellectual atmosphere without being tied to the stabilising kite-tails of adequate definitions and philosophical vocabulary. He wanted to create what Bacon lamented did not exist, a "science that doth properly or fitly pertain to the imagination".

It is hard to say which previous analyses Coleridge is reflecting most in the *Biographia*. They overlap like bricks in a wall. In wording and in concept the distinctions among the functions of the imagination made by Tetens and Schelling seem the best candidates. But here, as in many cases, if Coleridge had a main source he also had many other sources—and his own thoughts as well. He was more aware of all the degrees of imagination already detected than anyone else who had made similar distinctions. (Kant is a possible exception.) Coleridge's method here is an example of his desire to incorporate, assimilate, and clarify.

---

[1] *Advancement of Learning* bk II xii. i.

An analysis of the primary and secondary levels of imagination is the only conclusive point Coleridge salvages from the promised "deduction" of that power in Chapter 13. The "primary" imagination is the power behind what Coleridge elsewhere calls "the mystery of perception". It is "the living Power and prime Agent of all human Perception". Its synthetic power operates through the most direct contact of the mind and nature. From a series of sense images not necessarily visual the primary imagination forms an intelligible view of the world. Organising and sifting disparate sensations and stimuli, something that the senses alone could never do, it presents the self with larger units and complex associations of what we experience. We begin, as Wordsworth says, half to create what we half perceive. The subjective mind receives and acts on the separate impressions of external nature, and, operating on these, it fashions them into larger wholes. The "association of ideas" comes into play, but Coleridge warns that neither materialism nor "any possible theory of association, supplies or supersedes a theory of perception, or explains the formation of the associable".[1] It is the primary imagination that creates or repeats "in the finite mind" what we do associate, the objects and process of nature, which themselves are products of "the eternal act of creation in the infinite I AM". The bit-by-bit pattern of sensory information becomes a comprehension of the creation of God. We learn, too, the symbols of language, of music, and of facial expressions— of those things, created by others, that have merged into everyday experience. The primary imagination is spontaneous, involuntary, what Coleridge calls "the *necessary* Imagination".[2] It is a reflex or instinct of the mind and what Kant calls an empirical—as distinct from a transcendental—degree of the imagination. It "unifies" by bringing together sensory data into larger units of understanding, a process that in Coleridge parallels Kant's "unity of the manifold".

The "secondary" imagination is basically the creative or poetic imagination. Coleridge knew that using "imagination" (even when qualified by "primary") to explain perception was by no means common usage. It implied a knowledge of psychology and some sophisticated background reading on the part of his audience. So in Chapter 7 when he mentions the imagination "in all its degrees and

---

[1] Ch 8 headnote, below, I 129.   [2] See *Friend (CC)* I 440n.

determinations", he anticipates his own distinction of primary and secondary in Chapter 13 and remarks that "in common language, and especially on the subject of poetry, we appropriate the name [imagination] to a superior degree of the faculty, joined to a superior voluntary controul over it", which is another way of saying that the poetic or secondary imagination co-exists "with the conscious will". Actually, then, the distinction occurs in Chapter 7 but without the specific terms "primary" and "secondary".[1] In Chapter 13 Coleridge reiterates that this wilful and poetic imagination differs "only in *degree*" from the primary. And in the next chapter (14) he re-emphasises the instigation and control of the will, saying that, in the poet, "this power" is "first put in action by the will and understanding".[2] Related to this self-will, a true exercise or exertion, the secondary imagination limits itself to a select number of individuals. Such exclusivity bothered Coleridge, who asserts a broader *moral* sense of the heart capable of leading all individuals to a higher spiritual life and salvation. The spiritual organs show themselves first in the *moral* being and, though not equally developed in all, exist in all.[3]

The poetic or secondary imagination becomes the fullest exercise of the self and of its inner powers. It is "the free-will, our only absolute *self*", that controls and directs the creative activity of art.[4] This gives poetry—and all human creation—a moral dimension, a moral responsibility. The secondary imagination creates new images and symbols and through these it reconciles the self-conscious mind to that picture of the world already formed involuntarily and provided by the primary imagination. The process of art joins nature with the self-conscious mind in one seamless product. The common man, equipped with only the primary imagination, cannot create (although he may appreciate) this complex and richer degree of imaginative vision. This is part of Coleridge's argument against Wordsworth's "rustic" and against the language that rustics use. The best part of human language is not a product of the primary imagination, but of a "voluntary" act performed by a mind self-consciously aware of its own imaginative potential:

[1] Ch 7, below, I 125, ch 13, I 304.
[2] Ch 14, below, II 16; cf ch 18, II 64–6, on the voluntary, i.e. willed or wilful, process of composition.
[3] Ch 12, below, I 242.
[4] Ch 6, below, I 114

The best part of human language . . . is derived from reflection on the acts of the mind itself. It is formed by a voluntary appropriation of fixed symbols to internal acts, to processes and results of imagination, the greater part of which have no place in the consciousness of uneducated man . . .[1]

Then Coleridge makes an interesting qualification: "though in civilized society, by . . . passive remembrance of what they hear from their religious instructors and other superiors, the most uneducated share in the harvest which they neither sowed or reaped". That is, the primary imagination of the uneducated "rustic" supplies him with what has previously been created by the secondary imaginations of poets and creative thinkers. Thus, social implications (or rather what one inherits and cultivates in talent and genius, not in birth or wealth) become germane to any theory of language and diction.

Furthermore, as a "repetition" in the finite mind and operating in conjunction with "passive remembrance", the primary imagination, the agent of perception, basically produces a *copy* of what has been created in nature or by other individuals. Once we "perceive" or experience the *Iliad*, for example, we can more or less reproduce it, especially if gifted with a full memory. There is no originality in the primary imagination; it repeats and copies. But the secondary or poetic imagination "dissolves, diffuses, and dissipates" what has been perceived "in order to recreate", "to idealize and to unify". The secondary imagination produces a true *imitation*, not a mere copy. This distinction, again, holds an essential key to understanding Coleridge's theory of productivity and originality in the arts. The contrast between copy and imitation, essentially reflecting the distinction between the primary and secondary imagination, thus becomes crucial for an understanding of the controversy with Wordsworth and the question of poetic language.

Coleridge reminds us that the primary and secondary imaginations are still of one "kind". They are not independent. The secondary imagination must rely on the primary or "necessary" imagination for its raw materials. In this sense it is an "echo" of the primary. It takes the perceptions supplied by the more basic primary imagination and reconciles these perceptions with the full mind, not just with the understanding, but with the "self-circling

[1] Ch 17, below, II 54.

energies of the reason", with "the whole man". The primary
imagination serves as a foundation in the way that primary grades
precede secondary schools. The primary imagination is more
"primitive", that is, it must come first ("primary colors" are an
example). There is a chronological implication too. The poet's
mind must grow from the primary to the secondary; and, this is
one theme in Wordsworth's *Prelude*, the growth of creative and
productive powers is built upon the earlier powers of perception
and realisation. The poet's secondary imagination permits him to
be, in the old cliché (popular during the Renaissance), "a second
maker under Jove" who creates—as Kant says in the *Kritik der
Urtheilskraft*—a second nature, a new world.[1]

"There is," Coleridge says also, "a philosophic, no less than a
poetic genius, which is differenced from the highest perfection of
talent, not by degree but by kind".[2] And, though he distinguishes
the imagination as either primary or secondary, he speaks earlier
of the imagination "in *all* its degrees and determinations" and calls
the poetic imagination "a [not "the"] superior degree" of that
faculty. In fact, Chapters 12 and 13 are filled with hints concerning
a *"philosophic consciousness"*. Whatever else is involved, this
philosophic consciousness or philosophic imagination relies on (or
actually is) a form of intuition directed inward to the conscious
self. It is essentially a transcendental power of which the object and
the "sources must be far higher and far inward". The philosophic
imagination becomes at one point the equivalent of "the sacred
power of self-intuition", one version of the command "Know
thyself", in which "intuitive knowledge" of the world comes to the
self "by contemplating intuitively" its own consciousness in relationship to nature.[3] Realising that the self and nature are constitutive in the laws of their being, the self-conscious mind will then
discover that in contemplating itself in relationship to nature it has
been contemplating nature itself, and not just nature but the
process and form of nature, its living principles of *natura naturans*;
for all knowledge rests in a meeting of subjective and objective.

Just as "the armed vision" is a powerful form of perception
magnifying the razor's edge until it looks like a saw, so "the
ascertaining vision" of philosophy unlocks the processes and forms

---

[1] § 49.
[2] Ch 12, below, I 241, ch 13, I
299–300.

[3] Ch 12, below, I 239–41, ch 13, I
299.

of the self-conscious mind and consequently of nature as well.[1]
It was just this ascertaining vision, something not quite like either
the "armed vision" of perception or the "poetic" vision of a damsel
with a dulcimer, that Wordsworth seemed to possess. So Coleridge
proclaims Wordsworth capable of writing "the first genuine philosophic poem", and in discussing "the highest and intuitive knowledge" in Chapter 12 he describes it by using Wordsworth's line

> The vision and the faculty divine.

When Coleridge quotes this a second time,[2] there again is the
implication that this special vision may accompany poetic genius
(as it does in Wordsworth) but is not to be equated with it.

We might tentatively interpret Coleridge's scattered references
to a philosophic imagination in the following way. This level of
imagination gives us an understanding of ideas either by intuiting
these ideas or by receiving them from an intuitive reason and then
transferring them to the understanding. This process is the ideal
counterpart of the way in which the primary imagination gives us
an awareness of nature experienced through our senses. It operates
on ideas in the same way that the primary imagination operates on
sense impressions. The philosophic imagination works through "all
the organs of spirit" that "are framed for a correspondent world
of spirit".[3] (These spiritual organs suggest not only reason but the
long-established concept of "inner sense", Leibniz's "sens interne",
used by Kant, Schelling, and others.) Even Locke had not denied
the possibility of intuitive knowledge. And the passage from *Paradise Lost* that Coleridge is fond of quoting, and uses to begin
Chapter 13, ends with a scale of being that aspires to a place

> whence the soule
> Reason receives, and reason is her being,
> Discursive, or Intuitive . . .

It is in reference to this quotation earlier in Chapter 10 that Coleridge proclaims, with a tone of hopeful prophecy, that "Philosophy
has *hitherto* been DISCURSIVE", the implication being that with
a new philosophy, with transcendentalism in particular, philosophy
will become, at least in one of its aspects, intuitive.[4] The ideas

---

[1] Ch 7, below, I 118, ch 12, I 239.   [3] Ch 12, below, I 242.
[2] Ch 18, below, II 60.   [4] Ch 10, below, I 174, C's n.

that the mind receives and that are made intelligible to it through
the philosophic imagination permit it to see nature as the symbolic
work of an imaginative Creator. And so the philosophic imagination shapes ideas and forms them into a large unity.

Such a philosophy, the equatorial point of all subjectivity and
all objectivity, thus emerges from a reconciliation brought about
by a philosophic imagination. By penetrating the spirit of nature
and approaching the source of all creativity, the speculative intellect leads to God, and philosophy to religion. This had already
been suggested by Coleridge in a note for a lecture on Shakespeare,
in which he says that imagination at last will "produce that ultimate
end of human Thought, and human Feeling, Unity and thereby the
reduction of the Spirit to its Principle & Fountain, who alone is
truly *one*".[1] The final significance is religious. The process of the
imagination, of the encounter between mind and nature, between
the mind and its own "inner nature", results in a confrontation
with the creative force of the cosmos.

In looking at objects of Nature while I am thinking, as at yonder moon
dimglimmering thro' the dewy window-pane, I seem rather to be
seeking, as it were *asking*, a symbolical language for something within
me that already and forever exists, than observing any thing new. Even
when that latter is the case, yet still I have always an obscure feeling
as if that new phaenomenon were the dim Awaking of a forgotten or
hidden Truth of my inner Nature/ It is still interesting as a Word, a
Symbol! It is Λογος, the Creator! ⟨and the Evolver!⟩ [2]

Just as Coleridge criticised the mechanical philosophers and
mere logicians for their "notions" and for their "impressions, ideas,
sensations", he realised that the philosophic imagination, with its
power of self-intuition, had to be rescued from an abstract plane
of words, of idealism without a corresponding realism. It had no
direct contact with experience of the world in a sensuous and
empirical way. That was the trouble with Fichte—in his system
self-intuition and philosophic imagination dominated too much and
created a "crude egoismus" without reference to a real nature,
without the *Naturphilosophie* that Schelling offered as a necessary
supplement. Fichte's system of idealism showed "a boastful and
hyperstoic hostility to N A T U R E", indicating that the philosophic
imagination could not stand alone.[3]

[1] *CN* iii 3247.   [3] Ch 9, below, i 158–9.
[2] *CN* ii 2546.

Here, again, the mediation of art and of the poetic imagination enters. The imitation that is art (and is there not, as Coleridge asked, a connection between imitation and imagination?) combines sensuous experience and matter with the forms and intuitions of the self-conscious mind. In other words, the poetic imagination stands between and connects—it provides the only true link between—the "primary" imagination, our outward perception, and the philosophic imagination, our inner intuition. It symbolises them together in art, which is accessible to everyone's perception. The creative imagination of art becomes a completing power. It is synthetic in the highest sense. The synthesis of syntheses, it reconciles the products of perception with those of inner perception or intuition, consciousness with self-consciousness, and the whole mind—on every level—with the whole of nature, a symbolic presence itself, the artwork of God.[1]

Definite similarities exist between this view of the philosophic imagination in Coleridge (and his relating of this level of imagination to perception, art, and religion) and the concept of "intellectual intuition" or "productive" imagination in Schelling. The similarities are strong especially if we include not only the *System des transscendentalen Idealismus* but go beyond this to Schelling's *Vorlesungen über die Methode des akademischen Studiums* (1802), the *Philosophie der Kunst* (1802), *Fernere Darstellungen* (1803), *Philosophie und Religion* (1804), and his contributions to the *Jahrbücher der Medicin als Wissenschaft* (1806). Schelling's levels (*Potenzen*) of the imagination find a parallel in Coleridge's. For Schelling these three *Potenzen* are the sensuous or perceptive, the productive or the intellectual, and the aesthetic or artistic. But the separate perceptive and artistically creative rôles of imagination were well established before either Coleridge or Schelling, as we have seen. Furthermore, Schelling cannot be credited with the concept of "the philosophic imagination". Kant suggested it, or rather brought up the subject of intellectual intuition, but does not rely on it in any definite way. The intuition that the individual has of his inner self—according to Kant—gives him only a picture of

---

[1] In this context we might remember Goethe's lines:

Wer Wissenschaft und Kunst besitzt, hat auch Religion;
Wer jene beide nicht besitzt, der habe Religion!

Who has science and art has also religion;
Who neither has, let him have religion!
Zahme Xenien ix: *Gedichte aus dem Nachlass*

what he seems to be to himself, not what he really is. There is no guarantee of knowledge. However, as a *transcendental* concept (this is stressed by Coleridge in Chapter 12), the philosophic imagination, the power of "self-intuition", could be said to originate with Kant. Then it is Fichte, not Schelling, who capitalises on it and makes it the central organ of his own philosophy. At the expense of the perceptive, but especially at the expense of the artistic or aesthetic, imagination, Fichte places the philosophic imagination on a singularly high pedestal and proclaims that only those who have it can even understand and appreciate what it is. It is interesting, too, that although Coleridge relies on Schelling in Chapter 12 and at the beginning of Chapter 13 he seems, at the point where Chapter 13 breaks off and the letter from "a friend" intervenes, to be turning more to Fichte for help in the philosophical deduction of the imagination. Schelling himself, after all, had been a disciple of Fichte's throughout the mid-1790s, and much of Schelling's concept of a productive and philosophical imagination, and of intellectual intuition, came from Fichte and had its first roots in Kant.

Though the philosophic imagination was a natural product of transcendentalism, Coleridge felt he was also reaching back farther.[1] Religious figures had always spoken of intuitions or visions. Milton endorsed intuitive reason, and Bacon recognised "imaginative or insinuative reason", a close approximation of intuition, as well as religious visions transmitted by the imagination. Certainly the idea of intuition and its connection with the imaginative faculty was old. It was one of the attractions of Plotinus for Coleridge, and he turns to Plotinus in Chapter 12 when he introduces and names the philosophic imagination. In the passage Coleridge cites and translates from the *Enneads*, the key is intuition, and Coleridge thinks of it as a "sacred power". Our intuitions, our philosophic imaginations, meet the divine on a middle ground where the divine chooses to appear to us. This is the message of the lines from Synesius that form the third epigraph to Chapter 13. So while the immediate stimulus of the concept of the "philosophic imagination" is German transcendentalism, originally for Coleridge, as long ago

[1] The phrase "philosophic imagination", not uncommon, occurs in Gerard's *Essay on Genius* (1774), but the transcendental treatment of it was something new.

as Christ's Hospital days, his stream of thought went back through the centuries.

THE DISTINCTION BETWEEN FANCY AND IMAGINATION

No aspect or subject of Coleridge's criticism is more famous than this distinction.[1] Even readers unfamiliar with his critical writing know that he made the distinction. In countless books and articles it is mentioned, interpreted, and reinterpreted. Its background—for there is a considerable background—has been less clear. One reason is that the distinction between fancy and imagination as Coleridge made it (and as it was made by those of his immediate predecessors and contemporaries on whom he drew) is almost the reverse of that found in classical and mediaeval thought, and which, in fact, persisted into the eighteenth century. In this older distinction, the Greek *phantasia*, with its suggestion of a free play of mind, was the higher or more creative power. The Latin *imaginatio*, with its stress on the concrete and sensory (from the root-word "image"), was the inferior power.[2] We still find echoes of this as late as the early 1800s.[3]

Two factors explain the reversal. At the height of seventeenth-century rationalism, *phantasia* with its related words, because of the freer play of mind connoted, was especially an object of rationalistic distrust. It became associated with chimeras, unrealistic fantasies. Meanwhile British psychological empiricism, with its potential distrust of all except the sensory, increasingly found in "imagination" a ready term for the mind's reception and modification of the sensory. Indications that, in England, "imagination" was becoming the more comprehensive and serious word are found in Dryden's letter to Sir Robert Howard prefatory to *Annus Mirabilis* (1667), Shaftesbury's *Characteristics* (1711)—in a passage Coleridge possibly echoes (see below, I 84)—and in John-

[1] For more detailed discussion of the subject, especially the German uses of the distinction, see Engell *CI* 172–83, 211, 274.

[2] See e.g. Murray Wright Bundy *Theory of Imagination in Classical and Mediaeval Thought* (Urbana, Ill 1927) 34–6, 140–1, 192–5, 277–8.

[3] An example in Germany would be J. P. Richter *Vorschule der Aesthetik* (1804) §§ 6–8 and, in England, William Taylor *British Synonyms Discriminated* (1813).

Biographia Literaria

son's *Dictionary* (1755). Several remarks could be cited to show
that by the 1780s, as James Beattie said, "According to the common use of words, Imagination and Fancy are not perfectly
synonymous"—the first being applied to stronger, "more solemn"
exertions of mind, and "the latter to the more trivial": [1] a remark
that Hester Thrale Piozzi, in her *British Synonymy* (1794), confirms and elaborates.[2] Nor is it only popular speech alone that
reflects the widening difference in the terms. William Duff's *Essay
on Original Genius* (1767) analyses the two concepts in a way that
begins to approach Coleridge. "Fancy", like "wit", is an unusually
lively form of association, whether of ideas or images; while
"imagination" is "inventive and plastic".[3] Duff's distinction is
further developed by Dugald Stewart (1792), who conceives
"imagination" as a comprehensive function of mind that combines
"fancy" with "conception", "abstraction", and "judgment or
taste".[4]

In criticism there is often an implied distinction like that found
in John Moir's *Gleanings; or, Fugitive Pieces* (1785). Fancy, he
says, does not feign objects "unknown to the senses" but is concerned with "embellishing them . . . connecting them . . . disposing
them in attitudes and groups" and giving "arrangements" and
"new combinations". It is the imagination, however, that actually
"creates or fabricates".[5]

Until a few of these previous distinctions in England were called
to Coleridge's attention (mainly by Wordsworth's 1815 Preface),
he does not seem to have been conscious of them, though he had at
one time or other read most of the authors cited above. Yet he
implies that he had always avoided claiming originality for his
own distinction, remarking in the *Biographia* that "There was a
time, certainly, in which I took some little credit to myself, in the
belief that I had been the first of my countrymen, who had pointed
out the diverse meaning of which the two terms were capable".[6]
"*Of my countrymen*" is the deliberate and important qualification.
He obviously has in mind—and had in mind from the first time he
had made his distinction—that there were earlier ones in other

---

[1] James Beattie *Dissertations Moral and Critical* (1783) 72.
[2] See J. Bullitt and W. J. Bate *MLN* LX (1945) 8–15; and Engell *CI* 174–6.
[3] Pp 6–7, 52, 70–1, 89.

[4] *Elements of the Philosophy of the Human Mind* (1792) 284–5, 305–9, 477.
[5] I 107.
[6] Ch 4, below, I 85–6.

countries. He mentions first the Latin and the latinised Greek, *imaginatio* and *phantasia,* and himself points out this distinction and its "reversed" effect in Ludovico Vives.[1] The distinction runs back at least to Boethius and Macrobius. It can be found in writers like Froissart. In all these, as we have noted above, *imaginatio* is usually the power of recalling images not present to the senses and *phantasia* is given the more active and creative rôle.

But in Chapter 4 Coleridge also mentions that German, as a "homogeneous" language, maintains a distinctness of terms. And in a number of German thinkers Coleridge encountered a wealth of distinctions between imagination and fancy, relatively recent and relatively consistent with each other, and all giving imagination the more creative rôle and fancy the important but basically inferior power of selecting and connecting images without actually creating new ones. These German distinctions aided Coleridge to make his own.

The German distinctions are naturally complicated (and enriched) by the multiplicity of terms used for "imagination" and "fancy". Aside from *Einbildungskraft* and *Phantasie,* German thinkers employed *Vorstellungskraft* (and *Wiedervorstellungskraft*), *Perceptionsvermögen, Dichtkraft* (and *Dichtungskraft* or *Dichtungsvermögen*), *Fassungskraft,* and adjectives qualifying the general power of imagination as *reproduktive, produktive,* or *ästhetische.* These adjectives for imagination often lead to a distinction between what others, not employing them, meant by distinguishing fancy from one or more levels of the imagination. In other words, the problem is semantic as well as conceptual. Yet, in a way that attracted Coleridge, the thinking behind these terms is often nuanced and exact, or tries to be, and produces deep psychological and philosophical implications with potentially rich uses for the arts and criticism.

However, as early as 1772, with Ernst Platner's *Anthropologie für Aerzte und Weltweise,* there is a general drive to simplify the welter of terms, increasingly confusing as well as insightful, and to rely more heavily on the two words *Phantasie* (for fancy) and *Einbildungskraft* (for imagination). There are exceptions—for example, Tetens. But by the 1790s *Phantasie* and *Einbildungskraft* emerge as the most common, and also as the most commonly

[1] Ch 5, below, I 99.

contrasted or differentiated terms. This is partially owing to the
rise of transcendental philosophers, who did not have as much use
for the *Dicht-* terms associated primarily with art, or for words,
like *Fassungskraft*, that could recall empirical psychology on its
own terms.

When Christian Wolff distinguished between *imaginatio* and the
facultas fingendi in his works of the 1730s (especially the *Psychologia empirica* and the *Psychologia rationalis*), he reverted to
the older use of *imaginatio* simply as the power of supplying and
reordering images already experienced. The *facultas fingendi* is, on
the other hand, creative. His distinction really amounts to what
later thinkers would distinguish as *Phantasie* (Wolff's *imaginatio*,
which works with *phantasmata* and connects and rearranges them)
and *Einbildungskraft* in the creative sense (Wolff's *facultas
fingendi*). Extremely popular throughout the century, Wolff stood
as a turning-point in reversing the older classical and mediaeval
distinction. He does not merely imply a difference in his terms but
is at pains to explain it.

In his *Philosophische Versuche*, Tetens equates *Phantasie* and
Einbildungskraft, but only superficially. Because he recognises
levels of the imagination (his most general term for the combined
general power of all imagination and fancy actually is *Vorstellungskraft*), he also distinguishes between *Phantasie* and *Perceptionsvermögen* and between *Phantasie* and *Dichtungskraft*. *Phantasie*
newly arranges the images that perception provides, whereas
Dichtungskraft creates new ones altogether. "Fancy" thus becomes
an intermediate power positioned above a perceiving imagination
and below a creative one. For the idea of imaginative genius that
adds body to this distinction, Tetens, as we have noted, credits
Alexander Gerard's *Essay on Genius*.

In 1772, the year Coleridge was born, Ernst Platner made a
remarkable and clear-cut distinction between *Phantasie* and *Einbildungskraft*, the words that were to gain such currency in the
1790s and afterward. Platner's distinction is of special importance
for several reasons: (1) It predates Tetens's distinction by four or
five years and Gerard's *Essay* by two. (Platner may have read
William Duff's 1767 *Essay on Original Genius*.) (2) Platner extends
his distinction beyond the more purely psychological interests of
Wolff. (3) Coleridge read the *Anthropologie für Aerzte und
Weltweise* (1772), the popular book in which Platner makes his

distinction.[1] (4) Platner, like Tetens, discernibly influenced Kant and the philosopher-critics of the last twenty-five years of the eighteenth century and of the early 1800s. For example, Fichte made extensive notes on Platner's *Philosophische Aphorismen* (1776).

For Platner, *Phantasie* is a presentation, a "mechanical" association and juxtaposition of images that does not transform them. It is relatively ungoverned by fact or reality. *Einbildungskraft* is the mother of creative invention because it creates compact clusters of associations—it makes them seamless (the literal meaning of *dichten* that lies behind the *Dicht-* terms used for the creative imagination)—so that a new unity and new images are formed by a melting or fusing process. First, then, "The presentation of ideas [or images] without reference to reality and without the test of possibility, verisimilitude, and proportion is fancy." Platner continues, "I distinguish the imagination from fancy on good grounds". Whereas fancy "occurs by the law of mechanical association", there comes a point when the associations (the "objects") are so packed together that "by gradual compounding or cohesiveness", new wholes are formed. This is the work of the imagination and shows "more genius" than the products of fancy, which rely on images experienced and then "exactly [and selectively] remembered". Fancy is the more mechanical operation. Useful in itself, ✓ especially for comic writers, it provides image combinations that the imagination then joins into new and *lively* wholes. Fancy deals mechanically with "objects" according to the law of association. Imagination unifies and is a vital (*lebhaft*), living power.[2]

For Maass *Einbildungskraft* has two levels, its "widest meaning" in the act of perception and its higher stage of chemical-like mixture and creativity (similar to Friedrich Schlegel's *chemischer Witz*, Thomas Brown's "chemistry of mind", and later J. S. Mill's "mental chemistry"). Maass places *Phantasie* between these two levels. Fancy can alter images but cannot unify them into one new simple image or symbol. Maass's distinction appears in his *Versuch über die Einbildungskraft* (1792, 1797), which Coleridge draws on in Chapters 5–7.

With Kant, the usual approach is to equate his "reproductive imagination" with fancy and his "productive imagination" with

[1] See *CL* iv 613 (late Dec 1815).   [2] *Anthropologie* (1772) 159, 262–3, 276.

the creative power. (There is much truth to this, especially since Schelling, following Kant, calls *Phantasie* reproductive and *Einbildungskraft* productive.) But if we look beyond the *Critiques*, we find that Kant does distinguish *Phantasie* from *Einbildungskraft*. This is in the *Anthropologie in pragmatischer Hinsicht*. Coleridge owned and annotated the 1798 edition and also annotated J. H. Green's copy of the 1800 edition.

Here again, Kant speaks of a productive imagination in contrast to a derivative and reproductive one. But imagination, "in so far as it presents images spontaneously, is called fancy [*Phantasie*]". He goes on to speak of a creative imagination (differing from the productive), which also is distinguished from fancy in a similar way. We have control over the imagination and "we often play with imagination". But fancy is not under our control and "plays ... with us": "aber die Einbildungskraft (als Phantasie) spielt eben so oft und bisweilen sehr ungelegen auch mit uns". Yet it proves increasingly difficult to disentangle Kant's terms, for—like Fichte—he mentions a creative imagination again (*schöpferische Einbildungskraft*) and then equates this, in at least one instance, with fancy! ("Phantasie, d.i. schöpferische Einbildungskraft").[1]

Schelling follows in a slightly different vein. Among the Schelling works Coleridge read, the *Darstellung meines Systems* (1801) connects the imagination with reason and with the active forming and perfecting of art. Fancy, more in tune with reproductive faculties and with the understanding, nevertheless provides for art an "intellectual intuition", presumably as a kind of groundwork or basis for the work of the imagination. Another way to look at this reminds us of earlier distinctions: fancy provides the raw materials that imagination then shapes into works of art.[2] In addition to these important distinctions, Fichte, Schiller, and Goethe all tend to separate fancy from imagination. Fichte essentially denigrates fancy; Schiller and Goethe follow more nearly the line represented by Platner, Tetens, Kant, Maass, and Schelling.

It is the distinctions of these five writers that bear most similarity to Coleridge's. He had read them all and found a sophisticated

1 *Anthropologie in pragmatischer Hinsicht* (1800) pt I bk I §§ 28–9 (pp 80ff), § 31 (p 93). Kant makes essentially the same point, with reference to Alexander Gerard, in *Menschenkunde oder philosophische Anthropologie: Nach handschriftlichen Vorlesungen* ed F. C. Starke (Leipzig 1831) 107–8.

2 Schelling *SW* IV 115n, V 393–6, esp 395.

series of distinctions showing only marginal differences. With the exception of Maass, the words used by these writers are *Phantasie* and *Einbildungskraft*. Fancy is "mechanical", deals with "objects", and follows the rules of association. *Einbildungskraft*, more specifically a creative level of imagination, is a living and productive power that deliberately shapes a new object or image that is unified and original, still possessing a sense of reality often lacking in the realm of fancy. Fancy tends, with its comparisons and comic incongruities—with its delight in difference thrown together in a heterogeneous way—to be the mainspring of wit and humour. Imagination creates metaphor and symbol by a unifying metamorphosis. It is a characteristic of genius.

Following the general trend in the distinction that is represented by Platner and Tetens, and later by Kant (though in Kant to a less clear extent), Maass, and Schelling, Coleridge selects points of his own on which to lay particular stress. Fancy still deals with "fixities and definites" and, like memory, receives "its materials ready made from the law of association", but "is blended with, and modified by that empirical phenomenon of the will, which we express by the word CHOICE".[1] (It is the element of "choice" that distinguishes fancy from the extreme it would otherwise become, "delirium".) This "faculty of choice (*Germanice*, Willkür)"[2] apparently means a conscious choice, at least in *artistic* works that are fanciful. For example, Otway's "Lutes, lobsters, seas of milk, and ships of amber" is a deliberately chosen series of images associated in some special, even idiosyncratic way by the author's mind.[3] We can recall Coleridge's remark in Chapter 24 that our fancy is "always the ape, and too often the adulterator and counterfeit of our memory".[4] The imagination, however, in creating new wholes, *wills* them into being, designs their totality, and acts not as an "empirical phenomenon" but as a conscious desire for something not yet in existence, something to be created that, by definition, cannot be subject to choice, which selects and combines images from those already perceived. (Schelling, in the *System*, had thus given the will an important part to play in the productions of artistic genius.)

In short, Coleridge wanted to stress that fancy is tied to sensory

[1] Ch 13, below, I 305.
[2] Ch 12, below, I 293.
[3] Ch 4, below, I 84.
[4] Ch 24, below, II 235.

experience. It can aggregate and combine only what it has received. The choice of what it uses may be deliberate but it is
limited, empirically, by what we can remember that we have perceived or experienced. Fancy may produce unreal or impossible
combinations, but their component parts will all be part of the
experienced world. The rules of fancy are "from the law of association"; those of the imagination "are themselves the very powers
of growth and production".[1]

POETIC LANGUAGE AND THE CRITIQUE
OF WORDSWORTH

The whole discussion of the language of poetry and the critique of
Wordsworth is a section of which Coleridge was justly proud. It
was written with ease and fluency, and we do not face the need,
as we so often do in the difficult earlier chapters, to turn to
Coleridge's other writings for supplementary help in filling out
interstices or explaining what he leaves incomplete or ambiguous.
As a result, readers for generations have naturally been tempted
to view this entire section as a relatively self-contained unit, and
parts of it have been repeatedly excerpted and anthologised with
the confidence that they are reasonably self-explanatory. Within
limits this confidence is justified. But we should stress that these
famous chapters on poetic language and on Wordsworth in particular, even though they were written before the "philosophical
chapters", are nonetheless an extension—an application both theoretical and practical—of the larger premises of the book as a
whole, and that the earlier chapters were inserted not as an after-
thought to a work already viewed by Coleridge as self-sufficient but
as an attempt to provide a broader foundation and a richer background to what he had already written. In doing this he was
fulfilling the intention he had expressed years before to Humphry
Davy (9 October 1800) to write "an Essay on the Elements of
Poetry" of such range of implication that it "would in reality be
a *disguised* System of Morals & Politics".[2]
    The fundamental premise is already implied in the discussion of
Coleridge's ideal of "the undivided philosophy": the essence of
human experience is an active and productive co-operation of the

---

[1] Ch 13, below, I 305, ch 18, II 84.   [2] *CL* I 632.

perceiving (and conceiving) mind with the given data of what is external to us. In this co-operation, through what Keats called "a greeting of the spirit", we have in miniature (in and through the "finite mind") an activity analogous to the eternal act of creation itself—as Coleridge says at the close of Chapter 13—emanating from the "infinite I A M": in short, an extension or "echo", in the finite and specifically human realm, of the creative process of nature. Poetry (and, for that matter, art generally) is a uniquely and profoundly human expression of this greeting and union of the *Ich bin* with the *Es gibt*. Specifically relevant at this point is the famous opening of Coleridge's Schellingesque "On Poesy or Art": [1] that art, in its broadest sense, is "the mediatress between, and reconciler of, nature and man", involving "the power of humanizing nature, of infusing the thoughts and passions of man into every thing which is the object of his contemplation; color, form, motion, and sound, are the elements which it combines, and it stamps them into unity in the mould of a moral idea".[2] Language, especially (as an even more distinctively and elaborately human construct than our perception of colours and shapes used in the visual arts or our perception of the sounds used in music), involves this "infusion" of the human—presenting, in itself, a kind of "second nature", different from the primary nature external to us; and what is true of language generally is far truer of the language of *poetry*.

Hence the essence of Coleridge's approach to the subject, and of the critique of Wordsworth's theory, is to be found in Coleridge's crucial distinction between "copy" and "imitation": an approach that is not only congenial to but seminal for concepts and studies of poetic language and metrics during the generation since World War II.[3] For Coleridge the essential flaw in Wordsworth's theory —the disagreement he had resolved back in 1802 to "get to the bottom of"—is that Wordsworth is regarding the language of poetry as, in effect, a "copy", a reproduction of ordinary speech. On the contrary, it is a form of "imitation". The distinction is radical. For an indispensable element in all genuine "imitation", as contrasted with mere "copy", is an "acknowledged sense of differ-

---

[1] This essay, posthumously published with that title, was actually a notebook entry dated 10 Mar 1818 (*CN* III 4397); it was much added to and altered in *LR* I 216–20. See *CN* III 4397n.

[2] *PA: BL* (1907) II 253.

[3] See Emerson Marks *Coleridge on the Language of Verse* (Princeton, N.J. 1981) 42–59.

ence", in the materials and indeed the entire nature of the medium, from what is being "imitated". The emerging "form" of these different materials will proceed in and from them (from the "multëity", in other words, provided by the medium itself) rather than be something "superimposed", as is futilely attempted in a mere "copy". Moreover, the human mind in confronting a true "imitation" is able to proceed creatively—moving from the "acknowledged sense of difference" toward the sense of "sameness" or, in other words, from diversity to unity. In a "copy" this procedure is reversed. As in wax-figures or a "marble peach" we start with a mistaken sense of "sameness" and then, as we consider the work more closely, begin to note difference. Hence the disappointment felt as we move from unity (or rather a spurious form of unity) or from "sameness" to "difference". "Imitation", both in itself and in its effect on the mind, presents development, and also arouses the sense of development in the observing imagination, whereas "copy" produces the opposite effect.

To sum up: as speech itself is not a "copy" but an "imitation" of human thoughts and feelings expressed in words, so a poem is not a "copy" but an *imitation* of ordinary human utterance. Poetry is speech raised and transformed into something else, which, as Coleridge had said long ago to William Sotheby (1802), necessitates "some new combination of Language, & *commands* the omission of many others allowable in other composition".[1] Coleridge's discussion of metre is part and parcel of his general approach to poetic expression as a form of creative *mimesis*.

With this broad premise in mind—a premise that underlies much of the semantic, structuralist, and metrical analysis of the past generation—we may quickly touch on the principal points of Coleridge's discussion. Of special interest is the norm for the language of poetry implied throughout the three opening chapters (14–16) and ramified throughout the following three before Coleridge turns more specifically to Wordsworth's actual practice as a poet. It is a norm at once classical (even Aristotelian), oriented to Shakespeare and the Renaissance, and expressive of the later eighteenth-century and Romantic ideal that looks back nostalgically to the Renaissance (in England specifically the Elizabethan period and the earlier seventeenth century) as a golden age of poetic

[1] *CL* ii 812.

language. The values associated with it are naturalness, simplicity, compatibility with "good sense", cleanliness of idiom, united with metaphoric strength and "passion" and freedom from anxiety for novelty of expression. It could be described by a combination of two phrases: Spenser's remark about Chaucer, which critics from Johnson to Coleridge applied to Spenser's own age, a "well of English undefiled"; and Milton's ideal of poetry, which Coleridge is fond of quoting—"simple, sensuous, and passionate". Much the same values are championed a generation later by Matthew Arnold in contrasting the "classical" and the "modern", and again by the "High Modernist" mode associated with Pound and Eliot in contrasting eighteenth- and especially nineteenth-century idioms of poetry with those of pre-1660 England (pre-"dissociation of sensibility").

The norm, in short, is conservative in the best sense, cosmopolitan, antisubjective, and antiparochial. Associated with it is the moral and psychological idea of the arts as appealing, at their best, to the "total self"—the senses, the emotions, and the imagination, as well as the intellect and judgement. This again is classical and Renaissance, especially as the later eighteenth century and the Romantics viewed the "classical" and the "Renaissance" in reacting to their own fear that "modern" poetry was becoming too defensive, specialised, and restricted. It is typical both of himself and of the more serious criticism of the time, British and German, that Coleridge, preparing to concentrate on poetic language, inserts here (Chapter 14) the famous paragraph that states: "The poet, described in *ideal* perfection, brings the whole soul of man into activity . . . [blending and fusing through the imagination] the general, with the concrete; the idea, with the image; the individual, with the representative . . . ".[1]

What is wanted, above all, is the active coalescence of the "parts to the whole", the traditional classical ideal of "decorum". But it is strengthened and given a new direction by the profound emphasis on the "organic" in British and especially German thought, from the 1760s to the 1820s, which Coleridge embraced and sympathised with so eagerly. More significant by far than the routine distinction between "poetry" and "prose" is the distinction between "poetry" and "science":

[1] See below, II 15–17.

A poem is that species of composition, which is opposed to works of science, by proposing for its *immediate* object pleasure, not truth; and from all other species (having *this* object in common with it) it is discriminated by proposing to itself such delight from the *whole*, as is compatible with a distinct gratification from each component *part*.[1]

"Truth", broadly conceived, may very well be the *ultimate* object of poetry. ("The mind," as Johnson said, "can only repose on the stability of truth.") When we say that pleasure is the immediate object, we mean that each "part" (each phrase, cadence, image, metaphor, episode) is, ideally speaking, providing a pleasure in and through itself as well as contributing a further pleasure as it adds architectonically to the "whole". He is speaking, in other words, of what for almost a half century we have called "texture", though of a texture that is "compatible" and contributory to the structure emerging through and by means of it into an increasingly weighted richness as the totality emerges. It is this heightened, enriched texture that distinguishes poetry from, say, a tale or novel in which the language is not equally heightened. In poetry the reader is carried forward "not merely or chiefly by the mechanical impulse of curiosity, or by a restless desire to arrive at the final solution; but by the pleasurable activity of mind excited by the attractions of the journey itself". An "infallible test" is the "untranslatableness" of the words. For in the rich nexus of which we are speaking, so many associations and implications are present in solution (in phrase and idiom, in suggestion, in cadence) that the subtler, at very least, are inevitably lost in translation or paraphrase.

It is the lucidity with which Coleridge expresses this concept of style, and, in his practical criticism, exemplifies it, that has particularly endeared him to writers and critics of the last two generations, more especially since he is constantly offering a counterpart in his psychology of poetry (and of art generally) through his concept of the imagination. For the active coalescence of the "parts to the whole" applies not only to "style" or the language of poetry but also to the interplay and unification of the human psyche as it creates or shares the experience of poetry.

In rescuing and reinterpreting this classical ideal through the Romantic ideal of the organic (or, to put it another way, in lifting the ideal of the organic—which Wordsworth himself shared—to

[1] See below, II 13.

the classical plane) Coleridge is also gaining distance through which he can dissociate himself from Wordsworth's theory of poetry, but also, though to a lesser extent, from Wordsworth's practice. He is taking a broader stance. And there was certainly some thought of Wordsworth's comparatively specialised "subjectivity" as Coleridge turns to Shakespeare (Chapter 15). Using Shakespeare as a prototype, Coleridge emphasises the central importance for poetry of four qualities in particular, as "promises and specific symptoms of poetic power", in only the last two of which Wordsworth is pre-eminent: (1) The "sense of musical delight". (2) The fact that poetic genius is at its greatest when it involves sympathetic imagination—the capacity to enter into the feelings and experience of another, and submerge one's own identity in the process (which is not Wordsworth's own poetic gift). (3) The modification of images and thoughts by a "predominant passion". The powerful centrality achieved through the creative uses of "passion" is one of the surest "proofs of original genius", giving organic unity to the work and at the same time giving us a dramatic encounter with a living, creative spirit. Here Wordsworth, as Coleridge is to show later, is superb in his greatest poetry, though by no means with the panoramic range and flexibility, the dramatic three-dimensionality, of a Shakespeare. (4) "Depth, and energy of thought": knowledge genuinely digested and absorbed into "habitual feelings". This again is a quality Wordsworth possesses, though, when compared with the greatest poets, only in a limited compass.

His "practical criticism" of Wordsworth (the phrase is Coleridge's own) proceeds from these standards and implicitly measures the result against them, while at the same time the criticism avoids doctrinaire or theoretical rigidity. One of his primary purposes is to separate Wordsworth's 1800 Preface and his actual practice as a poet. Coleridge was right in taking this for granted as a necessary task. Every major poet who has ever written a manifesto has had it applied and reapplied to his own work. Whether for rebuke, praise, or merely because of the human eagerness to "label" and categorise, we continue to do this even after we have been shown, repeatedly and in detail, that we are oversimplifying. Coleridge admits that the Preface is not a fixed and literal *credo*. Wordsworth's purpose was to correct abuses in poetic style that he thought had been common (though by no means always prevalent) since the mid-seventeenth century and that had progressively removed the poetic idiom from the genius or spirit of common speech. Wordsworth's equation of "natural" language with rustic and humble life might conceivably have a point if what we mean by language is merely "vocabulary" (though the vocabulary, if "selected" and "purified" as Wordsworth admits that it should be, would not then be the vocabulary of a specific "class" or group). But the fundamental point that Coleridge is making, in answer, is that the essence of style, of language, is its character in and as *Gestalt*, totality of form and impact. It is the *order* of the words, the "surview of mind" arranging them, that distinguishes the educated from the uneducated, or, even apart from education, the intelligent from the unintelligent. The latter, in each case, express themselves in a series of insulated facts, as Shakespeare has Dame Quickly do in her long circumstantial account to Falstaff of the occasion when he offered her marriage (a favourite example not only of Coleridge but of the eighteenth-century associationists). As the generally intelligent (or educated) are to the unintelligent (or uneducated), so is genius to ordinary intelligence. To reduce "style" to mere "vocabulary" is like equating the architecture of West-minster Abbey and St Paul's because the stones might be similar (or even drawn from the same quarry). Deepening the implication of what Coleridge is saying is the concept of "organic unity", in which the "parts"—the individual words—are changed and as it were melted into each other in and through context, in and through the "surview" of the imagination (and, he would add, of the "fusive" power of "passion").

Turning specifically to Wordsworth's own poetry, after disso-ciating it from his "theory" (as expressed in Wordsworth's Preface), Coleridge discusses succinctly and with admirable impersonality (Chapter 22) its defects. Of these "defects"—ranging from exces-sive "matter-of-factness" to occasional disproportion between the feeling he expresses and the importance (value, interest) of the sub-ject—the really essential one, as critics have noticed, is "an undue predilection for the *dramatic* form in certain poems".[1] He would succeed better if he simply wrote in his own person as (what he in effect is) a "philosophical poet".[2] Wordsworth's genius, to quote Hazlitt, is "the reverse of the dramatic".[3] Wordsworth certainly

[1] Ch 22, below, II 135.   [3] *H Works* IV 113.
[2] Stephen Maxfield Parrish *PM-LA* 73 (1958) esp 370–4.

possesses "sympathy", as Coleridge says elsewhere, but it is a sympathy "*ab extra*". Wordsworth can "feel *for*" but not "feel *with*". His confidence that he is being dramatic as he characterises individuals and creates their language results only in a form of "ventriloquism". The "Protean" ideal of the sympathetic imagination, as it was developed in the eighteenth century, is not the same as the Renaissance ideal of the universal man, curious about and gifted in everything. Hence even Goethe, to Coleridge, is—like Wordsworth—a "spectator *ab extra*", at most feeling "for" but not "with". The "Protean" ideal is to "become that on which it meditates". What is wanted (as in Keats's ideal of "negative capability") is the capacity to lose the sense of self-identity, so firm in poets as diverse as Wordsworth and Goethe, in something beyond the self. Hence Coleridge's familiar contrast of Shakespeare, the true "Proteus", with Milton, who "attracts all forms and things to himself, into the unity of his own IDEAL".[1]

Coleridge then sums up superbly the virtues of Wordsworth: the "perfect appropriateness of the words to the meaning" that shows itself in the "untranslatableness" into other words without loss to the meaning; the "weight and sanity" of his moral reflections as expressed in poetry, especially in single lines or great passages; more uniquely meditative pathos—feeling that turns into thought, thought domesticated into feeling—though admittedly this is done as a "contemplator" rather than as a Shakespearian active sharer; and finally "imaginative power"—"fusive", integrative, yielding a genuine and earned vision of life—to such a degree that "he stands nearest of all modern writers to Shakespear and Milton; and yet in a kind perfectly unborrowed and his own".[2]

Interspersed throughout these chapters are observations that sum up fifty to seventy years of psychological insight into style. An example would be the discussion of "poetic illusion". Another would be the concept of "suggestiveness", through which, in the half-declared, the imagination is induced to fill out the picture (rather than to receive it passively) in elaborated detail, an act that also involves the interplay of the senses: e.g., the excitement of the sense of sight through sound, or *vice versa*. Allied with both of these is the distinction between genuine "imitation" and mere "copy". We should also note the modified "primitivism" in Cole-

---

[1] Ch 15, below, II 27–8.   [2] *TT* 16 Feb 1833; see below, II 151.

ridge's approach to poetic language. The term "primitivism" is misleadingly simplistic, but as a convenient short-hand term it applies to the common eighteenth-century belief, which had become psychologically and historically sophisticated by the 1770s and 1780s, that language in its earlier stages is naturally more "poetic". With a smaller vocabulary, language is less denotative, more connotative and metaphorical. A central work concerned with the subject is Adam Smith's *Considerations Concerning the First Formation of Languages* (1767). The belief that poetry is inevitably eviscerated by progressive refinement from concrete to abstract, from metaphor to denotation, is commonplace after the 1760s. The protests against the refinement of poetic diction since the mid-seventeenth century sometimes reflected a frank predilection for the humble, the rustic, or any other modern approximation we might have to the "primitive" (Wordsworth's *theoretical* attitude is, in a highly qualified way, in this vein). More useful and lasting was the interest in a "second" early period, truly "classical", a "golden age" following an "iron age": [1] for example, the great era of Greek drama and poetry, among the ancients, or the Renaissance (fifteenth to early seventeenth century) among the moderns. Coleridge's discussion of the language of poetry should be viewed partly in the light of these interests or premises, which he certainly shared. But every serious thinker about poetry since his time has also shared them; and when attempts have been made to "modernise", and even to introduce a modern colloquial language, it is often with the thought of what poetry could and did mean in those earlier societies where, however we exaggerate and overidealise, it was more often a central part of human experience than it was appearing to be in the period from 1650 to 1800, and certainly more central than it became after the mid-nineteenth century.

Whereas traditional metrics rarely went beyond the concept of metre as a form of "uniformity and variety", Coleridge concentrated on the psychological effects of metrical rhythm in a twofold way that, simply because it is twofold, opens the door to implications to which others had been theoretically blind, however frequently they had experienced the effects. Metre, he says, arises from the balance-loving, balance-needing aspects of the human

[1] Bate *BP* 51–2, 62–71.

psyche (here, as elsewhere, he draws on Schiller and other German writers, but is more specific in his practical application to metre). It expresses our instinctive effort to hold in check the workings of passion through rhythmic ordering, while at the same time it arouses an expectant tension. The check is simultaneously a spur; at once an incitement and a satisfaction. What we are describing is, in ordinary logic, an apparent contradiction in terms, as are so many other things in art or in life generally. In each of these two operations, metrical rhythm is inevitably of a chameleon nature, dependent on what else accompanies it. If body of thought, passion, and figurative language are present, metre (or rhythm generally) operates like a "medicated atmosphere", or like wine during animated conversation: it intensifies (to use a word Coleridge coined) expectancy and alertness. If sufficient body or "food" is lacking, however, there is an inevitable sense of "disappointment", a drop, a feeling that the rhythm has become mere thump. So with the function of rhythm as a "checking" and ordering of passion. By definition this implies the existence of something to be checked and ordered, just as the alertness and expectancy incited by metre imply something for which the aroused attention is prepared. The "pleasure" of metre, in short, is *conditional* on what is being presented in the *Gestalt*. During the half century of prosodic theory before Coleridge (1750–1800), much of it extraordinarily ingenious, this sense of *Gestalt* was by no means common. A notable exception was Johnson, who, in two of his discussions of the effect of metre, says much the same thing in a briefer, less subtle way.[1] (Johnson, with whom Coleridge often takes issue, sometimes anticipates him more closely than Coleridge would care to admit.) Coleridge's ideas on metre were resurrected and developed in I. A. Richards's chapter on "Rhythm and Metre" in *Principles of Literary Criticism* (1924), especially in the contention that "Through its very appearance of artificiality metre produces in the highest degree the 'frame' effect, isolating the poetic experience from the accidents and irrelevancies of everyday existence."[2]

To put it briefly: in many of his values, when he speaks of the

---

[1] *Rambler* Nos 92 and 94; *Lives* "Pope" III 232.

[2] This, in effect, is what John Hollander and other recent metrists mean by "the contractual basis of metrical choice": "a choice conditioned by variables of expectation on the part of an audience—a modern literary-historical concept, in short, of convention". Hollander *Vision and Resonance* (1975) 194.

language of poetry, Coleridge serves as a barometer of almost every central issue raised from the 1750s to the early 1800s. At the same time he coalesces them, often in luminous phrasing, with an originality of personal insight and experience that allows him to anticipate our twentieth-century reopening of the issues. One of the manifestos of the new movement in criticism, as it began to take systematic shape after World War II, could therefore state at the start that the *Biographia* "is almost the bible of modern criticism" and Coleridge himself "the first really great modern critic".[1] To the extent that this is true, it is because of the combination of several things. As a *reader* of poetry, Coleridge is almost unrivalled in his sense for nuance and implication in poetic language, with only one major block (the "High Neoclassic Mode"). At the same time, his intellectual interests are as wide and strong as those of such critics as Johnson and Goethe. Still more important was the fertility with which these interests could come to focus in "practical criticism". However incomplete we may regard his effort to find an all-embracing philosophical or theological framework to express it, the ideal of unity that haunted him was not a matter of mere theory but a living, formative instinct constantly awake to connections. In approaching the language of poetry, he is able at once to see the image, the metaphor, the structure, the cadence, with what (in a fine phrase he anglicises from the German) he himself calls the "armed vision" of broad and diverse knowledge, exemplifying as a critic what he said of the poet to William Sotheby in July 1802:

> A great Poet must be, implicitè if not explicitè, a profound Metaphysician. He may not have it in logical coherence, in his Brain & Tongue; but he must have it by *Tact*/ For all sounds, & forms of human nature he must have the *ear* of a wild Arab listening in the silent Desart, the eye of a North American Indian tracing the footsteps of an Enemy upon the Leaves that strew the Forest—; the *Touch* of a Blind Man feeling the face of a darling Child.[2]

THE GERMAN BORROWINGS AND THE ISSUE OF PLAGIARISM

A major obligation in editing the *Biographia* is to face directly the complicated problem of Coleridge's unacknowledged appropri-

---

[1] Stanley E. Hyman *The Armed Vision: a Study in Methods of Modern Criticism* (1948) 11

[2] *CL* II 810.

ations of German philosophical writing (notably in Chapters 5–9 and 12–13). Nothing quite like this problem, both in degree and in kind, exists for any classic comparable to the *Biographia* in importance. Yet the subject remains shadowy for the majority of the readers of the book, however curious they may be. Several reasons combine to explain this. One is the relative unfamiliarity of many of the German writings in the English-speaking world. A second reason is the comparative generality with which the subject has often been discussed. General charges of plagiarism are made, with a few passages cited as "examples" or with simple page numbers. When we face the issue of plagiarism, at least in an important work, there is no substitute for presenting parallel passages in full. Otherwise it would be to the reader's disposition to exaggerate or to minimise.

Tangled motives, defensive and accusatory, persist throughout the long history of the discussion of Coleridge's "plagiarisms". If the history of this discussion had not been authoritatively presented by Thomas McFarland, it would be appropriate to devote several paragraphs to it here, since the *Biographia* is the only work of Coleridge published by himself (as contrasted with lectures and unpublished manuscripts) in which the issue of plagiarism is important. It is sufficient now, after referring to McFarland's discussion, to mention: Thomas De Quincey's article (*Tait's Edinburgh Magazine* September 1834), published almost immediately after Coleridge's death, pointing to some of the borrowings from Schelling in Chapter 12; J. F. Ferrier's vindictive, more detailed attack in *Blackwood's* (March 1840); and the attention called to some of Coleridge's use of Johann G. E. Maass's *Versuch über die Einbildungskraft* for the history of the associationist psychology in Chapters 5 and 6. The last charge of plagiarism was published by William Hamilton in a "Supplementary Dissertation" to his edition of *The Works of Thomas Reid* (1846).

It was in order to meet these accusations that Coleridge's daughter Sara, in the 1847 edition of the *Biographia*, conscientiously tried to document her father's unacknowledged borrowings from the German. The editors of the present edition have great admiration for her courage in trying to meet this problem. She is on occasion forgivably a little vague judged by modern standards of editing. She at moments, perhaps unconsciously, minimises the directness with which Coleridge translates. Nor did she notice the extent of Coleridge's indebtedness to Maass or Jacobi. Shawcross, in his edition (1907), relies almost wholly on the 1847 edition in this matter and, as a rule, transcribes his page numbers from Sara Coleridge's notes.

Probably because Shawcross's edition (1907) largely superseded the 1847 edition, and because relatively unannotated editions and reprints were becoming common, the direct appropriation of German material became lost sight of, or minimised, except among specialists. The writings of René Wellek, beginning with his *Immanuel Kant in England* (1931), cited in detail Coleridge's use, in a variety of works, of German writers. In part because of the impetus given by Wellek, the subject was further examined in G. N. G. Orsini's *Coleridge and German Idealism* (1969), in the more comprehensive *Coleridge and the Pantheist Tradition* (1969) by Thomas McFarland, and in Norman Fruman's *Coleridge: The Damaged Archangel* (1971).

For the *Collected Works*, there was no alternative except to pursue this subject as exhaustively as we could for the *Biographia*. As we proceeded, we found the subject increasingly complex. For example, Coleridge at times translates or paraphrases from an author who, in turn, was himself quoting or paraphrasing from another writer. Moreover, Coleridge's use of German books and his own marginalia in them was often so fluid and intertwined— a sentence here, then two or three sentences elsewhere—that our experience repeatedly confirmed what McFarland calls the "mosaic" form of composition in Coleridge. There would be a passage from, say, Maass or Schelling, and then—before going on—he would leap ahead, or he would follow up sources they used, or he would suddenly intermix still other sources or his own marginal notes. Unquestionably, when he was not dictating to John Morgan, Coleridge would select passages to use, organising them himself, jumping from one to another many pages before or later, then back; or remembering another work, inevitably returning several times to pages or sections that especially interested him. The procedure is fascinating to speculate about as he tried in August (1815) to expand his *Biographia*, his "apology", his "literary life", within three or four weeks.

To face directly the problem of plagiarism there is no alternative to parallel passages; this complex situation entails a direct presentation of sources, page by page, sometimes line by line. If Coleridge translates directly, the German is supplied. Variations are noted in brackets. If Coleridge paraphrases heavily, the original German is given, followed by a literal English translation. With loose paraphrases there is generally given only an English translation of the material Coleridge is using. For in these instances, Coleridge expresses ideas and sentiments without repeating the particular wording or phrases of the original. If he very loosely summarises and condenses, this is simply noted and at times an English translation is given of at least some of the material he presents in shortened form.

To establish a clear idea of the *amount* of material that Coleridge used but did not acknowledge, we present a simple table. It measures the bulk of material, quantitatively, in Chapters 5–9 and 12–13 that Coleridge did not credit to German authors. (See Appendix A.) What generalisations should be made? A maximum of a quarter of the total material in the philosophical chapters is used without citing its source; if we put aside the category of summary, then just over one-fifth of the pages covered by these chapters is either translated or paraphrased. Chapters 9 and 12 each contains a long passage for which Coleridge gives a partial but potentially misleading reference (see below, I 147 and n 5, 248 and n 1). If these two passages together are, in fact, considered as "unacknowledged", they then account for almost one-third of the unacknowledged direct translation. The largest percentage of unacknowledged material per chapter falls in Chapters 8 and 12. Chapter 7 contains none.

Coleridge anticipates the question of plagiarism. Twice in the *Biographia* he mentions the "charge of plagiarism" or of "an ungenerous concealment or intentional plagiarism".[1] His remarks are more than an early defence against the inevitable. Certainly he felt uneasy about the passages he appropriated. His motives were tangled. In Chapter 9 he states that "an identity of thought, or even similarity of phrase will not be at all times a certain proof that the passage has been borrowed from Schelling"; that "many of the most striking resemblances, indeed all the main and fundamental ideas, were born and matured in my mind before I had ever seen a single page of the German Philosopher [Schelling]". Yet later in the same paragraph, Coleridge claims, "To me it will be happiness and honor enough, should I succeed in rendering the system itself [Schelling's completion of what Kant and Fichte

[1] Ch 9, below, I 161, 164.

started] intelligible to my countrymen". It is still in this paragraph, one sentence later, that Coleridge makes the statement that:

> For readers in general, let whatever shall be found in this or any future work of mine, that resembles, or coincides with, the doctrines of my German predecessor, though contemporary, be wholly attributed to *him*: provided, that the absence of distinct references to his books, which I could not at all times make with truth as designating citations or thoughts actually *derived* from him; and which, I trust, would, after this general acknowledgment be superfluous; be not charged on me as an ungenerous concealment or intentional plagiarism.

Near the close of this remarkable and long paragraph comes the equally famous remark that he regards truth "as a divine ventriloquist".[1] Coleridge veers a delicate, an almost contradictory course; he appears at once to give a great deal of credit to Schelling and to reserve a good deal for himself. On the one hand he thinks it "happiness and honor enough" to communicate Schelling's system to the English, and that "whatever shall be found" in his works to "be wholly attributed to *him*". On the other hand, Coleridge claims that identities of thought and phrase "will not be at all times a certain proof that the passage has been borrowed from Schelling". The close of Chapter 9, with this extraordinary paragraph, then ends with "a cluster of citations" in order "to conclude the subject of citation".[2] The matter is important and troubling to Coleridge—more so if we consider the possibility that Chapter 10, beginning with a short dissertation on the meaning of "esemplastic", may itself have started out, as he was dictating, to be the crucial chapter "on the nature and genesis of the imagination". Such a chapter (postponed to Chapters 12 and 13) would involve the German writers and necessitate treating "the subject of citation".

What we have done is to identify exactly what (and what amount) Coleridge used where he himself gave no specific citation. We present the facts, without the rhetoric of either defence or accusation. What is most eloquent are the detailed annotations. They speak for themselves. How Coleridge used his material and wove it into a larger context of his own, where "the organic Whole" is greater than the sum of its parts, is discussed below, in Coleridge's "Method of Composition", for the issue of plagiarism needs to be supplemented by understanding how Coleridge shaped all

[1] Ch 9, below, I 164.   [2] Ch 9, below, I 165.

materials into a body whose message and shape could not be extrapolated from its separate sections. The following discussion of Coleridge's use of German authors is a mere preliminary to the tortuous and fascinating trail marked in the notes.

Schelling

It has long been known that Coleridge relies more heavily on Schelling in the *Biographia* than on any other German writer. He translates literally, or with minor changes, at length, and also paraphrases both closely and loosely; he summarises or condenses or even lets a few words stand for an idea that Schelling takes great pains and many pages to develop. Coleridge extends and answers or disagrees with Schelling. Two or three times—as once in Chapter 12 for a particularly long section translated almost verbatim—Coleridge names the title of Schelling's book. In short, Coleridge places Schelling's line of thought in a new context—not always, but to a greater extent than with any other German writer. His ready knowledge of Schelling in 1815 probably exceeded his familiarity with the other Germans, with the exception of Kant; he seems, and by his own admission as well, more attracted to and involved intellectually with a larger range of ideas and titles in Schelling's works. Schelling is the only German writer of whom we know that Coleridge ordered—or even wished to pursue—"*all the* works".[1] He is more likely to vary his translations and paraphrases from Schelling than his ones from Maass and Jacobi.

Except for influences and parallels of general conception and subject matter, Coleridge's use of Schelling comes in four chapters: 8, 9, 12, and 13. In Chapter 8, for instance, Coleridge uses Schelling's *System des transscendentalen Idealismus*, and in four different places translates or paraphrases from one continuous section of the *System* for a total of about two hundred words. But Coleridge intersperses these parts with use of another section from the *System*, one that he also splits, this time into two separate translations of about fifty words each and one fifty-word paraphrase. He jumps back and forth between the sections, returning frequently to the place he had left off. Furthermore, he intermixes and adds passages, variously handled in their reproduction, from the *Abhandlungen zur Erläuterung des Idealismus*. This borrowing

---

[1] See ch 9, below, I 164 n 3.

from the *Abhandlungen* is usually general in nature. Coleridge translates or paraphrases about twenty-five words. Lastly, he takes about fifty words from two different places in the Introduction to *Ideen zu einer Philosophie der Natur*. Thus five or six passages in three separate works of Schelling are used in Chapter 8, but Coleridge splinters these passages into almost triple that number of shorter translations and paraphrases. The example of Chapter 8 is complex enough but is simplicity itself compared with the intricacies of Chapter 12. (See below on Coleridge's "Method of Composition".)

We are not dealing—or at least not dealing primarily—with orderly blocks of verbatim translation, but something more like a chemical compound. In Chapters 9 and 12 the situation becomes extremely intricate. Schelling is not the only author involved, though he is easily the major one. No attempt has been made to summarise here the borrowings in those chapters. The nature of Coleridge's sources, especially in Chapter 12, can really not be "summarised" or described accurately in a few pages. Only extensive notes do justice to the facts. Although nearly all that Coleridge takes from Maass has already been presented by Chapter 8, in which Schelling first becomes important as a source, Coleridge does not exhaust one German writer and then proceed to another. The sources of his borrowings, acknowledged and unacknowledged, are mixed. And the forms of the borrowings (translations, paraphrase, summary, terms adopted, ideas echoed) are equally mixed. Given all the works and several ways of using each, the combinations and permutations of them are many. Coleridge manages to employ a remarkably large number of them. He even translates and strings together three quotations that have been separately quoted and translated from French into German in two or three places in another book.[1] As many notes show graphically, he often follows the typography, especially of Schelling, and italicises words and phrases that Schelling puts in widely spaced fraktur, and italicises no others.

It may be a help to list those books by Schelling that pertain most to the *Biographia*. In the first rank, unquestionably, come two, and it is hard to judge the precedence between them: the *System des transscendentalen Idealismus* (1800) and the *Abhand-*

[1] See ch 12, below, I 244 and n 2.

lungen zur Erläuterung des Idealismus der Wissenschaftslehre
(1796–7). Coleridge names both titles in full (Chapters 9 and 12).
Next should be placed the *Vom Ich als Princip der Philosophie*
(1795), which he does not mention by name. But Coleridge says
that he has procured the first volume of Schelling's collected tracts,
and this includes the *Vom Ich*. The first volume of tracts, mentioned in Chapter 9, is *Philosophische Schriften* (Vol I 1809; no
further vols published). (This also contains *Über das Verhältniss
der bildenden Künste zu der Natur*—1807—used in *CN* III 4397,
the basis of "On Poesy or Art".) Then, sharing nearly the same
magnitude of use, come the *Ideen zu einer Philosophie der Natur*
(1797) and the *Darlegung des wahren Verhältnisses der Natur-
philosophie zur verbesserten Fichte'schen Lehre* (1806). The first
may be what Coleridge is referring to when he names the "*Natur-
Philosophie*". The second he identifies as the "small pamphlet
against Fichte".[1] When we descend (in rough order) to *Ueber
das Wesen der menschlichen Freyheit* (1809), *Philosophische Briefe
über Dogmatismus und Kritizismus* (1795), *Philosophie und Religion* (1804), and *Ueber die Möglichkeit einer Form der Philosophie überhaupt* (1794), the first two of which are in the *Philosophische Schriften*, we are distinctly fading out of the range of
strict verbal parallels. Either directly, by stating the title, or indirectly, by referring to the "*Natur-Philosophie*" or to "the 1st
volume of his collected Tracts", Coleridge names in the *Biographia*
itself *every work* of Schelling with which there are strong verbal
similarities or outright questions of plagiarism for the *Biographia*.

With Coleridge's use of Schelling we meet in acute form three
problems associated with his use of the Germans as a whole, and
particularly in those instances where we are not encountering
translation or obvious paraphrase.

(1) Coleridge uses terms, single words, phrases, and occasional
images that reflect or repeat terms and phrases in his reading. This
is a matter of course for all philosophical writing. Examples include: objectivise, potence, subject and object, multeity, "two
opposing forces", postulate, substrate, "evolution of self-consciousness", self-affirmation, the dynamic philosophy, intuition and
self-intuition, "armed vision" and distinctions between talent and
genius, fancy and imagination, transcendental and transcendent,

[1] Ch 9, below, I 147, 164.

and mediate and immediate truths. Some of these were recognisably common property in Coleridge's time. A few have an esoteric flavour, a gnarled history; a few are unique to Schelling or enjoy an especially marked importance in his thinking. On the whole, Coleridge seeks to expand the philosophic vocabulary of the British, to make it less materialistic, and to introduce to British thought the key words of Continental (especially German) thought.

(2) There are multiple, overlapping sources. This problem is difficult when Coleridge appears to be using the early Schelling, especially the *Vom Ich* (though not that alone). Schelling at times closely paraphrases Fichte and is also strongly influenced by Jacobi, Bruno, and Kant. When Coleridge is summarising or even paraphrasing, it is frequently hard to tell which of two or several authors he is remembering and using; for Coleridge read and interpreted them all together, and they were not "clear and distinct" ideas in his mind.

(3) Schelling, Jacobi, Maass, Fichte, and to some extent Kant—but especially Schelling—repeat themselves, often closely. Two or three sentences in two or more different places become candidates for what Coleridge uses only once. This situation arises most often when Coleridge is paraphrasing. It is sometimes involved with and aggravated by the problem discussed under (2) in the paragraph above.

Maass

Johann G. E. Maass's *Versuch über die Einbildungskraft* (1792; Coleridge used the revised edition of 1797) is 453 pages long. Its final part on the history of the association of ideas ("Beiträge zur Geschichte der Lehre von der Vergesellschaftung der Vorstellungen", pp 311–453) could still be recommended as the best history of the subject from Plato to the early nineteenth century. The passages and information that Coleridge draws on occur in this part (especially 320–9, 343–58) and also in Maass's discussion of the general law of association itself ("Von dem höchsten Gesetze", pp 13–54; Coleridge concentrates on pp 25–35). Coleridge gives Maass's name at the beginning of Chapter 6. In Chapter 7, when Coleridge formulates his own general law of the association of ideas, he also uses his marginalia and earlier reactions to Maass, and in Chapter 9 Coleridge's criticism of Locke closely echoes Maass's opinion in wording; but by far the main use of

Maass, consisting of translation, paraphrase, and a summary that condenses and conflates Maass's discussions, is in Chapters 5 and 6. Coleridge's opinions of Aristotle, Hobbes, and Locke seem generally reinforced by what Maass says.

Coleridge, as usual, leaps ahead or behind and then returns to passages where he had earlier left off. He uses Maass for history, facts, and summary judgements. In effect he presents Maass's material, often in Maass's wording, as an authority to refute James Mackintosh and, in general, all materialists or mechanists who, ignoring the power of the will, explain association of ideas as a phaenomenon purely passive and physiological. Coleridge alters or changes little in the sentences he appropriates. Mackintosh—and other associationists—were obviously challenged by the erudition in Chapters 5 and 6 of the *Biographia*, and their attempts to charge Coleridge with theft of the material in these chapters did nothing to change the fact that Maass (and Coleridge) were essentially correct in their judgements.

The appeal of Maass lay in his powers of analysis, his extensive knowledge and ability to push the history of the association of ideas back to its earliest or "pure" origins, with emphasis on Aristotle, a fact that pleased Coleridge. Such an erudite search for the complete story of a concept that had fired him as a younger man now caught his attention strongly. Maass came to represent detailed scholarship and knowledge of a kind that many British empiricists and psychologists lacked, a shortcoming that made them seem to Coleridge proud, superficial, or—like Hartley—pious but misguided and inconsistent.

Coleridge never seems to agree completely with the book in front of him, and the *Versuch* is no exception. Coleridge's own "general law of association"[1] stems from marginalia of his own that are critical of (or at least meant to correct) Maass. Hence, when we arrive at what might be called the climax of Chapters 5–7, Coleridge's reformulation of this law, he rejects the law stated by Maass as being so universal that it proves nugatory and effectively useless. On this crucial point concerning associationism Maass becomes a sounding or springboard from which Coleridge rebounds in order to arrive at a new, unique position that reflects his own understanding and acquaintance of more than twenty years with the subject. Coleridge uses Maass to arrive at his own concept of

[1] See esp ch 7, below, I 126–8.

the imagination in which, as in Maass's, the association of ideas plays an important rôle. But whereas Maass essentially sees *Einbildungskraft* as a broad view of association itself, Coleridge conceives of imagination as responsible for the original perception that makes all association possible. Maass touches very little on literary and artistic ideas of the creative imagination. Coleridge thus uses Maass on association *per se*, but not on association as a basis for the imagination, for Coleridge senses that Maass is much too limited in that area.

Jacobi

Coleridge relied on Jacobi's *Ueber die Lehre des Spinoza* in a way altogether unique. A work congenial and suggestive, written by one like-minded, *Ueber die Lehre* attracted him for a number of reasons, especially its deeply Christian context. In the *Biographia* he uses it (the second and expanded edition of 1789) as a source for quotations from Kant and especially from Leibniz. He does not name the book in the *Biographia* but mentions its author when he relates an anecdote from *Ueber die Lehre* in Chapter 22. In addition to repeating quotations he found in *Ueber die Lehre* (repeating them sometimes with acknowledgement to the original source and sometimes translating the German of Jacobi, itself a translation of Leibniz's French, into English), Coleridge absorbed the larger sections of the book, particularly the discussions of Bruno and of "pre-established harmony". Awareness of these sections generally appears in Chapters 8–13, 22, and 24 of the *Biographia*. For example, in Chapter 12, the theses I–III, VI, VII, IX, and X all reflect, in part, points made by Jacobi. The appeal to Coleridge here was Jacobi's infusion of religion and of moral belief into the realm of speculative or theoretical philosophy established in the earlier critical writings of Kant, Schelling, and Fichte. There is, too, an influence of Jacobi on Coleridge through the medium of Schelling.

Coleridge takes directly no more than an occasional phrase of two or three words from Jacobi's own prose. More fascinating is the way Coleridge appropriates quotations given by Jacobi from Leibniz and Kant (and also one verse paraphrase from the book of Job, which he translates from Jacobi himself).[1] The special

[1] See the nn to chs 10, 12, and 13.

nature of *Ueber die Lehre*, its long letters, extracts, dialogues, and numerous quotations, many in notes and many printed in both the original and a German translation, make it an ideal source-book, one totally different in composition and format from the works of Schelling, Kant, Maass, Lessing, and Fichte. But it is still interesting to speculate why Coleridge chose to use Jacobi's quotations from Leibniz and Kant and passed over the many from Bruno and Spinoza. Was it because of their pantheistic implications?

Yet, Coleridge digested *Ueber die Lehre* thoroughly because Spinozism offered the greatest hopes, yet harboured grave dangers that had to be faced. Spinoza promised unity and coherent order, but his system lacked a personal god. Jacobi's book offered much in the way of approaching Spinozism and rescuing it from the dangers of materialism and atheism. The book did not, finally, argue for Spinozism, but presented pantheistic arguments to advantage. It was a reasoned dialogue, full of admiration for Spinoza as well as for his system, yet deeper still in the belief of a personal God and His Son. The book was philosophical, enlightened, kind, and tolerant. About a Jew whom many scorned and called an atheist, it was written by an appreciative Christian who apprehended truths in the heart and mind of Spinoza that went deeper than the logic of his system.

Kant

Kant, as the founder and central figure of the critical philosophy, touched almost every important intellectual topic of the period. Coleridge could not—nor could anyone else—take up issues and ideas raised and introduced by the new philosophy without everywhere encountering Kant. Kant's ideas and attitudes inform Chapters 7–13 generally, but especially 8, 9, 12, and 13. When Coleridge quotes, paraphrases, or summarises Kant in the *Biographia*, he always names him and gives the title of the work used and—in several instances—the page numbers that are relevant. There are two exceptions, both minor. In Chapter 8 Coleridge quotes without acknowledgement (perhaps from memory) one sentence from the *Metaphysische Anfangsgründe der Naturwissenschaft*, a book he names in the next chapter. In Chapter 9 he quotes, almost certainly from memory, one sentence from a letter or *Erklärung* by Kant published in a German periodical. Coleridge uses quotation marks but does not name the exact source.

Coleridge quotes from both Kant's German and Latin and translates the texts into English in footnotes. When he puts an English translation in his own text he uses quotation marks. Coleridge identifies by name the one relatively short section in the *Kritik der reinen Vernunft* that influences parts of Chapters 9 and 12.[1]

Even by today's standards, Coleridge was, in the *Biographia*, careful to cite Kant. This is indicative of his high opinion (or at least one important side of his opinion) concerning the man whose name, as Coleridge said, was "buzzing about" all Germany when he arrived there in 1798. Professors Wellek and Orsini state that Coleridge sometimes criticises Kant by quietly adopting Schelling's views. Yet Coleridge, in observations he never intended for publication, criticised Fichte and Schelling for claiming too much for themselves and diminishing Kant. Kant remained for Coleridge a central figure for whom he had special reverence. He felt the same need as Kant's German followers to correct, ramify, interpret, and expand Kant, a need to engage Kant's ideas in a dialectic that built new positions and systems, some even seeming to disagree with Kant himself.

Fichte; Minor Sources

With a few exceptions, Coleridge does not borrow directly from Fichte. Often he turns to the early Schelling instead, to the Fichtean *Vom Ich* for example, a book highly dependent on Fichte's *Wissenschaftslehre*. Coleridge's own reading in the *Grundlage der gesammten Wissenschaftslehre* and the *Grundriss des Eigenthümlichen der Wissenschaftslehre* unmistakably shows through. Crucial ideas in the "philosophical chapters"—the deduction of the imagination, the search for a first principle of all knowledge, the idea of self-consciousness, of philosophical "freedom" and "spirit"—have parallels in Fichte. A perusal of the notes reveals how often, and at times how specifically, Fichte appears necessary for what Coleridge is saying. The fascinating thing is that one could make a strong case that for much of the intellectual content of Chapters 8–13 Coleridge could just have easily used Fichte instead of Schelling; he could have quoted and paraphrased from Fichte and used Fichte's examples. Why, then, did he turn to Schelling in these cases? There

---

[1] The section on "original apperception": see ch 9, below, I 153; C used a reprint (1799) of the 2nd ed of the first *Kritik* (1787).

is something very telling in Coleridge's reaction to Fichte's philosophy as "crude egoismus", and although he knew that this was a harsh judgement, it seems almost certain that Fichte's personality, not only as Coleridge encountered it in Fichte's books, but as he heard about it while in Germany, blocked him from approaching Fichte with the same air of congeniality that he did Schelling. Furthermore, Schelling's later works, beginning with *Philosophie und Religion* (1804), seemed to be leading philosophy more in the direction Coleridge hoped it would go. A philosophy like Fichte's, stringently built on the "I" and on individual will, would attract Coleridge at first. But then, as it seemed to stress unremittingly only the self, it could prey on his self-conscious anxieties, moral conscience, and sense of religious piety. Fichte's logic appeared at times strained and even ridiculous.[1]

The extent of Coleridge's German reading as it is seen in the *Biographia* has often been darkened by the issue of plagiarism. Much of the time acknowledging his source, Coleridge turned to Lessing, Herder, Leibniz, Schiller, Richter, Garve, Steffens, Luther, and Ottfried. In 1817, the *Biographia* showed more personal acquaintance with a range of German literature and philosophy than any book previously published in English.

COLERIDGE'S SENSE OF AUDIENCE

Aside from his remarks near the end of Chapter 9 on "the charge of plagiarism", Coleridge felt general uneasiness about the public reception of the *Biographia*, particularly of the first volume. Fourteen months after the book was published, while discouraging his philosophical disciple J. H. Green from considering Schelling too seriously (Coleridge said, "from the tendency of my mind to confidence in others I was myself *taken in*" by Schelling's inconsistencies), he also expressed dissatisfaction with "the metaphysical chapters of my Literary Life".[2] Within another five months, he wrote Britton: "were it in my power, my works should be confined to the second volume of my 'Literary Life,' the Essays of the third volume of the 'Friend,' from page 67 to page 265, with about fifty or sixty pages from the two former volumes, and some half-dozen

[1] *CL* II 673–4.   [2] 30 Sept 1818: *CL* IV 874; cf also 792–3, 873–6.

of my poems".[1] And there is the famous remark shortly before his death: "The metaphysical disquisition at the end of the first volume . . . is unformed and immature; it contains the fragments of the truth, but it is not fully thought out. It is wonderful to myself to think how infinitely more profound my views now are, and yet how much clearer they are withal."[2]

Even while writing the *Biographia* Coleridge was apprehensive about "the multitudinous PUBLIC", which "shaped into personal unity by the magic of abstraction, sits nominal despot on the throne of criticism". The fear of rejection on grounds of being abstruse aggravated two already conflicting ideals in Coleridge's mind, the moral and religious desire to serve, lead, and educate as many people as possible, and the profound interest in highly intellectual and even esoteric subjects. The first one-fifth of Chapter 12 is essentially a pre-emptive defence against ignorant critics, those "invisible ministers, whose intellectual claims to the guardianship of the muses seem . . . analogous to the physical qualifications which adapt their oriental brethren for the superintendence of the Harem".[3] Then, just prior to the main philosophical discussion in Chapter 12 Coleridge makes a remarkable statement, remarkable because many writers on intellectual topics would take it for granted and would not be disturbed by its implications. But Coleridge says something that he seems to have wanted to say for most of the first volume; his tone is dramatic, almost as if he were throwing down the glove, yet also strangely guilty, too, as if confessing a regrettable truth.

> But it is time to tell the truth; though it requires some courage to avow it in an age and country, in which disquisitions on all subjects, not privileged to adopt technical terms or scientific symbols, must be addressed to the PUBLIC. I say then, that it is neither possible or necessary for all men, or for many, to be PHILOSOPHERS.[4]

It is not necessary for all men to be philosophers, because, as Coleridge explains a few pages later, it is "the *moral* being", which all men possess, that holds the key to "a prophecy of universal fulfilment".[5] Yet the point is that philosophy and criticism are not, and cannot, be open to all. This exclusive quality troubled Coleridge and perhaps angered him—angered him against pre-

[1] 28 Feb 1819: *CL* iv 925.   [4] Ch 12, below, i 235–6.
[2] *TT* 28 Jun 1834.   [5] Ch 12, below, i 242.
[3] Ch 3, below, i 59.

sumptuous or ignorant critics, but also split him against himself. Earlier in the *Biographia*, he confessed that "a tried experience of twenty years, has taught me, that the original sin of my character consists in a careless indifference to public opinion".[1] When this conflict is added to his qualms about his work in the first volume, the result is a tentative or hesitant approach. Certainly this helps to explain why he abandoned the thirteenth chapter. It would hold "the same relation in abstruseness to Plotinus, as Plotinus does to Plato",[2] a condition strong enough to stymie all but the most unwary. Yet repeatedly Coleridge feels the need to explain himself, to go out of the way to define his neologisms and his vocabulary—to make things as clear as he can to "the multitudinous P U B L I C".

There is a Quixotic element in the *Biographia*, a self-conscious one.[3] Coleridge senses the high comedy—the incongruity of scope—in trying to do so much in one part (the philosophical chapters) of his "immethodical miscellany", combining philosophy, religion, morality, and criticism. The task was as large, as "foolish" as any that a knight errant had faced. The spirit and the humour Coleridge expresses come from a modern crusader of great causes who, looking to philosophical and literary figures of the past in a way that Don Quixote looked to chivalric ones, is all too aware of his own troubles, and keenly aware that his hopes and high purposes can make him seem ridiculous or, at the very least, obscure to most people. While at times this forces a tone of stiffness or of defensiveness ("Anxiety", he said, "makes us all ceremonious"), it also reveals a deep human feeling. The way in which his thought was troubled and his hope tempered indicates a large measure of humility.

METHOD OF COMPOSITION

Coleridge's method of composing the *Biographia*, especially in his use of German writers, is fascinating and complex. The text is an amazing trail left by his active mind. In reading the text and in reading what he himself read, we will, as he said, "trace or if you

[1] Ch 2, below, I 44.
[2] Ch 13, below, I 303.
[3] The curious extended metaphor of ch 21, "Should any literary Quixote . . ." (below, II 111), may be regarded as a kind of autobiographical statement on C's part, a warning from one who had taken such a Quixotic path "on which", as he translates the epigraph for *BL*, "he himself had lost his way".

are on the hunt, track me".[1] There are actually a number of interconnected trails. Coleridge had a highly associative and amalgamating mind: a proper name or single word often sends him in pursuit of related ideas with the result that he connects these to the main body of his discourse and, in the process, discovers ("half-perceives" and "half-creates") more than the one initial and suggestive association. Many conversations and letters from the twenty years leading up to the *Biographia* find a vent, a resting-place, in the book. He mines his notebooks for materials and suggestions as, for example, in the Theses of Chapter 12. It seems likely that he also had some books, German and English, ready at hand while he dictated and composed. Many of these books include marginalia, and at times he incorporates parts of these into the text (e.g. Chapters 6, 7). Blessed with an almost photographic memory (he once repeated a speech of Burke after reading through it a single time), Coleridge was also recalling materials not immediately in front of him, books, conversations, marginal notes, or his own notebooks. Finally, he had fifteen years to consider, plan, revise, and disagree with himself about the *Biographia*, for it was in 1803 that he decided "to write my metaphysical works, as *my Life, & in my Life*".[2]

Nothing like the overall plan of the philosophical chapters, moving through materialism and associationism to transcendentalism, to the question of philosophical intuition, and to a final vision of synthesis that passes into religious thought, exists in any one of the German or English books Coleridge read. Nothing so drastically and accurately *condensed* as Coleridge's discussion in Chapters 5–9 and 12 appears in any of his reading. And the application to poetry of philosophical principles developed in the chapters on "metaphysics", especially the stress on the imagination as distinguished from fancy, is an effort that Coleridge, in the practical criticism of the second volume, pushes far beyond what he found in other works. Even apart from its unique biographical interest, the aims and the composition of the *Biographia* are uniquely Coleridge's.

The books Coleridge read almost always prompted in him a mental or marginal editing. This was not the drudgery of sources, dates, parallels, and controversies that too often embroils scholars.

[1] *CN* II 2375.   [2] *CN* I 1515.

It was a dialogue and commentary—a creative variorum—that could be written only by one saturated with the subject, with many subjects and knowledges, only by one who, as Coleridge remarks, read books not in order to write one, but to find truth. For instance, in reading Schelling's *System* Coleridge becomes frustrated by the symbolic logic and the awkward definitions and asks tartly in the margin, "*What do you mean? Give me an instance*". The text had become too abstract. Coleridge criticises Schelling for verbose terminology and protests that Schelling could have made his points clearer if he had used "simple common-life Words".

While reading Schelling's *System*, Coleridge encountered the assertion that intelligence, in its productive capacity, has consciousness whereas nature, in hers, is without consciousness. His reaction, actually a series of reactions, is typical of the way he approached his reading:

I deny it: & for the reasons above stated. ⟨i.e. at this moment.⟩ A book, I value, I reason & quarrel wit[h] as with myself when I am reason[ing] S. T. [C.]

He states that much of Schelling's idealism becomes "0=0!" but suddenly, catching himself, he revokes his own objections and says, "No! I am wrong".[1] Coleridge's act of reading was a perpetual stream of mind, more active than passive; what he read became part of his being. It was a transfusive process through which he could feel that he had earned the right to consider ideas "my own". No idea remained inert in the atmosphere of his thought, and composition and reading were for him ways of thinking.

How Coleridge uses several different passages in Maass's *Versuch* (often separated by 350 pages or more) and also anywhere from one to a half-dozen passages in each of four or five of Schelling's different books has already been mentioned. In addition, he uses parts of his own marginal notes to these writers, and even divides his own notes and places their parts in different paragraphs (even chapters) of the *Biographia*. As a passage in Maass or Schelling renews his thinking, he will launch into a discourse on that point, an example or a ramification—often informed by other reading. Then he will return to where he left off in the German book. This evokes new thoughts and reactions, sometimes a difference of

[1] Annotations on a front flyleaf, referring to pp 15–16, and on the title-page, referring to p 17: *CM* (*CC*) IV.

opinion, and often causes him to skip ahead or backward to a related passage in that same book, or to one in a different volume—Jacobi's *Ueber die Lehre des Spinoza*, for instance—from which he uses a footnote that quotes Leibniz or Kant. And this in turn will send him to another place in Jacobi—and then back again to Schelling, or to his own thoughts.

UNITY OF THE *BIOGRAPHIA*

If we look for a simple unity that dominates the *Biographia* we are thwarted. The book actually presents a series of interlocking unities: biographical, critical, philosophical, and religious. The first volume also has chronological unity throughout. In addition, the two volumes together form a response to Wordsworth, especially to the 1815 Preface, a fact that strongly prescribes the pattern of philosophical and critical discussion in Volume I and its transition to Chapters 14–22. Coleridge in Volume I seeks to establish "my principles" and, with these, a philosophic idea of the imagination. Volume II is an "application of the rules, deduced from philosophical principles, to poetry and criticism", the test of the *poetic* imagination.[1] As Chapter 15 states at the beginning, Coleridge is there embarking on "the application of these principles to purposes of practical criticism".

In considering the unity of the *Biographia*, one must realise at the start that "Satyrane's Letters" and the critique of *Bertram* had no place in Coleridge's original scheme. They were added when he was obliged to find more than a hundred pages to fill out the second volume, owing to the publisher's miscalculation. The main problem of "unity" rests in the first thirteen chapters: how they stand together and how they relate to the critical observations in the second volume. Yet it is within the first volume (and taken as a prelude to the second) that Coleridge's unified intentions are revealed most completely.

In biography and chronology, Chapters 1–13 provide an unbroken chain of development. At first this may sound untenable, since the philosophical chapters seem to differ significantly in their nature and subject. But there is an unshaken continuity. Chapters 1–4 carry Coleridge through the *Lyrical Ballads* and 1798; he

[1] Ch 1, below, I 5.

relates his school experiences, early poems, the admiration of Bowles, and associations with Southey, Wordsworth, and others in the 1790s. The falling out with critics at large and his first public receptions have their roots in early reviews and encounters of the 1790s. Thus, discussion of critics and of Southey, Bowles, and Wordsworth all fall into these first four chapters, too. Chapters 5–9 and 12–13 do not, by contrast, seem "biographical" at all. But they are, because when Coleridge sailed to Germany in 1798— and for several years afterwards—he was in the process of extricating himself from a primary reliance on materialism, from a view of mind and of poetry as largely built on an associative rather than an imaginative faculty. From 1799, slowly at first, and then more surely by 1803–4, he was discovering and exploring the transcendental philosophy. This central and biographical fact runs through the philosophical chapters. These provide an odyssey of his own metaphysical journey of nearly twenty years. It was during the fifteen years after his return from Germany in 1799 that Coleridge, transient and often unhappy in his personal circumstances (which he understandably omits for the most part), read for the first time—or continued to read—Kant, Tetens, Leibniz, Jacobi, Schelling, Bruno, and others. His philosophical liberation and the growth of his metaphysical views he thus considers the essential and important part of his life from 1799 to 1815.[1] Chapters 5–9 reflect this, as do 12 and 13. Actually, Chapter 10, beginning with an effort to explain "esemplastic", is probably a false start on the goal of the philosophical chapters, the deduction of the imagination. As he started to write it he may have even intended Chapter 10 to be the final philosophical chapter. But he postponed the deduction and the "esemplastic power" for a later chapter (to become 13) and reverted to the style of the first four chapters. Chapter 11 is a brief lament for the lack of a profession to keep him on the track of a regular life and also a caveat to budding authors "never [to] pursue literature as a trade".

Volume I, then, is almost strictly chronological, with Chapters 1–4 presenting a mixture of biography (in the sense of events) and of intellectual development. Chapters 5–13 then swing more exclusively (yet chronologically) to the life of his mind. Throughout

[1] See *CN* I 1515: ". . . to write my metaphysical works, as *my Life, & in* my Life—intermixed with all the other events/ or history of the mind & fortunes of S. T. Coleridge".

these philosophical chapters, and in the critical applications of Volume II, Coleridge also dissociates himself, to some extent, from Wordsworth and from any notion of a school of Lake Poets by showing that his own principles as a philosopher-poet and as a critic rest on a deeper study of nature and of the faculties of the mind. The first volume establishes philosophical principles—especially that of the imagination and its difference from fancy. In Volume II, Coleridge embodies his principles in the critical observations that begin in Chapters 14 and 15, on the imagination as exercised by specific poets in specific poems, its "*poetic* fruitage".[1] The logical break in the book occurs exactly where it is, after Chapter 13.

The "esemplastic power," in "all its degrees and determinations", is the culmination of Volume I; it had become the central pillar of Coleridge's investigations from 1800 (or even earlier) until the time of the *Biographia*. Yet it was also to be the imagination as differentiated from fancy in a special way, not in the way Wordsworth differentiated them in the 1815 Preface. This is an important point of cohesion for the book as a whole. Coleridge first comes to this point at the end of Chapter 4 and again at the end of Chapter 13. Significantly, these two places mark the "entrance" and "exit" of the philosophical chapters, their beginning and end. And it is at these very places that Wordsworth enters the picture, specifically on the very subject of fancy and imagination, for Coleridge is answering him. When Coleridge first discusses this at the end of Chapter 4, we should remember that he begins this chapter by saying, "I have wandered far from the object in view", which involves, as the headnote explains, "The lyrical ballads with the preface . . . On fancy and imagination—The investigation of the distinction important to the fine arts". By the end of this chapter, Coleridge has become engaged in a dialogue with Wordsworth about fancy and imagination. And while he does not mention Wordsworth by name in Chapter 13, in which Coleridge makes his firm distinction, it is obvious that the last three paragraphs of Chapter 13 are meant to continue that dialogue with Wordsworth. There are two reasons for this. First, Coleridge ends Chapter 13 (and Volume I) with a reference to the *Ancient Mariner*, his significant contribution to the *Lyrical Ballads*. He intends to dissociate

[1] Ch 4, below, I 88.

this poem from the *Lyrical Ballads* by republishing it separately and writing for it his own preface or "critical essay" that will explain *his* theory "concerning the powers and privileges of the imagination".[1] Second, the whole of Chapter 13 is introduced by the last paragraph of Chapter 12, in which Coleridge dwells again (as in Chapter 4) on the difference between his view of imagination *vs* fancy and the view expressed by Wordsworth in the 1815 Preface. Coleridge says, "I have attached a meaning to both fancy and imagination, which he had not in view, at least while he was writing that preface [1815]".[2] The effective cause of the *Biographia* is Wordsworth's 1815 Preface: as we trace the unity and structure of the *Biographia*, we find that it hinges—at every crucial point and transition (Chapters 4–5, 12–13, and 13 to the second volume as a whole)—on the dialogue between Coleridge and Wordsworth and on Coleridge's reply to Wordsworth concerning the subject of imagination and fancy.

There is another axis or line of unity in the *Biographia*, one that joins with the others. The book is a religious testament, and Coleridge's religious beliefs and thoughts intwine and are part of his "total and undivided philosophy". For him a strong relation exists also between religion and poetry. And finally, in the *Biographia* Coleridge relates changes in his own beliefs—his religious biography in miniature up to 1817.

When he announces the contents of the book in its first pages, he includes "my principles in . . . Religion".[3] At strategic points he introduces these principles and, with them, what might be called the history of his belief. Chapter 10, at the heart of the philosophical chapters, is crucial for this history, and in Chapter 11 Coleridge indirectly laments that he did not settle on the clerical calling. The last chapter of the book concludes on a strong, even a fervent, religious crescendo. Coleridge's metaphysics, after all, grew *with* his moral and religious convictions, the keeping alive, as he called it, of the *heart* in the *head*.[4] For him this seemed natural and violated no intellectual or scientific principles. When he says in Chapter 9 that he will use the new "revolution in philosophy" and apply it "to the most awful of subjects for the most important of purposes", he means for profound religious inquiry.[5] And

---

[1] Ch 13, below, I 306.
[2] Ch 12, below, I 294.
[3] Ch 1, below, I 5.

[4] Ch 9, below, I 152.
[5] Ch 9, below, I 163–4.

when he jokes about his fear that his deduction of the imagination would, if printed in full, be compared with Berkeley's essay, "which beginning with Tar ends with the Trinity",[1] this uneasy joking comes from his awareness that his philosophical and religious thoughts are deeply inseparable and can be discussed only as one large unit or not at all.

In a way, then, the *Biographia* is a book whose circumference is everywhere and whose centre is nowhere. Its many unities ("Sketches") of biography, chronology, philosophy, criticism, and religion create a dynamic nucleus of fundamentals that are dependent on each other and fuse into one. The book has no single-minded unity but a myriad-minded one. We might even characterise it as multeity in unity. If Coleridge had written only a more orthodox autobiography of events, a philosophical monograph, a series of critical essays, or a statement of religious or political beliefs, then the "unity" would be obvious and easy. But for his own literary life, his life of experience and thought and feeling, such single unities could not be. They were parts of the whole. The unity that does emerge from the book is more inclusive than any of these parts because it connects all of them, and in doing this the book calls on the life of the whole man.

[1] Ch 13, below, I 303.

Josiah Wade, Esqr
in testimony of grateful regard
from the
obliged
Author.

BIOGRAPHIA LITERARIA;

OR

Biographical Sketches

OF

MY LITERARY LIFE

AND

OPINIONS.

BY S. T. COLERIDGE, Esq.

....

VOL. I.

....

LONDON:

REST FENNER, 23, PATERNOSTER ROW

—

1817.

2. *Biographia Literaria* (1817). Title-page, from the copy
inscribed by Coleridge to Josiah Wade
reproduced by kind permission of the Houghton Library,
Harvard University

BIOGRAPHIA LITERARIA
VOLUME I

So wenig er auch bestimmt seyn mag andere zu belehren, so wünscht er doch sich denen mitzutheilen, die er sich gleichgesinnt weiss oder hofft, deren Anzahl aber in der Breite der Welt zerstreut ist: er wünscht sein Verhältniss zu den ältesten Freunden wieder anzuknüpfen, mit neuen es fortzusetzen, und in der letzen Generation sich wieder andere für sein übrige Lebenszeit zu gewinnen. Er wünscht der Jugend die Umwege zu ersparen, auf denen er sich selbst verirrte.

GOETHE.[1]

TRANSLATION. Little call as he may have to instruct others, he wishes nevertheless to open out his heart to such as he either knows or hopes to be of like mind with himself, but who are widely scattered in the world: he wishes to knit anew his connections with his oldest friends, to continue those recently formed, and to win other friends among the rising generation for the remaining course of his life. He wishes to spare the young those circuitous paths, on which he himself had lost his way.

---

[1] *Propyläen* Einleitung (Tübingen 1798) i i viii–ix (var). C may have read the periodical while in Germany. He copied the passage into a notebook in 1807–8: see *CN* ii 3221 and n. His translation varies the literal sense of one or two phrases.

CHAPTER 1

The motives of the present work—Reception of the Author's first publication—The discipline of his taste at school—The effect of contemporary writers on youthful minds—Bowles's sonnets—Comparison between the Poets before and since Mr. Pope

IT HAS BEEN my lot to have had my name introduced both in conversation, and in print, more frequently than I find it easy to explain, whether I consider the fewness, unimportance, and limited circulation of my writings, or the retirement and distance, in which I have lived, both from the literary and political world. Most often it has been connected with some charge, which I could not acknowledge, or some principle which I had never entertained. Nevertheless, had I had no other motive, or incitement, the reader would not have been troubled with this exculpation. What my additional purposes were, will be seen in the following pages. It will be found, that the least of what I have written concerns myself personally. I have used the narration chiefly for the purpose of giving a continuity to the work, in part for the sake of the miscellaneous reflections suggested to me by particular events, but still more as introductory to the statement of my principles in Politics, Religion, and Philosophy, and the application of the rules, deduced from philosophical principles, to poetry and criticism. But of the objects, which I proposed to myself, it was not the least important to effect, as far as possible, a settlement of the long continued controversy concerning the true nature of poetic diction: and at the same time to define with the utmost impartiality the real *poetic* character of the poet, by whose writings this controversy was first kindled, and has been since fuelled and fanned.

In 1794, when I had barely passed the verge of manhood, I published a small volume of juvenile poems.[1] They were received

---

[1] Actually 16 Apr 1796: *Poems on Various Subjects.* Among the poems are *Monody on the Death of Chatterton, Religious Musings,* and *Effusion XXXV,* which C later entitled (1817) *The Eolian Harp.* Lamb contributed three of the sonnets (XI–XIII) and parts of two others (VII and XIV), and RS wrote the first part of XV. But C had published, in 1795, *The Fall of Robespierre,* his collaboration with RS.

with a degree of favor, which, young as I was, I well knew, was bestowed on them not so much for any positive merit, as because they were considered buds of hope, and promises of better works to come. The critics of that day, the most flattering, equally with the severest, concurred in objecting to them, obscurity, a general turgidness of diction, and a profusion of new coined double epithets.[1]* The first is the fault which a writer is the least able to

* The authority of Milton and Shakspeare may be usefully pointed out to young authors. In the Comus, and earlier Poems of Milton there is a superfluity of double epithets; while in the Paradise Lost we find very few, in the Paradise Regained scarce any. The same remark holds almost equally true, of the Love's Labour Lost, Romeo and Juliet, Venus and Adonis, and Lucrece compared with the Lear, Macbeth, Othello, and Hamlet of our great Dramatist.[2] The rule for the admission of double epithets seems to be this: either that they should be already denizens of our Language, such as blood-stained, terror-stricken, self-applauding: or when a new epithet, or one found in books only, is hazarded, that it, at least, be one word, not two words made one by mere virtue of the printer's hyphen. A language which, like the English, is almost without cases, is indeed in its very genius unfitted for compounds. If a writer, every time a compounded word suggests itself to him, would seek for some other mode of expressing the same sense, the chances are always greatly in favor of his finding a better word. "Tanquam scopulum sic vites insolens verbum,"[3] is the wise advice of Cæsar to the

[1] "The Reviews have been wonderful", C wrote to Estlin (4 Jul 1796). "The Monthly [Review] has *cataracted* panegyric on my poems; the Critical has *cascaded* it; and the Analytical has *dribbled* it with very tolerable civility. The Monthly has at least done justice to my Religious Musings—They place it 'on the very top of the scale of Sublimity.'—!—!—!" *CL* I 224. C in this letter refers to the reviews (all in 1796) in *M Rev* NS XX 194–9, *C Rev* NS XVII 209–12, and *Analytical* XXIII 610–12. He was also doubtless thinking of those in *B Critic* VII 549–50, *Free-Mason's Review* VII 52–3, *Monthly Mirror* II 97, and (in 1797) *A Reg* XVII 265. C is oversensitive to the adverse criticism of his compound epithets, which appeared in the *Analytical* and esp *English Review* XXVIII 172–5.
[2] Cf C's Lect 7 of 9 Dec 1811: "It would be a hopeless symptom in Coleridge's mind if he found a young man with perfect taste. In the early works of Shakespeare a profusion of double epithets would be found . . .". *Lects 1808–19 (CC)* ms. Cf also "We want, methinks, a little treatise from some man of flexible good sense, and well versed in the Greek poets . . . containing first a history of compound epithets, and then the laws and licenses." Annotation on Thomas Gray *Works* (2 vols 1814) I 9: *CM (CC)* II.
[3] Aulus Gellius *Noctes Atticae* 1.10.4. C abbreviates the injunction attributed by Gellius to Caesar in bk I of *De analogia*, i.e. the "treatise" to which C refers in the next sentence: ". . . habe semper in memoria atque in pectore, ut tamquam scopulum, sic fugias inauditum atque insolens verbum" ("have ever in mind and heart to avoid, as you would a rock, a strange and unfamiliar word"). *BL* (1907) I 204. C had copied the remark into a notebook in 1799: *CN* I 384 and n. (Cf *CN* III 3245.) Later also used in the 1818 *Friend (CC)* I 449.

detect in his own compositions: and my mind was not then sufficiently disciplined to receive the authority of others, as a substitute
for my own conviction. Satisfied that the thoughts, such as they
were, could not have been expressed otherwise, or at least more
perspicuously, I forgot to enquire, whether the thoughts themselves
did not demand a degree of attention unsuitable to the nature and
objects of poetry. This remark however applies chiefly, though not
exclusively to the *Religious Musings*. The remainder of the charge
I admitted to its full extent, and not without sincere acknowledg-
ments to both my private and public censors for their friendly
admonitions. In the after editions, I pruned the double epithets with
no sparing hand, and used my best efforts to tame the swell and
glitter both of thought and diction; though in truth, these parasite
plants of youthful poetry had insinuated themselves into my longer
poems with such intricacy of union, that I was often obliged to
omit disentangling the weed, from the fear of snapping the
flower.[1] From that period to the date of the present work I have
published nothing, with my name, which could by any possibility
have come before the board of anonymous criticism.[2] Even the
three or four poems, printed with the works of a friend,[3] as far as

---

Roman Orators, and the precept applies with double force to the writers in
our own language. But it must not be forgotten, that the same Cæsar wrote a
grammatical treatise for the purpose of reforming the ordinary language by
bringing it to a greater accordance with the principles of Logic or universal
Grammar.

[1] C in the above sentences is repeating, in almost identical language,
the apologetic opening of the Preface
to the 2nd ed of *Poems* (pub 28 Oct
1797) xvii. See *PW* (EHC) II 1145.
C "pruned" relatively few "double
epithets". But he did omit twenty-
three of the poems published in the
first edition, and added twelve,
among them the *Dedication* (to his
brother George), *Ode on the Departing Year,* and *Reflections on
Having Left a Place of Retirement.*
Also included in the 2nd ed were
fifteen poems by Lamb and twenty-
nine by Charles Lloyd. The 3rd ed
(1803) was substantially a reprint of
the 2nd, except for the omission of
the poems by Lamb and Lloyd and
six by C himself.

[2] Thinking of non-dramatic verse,
C hence does not mention his translation of Schiller's *Wallenstein*
(1800), *The Friend* (1809–10), or
his tragedy *Remorse* (1813). But he
is forgetting *Fears in Solitude . . .
To which are added, France, an Ode;
and Frost at Midnight* (1798). The
contributions to *LB* (1798) were
anonymous. At the time he is writing
(1815), *Christabel* (1816) and *SL*
(1817) had not yet been published.
Cf C's remark, below, I 50–3.

[3] C's four poems in *LB: The Rime
of the Ancyent Marinere, The Foster-
Mother's Tale, The Nightingale,* and
The Dungeon. Reviewers in general
assumed that the volume was written
by a single author. The adverse
comments C has in mind appeared

they were censured at all, were charged with the same or similar defects, though I am persuaded not with equal justice: with an EXCESS OF ORNAMENT, in addition to STRAINED AND ELABORATE DICTION. *(Vide the criticisms on the* "Ancient Mariner," *in the Monthly and Critical Reviews of the first volume of the Lyrical Ballads.)* May I be permitted to add, that, even at the early period of my juvenile poems, I saw and admitted the superiority of an austerer, and more natural style, with an insight not less clear, than I at present possess. My judgment was stronger, than were my powers of realizing its dictates; and the faults of my language, though indeed partly owing to a wrong choice of subjects, and the desire of giving a poetic colouring to abstract and metaphysical truths, in which a new world then seemed to open upon me, did yet, in part likewise, originate in unfeigned diffidence of my own comparative talent.—During several years of my youth and early manhood, I reverenced those, who had re-introduced the manly simplicity of the Grecian, and of our own elder poets, with such enthusiasm, as made the hope seem presumptuous of writing successfully in the same style. Perhaps a similar process has happened to others; but my earliest poems were marked by an ease and simplicity, which I have studied, perhaps with inferior success, to impress on my later compositions.

At school I enjoyed the inestimable advantage of a very sensible, though at the same time, a very severe master. He* early moulded my taste to the preference of Demosthenes to Cicero, of Homer and Theocritus to Virgil, and again of Virgil to Ovid. He habituated me to compare Lucretius, (in such extracts as I then read) Terence, and above all the chaster poems of Catullus, not only with

---

* The Rev. James Bowyer, many years Head Master of the Grammar-School, Christ's[a] Hospital.[1]

[a] *BL* (1817): Christ

---

mainly in *A Rev* XXVIII (1798) 583–7, *M Rev* NS XXIX (1798) 202–10, and (by RS) *C Rev* NS XXIV (1798) 197–204.

[1] James Boyer (1736–1814), an alumnus of Balliol, had become Upper Grammar Master at Christ's Hospital in 1776. His severity and his fondness for the birch-rod were a legend. Cf the famous account in Lamb's "Christ's Hospital Five and Thirty Years Ago" (*L Works* II 18–20) and De Q's more caustic description ("Coleridge and Opium-Eating" *De Q Works* II 197–8). For C's account of his one flogging by Boyer (because at thirteen he announced "I am an infidel") see *TT* 27 May 1830.

the Roman poets of the, so called, silver and brazen ages;[1] but with even those of the Augustan era: and on grounds of plain sense and universal logic to see and assert the superiority of the former, in the truth and nativeness, both of their thoughts and diction. At the same time that we were studying the Greek Tragic Poets, he made us read Shakspeare and Milton as lessons: and they were the lessons too, which required most time and trouble to *bring up*, so as to escape his censure. I learnt from him, that Poetry, even that of the loftiest, and, seemingly, that of the wildest odes, had a logic of its own, as severe as that of science;[2] and more difficult, because more subtle, more complex, and dependent on more, and more fugitive causes. In the truly great poets, he would say, there is a reason assignable, not only for every word, but for the position of every word; and I well remember, that availing himself of the synonimes to[a] Homer of Didymus,[3] he made us attempt to show, with regard to each, *why* it would not have answered the same purpose; and *wherein* consisted the peculiar fitness of the word in the original text.

In our own English compositions (at least for the last three years of our school education) he showed no mercy to phrase, metaphor,

[a] *BL* (1817): to the

[1] The Silver Age of Latin literature was generally regarded as from A.D. 14 (the death of Augustus) to A.D. 117 (the death of Trajan) and the Bronze Age from A.D. 117 to A.D. 410 (the sack of Rome by the Goths). Cf Robert Ainsworth *Thesaurus linguae latinae* (1736) xxx.

[2] Cf "Young somewhere in one of his prose works remarks that there is as profound a Logic in the most daring & dithyrambic parts of Pindar, as in the Ὄργανον [Logic] of Aristotle—the remark is a valuable one". To William Sotheby 10 Sept 1802: *CL* II 864. The passage in Edward Young actually reads: "Thus Pindar, who has as much logic at the bottom as Aristotle or Euclid, to some critics has appeared as mad; and must appear so to all, who enjoy no portion of his own divine spirit." "On Lyric Poetry", appended to *An Ode to the King, 1728: Works* (1774–8) VI 130. C had read

Young's essay and taken notes from it in 1795 (*CN* I 33–6 and nn). On the remark generally, cf C's note on John Selden *Table Talk* (ed not identified): "They, that is, verses, are not logic; but they are, or ought to be, the envoys and representatives of that vital passion, which is the practical cement of logic; and without which logic must remain inert." *CM* (*CC*) IV; *Misc C* 277. See Mc-Farland 113.

[3] That is, the ancient scholia, previously attributed to the Alexandrian scholar Didymus Chalcenterus (c 80–10 B.C.). Boyer may have been using the Elzevir Homer, *Ilias et Odyssea et in easdem scholia sive interpretatio Didymi* ed Cornelius Schrevelius (Amsterdam 1655–6). A copy of this appears in *Catalogue of the Books in the Library of Christ's Hospital* (1874). The date 1654 in the catalogue appears to be an error.

or image, unsupported by a sound sense, or where the same sense might have been conveyed with equal force and dignity in plainer words.[1] Lute, harp, and lyre, muse, muses, and inspirations, Pegasus, Parnassus, and Hippocrene, were all an abomination to him. In fancy I can almost hear him now, exclaiming *"Harp? Harp? Lyre? Pen and ink, boy, you mean! Muse, boy, Muse? your Nurse's daughter, you mean! Pierian spring? Oh 'aye! the cloister-pump, I suppose!"* Nay certain introductions, similies, and examples, were placed by name on a list of interdiction. Among the similies, there was, I remember, that of the Manchineel fruit,[2] as suiting equally well with too many subjects; in which however it yielded the palm at once to the example of Alexander and Clytus,[3] which was equally good and apt, whatever might be the theme. Was it ambition? Alexander and Clytus!—Flattery? Alexander and Clytus!—Anger? Drunkenness? Pride? Friendship? Ingratitude? Late repentance? Still, still Alexander and Clytus! At length, the praises of agriculture having been exemplified in the sagacious observation, that had Alexander been holding the plough, he would not have run his friend Clytus through with a spear, this tried, and serviceable old friend was banished by public edict in secula

[1] Cf "High-flown epithets and violent metaphors, conveyed in inflated language, is not poetry. Simplicity is indispensable . . .". Lect 2 of 1811: *Sh C* II 66. "For works of imagination should be written in very plain language; the more purely imaginative they are the more necessary it is to be plain." *TT* 31 May 1830. *BL* (1847) I 7n prints a note to this passage, presumably an annotation from C's copy of *BL* from which the eds were working: "This is worthy of ranking as a maxim, (*regula maxima,*) of criticism. Whatever is translatable in other and simpler words of the same language, without loss of sense or dignity, is bad. N.B. By dignity I mean the absence of ludicrous and debasing associations."

[2] A West Indian tree, attractive-looking but with poisonous sap. Boyer's dislike of it as a stock image impressed itself also on Lamb, who told C in a letter (?20 Sept 1797): "I shall get angry, & call you hard names, Manchineel, & I don't know what else". *LL* I 123. On one occasion, however, C yielded to the temptation to use the image, in the *Dedication* (line 26) of the 2nd ed of his *Poems* (1797): "False and fair-foliag'd as the manchineel", and possibly alludes to it in ch 10, below, I 197.

[3] For Alexander's slaying of his frankly speaking friend, Clitus, while both were intoxicated at a banquet, and his impassioned remorse afterwards, see Plutarch *Lives:* "Alexander" 50–2. According to De Q, C, presumably in conversation, "used the image of a man 'sleeping under a manchineel tree' alternately with the case of Alexander killing Clytus as resources for illustration which Providence had bountifully made exhaustless in their application". *De Q Works* XI 378.

seculorum.[1] I have sometimes ventured to think, that a list of this kind, or an index expurgatorius of certain well known and ever returning phrases, both introductory, and transitional, including the large assortment of modest egotisms, and flattering illeisms,[2] &c. &c. might be hung up in our law-courts, and both houses of parliament, with great advantage to the public, as an important saving of national time, an incalculable relief to his Majesty's ministers, but above all, as insuring the thanks of country attornies, and their clients, who have private bills to carry through the house.

Be this as it may, there was one custom of our master's, which I cannot pass over in silence, because I think it imitable and worthy of imitation. He would often permit our theme exercises, under some pretext of want of time, to accumulate, till each lad had four or five to be looked over. Then placing the whole number *abreast* on his desk, he would ask the writer, why this or that sentence might not have found as appropriate a place under this or that other thesis; and if no satisfying answer could be returned, and two faults of the same kind were found in one exercise, the irrevocable verdict followed, the exercise was torn up, and another on the same subject to be produced, in addition to the tasks of the day. The reader will, I trust, excuse this tribute of recollection to a man, whose severities, even now, not seldom furnish the dreams, by which the blind fancy would fain interpret to the mind the painful sensations of distempered sleep; but neither lessen nor dim the deep sense of my moral and intellectual obligations. He sent us to the University excellent Latin and Greek scholars, and tolerable Hebraists.[3] Yet our classical knowledge was the least of the good gifts, which we derived from his zealous and conscientious tutorage. He is now gone to his final reward, full of years, and full of honors, even of those honors, which were dearest to his heart, as gratefully bestowed by that school, and still binding him to the interests of that school, in which he had been himself educated, and to which during his whole life he was a dedicated thing.

From causes, which this is not the place to investigate, no models of past times, however perfect, can have the same vivid

---

[1] Tr "For ever and ever" in the Bible (AV).

[2] C's coinage. Literally "that-ism" or "that-personism". In other words, a "flattering" cliché or polite tag referring to another person. Cf *Friend (CC)* I 26 and n, II 32.

[3] C's early knowledge of Hebrew was at best only "tolerable". But he returned to the study of it in 1817.

effect on the youthful mind, as the productions of contemporary genius. The Discipline, my mind had undergone, "Ne falleretur rotundo sono et versuum cursu, cincinnis et floribus; sed ut inspiceret quidnam subesset, quæ sedes, quod firmamentum, quis fundus verbis; an figuræ essent mera ornatura et orationis fucus: vel sanguinis e materiæ ipsius corde effluentis rubor quidam nativus et incalescentia genuina;"[1] removed all obstacles to the appreciation of excellence in style without diminishing my delight. That I was thus prepared for the perusal of Mr. Bowles's sonnets and earlier poems,[2] at once increased *their* influence, and *my* enthusiasm. The great works of past ages seem to a young man things of another race, in respect to which his faculties must remain passive and submiss, even as to the stars and mountains. But the writings of a contemporary, perhaps not many years elder than himself, surrounded by the same circumstances, and disciplined by the same manners, possess a *reality* for him, and inspire an actual friendship as of a man for a man. His very admiration is the wind which fans and feeds his hope. The poems themselves assume the properties of flesh and blood. To recite, to extol, to contend for them is but the payment of a debt due to one, who exists to receive it.

There are indeed modes of teaching which have produced, and are producing, youths of a very different stamp; modes of teaching, in comparison with which we have been called on to despise our great public schools, and universities

> In whose halls are hung
> Armoury of the invincible knights of old—[3]

modes, by which children are to be metamorphosed into prodigies. And prodigies with a vengeance have I known thus produced!

[1] No source has been traced. *BL* (1847) I 10n conjectured that the Latin was C's and (now confirmed by *Thesaurus linguae latinae*—Leipzig 1900) that *incalescentia* is not a classical word; *BL* (1975) 5n that the Latin was from a Renaissance treatise on rhetoric. Tr: "So that it [i.e. my mind] was not misled by the smooth sound and flow of the verses, their ringlets and flowers, but examined what lay beneath them, what was their ground, their firmament, their foundation; whether the figures were mere ornamentation and the paint of rhetoric, or a natural flush and genuine warmth of the blood flowing from the heart of the matter itself."

[2] William Lisle Bowles (1762–1850), vicar of Bremhill from 1804. See below, I 13–17. C. visited Bowles in Bremhill in 1814 and 1815. See *CN* III 4300 and n.

[3] WW *Poems Dedicated to National Independence* Sonnet XVI ("It is not to be thought of") lines 9–10 (var).

Prodigies of self-conceit, shallowness, arrogance, and infidelity! Instead of storing the memory, during the period when the memory is the predominant faculty, with facts for the after exercise of the judgement; and instead of awakening by the noblest models the fond and unmixed LOVE and ADMIRATION, which is the natural and graceful temper of early youth; *these* nurselings of improved pedagogy are taught to dispute and decide; to suspect all, but their own and their lecturer's wisdom; and to hold nothing sacred from their contempt, but their own contemptible arrogance: boy-graduates in all the technicals, and in all the dirty passions and impudence, of anonymous criticism.[1] To such dispositions alone can the admonition of Pliny be requisite, "Neque enim debet operibus ejus obesse, quod vivit. An si inter eos, quos nunquam vidimus, floruisset, non solum libros ejus, verum etiam imagines conquireremus, ejusdem nunc honor præsentis, et gratia quasi satietate languescet? At hoc pravum, malignumque est, non admirari hominem admiratione dignissimum, quia videre, complecti, nec laudare tantum, verum etiam amare contingit." *Plin. Epist. Lib. I.*[2]

I had just entered on my seventeenth year, when the sonnets of Mr. Bowles, twenty in number, and just then published in a quarto pamphlet, were first made known and presented to me, by a school-fellow who had quitted us for the University, and who, during the whole time that he was in our first form (or in our school language a GRECIAN) had been my patron and protector. I refer to Dr. Middleton, the truly learned, and every way excellent Bishop of Calcutta:[3]

[1] C possibly refers to "the Education of the Dissenters and of the Scotch Universities . . . for nothing can surpass their eagerness to dispute and criticize in their Pupillage . . .". *CN* III 3243.

[2] Pliny *Letters* 1.16, from which C omits two inessential words; tr (LCL): "Let it not be any prejudice to his merit that he is a contemporary writer. Had he flourished in some distant age, not only his works, but the very pictures and statues of him would have been passionately inquired after; and shall we then, from a sort of satiety, and merely because he is present among us, suffer his talents to languish and fade away unhonoured and unadmired? It is surely a very perverse and envious disposition, to look with indifference upon a man worthy of the highest approbation, for no other reason but because we have it in our power to see him and to converse familiarly with him, and not only to give him our applause, but to receive him into our friendship." C had copied the passage into a notebook in 1804 (*CN* II 1944) and first applied it to WW in *Friend* No 7: *Friend* (*CC*) II 108n (I 183n).

[3] C refers to Bowles's 2nd ed, *Sonnets, Written Chiefly in Picturesque Spots, During a Tour* (Bath

Qui laudibus amplis
Ingenium celebrare meum, calamumque solebat,
Calcar agens animo validum. Non omnia terræ
Obruta! Vivit amor, vivit dolor! Ora negatur
Dulcia conspicere; at flere et meminisse * relictum est.
                              Petr. Ep. Lib. I. Ep. I.[1]

It was a double pleasure to me, and still remains a tender recollection, that I should have received from a friend so revered the
first knowledge of a poet, by whose works, year after year, I was so
enthusiastically delighted and inspired.[2] My earliest acquaintances

---

* I am most happy to have the necessity of informing the reader, that
since this passage was written, the report of Dr. Middleton's death on his
voyage to India has been proved erroneous. He lives and long may he live;
for I dare prophesy, that with his life only will his exertions for the temporal
and spiritual welfare of his fellow men be limited.

1789), which contained twenty-one sonnets.

Thomas Fanshaw Middleton (1769–1822), who had called C's attention to Bowles, had left for Cambridge in 1788. He continued to befriend C during C's first year in Cambridge (1791–2). He was appointed bp of Calcutta in 1814. For C's reaction to his *Doctrine of the Greek Article; Applied to the Criticism and the Illustration of the New Testament* (1808), see *CN* III 3275 and n.

[1] Petrarch *Epistola Barbato Sulmonensi* lines 12–16 (var). C had copied the lines into a notebook in 1813, from Petrarch *Opera* (Basle 1581) III 76: *CN* III 4178 and n. Tr: "Who, with lavish praises, was wont to celebrate my genius and my pen, setting a sharp spur to my spirit. Not everything is buried in the earth. Love lives, grief lives on! We are denied the sight of those sweet features; but it is left for us to weep and to remember." C later combined the lines with Latin lines from Milton to make a motto for an essay in the 1818 *Friend: Friend (CC)* I 144. For other quotations from Petrarch's verse letter see ch 10, below, I 222, and ch 14, below, II 16 n 6.

[2] What most struck C in Bowles was the union of direct, heartfelt sentiment with moral reflection. Cf remarks in the letters 1792–6: "the exquisite Bowles"; "descriptive, dignified, tender, sublime"; "the bard of my idolatry"; and his sonnet *To the Rev. W. L. Bowles* in *M Chron* 26 Dec 1794 ("My heart has thank'd thee, Bowles! for those soft strains"): *PW* (EHC) I 84–5. In C's *Poems* (1796) he diffidently entitled his own sonnets "effusions" partly, as he said in his Preface (p x), because "I was fearful that the title 'Sonnet' might have reminded my reader of the Poems of the Rev. W. L. Bowles—a comparison with whom would have sunk me below that mediocrity, on the surface of which I am at present enabled to float". *PW* (EHC) II 1137. After a visit to Bowles in 1797 C's friends noticed that he spoke of Bowles with less ardour. By 1802 he confessed to Sotheby: "Bowles has indeed the *sensibility* of a poet; but he has not the *Passion* of a great Poet", and, in addition, "he is not a Thinker". *CL* II 864. Several years later, during a visit with Bowles, C felt "I injured myself irreparably with him by devoting a fortnight to the correction" of one of his poems. Bowles "took

will not have forgotten the undisciplined eagerness and impetuous zeal, with which I laboured to make proselytes, not only of my companions, but of all with whom I conversed, of whatever rank, and in whatever place. As my school finances did not permit me to purchase copies, I made, within less than a year and an half, more than forty transcriptions, as the best presents I could offer to those, who had in any way won my regard. And with almost equal delight did I receive the three or four following publications of the same author.[1]

Though I have seen and known enough of mankind to be well aware, that I shall perhaps stand alone in my creed, and that it will be well, if I subject myself to no worse charge than that of singularity; I am not therefore deterred from avowing, that I regard, and ever have regarded the obligations of intellect among the most sacred of the claims of gratitude. A valuable thought, or a particular train of thoughts, gives me additional pleasure, when I can safely refer and attribute it to the conversation or correspondence of another. My obligations to Mr. Bowles were indeed important and for radical good. At a very premature age, even before my fifteenth year, I had bewildered myself in metaphysicks, and in theological controversy.[2] Nothing else pleased me. History, and

---

the corrections and never forgave the Corrector". *CL* IV 694. Cf *CN* III 3644n, 4233, 4276n, 4300, and nn.

[1] Presumably *The Grave of Howard* (1790), *Verses on the Benevolent Institution of the Philanthropic Society* (1790), and the 3rd, 4th, and 5th eds of the *Sonnets* (1794, 1796), and possibly *Hope, an Allegorical Sketch* (1796). Bowles's *Elegiac Stanzas* (1796) C considered "unworthy" of him. *CL* I 203. In the autumn of 1796 C, to amuse himself, selected 28 sonnets to be bound with Bowles's sonnets, had 200 copies printed, and sold them to his friends for sixpence each. One surviving copy of "A Sheet of Sonnets", bound with Bowles *Sonnets* (4th ed 1796), is in the V & A, another, with Bowles *Sonnets* (3rd ed 1794), is in HEHL. See *CL* I 152, 285.

[2] Cf Lamb's famous passage: "Come back into memory, like as thou wert in the day-spring of thy fancies, with hope like a fiery column before thee—the dark pillar not yet turned—Samuel Taylor Coleridge—Logician, Metaphysician, Bard!—How have I seen the casual passer through the Cloisters stand still, intranced with admiration (while he weighed the disproportion between the *speech* and the *garb* of the young Mirandula), to hear thee unfold, in thy deep and sweet intonations, the mysteries of Jamblichus, or Plotinus (for even in those years thou waxedst not pale at such philosophic draughts), or reciting Homer in his Greek, or Pindar—while the walls of the old Grey Friars re-echoed to the accents of the *inspired charity-boy!*" "Christ's Hospital Five and Thirty Years Ago" *L Works* II 24–5. Cf C's later remark that he translated "the eight Hymns of Synesius . . . before my 15th

particular facts, lost all interest in my mind. Poetry (though for a school-boy of that age, I was above par in English versification, and had already produced two or three compositions which, I may venture to say, without reference to my age, were somewhat above mediocrity, and which had gained me more credit, than the sound, good sense of my old master was at all pleased with)[1] poetry itself, yea novels and romances, became insipid to me. In my friendless wanderings on our *leave-*days,* (for I was an orphan, and had scarce any connections in London)[2] highly was I delighted, if any passenger, especially if he were drest in black,[3] would enter into conversation with me. For I soon found the means of directing it to my favorite subjects

> Of providence, fore-knowledge, will, and fate,
> Fix'd fate, free will, fore-knowledge absolute,
> And found no end in wandering mazes lost.[4]

This preposterous pursuit was, beyond doubt, injurious, both to my natural powers, and to the progress of my education. It would perhaps have been destructive, had it been continued; but from this I was auspiciously withdrawn, partly indeed by an accidental intro-

---

* The Christ's[a] Hospital phrase, not for holidays altogether, but for those on which the boys are permitted to go beyond the precincts of the school.

[a] *BL* (1817): Christ

---

year" into English Anacreontics, which would have been something of a feat. Ch 12, below, I 247 n 2.

[1] Boyer kept a *Liber Aureus* containing what he considered his students' best exercises. (It is now in the BM.) Cf *CN* I 1706, II 2647. Included in it are C's *Nil Pejus Est Caelibe Vita, Quae Nocent Docent, Progress of Vice,* and particularly *Monody on the Death of Chatterton.* To one poem Boyer did not include, *Dura Navis,* written in C's fifteenth year, C in later years appended a note: "I well remember old Jemmy Bowyer . . . bade me leave out as many epithets as would turn the whole into eight-syllable lines, and then ask myself if the exercise would not be greatly improved. How often have I thought of the proposal since then, and how many thousand

bloated and puffing lines have I read, that, by this process, would have tripped over the tongue excellently. Likewise, I remember that he told me on the same occasion—'Coleridge! the connections of a Declamation are not the transitions of Poetry—bad, however, as they are, they are better than "Apostrophes" and "O thou's", for at the worst they are something like common sense. The others are the grimaces of Lunacy.'" *PW* (EHC) I 3n.

[2] C's father had died in 1781, but his mother lived until 1809. His mother's brother, a tobacconist and clerk to an underwriter, treated him with affection when he first went to London. See *CL* I 388.

[3] In other words, a clergyman.

[4] Milton *Paradise Lost* II 559–61.

duction to an amiable family,[1] chiefly however, by the genial influence of a style of poetry, so tender, and yet so manly, so natural and real, and yet so dignified, and harmonious, as the sonnets, &c. of Mr. Bowles! [2] Well were it for me perhaps, had I never relapsed into the same mental disease; if I had continued to pluck the flower and reap the harvest from the cultivated surface, instead of delving in the unwholesome quicksilver mines of metaphysic depths.[3] But if in after time I have sought a refuge from bodily pain and mismanaged sensibility in abstruse researches,[4] which exercised the strength and subtlety of the understanding without awakening the feelings of the heart; still there was a long and blessed interval,[5] during which my natural faculties were allowed to expand, and my original tendencies to develope themselves: my fancy, and the love of nature, and the sense of beauty in forms and sounds.

The second advantage, which I owe to my early perusal, and admiration of these poems (to which let me add, though known to me at a somewhat later period, the Lewsdon Hill of Mr.

[1] His school friend, William Evans, introduced C in 1788 to his widowed mother and three sisters (Mary, Anne, and Elizabeth). Mrs Evans created an atmosphere of affectionate humour and good sense. C was captivated by the friendly warmth, became known as "Brother Coly", and fell in love with the eldest sister, Mary. Though his feelings appear to have been sentimental rather than passionate, they were durable, as most of C's emotional attachments were. But Mary did not return them and finally brought herself to refuse him with kindliness but firmness. *C Life* (H) 22–3, 27–31, 54, 56, 60.

[2] Cf ". . . Bowles, the most tender, and, with the exception of Burns, the only *always-natural* poet in our Language". To John Thelwall 17 Dec 1796: *CL* I 278.

[3] "Believe me, Southey! a metaphysical Solution that does not instantly *tell* for something in the Heart, is grievously to be suspected as apocry[p]hal." To RS [7 Aug

1803]: *CL* II 961. "Our quaint metaphysical opinions in an hour of anguish like playthings by the bedside of a child deadly sick." *CN* I 182 (Sept–Oct 1796).

[4] Cf

For not to think of what I needs
    must feel,
    But to be still and patient,
    all I can;
And haply by abstruse research
    to steal
    From my own nature all
    the natural man—
    This was my sole resource,
    my only plan:
Till that which suits a part
    infects the whole,
And now is almost grown the
    habit of my soul.

Dejection: an Ode lines 87–93: *PW* (EHC) I 367. Cf also *CL* IV 893.

[5] Until 1800–2, when he was twenty-eight or thirty, and when his growing unhappiness and his addiction to opium seem to have become more pronounced.

CROW)[1] bears more immediately on my present subject. Among those with whom I conversed, there were, of course, very many who had formed their taste, and their notions of poetry, from the writings of Mr. Pope and his followers: or to speak more generally, in that school of French poetry, condensed and invigorated by English understanding, which had predominated from the last century. I was not blind to the merits of this school, yet as from inexperience of the world, and consequent want of sympathy with the general subjects of these poems, they gave me little pleasure, I doubtless undervalued the *kind*, and with the presumption of youth withheld from its masters the legitimate name of poets. I saw, that the excellence of this kind consisted in just and acute observations on men and manners in an artificial[2] state of society, as its matter and substance: and in the logic of wit,[3] conveyed in smooth and strong epigrammatic couplets, as its *form*.[4] Even when the subject was addressed to the fancy, or the intellect, as in the Rape of the Lock, or the Essay on Man; nay, when it was a consecutive narration, as in that astonishing product of matchless talent and ingenuity, Pope's Translation of the Iliad; still a *point* was looked for at the end of each second line, and the whole was as it were a sorites,[5] or, if I may exchange a logical for a gram-

[1] William Crowe (1745–1829), who held the position of Public Orator at Oxford from 1784 to his death. His *Lewesdon Hill* (1788) is in the sentimental-reflective vein of Bowles and C's own early verse. C had borrowed a copy of it from the Bristol Library 2–10 Mar 1795: *Bristol LB* 119.

[2] By the 1780s the older meaning of "artificial" (e.g. in Johnson's *Dictionary*, "made by art . . . contrived with skill") was being driven out by the conception of it as something "not natural or genuine". Significantly the conservative Johnson is among the first to apply it to "society", as indicating specialised and transitory customs, in a famous remark in the "Preface" to Shakespeare (1765) par 5, which C may be echoing: "Every topick of merriment, or motive of sorrow, which

the *modes of artificial life* afforded him, now only obscure the scenes which they once illuminated."

[3] Not in the traditional sense of "wit" (cf Johnson: "powers of the mind . . . the intellect") but in the more limited sense of what Dryden called "pointed wit" (Preface to *Troilus and Cressida*), which by the later eighteenth century becomes the dominant meaning in critical writing. The subject of one of C's 1808 lectures was "Dryden and Pope, including the origin and after history of poetry of witty logic". *Sh C* II 5.

[4] Cf *CN* II 1889n, and below, I 39.

[5] Literally something "heaped together". In logic a technical term for a group of two or more syllogisms in which the conclusion of the preceding one serves as the premise for the next.

matical metaphor, a *conjunction disjunctive*,[1] of epigrams. Meantime the matter and diction seemed to me characterized not so much by poetic thoughts, as by thoughts *translated* into the language of poetry.[2] On this last point, I had occasion to render my own thoughts gradually more and more plain to myself, by frequent amicable disputes concerning Darwin's BOTANIC GARDEN, which, for some years, was greatly extolled, not only by the *reading* public in general, but even by those, whose genius and natural robustness of understanding enabled them afterwards to act foremost in dissipating these "painted mists" that occasionally rise from the marshes at the foot of Parnassus.[3] During my first Cambridge vacation, I assisted a friend in a contribution for a literary society in Devonshire: [4] and in this I remember to have

[1] On the "conjunction disjunctive of Wit", typified by Samuel Butler's *Hudibras*, cf *CN* II 2112 and n.

[2] Cf "Difference of Form as proceeding and Shape as superinduced—the latter either the Death or the imprisonment of the Thing; the former, its self-witnessing, and self-effected sphere of agency—". *CN* III 4397 f 53ᵛ.

[3] *The Botanic Garden* (1789–92) was an attempt by Erasmus Darwin (1731–1802)—physician, naturalist, grandfather of the famous Charles—to incorporate science as part of the subject matter of poetry. It consisted of two Parts, "The Economy of Vegetation" and "Loves of the Plants", with long prose notes amplifying scientific details and, in Pt II, three "interludes" discussing poetic style. The poem is written in the closed heroic couplet perfected by Pope, and, without inspiration, makes painstaking use of stylistic devices, especially periphrasis and personification, associated with conventional neoclassic verse. The style was for C a prototype of all he reacted against in commonplace poetry of the time. "I absolutely nauseate Darwin's Poem", he wrote in 1796 (*CL* I 216); and he kept recurring to it and Darwin's ideas about the relation of poetry and painting (e.g. *CN* I 132 and n). Cf his remark that young poets "seek for reputation. . . . It was into this error that the Author of the Botanic Garden had fallen . . . there were not to be found 20 images described . . . in a state of excitement. It was written with all the industry of a Milliner or tradesman, who was anxious to dress his ideas in silks & satins and by collecting all the sonorous & handsome-looking words." Lect 2 of 21 Nov 1811: *Lects 1808–19 (CC)* ms. Actually *The Botanic Garden* was less "extolled" by the reading public than C says. It was popular largely as a curiosity, and most of its readers enjoyed George Canning's parody, *The Loves of the Triangles* (1798). The "amicable disputes" were probably those C had with friends at Cambridge. Christopher Wordsworth tells of one in his college diary for 5 Nov 1793, printed at the end of his *Social Life at the English Universities* (1874) 589.

[4] Presumably a group calling itself "A Society of Gentlemen at Exeter", founded by Dr Hugh Downman about 1790 and lasting until 1808. It is described in the obituary for Downman in *G Mag*

compared Darwin's work to the Russian palace of ice, glittering, cold and transitory.[1] In the same essay too, I assigned sundry reasons, chiefly drawn from a comparison of passages in the Latin poets with the original Greek, from which they were borrowed, for the preference of Collins's odes to those of Gray;[2] and of the simile in Shakspeare

> How like a younker or a prodigal,
> The skarfed bark puts from her native bay
> Hugg'd and embraced by the strumpet wind!
> How like a prodigal doth she return,
> With over-weather'd ribs and ragged sails,
> Lean, rent, and beggar'd by the strumpet wind![3]

to the imitation in the bard;

> Fair laughs the morn, and soft the zephyr blows
> While proudly riding o'er the azure realm
> In gallant trim the gilded vessel goes,
> Y O U T H at the prow and P L E A S U R E at the helm,
> Regardless of the sweeping whirlwind's sway,
> That hush'd in grim repose, expects it's evening prey.[4]

(In which, by the bye, the words "realm" and "sway" are rhymes dearly purchased.) I preferred the original on the ground, that in the imitation it depended wholly in the compositor's putting, or not putting a *small Capital*, both in this, and in many other passages of the same poet, whether the words should be personifications, or mere abstracts.[5] I mention this, because in referring various lines in Gray to their original in Shakspeare and Milton; and in the clear perception how completely all the propriety was lost in the transfer; I was, at that early period, led to a conjecture, which, many years afterwards was recalled to me from the same thought

LXXX (1810) 81–4, which states that its dozen members—C was not a regular member—met "to unite talents of different descriptions, and genius directed to different pursuits". It published a volume in 1796, *Essays by a Society of Gentlemen, at Exeter*. The essay mentioned by C does not appear in it, but the preface notes that "materials for another" volume "have been preserved".

[1] The ice palace built at St Petersburg by the Empress Anna in the winter of 1739–40, which melted the following March.

[2] "He thought Collins had more genius than Gray, who was a singular instance of a man of taste, poetic feeling, and fancy, without imagination." *TT* 21 Apr 1811.

[3] *Merchant of Venice* II vi 14–19.

[4] Gray *The Bard* lines 71–6.

[5] "Gray's personifications, he said, were mere printer's devils' personifications—persons with a capital letter, abstract qualities with a small one." *TT* 21 Apr 1811.

having been started in conversation, but far more ably, and developed more fully, by Mr. WORDSWORTH; namely, that this style of poetry, which I have characterised above, as translations of prose thoughts into poetic language, had been kept up by, if it did not wholly arise from, the custom of writing Latin verses, and the great importance attached to these exercises, in our public schools. Whatever might have been the case in the fifteenth century, when the use of the Latin tongue was so general among learned men, that Erasmus is said to have forgotten his native language; yet in the present day it is not to be supposed, that a youth can *think* in Latin, or that he can have any other reliance on the force or fitness of his phrases, but the authority of the author from whence he has adopted them. Consequently he must first prepare his thoughts, and then pick out, from Virgil, Horace, Ovid, or perhaps more compendiously from his * Gradus, halves and quarters of lines, in which to embody them.

I never object to a certain degree of disputatiousness in a young man from the age of seventeen to that of four or five and twenty, provided I find him always arguing on one side of the question. The controversies, occasioned by my unfeigned zeal for the honor of a favorite contemporary, then known to me only by his works,[4] were of great advantage in the formation and establish-

---

* In the Nutricia of Politian there occurs this line:
  Pura coloratos interstrepit unda lapillos.[1]
Casting my eye on a University prize-poem, I met this line,
  Lactea purpureos interstrepit unda lapillos.
Now look out in the Gradus for *Purus*, and you find as the first synonime, *lacteus*; for *coloratus*, and the first synonime is *purpureus*.[2] I mention this by way of elucidating one of the most ordinary processes in the *ferrumination*[3] of these centos.

[1] Poliziano (or Politianus): the name given Angelo Ambrogini (1454–94) from his birthplace, Montepulciano. The line is not in his *Nutricia* but in his *Rusticus* (line 14). In 1803 C copied the first two words (as well as the Latin line, below) into a notebook: see *CN* I 1673 and n. Tr: "The clear stream murmurs on amid the little coloured stones."

[2] C refers to the famous handbook of Latin prosody by Paul Aler (1656–1727), *Gradus ad Parnassum*, which first appeared in 1687 and was widely used in English schools for over a century and a half. But he makes a slip in citing the examples he does. Though the words could easily be imagined as routinely appropriate in school exercises, *lacteus* is not listed at all under *purus* in the *Gradus*, nor is *purpureus* under *coloratus*.

[3] "Gluing together" or, here, "Cementing together"; C is probably thinking of fitting together a wall from various shapes of stone.

[4] Bowles.

ment of my taste and critical opinions. In my defence of the lines running into each other, instead of closing at each couplet; and of natural language, neither bookish, nor vulgar, neither redolent of the lamp, or of the kennel, such as *I will remember thee*;[1] instead of the same thought tricked up in the rag-fair finery of,

—— Thy image on her wing
Before my FANCY'S eye shall MEMORY bring,[2]

I had continually to adduce the metre and diction of the Greek Poets from Homer to Theocritus inclusive; and still more of our elder English poets from Chaucer to Milton. Nor was this all. But as it was my constant reply to authorities brought against me from later poets of great name, that no authority could avail in opposition to TRUTH, NATURE, LOGIC, and the LAWS of UNIVERSAL GRAMMAR; actuated too by my former passion for metaphysical investigations; I labored at a solid foundation, on which permanently to ground my opinions, in the component faculties of the human mind itself, and their comparative dignity and importance.[3] According to the faculty or source, from which

[1] Cf ". . . he will remember you". Bowles Sonnet III "To the River Wisbeck" line 14: *Sonnets* (3rd ed 1794) 6.

[2] C is partly reacting from his own youthful fondness for the image, as in "On Memory's wing, like shadows fly" (*Absence* line 10), "On shadowy Memory's wings" (*Effusion at Evening* line 8), and "Hover around me on sad Memory's wings" (*Fall of Robespierre* I 46). *PW* (EHC) I 29, 49, II 497.

[3] On judging poetry according to its derivation from and its effect upon the "component faculties of the . . . mind", cf Lect 5 of 11 Nov 1813 in Bristol: "The only nomenclature of criticism should be the classification of the faculties of the mind, how they are placed, how they are subordinate, whether they do or do not appeal to the worthy feelings of our nature." *Lects 1808–19 (CC); Sh C* II 280. Explaining the similarity of his observations on Shakespeare to those of Schlegel, C

remarked, "For Schlegel & myself had both studied . . . the philosophy of Kant, the distinguishing feature of which [is] to treat every subject in reference to the operation of the mental Faculties, to which it specially appertains . . ." To an unknown correspondent [c 15–21 Dec 1811]: *CL* III 360. (To exemplify a psychological approach to criticism C could have picked many other writers, including Lord Kames, Joseph Priestley, Hugh Blair, Alexander Gerard, James Beattie, Daniel Webb, Lessing, Herder, or Schiller.) Cf WW's classification, undoubtedly influenced by C, in 1815 and later eds, in which many of the poems "are placed according to the powers of mind, in the Author's conception, predominant in the production of them". *Poems* Preface (1815) I xv: *W Prose* III 29.

Ch 18, below, is the best explanation in *BL* of the above on "principles" of writing rather than of "judging".

the pleasure given by any poem or passage was derived, I estimated the merit of such poem or passage. As the result of all my reading and meditation, I abstracted two critical aphorisms, deeming them to comprize the conditions and criteria of poetic style; first, that not the poem which we have *read*, but that to which we *return*, with the greatest pleasure, possesses the genuine power, and claims the name of *essential poetry*. Second, that whatever lines can be translated into other words of the same language, without diminution of their significance, either in sense, or association, or in any worthy feeling, are so far vicious in their diction. Be it however observed, that I excluded from the list of worthy feelings, the pleasure derived from mere novelty, in the reader, and the desire of exciting wonderment at his powers in the author. Oftentimes since then, in perusing French tragedies, I have fancied two marks of admiration at the end of each line, as hieroglyphics of the author's own admiration at his own cleverness.[1] Our genuine admiration of a great poet is a continuous *under-current* of feeling; it is every where present, but seldom any where as a separate excitement. I was wont boldly to affirm, that it would be scarcely more difficult to push a stone out from the pyramids with the bare hand, than to alter a word, or the position of a word, in Milton or Shakspeare, (in their most important works at least) without making the author say something else, or something worse, than he does say.[2] One great distinction, I appeared to myself to see plainly, between, even the characteristic faults of our elder poets, and the false beauty of the moderns. In the former, from DONNE to COWLEY, we find the most fantastic out-of-the-way thoughts, but in the most pure and genuine mother English; in the latter, the most obvious thoughts, in language the most fantastic and arbitrary.[3] Our faulty elder poets sacrificed the

[1] For C's persistent prejudice against French literature, cf ". . . spite of Paschal, Madame Guyon, and Moliere France is my Babylon, the Mother of Whoredoms in Morality, Philosophy, Taste/ the French themselves feel a foreignness in these Writers". *CN* ii 2598. Cf also *CN* iii 4264 and n and *Sh C* ii 84, 159.

[2] Cf "The collocation of words is so artificial in Shakspere and Milton, that you may as well think of push-ing a brick out of a wall with your fore-finger, as attempt to remove a word out of any of their finished passages." *TT* 3 Jul 1833.

[3] "Wonder-exciting vigour, intenseness and peculiarity of thought, using at will the almost boundless stores of a capacious memory, and exercised on subjects, where we have no right to expect it—this is the wit of Donne!" C's annotation on Donne in Alexander Chalmers *The Works of*

passion, and passionate flow of poetry, to the subtleties of intellect, and to the starts of wit; the moderns to the glare and glitter of a perpetual, yet broken and heterogeneous imagery, or rather to an amphibious something, made up, half of image, and half of abstract * meaning. The one sacrificed the heart to the head; the other both heart and head to point and drapery.

The reader must make himself acquainted with the general style of composition that was at that time deemed poetry, in order to understand and account for the effect produced on me by the SONNETS, the MONODY at MATLOCK, and the HOPE, of Mr. Bowles;[1] for it is peculiar to original genius to become less and less *striking*, in proportion to its success in improving the taste and judgement of its contemporaries.[2] The poems of WEST indeed had the merit of chaste and manly diction, but they were cold, and, if I may so express it, only *dead-coloured*;[3] while in the best of Warton's there is a stiffness, which too often gives them the appearance of imitations from the Greek.[4] Whatever relation

---

* I remember a ludicrous instance in the poem of a young tradesman:
No more will I endure love's pleasing pain,
Or round my *heart's leg* tie his galling chain.

---

the *English Poets* (1810) vol v. *CM (CC)* II. "How legitimate a child was not Cowley of Donne; but C. had a Soul-*mother* as well as Soul-*father*—& who was she? what was that?—Perhaps, sickly Court-Loyalty . . . a discursive Intellect, *naturaly* less vigorous, & daring—& then *cowed* by King-Worship." Part of C's annotation on *The Indifferent* in Donne *Poems* (1669) 7–10. *CM (CC)* II.

[1] Cf above, I 15 n 1. Of *Hope* C wrote to Thelwall (19 Nov 1796): Bowles "has written a poem lately without plan or meaning—but the component parts are divine". *CL* I 259.

[2] Cf ". . . every author, as far as he is great and at the same time *original,* has had the task of *creating* the taste by which he is to be enjoyed: so has it been, so will it continue to be. This remark was long since made to me by the philosophical Friend [C] for the separation of whose poems from my own I

have previously expressed my regret." WW "Essay Supplementary to the Preface" *Poems* (1815): *W Prose* III 80.

[3] Gilbert West (1703–56), remembered for his imitations of Spenser (1739, 1751) and his translation of Pindar (1749). "Dead-coloured", a term in painting, the first layer of paint on a canvas—pale and lifeless: see *OED*.

[4] Probably Thomas Warton (1728–90), the poet laureate and editor of Theocritus, rather than his brother Joseph (1722–1800). Cf Dr Johnson on Thomas Warton:
Uncouth words in disarray,
Trick'd in antique ruff and bonnet,
Ode, and elegy, and sonnet.
In his introduction to "A Sheet of Sonnets" (which included one of Thomas Warton's, "When late the trees . . .") C noted: "The greater part of Wharton's Sonnets are severe and masterly likenesses of the style

therefore of cause or impulse Percy's collection of Ballads may bear to the most *popular* poems of the present day;[1] yet in the more sustained and elevated style, of the then living poets Bowles and Cowper* were, to the best of my knowledge, the first who combined natural thoughts with natural diction; the first who reconciled the heart with the head.

It is true, as I have before mentioned, that from diffidence in my own powers, I for a short time adopted a laborious and florid diction, which I myself deemed, if not absolutely vicious, yet of very inferior worth. Gradually, however, my practice conformed to my better judgement; and the compositions of my twenty-fourth and twenty-fifth year (*ex. gr.* the shorter blank verse poems, the lines which are now adopted in the introductory part of the VISION in the present collection in Mr. Southey's Joan of Arc,

---

* Cowper's Task was published some time before the sonnets of Mr. Bowles; but I was not familiar with it till many years afterwards.[2] The vein of Satire which runs through that excellent poem, together with the sombre hue of its religious opinions, would probably, *at that time,* have prevented its laying any strong hold on my affections. The love of nature seems to have led Thomson[a] to a chearful religion; and a gloomy religion to have led Cowper to a love of nature. The one would carry his fellow-men along with him into nature; the other flies to nature from his fellow-men. In chastity of diction however, and the harmony of blank verse, Cowper leaves Thomson[a] unmeasureably below him; yet still I feel the latter to have been the *born poet.*[3]

[a] *BL* (1817): Thompson

---

of the Greek επιγραμματα." *PW* (EHC) II 1139.

[1] The famous *Reliques of Ancient English Poetry* (1765) by Bishop Thomas Percy (1729–1811), which—despite Percy's alterations and retouching of his texts—remained the primary source of ballad literature until F. J. Child's first version of his *English and Scottish Popular Ballads* (8 vols 1857–8). C, especially in *AM,* was strongly influenced by Percy's ballads (see e.g. *RX* 173, 244, 249, 331–2, 336, 498). "I do not think that there is an able writer in verse of the present day who would not be proud to acknowledge his obligations to the Reliques; I know that it is so with my friends; and, for myself, I am happy in this occasion to make a public avowal of my own." WW *Poems* (1815) "Essay, Supplementary to the Preface": *W Prose* III 78.

[2] William Cowper's *The Task* was published four years before Bowles's *Sonnets* (1789). In a letter of 1796 C praised "the divine Chit chat of Cowper" (*CL* I 279), and in 1801 entered a line from *The Task* into a notebook: *CN* I 1055. Cf also *CN* II 2484. Cowper's blank verse was one of C's principal models for the style of his conversation poems. *C Life* (B) 43–51.

[3] In an annotation on *B Poets* C called James Thomson (1700–48) "the Honor, yea, the Redeemer of Scotland". *CM (CC)* I 74.

2nd book, 1st edition, and the Tragedy of R E M O R S E) are not more below my present ideal in respect of the general tissue of the style, than those of the latest date.[1] Their faults were at least a remnant of the former leaven, and among the many who have done me the honor of putting my poems in the same class with those of my betters, the one or two, who have pretended to bring examples of affected simplicity from my volume, have been able to adduce but one instance, and that out of a copy of verses half ludicrous, half splenetic, which I intended, and had myself characterized, as *sermoni propriora.*[2]

Every reform, however necessary, will by weak minds be carried to an excess, that itself will need reforming.[3] The reader will excuse me for noticing, that I myself was the first to expose *risu honesto*[4] the three sins of poetry, one or the other of which is the most likely to beset a young writer. So long ago as the

---

[1] The blank-verse poems to which C refers include *To a Friend Who Had Declared His Intention of Writing No More Poetry, To the Rev. George Coleridge, This Lime-Tree Bower My Prison,* and *The Dungeon.* The lines "now adopted in the introductory part of the VISION" consist of 255 lines contributed by C to RS's *Joan of Arc, an Epic Poem* (1796) Bk II. To these C added others from an unpublished poem (variously entitled *The Progress of Liberty* or *The Vision of the Maid of Orleans*). With some revision the result was then published as *The Destiny of Nations: a Vision* in *SL* (1817), the "present collection" mentioned above, which C had at first planned to publish with *BL.* "The Tragedy of REMORSE" refers to the first version of the play, *Osorio,* which C in 1797 wrote at the invitation of R. B. Sheridan for performance at Drury Lane. Sheridan did not accept it. In 1812 C rewrote it as *Remorse,* and it was performed the following January at Drury Lane, where it ran for twenty nights.

[2] *Address to a Young Jackass and Its Tethered Mother,* pub *M Chron* 30 Dec 1794, and included in *Poems* (1796): *PW* (EHC) I 74–6. Actually it was not this poem C characterised as *Sermoni propriora,* "more suitable to prose/ conversation" (Horace *Satires* 1.4 reads *propriora,* "nearer to")—which Lamb puckishly translated as "properer for a sermon" (*TT* 25 Jul 1832)—but *Reflections on Having Left a Place of Retirement: PW* (EHC) I 106–8. The motto, which he prefixed to *Reflections* in 1797, could be described both as an apology and as a conscious aim for the style of the "conversation poems" generally. *C Life* (B) 42. C doubtless confused the poem to which he attached it because in *M Chron* his subtitle for the *Young Jackass* ("In familiar verse") had a similar implication.

[3] C may be thinking of the famous remark of Burke, whose writings he knew so well, that in hasty "reform"—"what men, more zealous than considerate, call *making clear work*"—things are carried so far that "Then some part of the abdicated grievance is recalled from its exile in order to become a corrective of the correction." Speech on the Oeconomical Reform 11 Feb 1780: *Works* (1803) III 248.

[4] "With honest laughter".

publication of the second number of the monthly magazine, under
the name of NEHEMIAH HIGGENBOTTOM I contributed three
sonnets, the first of which had for its object to excite a good-
natured laugh at the spirit of *doleful egotism*, and at the recurrence
of favorite phrases, with the double defect of being at once trite,
and licentious. The second, on low, creeping language and
thoughts, under the pretence of *simplicity*. And the third, the
phrases of which were borrowed entirely from my own poems, on
the indiscriminate use of elaborate and swelling language and
imagery. The reader will find them in the note * below, and will I

SONNET I

* PENSIVE at eve, on the *hard* world I mused,
And *my poor* heart was sad; so at the MOON
I gazed, and sighed, and sighed; for ah how soon
Eve saddens into night! mine eyes perused
With tearful vacancy the *dampy* grass
That wept and glitter'd in the *paly* ray:
And I *did pause me*, on my lonely way
And *mused me*, on the *wretched ones* that pass
O'er the bleak heath of sorrow. But alas!
Most of *myself* I thought! when it befel,
That the *soothe* spirit of the *breezy* wood
Breath'd in mine ear: "All this is very well,
But much of ONE thing, is for NO thing good."
Oh *my poor heart's* INEXPLICABLE SWELL!

SONNET II

OH I do love thee, meek SIMPLICITY!
For of thy lays the lulling simpleness
Goes to my heart, and soothes each small distress,
Distress tho' small, yet haply great to me,
'Tis true on Lady Fortune's gentlest pad
I amble on; and yet I know not why
So sad I am! but should a friend and I
Frown, pout and part, then I am *very* sad.
And then with sonnets and with sympathy
My dreamy bosom's mystic woes I pall;
Now of my false friend plaining plaintively,
Now raving at mankind in general;
But whether sad or fierce, 'tis simple all,
All very simple, meek SIMPLICITY!

SONNET III

AND this reft house is that, the which he built,
Lamented Jack! and here his malt he pil'd,
Cautious in vain! these rats, that squeak so wild,
Squeak not unconscious of their father's guilt.
Did he not see her gleaming thro' the glade!
Belike 'twas she, the maiden all forlorn.
What tho' she milk no cow with crumpled horn,

trust regard them as reprinted for biographical purposes, and not
for their poetic merits.[2] So general at that time, and so decided

> Yet, *aye* she haunts the dale where *erst* she stray'd:
> And *aye*, beside her stalks her amorous knight!
> Still on his thighs their wonted brogues are worn,
> And thro' those brogues, still tatter'd and betorn,
> His hindward charms gleam an unearthly white.
> Ah! thus thro' broken clouds at night's high Noon
> Peeps in fair fragments forth the full-orb'd harvest-moon!

The following anecdote will not be wholly out of place here, and may
perhaps amuse the reader. An amateur performer in verse expressed to a
common friend, a strong desire to be introduced to me, but hesitated in
accepting my friend's immediate offer, on the score that "he was, he must
acknowledge the author of a confounded severe epigram on my *ancient
mariner*, which had given me great pain. I assured my friend that if the
epigram was a good one, it would only increase my desire to become
acquainted with the author, and begg'd to hear it recited: when, to my no
less surprise than amusement, it proved to be one which I had myself some
time before written and inserted in the Morning Post.

> To the author of the Ancient Mariner.

> Your poem must eternal be,
> Dear sir! it cannot fail,
> For 'tis incomprehensible
> And without head or tail.[1]

[1] C's own lines (*M Post* 24 Jan 1800) were addressed not "to the author of the Ancient Mariner" but to Henry James Pye (1745–1813), poet laureate: *To Mr. Pye* "On his *Carmen Seculare* (a title which has by various persons who have heard it, been thus translated, 'A Poem an age long')". *PW* (EHC) II 959. C has been censured for implying, in his footnote above, that his own title in *M Post* was "To the author of the Ancient Mariner". But (though he may have invented the story) he is here supposedly quoting the epigram as it was entitled by the "amateur performer". In any case he does not mention his source. The epigram is suggested by Lessing's *Sinngedichte, Die Ewigkeit gewisser Gedichte* ("The Eternity of Certain Poems"): *Sämmtliche Schriften* (Berlin 1796) I 11:
Verse, wie sie Bassus schreibt,
Werden unvergänglich bleiben:—
Weil dergleichen Zeug zu schreiben,
Stets ein Stümper übrig bleibt.
("Verses such as Bassus writes | Will remain eternal: | For to write such stuff | There will always be one more bungler left.") Cf *CN* I 625 and n.

[2] The sonnets appeared in *M Mag* Nov 1797, with the title *Sonnets Attempted in the Manner of Contemporary Writers*. (See *PW*—EHC —I 209–11: all var.) "I sent three mock Sonnets", C meanwhile wrote Cottle, "in ridicule of my own, & Charles Lloyd's, & Lamb's, &c &c— in ridicule of that affectation of unaffectedness, of jumping & misplaced accent on common-place epithets, flat lines forced into poetry by Italics (signifying how well & *mouthis[h]ly* the Author would read them) puny pathos &c &c—the instances are almost all taken from mine & Lloyd's poems—I signed

was the opinion concerning the characteristic vices of my style, that a celebrated physician (now, alas! no more) [1] speaking of me in other respects with his usual kindness to a gentleman, who was about to meet me at a dinner party, could not however resist giving him a hint not to mention the *"House that Jack built"* in my presence, for "that I was *as sore as a boil* about that sonnet;" he not knowing, that I was myself the author of it.

them Nehemiah Higginbottom. I think they may do good to our young Bards." *CL* I 357–8. Though the first sonnet is certainly a parody of Lloyd (in the present version the capitals and especially the italics are exaggerated), and though the third could be viewed as a less convincing parody of himself, in the second C may have been thinking as much of RS as of Lamb. Certainly Lamb assumed this (*CL* I 404), and so did RS, to whom C wrote a passionate letter of denial (*CL* I 358–9). Later, still smarting, RS wrote four sonnets supposedly in C's most flaccid style and published them as by "Abel Shufflebottom".

[1] Probably C's friend Dr Thomas Beddoes (1760–1808), who in 1796 contributed to Poole's subscription to help C.

CHAPTER 2

Supposed irritability of men of Genius—Brought to the test of Facts—
Causes and Occasions of the charge—Its Injustice

I HAVE often thought, that it would be neither uninstructive nor unamusing to analyze, and bring forward into distinct consciousness, that complex feeling, with which readers in general take part against the author, in favor of the critic; and the readiness with which they apply to *all* poets the old sarcasm of Horace upon the scriblers of his time: "Genus irritabile vatum."[1] A debility and dimness of the imaginative power, and a consequent necessity of reliance on the immediate impressions of the senses, do, we well know, render the mind liable to superstition and fanaticism. Having a deficient portion of internal and proper warmth, minds of this class seek in the crowd *circum fana*[2] for a warmth in common, which they do not possess singly. Cold and phlegmatic in their own nature, like damp hay, they heat and inflame by co-acervation;[3] or like bees they become restless and irritable through the increased temperature of collected multitudes. Hence the German word for fanaticism (such at least was its original import) is derived from the swarming of bees, namely, Schwärmen, Schwärmerey.[4]

---

[1] Horace *Epistles* 2.2.102; tr "The touchy race of poets". "It is my Faith, that the 'Genus irritabile' is a phrase applicable only to *bad* poets—Men of great Genius have indeed, as an essential of their composition, great sensibility, but they have likewise great confidence in their own powers—and Fear must always precede anger, in the human mind." To Sotheby 10 Sept 1802: *CL* II 863. Cf esp *CN* I 979.

[2] "Around the temple". Cf *"Fanatici—qui circum fana furorem mutuo contrahunt et afflant*—those who in the same conventicle . . . heat and ferment by co-acervation"; also ". . .

those who catch heat best by crowding together round the same *Fane*". Annotations on Walter Birch *Sermon on Enthusiasm* (1818) and on Richard Baxter *Reliquiae Baxterianae: CM* (*CC*) I 496, 270.

[3] "The act of heaping": Johnson. The first recorded use (*OED*) is by the translator John Trevisa (1398).

[4] The use of *Schwärmerei* for "fanaticism" dates back at least as far as Luther (1527). The beehive is a recurring metaphor of C's for error or fanaticism. Cf below, I 197; *CN* II 2434 and n; *Friend* (*CC*) I 22 (II 152), 508; *C&S* (*CC*) 59 and n, 171.

The passion being in an inverse proportion to the insight, *that* the more vivid, as *this* the less distinct; anger is the inevitable consequence.[1] The absence of all foundation within their own minds for that, which they yet believe both true and indispensible for their safety and happiness, cannot but produce an uneasy state of feeling, an involuntary sense of fear from which nature has no means of rescuing herself but by anger.[2] Experience informs us that the first defence of weak minds is to recriminate.

> There's no Philosopher but sees,
> That rage and fear are one disease,
> Tho' that may burn, and this may freeze,
> They're both alike the ague.
>
> MAD OX.[3]

But where the ideas are vivid, and there exists an endless power of combining and modifying them, the feelings and affections blend more easily and intimately with these ideal creations, than with the objects of the senses; the mind is affected by thoughts, rather than by things; and only then feels the requisite interest even for the most important events, and accidents, when by means of meditation they have passed into *thoughts*. The sanity of the mind is between superstition with fanaticism on the one hand; and enthusiasm with indifference and a diseased slowness to action on the other.[4] For the conceptions of the mind may be so vivid and adequate, as to preclude that impulse to the realizing of them, which is strongest and most restless in those, who possess more than mere *talent* (or the faculty of appropriating and applying the knowledge of others) yet still want something of the creative, and self-sufficing power of absolute *Genius*.[5] For this reason therefore,

---

[1] For C on "the disproportion of human passions to their ordinary objects" see *Friend (CC)* I 35 (II 31).

[2] "In all perplexity there is a portion of fear, which predisposes the mind to anger." Below, I 71. Cf above, I 30 n 1.

[3] From C's own *Recantation: Illustrated in the Story of the Mad Ox* lines 63–6: *PW* (EHC) I 301. Cf C's "Essay on the Passions", on rage and fear, in which he also quoted his lines from *Recantation*. BM MS Egerton 2800 ff 43–5, quoted in *IS* 66–7.

[4] For C's distinction between fanaticism and enthusiasm cf also his annotation on Walter Birch *A Sermon on Enthusiasm* (1818)—*CM (CC)* I 495–6—and *SM (CC)* 23 and n.

[5] Alexander Gerard, Condillac, Kant, and others made a similar distinction between genius and talent. Cf e.g. Henry Fuseli, in his first lecture on painting at the Royal Academy, Mar 1801: "Of *genius* I shall speak with reserve, for no word has been more indiscriminately confounded; by genius I mean that

they are men of *commanding* genius.[1] While the former rest content between thought and reality, as it were in an intermundium[2] of which their own living spirit supplies the *substance,* and their imagination the ever-varying *form*; the latter must impress their preconceptions on the world without, in order to present them back to their own view with the satisfying degree of clearness, distinctness, and individuality. These in tranquil times are formed to exhibit a perfect poem in palace or temple or landscape-garden; or a tale of romance in canals that join sea with sea, or in walls of rock, which shouldering back the billows imitate the power, and supply the benevolence of nature to sheltered navies; or in aque-

power which enlarges the circle of human knowledge, which discovers new materials of nature, or combines the known with novelty; whilst *talent* arranges, cultivates, polishes the discoveries of genius." *Lectures on Painting* (1801) 6. In his translation of J. C. Lavater *Aphorisms on Man* (1793) 10, Fuseli had written: "Who in the same given time can produce more than many others, has *vigour;* who can produce more or better, has *talent;* who can produce what none else can, has *genius.*" C, according to John Payne Collier's report of a conversation of 17 Oct 1811, "drew the distinction between talent and genius by comparing the first to a watch and the last to an eye . . . one was a piece of only ingenious mechanism, while the other was a production above all art. . . . Nobody could make an eye, but anybody, duly instructed, could make a watch." *Sh C* II 124. ". . . I define GENIUS, as originality in intellectual construction: the moral accompaniment, and actuating principle of which consists, perhaps, in the carrying on of the freshness and feelings of childhood into the powers of manhood. By TALENT, on the other hand, I mean the comparative facility of acquiring, arranging, and applying the stock furnished by others and already existing in books or other conserva-

tories of intellect." *Friend (CC)* I 419. For this favourite distinction of C's cf esp ibid I 110, 415; *EOT (CC)* I 220; *C&S (CC)* 67 and n 4; *CL* IV 667; and below, I 42, 81, 224, 299–300.

[1] "Absolute Genius" manifests itself in the world of the arts and the intellect. "*Commanding* genius" shows itself in the world of practical affairs (e.g. politics and warfare), appearing in its most destructive form in the "mighty Hunters of Mankind, from NIMROD to NAPOLEON": "Hope in which there is no Chearfulness; Steadfastness within and immovable Resolve, with outward Restlessness and whirling Activity; Violence with Guile; Temerity with Cunning; and, as the result of all, Interminableness of Object with perfect Indifference of Means; these are the qualities that have constituted the COMMANDING GENIUS!" *SM (CC)* 65–6 and n 1, which cites Carl Woodring's argument that C took both the concept and term from Schiller's *Wallenstein: Politics in the Poetry of Coleridge* (Madison 1961) 87. Cf also *EOT (CC)* I 222 and n 6.

[2] A Latin word used by Cicero in describing Epicurean cosmology, and discussed by e.g. Gassendi *Opera* (1658) I 141. C owned some volumes of this and later sent for them from Keswick (*CL* V 328). Cf *OED,* "intermundium".

ducts that arching the wide vale from mountain to mountain give a Palmyra to the desert. But alas! in times of tumult they are the men destined to come forth as the shaping spirit of Ruin,[1] to destroy the wisdom of ages in order to substitute the fancies of a day, and to change kings and kingdoms, as the wind shifts and shapes the clouds.* The records of biography seem to confirm this theory. The men of the greatest genius, as far as we can judge from their own works or from the accounts of their contemporaries, appear to have been of calm and tranquil temper, in all that related to themselves.[3] In the inward assurance of permanent fame, they seem to have been either indifferent or resigned, with regard to immediate reputation.[4] Through all the works of Chaucer there reigns a chearfulness, a manly hilarity, which makes it almost impossible to doubt a correspondent habit of feeling in the author himself.[5] Shakspeare's evenness and sweetness of temper were almost proverbial in his own age. That this did not arise from ignorance of his own comparative greatness, we have

> * Of old things all are over old,
> Of good things none are good enough:—
> We'll show that we can help to frame
> A world of other stuff.
>
> I too will have my kings, that take
> From me the sign of life and death:
> Kingdoms shall shift about, like clouds,
> Obedient to my breath.
>   WORDSWORTH'S ROB ROY[2]

[1] Cf "For this great Monarch-spirit, if he fall, | Will drag a world into the ruin with him." *Piccolomini* III iii 62–3: *PW* (EHC) II 684. Cf also Burke's expression "architects of ruin": *EOT* (*CC*) I 230 and n 7.

[2] *Rob Roy's Grave* lines 85–92.

[3] "But it is no less an essential mark of true genius, that its sensibility is excited by any other cause more powerfully, than by its own personal interests . . .". See below, I 43.

[4] "By Fame . . . I mean any thing rather than 'Reputation'—I mean, the desire of working on the good & great permanently, thro' indefinite ages—the struggle to be promoted into the rank of God's Fellow-Labourers". *CN* III 3291. ". . . In the pursuit of literary Reputation, which a few disguise . . . as an honorable love of *Fame,* & betray the truth to all sharp-sighted minds by their undue Irritation & vehemence of Language concerning every Review which attacks them . . .". *CN* III 3325 ff 13–13ᵛ. Cf also a letter to Matilda Betham 4 Apr 1808: *CL* III 83–4.

[5] "I take increasing delight in Chaucer. His manly cheerfulness is especially delicious to me in my old age. How exquisitely tender he is, and yet how perfectly free from the least touch of sickly melancholy or morbid drooping!" *TT* 15 Mar 1834. On Chaucer cf II 92–3, 93 n 1.

abundant proof in his sonnets, which could scarcely have been known to Mr. Pope,* when he asserted, that our great bard "grew

* Mr. Pope was under the common error of his age, an error, far from being sufficiently exploded even at the present day. It consists (as I explained at large, and proved in detail in my public lectures) in mistaking for the *essentials* of the Greek stage certain rules, which the wise poets imposed upon themselves, in order to render all the remaining parts of the drama consistent with those, that had been forced upon them by circumstances independent of their will; out of which circumstances the drama itself arose.[1] The circumstances in the time of Shakspeare, which it was equally out of his power to alter, were different, and such as, in my opinion, allowed a far wider sphere, and a deeper and more human interest. Critics are too apt to forget, that *rules* are but means to an end; consequently where the ends are different, the rules must be likewise so. We must have ascertained what the end *is*, before we can determine what the rules *ought* to be.[2] Judging under this impression, I did not hesitate to declare my full conviction, that the consummate judgement of Shakspeare, not only in the general construction, but in all the *detail*, of his dramas impressed me with greater wonder, than even the might of his genius, or the depth of his philosophy. The substance of these lectures I hope soon to publish; and it is but a debt of justice to myself and my friends to notice, that the first course of lectures, which differed from the following courses only, by occasionally varying the illustrations of the same thoughts, was addressed to very numerous, and I need not add, respectable audiences at the royal institution, before Mr. Schlegel gave his lectures on the same subjects at Vienna.[3]

[1] C refers to Pope's "Preface" to his ed of Shakespeare (1725). But Pope does not censure Shakespeare for neglecting the "unities" of time and place, and in fact states that to judge Shakespeare "by Aristotle's rules, is like trying a man by the laws of one country, who acted under those of another". *Works* ed W. Elwin and W. J. Courthope (1871–86) x 537. Nor was the confusion of which C speaks "the common error" of Pope's age in England, as distinct from France. Long before Johnson's "Preface" to Shakespeare (1765) effectively undermined the arguments for the "unities", English critics were either championing or excusing Shakespeare's neglect of them. C is letting his dislike of French neo-classicism colour his conception of the critical views of English neo-classic writers, and of those of Pope in particular as the principal poet in that mode. For C's discussion of the "unities" in various

notes and lectures, see *Sh C* I 4–5, 50–1, 203–4; II 70–3, 82–3, 160–2, 263–4.

[2] "Imagine not I am about to oppose genius to rules. . . . The spirit of poetry, like all other living powers, must of necessity circumscribe itself by rules, were it only to unite power with beauty. It must embody in order to reveal itself; but a living body is of necessity an organized one,—and what is organization, but the connection of parts to a whole, so that each part is at once end and means!" *Sh C* I 223 (from BM MS Egerton 2800 f 24).

[3] C's "first course of lectures" was delivered in 1808 at the Royal Institution before an audience he estimated at 600 to 700, from 15 Jan to mid-Jun, when illness forced him to stop. *Sh C* I 18–19, II 3–23. Schlegel's lectures were delivered in Vienna in the spring of 1808 and published 1809–11 (*Vorlesungen über dramatische Kunst und Litteratur*). C, sensi-

immortal in his own despite."[1] Speaking of one whom he had celebrated,[2] and contrasting the duration of his works with that of his personal existence, Shakspeare adds:

> Your name from hence immortal life shall have,
> Tho' I once gone to all the world must die;
> The earth can yield me but a common grave,
> When you entombed in men's eyes shall lie.
> Your monument shall be my gentle verse,
> Which eyes not yet created shall o'er-read;
> And *tongues to be* your being shall rehearse,
> When all the breathers of this world are dead:
> You still shall live, such virtue hath my pen,
> Where breath most breathes, e'en in the mouth of men.
>
>   SONNET 81st.[3]

I have taken the first that occurred; but Shakspeare's readiness to praise his rivals, ore pleno,[4] and the confidence of his own equality with those whom he deem'd most worthy of his praise, are alike manifested in the 86th sonnet.

> Was it the proud full sail of his great verse
> Bound for the praise of all-too-precious you,
> That did my ripe thoughts in my brain inhearse,
> Making their tomb, the womb wherein they grew?

---

tive to the charge that he borrowed heavily from Schlegel in his later lectures of 1811–12, frequently stressed that he had made many of the same points in his own 1808 lectures, before he could possibly have read Schlegel's. Cf *CL* III 358–60. But too little of these lectures survives to verify either the charge or C's defence. With a few exceptions, later discussions have added little precise information and often, except for a few illustrations cited as "typical", substitute expressions of moral outrage for specific detail. For judicious general discussion, see G. N. G. Orsini in *Comparative Literature* XVI (1964) 97–118 and McFarland 256–61. C never published the lectures, and no complete report of what he said survives in his hand.

[1] *Imitations of Horace* bk II ep I line 72 (Shakespeare "For gain, not

glory, wing'd his roving flight, | And grew Immortal in his own despight"). Cf *Sh C* I 219, *CN* III 3288 f 10. C wishes to do away with this "popular notion".

[2] For C's uneasiness in admitting that Sonnets 1–126 were addressed to a man (hence the neutral "one whom he had celebrated", above), see *TT* 14 May 1833. Cf ". . . if thou wouldst understand these Sonnets, thou must read the Chapter in Potter's Antiquities on the Greek Lovers—of whom were that Theban Band of Brothers, over whom Philip, their victor, stood weeping . . .". C called it "This pure Love", which Shakespeare "appears to have felt". Annotation on *B Poets* II 665–8: *CM (CC)* I 42–3.

[3] Lines 5–14 (var).

[4] "With full voice". A common instruction in music books. Every choirboy would know it.

Was it his spirit, by spirits taught to write
Above a mortal pitch that struck me dead?
No, neither he, nor his compeers by night
Giving him aid, my verse astonished.
He, nor that affable familiar ghost,
Which nightly gulls him with intelligence,
As victors of my silence cannot boast;
I was not sick of any fear from thence!
But when your countenance fill'd up his line,
Then lack'd I matter, that enfeebled mine.[1]

In Spencer[a] indeed, we trace a mind constitutionally tender, delicate, and, in comparison with his three great compeers, I had almost said, *effeminate*;[2] and this additionally saddened by the unjust persecution of Burleigh, and the severe calamities, which overwhelmed his latter days. These causes have diffused over all his compositions "a melancholy grace,"[3] and have drawn forth occasional strains, the more pathetic from their gentleness. But no where do we find the least trace of irritability, and still less of quarrelsome or affected contempt of his censurers.

The same calmness, and even greater self-possession, may be affirmed of Milton, as far as his poems, and poetic character are concerned. He reserved his anger, for the enemies of religion,

a BL (1817): Spencer

[1] Substituting "praise" for "prize" (line 2). In an annotation on *B Poets* II C classified Sonnet 86 as of the "4th or highest" class: *CM (CC)* I 83, 84.

[2] C noted the "indescribable sweetness" of Spenser's verse, "Spenser's great character of mind. Fancy under the conditions of Imagination, with a feminine tenderness & almost maidenly purity—above all, deep moral earnestness". *CN* III 4501. For C's distinction between "feminine" and "effeminate" see *C&S (CC)* 24.

[3] C quotes the phrase from a variant ms version of *The Dark Ladie* line 42: *PW* (EHC) II 1055n. The belief, now discredited, that Spenser was persecuted by William Cecil, Lord Burghley (1520–98) was based on a misinterpretation of what Spenser wrote about him in *Mother Hubberds Tale* (1591). And C had read in *B Poets* II 3 that Burghley, "instead of promoting his interest with the Queen, is said to have intercepted her favour" and repulsed and opposed him (II 4). Nor did "severe calamities" affect the tone of his verse. C is thinking of Spenser's traumatic experience in Ireland, as sheriff of Cork, when his home was sacked and burned during Tyrone's Rebellion in Oct 1598 (but this was only three months before Spenser's death, and no extant verse was written during that brief time), and probably of *B Poets* II 4: "His fortune was now broken; his heart was wounded with calamity; and the evening of a day, in which he had seen but a few bright hours, was spent in the deep gloom of adversity."

freedom, and his country.[1] My mind is not capable of forming a more august conception, than arises from the contemplation of this great man in his latter days: poor, sick, old, blind, slandered, persecuted,

> Darkness before, and danger's voice behind,[2]

in an age in which he was as little understood by the party, *for* whom, as by that, *against* whom he had contended; and among men before whom he strode so far as to *dwarf* himself by the distance; yet still listening to the music of his own thoughts, or if additionally cheered, yet cheered only by the prophetic faith of two or three solitary individuals, he did nevertheless

> —— Argue not
> Against Heaven's hand or will, nor bate a jot
> Of heart or hope; but still bore up and steer'd
> Right onward.[3]

From others only do we derive our knowledge that Milton, in his latter day, had his scorners and detractors; and even in his day of youth and hope, that he had enemies would have been unknown to us, had they not been likewise the enemies of his country.

I am well aware, that in advanced stages of literature, when there exist many and excellent models, a high degree of talent, combined with taste and judgement, and employed in works of imagination, will acquire for a man the *name* of a great genius; though even that *analogon*[4] of genius, which, in certain states of society, may even render his writings more popular than the absolute reality could have done, would be sought for in vain in the mind and temper of the author himself. Yet even in instances of this kind, a close examination will often detect, that the irritability, which has been attributed to the author's *genius* as its cause, did really originate in an ill conformation of body, obtuse pain, or constitutional defect of pleasurable sensation. What is charged to the *author*, belongs to the *man*, who would probably have been still more impatient, but for the humanizing influences of the very pursuit, which yet bears the blame of his irritability.

---

[1] For C's defence of Milton's strong language in controversy, in some of the prose writings, see his "Apologetic Preface to *Fire, Famine, and Slaughter*": *PW* (EHC) II 1103–08.

[2] WW *Prelude* III 288.

[3] Milton *To Cyriack Skinner* (Sonnet 22) lines 6–9 (var).

[4] That is, "analogue". Cf *Friend* (CC) I 515. OED cites C as the first to use it as an English word.

How then are we to explain the easy credence generally given to this charge, if the charge itself be not, as we have endeavoured to show, supported by experience? This seems to me of no very difficult solution. In whatever country literature is widely diffused, there will be many who mistake an intense desire to possess the reputation of poetic genius, for the actual powers, and original tendencies which constitute it. But men, whose dearest wishes are fixed on objects wholly out of their own power, become in all cases more or less impatient and prone to anger. Besides, though it may be paradoxical to assert, that a man can know one thing, and believe the opposite, yet assuredly, a vain person may have so habitually indulged the wish, and persevered in the attempt to appear what he is not, as to become himself one of his own proselytes. Still, as this counterfeit and artificial persuasion must differ, even in the person's own feelings, from a real sense of inward power, what can be more natural, than that this difference should betray itself in suspicious and jealous irritability? Even as the flowery sod, which covers a hollow, may be often detected by its shaking and trembling.

But, alas! the multitude of books, and the general diffusion of literature, have produced other, and more lamentable effects in the world of letters, and such as are abundant to explain, tho' by no means to justify, the contempt with which the best grounded complaints of injured genius are rejected as frivolous, or entertained as matter of merriment. In the days of Chaucer and Gower, our language might (with due allowance for the imperfections of a simile) be compared to a wilderness of vocal reeds, from which the favorites only of Pan or Apollo could construct even the rude Syrinx; and from this the *constructors* alone could elicit strains of music. But now, partly by the labours of successive poets, and in part by the more artificial state of society and social intercourse, language, mechanized as it were into a barrel-organ, supplies at once both instrument and tune.[1] Thus even the deaf may play,

[1] Cf C's remark to Thomas Curnick 9 Apr 1814: "From the time of Pope's translation of Homer, inclusive, so countless have been the poetic metamorphoses of almost all possible thoughts and connections of thought, that it is scarcely practicable for a man to write in the ornamented style on any subject without finding his poem . . . a cento of lines that had pre-existed in other works; and this it is which makes poetry so very difficult, because so very easy, in the present day. I myself have for many years past given it up in despair." *CL* III 469–70. Cf also *CN* I 470, 1236.

so as to delight the many. Sometimes (for it is with similies, as it is with jests at a wine table, one is sure to suggest another) I have attempted to illustrate the present state of our language, in its relation to literature, by a press-room of larger and smaller stereotype pieces, which, in the present anglo-gallican fashion of unconnected, epigrammatic periods,[1] it requires but an ordinary portion of ingenuity to vary indefinitely, and yet still produce something, which, if *not* sense, will be so like it, as to do as well.[2] Perhaps better: for it spares the reader the trouble of thinking; prevents vacancy, while it indulges indolence; and secures the memory from all danger of an intellectual plethora. Hence of all trades, literature at present demands the least talent or information; and, of all modes of literature, the manufacturing of poems. The difference indeed between these and the works of genius, is not less than between an egg, and an egg-shell; yet at a distance they both look alike. Now it is no less remarkable than true, with how little examination works of polite literature are commonly perused, not only by the mass of readers, but by men of first rate ability, till some accident or chance * discussion have roused their attention,

---

* In the course of my lectures, I had occasion to point out the almost faultless position and choice of words, in Mr. Pope's *original* compositions, particularly in his satires and moral essays, for the purpose of comparing them with his translation of Homer, which [a] I do not stand alone in regarding as the main source of our pseudo-poetic diction.[3] And this, by the bye,

[a] *BL* (1817): which,

[1] Meaning the pointed epigrammatic style of Dryden, Pope, and their followers, which C and other Romantic writers associate with French influence. Cf above, I 18 n 3. Cf his "aversion to the epigrammatic unconnected periods of the fashionable *Anglo-Gallican* taste". *Friend (CC)* I 20.

[2] On the Stanhope process of stereotyping, introduced early in the nineteenth century, and its importance in producing cheap books, see *LS (CC)* 165–6n and 166 n 1.

[3] Though it has not survived, C probably refers to a lecture of 27 Jan 1812, in which, says HCR, "he analysed a passage in Pope's Homer (a description of moonlight) and shewed its want of propriety and

taste with great spirit. At the same time he introduced this censure with a very insincere eulogium." *Sh C* II 220–1. Cf *CN* II 1889n. Cf "She [Lady Beaumont] afterwards sd. to me, that Coleridge & Wordsworth thought the bad taste in writing which now prevails, is owing to works of two celebrated authors, *Popes translation of Homer, & the Odyssey,* and *Johnson's Lives of the Poets.* These models of art and an inflated style have been imitated to the destroying of all simplicity.— *The Old Testament,* they say, is the true model of simplicity of style." Joseph Farington *Diary* ed James Greig (8 vols 1922–8) v 132 (28 Mar 1809).

and put them on their guard. And hence individuals below mediocrity not less in natural power than in acquired knowledge;

---

is an additional confirmation of a remark made, I believe, by Sir Joshua Reynolds, that next to the man who formed and elevated the taste of the public, he that corrupted it, is commonly the greatest genius.[1] Among other passages, I analyzed sentence by sentence, and almost word by word, the popular lines,

> As when the moon, resplendent lamp of light, &c.[2]

much in the same way as has been since done, in an excellent article on Chalmers's British Poets in the Quarterly Review.[3] The impression on the audience in general was sudden and evident: and a number of enlightened and highly educated individuals, who at different times afterwards addressed me on the subject, expressed their wonder, that truth so obvious should not have struck them *before*; but at the same time acknowledged (so much had they been accustomed, in reading poetry, to receive pleasure from the separate images and phrases successively, without asking themselves whether the collective meaning was sense or nonsense) that they might in all probability have read the same passage again twenty times with undiminished admiration, and without once reflecting, that "ἄστρα φαεινὴν ἀμφὶ σελήνην φαίνετ' ἀριπρεπέα"[4] (i.e. the stars around, or near the full moon, shine pre-eminently bright) conveys a just and happy image of a moonlight sky: while it is difficult to determine whether in the lines,

> Around *her throne* the vivid planets *roll,*
> And stars *unnumber'd gild* the *glowing pole,*[5]

the sense, or the diction be the more absurd. My answer was; that tho' I had derived peculiar advantages from my school discipline, and tho' my *general* theory of poetry was the same then as now, I had yet experienced the same sensations myself, and felt almost as if I had been newly coached, when by Mr. Wordsworth's conversation, I had been induced to re-examine with impartial strictness Gray's[a] celebrated elegy. I had long before detected

_a *BL* (1817): Grey's

[1] Untraced.

[2] Pope *Iliad* VIII 687 (var). WW may be echoing C's opinion in his remark: "To what a low state knowledge of the most obvious and important phenomena had sunk, is evident from the style in which Dryden has executed a description of Night in one of his Tragedies, and Pope his translation of the celebrated moonlight scene in the Iliad." *Poems* (1815) "Essay, Supplementary to the Preface": *W Prose* III 73. In citing his earlier lecture (HCR 27 Jan 1812) C understandably wishes to establish his priority in discussing the subject and to indicate he is not borrowing from WW.

[3] The review by RS in *QR* XI (1814) 480–504 of *Works of the English Poets* (1810) by Alexander Chalmers (1759–1834). But RS does not touch on the subject C mentions. RS had suggested to John Murray that C review Chalmers—"in such criticism you must know, if you have heard him lecture, that he is unequalled: and the thing will be far better in his hands than mine". *S Letters* (Curry) II 29. No doubt they discussed the work, and perhaps C assumed that RS had carried out his kind of analysis.

[4] Homer *Iliad* 8.555–6.

[5] Pope *Iliad* VIII 691–2.

nay, bunglers that had failed in the lowest mechanic crafts,[2] and whose presumption is in due proportion to their want of sense and sensibility; men, who being first scriblers from idleness and ignorance next become libellers from envy and malevolence; have been able to drive a successful trade in the employment of the booksellers, nay have raised themselves into temporary name and reputation with the public at large, by that most powerful of all adulation, the appeal to the bad and malignant passions of mankind.* But as it is the nature of scorn, envy, and all malignant

---

the defects in "the Bard;"[1] but "the Elegy" I had considered as proof against all fair attacks; and to this day I cannot read either, without delight, and a portion of enthusiasm. At all events, whatever pleasure I may have lost by the clearer perception of the faults in certain passages, has been more than repaid to me, by the additional delight with which I read the remainder.

* Especially "in this AGE OF PERSONALITY, this age of literary and political GOSSIPING,[3] when the meanest insects are worshipped with a sort of Egyptian superstition, if only the brainless head be atoned for by the sting of personal malignity in the tail! When the most vapid satires have become the objects of a keen public interest, purely from the number of contemporary characters named in the patchwork notes (which possess, however, the comparative merit of being more poetical than the text) and because, to increase the stimulus, the author has sagaciously left his own name for whispers and conjectures! In an age, when even sermons are published with a double appendix stuffed with *names*—in a generation so transformed from the characteristic reserve of Britons, that from the ephemeral sheet of a London newspaper, to the everlasting Scotch Professorial Quarto, almost every publication exhibits or flatters the epidemic distemper; that the very "last year's rebuses" in the Ladies Diary, are answered in a serious elegy *"on my father's death"* with the name and habitat of the elegiac Œdipus subscribed; and *"other ingenious solutions were likewise given"* to the said *rebuses*—not as heretofore by Crito, Philander, A, B, Y, &c. but by fifty or sixty plain English sirnames at full length with their several places of abode! In an age, when a bashful *Philalethes*, or *Phileleutheros* is as rare on the title-pages, and among the signatures of our magazines, as a real name used to be in the days of our shy and notice-shunning grandfathers! When (more exquisite than all) I see an EPIC POEM (spirits of Maro and Mæonides make ready to welcome your new compeer!)

---

[1] In 1799 C wrote *"The Bard once intoxicated me, & now I read it without pleasure."* CN I 383. Again, as late as TT 23 Oct 1833: "I think there is something very majestic in Gray's Installation Ode; but as to the Bard and the rest of his lyrics, I must say I think them frigid and artificial." Cf also CN III 3415 and n, 4313.

[2] Probably a dig at William

Gifford (1756–1826), editor of QR, who had once been apprenticed to a shoemaker. Lamb wrote of Gifford's "Shoemaker phraseology" in a letter to WW 7 Jan 1815: LL III 129.

[3] We should recall C's well-known dislike of gossip generally and his tendency to leave the room when talk turned to gossip.

propensities to require a quick change of objects, such writers are sure, sooner or later to awake from their dream of vanity to disappointment and neglect with embittered and envenomed feelings. Even during their short-lived success, sensible in spite of themselves on what a shifting foundation it rested, they resent the mere refusal of praise, as a robbery, and at the justest censures kindle at once into violent and undisciplined abuse; till the acute disease changing into chronical, the more deadly as the less violent, they become the fit instruments of literary detraction, and moral slander. They are then no longer to be questioned without exposing the complainant to ridicule, because, forsooth, they are *anonymous* critics, and authorised as "synodical individuals" * [2] to speak of themselves plurali majestatico! [3] As if literature formed a cast like that of the PARIAS[a] in Hindostan,[4] who, however maltreated, must not dare to deem themselves wronged! As if that, which in all other cases adds a deeper dye to slander, the circumstance of its being anonymous, here acted only to make the slanderer inviolable! Thus, in *part*, from the accidental tempers of individuals (men of undoubted talent, but not men of genius)[5] tempers rendered yet more irritable by their desire to *appear* men of genius; but still more effectively by the excesses of the mere *counterfeits* both of talent and genius; the number too being so

---

advertised with the special recommendation, that the said EPIC POEM contains more than an hundred names of *living* persons."

FRIEND NO. 10.[1]

* A phrase of Andrew Marvel's.

[a] *BL* (1817): PARAS

[1] *Friend* (*CC*) II 138 (19 Oct 1809). For annotation see 1818 text (*CC*) I 210–11.

[2] *The Rehearsal Transpros'd . . .* (1672) 43, in which Marvell is speaking of Samuel Parker, bp of Oxford: "For he talks . . . as if he were a *Synodical Individuum;* nay if he had a fifth Council in his belly he could not dictate more dogmatically". C was struck by the phrase in 1800 (*CN* I 704) and used it also in *Friend* (*CC*) II 108n (I 183n).

[3] "With the royal plural" (i.e. the editorial "we"). By "*anony-* *mous* critics" C refers principally to those writing for *Ed Rev, QR,* and the *Examiner,* in particular Hazlitt, Francis Jeffrey, and William Gifford. With the general discussion of reviewers above, especially "anonymous critics", cf *Friend* (*CC*) I 49, 74, 125, 183, 277, 358; Lect 5 of 1811: *Sh C* II 105–6; and below, I 48, II 157, 239.

[4] The extensive lower caste in southern India; commonly used in English, though not by C above, for those of no caste at all.

[5] On genius vs talent, see above, I 31 and n 5.

incomparably greater of those who are *thought* to be, than of those who really *are* men of real genius; and in part from the natural, but not therefore the less partial and unjust distinction, made by the public itself between *literary*, and all other property; I believe the prejudice to have arisen, which considers an unusual irascibility concerning the reception of its products as characteristic of genius. It might correct the moral feelings of a numerous class of readers, to suppose a Review set on foot, the object of which was to criticise all the chief works presented to the public by our ribbon-weavers, calico-printers, cabinet-makers, and china-manufacturers; a Review conducted in the same spirit, and which should take the same freedom with personal character, as our literary journals. They would scarcely, I think, deny their belief, not only that the "genus irritabile"[1] would be found to include many other *species* besides that of bards; but that the irritability of *trade* would soon reduce the resentments of *poets* into mere shadow-fights (σκιομαχίας) in the comparison. Or is wealth the only rational object of human interest? Or even if this were admitted, has the poet no property in his works? Or is it a rare, or culpable case, that he who serves at the altar of the muses, should be compelled to derive his maintenance from the altar, when too he has perhaps deliberately abandoned the fairest prospects of rank and opulence in order to devote himself, an entire and undistracted man, to the instruction or refinement of his fellow-citizens? Or should we pass by all higher objects and motives, all disinterested benevolence, and even that ambition of lasting praise which is at once the crutch and ornament, which at once supports and betrays, the infirmity of human virtue; is the character and property of the individual, who labours for our intellectual pleasures, less entitled to a share of our fellow feeling, than that of the wine-merchant or milliner? Sensibility indeed, both quick and deep, is not only a characteristic feature, but may be deemed a component part, of genius. But it is no less an essential mark of true genius, that its sensibility is excited by any other cause more powerfully, than by its own personal interests; for this plain reason, that the man of genius lives most in the ideal world, in which the present is still constituted by the future or the past;[2] and because his feelings

[1] See above, i 30 n 1.
[2] Cf C's defence of RS in the *Courier* of 27 Mar 1817: ". . . a young Poet, in all his poetic moments, lives in an *ideal* World". *EOT (CC)* ii 470. Cf also Satyrane's

have been habitually associated with thoughts and images, to the number, clearness, and vivacity of which the sensation of *self* is always in an inverse proportion.[1] And yet, should he perchance have occasion to repel some false charge, or to rectify some erroneous censure, nothing is more common, than for the many to mistake the general liveliness of his manner and language *whatever* is the subject, for the effects of peculiar irritation from its accidental relation to himself.*

For myself, if from my own feelings, or from the less suspicious test of the observations of others, I had been made aware of any literary testiness or jealousy; I trust, that I should have been, however, neither silly or arrogant enough, to have burthened the imperfection on GENIUS. But an experience (and I should not need documents in abundance to prove my words, if I added) a tried experience of twenty years, has taught me, that the original sin of my character consists in a careless indifference to public opinion, and to the attacks of those who influence it; that praise and admiration have become yearly, less and less desirable, except as marks of sympathy; nay that it is difficult and distressing to me, to

---

* This is one instance among many of deception, by the telling the half of a fact, and omitting the other half, when it is from their mutual counter-action and neutralization, that the *whole* truth arises, as a tertium aliquid different from either.[2] Thus in Dryden's famous line "Great wit" (which here means genius) "to madness sure is near allied."[3] Now as far as the profound sensibility, which is doubtless *one* of the components of genius, were alone considered single and unbalanced, it might be fairly described as exposing the individual to a greater chance of mental derangement; but then a more than usual rapidity of association, a more than usual power of passing from thought to thought, and image to image, is a component equally essential; and in the due modification of each by the other the GENIUS itself consists; so that it would be as just as fair to describe the earth, as in imminent danger of exorbitating, or of falling into the sun, according as the assertor of the absurdity *confined* his attention either to the projectile or to the attractive force exclusively.

Letters II, below, on Lessing and the "ideal world".

[1] "Genius may co-exist with wildness, idleness, folly, even with crime; but not long, believe me, with selfishness . . .". *TT* 23 Jul 1827. Cf *BL*, below, II 20: "A second promise of genius is the choice of subjects very remote from the private interests and circumstances of the writer himself."

[2] On half truths as "the most inflammatory of all modes of falsehood", "the most dangerous of errors", see *EOT (CC)* II 377, *LS (CC)* 228. On *tertium aliquid* (the "third something") see below, I 300.

[3] *Absalom and Achitophel* I 163–4: "Great wits are sure to madness near allied, | And thin partitions do their bounds divide."

think with any interest even about the sale and profit of my works, important, as in my present circumstances, such considerations must needs be. Yet it never occurred to me to believe or fancy, that the quantum of intellectual power bestowed on me by nature or education was in any way connected with this habit of my feelings; or that it needed any other parents or fosterers, than constitutional indolence,[1] aggravated into languor by ill-health; the accumulating embarrassments of procrastination; the mental cowardice, which is the inseparable companion of procrastination, and which makes us anxious to think and converse on any thing rather than on what concerns ourselves; in fine, all those close vexations, whether chargeable on my faults or my fortunes which leave me but little grief to spare for evils comparatively distant and alien.

Indignation at literary wrongs, I leave to men born under happier stars. I cannot *afford it*. But so far from condemning those who can, I deem it a writer's duty, and think it creditable to his heart, to feel and express a resentment proportioned to the grossness of the provocation, and the importance of the object. There is no profession on earth, which requires an attention so early, so long, or so unintermitting as that of poetry; and indeed as that of literary composition in general, if it be such, as at all satisfies the demands both of taste and of sound logic. How difficult and delicate a task even the mere mechanism of verse is, may be conjectured from the failure of those, who have attempted poetry late in life. Where then a man has, from his earliest youth, devoted his whole being to an object, which by the admission of all civilized nations in all ages is honorable as a pursuit, and glorious as an attainment; what of all that relates to himself and his family, if only we except his moral character, can have fairer claims to his protection, or more authorise acts of self-defence, than the elaborate products of his intellect, and intellectual industry? Prudence itself would command us to *show*, even if defect or diversion of natural sensibility had prevented us from *feeling*, a due interest and qualified anxiety for the offspring and representatives of our nobler being. I know it, alas! by woeful experience! I have laid too

---

[1] Cf C's self-charge of "constitutional indolence" in the first two numbers of the 1809–10 *Friend (CC)* 16, 36, in the second of which he writes of collecting his poems and newspaper essays and publishing them in two volumes, to be "preceded by a sketch of my Life . . . concerning falsehoods and calumnies attached to my name".

many eggs in the hot sands of this wilderness the world, with
ostrich carelessness and ostrich oblivion.[1] The greater part indeed
have been trod under foot, and are forgotten; but yet no small
number have crept forth into life, some to furnish feathers for the
caps of others, and still more to plume the shafts in the quivers of
my enemies, of them that unprovoked have lain in wait against
my soul.

Sic vos, non vobis mellificatis, apes![2]

An instance in confirmation of the Note, p. 39, occurs to me as I am
correcting this sheet, with the FAITHFUL SHEPHERDESS open before
me.[3] Mr. Seward[4] first traces Fletcher's lines;

More foul diseases than e'er yet the hot
Sun bred thro' his burnings, while the dog
Pursues the raging lion, throwing the fog
And deadly vapor from his angry breath,
Filling the lower world with plague and death.—[5]

To Spenser's Shepherd's Calendar,

The rampant lion hunts he fast
With dogs of noisome breath;

[1] C's comparison of himself to an ostrich repeats an 1802 notebook entry made after reading George Sandys's *A Relation of a Journey . . . Containing a Description of the Turkish Empire, of Aegypt, of the Holy Land . . .* (4th ed 1632). *CN* I 1248 and n. Used later almost verbatim in letters to Poole (1803) and to both Jeffrey and Sir George Beaumont (1808): *CL* II 1011; III 126, 145. On C's general fondness for identifying with the ostrich and other ungainly birds, see *C Life* (B) 111.

[2] "So you, but not for yourselves, produce honey, O Bees." Virgil once wrote a couplet in honour of Augustus and fixed it, anonymously, on a door. A mediocre poet, Bathyllus, claimed to have written it. Virgil was annoyed and wrote four times beneath it, "Sic vos, non vobis". Augustus asked for the lines to be completed, and after others had tried in vain, Virgil wrote (tr): "I made these verses, Another took the honor. | So you, but not for yourselves, build nests, Birds; | So you, but not

for yourselves, bear fleeces, Sheep; | So you, but not for yourselves, produce honey, Bees; | So you, but not for yourselves, pull the plough, Cattle." C would be identifying himself with Virgil and comparing those about whom he is writing, especially reviewers, with Bathyllus. The story is told in the life of Virgil attributed to Donatus, which is still often prefixed to editions of Virgil. C quoted from it in *CN* III 4125.

[3] C had purchased *The Dramatic Works of Ben Jonson, and Beaumont and Fletcher* (4 vols 1811) 29 Mar 1815, the volumes dated and inscribed Calne, Wilts. See *CM (CC)* I 373. *The Faithful Shepherdess* is in vol II (C did not annotate the play, as he did several others).

[4] Thomas Seward (1708–90), canon of Lichfield and father of Anna Seward; his notes to Beaumont and Fletcher are reprinted at the foot of the pages of C's volumes. Here, *Works* II 376n.

[5] *The Faithful Shepherdess* I lines 263–7: *Works* II 376.

Whose baleful barking brings, in haste,
Pyne, plagues, and dreary death![1]

He then takes occasion to introduce Homer's simile of the sight of Achilles' shield to Priam compared with the Dog Star, literally thus—

"For this indeed is most splendid, but it was made an evil sign, and brings many a consuming disease to wretched mortals."[2] Nothing can be more simple as a description, or more accurate as a simile; which (says Mr. S.) is thus *finely* translated by Mr. Pope:

Terrific Glory! for his burning breath
Taints the *red* air with fevers, plagues, and death![3]

Now here (not to mention the tremendous bombast) the *Dog Star*, so called, is turned into a *real* Dog, a very odd Dog, a Fire, Fever, Plague, and death-breathing, *red*-air-tainting Dog: and the whole *visual* likeness is lost, while the likeness in the *effects* is rendered absurd by the exaggeration. In Spenser[a] and Fletcher the thought is justifiable; for the images are at least consistent, and it was the intention of the writers to mark the seasons by this allegory of visualized *Puns.*[4]

---

a BL (1817): Spencer

[1] *Shepherd's Calendar* VII (Jul) 21–4 (var).

[2] Seward quotes the Greek only: *Iliad* 22.30–1; the tr is supplied by C; πυρετόν in the original may be translated either "heat" or "fever".

[3] Pope *Iliad* XXII 41–2.

[4] C had once thought of writing an *Ode on Punning* and, because of his interest in the psychology of punning, had long planned to write an "Essay in Defence of Punning". See *CL* II 999 and *CN* III 3542, 3762, and 4444 and nn. See also, below, I 52 (C's n) and n 3, 193 n 3, 194.

CHAPTER 3

The author's obligations to critics, and the probable occasion—
Principles of modern criticism—Mr. Southey's works and character

To anonymous critics in reviews, magazines, and news-journals
of various name and rank, and to satirists with or without a
name, in verse or prose, or in verse-text aided by prose-comment,
I do seriously believe and profess, that I owe full two thirds of
whatever reputation and publicity I happen to possess. For when
the name of an individual has occurred so frequently, in so many
works, for so great a length of time, the readers of these works
(which with a shelf or two of B E A U T I E S, E L E G A N T E X T R A C T S
and A N A S,[1] form nine-tenths of the reading of the reading public *) cannot but be familiar with the name, without distinctly

* For as to the devotees of the circulating libraries,[2] I dare not compliment their *pass-time*, or rather *kill-time*, with the name of *reading*. Call it
rather a sort of beggarly daydreaming, during which the mind of the dreamer
furnishes for itself nothing but laziness and a little mawkish sensibility;
while the whole *materiel* and imagery of the doze is supplied *ab extra* by a
sort of mental *camera obscura* manufactured at the printing office,[3] which
pro tempore fixes, reflects and transmits the moving phantasms of one man's
delirium, so as to people the barrenness of an hundred other brains afflicted
with the same trance or suspension of all common sense and all definite
purpose. We should therefore transfer this species of *amusement*, (if indeed
those can be said to retire *a musis*, who were never in their company, or
relaxation be attributable to those, whose bows are never bent)[4] from the
genus, *reading*, to that comprehensive class characterized by the power of
reconciling the two contrary yet co-existing propensities of human nature,
namely; indulgence of sloth, and hatred of vacancy. In addition to novels

[1] See e.g. Vicesimus Knox *Elegant
Extracts . . . in Prose* (1784),
which C quotes for ironical effect
in *Friend (CC)* I 484n, and *The
Beauties of the Anti-Jacobin* (1799),
quoted at the end of ch 3, below, I
67n–8
[2] On circulating libraries, see e.g.
SM (CC) 36 and n, 38 and n.
[3] Cf a note on beauty, jotted
down in May 1815, of "the Poet

whose Paintings, like those of the
Camera obscura, have only a present
endurance to his own eyes". *CN* III
4250 and n.
[4] Cf "The same craving for
amusement, that is, to be away from
the Muses! for relaxation *i.e.* the
unbending of a Bow which in fact
had never been strung!" *AR* (1825)
221n.

remembering whether it was introduced for an eulogy or for censure. And this becomes the more likely, if (as I believe) the habit of perusing periodical works may be properly added to Averrhoe's* catalogue of ANTI-MNEMONICS, or weakeners of the memory.[3] But where this has not been the case, yet the

---

and tales of chivalry in prose or rhyme, (by which last I mean neither rhythm nor metre)[1] this genus comprizes as its species, gaming, swinging, or swaying on a chair or gate; spitting over a bridge; smoking; snuff-taking; tete a tete quarrels after dinner between husband and wife; conning word by word all the advertisements of the daily advertizer in a public house on a rainy day, &c. &c. &c.[2]

* Ex. gr. Pediculos e capillis excerptos in arenam jacere incontusos; eating of unripe fruit; gazing on the clouds, and (in genere) on moveable things suspended in the air; riding among a multitude of camels; frequent laughter; listening to a series of jests and humourous anecdotes, as when (so to modernise the learned Saracen's meaning) one man's droll story of an Irishman inevitably occasions another's droll story of a Scotchman, which again by the same sort of conjunction disjunctive leads to some etourderie of a Welchman, and that again to some sly hit of a Yorkshireman; the habit of reading tomb-stones in church-yards, &c. By the bye, this catalogue strange as it may appear, is not insusceptible of a sound psychological commentary.

[1] See C's "Recipe for Poems" such as Scott's *The Lady of the Lake*, in a letter to WW of early Oct 1810, and his remark that "a man accustomed to cast words in metre and familiar with descriptive Poets & Tourists, himself a Picturesque Tourist, must be troubled with a mental Strangury, if he could not lift up his leg six times at six different Corners, and each time p— a canto". *CL* III 294–5, 292.

[2] The parenthetical remark in the text, with this footnote, is a reworking of BM MS Egerton 2800 ff 89–90 (the footnote is printed in *IS* 206).

[3] Not Averroes, but Burhān al-Dīn. This misattribution may be owing to C's using his note in *CN* III 3750, in which he begins, "The Arabian Philosopher . . .", which in the common contemporary allusive style would imply Averroes (1126–98), the great Moslem Aristotelian. In his footnote he is expanding a passage from Jean Baptiste de Boyer, Marquis d'Argens *Kabbalistische*

Briefe . . . (8 vols Danzig 1773–7) IV 126–7, which states simply: "An Arabian writer has suggested some causes for loss of memory . . ." ("Ein arabischer Schriftsteller hat einige Ursachen von dem Verluste des Gedächtnisses . . ."), citing in a footnote *Semita sap.*, i.e. *Semita sapientiae* (Paris 1646), a Latin tr by Abraham Ecchellensis of an anonymous Arabic ms, later known to be by Burhān al-Dīn, al-Zarnūjī. Argens' list includes the words, after the mention of camels, "or cast lice upon the earth without killing them" ("oder Läuse auf die Erde würfe, ohne sie todt zu machen"). This particular remark was one of those C recorded in N 18 when he first read the passage, and it is doubtless what he most wanted to say about periodical reviewers (cf the comparison of them to eunuchs below, I 59), and he therefore puts it first in his footnote here. But when he feels hurt, C often becomes indirect. He therefore writes the remark in Latin, and ap-

reader will be apt to suspect, that there must be something more than usually strong and extensive in a reputation, that could either require or stand so merciless and long-continued a cannonading. Without any feeling of *anger* therefore (for which indeed, on my own account, I have no pretext) I may yet be allowed to express some degree of *surprize*, that after having run the critical gauntlet for a certain class of faults which I *had*, nothing having come before the judgement-seat in the interim, I should, year after year, quarter after quarter, month after month (not to mention sundry petty periodicals of still quicker revolution, "or weekly or diurnal") have been for at least 17 years consecutively dragged forth by them into the foremost ranks of the *proscribed*, and forced to abide the brunt of abuse, for faults directly opposite, and which I certainly had not.[1] How shall I explain this?

Whatever may have been the case with others, I certainly cannot attribute this persecution to personal dislike, or to envy, or to feelings of vindictive animosity. Not to the former, for, with the exception of a very few who are my intimate friends, and were so before they were known as authors, I have had little other acquaintance with literary characters, than what may be implied in an accidental introduction, or casual meeting in a mixt company. And, as far as words and looks can be trusted, I must believe that, even in these instances, I had excited no unfriendly disposition.*

* Some years ago, a gentleman, the chief writer and conductor of a celebrated review, distinguished by its hostility to Mr. Southey, spent a day or two at Keswick.[2] That he was, without diminution on this account,

pears to toss it in casually as though it were an amusing quote from Averroes or someone else ("Throwing to the ground lice picked from the hair, without crushing them"). On reviewers generally as unauthorised, self-appointed "door-keepers", see also *Friend (CC)* I 276–8.

[1] There are over ninety extant articles and reviews from 1798 to the end of 1814 that discuss or mention C in specific detail. *C Bibl* (Haven & Adams) I 5–24. Of them at least sixty-three are favourable, often eulogistic; another ten or twelve strike a middle note; and in the remainder the adverse criticism is for the most part less abusive than C implies.

Curiously one of the most caustic discussions of any of C's works is that of *AM* by RS, whom C, in what Freud calls a "reaction formation", is now getting ready to defend against adverse reviews. RS, who described *AM* as "absurd or unintelligible . . . a Dutch attempt at German sublimity . . . a poem of little merit", reviewed *LB* in *C Rev* NS XXIV (1798) 197–204.

[2] Francis Jeffrey (1773–1850), the editor of *Ed Rev*, who in the first number of his magazine launched a general attack on the "Lake School" at the start of his review of RS's *Thalaba*. *Ed Rev* I (1802) 63–72. C is touched on very lightly,

Neither by letter, or in conversation, have I ever had dispute or controversy beyond the common social interchange of opinions.

treated with every hospitable attention by Mr. Southey and myself, I trust I need not say. But one thing I may venture to notice; that at no period of my life do I remember to have received so many, and such high coloured compliments in so short a space of time.[1] He was likewise circumstantially informed by what series of accidents it had happened, that Mr. Wordsworth, Mr. Southey, and I had become neighbours; and how utterly unfounded was the supposition, that we considered ourselves, as belonging to any common school, but that of good sense confirmed by the long-established models of the best times of Greece, Rome, Italy, and England; and still more groundless the notion, that Mr. Southey (for as to myself I have published so little, and that little, of so little importance, as to make it almost ludicrous to mention my name at all) could have been concerned in the formation of a poetic sect with Mr. Wordsworth, when so many of his works had been published not only previously to any acquaintance between them; but before Mr. Wordsworth himself had written any thing but in a diction ornate, and uniformly sustained; when too the slightest examination will make it evident, that between those and the after writings of Mr. Southey, there exists no other difference than that of a progressive degree of excellence from progressive developement of power, and progressive facility from habit and increase of experience. Yet among the first articles which this man wrote after his return from Keswick, we were characterized as "the School of whining and hypochondriacal poets that haunt the Lakes."[2] In reply to a letter from the same gentleman, in which he had asked me, whether I was in earnest in preferring the style of Hooker to that of Dr. Johnson; and Jeremy Taylor to Burke; I stated, somewhat at large, the comparative excellences and defects which characterized our best prose writers, from the reformation, to the first half of Charles 2nd; and that of those who had flourished during the present reign, and the preceding one.[3] About twelve

as also in Jeffrey's review of *The Dramatic Works of John Ford: Ed Rev* XVIII (1811) 283, in which C is named with WW, RS, and Joanna Baillie as poets who "copied the manner of our older poets"; "They do not write as those great poets would have written; they merely mimic their manner, and ape their peculiarities; — and consequently, though they profess to imitate the freest and most careless of all versifiers, their style is more remarkably and offensively artificial". Jeffrey, whose visit to Cumberland took place in 1810, answered C's above remarks in a long note appended to Hazlitt's review of *BL* in *Ed Rev* XXVIII (1817) 507–12, admitting he thought the poetry "whining and hypochondriacal" but denying in detail C's other charges. Significantly HNC suppressed C's footnote in *BL* (1847), though SC (I clix) defended the "main drift" of what C had said. Cf on Jeffrey, below, II 107 n 1.

[1] Cf Thomas Moore to Samuel Rogers 21 Oct 1810: "Jeffrey . . . lately in town . . . in his way hither . . . stopped at Keswick, and saw Southey and Coleridge. He seems to have been dazzled by the rhetoric of Coleridge, whom he had never seen before." *Memoirs, Journals, and Correspondence of Thomas Moore* ed Lord John Russell (8 vols 1853–6) VIII 89.

[2] Not located in *Ed Rev*.

[3] The letter has not survived. In his note to Hazlitt's review (see n above), Jeffrey denied that he had borrowed anything from it. Did his

Nay, where I had reason to suppose my convictions fundamentally different, it has been my habit, and I may add, the impulse of my nature, to assign the grounds of my belief, rather than the belief itself; and not to express dissent, till I could establish some points of complete sympathy, some grounds common to both sides, from which to commence its explanation.

Still less can I place these attacks to the charge of envy. The few pages, which I have published, are of too distant a date; and the extent of their sale a proof too conclusive against their having

---

months afterwards, a review appeared on the same subject,[1] in the concluding paragraph of which the reviewer asserts, that his chief motive for entering into the discussion was to separate a rational and qualified admiration of our elder writers, from the indiscriminate enthusiasm of a recent school, who praised what they did not understand, and caricatured what they were unable to imitate. And, that no doubt might be left concerning the persons alluded to, the writer annexes the names of Miss B A I L I E,[2] S O U T H E Y,[a] W O R D S W O R T H and C O L E R I D G E. For that which follows, I have only ear-say[3] evidence; but yet such as demands my belief; viz. that on being questioned concerning this apparently wanton attack, more especially with reference to Miss Bailie, the writer had stated as his motives, that this lady when at Edinburgh had declined a proposal of introducing him to her; that Mr. Southey had written against him; and Mr. Wordsworth had talked contemptuously of him; but that as to *Coleridge* he had noticed him merely because the names of Southey and Wordsworth and Coleridge always went together. But if it were worth while to mix together, as ingredients, half the anecdotes which I either myself know to be true, or which I have received from men incapable of intentional falsehood, concerning the characters, qualifications, and motives of our anonymous critics, whose decisions are oracles for our reading public; I might safely borrow the words of the apocryphal Daniel; "*Give me leave,* O S O V E R E I G N P U B L I C, *and I shall slay this dragon without sword or staff.*" For the compound would be as the "*Pitch, and fat, and hair, which Daniel took, and did seethe them together, and made lumps thereof, and put into the dragon's mouth, and so the dragon burst in sunder; and Daniel said* L O ; T H E S E A R E T H E G O D S Y E W O R S H I P."[4]

[a] *BL* (1817): W. S O U T H E Y,

---

praise of Jeremy Taylor as a writer with "more of the body and soul of poetry" in his works than all the odes and epics since produced echo C? For C on Taylor as a poet see e.g. *Friend (CC)* II 176n (I 347n) and "Apologetic Preface to *Fire, Famine, and Slaughter*": *PW* (EHC) II 1100, 1106.

[1] I.e. the review of *Ford* (see I 51 continuation of n 2, above).

[2] Joanna Baillie (1762–1851), Scottish poet and dramatist, admired for her songs but especially for her *Plays on the Passions* (1798, 1802, 1812).

[3] *OED*, under "ear-say", cites this passage, noting that it is an error for "hear-say", but C is probably punning.

[4] Apocrypha: Bel and the Dragon vv 26–7 (var, and C substituting "Sovereign Public" for "king").

been popular at any time; to render probable, I had almost said possible, the excitement of envy on *their* account; and the man who should envy me on any *other*, verily he must be *envy-mad!*

Lastly, with as little semblance of reason, could I suspect any animosity towards me from vindictive feelings as the cause. I have before said, that my acquaintance with literary men has been limited and distant; and that I have had neither dispute nor controversy. From my first entrance into life, I have, with few and short intervals, lived either abroad or in retirement.[1] My different essays on subjects of national interest, published at different times, first in the Morning Post and then in the Courier, with my courses of lectures on the principles of criticism as applied to Shakspeare and Milton, constitute my whole publicity;[2] the only occasions on which I *could* offend any member of the republic of letters. With one solitary exception in which my words were first misstated and then wantonly applied to an individual, I could never learn, that I had excited the displeasure of any among my literary contemporaries.[3] Having announced my intention to give a course of lectures on the characteristic merits and defects of English poetry in its different æras; first, from Chaucer to Milton; second, from

[1] By "retirement" C means that he had little to do with the active literary life of London but, after leaving Cambridge (Dec 1794), lived mainly in the west and later the north of England, except for a trip to Germany (Sept 1798 to Jul 1799) and to Malta and Italy (Apr 1804 to Aug 1806).

[2] C refers not to his entire list of publications (which would include his poems, his translation of *Wallenstein*, *The Friend*, *Remorse*) but writings that might arouse partisan feelings. Even so, aside from *M Post* (1797–1803) and the *Courier* (1804–14), he is overlooking *Conciones* (1795) and *The Watchman* (1796). In his *M Post* essays he offended the supporters of both Pitt and Fox, and in the essays in the *Courier* antagonised those who wanted peace with Napoleon and parliamentary reform.

[3] The "solitary exception" may refer to C's criticism of Joseph Lancaster and his plan of education, of which C "spoke in Terms of the utmost Asperity" in a lecture at the Royal Institution in 1808. *Sh C* II 20. C realised that he had given "great offence". See *CN* III 3291 and n, 4181 and n. More likely, C refers to his discussion, in Lect 5 of 1811, of poems such as *The Pleasures of Hope*, *The Pleasures of Fears*, etc, poems "made up by heaping together" images and thoughts. *Sh C* II 103–4. Samuel Rogers, author of *The Pleasures of Memory*, was among the audience: "Coleridge has attacked the *Pleasures of Hope*, and all other pleasures whatsoever. Mr. Rogers was present, and heard himself indirectly *rowed* by the lecturer." Byron to Francis Hodgson 8 Dec 1811: *Byron's Letters and Journals* ed Leslie A. Marchand II (1973) 140–1.

Dryden inclusive to Thomson;[a] and third, from Cowper to the present day; I changed my plan, and confined my disquisition to the two former æras,[1] that I might furnish no possible pretext for the unthinking to misconstrue, or the malignant to misapply my words, and having stampt their own meaning on them, to pass them as current coin in the marts of garrulity or detraction.

Praises of the unworthy are felt by ardent minds as robberies of the deserving; and it is too true, and too frequent, that Bacon, Harrington, Machiavel, and Spinosa, are *not* read,[2] because Hume, Condilliac, and Voltaire *are*.[3] But in promiscuous company no prudent man will oppugn the merits of a contemporary in his own supposed department; contenting himself with praising in his turn those whom *he* deems excellent. If I should ever deem it my duty at all to oppose the pretensions of individuals, I would oppose them in books which could be weighed and answered, in which I could evolve the whole of my reasons and feelings with their requisite limits and modifications; not in irrecoverable conversation, where however strong the reasons might be, the feelings that

[a] *BL* (1817): Thompson;

[1] The lectures of 1808, in which, as C told Humphry Davy (9 Sept 1807), he originally planned to continue beyond Milton to Dryden and Pope and to "Modern Poetry". *CL* III 30. But C is probably confusing those lectures with the lectures of 1811–12.

[2] Sir James Harrington (1611–77), the political philosopher, author of *The Commonwealth of Oceana* (1656), *Aphorisms Political* (1659), and *Political Discourses* (1660). C was reading him closely in 1804 and found him "prophetic". *CN* II 2223 and n. Harrington and Machiavelli were among the "red-letter names . . . in the almanacks of worldly wisdom". *SM (CC)* 17. C may be thinking primarily of Spinoza's political writing, e.g. *Tractatus politicus* (1677), quoted in *Friend (CC)* I 165. Hume with his *Inquiry Concerning Human Understanding* and Condillac with his *Logic* were among "the *flashy* moderns" (*CN* II 2139: see next n) C scorned. On

Condillac see also below, I 141 n 2. On Voltaire, cf: ". . . scarcely any one has a larger share of my aversion". *Friend (CC)* I 131.

[3] With this and the following two sentences, cf the closely similar remark in a notebook eleven years before (1804): "In company, indeed with all except a very chosen few, never dissent from any one as to the *merits* of another/ especially, in your own supposed department/ but content yourself with praising in your turn the really good. Praises of the unworthy are felt by a good man & man of genius as detractions from the worthy, as robberies . . . & Bacon & Harrington are *not* read because Hume & Condilliac are. . . . Oppose it, if at all, in books in which you can evolve the whole of your reasons & feelings (not in conversation, where it will be inevitably attributed to Envy)." *CN* II 2193. This is another example of the way in which C, in composing *BL,* constantly used his notebooks.

prompted them would assuredly be attributed by some one or other to envy and discontent. Besides I well know, and I trust, have acted on that knowledge, that it must be the ignorant and injudicious who extol the unworthy; and the eulogies of critics without taste or judgement are the natural reward of authors without feeling or genius. "Sint unicuique sua præmia." [1]

How then, dismissing, as I do, these three causes, am I to account for attacks, the long continuance and inveteracy of which it would require all three to explain. The solution may seem to have been given, or at least suggested, in a note to a preceding page. *I was in habits of intimacy with Mr. Wordsworth and Mr. Southey!* [2] This, however, transfers, rather than removes, the difficulty. Be it, that by an unconscionable extension of the old adage, "noscitur a socio," [a][3] my literary friends are never under the water-fall of criticism, but I must be wet through with the spray; yet how came the torrent to descend upon *them?*

First then, with regard to Mr. Southey. I well remember the general reception of his earlier publications: viz. the poems published with Mr. Lovell under the names of Moschus and Bion; the two volumes of poems under his own name, and the Joan of Arc.[4] The censures of the critics by profession are extant, and may be easily referred to:—careless lines, inequality in the merit of the different poems, and (in the lighter works) a predilection for the strange and whimsical; in short, such faults as might have been anticipated in a young and rapid writer, were indeed sufficiently

---

[a] *BL* (1817) omits comma

[1] "Let everyone have his own reward." Proverbial in this form. Cf 1 Cor 3.8, in which, however, the Latin of the Vulgate is quite different. Quoted in a similar context in *CN* II 2193.

[2] "But what can I say, when I have declared my abhorrence of the Ed. Review? . . . that on seeing my own name in their abuse I feel from it only as a symbol of Wordsworth & Southey—for in utter oblivion & disregard of any thing & all things which they *can* know of me—and from experience that my name is mentioned only because they have

heard, I am a friend of S. & W." *CN* III 3302 and n.

[3] Proverbial: "He is known by the company he keeps". Cf "Noscitur e socio, applied to me & W. with a vengeance in spite of direct proof to the contrary." *CN* I 1673 (Nov 1803).

[4] *Poems* by Robert Lovell and Robert Southey (Bath 1795) had the writers' names on the title page, but the individual poems were designated by "Bion" for RS and "Moschus" for Lovell. The other two publications by RS were *Poems* (2 vols Bristol 1797–9) and *Joan of Arc: an Epic Poem* (Bristol 1796).

enforced. Nor was there at that time wanting a party spirit to aggravate the defects of a poet, who with all the courage of uncorrupted youth had avowed his zeal for a cause, which he deemed that of liberty, and his abhorrence of oppression by whatever name consecrated. But it was as little objected by others, as dreamt of by the poet himself, that he *preferred* careless and prosaic lines on rule and of forethought, or indeed that he pretended to any other art or theory of poetic diction, besides that which we may all learn from Horace, Quintilian, the admirable dialogue de Causis Corruptæ Eloquentiæ,[1] or Strada's Prolusions;[2] if indeed natural good sense and the early study of the best models in his own language had not infused the same maxims more securely, and, if I may venture the expression, more vitally. All that could have been fairly deduced was that in his taste and estimation of writers Mr. Southey agreed far more with Warton,[3] than with Johnson. Nor do I mean to deny, that at all times Mr. Southey was of the same mind with Sir Philip Sidney in preferring an excellent ballad in the *humblest* style of poetry to twenty indifferent poems that strutted in the *highest*.[4] And by what have his works, published

[1] C refers to the *Dialogus de oratoribus* of Tacitus (c 55–120), to which he also refers in "Satyrane's Letters", below, II 176. The belief of Justus Lipsius (1579) that this was the lost *De causis corruptae eloquentiae* by Quintilian was not prevalent in C's time.

[2] The *Prolusiones academicae oratoriae, historicae, poeticae* (1617) by Famiano Strada (1572–1649), the Italian Jesuit historian known mainly for his *De bello belgico* (1632–47) on the Spanish–Dutch wars. See also *CN* III 3276 and n.

[3] Possibly Joseph Warton in his *Essay on the Genius and Writings of Pope* (2 vols 1756, 1782). The work is in part a protest on behalf of the "greater *genres*" (the epic, tragic drama, the "greater ode") vs satiric and didactic verse, and of the "pathetic" vs the stylised in diction. Actually Johnson took for granted much that Warton said, as is shown in his review of Warton's *Essay* in the *Literary Magazine* (1756). But

for C's generation Warton could seem a herald for their own critical values, whereas Johnson, viewed selectively, could superficially seem a supporter of the *status quo*. But more likely C refers to Thomas Warton (*BL* 1847 reads "Thomas Warton" in the text), whose *History of English Poetry* (1774–81) "helped to divert the stream of English verse from the formal and classical channels to which the prestige of Pope had for many years consigned it" (Sir Sidney Lee in *DNB*).

[4] "I never heard the old Song of *Percy* and *Duglas* that I founde not my heart mooved more than a Trumpet; and yet is it sung but by some blinde Crouder with no rougher voyce than rude stile." Sidney *Defence of Poesie* ed A. Feuillerat (Cambridge 1923) 24. C has exaggerated Sidney's remark. Cf the *Ed Rev* review of RS's *Curse of Kehama*: "While gravely preferring the tame vulgarity of our old ballads, to the nervous and refined verses of

since then, been characterized, each more strikingly than the preceding, but by greater splendor, a deeper pathos, profounder reflections, and a more sustained dignity of language and of metre?[1] Distant may the period be, but whenever the time shall come, when all his works shall be collected by some editor worthy to be his biographer, I trust that an excerpta of all the passages, in which his writings, name, and character have been attacked, from the pamphlets and periodical works of the last twenty years, may be an accompaniment. Yet that it would prove medicinal in after times, I dare not hope; for as long as there are readers to be delighted with calumny, there will be found reviewers to calumniate. And such readers will become in all probability more numerous, in proportion as a still greater diffusion of literature shall produce an increase of sciolists; and sciolism bring with it petulance and presumption.[2] In times of old, books were as religious oracles; as literature advanced, they next became venerable preceptors; they then descended to the rank of instructive friends; and as their numbers increased, they sunk still lower to that of entertaining companions; and at present they seem degraded into culprits to hold up their hands at the bar of every self-elected, yet not the less peremptory, judge,[3] who chuses to write from humour or interest, from enmity or arrogance, and to abide the decision (in the words

Pope or Johnson, they [the Lake Poets] lay claim, not to indulgence, but to admiration. . .". *Ed Rev* xvii (1811) 434.

[1] These would include *Thalaba the Destroyer* (2 vols 1801); the translation of Vasco de Lobeira's *Amadis of Gaul* (4 vols 1803); *Madoc: a Poem* (1805); *Metrical Tales and Other Poems* (1805); *The Curse of Kehama* (1810); *Omniana* (2 vols 1812), with contributions by C; and *Roderick: the Last of the Goths* (1814). The *Ed Rev* review of 1811 had objected to the "diffuseness and prolixity" of RS's style, accusing him of "perpetual artifice", "conceit and bad taste", and "childishness".

[2] C claimed that sciolism ("pretentious superficiality of knowledge": *OED*, citing C as earliest

example) caused an "epidemic of a proud ignorance" in the latter half of the eighteenth century. *SM (CC)* 94.

[3] A reworking of material in C's Lect 1 of 18 Nov 1811: ". . . the enormous multiplication of Authors & Books—At first Oracles, then preceptors, then agreeable Companions, but now Culprits by anticipation—& they act accordingly flattering basely the imaginary Word, *Public*—which is yet of pernicious effect by habituating every Reader to consider himself as the Judge & therefore the Superior of the Writer who yet if he has any justifiable claim to write ought to be his Superior . . .". Portions of Four Lectures f 11: ms in Berg Collection, in *Lects 1808–19 (CC)* ms. Cf *Sh C* ii 58.

of Jeremy Taylor) "of him that reads in malice, or him that reads after dinner."[1]

The same gradual retrograde movement may be traced, in the relation which the authors themselves have assumed towards their readers. From the lofty address of Bacon: "these are the meditations of Francis of Verulam, which that posterity should be possessed of, he deemed *their* interest:"[2] or from dedication to Monarch or Pontiff, in which the honor given was asserted in equipoise to the patronage acknowleged from PINDAR'S

$$\text{------} \; \epsilon\pi' \; \text{ἄλλοι-}$$

σι δ' ἄλλοι μεγάλοι. τὸ δ' ἔσχατον κορυ-
φοῦται βασιλεῦσι. μηκέτι
Πάπταινε πόρσιον.
Εἴη σέ τε τούτου
Ὑψοῦ χρόνον πατεῖν, ἐμέ
Τε τοσσάδε νικαφόροις
Ὁμιλεῖν, πρόφαντον σοφίαν καθ' Ἑλ-
λανας ἐόντα παντᾶ.

OLYMP. OD. I.[3]

a there was a gradual sinking in the etiquette or allowed style of pretension.*b*[4]

[1] Jeremy Taylor Σύμβολον θεολο-γικόν : or a *Collection of Polemicall Discourses* (1674) Epistle Dedicatory a1ᵛ (var). C prefaced the passage to lecture notes (BM MS Egerton 2800 f 89, the same ms that contains a version of the footnote at the beginning of ch 3, above, I 49 and n 2), and probably quoted more from the Epistle in his Lect 1 of 18 Nov 1811, for in Collier's notes to the lecture he wrote that "Coleridge here quoted from Bishop Jeremy Taylor . . . The passage related to the subject he was discussing & contained among others the following sentence. 'The favour of the people is as fickle as the smiles of children or the fall of a die' ", which precedes the above quotation (as does C's "from humour or interest"). See Collier's footnote in *Sh C* II 58n.

[2] C's tr of the Prooemium to the *Great Instauration.*

[3] *Olympian Odes* 1.113–16, the conclusion. Minor textual variations, lineation, and capitalisation suggest that this is from *Poetae graeci veteres, tragici, comici, lyrici, epigrammatarii* ed P. de la Rovière (Geneva 1614) II 4; see *CN* III 4189n. *Poetae graeci veteres* was the source of most of C's Greek quotations in *BL*. Tr LCL: "Some men are great in one thing; others in another: but the crowning summit is for kings. Refrain from peering too far. Heaven grant that thou mayest plant thy feet on high, so long as thou livest, and that I may consort with victors for all my days, and be foremost in the lore of song among Greeks in every land."

[4] Completed by C from Gillman's "corrected" copy: letter to Basil Montagu [1 May 1827]: *CL* VI 675. The sentence appears in *BL* (1847), an indication that HNC was using that annotated copy.

Poets and Philosophers, rendered diffident by their very number, addressed themselves to *"learned* readers;" then, aimed to conciliate the graces of "the *candid* reader;" till, the critic still rising as the author sunk, the amateurs of literature collectively were erected into a municipality of judges, and addressed as THE TOWN! And now finally, all men being supposed able to read, and all readers able to judge, the multitudinous PUBLIC, shaped into personal unity by the magic of abstraction, sits nominal despot on the throne of criticism. But, alas! as in other despotisms, it but echoes the decisions of its invisible ministers, whose intellectual claims to the guardianship of the muses seem, for the greater part, analogous to the physical qualifications which adapt their oriental brethren for the superintendence of the Harem. Thus it is said, that St. Nepomuc was installed the guardian of bridges because he had fallen over one, and sunk out of sight;[1] thus too St. Cecilia is said to have been first propitiated by musicians, because having failed in her own attempts, she had taken a dislike to the art, and all its successful professors.[2] But I shall probably have occasion hereafter to deliver my convictions more at large concerning this state of things, and its influences on taste, genius and morality.

In the "Thalaba,"[a] the "Madoc,"[a] and still more evidently in the unique * "Cid," the "Kehama," and as last, so best, the "Don

* I have ventured to call it "unique;" not only because I know no work of the kind in our language (if we except a few chapters of the old transla-

[a] *BL* (1817) omits comma

[1] St John of Nepomuc (c 1340–93) of Bohemia, who was drowned in the Moldau by order of Wenceslaus IV. C is here paraphrasing J. P. Richter *Blumen- Frucht- und Dornenstücke* (1796–7), in which Richter says (ch 5) that reviewers and critics, unable to write themselves, become the guardians of literature "for the same reason as St Nepomuc is the patron of bridges, and of those who pass over them,—because he once fell from one into the water". Tr E. H. Noel (1845) I 135. Cf *CN* III 4039n. C used the same illustration in Lect 5 of 2 Dec 1811: *Sh C* II 106.

[2] The association of St Cecilia (fl 2nd or 3rd cent) with the organ and instrumental music was late and was owing to a misreading of a phrase in the mediaeval text of her "Life and Acts". Forced to marry Valerian, then a pagan, she in the midst of the wedding-feast "while the organ was playing [*cantantibus organis*] sang to the only God in her heart" the song of David (Ps 119.80). *Cantantibus organis* was mistakenly applied to Cecilia herself ("she sang to [her own] playing of the organ"). *The Life of St. Cecilia* ed B. E. Lovewell (1898) 29, 72. C may be recalling Herder's account in *Zerstreute Blätter* (1792–7): *Sämmtliche Werke* ed B. Suphan (Berlin 1877–1913) XVI 253–67. Cf *CN* III 3337. For C's reading of "Verm. Blätter" before 1804 see *CM* (*CC*) II: Herder *Kalligone*.

Roderick;" Southey has given abundant proof, "se cogitâsse quám sit magnum dare aliquid in manus hominum: nec persuadere sibi posse, non sæpe tractandum quod placere et semper et omnibus cupiat." Plin. Ep. Lib. 7. Ep. 17.[3] But on the other [a]hand, I guess[b] that Mr. Southey was quite unable to comprehend, wherein could consist the crime or mischief of printing half a dozen or more playful poems;[4] or to speak more generally, compositions which would be enjoyed or passed over, according as the taste and humour of the reader might chance to be; provided they contained nothing immoral. In the present age "periturae parcere chartæ"[5] is emphatically an unreasonable demand. The merest trifle, he ever sent abroad, had tenfold better claims to its ink and paper, than all the silly criticisms, which prove no more, than that the critic was not one of those, for whom the trifle was written; and than all the grave exhortations to a greater reverence for the public. As if the passive page of a book, by having an epigram or doggrel[6] tale impressed on it, instantly assumed at once loco-motive power and a sort of ubiquity, so as to flutter and buz in the ear of the public

---

tion of Froissart)[1] none, which uniting the charms of romance and history, keeps the imagination so constantly on the wing, and yet leaves so much for after reflection; but likewise, and chiefly, because it is a compilation,[2] which in the various excellencies of translation, selection, and arrangement, required and proves greater genius in the compiler, as living in the present state of society, than in the original composers.

[a-b] *BL* (1817): hand I guess,

[1] *The Chronicle of Froissart* (1523–5) tr Sir John Bourchier, Lord Berners (1467–1533). Cf *CN* I 1075 and n.
[2] *The Chronicle of the Cid* (1808), published when RS was thirty-four, is a unified prose narrative translated from different sources and then interwoven. The basis is the part devoted to the Cid in the *Crónica general de España* compiled in the reign of Alfonso the Wise (1252–84) and the similar version known as the *Crónica del Cid*. To this RS added incidents and descriptions both from the earlier *Poema del Cid* (c 1140–90) and popular ballads about him.
[3] Slightly altered from Pliny's *Letters* (7.17) to fit in with the earlier part of C's sentence. Tr LCL: "[that he has thought] what a serious thing it is to place a work in the hands of the public; and he cannot help but be persuaded that he should constantly revise a work that he wants to please everyone for all time".
[4] Principally *The Devil's Walk*, on which RS and C collaborated, and the group of eight poems called "Nondescripts" (including *The Pig, The Dancing Bear*, and the famous *Cataract at Lodore*).
[5] Juvenal *Satires* 1.18. Tr LCL: "To spare paper that would be wasted anyway".
[6] Not a misprint. C (or Morgan) uses the common Elizabethan and seventeenth-century spelling.

to the sore annoyance of the said mysterious personage. But what gives an additional and more ludicrous absurdity to these lamentations is the curious fact, that if in a volume of poetry the critic should find poem or passage which he deems more especially worthless, he is sure to select and reprint it in the review; by which, on his own grounds, he wastes as much more paper than the author, as the copies of a fashionable review are more numerous than those of the original book; in some, and those the most prominent instances, as ten thousand to five hundred. I know nothing that surpasses the vileness of deciding on the merits of a poet or painter (not by characteristic defects; for where there is genius, *these* always point to his characteristic *beauties*;[1] but) by accidental failures or faulty passages; except the impudence of defending it, as the proper duty, and most instructive part, of criticism. Omit or pass slightly over, the expression, grace, and grouping of Raphael's *figures*; but ridicule in *detail* the knitting-needles and broom-twigs, that are to represent trees in his back grounds; and never let him hear the last of his *galli-pots!* Admit, that the Allegro and Penseroso of Milton are not *without merit*; but repay yourself for this concession, by reprinting at length the *two poems on the University Carrier!*[2] As a fair specimen of his sonnets, quote *"a Book was writ of late called Tetrachordon;"*[3]

[1] Cf C's resolve (Oct 1803): "Never to lose an opportunity of reasoning against the head-dimming, heart-damping Principle of Judging a work by its Defects, not its Beauties. *Every* work must have the former—we know it a priori—but every work has not the Latter/ & he therefore, who discovers them, tells you something that you could not with certainty or even with probability have anticipated." *CN* I 1551. Cf also Lect 6 of 5 Dec 1811: "To the young he would say that it was always wrong to judge of anything by its defects: the first attempt should be to discover its excellencies. When a man . . . began to abuse a book, while his invectives came down like water from a shower-bath, he told him no news because all works of course must have defects but if he shewed him beauties he had told him news indeed . . .". *Lects 1808–19 (CC)* ms.

[2] In Jan 1631 several Cambridge students wrote affectionate semi-jocose poems on the death of the aged Thomas Hobson, who kept a livery there. Milton, aged twenty-two, wrote two. Cf C's defence of them in answer to Richard Hurd: ". . . as if the two poor Copies of Verses had been a Dry-rot, threatening the whole life & beauty of the Comus, Lycidas, and other work in their vicinity! I confess that I have read these *Hobsons* 20 times, & always with amusement/ without the least injury to the higher & very different delight afforded by Milton's *poetry.*—These are the Junior Soph's very *learned* Jocularity . . .". Annotation on Milton *Poems upon Several Occasions* ed Thomas Warton (1791) 318–20: *CM (CC)* III.

[3] The first line of Sonnet XI (1645–6), distinctive in its combination of colloquial style and stiffly scornful humour.

and as characteristic of his rhythm and metre cite his literal translation of the first and second psalm! In order to justify yourself, you need only assert, that had you dwelt chiefly on the beauties and excellencies of the poet, the admiration of these might seduce the attention of future writers from the objects of their love and wonder, to an imitation of the few poems and passages in which the poet was most unlike himself.

But till reviews are conducted on far other principles, and with far other motives; till in the place of arbitrary dictation and petulant sneers, the reviewers support their decisions by reference to fixed canons of criticism, previously established and deduced from the nature of man; reflecting minds will pronounce it arrogance in them thus to announce themselves to men of letters, as the guides of their taste and judgment. To the purchaser and mere reader it is, at all events, an injustice. He who tells me that there are *defects* in a new work, tells me nothing which I should not have taken for granted without his information. But he, who points out and elucidates the *beauties* of an original work, does indeed give me interesting information, such as experience would not have authorised me in anticipating. And as to compositions which the authors themselves announce with "Hæc ipsi novimus esse nihil," [1] why should we judge by a different rule two printed works, only because the one author was alive, and the other in his grave? What literary man has not regretted the prudery of Spratt in refusing to let his friend Cowley appear in his slippers and dressing gown? [2] I am not perhaps the only one who had derived an innocent amusement from the riddles, conundrums, tri-syllable lines,[3] &c. &c. of Swift and his correspondents, in hours of languor

[1] Adapted from Martial 13.2.8: "Nos haec novimus esse nihil"; tr: "We ourselves know these things to be nothing". C on 19 Dec 1799 had advised RS to use this as a motto for "all the *light* pieces" (*CL* I 549), and RS did so for his *Minor Poems* (3 vols 1815).

[2] Thomas Sprat (1635–1713) in his "Account of the Life and Writings of Mr. Abraham Cowley" (which Johnson described as "a funeral oration rather than a history"), after praising Cowley's letters, stated that he thought it improper to print them. In private letters "the Souls of Men should appear undress'd: And in that negligent Habit, they may be fit to be seen by one or two in a Chamber, but not to go abroad into the Streets". Prefixed to Cowley *Works* (7th ed 1681) sig c 1 (C's annotated ed, now in Indiana University).

[3] C means to refer not to actual "lines" of three syllables but to Swift's use of Hudibrastic tri-syllabic rhymes (as in "merry Dan/ . . . Sheridan" or "Willy put/ . . . Lilliput").

when to have read his more finished works would have been useless to myself, and, in some sort, an act of injustice to the author. But I am at a loss to conceive by what perversity of judgement, these relaxations of his genius could be employed to diminish his fame as the writer of "Gulliver's travels," and the "Tale of a Tub."[1] Had Mr. Southey written twice as many poems of inferior merit, or partial interest, as have enlivened the journals of the day, they would have added to his honour with good and wise men, not merely or principally as proving the versatility of his talents, but as evidences of the purity of that mind, which even in its levities never wrote a line, which it need regret on any moral account.

I have in imagination transferred to the future biographer the duty of contrasting Southey's fixed and well-earned fame, with the abuse and indefatigable hostility of his anonymous critics from his early youth to his ripest manhood. But I cannot think so ill of human nature as not to believe, that these critics have already taken shame to themselves, whether they consider the object of their abuse in his moral or his literary character. For reflect but on the variety and extent of his acquirements! He stands second to no man, either as an historian or as a bibliographer; and when I regard him, as a popular essayist, (for the articles of his compositions in the reviews are for the greater part essays on subjects of deep or curious interest rather than criticisms on particular works *) I look in vain for any writer, who has conveyed so much information, from so many and such recondite sources, with so many just and original reflections, in a style so lively and poignant, yet so uniformly classical and perspicuous; no one in short who has combined so much wisdom with so much wit; so much truth and

---

* See the articles on Methodism, in the Quarterly Review; the small volume on the New System of Education, &c.[2]

[1] C considered *Gulliver's Travels* and *A Tale of a Tub* "the highest effort of Swift's genius". Annotation on Swift *Works* (13 vols 1768) v: *CM (CC)* IV; *Misc C* 130.

[2] Actually there was only one article: "On Evangelical Sects" *QR* IV (1810) (480–515, modifying the harsher opinions expressed in his earlier review of William Myles's *History of the Methodists* in *A Rev* I (1803) 210–13 and anticipating his sympathetic *Life of Wesley* (2 vols 1820). *The Origin, Nature, and Object, of the New System of Education* (1812), to which C refers, was an expansion of a review in *QR* VI (1811) 264–304 dealing with the educational methods of Andrew Bell (1753–1832) and Joseph Lancaster (1778–1838), which C mentions in ch 18, below, II 60n–1. Cf *Friend* (CC) II 29n; *CN* III 3291n, 4181n, and above, I 53 n 3.

knowledge with so much life and fancy. His prose is always intelligible and always entertaining. In poetry he has attempted almost every species of composition known before, and he has added new ones; and if we except the highest lyric, (in which how few, how very few even of the greatest minds have been fortunate) he has attempted every species successfully: from the political song of the day, thrown off in the playful overflow of honest joy and patriotic exultation, to the wild ballad;* from epistolary ease and graceful narrative, to the austere and impetuous moral declamation; from the pastoral charms*a* and wild streaming lights of the "Thalaba," in which sentiment and imagery have given permanence even to the excitement of curiosity; and from the full blaze of the "Kehama," (a gallery of finished pictures in one splendid fancy piece, in which, notwithstanding, the moral grandeur rises gradually above the brilliance of the colouring and the boldness and novelty of the machinery) to the more sober beauties of the "Madoc;" and lastly, from the Madoc to his "Roderic," in which, retaining all his former excellencies of a poet eminently inventive and picturesque, he has surpassed himself in language and metre, in the construction of the whole, and in the splendor of particular passages.

Here then shall I conclude? No! The characters of the deceased, like the encomia on tombstones, as they are described with religious tenderness, so are they read, with allowing sympathy indeed, but yet with rational deduction. There are men, who deserve a higher record; men with whose characters it is the interest of their contemporaries, no less than that of posterity, to be made acquainted; while it is yet possible for impartial censure, and even for quick-sighted envy, to cross-examine the tale without offence to the courtesies of humanity; and while the eulogist detected in

* See the incomparable "Return to Moscow," and the "Old Woman of Berkeley." 1

a BL (1817): claims

1 Appropriate enough for the first category ("patriotic exultation") is the bluff quasi-comic *March to Moscow* (1813): ("The Emperor Nap he would set off . . . Heigh-ho for Moscow!"). But "wild ballad" is so much an overstatement for the earlier *Old Woman of Berkeley* (1798) that one would suspect C of irony if irony were more endemic to his nature. Doubtless in his eagerness to praise RS's range, and having added the "wild ballad" as a category, he felt he would not be credited unless he gave an example.

exaggeration or falsehood must pay the full penalty of his baseness in the contempt which brands the convicted flatterer. Publicly has Mr. Southey been reviled by men, who (I would feign hope for the honor of human nature) hurled fire-brands against a figure of their own imagination, publicly have his talents been depreciated, his principles denounced; as publicly do I therefore, who have known him intimately, deem it my duty to leave recorded, that it is SOUTHEY'S almost unexampled felicity, to possess the best gifts of talent and genius free from all their characteristic defects.[1] To those who remember the state of our public schools and universities some twenty years past, it will appear no ordinary praise in any man to have passed from innocence into virtue, not only free from all vicious habit, but unstained by one act of intemperance, or the degradations akin to intemperance. That scheme of head, heart, and habitual demeanour, which in his early manhood, and first controversial writings, Milton, claiming the privilege of self-defence, asserts of himself, and challenges his calumniators to disprove;[2] this will his school-mates, his fellow-collegians, and his maturer friends, with a confidence proportioned to the intimacy of their knowledge, bear witness to, as again realized in the life of Robert Southey. But still more striking to those, who by biography or by their own experience are familiar with the general habits of genius, will appear the poet's matchless industry and perseverance in his pursuits;[3] the worthiness and dignity of those pursuits; his generous submission to tasks of transitory interest, or such as *his* genius alone could make otherwise; and that having thus more than satisfied the claims of affection or prudence, he should yet

---

[1] C's "public" praise of RS as a poet may be contrasted with some private misgivings. To J. P. Collier and others (1811–12) he said that neither RS, nor Scott, nor Thomas Campbell "would by their poetry survive much beyond the day when they lived and wrote", and even *The Curse of Kehama* he described "as a work of great talent, but not of much genius". *Sh C* II 44, 36 (though cf *TT* 20 Apr 1811). To HCR (1811) he said RS "wanted modifying power—he was a jewel-setter". As a poet C "did not seem inclined to place Southey above Scott. He considered neither of them as poets." *CRB* I 26, 48.

[2] Throughout the latter half, particularly at the close, of Milton's *Second Defence of the People of England: Works* (Columbia ed, 1931–40) VIII 119–225. In C's *Complete Collection of the Historical, Political and Miscellaneous Works* ed T. Birch (2 vols 1738) II 343–9.

[3] RS's industry was indeed phenomenal: over sixty volumes during his lifetime, not counting reprints and second editions; and almost thirty by the time C was writing *BL*.

have made for himself time and power, to achieve more, and in more various departments than almost any other writer has done, though employed wholly on subjects of his own choice and ambition. But as Southey possesses, and is not possessed by, his genius,[1] even so is he the master even of his virtues. The regular and methodical tenor of his daily labours, which would be deemed rare in the most mechanical pursuits, and might be envied by the mere man of business, loses all semblance of formality in the dignified simplicity of his manners, in the spring and healthful chearfulness of his spirits.[2] Always employed, his friends find him always at leisure. No less punctual in trifles, than stedfast in the performance of highest duties, he inflicts none of those small pains and discomforts which irregular men scatter about them, and which in the aggregate so often become formidable obstacles both to happiness and utility; while on the contrary he bestows all the pleasures, and inspires all that ease of mind on those around him or connected with him, which perfect consistency, and (if such a word might be framed) absolute *reliability*,[3] equally in small as in great concerns, cannot but inspire and bestow: when this too is softened without being weakened by kindness and gentleness. I know few men who so well deserve the character which an antient attributes to Marcus Cato, namely, that he was likest virtue, in as much as he seemed to act aright, not in obedience to any law or outward motive, but by the necessity of a happy nature, which could not act otherwise.[4] As son, brother, husband, father, master, friend, he moves with firm yet light steps, alike unostentatious, and alike exemplary. As a writer, he has uniformly made his talents subservient to the best interests of humanity, of public virtue, and domestic piety; his cause has ever been the cause of pure religion and of liberty, of national independence and

---

[1] Cf "Shakespeare . . . no passive vehicle of inspiration possessed by the spirit, not possessing it", ch 15, below, II 26–7.

[2] See *CN* I 1815 and n. Cf C's remark about RS to George Dyer (Feb 1795): "His Genius and acquirements are uncommonly great—yet they bear no proportion to his moral Excellence—He is truly a man of *perpendicular Virtue* . . .". *CL* I 152.

[3] *OED* cites C as the first to use the word.

[4] Cato "resembled Virtue herself, and in all his acts he revealed a character nearer to that of gods than of men. He never did a right action solely for the sake of seeming to do the right, but because he could not do otherwise." Velleius Paterculus 2.35.2, tr LCL. Cf WW's epigraph to *Ode to Duty* (added in 1837).

of national illumination. When future critics shall weigh out his guerdon of praise and censure, it will be Southey the poet only, that will supply them with the scanty materials for the latter. They will likewise not fail to record, that as no man was ever a more constant friend, never had poet more friends and honorers among the good of all parties; and that quacks in education, quacks in politics, and quacks in criticism were his only enemies.*

* It is not easy to estimate the effects which the example of a young man as highly distinguished for strict purity of disposition and conduct, as for intellectual power and literary acquirements, may produce on those of the same age with himself, especially on those of similar pursuits and congenial minds. For many years, my opportunities of intercourse with Mr. Southey have been rare, and at long intervals; but I dwell with unabated pleasure on the strong and sudden, yet I trust not fleeting influence, which my moral being underwent on my acquaintance with him at Oxford, whither I had gone at the commencement of our Cambridge vacation on a visit to an old school-fellow.[1] Not indeed on my moral or religious principles, for *they* had never been contaminated; but in awakening the sense of the duty and dignity of making my actions accord with those principles, both in word and deed. The irregularities only not universal among the young men of my standing, which I always *knew* to be *wrong*, I then learnt to feel as *degrading*; learnt to know that an opposite conduct, which was at that time considered by us as the easy virtue of cold and selfish prudence, might originate in the noblest emotions, in views the most disinterested and imaginative. It is not however from grateful recollections only, that I have been impelled thus to leave these, my deliberate sentiments on record; but in some sense as a debt of justice to the man, whose name has been so often connected with mine, for evil to which he is a stranger. As a specimen I subjoin part of a note, from "the Beauties of the Anti-jacobin," in which, having previously informed the public that I had been dishonor'd at Cambridge for preaching deism, at a time when for my youthful ardor in defence of christianity, I was decried as a bigot by the proselytes of French Phi- (or to speak more truly, Psi) losophy,[2] the writer concludes with these words; "since this time he has left his native country, commenced citizen of the world, *left his poor children fatherless, and his wife destitute. Ex his disce, his friends,* L A M B *and* S O U T H E Y ." With severest truth it may be asserted, that it would not be easy to select two men more exemplary in their domestic affections, than those whose names were thus printed at full length as in the same rank of morals with a denounced infidel and fugitive, who had left his children *fatherless and his wife destitute!* Is it surprising, that many good men remained longer than perhaps they otherwise would have done, adverse to a party, which encouraged and openly rewarded the authors of such atrocious calumnies! Qualis es, nescio; sed per quales agis, scio et doleo.[3]

[1] In Jun 1794.

[2] "Mere (or shallow) wisdom". ". . . from the Greek psilos slender, and Sophia Wisdom, in opposition to Philosophy, the Love of Wisdom and the Wisdom of Love, a thing still in some repute among your Country men [i.e. Germans] but long obsolete in England". To J. H. Bohte 27 Feb 1819: *CL* IV 922. Cf *CN* III 3244, 3507, 3935, 3975, 4401, and below, I 185.

[3] The "note" was appended to George Canning's poem *New Moral-*

ity in *The Beauties of the Anti-Jacobin* (1799) 306. The poem itself had previously appeared in the *A-J* of 9 Jul 1798 but without this note, which mentions C's non-attendance at chapel in college and adds: "To the disgrace of discipline, and a Christian University, this avowed Deist was not expelled for such sin. . . . He has since married, had children, and has now quitted the country, become a citizen of the world, left his little ones fatherless, and his wife destitute. 'Ex uno disce' his associates Southey and Lambe." C, whose gifts were not satiric, was distressed enough when he read the note (Nov 1799) to jot down a list of "Characters" for a satire he might write, listing "Canning & the Anti-Jacobins" first. *CN* I 567. Cf *Friend* No 2 of 8 Jun 1809, in which there is a similar passage quoting *The Beauties of the Anti-Jacobin* and including the Latin sentence at the end of the present note ("I do not know what sort of man you are; but I do know the sort of men through whom you act, and I regret it"), which was probably composed by C himself. *Friend (CC)* II 22–3n.

CHAPTER 4

The lyrical ballads with the preface—Mr. Wordsworth's earlier poems—On fancy and imagination—The investigation of the distinction ~ 86 15 *important to the fine arts*

I HAVE wandered far from the object in view, but as I fancied to myself readers who would respect the feelings that had tempted me from the main road; so I dare calculate on not a few, who will warmly sympathize with them. At present it will be sufficient for my purpose, if I have proved, that Mr. Southey's writings no more than my own, furnished the original occasion to this fiction of a *new school* of poetry, and of clamors against its supposed founders and proselytes.

As little do I believe that "Mr. WORDSWORTH'S Lyrical Ballads" were in *themselves* the cause. I speak exclusively of the two volumes so entitled.[1] A careful and repeated examination of these confirms me in the belief, that the omission of less than an hundred lines would have precluded nine-tenths of the criticism on this work.[2] I hazard this declaration, however, on the supposition, that the reader had taken it up, as he would have done any other collection of poems purporting to derive their subjects or interests from the incidents of domestic or ordinary life, intermingled with higher strains of meditation which the poet utters in his own person and character; with the proviso, that they were perused without knowledge of, or reference to, the author's peculiar opinions, and that the reader had not had his attention previously directed to those peculiarities. In these, as was actually the case with Mr. Southey's earlier works, the lines and passages which might have offended the general taste, would have been considered as mere

---

[1] C refers to the 2nd ed, containing the celebrated Preface: *Lyrical Ballads, with Other Poems* (2 vols 1800), "By W. Wordsworth". The 1st (1798) had been published anonymously in a single volume.

[2] Cf ch 22, below, II 126, speaking about just one of the "defects" of WW's poetry ("inconstancy of the style"): "I doubt whether the objectionable passages would amount in the whole to one hundred lines; not the eighth part of the number of pages".

inequalities, and attributed to inattention, not to perversity of judgement. The men of business who had passed their lives chiefly in cities, and who might therefore be expected to derive the highest pleasure from acute notices of men and manners conveyed in easy, yet correct and pointed language;[1] and all those who, reading but little poetry, are most stimulated with that species of it, which seems most distant from prose,[2] would probably have passed by the volume altogether. Others more catholic in their taste, and yet habituated to be most pleased when most excited, would have contented themselves with deciding, that the author had been successful in proportion to the elevation of his style and subject. Not a few perhaps, might by their admiration of "the lines written near Tintern Abbey," those "left upon a Seat under a Yew Tree," the "old Cumberland beggar," and "Ruth," have been gradually led to peruse with kindred feeling the "Brothers," the "Hart leap well," and whatever other poems in that collection may be described as holding a middle place between those written in the highest and those in the humblest style; as for instance between the "Tintern Abbey," and "the Thorn," or the "Simon Lee."[3] Should their taste submit to no further change, and still remain unreconciled to the colloquial phrases, or the imitations of them, that are, more or less, scattered through the class last mentioned; yet even from the small number of the latter, they would have deemed them but an inconsiderable subtraction from the merit of the whole work; or, what is sometimes not unpleasing in the publication of a new writer, as serving to ascertain the natural tendency, and consequently the proper direction of the author's genius.

In the critical remarks therefore, prefixed and annexed to the "Lyrical Ballads," I believe, that we may safely rest, as the true

[1] Cf ch 1, above, I 18, on "the writings of Mr. Pope and his followers": "I saw, that the excellence of this kind consisted in just and acute observations on men and manners in an artificial state of society, as its matter and substance: and in the logic of wit, conveyed in smooth and strong epigrammatic couplets, as its *form*."
[2] On the assumption that (in Johnson's phrase) "not to write prose is certainly to write poetry" (Johnson *Lives* "Collins" III 341), see ch 16, below, II 29–30.
[3] *Lines . . . Tintern Abbey, Lines Left upon a Seat in a Yew-Tree, The Thorn,* and *Simon Lee* were all published in *LB* (1798). The rest were added in *LB* (1800). For C's remarks on some of them, see below, II 45–52, 59, 68, 145, 151–2.

origin of the unexampled opposition which Mr. Wordsworth's writings have been since doomed to encounter.[1] The humbler passages in the poems themselves were dwelt on and cited to justify the rejection of the theory. What in and for themselves would have been either forgotten or forgiven as imperfections, or at least comparative failures, provoked direct hostility when announced as intentional, as the result of choice after full deliberation. Thus the poems, admitted by *all* as excellent, joined with those which had pleased the far *greater* number, though they formed two-thirds of the whole work, instead of being deemed (as in all right they should have been, even if we take for granted that the reader judged aright) an atonement for the few exceptions, gave wind and fuel to the animosity against both the poems and the poet. In all perplexity there is a portion of fear, which predisposes the mind to anger.[2] Not able to deny that the author possessed both genius and a powerful intellect, they felt *very positive*, but were not *quite certain*,[3] that he might not be in the right, and they themselves in the wrong; an unquiet state of mind, which seeks alleviation by quarrelling with the occasion of it, and by wondering

[1] C is thinking particularly of the attacks by Jeffrey (*Ed Rev* Oct 1802, Oct 1807). E.g., speaking of the "Lake poets" generally in his review of RS's *Thalaba:* "One of their own authors, indeed, has very ingenuously set forth, (in a kind of manifesto that preceded one of their most flagrant acts of hostility), that it was their capital object 'to adapt to the uses of poetry, the ordinary language . . . among the middling and lower orders of the people.' . . . The arts that aim at exciting admiration and delight, do not take their models from what is ordinary . . .". *Ed Rev* I (1802) 65–7. The review of WW's *Poems* (1807) emphasises the extent to which "Mr. Wordsworth and his friends . . . write as they do, upon principle and system; and it evidently costs them much pains to keep *down* to the standard which they have proposed to themselves." Jeffrey's adverse criticism is almost entirely focussed on ludicrous or pedestrian passages that seem written according to WW's theories, whereas Jeffrey considers WW's poetry to rise in quality, especially in the sonnets, "when, by any accident, he is led to abandon his system . . .". *Ed Rev* XI (1807) 214–31. Cf below, II 156–8. In addition to Jeffrey, C may also be remembering Peter Bayley's parody of *The Idiot Boy* with its note on "that most simple of all poets, Mr. W." that annoyed WW, RS, and C. See *WL* (*E*) 413, 424, 455, *CN* I 1673.

[2] See above, I 31 and n 2.

[3] The distinction between "positiveness" and "certainty"—"the blessedness of Certainty contrasted with the Bubble-bubble of *Positiveness*"—is another of C's favourite distinctions. Cf *CN* I 1410, II 2196, 2643, 3095, III 3592 and n; *CL* III 48, IV 571, 750; *Friend* (*CC*) II 7, 7n, 76n; *LS* (*CC*) 175 and n; *C&S* (*CC*) 21n.

at the perverseness of the man, who had written a long and argumentative essay to persuade them, that

Fair is foul, and foul is fair;[1]

in other words, that they had been all their lives admiring without judgement, and were now about to censure without reason.*

* In opinions of long continuance, and in which we had never before been molested by a single doubt, to be suddenly *convinced* of an *error*, is almost like being *convicted* of a fault. There is a state of mind, which is the direct antithesis of that, which takes place when we maĸ: a bull.[2] *The bull* namely consists in the bringing together two incompatible thoughts, with the *sensation*, but without the *sense*, of their connection. The psychological condition, or that which constitutes the possibility of this state, being such disproportionate vividness of two distant thoughts, as extinguishes or obscures the consciousness of the intermediate images or conceptions, or wholly abstracts the attention from them. Thus in the well known bull, "*I was a fine child, but they changed me;*" the first conception expressed in the word "*I,*" is that of personal identity—*Ego contemplans*: the second expressed in the word "*me,*" is the visual image or object by which the mind represents to itself its past condition, or rather, its personal identity under the form in which it imagined itself previously to have existed.—Ego contemplatus.[3] Now the change of one visual image for another involves in itself no absurdity, and becomes absurd only by its immediate juxta-position with the first thought, which is rendered possible by the whole attention being successively ab-

[1] Shakespeare *Macbeth* I i 11.

[2] In the simplest sense a "bull" (probably from MF *bouler,* meaning to "roll" [as in playing bowls] and later to "deceive") is a statement with apparent congruity but with a fundamental incongruity of ideas of which the speaker is presumably unaware. This was particularly the case with "Irish bulls" (e.g. "He said it was an inherited trait of his family not to have children"), which were popular in C's time. Cf Richard and Maria Edgeworth *Essay on Irish Bulls* (1802). C, wrestling to explain bulls, was interested in them as an example of the way emotion can make a connection for the mind however impossible in fact. E.g. a notebook entry for Nov 1803: DC, coming in for tea and noticing the cake was already eaten, cried out: "O but don't eat the Cake! You have eat the cake! O but don't eat up all the cakes!" C observes: "His Passion had compleatly confounded his Sense of Time, & its Consequences—He saw that it was done; & yet he passionately entreated you not to do it—& not for the time to come/ but for the Present & the Past. 'O but you have! O but don't now!' This Mem. for the effect of the Passions on the reasoning power imprimis in producing *Bulls.*" *CN* I 1643; cf I 915; 1620 and n, 1645; II 2807; *Omniana* I 219–21; *SM* (*CC*) 153 and n.

[3] Cf *CN* II 2057, 2389 and n on "I contemplating" as "intimate Synthesis with the principle of Co-adunation", the sum total of what we value outside us (e.g. those we love) in a process of active experience, whereas the "I contemplated", as object, is by definition an extrapolation. Needless to say, both *ego contemplans* and *ego contemplatus* are involved in our sense of personal identity, though not in the same degree.

The Lyrical Ballads

That this conjecture is not wide from the mark, I am induced to believe from the noticeable fact, which I can state on my own knowledge, that the same general censure should have been grounded almost by each different person on some different poem. Among those, whose candour and judgement I estimate highly, I distinctly remember six who expressed their objections to the "Lyrical Ballads" almost in the same words, and altogether to the same purport, at the same time admitting, that several of the poems had given them great pleasure; and, strange as it might seem, the composition which one had cited as execrable, another had quoted as his favorite.[1] I am indeed convinced in my own mind, that could the same experiment have been tried with these volumes, as was made in the well known story of the picture, the result would have been the same; the parts which had been covered by the number of the *black* spots on the one day, would be found equally *albo* lapide notatæ[2] on the succeeding.

However this may be, it is assuredly hard and unjust to fix the attention on a few separate and insulated poems with as much

---

sorbed in each singly, so as not to notice the interjacent notion, "changed" which by its incongruity with the first thought, "*I*," constitutes the bull. Add only, that this process is facilitated by the circumstance of the words "*I*," and "*me*," being sometimes equivalent, and sometimes having a distinct meaning; sometimes, namely, signifying the act of self-consciousness, sometimes the external image in and by which the mind represents that act to itself, the result and symbol of its individuality. Now suppose the direct contrary state, and you will have a distinct sense of the connection between two conceptions, without that *sensation* of such connection which is supplied by habit. The man *feels*, as if he were standing on his head, though he cannot but *see*, that he is truly standing on his feet. This, as a painful sensation, will of course have a tendency to associate itself with the person who occasions it; even as persons, who have been by painful means restored from derangement, are known to feel an involuntary dislike towards their physician.

[1] WW had passed on to C some examples of such directly opposite opinions. E.g. of *Nutting:* "Mr. C. W.: 'Worth its weight in gold.' Mr. S.: 'Can make neither head nor tail of it.'" Of *Poet's Epitaph:* "Mr. Charles Lamb: 'The latter part preeminently good and your own.' Mr. S.: 'The latter part very ill written.'" *Cumberland Beggar:* "Mr. J. W.: 'Everybody seems delighted.' Mr. Charles Lamb: 'You seem to presume your readers are stupid . . .' ."

Christopher Wordsworth *Memoirs of William Wordsworth* (1851) I 174–5.

[2] The parts of the picture would be "marked with a *white* stone". Cf e.g. Catullus 68.148. The "well known story" is untraced. C refers to the Roman custom of using white and black pebbles to note favourable or unfavourable days (and also to vote for or against, from which descends the practice of "blackballing").

aversion, as if they had been so many plague-spots on the whole work, instead of passing them over in silence, as so much blank paper, or leaves of bookseller's catalogue; especially, as no one pretends to have found immorality or indelicacy; and the poems therefore, at the worst, could only be regarded as so many light or inferior coins in a roleau of gold, not as so much alloy in a weight of bullion. A friend whose *talents* I hold in the highest respect, but whose *judgement* and strong sound sense I have had almost continued occasion to *revere*,[1] making the usual complaints to me concerning both the style and subjects of Mr. Wordsworth's minor poems; I admitted that there were some few of the tales and incidents, in which I could not myself find a sufficient cause for their having been recorded in metre. I mentioned the "Alice Fell" as an instance; "nay," replied my friend with more than usual quickness of manner, "I cannot agree with you *there!* that I own *does* seem to me a remarkably pleasing poem." In the "Lyrical Ballads" (for my experience does not enable me to extend the remark equally unqualified to the two subsequent volumes)[2] I have heard at different times, and from different individuals every single poem *extolled* and *reprobated*, with the exception of those of loftier kind, which as was before observed, seem to have won universal praise. This fact of itself would have made me diffident in my censures, had not a still stronger ground been furnished by the strange contrast of the heat and long continuance of the opposition, with the nature of the faults stated as justifying it. The seductive faults, the dulcia vitia[3] of Cowley, Marini,[4] or Darwin might reasonably be thought capable of corrupting the public judgement for half a century, and require a twenty years war, campaign after campaign, in order to dethrone the usurper and re-establish the

---

[1] Tom Poole? Lamb?

[2] WW's *Poems in Two Volumes* (1807), in which *Alice Fell* (written in 1802) first appeared.

[3] C probably recalls Quintilian 10.1.129, speaking of Seneca the Younger: "His style is for the most part corrupt and exceedingly dangerous, for the very reason that [his works] abound in attractive faults ['quod abundant dulcibus vitiis']." Cf Cicero *De Senectute* 65, on the faults of old age (speaking of Cato the Elder): "Those faults all become attractive both by good character and arts"—"ea vitia . . . omnia dulcia [dulciora] fiunt et moribus bonis et artibus".

[4] Giambattista Marino (or Marini) (1569–1625), founder of the school of poetry named after him, *Marinismo* (later *Secentismo*); noted for his brilliantly elaborate use of conceit and metaphor. C had studied his sonnets closely in 1805. *CN* II 2625 and n. For C on Cowley and Darwin, see above, I 19–20, 23.

legitimate taste. But that a downright simpleness, under the affectation of simplicity, prosaic words in feeble metre, silly thoughts in childish phrases, and a preference of mean, degrading, or at best trivial associations and characters, should succeed in forming a school of imitators, a company of almost *religious* admirers, and this too among young men of ardent minds, liberal education, and not

with academic laurels unbestowed;[1]

and that this bare and bald *counterfeit* of poetry, which is characterized as *below* criticism, should for nearly twenty years have well-nigh *engrossed* criticism, as the main, if not the only, *butt* of review, magazine, pamphlets, poem, and paragraph;—this is indeed matter of wonder! Of yet greater is it, that the contest should still continue as * undecided as that between Bacchus and the frogs in

* Without however the apprehensions attributed to the *Pagan* reformer of the poetic republic. If we may judge from the preface to the recent collection of his poems,[2] Mr. W. would have answered with Xanthias—

Σὺ δ' οὐκ ἔδεισας τὸν ψόφον τῶν ῥημάτων,
Καὶ τὰς ἀπειλάς; ΞΑΝ. οὐ μὰ Δί', οὐδ' ἐφρόντισα.[3]

And here let me dare hint to the authors of the numerous parodies, and pretended imitations of Mr. Wordsworth's style,[4] that at once to conceal and convey wit and wisdom in the semblance of folly and dulness, as is done in the clowns and fools, nay even in the Dogberry, of our Shakespear,

[1] C is quoting from memory the last line in Thomas Warton's sonnet *To the River Lodon:* "Nor with the Muse's laurel unbestow'd". C's early sonnet *To the River Otter* may have been suggested by this sonnet as well as by Bowles's *To the Itchen.*

[2] ". . . justified by recollection of the insults which the ignorant, the incapable, and the presumptuous, have heaped upon these and my other writings, I may be permitted to anticipate the judgment of posterity upon myself, I shall declare . . . that I have given in these unfavourable times, evidence of exertions of this faculty [the imagination] upon its worthiest objects, the external universe, the moral and religious sentiments of Man . . . worthy to be holden in undying remembrance". *Poems* Preface (1815): *W Prose* III 35.

[3] Aristophanes *Frogs* 492–3. In *Poetae graeci veteres* ed P. de la Rovière I 781. Tr LCL:

DIONYSUS: But weren't *you* frightened at those dreadful t h r e a t s And shoutings?
XANTHIAS: Frightened? Not a bit. I cared not.

In the summer of 1816 (after this chapter was written but before *BL* was published) C was reading his old Cambridge acquaintance's tr of Aristophanes, privately printed by John Hookham Frere for distribution to his friends; it was not published until 1839. See *CL* IV 647, 649; *CN* III 4331 and n.

[4] Parodies such as those of Peter Bayley (see above, I 71 n 1) and of James and Horace Smith in *Rejected Addresses* (1812).

Aristophanes; when the former descended to the realms of the departed to bring back the spirit of old and genuine poesy.

Χορὸς Βατράχων· Διόνυσος

X.　βρεκεκεκέξ, κοάξ, κοάξ.

Δ.　ἀλλ᾽ ἐξόλοισθ᾽ αὐτῷ κοάξ.
　　οὐδὲν γάρ ἐστι, ἢ κοάξ.
　　οἰμώζετ᾽· οὐ μοι μέλει.

X.　ἀλλὰ μὴν κεκραξόμεσθά
　　γ᾽, ὁπόσον ἡ φάρυγξ ἂν ἡμῶν
　　χανδάνῃ δι᾽ ἡμέρας,
　　βρεκεκεκέξ, κοάξ, κοάξ!

Δ.　τούτῳ γὰρ οὐ νικήσετε.

X.　οὐδὲ μὲν ἡμᾶς σὺ πάντως.

Δ.　οὐδὲ μὲν ὑμεῖς γε δή με
　　οὐδέποτε· κεκράξομαι γάρ,
　　κἄν με δεῖ, δι᾽ ἡμέρας,
　　ἕως ἂν ὑμῶν ἐπικρατήσω τῷ κοάξ!

X.　βρεκεκεκέξ, ΚΟΆΞ, ΚΟΆΞ![3]

---

is doubtless a proof of genius, or at all events, of satiric talent; but that the attempt to ridicule a silly and childish poem, by writing another still sillier and still more childish, can only prove (if it prove any thing at all) that the parodist is a still greater blockhead than the original writer, and what is far worse, a *malignant* coxcomb to boot. The talent for mimicry seems strongest where the human race are most degraded. The poor, naked, half human savages of New Holland[1] were found excellent mimics: and in civilized society, minds of the very lowest stamp alone satirize by *copying*.[2] At least the difference, which must blend with and balance the likeness, in order to constitute a just imitation, existing here merely in caricature, detracts from the libeller's heart, without adding an iota to the credit of his understanding.

---

[1] Australia. Cf C's Lect 1 of 15 Jan 1808: ". . . at all times, but more especially in the less artificial state of manners, Ridicule disposes men to mimicry—The new Hollanders, whose dullness of apprehension has made many philanthropic observers melancholy, are yet perfect masters of mimicry". Portions of Four Lectures f 7ᵛ (ms in Berg Collection, NYPL): *Lects 1808–19* (*CC*) ms.

[2] On "copy" vs "imitation" see below, II 72 and n 4.

[3] *Frogs* 227–9, 256–68 (var). C's text corresponds significantly in three places to that of *Poetae graeci veteres* I 784–5. In line 3 of his quotation C omits ἀλλ᾽ ("but"), without really altering the sense; there are other slight changes. Tr LCL:

	Chorus of Frogs; Dionysus
FROGS:	Brekekekex, ko-ax, ko-ax.
DIONYSUS:	Hang you, and your ko-axing too! There's nothing but ko-ax with you.
	. . . . . . Go hang yourselves, for what care I?
FROGS:	All the same we'll shout and cry, Stretching all our throats with song, Shouting, crying, all day long,

During the last year of my residence at Cambridge, I became acquainted with Mr. Wordsworth's first publication entitled "Descriptive Sketches;"[1] and seldom, if ever, was the emergence of an original poetic genius above the literary horizon more evidently announced. In the form, style, and manner of the whole poem, and in the structure of the particular lines and periods, there is an harshness and acerbity connected and combined with words and images all a-glow, which might recall those products of the vegetable world, where gorgeous blossoms rise out of the hard and thorny rind and shell, within which the rich fruit was elaborating. The language was not only peculiar and strong, but at times knotty and contorted, as by its own impatient strength; while the novelty and struggling crowd of images acting in conjunction with the difficulties of the style, demanded always a greater closeness of attention, than poetry, (at all events, than descriptive poetry) has a right to claim.[2] It not seldom therefore justified the complaint of obscurity. In the following extract I have sometimes fancied, that I saw an emblem of the poem itself, and of the author's genius as it was then displayed.

> 'Tis storm; and hid in mist from hour to hour,
> All day the floods a deepening murmur pour;
> The sky is veiled, and every cheerful sight:
> Dark is the region as with coming night;
> And yet what frequent bursts of overpowering light!
> Triumphant on the bosom of the storm,
> Glances the fire-clad eagle's wheeling form;

FR. and DI: Brekekekex, ko-ax, ko-ax.

DIONYSUS: In this you'll never, never win.

FROGS: This you shall not beat us in.

DIONYSUS: No, nor ye prevail o'er me. Never! never! I'll my song Shout, if need be, all day long, Until I've learned to master your ko-ax. Brekekekex, ko-ax, ko-ax.

[1] *Descriptive Sketches in Verse. Taken During a Pedestrian Tour in the Italian, Grison, Swiss, and Savoyard Alps* (1793). Actually it was WW's second publication, being preceded the same year by *An Evening Walk* (1793). C's "last year" of residence at Cambridge was 1794. He left in Dec.

[2] Cf C's remark in ch 1, above, I 7, speaking of his own early poems: ". . . I forgot to enquire, whether the thoughts themselves did not demand a degree of attention unsuitable to the nature and objects of poetry. This remark however applies chiefly, though not exclusively to the *Religious Musings.*"

Eastward, in long perspective glittering, shine
The wood-crowned cliffs that o'er the lake recline;
Wide o'er the Alps a hundred streams unfold,
At once to pillars turn'd that flame with gold;
Behind his sail the peasant strives to shun
The West, that burns like one dilated sun,
Where in a mighty crucible expire
The mountain, glowing hot, like coals of fire.[1]

The poetic P S Y C H E , in its process to full developement, under-
goes as many changes as its Greek name-sake, the * butterfly.
And it is remarkable how soon genius clears and purifies itself
from the faults and errors of its earliest products; faults which, in
its earliest compositions, are the more obtrusive and confluent,
because as heterogeneous elements, which had only a temporary
use, they constitute the very *ferment*, by which themselves are
carried off. Or we may compare them to some diseases, which
must work on the humours, and be thrown out on the surface, in
order to secure the patient from their future recurrence. I was in
my twenty-fourth year, when I had the happiness of knowing Mr.
Wordsworth personally,[3] and while memory lasts, I shall hardly
forget the sudden effect produced on my mind, by his recitation

* The fact, that in Greek Psyche is the common name for the soul, and
the butterfly, is thus alluded to in the following stanza from an unpublished
poem of the author;

    The butterfly the ancient Grecians made
    The soul's fair emblem, and its only name—
    But of the soul, escaped the slavish trade
    Of mortal life! For in this earthly frame
    Our's is the reptile's lot, much toil, much blame,
    Manifold motions making little speed,
    And to deform and kill the things, whereon we feed.

                                S. T. C.[2]

[1] C quotes the passage not as he
had read it in the 1793 text (lines
332–47) but from a group of revised
selections from *Descriptive Sketches*
in *Poems* (1815) I 79–80. The
original version begins:
'Tis storm; and hid in mist from
   hour to hour
All day the floods a deeper
   murmur pour,
And mournful sounds, as of a
   spirit lost,
Pipe wild along the hollow-
   blustering coast,

Till the Sun walking on his
   western field
Shakes from behind the clouds
   his flashing shield.
Then follow the lines in the above
passage beginning: "Triumphant on
the bosom of the storm . . .".
[2] This is the first appearance of
the poem in print. *PW* (EHC) I
412.
[3] Their first meeting was on or
about 1 Sept 1795. *CN* I 6n and 9n;
Reed 167.

of a manuscript poem, which still remains unpublished, but of which the stanza, and tone of style, were the same as those of the "Female Vagrant" as originally printed in the first volume of the "Lyrical Ballads." [1] There was here, no mark of strained thought, or forced diction, no crowd or turbulence of imagery, and, as the poet hath himself well described in his lines "on re-visiting the Wye," [2] manly reflection, and human associations had given both variety, and an additional interest to natural objects, which in the passion and appetite of the first love they had seemed to him neither to need or permit. The occasional obscurities, which had risen from an imperfect controul over the resources of his native language, had almost wholly disappeared, together with that worse defect of arbitrary and illogical phrases, at once hackneyed, and fantastic, which hold so distinguished a place in the *technique* of ordinary poetry, and will, more or less, alloy the earlier poems of the truest genius, unless the attention has been specifically directed to their worthlessness and incongruity.* I did not perceive

---

* Mr. Wordsworth, even in his two earliest "the Evening Walk and the Descriptive Sketches," is more free from this latter defect than most of the young poets his contemporaries. It may however be exemplified, together with the harsh and obscure construction, in which he more often offended, in the following lines:—

'Mid stormy vapours ever driving by,
Where ospreys, cormorants, and herons cry;
Where hardly given the hopeless waste to cheer,
Denied the bread of life the foodful ear,
Dwindles the pear on autumn's latest spray,
And *apple sickens* pale in summer's ray;
Ev'n here content has fixed her smiling reign
With independence, child of high disdain.[3]

[1] C refers to *Guilt and Sorrow; or Incidents upon Salisbury Plain,* written 1791–4 but not published in its entirety until 1842. A version of stanzas 23–50 was published under the title *The Female Vagrant* in *LB* (1798). Cf WW's later (IF) note: "Mr. Coleridge, when I first became acquainted with him, was so impressed with this poem, that he would have encouraged me to publish the whole as it then stood; but the mariner's fate appeared to me so tragical as to require a treatment more subdued and yet more strictly applicable in expression than I had at first given to it. This fault was corrected nearly fifty years afterwards, when I determined to publish the whole." *WPW* I 330.

[2] *Lines . . . Tintern Abbey* lines 22–102, esp (88–91):

For I have learned
To look on nature, not as in the hour
Of thoughtless youth; but hearing oftentimes
The still, sad music of humanity . . .

[3] *Descriptive Sketches* lines 317–24 (C's italics). Cf the 1849 text (lines 254–61), revised in deference to C's remarks above:

any thing particular in the mere style of the poem alluded to during its recitation, except indeed such difference as was not separable from the thought and manner; and the Spenserian*[a]* stanza, which always, more or less, recalls to the reader's mind Spenser's*[b]* own style, would doubtless have authorized in my then opinion a more frequent descent to the phrases of ordinary life, than could without an ill effect have been hazarded in the heroic couplet. It was not however the freedom from false taste, whether as to common defects, or to those more properly his own, which made so unusual an impression on my feelings immediately, and subsequently on my judgement. It was the union of deep feeling with profound thought; the fine balance of truth in observing with the imaginative faculty in modifying the objects observed; and above all the original gift of spreading the tone, the *atmosphere*, and with it the depth and height of the ideal world [1] around forms, incidents, and situations, of which, for the common view, custom had bedimmed all the lustre, had dried up the sparkle and the dew drops.[2] "To find no contradiction in the union of old and new; to contemplate the ANCIENT of days and all his works with feelings as fresh, as if all had then sprang forth at the first creative fiat; characterizes the mind that feels the riddle of the world, and may help to unravel it.[3] To carry on the feelings of

I hope, I need not say, that I have quoted these lines for no other purpose than to make my meaning fully understood. It is to be regretted that Mr. Wordsworth has not republished these two poems entire.

[a] BL (1817): Spencerian   *[b] BL* (1817): Spencer's

And what if ospreys, cormorants, herons cry,
Amid tempestuous vapours driving by,
Or hovering over wastes too bleak to rear
That common growth of earth, the foodful ear;
Where the green apple shrivels on the spray,
And pines the unripened pear in summer's kindliest ray;
Contentment shares the desolate domain
With Independence, child of high Disdain.

[1] Cf above, I 43, "the man of genius who lives most in the ideal world".

[2] Cf on WW's purpose in *LB:* "to give the charm of novelty to things of every day . . . by awakening the mind's attention from the lethargy of custom, and directing it to the loveliness and the wonders of the world before us; an inexhaustible treasure, but for which in consequence of the film of familiarity and selfish solicitude we have eyes, yet see not . . .". Below, ch 14, II 7.

[3] This sentence is taken almost verbatim from a notebook entry of Oct 1803 (*CN* I 1622) and also used in *SM* (*CC*) 25. The entire passage in quotation marks is extracted from the 1809–10 *Friend: Friend* (*CC*) II 73–4.

childhood into the powers of manhood; to combine the child's sense of wonder and novelty[1] with the appearances, which every day for perhaps forty years had rendered familiar;

> With sun and moon and stars throughout the year,
> And man and woman;[2]

this is the character and privilege of genius, and one of the marks which distinguish genius from talents.[3] And therefore is it the prime merit of genius and its most unequivocal mode of manifestation, so to represent familiar objects as to awaken in the minds of others a kindred feeling concerning them and that freshness of sensation which is the constant accompaniment of mental, no less than of bodily, convalescence. Who has not a thousand times seen snow fall on water? Who has not watched it with a new feeling, from the time that he has read Burns' comparison of sensual pleasure

> To snow that falls upon a river
> A moment white—then gone for ever![4]

"In poems, equally as in philosophic disquisitions, genius pro-

[1] Cf C's Lect 8 of 12 Dec 1811: "In the Poet was comprehended the man who carries the feelings of childhood into the powers of manhood: who with a soul unsubdued, unshackled by custom can contemplate all things with the freshness and wonder of a child & connecting with it the inquisitive powers of his manhood, adds as far as he can find knowledge, admiration & where knowledge no longer permits admiration gladly sinks back again into the childlike feeling of devout wonder." *Lects 1808–19* (*CC*) ms. Cf also "I define GENIUS, as originality of intellectual construction: the moral accompaniment, and actuating principle of which consists, perhaps, in the carrying on of the freshness and feelings of childhood into the powers of manhood." *Friend* (*CC*) I 419.

[2] Milton Sonnet XXII ("To Mr. Cyriack Skinner upon his Blindness") lines 5–6: "Of Sun, or Moon, or Starre throughout the year, | Or man or woman."

[3] On the distinction between "genius" and "talent" see ch 2, above, I 31 n 5.

[4] Robert Burns *Tam o'Shanter* lines 59–62:

> But pleasures are like poppies spread,
> You seize the flow'r, its bloom is shed:
> Or like the snow falls in the river—
> A moment white, then melts for ever.

"I would rather have written one simile by Burns [C then quotes the last two lines] than all the poetry that his countryman Scott—as far as I am yet able to form an estimate—is likely to produce." From J. P. Collier's Diary, quoted in his *Seven Lectures on Shakespeare and Milton* Preface (1856): *Sh C* II 38. Cf *Sh C* II 98, 203, and C's half-parody of the lines, speaking of his own conversation as contrasted with Johnson's: "Sparks that fall upon the River, | A moment bright, then lost for ever." *IS* 185.

See p. 32

duces the strongest impressions of novelty, while it rescues the most admitted truths from the impotence caused by the very circumstance of their universal admission. Truths of all others the most awful and mysterious, yet being at the same time of universal interest, are too often considered as *so* true, that they lose all the life and efficiency of truth, and lie bed-ridden in the dormitory of the soul, side by side, with the most despised and exploded errors." THE FRIEND,* page 76, No. 5.

This excellence, which in all Mr. Wordsworth's writings is more or less predominant, and which constitutes the character of his mind, I no sooner felt, than I sought to understand. Repeated meditations led me first to suspect, (and a more intimate analysis of the human faculties, their appropriate marks, functions, and effects matured my conjecture into full conviction) that fancy and imagination were two distinct and widely different faculties, instead of being, according to the general belief, either two names with one meaning, or at furthest, the lower and higher degree of one and the same power. It is not, I own, easy to conceive a more apposite*a* translation of the Greek *Phantasia,* than the Latin Imaginatio; but it is equally true that in all societies there exists an instinct of growth, a certain collective, unconscious good sense working progressively to desynonymize[2] † those words originally

* As "the Friend" was printed on stampt sheets, and sent only by the post to a very limited number of subscribers, the author has felt less objection to quote from it, though a work of his own. To the public at large indeed it is the same as a volume in manuscript.[1]

† This is effected either by giving to the one word a general, and to the other an exclusive use; as "to put on the back" and "to indorse;"[3] or by

a BL (1817): opposite

[1] ". . . A work, which was printed rather than published, or so published that it had been well for the unfortunate author, if it had remained in manuscript!" Ch 10, below, I 175. For discussion of its reception, see *Friend (CC)* I ix–xv, ciii–cv.

[2] *OED* cites this as the first use of the word. ". . . The whole process of human intellect is gradually to desynonymize terms . . .". *P Lects* Lect 5 (1949) 173; cf 47–51, 152–3, 184–5, 199–201, 368–9; *CN* III 3312n, 4397 f 49ᵛ, 4422 and n.

"His [C's] word, to *desynonymize* . . . is a truly valuable one, as designating a process very common in the history of language, and bringing a new thought into circulation." J. C. Hare *Guesses at Truth* (1867) 220.

[3] From *in-dorsum* (on the back of). Cf *Paradise Regained* III 329: "Elephants indorsed with towers". C used this as an example of "the laxity in the use of terms" by modern poets, in Lect 2 of 21 Nov 1811: *Sh C* II 64.

of the same meaning, which the conflux of dialects had supplied to the more homogeneous languages, as the Greek and German: and which the same cause, joined with accidents of translation from original works of different countries, occasion in mixt languages like our own. The first and most important point to be proved is, that two conceptions perfectly distinct are confused

---

an actual distinction of meanings as "naturalist," and "physician;" or by difference of relation as "I" and "Me;" (each of which the rustics of our different provinces still use in all the cases singular of the first personal pronoun).[1] Even the mere difference, or corruption, in the *pronunciation* of the same word, if it have become general, will produce a new word with a distinct signification; thus "property" and "propriety;" the latter of which, even to the time of Charles II. was the *written* word for all the senses of both.[2] Thus too "mister" and "master" both hasty pronounciations of the same word "magister," "mistress," and "miss," "if," and "give," &c. &c.[3] There is a sort of *minim immortal* among the animalcula infusoria[4] which has not naturally either birth, or death, absolute beginning, or absolute end: for at a certain period a small point appears on its back, which deepens and lengthens till the creature divides into two, and the same process recommences in each of the halves now become integral. This may be a fanciful, but it is by no means a bad emblem of the formation of words, and may facilitate the conception, how immense a nomenclature may be organized from a few simple sounds by rational beings in a social state. For each new application, or excitement of the same sound, will call forth a different sensation, which cannot but affect the pronunciation. The after recollection of the sound, without the same vivid sensation, will modify it still further; till at length all trace of the original likeness is worn away.

---

[1] C is remembering the Devon use of pronouns, which he commonly heard as a boy.

[2] "Propriety" (OF *propriété*), as a word that includes the idea of "property", continued to be used into the 1700's. Cf Johnson's two definitions of it (1755): "peculiarity of possession; exclusive right" and "accuracy, justness". For C's later use of "propriety" as distinguished from "nationalty" see *C&S* (*CC*) 35. For several of the terms in this note cf *CN* III 4397 f 49ᵛ.

[3] In a marginal note in his copy of *BL* (now in NYUL) John Thelwall charged that the reader "acquainted with [Horne Tooke's] Diversions of Purley [1786–98] will not fail to discover that the fountain of all this reasoning is in that book". Actually Tooke, whose work C knew

well (cf e.g. *CN* III 3587n, 3834n, 4237n, 4436n), lists none of the examples, except C's "if" and "give", arguing that all conjunctions are derived from verbs. Since Adam Smith's *Considerations Concerning the First Formation of Languages* (1767), it had become a commonplace of literary criticism and linguistic studies that languages, developing from the concrete to the abstract, become more denotative and hence tend progressively, in C's word, to "desynonymize".

[4] I.e. "a sort of 'barely-there immortality' among the tiny organisms . . .". C is speaking of the reproduction by division (mitosis) of one-cell organisms. The "small point" two lines later is the cell's nucleus.

under one and the same word, and (this done) to appropriate that word exclusively to one meaning, and the synonyme (should there be one) to the other. But if (as will be often the case in the arts and sciences) no synonyme exists, we must either invent or borrow a word. In the present instance the appropriation had already begun, and been legitimated in the derivative adjective: Milton had a highly *imaginative*, Cowley a very *fanciful* mind. If therefore I should succeed in establishing the actual existences of two faculties generally different, the nomenclature would be at once determined. To the faculty by which I had characterized Milton, we should confine the term *imagination*; while the other would be contra-distinguished as *fancy*.[1] Now were it once fully ascertained, that this division is no less grounded in nature, than that of delirium from mania, or Otway's

> Lutes, lobsters, seas of milk, and ships of amber,[2]

[1] HCR, after a discussion with C on fancy vs imagination (21 Dec 1816), found WW's "obscure discrimination" between the terms in his 1815 Preface "greatly illustrated". *CRD* I 200.

[2] Thomas Otway (1652–85) *Venice Preserved* (1682) v 369: "Lutes, laurels, seas of milk and ships of amber". The "lobsters" are a transference from lines in Butler's *Hudibras* that C also uses to illustrate "fancy" (see below). In citing the lines from Otway, C may have been thinking of Shaftesbury's remark in "Advice to an Author", in which "Fancy" is associated with "mental abandon". Subjected to "Fancy", "I must then join voices with her and cry . . . *Seas of milk, and ships of amber*". *Characteristics* ed J. Robertson (2 vols 1900) I 209–11. On "delirium" see the discussion of Hartley's theory of association in ch 6, below, I 111. Cf HCR 14 Nov 1810: "He [C] made an elaborate distinction between fancy and imagination. The excess of fancy is delirium, of imagination mania. Fancy is the arbitrarily bringing together of things that lie remote, and forming them into a unity. The materials lie ready for the fancy, which acts by a sort of juxtaposition. On the other hand, the imagination under excitement generates and produces a form of its own. The 'seas of milk and ships of amber' he quoted as fanciful delirium. He related, as a sort of disease of imagination, what occurred to himself. He had been watching intently the motions of a kite among the mountains of Westmoreland, when on a sudden he saw two kites in an opposite direction. This delusion lasted some time. At last he discovered that the two kites were the fluttering branches of a tree beyond a wall." *CRD* I 306. The distinction is one of the last discussions recorded in *TT* (23 Jun 1834): "You may conceive the difference in kind between the Fancy and the Imagination in this way,— that if the check of the senses and the reason were withdrawn, the first would become delirium, and the last mania. The Fancy brings together images which have no connection natural or moral, but are yoked together by the poet by means of some accidental coincidence; as in the well-known passage in Hudibras:—

from Shakespear's

> What! have his daughters brought him to this pass?[1]

or from the preceding apostrophe to the elements;[2] the theory of the fine arts, and of poetry in particular, could not, I thought, but derive some additional and important light. It would in its immediate effects furnish a torch of guidance to the philosophical critic; and ultimately to the poet himself. In energetic minds, truth soon changes by domestication into power;[3] and from directing in the discrimination and appraisal of the product, becomes influencive in the production. To admire on principle, is the only way to imitate without loss of originality.

It has been already hinted, that metaphysics and psychology have long been my hobby-horse. But to have a hobby-horse, and to be vain of it, are so commonly found together, that they pass almost for the same. I trust therefore, that there will be more good humour than contempt, in the smile with which the reader chastises my self-complacency, if I confess myself uncertain, whether the satisfaction from the perception of a truth new to myself may not have been rendered more poignant by the conceit, that it would be equally so to the public.[4] There was a time, certainly, in which I took some little credit to myself, in the belief that I had been the first of my countrymen, who had pointed out the diverse meaning

---

'The sun had long since in the lap
Of Thetis taken out his nap,
And like a lobster boyl'd, the morn
From black to red began to turn.' [*Hudibras* ii ii 29–32]
The Imagination modifies images, and gives unity to variety; it sees all things in one, *il più nell' uno*. There is the epic imagination, the perfection of which is in Milton; and the dramatic, of which Shakspere is the absolute master."

[1] *King Lear* iii iv 63 (var).

[2] *King Lear* iii ii 16–17:
I tax you not, you elements, with unkindness;
I never gave you kingdom, call'd you children.
Cf C's 1808 lecture notes: ". . . we find undoubted proof in his [Shakespeare's] mind of Imagination or the power by which one image or feeling is made to modify many others, & by a sort of *fusion to force many into one*—that which after shewed itself in such might & energy in Lear, where the deep anguish of a Father spreads the feeling of Ingratitude & Cruelty over the very Elements of Heaven". *CN* iii 3290. In the Preface to *Poems* (1815) WW also cites the passage in discussing the imagination: *W Prose* iii 35.

[3] Cf ". . . that sublime faculty, by which a great mind becomes that which it meditates on". *CN* iii 3290.

[4] Cf C's "delight" in "the distinct perception of a fundamental Truth" and his hope of a "Public . . . of persons susceptible of the same Delight." *Friend* (*CC*) ii 276 (i 15, 16).

of which the two terms were capable, and analyzed the faculties to which they should be appropriated.[1] Mr. W. Taylor's recent volume of synonimes[2] I have not yet seen; * but his specification

* I ought to have added, with the exception of a single sheet which I accidentally met with at the printer's. Even from this scanty specimen, I found it impossible to doubt the talent, or not to admire the ingenuity of the author. That his distinctions were for the greater part unsatisfactory to *my* mind, proves nothing against their accuracy; but it may possibly be serviceable to him in case of a second edition, if I take this opportunity of suggesting the query; whether he may not have been occasionally misled, by having assumed, as to me he appeared to have done, the non-existence of *any* absolute synonimes in our language? Now I cannot but think, that there are many which remain for our posterity to distinguish and appropriate, and which I regard as so much reversionary wealth in our mother-tongue. When two distinct meanings are confounded under one or more words, (and such must be the case, as sure as our knowledge is progressive and of course imperfect) erroneous consequences will be drawn, and what is true in one sense of the word, will be affirmed as true in toto. Men of research startled by the consequences, seek in the things themselves (whether in or out of the mind) for a knowledge of the fact, and having discovered the difference, remove the equivocation either by the substitution of a new word, or by the appropriation of one of the two or more words, that had before been used promiscuously. When this distinction has been so naturalized and of such general currency, that the language itself does as it were *think* for us (like the sliding rule which is the mechanic's safe substitute for arithmetical knowledge) we then say, that it is evident to *common sense*.[3] Common sense, therefore, differs in different ages. What was born and christened

[1] By no means the first. Several English and Scottish writers had anticipated him, particularly William Duff and Dugald Stewart. But the phrase "first of my countrymen", despite the inference of Shawcross, *BL* (1907) I 226, suggests that C is fully aware of German distinctions. For general discussion, see Introd, above, I xcvii–civ.

[2] William Taylor (1765–1836), RS's friend, reverted to the old distinction (see Introd, above, I xcvii) in his *English Synonyms Discriminated* (1813): imagination is simply "the faculty which *images* within the mind the phenomena of sensation. A man has fancy in proportion as he can call up, connect, or associate, at pleasure, those internal images . . . so as to complete ideal representations of absent objects". (Quoted from WW's Preface to *Poems* 1815.) Taylor, WW replies, is imprisoned by etymology, restricting the words narrowly to their original significance, and then argues for a conception of the imagination that will stress its ability to "modify", "shape", and "create". WW's position is nearer C's than is implied above, though WW's focus, as C goes on to say, is entirely on poetic style. *W Prose* III 30–5.

[3] "What is common sense?—It is when the Language has been so determined in its meanings by great men (being in itself mere arbitrary counters, or physical equivalents, as compulsion & obligation &c) that the very words of a language as used in common Life carry with them the confutation of an error or establishment of a Truth, then we call convictions so received common sense, bearing to the original reason the same relations as operations by an Arithmetical Rule to those by universal Arithmetic." *CN* III 3549; cf I 1700.

of the terms in question has been clearly shown to be both insufficient and erroneous by Mr. Wordsworth in the preface added to the late collection of his "Lyrical Ballads and other poems." The explanation which Mr. Wordsworth has himself given, will be found to differ from mine, chiefly perhaps, as our objects are different. It could scarcely indeed happen otherwise, from the advantage I have enjoyed of frequent conversation with him on a subject to which a poem of his own first directed my attention,[2] and my conclusions concerning which, he had made more lucid to myself by many happy instances drawn from the operation of natural objects on the mind. But it was Mr. Wordsworth's purpose

in the schools passes by degrees into the world at large, and becomes the property of the market and the tea-table. At least I can discover no other meaning of the term, *common sense*, if it is to convey any specific difference from sense and judgement in genere, and where it is not used scholastically for the *universal reason*. Thus in the reign of Charles II. the philosophic world was called to arms by the moral sophisms of Hobbs, and the ablest writers exerted themselves in the detection of an error, which a school-boy would now be able to confute by the mere recollection, that *compulsion* and *obligation* conveyed two ideas perfectly disparate, and that what appertained to the one, had been falsely transferred to the other by a mere confusion of terms.[1]

[1] Cf *P Lects* Lect 5 (1949) 174: "Even so late as the time of Charles the First and the Republic of England, the words 'compelled' and 'obliged' were perfectly synonymous. Hobbes and other men of his mind took advantage of this one term and contended therefore, that as everybody acknowledged that men were obliged to do such and such things, and that if a man were *obliged* it was synonymous to say he was *compelled*, there could never arise anything like guilt. For who could blame a man for doing what he was obliged to do since he was compelled to do it. . . . In this instance they are two perfectly different things and every man feels them to be different, and the best way is to use the word 'obliged' when we mean what a man ought to do, and the word 'compelled' when we mean what a man must do whether he likes it or not. And with this single clearing up of the terms the whole basis fell at once, as far at least as *that* argument

was convincing." *BL* (1847) mistakenly assumed that C was in error, that Hobbes did not use "obligation" in the sense of "compulsion". Cf, however, "The *promises* therefore which are made for some *benefit* received (which are also Covenants) are Tokens of the Will; that is . . . of the last act of deliberating, whereby the liberty of non-performance is abolished, and by consequence are obligatory. For where Liberty ceaseth there beginneth Obligation." *Philosophicall Rudiments Concerning Government and Society* pt i ch 2 § 10 (1651; later known as *De Cive, or the Citizen*) 25. Cf also ". . . the openly declar'd Will of the obliger is requisite to make an Obligation by *Vow* . . . Now I call him the *Obliger*, to whom any one is tyed, and the *Obliged*, him who is tyed". Pt i ch 2 § 13 p 27. Cf also pt i ch 2 §§ 14, 16, 17, 19, pt 2 ch 6 §§ 14, 20, ch 7 §§ 7, 8, 12.

[2] Probably, *The Prelude*.

to consider the influences of fancy and imagination as they are manifested in poetry, and from the different effects to conclude their diversity in kind; while it is my object to investigate the seminal principle, and then from the kind to deduce the degree. My friend has drawn a masterly sketch of the branches with their *poetic* fruitage. I wish to add the trunk, and even the roots as far as they lift themselves above ground, and are visible to the naked eye of our common consciousness.

Yet even in this attempt I am aware, that I shall be obliged to draw more largely on the reader's attention, than so immethodical a miscellany can authorize; when in such a work (*the Ecclesiastical Policy*) of such a mind as Hooker's, the judicious author, though no less admirable for the perspicuity than for the port and dignity of his language; and though he wrote for men of learning in a learned age; saw nevertheless occasion to anticipate and guard against "complaints of obscurity," as often as he was to trace his subject "to the highest well-spring and fountain." Which, (continues he) "because men are not accustomed to, the pains we take are more needful a great deal, than acceptable; and the matters we handle, seem by reason of newness (till the mind grow better acquainted with them) dark and intricate." [1] I would gladly therefore spare both myself and others this labor, if I knew how without it to present an intelligible statement of my poetic creed; not as my *opinions*, which weigh for nothing, but as deductions from established premises conveyed in such a form, as is calculated either to effect a fundamental conviction, or to receive a fundamental confutation. If I may dare once more adopt the words of Hooker, "they, unto whom we shall seem tedious, are in no wise injured by us, because it is in their own hands to spare that labour, which they are not willing to endure." Those at least, let me be permitted to add, who have taken so much pains to render me ridiculous for a perversion of taste, and have supported the charge by attributing strange notions to me on no other authority than their own conjectures, owe it to themselves as well as to me not to refuse their attention to my own statement of the theory, which I *do* acknowledge; or shrink from the trouble of examining the grounds on which I rest it, or the arguments which I offer in its justification.

[1] This and the quotation below are from Richard Hooker *Of the Laws of Ecclesiastical Polity* I i (var): *Works* (1682) 70. In Hooker the second passage precedes the first.

CHAPTER 5[1]

On the law[2] of association—Its history traced from Aristotle to Hartley

THERE have been men in all ages, who have been impelled as by an instinct to propose their own nature as a problem, and who devote their attempts to its solution. The first step was to construct a table of distinctions, which they seem to have formed on the principle of the absence or presence of the WILL.[3] Our   ✳ H.M.!

---

[1] C's purpose in the following four chapters is indicated by his remark to R. H. Brabant (29 Jul 1815), though he could have been speaking of a prefatory or abbreviated form of the discussion: "One long passage—a disquisition on the powers of association, with the History of the Opinions on this subject from Aristotle to Hartley, and on the generic difference between the faculties of Fancy and Imagination —I did not indeed altogether insert, but I certainly extended and elaborated, with a view to your perusal— as laying the foundation Stones of the Constructive or Dynamic Philosophy in opposition to the merely mechanic—." *CL* IV 579. In this chapter and the next two chapters C draws extensively from Johann Gebhard Ehrenreich Maass (1766– 1823) *Versuch über die Einbildungskraft* (2nd ed Halle & Leipzig 1797), which he owned and annotated. The *Versuch* is largely about the association of ideas and extends Maass's first work, *Dissertatio exhibens paralipomena ad historiam doctrinae de associatione idearum* (1787). He became professor of philosophy at Halle and wrote books on mathematics, logic, religion, philosophy, and psychology and in

1813 published a four-volume novel. Maass belonged to the Leibniz–Wolff school and opposed Kant in general principles. Cf McFarland 333. C may have read Maass's *Versuch* as early as 1801: "I shall . . . send off some Letters . . . respecting Locke & Des Cartes, & likewise concerning the supposed Discovery of the Law of Association by Hobbes.—Since I have been at Keswick, I have read a great deal/ and my Reading has furnished me with many reasons for being exceedingly suspicious of *supposed Discoveries* in Metaphysics." To Thomas Poole 13 Feb 1801: *CL* II 675.

[2] C's use of the singular "law" may follow Maass's "allgemeine Gesetz". Maass's pt III of the *Versuch* (pp 311–453) is entitled "Beiträge zur Geschichte der Lehre von der Vergesellschaftung der Vorstellungen", but a "history" of associationism was not a novel idea. Cf *Geschichte der Lehre von der Association der Ideen* by Michael Hissmann (Göttingen 1777).

[3] C's division into absence or presence of will has a rough analogy in Maass pt I ch 2 sects i and ii (§§ 23–43: pp 62–163, 163–70): "Von der unwillkührlichen Reihe

89

various sensations, perceptions, and movements were classed as active or passive, or as media partaking of both. A still finer distinction was soon established between the voluntary and the spontaneous. In our perceptions we seem to ourselves merely passive to an external power, whether as a mirror reflecting the landscape, or as a blank canvas on which some unknown hand paints it.[1] For it is worthy of notice, that the latter, or the system of idealism may be traced to sources equally remote with the former, or materialism; and Berkeley can boast an ancestry at least as venerable as Gassendi[2] or Hobbs. These conjectures, however, concerning the mode in which our perceptions originated, could not alter the natural differences of *things* and *thoughts*.[3] In the former, the cause appeared wholly external, while in the latter, sometimes our will interfered as the producing or determining cause, and sometimes our nature seemed to act by a mechanism of its own, without any conscious effort of the will, or even against it. Our inward experiences were thus arranged in three separate classes, the passive sense, or what the school-men call the merely receptive quality of the mind; the voluntary, and the spontaneous, which holds the middle place between both. But it is not in human nature to meditate on any mode of action, without enquiring after the law that governs it; and in the explanation of the spontaneous movements of our being, the metaphysician took the lead of the anatomist and natural philosopher.[4] In Egypt, Palestine, Greece,

---

der Einbildungen" and "Von der willkührlichen Reihe der Einbildungen". But such a division was common. Maass often discusses the will and its relation to imagination and association. E.g. pp 50–1, 351–7, 360–5. As early as 1801, however, C had discussed the absence or presence of will in Descartes' philosophy; see his letter to Josiah Wedgwood of 24 Feb 1801: *CL* ii 688.

[1] Cf C's illustration of Berkeley's idealism, the image in the mirror and the picture on the canvas, in *CN* iii 3605 f 120ᵛ (Aug–Sept 1809), and his early image of the landscape miniatured on a convex mirror, in LRR vi: *Lects 1795* (*CC*) 224.

[2] Pierre Gassendi or Gassend (1592–1655) attempted to revive

and extend Epicurean philosophy and wrote against Descartes. His interest and works were prolific and included studies in astronomy and medicine. In their principles of methodical observation Hobbes and Gassendi personally expressed agreement with each other. C links them together again in *P Lects* Lect 12 (1949) 345 (see also 455 n 16). In France Gassendi is occasionally credited with founding empirical psychology.

[3] On C's distinction between "things" and "thoughts" see *CN* ii 2784, iii 3787, and above, i 31.

[4] Cf Maass p 358 (§ 102): "Nun fragte die Metaphysik weiter: wie geht es zu, dass die Bewegung der Lebensgeister eine Vorstellung, dass überhaupt eine Veränderung des

and India the analysis of the mind had reached its noon and man-   *zenith !*
hood, while experimental research was still in its dawn and infancy.
For many, very many centuries, it has been difficult to advance a
new truth, or even a new error, in the philosophy of the intellect
or morals. With regard, however, to the laws that direct the spontaneous movements of thought and the principle of their intellectual mechanism there exists, it has been asserted, an important
exception most honorable to the moderns, and in the merit of
which our own country claims the largest share. Sir James Mackintosh (who amid the variety of his talents and attainments is not
of less repute for the depth and accuracy of his philosophical
enquiries, than for the eloquence with which he is said to render
their most difficult results perspicuous, and the driest attractive)
affirmed in the lectures, delivered by him at Lincoln's Inn Hall,[1]
that the law of association as established in the contemporaneity
of the original impressions,[2] formed the basis of all true psychology;

Körpers eine Veränderung in der
Seele wirken kann?" ("Now metaphysics asked further how it comes
about that the motion of the 'animal
spirits' can produce a representation; above all, that a bodily change
can effect a change in the soul?")
But the context of C's similar remark
is considerably different.

[1] Sir James Mackintosh (1765–
1832), publicist, lawyer, and philosophical writer. His lectures given in
1799 (the introduction or prolegom-
enon to the lectures was published
as *A Discourse on the Study of the
Law of Nature and Nations* [1799])
were repeated by him in Jan–Mar
1800. C attended five and disliked
them. *CN* I 634 and n convincingly
suggests that C's "philosophical"
letters to Josiah Wedgwood (Feb
1801: *CL* II 677–703) were in part
an answer to Mackintosh. In taking
Mackintosh's lectures of fifteen years
before as a jumping-off point for the
philosophical discussions that follow,
C reveals the extent to which he is
pressed for time (see Introd, above,
I cxxiii). But in addition Mackintosh
was a well-known man; and for C
he had always seemed a symbol,

both personally and intellectually, of
what C considered the parochially
positivistic, quasi-commercial, and
legalistic strain of British empirical
thinking that needed to be corrected
by the broader philosophical stance
of the Continent, especially Germany. As such a symbol Mackintosh
continued to annoy C, who often
expressed his reaction. In his *Memoirs*—ed R. J. Mackintosh (1835) I
326—Mackintosh notes that C "was
well known to have (capriciously)
disliked me"; and C's private remarks about him could be caustic
(e.g. the reference to him in *CL* I
588 as "the great Dung-fly"). Cf
Carlyon (1836) I 68–9; *CN* II 2618
and n; *TT* 27 Apr 1823, in which he
states one "might not improperly
write on his forehead, 'Warehouse to
let!' ". For C's relations with Mackintosh see also the entries under
"Coleridge (4)" and "Mackintosh"
in *EOT* (*CC*) III 355, 439.

[2] This "contemporaneity" C describes is not for C himself the
"general law" of association. Hartley
and Hobbes, as materialists, err,
thinks C, when they see "one law of
time" as the sole cause of associa-

and any ontological or metaphysical science not contained in such (i.e. empirical) psychology was but a web of abstractions and generalizations. Of this prolific truth, of this great fundamental law, he declared HOBBS to have been the original *discoverer*, while its full application to the whole intellectual system we owe to David Hartley; who stood in the same relation to Hobbs as Newton to Kepler; the law of association being that to the mind, which gravitation is to matter.

Of the former clause in this assertion, as it respects the comparative merits of the ancient metaphysicians, including their commentators, the school-men, and of the modern French and British philosophers from Hobbs to Hume, Hartley and Condilliac, this is not the place to speak. So wide indeed is the chasm between this gentleman's philosophical creed and mine, that so far from being able to join hands, we could scarce make our voices intelligible to each other: and to *bridge* it over, would require more time, skill and power than I believe myself to possess. But the latter clause involves for the greater part a mere question of fact and history, and the accuracy of the statement is to be tried by documents rather than reasoning.[1]

First then, I deny Hobbs's claim in toto: for he had been anticipated by Des Cartes whose work "De Methodo" preceded Hobbs's "De Natura Humana," by more than a year.[2] But what is of much more importance, Hobbs builds nothing on the principle

tion. See below, I 110. Throughout C opposes equating the "law" of contemporaneity or time with the "general" or one "effective law" of association at large. See ch 7 for C's statement of "the true practical general law of association". Therefore C disagrees with Mackintosh on this point. C also denies Mackintosh's claims about even the originality of Hobbes and Hartley in their discussions of contemporaneity. As C draws on Maass, he is using him to refute Mackintosh. SC implies as much: *BL* (1847) I 111–12.

[1] As the two clauses are stated above ("Of this prolific truth, of this great fundamental law") the "latter" involves the contemporaneity of impressions stated as *the* law of association. C prepares to take issue

with this as "a mere question of fact".

[2] Thomas Hobbes (1588–1679) *Human Nature,* though possibly written in the 1630s, was published 1650. René Descartes (1596–1650) *Discours de la méthode* was published 1637. C is probably thinking of the Latin version published 1644. Neither ed, as HNC points out, deals with the subject mentioned above. The nearest approach is a passage in Descartes' posthumous *De homine* (Leyden 1662) § 73. *BL* (1847) I 91n. For C's early study of Descartes, see the four "philosophical" letters to Josiah Wedgwood (Feb 1801) *CL* II 677–703; J. I. Lindsay "Coleridge Marginalia in a Volume of Descartes" *PMLA* XLIX (1934) 184–95; McFarland 320–3.

which he had announced.[1] He does not even announce it, as differing in any respect from the general laws of material motion and impact: nor was it, indeed, possible for him so to do, compatibly with his system, which was exclusively material and mechanical.[2] Far otherwise is it with Des Cartes;[3] greatly as he too in his after writings (and still more egregiously his followers De la Forge,[4] and others) obscured the truth by their attempts to explain

[1] Actually it is a fundamental premise of Hobbes, who, as Mackintosh stated in reply to C, builds "a general theory of the human understanding, of which reasoning is only a particular case". "Dissertation Second: Exhibiting a General View of the Progress of Ethical Philosophy, Chiefly During the Seventeenth and Eighteenth Centuries" prefixed to *EB* (7th ed 1842) I 428. Mackintosh's reply is a commonplace in the history of philosophy, as he well recognised, and C is hurriedly and inaccurately urging a case because of his antipathy to the materialism of Hobbes and his followers. Cf Hazlitt's strictures on C's position here in his review (1817) of *BL. H Works* XVI 123.

[2] C continues to distort Hobbes, who speaks of an active principle in the "compounded imagination" and of the influence of conscious design on association: "In sum, the discourse of the mind, when it is governed by design, is . . . the faculty of invention." See Hobbes *Leviathan* pt I chs 2, 3: *English Works* ed W. Molesworth (1839) III 6, 11–15. C's specific critique of Hobbes seems coloured by Maass (§ 99 p 350), who denies that Hobbes actually states the general law of association: "Inzwischen gab doch Hobbes ein Gesetz an, und die fehlerhafte Unvollständigkeit desselben scheint mit seinem Materialismus zusammen zu hangen. Nach diesem waren alle Vorstellungen ursprünglich Empfindungen." ("Meanwhile Hobbes still asserted a law, and the faulty incompleteness of it seems to hang together with his materialism. According to it, all representations were originally sense impressions.")

[3] C's preference for Descartes over Hobbes accords with Maass's opinion (§ 100 p 351): "Bald nach Hobbes trat der grosse *Cartesius* auf, der, soweit ihn sein Genie über den erstern erhob, doch so gut wie dieser die Vergesellschaftung der Vorstellungen aus physiologischen und mechanischen Gründen zu erklären suchte. Allerdings aber ist sein System mit grösserm Scharfsinn erbaut und es verdient eine genauere Erwägung." ("Soon after Hobbes the great Descartes appeared, who, so far as his genius raised him above the first, still sought as well as Hobbes to explain the association of ideas on physiological and mechanical grounds. But, to be sure, his system is constructed with greater insight and it deserves a close consideration.") In his copy of Maass, C underlined "nach . . . grosse" and commented: "No!! DeC. died long before Hobbes". *CM* (*CC*) III. From "Far otherwise is it with Descartes . . .", including the following six sentences (to ". . . may represent a whole class"), C may have Maass 351–5 in mind but is not paraphrasing or translating. Unlike Maass, C gives Descartes chronological primacy. Cf C on Hobbes in 1801 in *CN* I 937F, 937G.

[4] Louis de la Forge (fl 1650–70), physician and friend of Descartes. His *Traité de l'esprit de l'homme* (Paris 1661), as *BL* (1907) II 229 notes, carried Descartes' concepts

it on the theory of nervous fluids, and material configurations. But in his interesting work "De Methodo," Des Cartes relates the circumstance which first led him to meditate on this subject, and which since then has been often noticed and employed as an instance and illustration of the law.[1] A child who with its eyes bandaged had lost several of his fingers by amputation, continued to complain for many days successively of pains, now in this[a] joint and now in that of the very fingers which had been cut off. Des Cartes was led by this incident to reflect on the uncertainty with which we attribute any particular place to any inward pain or uneasiness, and proceeded after long consideration to establish it as a general law; that contemporaneous impressions, whether images or sensations, recal each other mechanically. On this principle, as a ground work, he built up the whole system of human language, as one continued process of association. He showed, in what sense not only general terms, but generic images (under the name of abstract ideas) actually existed, and in what consists their nature and power. As one word may become the general exponent of many, so by association a simple image may

a BL (1817): his

further toward "occasionalism" (i.e. an act of will is taken by God as an "occasion" for producing bodily reactions that correspond, and vice versa). See Maass 352, 357–8 and Heinrich Seyfarth *L. de la Forge und seine Stellung im Occasionalismus* (Jena 1887) pt III. In *TL* (1848) 31, C says, "Should the reader chance to put his hand on the 'Principles of Philosophy,' by La Forge, an immediate disciple of Descartes, he may see the phenomena of sleep solved in a copper-plate engraving, with all the figures into which the globules of the blood shaped themselves, and the results demonstrated by mathematical calculations." Cf *P Lects* Lect 12 (1949) 342. But La Forge did not write the *Principles of Philosophy*. C has taken his examples from La Forge's *Traité* and perhaps mixed it up with Descartes' *Principia philosophiae* (1644). See

P Lects 455 n 9. C probably encountered La Forge's name in Maass 352, 359, who describes La Forge's system of "animal spirits" of fluids travelling through both arteries and small hollow canals between the nerve centre in the brain (*conarium*) and the muscles of the whole body. The system is a kind of nervous hydraulics to explain all thought and physical movement. Maass mentions La Forge in direct connection with Descartes. See also Maass 32–50 for general discussion.

[1] As *BL* (1847) notes (I 93n), this is not in *De methodo* but in Descartes *Principia philosophiae* (1644) pt IV § 196. In C's annotated copy, *Opera philosophica* (3 pts Amsterdam 1685) i 216. In 1801 C had the correct source, "the fourth Part of his Principia", and quoted the passage. Letter to Wedgwood 24 Feb 1801: *CL* II 687–8.

represent a whole class.[1] But in truth Hobbs himself makes no claims to any discovery, and introduces this law of association, or (in his own language) discursûs mentalis, as an admitted fact, in the *solution* alone of which, this by causes purely physiological, he arrogates any originality.[2] His system is briefly this;[3] when-

[1] On "Words (according to Des Cartes)" cf C's later letter to Wedgwood [Feb 1801]: *CL* ii 697–8.

[2] C continues to echo Maass's estimate of Hobbes: "Hobbes nannte die Vergesellschaftung der Vorstellungen eine Reihe oder Folge von Einbildungen, auch einen *discursus mentalis*" (§ 99 p 349); "Er war . . . ein psychologischer Materialist. Daher musste er auch die Association der Vorstellungen aus physiologischen oder körperlichen Ursachen erklären. . . ." (p 348) ("Hobbes called the association of ideas a series or train of images, also a mental discourse." "He was . . . a psychological materialist. Because of that he also had to explain the association of ideas on physiological or anatomical principles . . .".) C's view of Hobbes had religious overtones. C, figuratively speaking, said he was "burning" him—along with Locke and Hume—"under his [Duns Scotus'] Nose" (*CL* ii 746) in 1801, and often attacked Hobbes for materialism, atheistic tendencies, or political absolutism. See *P Lects* (1949) 456 n 19 and cf i 96 n 1, below; also *EOT* (*CC*) ii 311–12.

[3] From here to the end of the paragraph C—with the exception of a few phrases and his footnote on "idea"—is translating from Maass § 99 (pp 348–50): ". . . und seine Theorie . . . ist kürzlich diese.

"Wenn ein Gegenstand unsere Sinne afficirt [C here adds, "whether by the rays of light reflected from them, or by effluxes of their finer particles", and his plural pronouns refer to "external objects", which he uses to translate Maass's "ein Gegenstand"]; so entsteht eine Bewegung der innersten und feinsten Organe. Diese Bewegung macht die Vorstellung aus, und es bleibt ein Eindruck von derselben, eine gewisse Disposition zu dieser Bewegung zurück. Empfinden wir mehrere Gegenstände zusammen; so werden die zurückbleibenden Eindrücke [C here adds parenthetically, and leaps ahead to Maass § 110 (p 383) for his parenthesis: "Eine Einbildung heisst bei ihm [Hartley] nach dem Humischen Sprachgebrauche eine Idee", "or in the language of Mr. Hume, the *ideas*"] mit einander verbunden. Wird also das Organ einmal wieder in eine von jenen Bewegungen gesetzt; so entsteht daraus die andre. [C's translation of this last sentence having implied what Maass says in his next, C moves on. In C's next sentence the part "who derive association . . . constitute our thoughts" is taken from part of the final sentence in Maass's paragraph:] "Die Association gründet sich also auf den Zusammenhang der Materie, deren Bewegungen unsre Vorstellungen ausmachen . . .".

Beginning then with his next sentence ("But even the merit") and until the end of his paragraph, C continues to draw from Maass in a slightly freer translation. Maass (p 349) says that Hobbes discovered the working principle of association "aber gar nicht das allgemeine Gesetz." On the next page (350) is a new paragraph in which Maass continues to discuss Hobbes and which C translates to end his own: "Freilich ist dieses Gesetz nicht allgemein genug ausgedrückt. Denn die Gegenstände zweier Vorstel-

ever the senses are impinged on by external objects, whether by the rays of light reflected from them, or by effluxes of their finer particles, there results a correspondent motion of the innermost and subtlest organs. This motion constitutes a *representation*, and there remains an *impression* of the same, or a certain disposition to repeat the same motion. Whenever we feel several objects at the same time, the *impressions* that are left (or in the language of Mr. Hume, the *ideas*) are linked together. Whenever therefore any one of the movements, which constitute a complex impression, are renewed through the senses, the others succeed mechanically. It follows of necessity therefore that Hobbs, as well as Hartley and all others who derive association from the connection and inter-dependence of the supposed matter, the movements of which con-stitute our thoughts, *must* have reduced all its forms to the one law of time.[1] But even the merit of announcing this law with philo-sophic precision cannot be fairly conceded to him. For the objects of any two ideas * need not have co-existed in the same sensation

* I here use the word "idea"[2] in Mr. Hume's sense on account of its

lungen [C translates *Vorstellungen* here as "ideas"; where above he used "thoughts", hence his footnote] brauchen nicht gerade zusammen empfunden zu werden, wenn die letztern associabel werden sollen. Dieser Erfolg entsteht auch, wenn die Objekte auf eine andre Art zusammen vorgestellt werden, als durch die Sinne." C substitutes "memory" for "eine andre Art," a logical choice, and does not give a literal translation of this last sen-tence. C suggests that one "idea" may come through the senses and the other from memory, whereas Maass simply states that neither has to come through the senses but both may come "by another manner". Maass gives examples and discusses this on pp 26–8.

[1] Maass says that Hobbes un-covers only the "working ground" of association and not its basic law (p 349). On p 350 Maass explains that this "working ground" is essen-tially the principle of contempora-neity. C claims that "the one law of time" belongs to *all* the materialists and falls short of the larger general and true law of association, though it is a part of it. See chs 6 and 7, below, I 110, 123–7.

[2] C's long note is essentially an apology for the common English phrase "association of ideas". He believes it debases the historical context and higher meanings of "idea". Handcuffed by current usage, C would ideally prefer a more pre-cise phrase like Maass's "association of representations" ("Vergesellschaf-tung der Vorstellungen"). Note should be taken of C's struggle with the word "idea", e.g. *CN* III 3268 ("that abominable word"); cf *SM* (*CC*) 100–3. In a letter to Davy of 3 Feb 1801 C wrote that the subject of his meditations "ha[s] been the Relations of Thoughts to Things, in the language of Hume, of Ideas to Impressions". *CL* II 672. Cf also C's remarks on "the unphilosophical jargon" of Hume, in a letter to Clarkson of 13 Oct 1806: *CL* II 1194–5.

in order to become mutually associable. The same result will follow when one only of the two ideas has been represented by the senses, and the other by the memory.

---

general currency among the English metaphysicians; though against my own judgement, for I believe that the vague use of this word has been the cause of much error and more confusion. The word, 'Ἰδέα, in its original sense as used by Pindar, Aristophanes, and in the gospel of Matthew, represented the visual abstraction of a distant object, when we see the whole without distinguishing its parts.[1] Plato adopted it as a technical term, and as the antithesis to εἴδωλα, or sensuous images; the transient and perishable emblems, or mental words, of ideas. The ideas themselves he considered as mysterious powers, living, seminal, formative, and exempt from time. In this sense the word became the property of the Platonic school; and it seldom occurs in Aristotle, without some such phrase annexed to it, as according to Plato, or as Plato says.[2] Our English writers to the end of Charles 2nd's reign, or somewhat later, employed it either in the original sense, or platonically, or in a sense nearly correspondent to our present use of the substantive, Ideal, always however opposing it, more or less, to image, whether of present or absent objects. The reader will not be displeased with the following interesting exemplification from Bishop Jeremy Taylor. "St. Lewis the King sent Ivo Bishop of Chartres on an embassy, and he told, that he met a grave and stately matron on the way with a censor of fire in one hand, and a vessel of water in the other; and observing her to have a melancholy, religious, and phantastic deportment and look, he asked her what those symbols meant, and what she meant to do with her fire and water; she answered, my purpose is with the fire to burn paradise, and with my water to quench the flames of hell, that men may serve God purely for the love of God. But we rarely meet with such spirits which love virtue so metaphysically as *to abstract her*

---

[1] Pindar uses ἰδέα once (*Olympian Odes* 10.103). For Aristophanes see *Clouds* 289 and *Plutus* 559. In Matt the word appears only in 28.3. C is alluding, as so often, to the derivation of the word, the root ἰδ, like the Latin vid-, meaning "see". (The cognate εἶδος is more common and can have the same meanings as ἰδέα.)

[2] Plato used ἰδέα and εἶδος indiscriminately, and it is necessary to deduce from the context whether he was using them in his own specialised sense, which he often expressed in other ways, e.g. the idea of beauty as "beauty itself in itself". The Greek Neoplatonists did the same, and it was no doubt the greater ease of fitting ἰδέα into Latin, and into modern languages, that fixed it as the technical term for the later Platonists. Relevant passages in Plato include, for the contrast with εἴδωλον, *Symposium* 211D–212A and *Republic* 601B–C; Neoplatonic teaching on the ideas as *living* was based on *Sophist* 248E–249B; for the ideas in general, *Phaedo* 73–9, *Phaedrus* 250, *Timaeus* 51Bff (these without the word ἰδέα, except in a non-technical sense at 251A), *Parmenides* 128E–131A and passim, *Republic* 507–9 (ἰδέα at 507B, 508E), 596–7 (ἰδέα at 596B).

Aristotle, too, used both terms in their everyday meanings, and did not discriminate clearly when summarising Plato (e.g. *Metaphysics* 987b–988a, 990a–992b), though he tended to prefer εἶδος as his own technical term (usually translated "form").

Long however before either Hobbs or Des Cartes the law of
association had been defined, and its important functions set forth
by Melanchthon,[5] Ammerbach, and Ludovicus Vives;[6] more

---

from all sensible compositions, and love the purity of the idea."[1] Des
Cartes having introduced into his philosophy the fanciful hypothesis of
material ideas, or certain configurations of the brain, which were as so
many moulds to the influxes of the external world;[2] Mr. Locke[a] adopted
the term, but extended its signification to whatever is the immediate object
of the mind's attention or consciousness.[3] Mr. Hume distinguishing those
representations which are accompanied with a sense of a present object,
from those reproduced by the mind itself, designated the former by *impressions,* and confined the word *idea* to the latter.[4]

a BL (1817): Lock

[1] XXVII *Sermons Preached at
Golden Grove* Sermon XII: 'Ἐνιαυτὸς.
A Course of Sermons . . . (1668)
ii 116 (var). The final sentence is
untraced. When C had SH copy the
passage into a notebook in Dec 1800
(*CN* I 872), this final sentence appeared first, probably dictated by C
as a prefatory thought (based on
his general reading of the idea in
Taylor),· and now, rereading his
notebook, C assumes that the entire
passage is by Taylor.

[2] Put most explicitly in *De
homine* (Leyden 1662) §§ LXVI–
LXXII, and in the French version
L'Homme de René Descartes (Paris
1664) 71–5. Descartes provides
conjectural diagrams of the process.
See also the richly annotated English
version, *Treatise of Man* tr and ed
Thomas S. Hall (Cambridge, Mass
1972) 84–8.

[3] Locke *Essay Concerning Human Understanding* bk II passim.
(C's edition is not known.) A suc-
cinct general definition is given in
Introd § 8: "It being that term
which, I think, serves best to stand
for whatsoever is the *object* of the
understanding when a man thinks,
I have used it to express whatever
is meant by *phantasm, notion, species, or whatever it is which the mind
can be employed about thinking.*"
Essay ed A. C. Fraser (Oxford
1894) I 32.

[4] Hume's famous distinction oc-

curs at the start of *A Treatise of
Human Nature* (1739–40) bk I pt 1
§ 1: "All the perceptions of the
human mind resolve themselves into
two distinct kinds, which I shall call
IMPRESSIONS and IDEAS. . . . Those
perceptions which enter with most
force and violence, we may name
impressions; and, under this name,
I comprehend all our sensations,
passions and emotions . . . By *ideas,*
I mean the faint images of these in
thinking and reasoning . . .". *Philosophical Works* (1845) I 15. In *P
Lects* Lect 13 (1949) 378 C berates
the abuse of "idea" by Descartes and
by Locke, who originated the phrase
"association of ideas". C says in a
note on John Petvin *Letters Concerning Mind* (1750) 105–6 that
Locke's conception of idea and
Plato's were no more alike than "a
Syllogism & an Apple-dumpling".
CM (CC) III.

[5] Philipp Melanchthon (1497–
1560), the German religious re-
formist, who adopted a mediating
position on the subject of freedom of
the will and God's grace ("syner-
gism"): the primary cause of regeneration is God's grace, but
regeneration is not genuine or effective without the co-operation of
man's will. But Maass and C are
thinking primarily of Melanchthon's
De anima (1540).

[6] Veit (Vitus) Amerbach (1487–
1557), professor at Ingolstadt, au-

especially by the last.[1] Phantasia, it is to be noticed, is employed by Vives to express the mental power of comprehension, or the *active* function of the mind; and imaginatio for the receptivity (vis receptiva) of impressions, or for the *passive* perception.[2] The power of combination he appropriates to the former: "quæ singula et simpliciter acceperat imaginatio, ea conjungit et disjungit phantasia."[3] And the law by which the thoughts are spontaneously presented follows thus; "quæ simul sunt a phantasia comprehensa si alterutrum occurrat, solet secum alterum repræsentare."[4] To time therefore he subordinates all the other exciting causes of association. The soul proceeds "a causa ad effectum, ab hoc ad instrumentum, a parte ad totum;"[5] thence to the place, from

---

thor of *De anima* (1542) and *De philosophia naturali* (1549). C, like Maass, spells Amerbach's name with two *m*'s. Juan Luis (Ludovicus) Vives (1492–1540), the Spanish humanist and follower of Erasmus, taught in England for many years (serving as tutor to Princess Mary and lecturing at Oxford) until he came under the displeasure of Henry VIII for opposing the divorce from Catherine of Aragon. His *De anima et vita* (1538) ranks as one of the first modern works on psychology.

[1] This whole paragraph is a conflation of Maass § 98 (pp 343–6) from "Zu den ersten" to "völlig deutlich". All of C's Latin quotations he copies from Maass with slight rearrangement. C's intervening matter is a selectively condensed translation, to a third of the length, of the material in Maass. The sentences and phrases translated verbatim—or nearly so—are: ". . . *Melanchthon, Ammerbach* und *Lud. Vives.* . . . Bei weitem das meiste aber leistete *Vives*" (p 343). ". . . ferner vom Theile zum Ganzen, von diesem zu dem Orte wo es war, von dem Orte zur Person, von dieser zu dem, was vor ihr und nach ihr war . . ." (p 344). ". . . welche die Einbildungskraft zusammen aufgefasst hat . . . so wird dadurch auch die andre wieder hervorgerufen" (pp 344–5). ". . . dass er unter einem Sprunge

nur eine Assation [for "Association"] zweier Vorstellungen verstanden habe . . ." (p 346).

C's observation on Vives, "To time therefore he subordinates all the other exciting causes of association", seems his only contribution to the substance of the paragraph, but also the very point he is most eager to make.

[2] On p 344n Maass also draws attention to the fact that in Vives the imagination means the power to perceive (passively) an impression: "*Imaginatio* heisst beim Vives das Vermögen, einen Eindruck zu percipiren." Maass cites *De anima* I sect. d[e] cogn[itione] intern[a].

[3] Slightly altered from Maass's citation (p 344n) of Vives *De anima* I sect. d. cogn. intern. Tr: "Things the imagination had received simply and one at a time the fancy joins and unjoins".

[4] Maass's citation (p 344n) of Vives *De anima* II sect. d[e] mem[oria] et record[atione]. Tr: "If one of two things that fancy has grasped at the same time offers itself, the other usually presents itself with it".

[5] Maass's citation (p 344n) of Vives *De anima* II sect. d. mem. et record. Tr: "From cause to effect, from this to the instrument, from a part to the whole".

place to person, and from this to whatever preceded or followed, all as being parts of a total impression, each of which may recal the other. The apparent springs[1] "Saltus vel transitus etiam longissimos,"[2] he explains by the same thought having been a component part of two or more total impressions. Thus "ex Scipione venio in cogitationem potentiæ Turcicæ propter victorias ejus in eâ parte Asiæ in qua regnabat Antiochus."[3]

But from Vives I pass at once to the source of his doctrines, and (as far as we can judge from the remains yet extant of Greek philosophy) as to the first, so to the fullest and most perfect enunciation of the associative principle, viz. to the writings of Aristotle;[4] and of these principally to the books "De Anima," "De Memoria," and that which is entitled in the old translations "Parva Naturalia."[5] In as much as later writers have either deviated from, or added to his doctrines, they appear to me to have introduced either error or groundless supposition.[6]

In the first place it is to be observed, that Aristotle's positions on

[1] That the springs are "apparent" Maass explains in five sentences (pp 345-6) from "Das heisst" to "Sprung ausmachte".

[2] Maass's citation (p 345) from Vives *De anima* II sect. d. mem. et record. C slightly alters it. Tr: "The very longest leaps and transitions".

[3] Maass's citation (p 346) from Vives *De anima* II sect. d. mem. et record. (var). Tr: "From Scipio I pass to the thought of the Turkish power, because his victories were in the region of Asia in which Antiochus ruled".

[4] C's stress on Aristotle seems to derive from Maass. For example, Maass p 345: "Man sieht also, dass Vives von dem allgemeinen Associationsgesetze einen richtigen Begriff hatte, und nach dem Stagiriten der erste war, der dasselbe deutlich ausdrückte. . . . Wahrscheinlich . . . nahm er es aus dem Aristoteles. . . . Ueberdem aber, was die Hauptsache ist, war er mit der Theorie des Associationsgesetzes, ob er gleich dasselbe richtig angab, doch nicht ganz so aufs Reine gekommen, als Aristoteles." ("One thus sees that

Vives had a proper grasp of the general law of association, and after the Stagirite was the first who clearly expressed it. . . . Probably he took it from Aristotle. . . . But above all, and what is most important, although he gave it correctly he did not arrive at such a complete understanding of the theory of the law of association as Aristotle.") Cf *P Lects* Lect 5 (1949) 189–90, also *CN* I 973A and n.

[5] A collection, given this title in the thirteenth century, of relatively short treatises: *De sensu, De memoria* (mentioned by C above as something separate), *De somno, De insomniis, De divinatione per somnum, De longitudine vitae,* and *De juventute.*

[6] However, C will deny that Aristotle, Vives, Descartes, Hobbes, or Hartley ever state the "true practical general law of association". In the order listed, with Aristotle first, they approach the law and set down the common conditions of association. But all fall short of the law itself—including Maass—as C states it in ch 7, below, I 126–7.

this subject are unmixed with fiction.[1] The wise Stagyrite speaks of no successive particles propagating motion like billiard balls (as Hobbs;)[2] nor of nervous or animal spirits, where inanimate and irrational solids are thawed down, and distilled, or filtrated by ascension, into living and intelligent fluids, that etch and re-etch engravings on the brain, (as the followers of Des Cartes, and the humoral pathologists in general;) nor of an oscillating ether which was to effect the same service for the nerves of the brain considered as solid fibres, as the animal spirits perform for them under the notion of hollow tubes (as *Hartley* teaches)—nor finally, (with yet more recent dreamers) of chemical compositions by elective affinity, or of an electric light at once the immediate object and the ultimate organ of inward vision, which rises to the brain like an Aurora Borealis, and there disporting in various shapes (as the balance of plus and minus, or negative and positive, is destroyed or re-established) images out both past and present.[3] Aristotle delivers a just *theory* without pretending to an *hypothesis*; or in other words a comprehensive survey of the different facts, and of their relations to each other without *supposition*, i.e. a fact *placed under* a number of facts, as their common support and explanation;[4] tho' in the majority of instances these hypotheses or suppo-

---

[1] C now greatly extends Maass's comparison between Aristotle and Vives to one between Aristotle and modern materialists. C "is objecting to the physical dreams . . . introduced into the survey of psychological facts delivered by" Aristotle. *BL* (1847) I 102n.

[2] HNC and SC rightly note that the image is not in Hobbes's discussion of the subject in *Human Nature* (1650) chs 2 and 3. C is probably recalling Hume *An Inquiry Concerning Human Understanding* (1748) sect IV pt i: "We fancy, that were we brought, on a sudden, into this world, we could at first have inferred, that one Billiard-ball would communicate motion to another upon impulse . . ."; cf also sect IV pt ii and sect VII. C made the same error in Lect 12 of *P Lects* (1949) 348. Cf *CN* III 4452 and n. See below, I 108.

[3] C essentially repeats this long sentence in *P Lects* Lect 12 (1949) 348, but with a few changes. There C drops mention of Hartley as teaching the system of hollow tubes, perhaps because he realised this statement was in error. Hartley in *Observations on Man* pt I ch 1 sect I Prop V (1791) 17–18 follows Newton and rejects the theory, attributing it to Boerhaave. See also *P Lects* (1949) 456 n 23. But the theory had persisted in popular works like Ernst Platner *Anthropologie für Aerzte und Weltweise* (Leipzig 1772) 39–49. Platner may have taken it from Albrecht von Haller.

[4] In other words "supposition" in the literal sense—as being "placed under".

sitions better deserve the name of ὑποποιήσεις, or *suffictions*.[1] He uses indeed the word κινήσεις,[2] to express what we call representations or ideas,[3] but he carefully distinguishes them from material motion, designating the latter always by annexing the words ἐν τόπῳ, or κατὰ τόπον.[4] On the contrary in his treatise "De Anima," he excludes place and motion from all the operations of thought, whether representations or volitions, as attributes utterly and absurdly heterogeneous.[5]

The *general law* of association, or more accurately, the *common condition* under which all exciting causes act, and in which they may be generalized, according to Aristotle is this.[6] Ideas by having

---

[1] C's coinages—Greek ὑποποίησις, literally "a making under", and *suffiction*, "an inventing under"—would imply clearly, as "hypothesis" and its exact Latin-derived equivalent, "supposition", do not, that a theory is based on fiction, not on fact. For more detailed discussion, which C is here condensing, see his notebook entry (1809) in *CN* III 3587 and n. For "suffictions" cf *P Lects* Lect 12 (1949) 361, *TT* 29 Jun 1833.

[2] "Movements".

[3] Paraphrased (with an eye to Maass §§ 90–2 pp 320–4 generally) from § 91 p 321: ". . . das Wort κίνησις beim Aristoteles eine Veränderung überhaupt bedeuten könne, und nicht nothwendig eine Veränderung des Orts, oder Bewegung anzeige. Denn wenn es das letztere heissen soll; so setzt er ausdrücklich hinzu: ἐν τόπῳ, oder κατα τόπον."

[4] "In space" or "as regards space". Aristotle *De anima* 1.3 and 2.3, cited by Maass pp 322n, 321n.

[5] C draws from Aristotle (*De anima* 1.3) as quoted by Maass § 91 (p 322). Tr SC: "For perhaps not only it is false that the being of the soul is such as they suppose, who affirm that it is a thing which moves or is able to move itself; but it may be that it is a thing to which motion cannot possibly belong." *BL* (1847) I 104n.

[6] The first three sentences of C's paragraph ("The *general law*") are

substantially compacted from Maass pp 28–9, 325–9. On pp 28–9 (§ 13) Maass defines *Totalvorstellung, Partialvorstellung*, and *das allgemeine Associationsgesetz*. With this and p 325 probably in mind C writes his first sentence and then translates his second sentence ("Ideas by having") from p 326 (§ 92): ". . . Vorstellungen, die zusammen gewesen sind, rufen sich einander hervor, oder jede Partialvorstellung erweckt ihre Totalvorstellung." Maass then continues to credit Aristotle for catching the essence of the general law, as C does in his first sentence. C's third sentence ("In the practical determination") begins with a brief and loose summary of Maass pp 326–7 and then, at "he admits", C again starts to paraphrase in a condensed way from pp 327–8 (§ 92):

"Er erkennt also vier [C adds a fifth and makes it the "3rd", so Maass's nos 1, 2, 3, and 4 match C's 1, 2, 4, and 5] besondre Regeln für die Association. . . .

1) Wenn ihre Gegenstände in der Zeit verbunden sind. . . . und zwar derjenigen, die in jener Zeit existirten, oder vor ihr voraufgiengen oder auf sie folgten" (p 327).

2) wenn ihre Gegenstände im Raume nebeneinander waren . . .

[C here inserts his "3rd" agent of "interdependence or necessary connection"]

been together acquire a power of recalling each other; or every partial representation awakes the total representation of which it had been a part. In the practical determinaiton of this common principle to particular recollections, he admits five agents or occasioning causes:[1] 1st, connection in time, whether simultaneous, preceding or successive; 2nd, vicinity or connection in space; 3rd, interdependence or necessary connection, as cause and effect; 4th, likeness; and 5th, contrast.[2] As an additional solution of the occasional seeming chasms in the continuity of reproduction he proves, that movements or ideas possessing one or the other of these five characters had passed through the mind as intermediate links, sufficiently clear to recal other parts of the same total impressions with which they had co-existed, though not vivid enough to excite that degree of attention which is requisite for distinct recollection, or as we may aptly express it, *after-consciousness*.[3] In association then consists the whole mechanism of the reproduction of impressions, in the Aristolelian Psychology.[4] It is the

---

3) wenn ihre Gegenstände einander ähnlich, und

4) wenn sie entgegengesetzt sind, oder miteinander kontrastiren" (p 328).

[1] C does not believe that even these agents constitute the general law, which he states finally in ch 7, below, I 126–7. What Aristotle states C thinks of more accurately as the common condition of association, expressed by Aristotle more clearly than by Vives, Descartes, Hobbes, or Hartley.

[2] The four rules of Aristotle as Maass lists them are from *De memoria* ch 2: Tr SC: "Therefore in trying to remember we search (our minds) in regular order, proceeding from the present or some other time (to the time in which what we want to recollect occurred); or from something like, or directly opposite, or near in place." *BL* (1847) I 106n. C's insertion of "interdependence and necessary connection" may have come from reading Hume.

[3] As *BL* (1847) I 107n points out, C summarises a long example in Maass p 27 (§ 12), which he "seems to have mixed up" with Aristotle's work. But Maass p 328, cited in previous notes above, may have led C to recall the earlier example. *"After-consciousness"* may be a translation of Maass's *Nachdenken* (e.g. p 52) or *Wiedererweckung* (e.g. p 331). In his example on p 27 Maass refers to ideas or representations entering the consciousness (*Bewusstseyn*) and C may simply be extending this usage. McFarland ("SI" 235 n 65) also suggests Tetens' *Nachempfindung*.

[4] C wants to stress that Aristotle studied the mind as a phenomenon, not as a physical mechanism similar to those attacked in the previous paragraph. Cf Maass p 329 (§ 93), which follows Maass's list of Aristotle's rules and hence parallels the progress of C's remarks: ". . . dass Aristoteles die Vergesellschaftung der Vorstellungen aus psychologischen, nicht aus physiologischen Gründen erkläre . . ." (". . . that Aristotle explains the association of ideas on psychological, not physiological grounds . . .").

universal law of the *passive* fancy and *mechanical* memory; that which supplies to all other faculties their objects, to all thought the elements of its materials.

In consulting the excellent commentary of St. Thomas Aquinas on the Parva Naturalia of Aristotle, I was struck at once with its close resemblance to Hume's essay on association. The main thoughts were the same in both, the *order* of the thoughts was the same, and even the illustrations differed only by Hume's occasional substitution of more modern examples.[1] I mentioned the circumstance to several of my literary acquaintances, who admitted the closeness of the resemblance, and that it seemed too great to be explained by mere coincidence; but they thought it improbable that Hume should have held the pages of the angelic Doctor worth turning over. But some time after Mr. Payne,[2] of the King's mews, shewed Sir James Mackintosh some odd volumes of St. Thomas Aquinas, partly perhaps from having heard that Sir James (then Mr.) Mackintosh had in his lectures past a high encomium on this canonized philosopher, but chiefly from the fact, that the volumes had belonged to Mr. Hume, and had here and there marginal marks and notes of reference in his own hand writing. Among these volumes was that which contains the *Parva Naturalia*, in the old latin version, swathed and swaddled in the commentary afore mentioned![3]

[1] C's remark that Hume essentially drew his discussion from Aquinas evoked justifiably stern rebuttals, beginning with an article in *Bl Mag* III (Mar 1818) 653–7. This points out that, despite a general similarity in a few sentences, there are fundamental differences. Aquinas had stressed three principal connections among ideas: resemblance, contiguity, and contrariety. Hume adds cause and effect, and considers contrariety as little more than "a mixture of causation and resemblance". A further answer is provided by J. H. Burton *Life and Correspondence of David Hume* (1846) I 287–8, which shows that Aquinas is referring to the recall of images in memory "not to the formation of new association", and adds that C is also forgetting that the classification was Aristotle's and not that of Aquinas. For the relevant passage from Aquinas (*Comment. in Arist. de memoria et reminiscentia*), which C had SH copy out for him in 1801 from *Opera omnia* (1612) II, borrowed from the library of Durham Cathedral, and for an English translation, see *CN* I 973A and n.

[2] Thomas Payne (1752–1843) was a well-known bookseller in Castle St, near the entrance of King's Mews. In 1806 he moved to Schomberg House, Pall Mall.

[3] In reply to C, Mackintosh some years later ("Dissertation Second", cited above, I 93 n 1) wrote: "I must add, that the manuscript of a part of Aquinas which I bought many years ago (on the faith of a bookseller's catalogue) as being written by Mr Hume, was not a

It remains then for me, first to state wherein Hartley differs from Aristotle;[1] then, to exhibit the grounds of my conviction, that he differed only to err; and next as the result, to shew, by what influences of the choice and judgment the associative power becomes either memory or fancy; and, in conclusion, to appropriate the remaining offices of the mind to the reason, and the imagination. With my best efforts to be as perspicuous as the nature of language will permit on such a subject, I earnestly solicit the good wishes and friendly patience of my readers, while I thus go "sounding on my dim and perilous way."[2]

copy of the Commentary on the *Parva Naturalia*, but of Aquinas's own *Secunda Secundae*; and that, on examination, it proves not to be the handwriting of Mr Hume, and to contain nothing written by him." In an admittedly very partial extenuation of C, we can remind ourselves that, though he was wrong about the particular work and was pushing the matter too far, the bookseller's catalogue had stated that the ms was by Hume, and that there is no indication that Mackintosh, later discovering that the writing was not Hume's, imparted the information to C. C became convinced that Hume borrowed "without acknowledgement a much more correct statement of the laws of association from Aquinas' commentaries on the *Parva naturalia* of Aristotle". *Logic* (*CC*) 186. He may have been mixing up his 1801 reading of Aquinas's commentaries on part of the *Parva naturalia* (see

I 104 n 1, above) with his examination of Mackintosh's ms. See *P Lects* (1949) 436 n 28 and 437 n 37, in which Kathleen Coburn quotes C's marginal note to Tennemann *Geschichte der Philosophie* (Leipzig 1798–1817) IX 20; C is defending Aquinas and the religious Schoolmen against a materialistic deism or scepticism: "I have *looked* into Thom. Aquinas's Commentaries and the Translation which is *swaddled* on them; & found nothing to confirm so harsh a charge [of Tennemann's against Aquinas]." The phrase "*swaddled* on them" echoes *BL*. But C's marginalia in Tennemann, written 1818–27, say little about Hume. Perhaps by then C was less sure about Hume's indebtedness. And C could defend Hume, e.g. *P Lects* Lect 6 (1949) 202–3.

[1] For C's use of Maass on Hartley see below, ch 7.

[2] WW *Excursion* III 701 (var).

CHAPTER 6

*That Hartley's system, as far as it differs from that of Aristotle, is
neither tenable in theory, nor founded in facts*

O F Hartley's hypothetical vibrations in his hypothetical oscillating ether of the nerves, which is the first and most obvious
distinction between his system and that of Aristotle, I shall say
little.[1] This, with all other similar attempts to render *that* an object
of the sight which has no relation to sight, has been already sufficiently exposed by the younger Reimarus,[2] Maass,[a] &c. as outraging
the very axioms of mechanics in a scheme, the merit of which
consists in its being mechanical. Whether any other philosophy be
possible, but the mechanical; and again, whether the mechanical
system can have any claim to be called philosophy; are questions

---

[a] *BL* (1817): Maasse,

[1] *Observations on Man* (1749;
1791 was C's ed) pt I ch 1 by David
Hartley (1705–57), physician and
systematiser of the British school of
associationism and C's first great
enthusiasm, as a college student,
among modern philosophers. C
named his first son after him. *C
Life* (B) 12–13 and *C Life* (H) 63,
65, 295–300, 304–5. Briefly, in
Hartley's physiological theory, sensation results through "vibrations"
that carry an impression through the
white medullary substance of the
nerves to the brain. These in turn
create fainter vibrations ("vibrati-
uncles"), which are left behind in the
brain, ready to combine with each
other and create more complex
reactions.

[2] Johann Albert Heinrich Reimarus (1729–1814), physician and
professor at the Hamburg Gymna-
sium and son of the more famous

Hermann Samuel Reimarus (1694–
1768). SC suggests that C has in
mind a passing refutation of materialism at the beginning of J. A. H.
Reimarus's treatise *Ueber die
Gründe der menschlichen Erkenntniss und der natürlichen Religion*
(Hamburg 1787) §§ 3–7. *BL* (1847)
I 330n. C owned and annotated a
copy of the Reimarus work, and in
an annotation on § 26 called Reimarus a "good and sensible man, a
worthy Son of a worthy Father".
In an annotation on Fichte *Die
Bestimmung des Menschen* (Berlin
1800) he remarked on "the sensible
Treatise by the younger Reimarus,
in answer to Jacobi, and the Super-
naturalists". *CM* (*CC*) II, III. Maass
also mentions the treatise and summarises Reimarus's views on the
rules of association in general,
though not on materialism as a
whole (§ 119 pp 433–4).

for another place.[1] It is, however, certain, that as long as we deny the former, and affirm the latter, we must bewilder ourselves, whenever we would pierce into the *adyta*[2] of causation; and all that laborious conjecture can do, is to fill up the gaps of fancy.[3] Under that despotism of the eye (the emancipation from which Pythagoras by his *numeral*, and Plato by his *musical*, symbols,[4] and both by geometric discipline, aimed at, as the first προπαιδευτικόν[5] of the mind)[6]—under this strong sensuous influence, we are restless because invisible things are not the objects of vision; and metaphysical systems, for the most part, become popular, not for their truth, but in proportion as they attribute to causes a susceptibility of being *seen*, if only our visual organs were sufficiently powerful.[7]

From a hundred possible confutations let one suffice. Accord-

---

[1] Maass in several places points out in detail the contradictions and difficulties with Hartley's system: pp 30, 41–2, 382–96. The key conclusion with which C agrees is on Maass p 387 (§ 110): "Dadurch aber geräht Hartleys System in einen Widerspruch . . ." ("But in this way Hartley's system falls into a contradiction . . .").

[2] *Adyton/adytum* in both Greek and Latin forms means "innermost sanctuary" (more literally "not to be entered"). Cf *EOT* (*CC*) I 113, III 224; *CN* III 4166 and n; and ch 10, below, I 197.

[3] C here repeats, to the end of the paragraph, almost verbatim a note he attached to lines he contributed to RS *Joan of Arc* (1796) 42n, but substituting the word "fancy" for "imagination".

[4] For Pythagoras (c 587–c 507 B.C.) the essence of all things—not only matter but all relationships in the universe—is found in number. For Plato on mathematical and musical symbols, see e.g. *Timaeus* 35B–36B and *Republic* 398–403, 443D–E, 522–32. For C on emancipating the mind from "the despotism of the eye" and on the importance of the "power of abstraction", in relation to Pythagoras and Plato, see *Logic* (*CC*) 242–3.

[5] "Preparatory education". With C a favourite word in various forms. Cf Plato *Republic* 536D, in which Plato uses the word προπαιδεία. Both forms of the word were common in English and German writings in C's day.

[6] In a marginal note to Tennemann *Geschichte* I 120, C equates Pythagorean number and the Platonic idea: "The arithmoi of Pyth. were evidently the very same as the *Ideas* of Plato." *CM* (*CC*) IV. C thus identifies Pythagoras and Plato with the first philosophical attempt to acknowledge and use "the whole Man, the free Will . . .". BM MS Egerton 2826 ff 393–4. This was crucial to C. See *P Lects* Lect 2 (1949) 107–9, 403 nn 45, 46; also below, I 114.

[7] Cf C's second sentence in this chapter. On the back flyleaf of his copy of Joannes Scotus Erigena *De divisione naturae* (Oxford 1681), C remarks on "that Slavery (of the Mind) to the Eye and ⟨the⟩ visual Imagination (or Fancy), ⟨under the influence of⟩ which ⟨the Reasoner⟩ must have a *picture* and mistakes surface for substance". *CM* (*CC*) III. C's objection to the "popular" systems of metaphysics seems to originate in his religious convictions. Cf below, I 133–6.

ing[1] to this system the idea or vibration *a* from the external object
A becomes associable with the idea or vibration *m* from the
external object M, because the oscillation *a* propagated itself so as
to re-produce the oscillation *m*. But the original impression from
M was essentially different from the impression A: unless therefore
different causes may produce the same effect, the vibration *a* could
never produce the vibration *m*: and this therefore could never be
the means, by which *a* and *m* are associated. To understand this,
the attentive reader need only be reminded, that the ideas are
themselves, in Hartley's system, nothing more than their appropriate configurative vibrations. It is a mere delusion of the fancy[2]
to conceive the pre-existence of the ideas, in any chain of association, as so many differently colored billiard-balls in contact, so that
when an object, the billiard-stick, strikes the first or white ball, the
same motion propagates itself through the red, green, blue, black,
&c. and sets the whole in motion. No! we must suppose the very
same force, which *constitutes* the white ball, to *constitute* the red
or black; or the idea of a circle to *constitute* the idea of a triangle;
which is impossible.[3]

But it may be said, that, by the sensations from the objects A
and M, the nerves have acquired a disposition to the vibrations *a*
and *m*, and therefore *a* need only be repeated in order to re-
produce *m*.[4] Now we will grant, for a moment, the possibility of

[1] Here C translates closely but not verbatim from Maass § 15 (pp 32–3): "Die Ursach, wodurch α bei der sich associirenden Einbildung hervorgebracht werden soll, ist irgend eine andre Nervenschwingung π, die sich dergestalt fortpflanzt, dass die erste entsteht; π aber ist etwas von dem Eindrucke wesentlich Verschiednes, den *A* hervorbrachte, als die Oscillation α bei der Empfindung entstand. Wenn nun wesentlich verschiedne Ursachen nicht einerlei Wirkungen haben; so kann auch α nicht durch π erzeugt werden, und Einbildungen können sich nicht durch fortgepflanzte Nervenschwingungen vergesellschaften." (C has changed the alphabetic characters used in the example.)
[2] That is, according to Hartley's system. From here to the end of this

paragraph C outlines the full implications of the example taken from Maass and what must be assumed if Hartley's system is accepted, which leads to an impossibility.
[3] But C was nevertheless fascinated by an immaterial force or *Kraft* rescuing materialism into a larger spiritual system or philosophy. This is part of the reason the word *Einbildungskraft* appealed to him so much. Cf the quotation from Leibniz at the beginning of ch 13, below, which deals with a pervading and constitutive force.
[4] C for this sentence returns to Maass p 33 exactly where he had left off in the above paragraph. "Aber man könnte sagen: Die Nerven haben durch die Empfindung des Gegenstandes *A* eine Disposition zu der Schwingung α erhalten: dürfen

such a disposition in a material nerve, which yet seems scarcely less absurd than to say, that a weather-cock had acquired a *habit* of turning to the east, from the wind having been so long in that quarter: for if it be replied, that we must take in the circumstance of *life*, what then becomes of the mechanical philosophy? And what is the *nerve*, but the flint which the wag placed in the pot as the first ingredient of his stone-broth, requiring only salt, turnips and mutton, for the remainder! [1] But if we waive this, and pre-suppose the actual existence of such a disposition; two cases are possible. [2] Either, every idea has its own nerve and correspondent oscillation, or this is not the case. If the latter be the truth, we should gain nothing by these dispositions; for then, every nerve having several dispositions, when the motion of any other nerve is propagated into it, there will be no ground or cause present, why exactly the oscillation *m* should arise, rather than any other to which it was equally pre-disposed. But if we take the former, and let every idea have a nerve of its own, then every nerve must be capable of propagating its motion into many other nerves; and again, there is no reason assignable, why the vibration *m* should arise, rather than any other ad libitum.

---

folglich nur überhaupt in Bewegung gesetzt werden, um α hervorzu-bringen." But C has expanded Maass to include *both* of the objects and their vibrations (A, *a* and M, *m*), not just Maass's A, α.

[1] C refers to a folk tale common in several European languages and usually known as "The Soup Stone Sold". Stith Thompson *Motif-Index of Folk-Literature* (Bloomington & London 1975) iv 244 (no K 112.2). A familiar seventeenth-century English version is "The Friar and the Whetstone" in *The Sack-Full of News* (1673).

[2] From here until the end of this paragraph C again returns to Maass pp 33–4 where he had left off at the end of the first sentence in the paragraph, so that in the whole of ch 6 C translates, in three of his own separate sections, just over one continuous page of Maass. "Wenn man die Frage über die Möglichkeit einer solchen Disposition bei Seite setzt; so giebt es, unter Voraussetzung ihrer Wirklichkeit, zwei Fälle. Entweder *a*) hat jede Vorstellung ihren eignen Nerven, dessen Oscillation ihr entspricht, oder *b*) es ist das nicht. Im letztern Falle würde man durch die Dispositionen nicht das mindeste gewinnen. Denn alsdann hat jeder Nerve mehrere Dispositionen, und wenn sich die Bewegung eines andern auf ihn fortpflanzt; so ist überall kein Grund vorhanden, warum grade die Oscillation α entstehen sollte. [C here adds the qualification "rather than any other to which it was equally pre-disposed".] Im erstern Falle, wenn jede Vorstellung ihren eignen Nerven hat; so muss jeder Nerve seine Bewegung auf viele andre fortpflanzen können, und es ist wiederum kein Grund da, warum die Schwingung α und nicht irgend eine andre entstand."

It is fashionable to smile at Hartley's vibrations and vibra-
tiuncles; and his work has been re-edited by Priestley, with the
omission of the *material* hypothesis.[1] But Hartley was too great
a man, too coherent a thinker, for this to have been done, either
consistently or to any wise purpose. For all other parts of his
system, as far as they are peculiar to that system, once removed
from their mechanical basis, not only lose their main support, but
the very motive which led to their adoption. Thus the principle of
contemporaneity, which Aristotle had made the common *condition*
of all the laws of association, Hartley was constrained to represent
as being itself the sole *law*.[2] For to what law can the action of
material atoms be subject, but that of proximity in *place*? And to
what law can their *motions* be subjected, but that of *time*? Again,
from this results inevitably, that the will, the reason, the judgment,
and the understanding, instead of being the determining causes of
association, must needs be represented as its *creatures,* and among
its mechanical *effects.* Conceive, for instance, a broad stream,
winding through a mountainous country with an indefinite number
of currents, varying and running into each other according as the
gusts chance to blow from the opening of the mountains. The
temporary union of several currents in one, so as to form the main
current of the moment, would present an accurate image of
Hartley's theory of the will.[3]

[1] C refers to Joseph Priestley's *Hartley's Theory of the Human Mind, on the Principle of the Association of Ideas* (1775). Priestley, as SC points out, was not opposed to the doctrine of vibrations but wished to slim down Hartley's book to what was more strictly relevant to the association of ideas. *BL* (1847) I 115n.

[2] See Hartley *Observations on Man* pt I ch 1 sect II prop x. This sentence also derives from part of C's marginal note to Maass § 13 (pp 28–9), in which Maass discusses general principles of association and offers a "general law" of association. C writes, "Contemporëity seems to me the common condition under which all the determining Powers act rather than itself the effective Law— Maass sometimes forgets (as Hartley

seems never to have remembered) that all our Images are abstractions: and that in many cases of Likeness the Association is merely an Act of Recognition." For Maass's name in his marginal note C substitutes the mention of Aristotle in *BL*. But this is neither inaccurate nor any effort to cover "tracks", especially considering C's reference to Maass at the start of this chapter and Maass's discussion (p 326) of the general law in Aristotle. See below in this chapter, I 111–12. C is being consistent with his own discussions in chs 5, 6, and 7. See ch 7, below, I 126–7, esp 126 n 2, for C's use of more of his same marginal note to express his own "true practical" version of a general law of association. Cf *CN* III 4059 and n.

[3] Cf C's remark in 1809: "But

Had this been really the case, the consequence would have been, that our whole life would be divided between the despotism of outward impressions, and that of senseless and passive memory. Take his law in its highest abstraction and most philosophical form, viz. that every partial representation recalls the total representation of which it was a part;[1] and the law becomes nugatory, were it only from its universality.[2] In practice it would indeed be mere lawlessness. Consider, how immense must be the sphere of a total impression from the top of St. Paul's church; and how rapid and continuous the series of such total impressions.[3] If therefore we suppose the absence of all interference of the will, reason, and judgement, one or other of two consequences must result. Either the ideas (or relicts of such impression) will exactly imitate the order of the impression itself, which would be absolute *delirium*:[4]

it will be my business to set forth an orderly proof, that Atheism is the necessary Consequence or Corollary of the Hartleian Theory of the Will . . .". *CN* III 3587 and n.

[1] The law as C states it here is almost a verbatim translation from Maass p 29 or p 326 (see below in this n). C also continues to draw on his own marginal notes to Maass pp 28–9. Though apparently still discussing Hartley, C is thus referring to Maass's general law ("allegemeine Associationsgesetz": p 29): "With a given representation all [representations] can be associated, which belong with it to a total representation, but those *only* [which can be associated] *immediately;* or, as is also said, Every representation calls back into the mind its total representation." Tr SC *BL* (1847) I 116n. "Rather," says C in the margin, "is capable, under given conditions, of recalling: or else our whole Life would be divided between the Despotism of outward Impressions, and that of senseless Memory". Maass restates the general law on p 326, in which he summarises Aristotle: "Every partial representation awakens its total representation." Tr SC *BL* (1847) I 105n. For C's use of

this in his discussion of Aristotle see above, I 102–3. Thus C views both Hartley and Maass (whether by himself or in summarising Aristotle) as offering the "law in its highest abstraction and most philosophical form", where it unfortunately becomes nugatory. In Hartley the relevant passage is *Observations on Man* pt I ch 1 sect II Prop x, mentioned above, 110 n 2. In ch 7, below, C will present his own "true practical general law of association".

[2] C's marginal note on Maass p 29 criticises Maass's law for being too universal. But when Maass attributes the law to Aristotle (p 326) Maass himself remarks of Aristotle "in what universality he had conceived the law of association". (". . . in welcher Allgemeinheit er sich das Associationgesetz gedacht habe".) C had naturally read this.

[3] C continues to draw from his marginalia on Maass p 29, in which he gives this same example of a view from St Paul's: "Consider how immense the Sphere of a total Impression, from the Top of Sᵗ Paul's— & how rapid the series of total Impressions."

[4] See ch 4, above, I 84 and esp n 2.

or any one part of that impression might recal any other part, and (as from the law of continuity, there must exist in every total impression some one or more parts, which are components of some other following total impression, and so on ad infinitum) *any* part of *any* impression might recal *any* part of any *other*, without a cause present to determine *what* it should be. For to bring in the will, or reason, as causes of their own cause, that is, as at once causes and effects, can satisfy those only who in their pretended evidences of a God having first demanded organization, as the sole cause and ground of intellect, will then coolly demand the pre-existence of intellect, as the cause and ground-work of organization. There is in truth but one state to which this theory applies at all, namely, that of complete light-headedness; and even to this it applies but partially, because the will, and reason are perhaps never wholly suspended.

A case of this kind occurred in a Catholic town in Germany a year or two before my arrival at Göttingen, and had not then ceased to be a frequent subject of conversation. A young woman of four or five, and twenty, who could neither read, nor write, was seized with a nervous fever; during which, according to the asseverations of all the priests and monks of the neighbourhood, she became *possessed*, and, as it appeared, by a very learned devil. She continued incessantly talking Latin, Greek, and Hebrew, in very pompous tones and with most distinct enunciation.[1] This possession was rendered more probable by the known fact, that she was or had been an heretic. Voltaire humourously advises the devil to decline all acquaintance with medical men; and it would have been more to his reputation, if he had taken this advice in the present instance. The case had attracted the particular attention of a young physician, and by his statement many eminent physiologists and psychologists visited the town, and cross-examined the case on the spot. Sheets full of her ravings were taken down from her own mouth, and were found to consist of sentences, coherent and

---

[1] A somewhat similar report, which C may have read, is told by Graf von Grävenitz "Ueber das Band zwischen Geist und Körper" *Magazin zur Erfahrungsseelenkunde* VIII Pt I (Berlin 1791) 50–2. The Count tells of his own experience as a boy of fourteen. In a state of severe nervous disorder lasting three years he frequently spoke Greek, Hebrew, and "an unknown language" all together without having previously studied any of them. The source of C's story has not been found.

intelligible each for itself, but with little or no connection with each other. Of the Hebrew, a small portion only could be traced to the Bible; the remainder seemed to be in the rabbinical[a] dialect. All trick or conspiracy was out of the question. Not only had the young woman ever been an harmless, simple creature; but she was evidently labouring under a nervous fever. In the town, in which she had been resident for many years as a servant in different families, no solution presented itself. The young physician, however, determined to trace her past life step by step; for the patient herself was incapable of returning a rational answer. He at length succeeded in discovering the place, where her parents had lived: travelled thither, found *them* dead, but an uncle surviving; and from him learnt, that the patient had been charitably taken by an old protestant pastor at nine years old, and had remained with him some years, even till the old man's death. Of this pastor the uncle knew nothing, but that he was a very good man. With great difficulty, and after much search, our young medical philosopher discovered a niece of the pastor's, who had lived with him as his house-keeper, and had inherited his effects. She remembered the girl; related, that her venerable uncle had been too indulgent, and could not bear to hear the girl scolded; that she was willing to have kept her, but that after her patron's death, the girl herself refused to stay. Anxious enquiries were then, of course, made concerning the pastor's habits; and the solution of the phenomenon was soon obtained. For it appeared, that it had been the old man's custom, for years, to walk up and down a passage of his house into which the kitchen door opened, and to read to himself with a loud voice, out of his favorite books. A considerable number of these were still in the niece's possession. She added, that he was a very learned man and a great Hebraist. Among the books were found a collection of rabbinical writings, together with several of the Greek and Latin fathers; and the physician succeeded in identifying so many passages with those taken down at the young woman's bedside, that no doubt could remain in any rational mind concerning the true origin of the impressions made on her nervous system.

This authenticated case furnishes both proof and instance, that reliques of sensation may exist for an indefinite time in a latent state, in the very same order in which they were originally impressed; and as we cannot rationally suppose the feverish state of

[a] *BL* (1817): rabinical

the brain to act in any other way than as a stimulus, this fact (and it would not be difficult to adduce several of the same kind) con- tributes to make it even probable, that all thoughts are in them- selves imperishable;[1] and, that if the intelligent faculty should be rendered more comprehensive, it would require only a different and apportioned organization, *the body celestial* instead of *the body terrestrial*, to bring before every human soul the collective experi- ence of its whole past existence. And this, this, perchance, is the dread book of judgement, in whose mysterious hieroglyphics every idle word is recorded![2] Yea, in the very nature of a living spirit, it may be more possible that heaven and earth should pass away,[3] than that a single act, a single thought, should be loosened or lost from that living chain of causes, to all whose links, conscious or unconscious, the free-will, our only absolute *self*, is co-extensive and co-present.[4] But[5] not now dare I longer discourse of this, waiting for a loftier mood, and a nobler subject, warned from within and from without, that it is profanation to speak of these mysteries * τοῖς μηδέποτε φαντασθεῖσιν, ὡς καλὸν τὸ τῆς δικαιοσύνης καὶ

* "To those to whose imagination it has never been presented, how beautiful is the countenance of justice and wisdom; and that neither the morning nor the evening star are so fair. For in order to direct the view

[1] Cf *CN* I 576 and n, 1575.

[2] Cf HCR on 12 Jul 1819: "Coleridge has the striking thought that possibly the punishment of a future life may consist in bringing back the consciousness of the past." *CRD* II 129. C's idea (though not its place in an after-life) has been the subject of neurological research for many years. Cf also a letter to RS of 7 Aug 1803: ". . . I hold, that association depends in a much greater degree on the recurrence of resembling states of Feeling, than on Trains of Idea/that the recollection of early childhood in latest old age depends on, & is explicable by this— & if this be true, Hartley's System totters." *CL* II 961.

[3] Mark 13.31; Luke 21.33.

[4] C connects free-will (as op- posed to passive materialism) with the essence of individuality. It is the evidence of the divine in man and hence the fear of "profanation"

expressed immediately below. The apposition "our absolute *self*" may be an echo of Fichte's *das absolute* or *reine Ich*. But whereas Fichte sees this absolute ego or pure self as supra-personal or even divine, C wants to emphasise the free agency and will of the individual human being while expressly avoiding the naming of God Himself by any form of "I" or "ego", even if modified by "pure" or "absolute". See ch 9, below, I 158–60, C's n; also above, I 110 n 3.

[5] C in this sentence repeats al- most verbatim the close of *PGC* (in which he also cites the same passage from Plotinus). *BL* (1907) II 246. The remark suggests the funda- mentally religious and spiritual impetus of these chapters as they will move from materialism to a spiritual or transcendental concep- tion. C feels already he is beginning to tread on holy ground.

σωφροσύνης πρόσωπον, καὶ οὔτε ἔσπερος οὔτε ἑῷος οὕτω καλά. Τὸν γὰρ ὁρῶντα πρὸς τὸ ὁρώμενον συγγενὲς καὶ ὅμοιον ποιησάμενον δεῖ ἐπιβάλλειν τῇ[θ]έᾳ· οὐ γὰρ ἂν πώποτε εἶδεν 'Οφθαλμὸς "Ηλιον ἡλιοειδὴς μὴ γεγενημένος, οὐδὲ τὸ Καλὸν ἂν ἴδῃ Ψυχὴ μὴ καλὴ γενομένη.— PLOTINUS.[1]

aright, it behoves that the beholder should have made himself congenerous and similar to the object beheld. Never could the eye have beheld the sun, had not its own essence been soliform," (*i.e. pre-configured to light by a similarity of essence with that of light*) "neither can a soul not beautiful ✓✓ attain to an intuition of beauty."

[1] *Ennead* 1.6.4 and (concluding sentence) 9 (var). C has made "the beholder" a male person instead of an object (the eye). There are other minor variations from the edition of Plotinus (Basle 1580), which C owned and annotated. See also below, ch 12, I 240 n 3.

CHAPTER 7

Of the necessary consequences of the Hartleian theory—Of the original mistake or equivocation which procured admission for the theory—Memoria Technica

WE WILL pass by the utter incompatibility of such a law (if law it may be called, which would itself be the slave of chances)[1] with even that *appearance* of rationality forced upon us by the outward phænomena of human conduct, abstracted from our own consciousness. We will agree to forget this for the moment, in order to fix our attention on that subordination of final to efficient causes in the human being,[2] which flows of necessity from the assumption, that the will, and with the will all acts of thought and attention, are parts and products of this blind mechanism, instead of being distinct powers, whose function it is to controul, determine, and modify[3] the phantasmal[a] chaos[4] of association.

---

[a] *BL* (1817): phantasma

[1] The law is the one C cited and criticised for its automatic, universal despotism of mechanical association, over which the will or self has no active control. See ch 6, above, I 111–12.

[2] Referring to two of Aristotle's four "causes": the material, formal, efficient, and final. *Physics* 194b–195a.

[3] The idea that a conscious will, innate and even synonymous with the individual self (but subject to a holy will), exerts directing influence over association and the imagination is central to C's concept of these two processes. The idea was not new to British thought; Hobbes, Locke, Berkeley, Addison, Akenside, Burke, Priestley, and others remark how the mind selects and voluntarily fashions particulars into larger units. But the term "will", used by Locke and Berkeley in speaking about the formation of complex ideas, had been mostly dropped in eighteenth-century British psychology, though it remained generally used in religious writing and discussion. The idea of the will directing association or the imaginative process and the terms *Wille, Absicht,* or *Selbstätigkeit* appear in numerous places in German writers whom C read. This reading probably helped C free himself from Hartley's mechanical concept of the will. E.g. J. N. Tetens *Philosophische Versuche* (1777) I 107, 115, 160 (see *CN* II 2375, 2382 and nn); Kant *KRV* pt I bk II §§ VIII–IX and *Grundlegung zur Metaphysik der Sitten* (Riga 1797) 7–10 (see *CN* I 1705, 1717 and nn; *P Lects* Lect 12—1949—360–6, 459, and McFarland "SI" 245–6); Schiller *AE* 134, 208, 210; Maass

116

The soul becomes a mere ens logicum; for as a real separable being, it would be more worthless and ludicrous, than the Grimalkins in the Cat-harpsichord, described in the Spectator.[1] For these did form a part of the process; but in Hartley's scheme the soul is present only to be pinched or *stroked*, while the very squeals or purring are produced by an agency wholly independent and alien. It involves all the difficulties, all the incomprehensibility (if it be not indeed, ὡς ἔμοιγε δοκεῖ,[2] the absurdity) of intercommunion between substances that have no one property in common, without any of the convenient consequences that bribed the judgement to the admission of the *dualistic* hypothesis.[3] Accordingly, this caput mortuum[4] of the Hartleian process has been rejected by his followers,[5] and the consciousness considered as a *result*, as a *tune*, the common product of the breeze and the harp: tho' this again is the mere remotion of one absurdity to make way for another, equally preposterous.[6] For what is harmony but a mode

---

50–1, 61–2, 163–70 passim; Schelling *STI* 322–404 (*SW* III 532–82). In his copy of Jacobi *Ueber die Lehre des Spinoza* (Breslau 1789), bound with Maass, C in a marginal note queries Jacobi's definition, "Wille ist reine Selbsthätigkeit, erhoben zu dem Grade des Bewusstseyns, welchen wir Vernunft nennen" (xxxviii). C is worried that here perhaps "spontaneity = *Selbsthätigkeit*" (which it is not, at least for Jacobi in a materialistic or physiological sense), because if it were, then the will would be another nervous type of reaction. Almost all the Germans discuss the part played by the will in the simplest associations up to the higher acts of creativity.

[4] For "phantasmal chaos" cf Schiller *AE* 208 and n, and for a possible connection with Kant see Orsini 93. Contrast C's own "harmonized Chaos" in *CN* III 4397 f 53ᵛ. For the final goal of C's insistence on the will and the *moral* will see *P Lects* Lects 11, 12 (1949) 333–4, 364–7; *BL* (1907) I 236; *Friend* (*CC*) I 500, 516; *AR* (1825) 27;

CN II 2441. See also Introd, above, I xc–xci.

[1] *Spectator* No 361 (24 Apr 1712) on "the Cat-call".

[2] "As it seems to me, at least".

[3] For C on dualism see below, I 129–31.

[4] Defined by *OED* as the residuum remaining after the distillation or sublimation of any substance, or, figuratively, any worthless residue. The transferred use was current in C's day. Cf *SM* (*CC*) 77 and n 2 and *TL* 70–1.

[5] By "followers" C means primarily Priestley. See above, I 110.

[6] C objects to consciousness viewed as a product of material interaction. For C it is more the breeze itself that is the spirit or consciousness (and, by ultimate connection, the Holy Spirit). Cf a letter to RS 7 Aug 1803: "I almost think, that Ideas *never* recall Ideas . . . any more than Leaves in a forest create each other's motion— The Breeze it is that runs thro' them/ it is the Soul, the state of Feeling—." *CL* II 961. On C's imagery of the Aeolian harp cf *Logic* (*CC*) 38, 142.

of relation, the very *esse* of which is *percipi*?[1] An ens rationale, which pre-supposes the power, that by perceiving creates it?[2] The razor's edge becomes a saw to the armed vision;[3] and the delicious melodies of Purcell or Cimarosa[4] might be disjointed stammerings to a hearer, whose partition of time should be a thousand times subtler than ours. But this obstacle too let us imagine ourselves to have surmounted, and "at one bound high overleap all bound!"[5] Yet according to this hypothesis the disquisition, to which I am at present soliciting the reader's attention, may be as truly said to be written by Saint Paul's church, as by *me*: for it is the mere motion of my muscles and nerves;[6] and these again are set in motion

[1] The "esse is percipi" formula C is probably quoting from George Berkeley (1685–1753) *A Treatise Concerning the Principles of Human Knowledge* (1710), which C read. See *B Works* II 42ff; cf I 5, 35, 119. Cf *Logic* (*CC*) 66. For this formula and its connection with C's view of subjective idealism see *CN* I 1842 and n, III 4186 and n; *P Lects* (1949) 60 (Introd and quotation from N 27), 371–2 (Lect 13), and Orsini 29–31. See also ch 8, below, I 137–8.

[2] C is saying that our perceptions actively create at least some of the harmonies and relationships evident to us; these harmonies and appearances are not necessarily innate to the things or phenomena themselves, as C exemplifies in the next sentence.

[3] I.e. the aided as opposed to the unaided eye. Common examples are vision through a microscope or telescope. "Bewaffnetes Auge" is a German idiom. C may be echoing Schiller *AE* 42: ". . . ihren Blick ins Unbedingte bewaffnet hätte" (". . . armed their eyes with a glass for peering into the Absolute"); or J. J. Engel's "mit unbewaffnetem Auge" ("with the unaided eye") in "Traum des Galilei" *Der Philosoph für die Welt: Schriften* (12 vols Berlin 1801–6) II 1239–40; see *CN* III 4065n and 3585 and n. Another possible "source", especially since C

later in this chapter will continue to use Maass (see below), is Maass p 170: ". . . die *Herschels* bewaffnet[t]es Auge in Sterne aufgelösst . . . hat . . ." (". . . which Herschel's aided vision has resolved in the stars . . ."). Both Schiller and Maass use the idiom in reference to William Herschel's (1738–1822) discoveries with the aid of a telescope as a physical paradigm for what can be achieved by purely intellectual means. Cf below, II 83.

[4] For C's fondness for the music of Henry Purcell (c 1658–95) and Domenico Cimarosa (1749–1801), the English and Italian composers, see esp *Friend* (*CC*) I 129 and n, *IS* 156, and *TT* 6 Jul 1833; also *P Lects* Lect 10 (1949) 305–6, 412 n 34, and *Sh C* II 77 (Lect 3 of 1811).

[5] Milton *Paradise Lost* IV 181: "At one slight bound high overleap'd all bound".

[6] C's example of St Paul's, or of his own muscles and nerves, actually producing his prose (and the examples involving RS, Byron, and "all things", below, I 120) has a close analogue in Jacobi *ULS* 143–4: "What you adopt from the doctrine of fatalism is enough for me; since one needs no more than to establish that St Peter's in Rome built itself; that Newton's discoveries were made by his body; and that in all such instances the soul is occupied only with looking on."

from external causes equally passive, which external causes stand themselves in interdependent connection with every thing that exists or has existed.[1] Thus the whole universe co-operates to produce the minutest stroke of every letter, save only that I myself, and I alone, have nothing to do with it, but merely the causeless and *effectless* beholding of it when it is done. Yet scarcely can it be called a beholding; for it is neither an act nor an effect; but an impossible creation of a *something–nothing* out of its very contrary! It is the mere quick-silver plating behind a looking-glass;[2] and in this alone consists the poor worthless I![3] The sum total of my moral and intellectual intercourse dissolved into its elements are reduced to *extension, motion, degrees of velocity*, and those diminished *copies* of configurative motion, which form what we call notions, and notions of notions. Of such philosophy well might Butler say—

> The metaphysic's but a puppet motion
> That goes with screws, the notion of a notion;
> The copy of a copy and lame draught
> Unnaturally taken from a thought:
> That counterfeits all pantomimic tricks,
> And turns the eyes, like an old crucifix;
> That counterchanges whatsoe'er it calls
> B' another name, and makes it true or false;
> Turns truth to falsehood, falsehood into truth,
> By virtue of the Babylonian's tooth.
>   MISCELLANEOUS THOUGHTS.[4]

The inventor of the watch did not in reality invent it; he only look'd on, while the blind causes, the only true artists, were unfold-

---

[1] Of interest here is C's note on a back flyleaf of Kant's *KRV*, a note written when C was discovering Kant: ". . . not the system of mere *Receptivity*, like that of Epicurus and Hartley". *CM (CC)* III. Kant probably helped lead C away from Hartley's theory of association. Orsini 47–9 presents the case that C's early study of Kant resulted in C's claim that "I have . . . overthrown the doctrine of Association, as taught by Hartley, and with it all the irreligious metaphysics of modern Infidels". To T. Poole [16 Mar 1801]: *CL* II 706. Cf *P Lects* Lect 12 (1949) 346–8.

[2] C refers to the thin film of solid mercury (or similar material) that gives a mirror its reflective property, the epitome of a passive copyist. Cf *CL* II 709.

[3] But while C rejects the purely passive "I" or self, he also steers clear of its opposite, the "crude egoismus" of a totally active and dominant self. For C and the "I" or self, see ch 9, below, I 145–6, 158–60.

[4] Lines 93–102.

ing themselves.[1] So must it have been too with my friend ALLSTON, when he sketched his picture of the dead man revived by the bones of the prophet Elijah.[2] So must it have been with Mr. SOUTHEY and LORD BYRON, when the one *fancied* himself composing his "RODERICK," and the other his "CHILD HAROLD."[3] The same must hold good of all systems of philosophy; of all arts, governments, wars by sea and by land; in short, of all things that ever have been or that ever will be produced. For according to this system it is not the affections and passions that are at work, in as far as they are *sensations* or *thoughts*. We only *fancy*, that we act from rational resolves, or prudent motives, or from impulses of anger, love, or generosity. In all these cases the real agent is a *something-nothing-every-thing*, which does all of which we know, and knows nothing of all that itself does.[4]

The existence of an infinite spirit, of an intelligent and holy will, must on this system be mere articulated motions of the air.[5] For as the function of the human understanding is no other than

---

[1] In this paragraph C remarks that if Hartley's or similar systems alone are believed, we must exclude acts of personal creativity and foreclose any active principle of genius in the fine arts.

[2] Washington Allston (1779–1843), the American historical painter whom C first met in Rome (1806) and in whose support he wrote *PGC* (1814). C refers to *The Dead Man Touching Elisha's Bones* (1810–11), for which Allston was given the prize of the British Institution (1811) and which is in the Pennsylvania Academy of Fine Arts (Philadelphia). C, who used the correct title in *PGC—BL* (1907) II 234—knew the Bible too well to forget that Elijah was transported to heaven and therefore left no bones. "Elijah" could have been Morgan's mistake or a slip of the tongue on C's part as he dictated. For C's relations with Allston see esp *CN* II 2785, 2794, and 2796 and nn; J. R. Welsh *Journal of American Studies* v (1971) 81–91. Cf ch 10, below, I 216 n 3. Allston's touching sonnet on C is quoted in *BL* (1847) I 123n.

[3] RS's *Roderick, the Last of the Goths* (1814) and the first two cantos of Byron's *Childe Harold's Piilgrimage* (1812), the third canto of which appeared in 1816 and the fourth in 1818.

[4] Cf C on assigning everything to association and leaving nothing for choice, the will, or even degrees of intensity in association: "Association in philosophy is like the term stimulus in medicine; explaining every thing, it explains nothing; and above all, leaves itself unexplained." *PGC*: *BL* (1907) II 222.

[5] For elaboration on this central objection to material association unsupported by faith in a Supreme Being, cf *P Lects* Lect 12 (1949) 361–3. Although influences are here tangled, Kant seems worth mention. In several places he matches C's general plane of discussion. E.g. "the freedom of the will, the immortality of the soul, and the existence of God" Kant avows in a way that apparently impressed C deeply. See McFarland "SI" 226. Cf *Friend* (*CC*) I 112. For "articulated motions" cf *EOT* (*CC*) II 249 and n 4.

merely (to appear to itself) to combine and to apply the phænomena of the association; and as these derive all their reality from the primary sensations; and the sensations again all *their* reality from the impressions ab extra; a God not visible, audible, or tangible, can exist only in the sounds and letters that form his name and attributes. If in *ourselves* there be no such faculties as those of the will, and the scientific reason, we must either have an *innate* idea of them, which would overthrow the whole system; or we can have no idea at all. The process, by which Hume degraded the notion of cause and effect into a blind product of delusion and habit, into the mere sensation of *proceeding* life (nisus vitalis) [1] associated with the images of the memory; [2] this same process must be repeated to the equal degradation of every *fundamental* idea in ethics or theology. [3]

Far, very far am I from burthening with the odium of these consequences the moral characters of those who first formed, or have since adopted the system! It is most noticeable of the excellent and pious Hartley, that in the proofs of the existence and attributes of God, with which his second volume commences, he

[1] "Vital impulse", "instinctive life". See also, for another important use of the word *nisus, Friend* (*CC*) I 492 and *CN* III 3744 and n.

[2] *Treatise of Human Nature* (1739–40) pt III sects XIV ("Of the Idea of Necessary Connexion") and XV ("Rules by Which to Judge of Causes and Effects"). Cf *An Inquiry Concerning Human Understanding* sect VII ("Of the Idea of Necessary Connexion").

[3] The last two sentences in this paragraph return to what C conceives as the necessary idea of will and reason "in *ourselves*", which—according to him—are innate and do not square with modern material systems and their corresponding theories of association. Cf C's annotation on a back flyleaf of Schelling's *Philosophische Schriften* [Landshut 1809] (on *Philosophische Untersuchungen über das Wesen der menschlichen Freyheit*), which points to the goal of this line of thought:

"The whole Question of the origin of Evil resolves itself into one—Is the Holy Will good in & of itself or only relative, i.e. as a means, to Pleasure, Joy, Happiness, &c?—If the latter be the truth, no solution can be given of the origin of Evil compatible with the attributes of God—but (as in the problem of the Squaring of a Circle) we can demonstrate, that it is *impossible* to be solved. If the [former] be true, as I more than believe, the Solution is easy and almost self-evident. Man cannot be a moral Being without having had the Choice of Good & Evil . . .". *CM* (*CC*) IV. C argues against Hartley and other material associationists because, if followed strictly, they deny the will and moral choice. For C, any theory of association reflects its complementary moral and religious belief. But in the next paragraph C typically apologises for the obvious implication.

makes no reference to the principles or results of the first.[1] Nay, he assumes, as his foundations, ideas which, if we embrace the doctrines of his first volume, can exist no where but in the vibrations of the ethereal medium common to the nerves and to the atmosphere. Indeed the whole of the second volume is, with the fewest possible exceptions, independent of his peculiar system. So true is it, that the faith, which saves and sanctifies, is a collective energy, a total act of the whole moral being;[2] that its living sensorium is in the *heart*;[3] and that no errors of the understanding can be morally arraigned unless they have proceeded from the heart.—But whether they be such, no man can be certain in the case of another, scarcely perhaps even in his own. Hence it follows by inevitable consequence, that man may perchance determine, *what* is an heresy; but God only can know, *who* is a heretic. It does not, however, by any means follow, that opinions fundamentally false are harmless. An hundred causes may co-exist to form one complex antidote. Yet the sting of the adder remains venomous, though there are many who have taken up the evil thing; and it hurted them not![4] Some indeed there seem to have been, in an unfortunate neighbour-nation at least, who have embraced this system with a full view of all its moral and religious consequences; some—

——————————— who deem themselves most free,
When they within this gross and visible sphere
Chain down the winged thought, scoffing assent,
Proud in their meanness; and themselves they cheat
With noisy emptiness of learned phrase,
Their subtle fluids, impacts, essences,
Self-working tools, uncaus'd effects, and all

[1] Pt II ch I "Of the Being and Attributes of God, and of Natural Religion". Cf a notebook entry of Jun 1810 (*CN* III 3907) on the difference between the "second Vol. of Hartley compared with the inevitable consequences (in logic) of his first Vol.". C is naturally hesitant to judge any man's soul, but will continue to identify materialism with "infidelity". E.g. *P Lects* Lect 13 (1949) 379.

[2] Cf "But faith is a *total* act of the soul . . .". *Friend* (*CC*) II 314 (I 315).

[3] A common feeling in C. Cf ch 10, below, I 217, on "that fortunate inconsequence of our nature, which permits the heart to rectify the errors of the understanding". Also cf ch 1, above, I 13, 17; *CL* II 961; *Friend* (*CC*) I 524; *AR* (1825) 87, 184.

[4] C paraphrases Mark 16.18: "They shall take up serpents; and if they drink any deadly thing, it shall not hurt them . . .". Cf *CN* III 3907 and n.

> Those blind omniscients, those Almighty slaves,
> Untenanting Creation of its God![1]

Such men need discipline, not argument; they must be made better men, before they can become wiser.

The attention will be more profitably employed in attempting to discover and expose the paralogisms, by the magic of which such a faith could find admission into minds framed for a nobler creed. These, it appears to me, may be all reduced to one sophism as their common genus; the mistaking the *conditions* of a thing for its *causes* and *essence*;[2] and the process by which we arrive at the knowledge of a faculty, for the faculty itself. The air I breathe, is the *condition* of my life, not its cause. We could never have learnt that we had eyes but by the process of seeing; yet having seen we know that the eyes must have pre-existed in order to render the process of sight possible. Let us cross-examine Hartley's scheme under the guidance of this distinction; and we shall discover, that contemporaneity (Leibnitz's *Lex Continui*)[3] is the *limit and condition* of the laws of mind, itself being rather a law of matter, at least of phænomena considered as material. At the utmost, it is to *thought* the same, as the law of gravitation is to loco-motion.[4]

---

[1] C's *The Destiny of Nations* lines 27–35: *PW* (*EHC*) I 132. These are among the 255 lines contributed by C to RS's epic *Joan of Arc* (1796) and later removed. Much of the remainder of the poem was also written in 1796, though not published in its entirety until *SL* (1817). *PW* (*EHC*) I 131n. The "unfortunate neighbour-nation" is France.

[2] On C's distinction between "cause" and "mere condition" see *CN* III 3886, 4047 and nn; a letter to R. H. Brabant [? Jun 1815]: *CL* VI 1036; and cf below, I 125.

[3] First stated in his *Lettre à M. Bayle sur un principe général: Opera* ed J. E. Erdmann (Berlin 1840) I 104–6. Cf *CN* III 4455 and n. The law essentially states that all causes and effects are ultimately interconnected (and hence joined by a series of successive, contemporaneous events) and is a basic principle of Leibniz's. "It is one of my great maxims, and one of the most truthful, that nature never makes leaps. I have called this the law of continuity . . .". *Nouveaux essais: Opera* I 198. C could also have come across the principle of *Continuität* in Schelling (*Von der Weltseele: SW* II 568–9; or in *Abhandlungen* I 361, 388). See also below, the quotation from Kant *De mundi sensibilis et intelligibilis forma et principiis* and C's tr, I 288–9 and nn. Cf *CL* IV 769. But the concept of the *lex continui* goes back as far as Aristotle: see A. O. Lovejoy *The Great Chain of Being* (Cambridge, Mass 1936) 55–8, 79–81, 144–5.

[4] The force of gravity constitutes the *total* vector of "loco-motion" only in those bodies which are free-falling; in all other moving bodies gravity is a force or condition constantly affecting every body that moves by another cause (muscles, wind, motor, etc). Early in the *KRV* Kant asserts that time is not an experienced fact or "cause" of such

In every voluntary movement we first counteract gravitation, in order to avail ourselves of it. It must exist, that there may be a something to be counteracted, and which by its re-action, aids the force that is exerted to resist it. Let us consider, what we do when we leap. We first resist the gravitating power by an act purely voluntary, and then by another act, voluntary in part, we yield to it in order to light on the spot, which we had previously proposed to ourselves. Now let a man watch his mind while he is composing; or, to take a still more common case, while he is trying to recollect a name; and he will find the process completely analogous. Most of my readers will have observed a small water-insect on the surface of rivulets, which throws a cinque-spotted shadow fringed with prismatic colours on the sunny bottom of the brook; and will have noticed, how the little animal *wins* its way up against the stream, by alternate pulses of active and passive motion, now resisting the current, and now yielding to it in order to gather strength and a momentary *fulcrum* for a further propulsion. This is no unapt emblem of the mind's self-experience in the act of thinking. There are evidently two powers at work, which relatively to each other are active and passive; and this is not possible without an intermediate faculty, which is at once both active and passive.[1] (In philosophical language, we must denominate this

facts but is a condition affecting all experience ("Transscendentalen Aesthetik" Abschn 1–2).

[1] The intermediary and the dual active-passive nature of the imagination were common observations by 1815. Locke, Hobbes, and Addison remark how the mind actively and "voluntarily" joins ideas; Vives, Wolff, Tetens, and Fichte also express the active-passive quality of the imagination. This idea may originally have come to C's attention through Kant (the transcendental synthetic of the imagination), Schelling (*Abhandlungen: SW* I 357, 411, 418; *Phil Briefe* IX: *SW* I 332 and n), Schiller (*AE* 150–2, 208–10) or Jacobi (*ULS* 118, 283). Maass first defines the imagination: "But all representations and modifications of the sense" (receptivity of impressions), "which are not really in it,

so far as it is affected by an object, must be produced through an active faculty of the same, which is distinguished from the Senses, and may be called the Imagination in the widest sense." Maass p 2 (§ 1), tr SC *BL* (1847) I 128. On p 326 (§ 92) Maass speaks of "the voluntary and involuntary series of imaginations", which may be taken as another way of expressing the active-passive quality. C's marginalia on Schelling *STI* show how crucial C thought the whole question, for the active power of the imagination would seem to rest on the direction of the will. Cf part of a note on a front flyleaf: ". . . so far that all Schelling's 'Contradictions' are reducible to the one difficulty of comprehending the co-existence of the Attributes, Agere et Pati, in the same subject . . ." (Schelling says that the imagination

intermediate faculty in all its degrees and determinations, the IMAGINATION.[1] But in common language, and especially on the subject of poetry, we appropriate the name to a superior degree of the faculty, joined to a superior voluntary controul over it.)

Contemporaneity then, being the common condition of all the laws of association, and a component element in all the materia subjecta,[2] the parts of which are to be associated, must needs be co-present with all. Nothing, therefore, can be more easy than to pass off on an incautious mind this constant companion of each, for the essential substance of all. But if we appeal to our own consciousness,[3] we shall find that even *time* itself, as the *cause* of a *particular* act of association, is distinct from contemporaneity, as the *condition* of *all* association.[4] Seeing a mackarel it may happen, that I immediately think of gooseberries, because I at the same time ate mackarel with gooseberries as the sauce. The first syllable of the latter word, being that which had co-existed with the image of the bird so called, I may then think of a goose. In the next moment the image of a swan may arise before me, though I had never seen the two birds together. In the two former instances, I am conscious that their co-existence in *time* was the circumstance, that enabled me to recollect them; and equally conscious am I, that the latter was recalled to me by the joint operation of likeness and contrast. So it is with *cause* and *effect*; so too with *order*. So

---

resolves all "contradictions" of experience and existence). Cf also two of C's back-flyleaf notes: "The whole difficulty lies in the co-existence of Agere et Pati as Predicates of the same Subject." ". . . What after all does the problem amount to more than the Fact, that the Will is a vis motrix, and the Mind a *directive* power . . .". *CM* (*CC*) IV. See Engell *CI* 338–9, 344–5, 359–61 and Introd, above, I lxxxiv, lxxxix–xcii.

[1] This and the next sentence point to the concluding paragraphs of ch 13, below, I 304–6. For C the active potential of the imagination seems determined by the will. Having noted the active-passive quality, C now proceeds to remark that there is a heightened "poetic" power and presumably a superior will or "superior voluntary controul" exercised in it.

This division of the imagination was fairly common in the Germans C had read (who in turn had been influenced by British writers like Alexander Gerard). See Introd, above, I lxxxi–xcvii, Engell *CI* 343–6, and McFarland "SI" 195–202, 208–26.

[2] "Subject matter".

[3] The appeal to consciousness is related to subjective idealism in general but is also a standard position of transcendental philosophers, especially Fichte and Kant and—somewhat less so—Schelling.

[4] In the same way that gravity causes a ball to fall when released, but is only one condition affecting a train moving uphill. See above, I 123. So "time" or contemporaneity is a condition of all associations but only *causes* some.

am I able to distinguish whether it was proximity in time, or continuity in space, that occasioned me to recall B. on the mention of A. They cannot be indeed *separated* from contemporaneity; for that would be to separate them from the mind itself. The act of consciousness is indeed identical with *time* considered in its essence. (I mean *time* per se, as contra-distinguished from our *notion* of time; for this is always blended with the idea of space, which as the *contrary* of time, is therefore its *measure*.)[1] Nevertheless the accident of seeing two objects at the same moment acts, as a distinguishable cause from that of having seen them in the same place: and the true practical general law of association is this;[2]

[1] Cf *CN* I 334, 1771 and n; *P Lects* Lect 13 (1949) 389–390. Schelling (*STI*) remarks how space and time limit and are a measure of each other. Cf also *Abhandlungen: SW* I 356. See *BL* (1847) I 129n. Kant *KRV* "Transscendentale Aesthetik" Abschn 1–2 discusses time and space in terms somewhat similar to C's but does not seem the direct source of his remarks. For C's more general indebtedness to Kant on this subject see Orsini 93–7.

[2] C's own general law of association (and his discussion in the middle third of this paragraph generally) can be traced directly to his marginal note on Maass pp 27–9. On pp 27–8 (§ 12) Maass gives an example in which only one part of a total representation "B" is connected with only one part of another total representation "A"; in consequence of which this one part of "A" calls up not only all of "A" but all of "B" as well. C comments, "This seems to me a proof, that Likeness as co-ordinate with, but not always subordinate to, Time exerts an influence per se on the Association. Thus too as to Cause and Effect— they can not of course be *separated* from Contemporëity, but yet act *distinctly* from it. Thus too Contrast: and even Order. In short, whatever makes certain parts of a total impression more vivid or distinct, will determine the mind to recall these rather than others. Contemporëity seems to me the common condition under which all the determining Powers act rather than itself the effective Law." *CM* (*CC*) III. C's own "true practical general law", thus taken from his marginal note on Maass, significantly qualifies and nuances Maass's law, which in ch 6 C called the "law in its highest abstraction and most philosophical form". (Maass p 326 § 92 restates the law vis-à-vis Aristotle.) Maass states his law first on p 29 (§ 13), on which C's note concludes, and it probably caused C to react and to formulate his own "general law" at the time he read Maass. For comparison, Maass's own "allgemeine Associationsgesetz" (p 29) should be repeated here (see also ch 6): "With a given representation all [representations] can be associated, which belong with it to one total representation, but those *only* [which can be associated] *immediately;* or, as is also said, Every representation calls back into the mind its total representation." Tr SC *BL* (1847) I 116n. Maass explains that "immediately" means all the associations must inherently belong together in a group. They are not any random string of associations but are interconnected by previous experience so each will recall the others "immediately" in the mind. C objects to Maass's general law as being too

that whatever makes certain parts of a total impression more vivid
or distinct than the rest, will determine the mind to recall these in
preference to others equally linked together by the common condition of contemporaneity, or (what I deem a more appropriate
and philosophical term) of *continuity*. But the will itself by confining and intensifying* the attention may arbitrarily give vividness
or distinctness to any object whatsoever; and from hence we may
deduce the uselessness if not the absurdity of certain recent
schemes which *promise* an artificial *memory*,[2] but which in reality

---

* I am aware, that this word occurs neither in Johnson's Dictionary or in
any classical writer. But the word, "*to intend*," which Newton and others
before him employ in this sense, is now so completely appropriated to
another meaning, that I could not use it without ambiguity:[1] while to
paraphrase the sense, as by *render intense*, would often break up the sentence
and destroy that harmony of the position of the words with the logical
position of the thoughts, which is a beauty in all composition, and more
especially desirable in a close philosophical investigation. I have therefore
hazarded the word, *intensify*; though, I confess, it sounds uncouth to my
own ear.

---

universal and in his marginal note
gives the example of a view from the
top of St Paul's. See ch 6, above, I
111 and n 3, in which C also has
Maass's general law in mind.

[1] *OED* credits C as the first to use
the word and quotes this footnote.
Cf *CN* III 3273, 3759 and n. C perhaps coined the word by thinking of
an equivalent for the German "in-
tensiv grösser sein"; Maass uses this
construction (p 387) to discuss how
two objects are related in their
intensity of association, a discussion
related to his points on pp 27–9 on
which C is essentially commenting
in the middle of this paragraph. C
may have encountered the idea that
the will intensifies certain parts of
associations in Aquinas's commentaries on Aristotle. *BL* (1847) I
109n. Johnson in his second definition of "intend" ("To enforce; to
make intense . . .") cites Newton's
Optics, which C read: "Magnetism
may be *intended* and remitted, and
is found only in the magnet and in
iron".

[2] Cf *CN* I 1768. *Memoria technica* is a method of using mechanical

association to recall ideas or objects.
This would "debase" fancy, the
higher associations of which might
involve wit, new images, and certain
types of artistic creation. Though
Memoria technica was an ancient
and arcane method of impressing
places and images on the memory
(see Frances Yates *The Art of
Memory*), the "recent schemes" C
has in mind are probably Richard
Grey *Memoria Technica: or, A New
Method of Artificial Memory*
(1730), which went through many
editions to the mid-nineteenth century, and Gregor von Feinaigle *The
New Art of Memory . . . to Which Is
Prefixed Some Account of the Principal Systems of Artificial Memory*
(1812), the "art" being applied to
"Chronology, Geography, History,
Language, Systematic Tables, and
Poetry and Prose". Preface p iii.
Feinaigle, who had visited England,
gave public experiments of his sys-
tem at the Royal Institution 22 Jun
1811 and at the Surrey Institution 6
Apr 1812, both reported in the *M
Post* (to which C was then con-
tributing). Another possible work,

can only produce a confusion and debasement of the *fancy*. Sound logic, as the habitual subordination of the individual to the species, and of the species to the genus;[1] philosophical knowledge of facts under the relation of cause and effect; a chearful and communicative temper that disposes us to notice the similarities and contrasts of things, that we may be able to illustrate the one by the other; a quiet conscience; a condition free from anxieties, sound health, and above all (as far as relates to passive remembrance) a healthy digestion; *these* are the best, these are the only ARTS OF MEMORY.[2]

---

written by a disciple of Feinaigle, was Thomas Coglan *An Improved System of Mnemonics; or Art of Assisting the Memory* (1813), the Introduction of which frequently mentions the association of ideas.

[1] The subordination of the individual to the species was by this time a *leitmotif* in German philosophy, especially in its view of history. Some opposed this view, but Kant, Schelling, and Schiller agree that when the individual becomes truly aware and creative he submerges himself in the species. E.g. Schelling *Über das Wesen* (*SW* VII 293) and *Vorlesungen* (*SW* V 280, 237–8), Schiller *AE* 82. C's reading would have repeatedly exposed him to this idea expressed in words similar to his own.

[2] CF *P Lects* Lect 14 (1949) 395.

CHAPTER 8

The system of D U A L I S M *introduced by Des Cartes—Refined first by Spinoza and afterwards by Leibnitz into the doctrine of Harmonia præstabilita—Hylozoism—Materialism—Neither of these systems, on any possible theory of association, supplies or supersedes a theory of perception, or explains the formation of the associable*

T o   t h e best of my knowledge Des Cartes was the first philosopher, who introduced the absolute and essential hetero-geneity of the soul as intelligence, and the body as matter.[1] The assumption, and the form of speaking, have remained, though the denial of all other properties to matter but that of extension, on which denial the whole system of dualism is grounded, has been long exploded.[2] For since impenetrability is intelligible only as a mode of resistance; its admission places the essence of *matter* in an act or power, which it possesses in common with *spirit*;[3] and

[1] See esp *Principia philosophiae* (1644) pt I §§ 8, 53, 63–4; pt II §§ 1–2; *Meditations* (1641) esp II and VI. C repeats this observation in *P Lects* Lect 12 (1949) 349; cf also Lect 13 pp 376–7: ". . . I believe . . . that Descartes was the first man who made nature utterly lifeless and godless, considered it as the subject of merely mechanical laws". But C later adds that Descartes "was a truly great man".

[2] In particular by Leibniz in his *Lettre sur la question si l'essence du corps consiste dans l'étendue* (Paris 1691): *Opera* I 113 (cf *Nouveaux essais: Opera* I 250), in which resistance is added to extension as a property of matter. *BL* (1907) I 238; see also *BL* (1847) I 131n. From this sentence to the end of the fourth paragraph of this chapter ("defunct substance"), C essentially repeats in *P Lects* Lect 12, in which, however, he does not follow Schel-

ling quite so closely (see below, I 130 n 2, 132–6 and nn). *P Lects* (1949) 349–52.

[3] For this conclusion C appears to be drawing on Kant's *Metaphysische Anfangsgründe der Naturwissenschaft* (2nd ed Riga 1787, the ed C read and annotated), a work from which he translates at the beginning of the next paragraph and which he names in ch 9, below, I 153. Kant states that impenetrability is a form of repulsion and that "all reality of objects of external sense . . . is to be conceived as a moving force" (p 81). Cited by Orsini 199–200. Schelling discusses and refers to Kant's *Anfangsgründe* in his own *Ideen zu einer Philosophie der Natur* (Landshut 1803) 326–7 (*SW* II 231–2). The idea is essential to what Schelling calls "the dynamic process" and helped C to formulate his own interpretation of a "dynamic philos-ophy" joining the realms of matter

body and spirit are therefore no longer absolutely heterogeneous, but *may* without any *absurdity* be supposed to be different modes, or degrees in perfection, of a common substratum.[1] To this possibility, however, it was not the fashion to advert. The soul was a *thinking* substance; and body a *space-filling* substance. Yet the apparent action of each on the other pressed heavy on the philosopher on the one hand; and no less heavily on the other hand pressed the evident truth, that the law of causality holds only between homogeneous things, i.e. things having some common property; and cannot extend from one world into another, its opposite.[2] A close analysis evinced it to be no less absurd, than the question whether a man's affection for his wife, lay North-east, or South-west of the love he bore towards his child?[3] Leibnitz's doctrine of a pre-established harmony, which he certainly borrowed from Spinoza,[4] who had himself taken the hint from Des Cartes's

---

and spirit. Today we know that matter *is* normally "impenetrable" because of atomic forces. When we touch something, the atoms in our hand never materially come in contact with the object. They are repulsed at a very small distance by electromagnetic forces on an atomic scale. Similarly light has both corpuscular and wave properties (both "matter" and "force"—or "spirit", as C calls it). The whole dualistic hypothesis and a search for "a common substratum" is still a fundamental question in physics and in neurophysiology.

[1] For "substratum", "substrate", and C's possible use of Schelling concerning these terms in this context see ch 9, below, I 143.

[2] This sentence, beginning "Yet the apparent action", C has loosely paraphrased from Schelling *STI* 112–13 (*SW* III 406–7), in which it appears in a similar context: "Gesetzt auch, dass ein Object auf das Ich, wie auf ein Object wirke, so könnte doch eine solche Affection immer nur etwas Homogenes, d.h. wiederum nur ein objectives Bestimmtseyn hervorbringen. Denn das Gesetz der Causalität gilt nur zwis-

chen gleichartigen Dingen (Dingen derselben Welt), und reicht nicht aus einer Welt in die andere." Tr SC *BL* (1847) I 134n, omitting the crucial second sentence of Schelling quoted here. Cf *P Lects* Lect 4 (1949) 145, in which C credits the germ of this idea to Pythagoras.

[3] A favourite illustration of C's, used e.g. in an annotation on John Petvin *Letters Concerning Mind* (1750) 41 (*CM—CC*—III) and in *P Lects* Lect 12 (1949) 350.

[4] Leibniz's doctrine of "pre-established harmony", to the complexity of which C is hardly doing justice, is in no way "borrowed from Spinoza". In fact, in a marginal note (ii 8) on Descartes' *Opera philosophica* (1685), referring to *De passionibus* pt I xvi, C himself had written: "Can the Bruckers and German Manualists have read this work of Des Cartes . . . that they should (one, I guess, copying from the other) talk of Spinoza's having given Leibnitz the *Hint* of his pre-established Harmony?—What is this XVIth Article if not a clear & distinct statement of the Theory?" *CM* (*CC*) II. C refers to Johann Jakob Brucker (1696–1770) and his *His-*

animal machines,[1] was in its *common* interpretation too strange to survive the inventor—too repugnant to our *common sense*[2] (which is not indeed entitled to a judicial voice in the courts of scientific philosophy; but whose whispers still exert a strong secret influence.) Even Wolf the admirer, and illustrious systematizer of the Leibnitzian doctrine, contents himself with defending the possibility of the idea, but does not adopt it as a part of the edifice.[3]

The hypothesis of Hylozoism[4] on the other side, is the death

toria critica philosophiae (4 vols Leipzig 1742–4) IV pt II. In the ed C borrowed from the Bristol Library in 1797 (6 vols Leipzig 1766–7) see esp IV pt II p 384. See also *BL* (1847) I 132–3 n 5.

C's opinion is no doubt coloured by Jacobi *ULS* Beylage VI (361–97), a section C quotes from in chs 12 and 13, below, I 244–7, 295–6, and which he read with great care. Jacobi minutely discusses Leibniz's debt to Spinoza and to Descartes' disciples for the principle of pre-established harmony. See esp pp 34–5, 361, 367, 375–6 and n, 381. C may also be drawing on Schelling *Ideen* Einleitung (which he uses later in this chapter) 14 (*SW* II 20): "Der *erste, der Geist und Materie mit vollem Bewusstseyn als Eines, Gedanke und Ausdehnung nur als Modifikationen desselben Princips ansah, war Spinoza.*"

[1] For Descartes' "animal machines" see *De methodo* v.

[2] The "*common* interpretation" of pre-established harmony that C refers to is superficially paralleled by Descartes' mechanism, especially as developed in the direction of "occasionalism" (see ch 5, I 93–4, above, on La Forge), in which object and subject are made to coincide by the direct interposition of God. *BL* (1907) I 238 mentions the Cartesian disciple Arnold Geulincx (1624–69), who, like Leibniz, uses the metaphor of two watches working in unison not because of any mutual influence but because they have been previously fashioned to synchronise. But

for Geulincx God's action is direct and constant, whereas for Leibniz (who thought the occasionalist concept of God a *deus ex machina*) the internal nature of things is so created as to mediate and carry out the will of God. Cf *BL* (1847) I 132n. Part of C's front flyleaf marginal note in Maass connects pre-established harmony, the watch metaphor, the imagination, and the phenomenon of perception: "In order to render the creative activity of the Imagination at all conceivable, we must necessarily have recourse to the Harmonia præstabilita of Spinoza and Leibnitz: in which case the automatism of the Imagination and Judgement would be Perception in the same sense, as a ⟨self-conscious⟩ Watch would be a Percipient of Time, and inclusively of the apparent motion of the Sun and Stars." *CM* (*CC*) III. But when C wrote this he expressed misgivings about pre-established harmony in favour of "the natural doctrine of physical influx". See below, I 137–8 n 6.

[3] Christian Wolff (1679–1754), professor of mathematics and natural philosophy at Halle (though see ch 9, below, I 154–5 n 3), who attempted to methodise the philosophy of Leibniz. In the process much that was distinctive in Leibniz was lost or discarded, particularly his concept of pre-established harmony. For C's interest and reading in Wolff see esp *CN* I 891, 902, 905; II 2219, 2382; III 3256, 3271, 3594 and nn.

[4] The doctrine that all matter is part of life or being; or, that life

of all rational physiology, and indeed of all physical science;[1] for that requires a limitation of terms, and cannot consist with the arbitrary power of multiplying attributes by occult qualities. Besides, it answers no purpose; unless indeed a difficulty can be solved by multiplying it, or that we can acquire a clearer notion of our soul, by being told that we have a million souls, and that every atom of our bodies has a soul of its own. Far more prudent is it to admit the difficulty once for all, and then let it lie at rest. There is a sediment indeed at the bottom of the vessel, but all the water above it is clear and transparent. The Hylozoist only shakes it up, and renders the whole turbid.[2]

But it is not either the nature of man, or the duty of the philosopher to despair concerning any important problem until, as in the squaring of the circle, the impossibility of a solution has been demonstrated.[3] How the *esse* assumed as originally distinct from the *scire*, can ever unite itself with it;[4] how *being* can transform

cannot exist without matter. From *hyle* (matter) and *zoē* (life).

[1] C in this sentence, as McFarland points out (356), is initially translating the second of the following two sentences from Kant's *Metaphysische Anfangsgründe:* "Auf dem Gesetze der Trägheit . . . beruht die Möglichkeit einer eigentliche Naturwissenschaft ganz und gar. Das Gegenteil des erstern, und daher auch der Tod aller Naturphilosophie, wäre der *Hylozism.*" In his copy (1787) 121, C wrote a brief note on the first sentence.

[2] C here echoes a notebook entry of 1801: "Materialists unwilling to admit the mysterious of our nature make it all mysterious—nothing mysterious in nerves, eyes, &c: but that nerves think &c!!—Stir up the sediment into the transparent water, & so make all opaque." *CN* ɪ 920 and n. C viewed modern materialism as stressing the organisation of atoms, whereas ancient materialists tended to consider each atom possessed with the complex qualities of matter at large. See *P Lects* Lect 12 (1949) 345–8 esp 348, and below, ɪ 133–4.

[3] A favourite example of logic in C—e.g. above, ch 7, ɪ 121 n 3.

[4] Most of this sentence and all of the next (from "How the *esse*" to "what it promises") are, with the exception of the two phrases "either as a property or attribute, or as an hypostasis or self subsistence", translated from Schelling *STI* 113 (*SW* ɪɪɪ 407), taken from the point where C left off in his paraphrase above, ɪ 130. By adding the two "i.e." phrases C makes the argument more subtle, but Schelling elsewhere dismisses the possibility that matter has self-subsistence. This second assumption of hypostasis or self-subsistence, which C does not discuss here, could lead to the pantheistic view that matter must be part of all "being" and hence of God. The sentence in *STI* from which C takes his two is: "Wie also ein ursprüngliches Seyn sich in ein Wissen verwandle, wäre nur dann begreiflich, wenn sich zeigen liesse, dass auch die Vorstellung selbst eine Art des Seyns sey, welches allerdings die Erklärung des Materialismus ist, ein System, das dem Philosophen erwünscht seyn müsste, wenn es nur wirklich leistete, was es

itself into a *knowing*, becomes conceivable on one only condition; namely, if it can be shown that the vis representativa, or the Sentient, is itself a species of being; i.e. either as a property or attribute, or as an hypostasis or self subsistence. The former is indeed the assumption of materialism; a system which could not but be patronized by the philosopher, if only it actually performed what it promises. But how any affection from without can metamorphose itself into perception or will; the materialist has hitherto left, not only as incomprehensible as he found it, but has aggravated it into a comprehensible absurdity. For, grant that an object from without could act upon the conscious *self*, as on a consubstantial object; yet such an affection could only engender something homogeneous with itself.[1] Motion could only propagate motion. Matter has no *Inward*.[2] We remove one surface, but to meet with another. We can but divide a particle into particles; and each atom comprehends in itself the properties of the material universe. Let any reflecting mind make the experiment of explaining to itself the evidence of our sensuous intuitions, from the hypothesis that in any given perception there is a something which has been communicated to it by an impact or an impression ab extra.[3] In the first place, by the impact on the percipient or ens representans not the object itself, but only its action or effect, will pass into the same.[4] Not the iron tongue, but its vibrations, pass into the metal

---

verspricht." For SC's translation, which differs slightly from C's, see *BL* (1847) I 134n. Cf also Schelling *Abhandlungen: Phil Schrift* 222 (*SW* I 365–6).

[1] The essence of this and the previous sentence is, again, from Schelling *STI* 112–13. In particular, C's last clause ("yet such . . . with itself") recapitulates Schelling's "so könnte doch eine solche Affection immer nur etwas Homogenes . . . hervorbringen". Cf above, I 130 n 2.

[2] This statement and its explanation, finishing with "particle into particles", are taken from several places in Schelling: *Abhandlungen: Phil Schrift* 240 (*SW* I 379): "Daher der Materie kein *Innres* zukommt." And earlier (same p): "Was *Materie* . . . ist, mögen wir in's Unendliche fort analysiren, mechanisch oder

chemisch theilen, wir kommen nie weiter als bis zu *Oberflächen* von Körpern." For a fuller quotation and translation see *BL* (1847) I 135n. But SC gives more than C uses. See also Schelling *Ideen* Einleitung 22 (*SW* II 25): "Ihr mögt theilen ins Unendliche, und kommt doch nie weiter, als bis zu Oberflächen der Körper." C may also have in mind a similar passage at p 17 (*SW* II 22).

[3] This sentence connects basic questions and terms C both formulated himself and picked up not only in Schelling but also in Tetens, Maass, Berkeley, Fichte, and Kant. Cf *TT* 15 May 1833.

[4] C here translates from Schelling *STI* 149 (*SW* III 428): "Vorerst wird durch Anstoss auf das vorstellende Wesen nicht der Gegenstand selbst, sondern nur seine Wirkung in

of the bell. Now in our immediate perception, it is not the mere power or act of the object, but the object itself, which is immediately present.[1] We might indeed attempt to explain this result by a chain of *deductions* and *conclusions*; but that, first, the very faculty of deducing and concluding would equally demand an explanation; and secondly, that there exists in fact no such intermediation by logical notions, such as those of cause and effect. It is the object itself, not the product of a syllogism, which is present to our consciousness. Or would we explain this supervention of the object to the sensation, by a productive faculty set in motion by an impulse; still the transition, into the percipient, of the object itself, from which the impulse proceeded, assumes a power that can permeate and wholly possess the soul,

> And like a God by spiritual art,
> Be all in all, and all in every part.
>   C O W L E Y.[2]

And how came the *percipient* here? And what is become of the wonder-promising M A T T E R, that was to perform all these marvels

---

dasselbe übergehen." Cf *Abhand-lungen: Phil Schrift* 237 *SW* I 377). Orsini 204.

[1] Translated from Schelling *STI* 149 (*SW* III 428), continuing from where C had used Schelling above but interpolating the image of the bell. In *STI:* "Nun ist aber in der Anschauung nicht die blosse Wirkung eines Gegenstands, sondern der *Gegenstand selbst* unmittelbar gegenwärtig." Orsini 204. Beginning with the next sentence ("We might indeed") and continuing until the two lines quoted from Cowley, C continues to draw from Schelling where he had left off in the previous sentence. But now C's translation is at once more condensed and somewhat looser (*STI* 149–50): "Wie nun zu dem Eindruck der Gegenstand ["this result"] hinzu komme, könnte man wohl etwa durch Schlüsse zu erklären versuchen, wenn nur nicht in der Anschauung selbst schlechthin nichts von einem Schlusse, oder einer Vermittlung durch Begriffe, etwa die der Ursache

und Wirkung vorkäme, und wenn es nicht der Gegenstand selbst, nicht ein blosses Product des Syllogismus wäre, was in der Anschauung vor uns steht. [C has changed the mood from the subjunctive to the indicative.] Oder man könnte das Hinzukommen des Gegenstands zur Empfindung aus einem producirenden Vermögen erklären, das durch äusseren Impuls in Bewegung gesetzt ist, so würde nie das unmittelbare Uebergehen des äussern Gegenstands, dessen, von welchem der Eindruck herrührt, in das Ich erklärt werden, man müsste denn den Eindruck oder den Anstoss von einer Kraft ableiten, welche die Seele ganz besitzen und gleichsam durchdringen könnte."

[2] *All-over Love* lines 9–10 (altered):

> But like a God by pow'rful Art,
> 'Twas *all* in *all*, and *all* in every *part*.

In C's ed, Abraham Cowley *Works* (1681) i 25.

by force of mere figure, weight, and motion?[1] The most consistent proceeding of the dogmatic materialist is to fall back into the common rank of *soul-and-bodyists*; to affect the mysterious, and declare the whole process a revelation *given*, and not to be *understood*, which it would be prophane to examine too closely. Datur non intelligitur.[2] But a revelation unconfirmed by miracles, and a faith not commanded by the conscience, a philosopher may venture to pass by, without suspecting himself of any irreligious tendency.

Thus as materialism has been generally taught, it is utterly unintelligible,[3] and owes all its proselytes to the propensity so common among men, to mistake distinct images for clear conceptions;[4] and vice versa, to reject as inconceivable whatever from its own nature is unimaginable. But as soon as it becomes intelligible, it ceases to be materialism.[5] In order to explain

[1] Parts of the following until "Datur non intelligitur" are translated from or have been suggested by the same passage in Schelling C has been using (*STI* 149–50: *SW* III 428–9). Where C says "The most consistent proceeding of the dogmatic materialist is to fall back" and "to affect the mysterious, and declare the whole process a revelation *given*, and not to be *understood*", Schelling says: "Es ist also immer noch das consequenteste Verfahren des Dogmatismus . . . in's Geheimnissvolle zu spielen, und davon als von einer Offenbarung zu sprechen, welche alle weitere Erklärung unmöglich macht . . .". This is the part of the last five sentences of C's paragraph that he translates more directly from Schelling; but all the first four sentences are expressive of Schelling's position and argument.
[2] "It is given, not understood".
[3] The first part of the sentence C has translated from Schelling *STI* 113. In this curious "hop-skip" process, C returns to precisely where he left off (at I 132–3 n 4, above); not a word has been omitted. In Schelling: "Allein so wie der Materialismus bis jetzt ist, ist er völlig unverständlich . . ." (*SW* III 407).

[4] For C on clear conceptions vs distinct images cf e.g. his letter to WW of 30 May 1815: ". . . for the philosophy of mechanism . . . in every thing that is most worthy of the human Intellect strikes *Death,* and cheats itself by mistaking clear Images for distinct conceptions, and . . . idly demands Conceptions where Intuitions alone are possible or adequate to the majesty of the Truth". *CL* IV 575. Cf also *Friend* (*CC*) II 71–2 (I 106), *EOT* (*CC*) I 370.
[5] For this and the next sentence C again, without omitting a word of Schelling's, returns to *STI* 113 and this time more loosely translates, substituting Schelling's contrast of materialism to transcendental idealism with the phrase "ceases to be materialism", and effectively altering "das Denken und die Materie" into *"perceiving"* and *"appearing"*. In Schelling: ". . . und so wie er [Materialismus] verständlich wird, ist er vom transscendentalen Idealismus in der That nicht mehr verschieden.—Das Denken als eine materielle Erscheinung zu erklären, ist nur dadurch möglich, dass man die Materie selbst zu einem Gespenst, zur blossen Modification einer Intelligenz macht,

thinking, as a material phænomenon, it is necessary to refine matter into a mere modification of intelligence, with the two-fold function of *appearing* and *perceiving.* Even so did Priestley in his controversy with Price![1] He stript matter of all its material properties; substituted spiritual powers; and when we expected to find a body, behold! we had nothing but its ghost! the *apparition* of a defunct substance!

I shall not dilate further on this subject; because it will (if God grant health and permission) be treated of at large and systematically in a work, which I have many years been preparing, on the PRODUCTIVE LOGOS human and divine; with, and as the introduction to, a full commentary on the Gospel of St. John.[2] To make myself intelligible as far as my present subject requires, it will be sufficient briefly to observe—1. That all association demands and presupposes the existence of the thoughts and images

deren gemeinschaftliche [C's "twofold"] Functionen das Denken und die Materie sind." Schelling's "matter as a ghost" ("Materie selbst zu einem Gespenst") appears in the penultimate exclamation of C's paragraph (*SW* III 407).

[1] C refers to the correspondence of Priestley and Richard Price (1723–91) published in *A Free Discussion of the Doctrines of Materialism and Philosophical Necessity, in a Correspondence Between Dr. Priestley and Dr. Price* (1778). Priestley's position was that of a materialistic determinist, whereas Price argued for the immateriality of the soul and for free will.

[2] C's *magnum opus* described to Daniel Stuart 12 Sept 1814 as "my most important work. . . . The title is: Christianity the one true Philosophy—or 5 Treatises on the Logos, or communicative Intelligence, Natural, Human, and Divine." The third treatise was to consist of "a full Commentary on the Gospel of St John". *CL* III 533. The following year, just as he completed *BL,* he described it again to John May (27 Sept 1815) as "a work, which has employed all my best thoughts &

efforts for the last twelve years and more, and on which I would ground my reputation. . . . This work will be entitled LOGOSOPHIA: or on the LOGOS, divine and human, in six Treatises." The first is to be a history of philosophy from Pythagoras to the modern "dynamic" philosophy; the second a study of logic and systematic reasoning; the third a work "on the Dynamic or Constructive Philosophy—preparatory to the IV. or a detailed Commentary on the Gospel of St John"; the fifth "on the Pantheists and Mystics; with the Lives and Systems of Giordano Bruno, Jacob Behmen, George Fox, and Benedict Spinoza"; the sixth "on the Causes & Consequences of modern Unitarianism". *CL* IV 589–90. On the plan of the *magnum opus* and the problems generally see McFarland ch 4 (esp 191–5) and *C Life* (B) 181–203. In writing such a work C would be following a pattern established in the eighteenth century by several writers who blend psychology, metaphysics, intellectual history, and Biblical commentary, especially on the Gospel of St John. See Engell *CI* 222, 348, 363.

to be associated.[1]—2. The hypothesis of an external world exactly correspondent to those images or modifications of our own being, which alone (according to this system) we actually behold, is as thorough idealism as Berkeley's, inasmuch as it equally (perhaps, in a more perfect degree) removes all reality and immediateness of perception, and places us in a dream-world of phantoms and spectres,[2] the inexplicable swarm and equivocal generation of motions in our own brains.[3]—3. That this hypothesis neither involves the explanation, nor precludes the necessity, of a mechanism and co-adequate forces in the percipient, which at the more than magic touch of the impulse from without is to create anew for itself the correspondent object. The formation of a copy is not solved by the mere pre-existence of an original;[4] the copyist of Raphael's Transfiguration must repeat more or less perfectly the process of Raphael.[5] It would be easy to explain a thought from the image on the retina, and that from the geometry of light, if this very light did not present the very same difficulty.[6] We might as

[1] In his *Abhandlungen: Phil Schrift* 237–8 (*SW* I 377–8) Schelling presents three distinct statements that discuss somewhat the same topics as C takes up in numbered observations 1 but especially 2 and 3. The parallel here is not, however, by translation or paraphrase; it is of the most general nature.

[2] Cf Schelling *Abhandlungen: Phil Schrift* 217 (*SW* I 362): "Der Idealist in diesem Sinn ist einsam und verlassen mitten in der Welt, von Gespenstern überall umgeben." ("The Idealist in this sense is left lonely and forsaken in the midst of the world, surrounded on all sides by spectres.") Tr SC *BL* (1847) I 139n.

[3] The criticism of Berkeley's subjective idealism in this sentence is expressed more fully by C in his front flyleaf marginal note to Schelling's *STI*, which itself may have helped prompt the tack of C's criticism here. The note reads in part: "Berkley's Scheme is merely an evolution of the positions—All perception is reducible to Sensation; and all Sensation is exclusively *subjective* . . . Ergo, all Perception is merely

subjective/ 'Perceptum = percipi': or 'Dum percipitur, est.' The principium *cognoscendi* is raised into the principium *essendi*. . . . Sensation, I would say, is never merely subjective . . . but of all the *known* Syntheses of Subject + Object it is the *least* Objective; but for that reason still objective." *CM* (*CC*) IV. This argument is reflected in ch 12, below, I 254–63.

[4] The use of "copy" and "original" in discussing perception and its original, external object is found in a similar context in *Abhandlungen: Phil Schrift* 218 and n, 240 (*SW* I 362 and n, 378–9). The German words Schelling uses are *Copie* and *Original*. C may also be recalling Jean Paul Richter's observations in his *Geist* anthology (1801) § 4 I 28–30, especially: "in short the atheist refuses to admit that the *copy* has any *original*". *CN* III 4087n.

[5] *The Transfiguration*, commissioned by Giulio de' Medici in 1517, was left uncompleted at Raphael's death (1520).

[6] Cf Schelling *Ideen* 440 (*SW* II 307–8) but esp *Abhandlungen: Phil*

rationally chant the Brahmin creed of the tortoise that supported the bear, that supported the elephant, that supported the world, to the tune of "This is the house that Jack built."[1] The *sic Deo placitum est*[2] we all admit as the sufficient cause, and the divine goodness as the sufficient reason; but an answer to the whence? and why? is no answer to the how? which alone is the physiologist's concern. It is a mere sophisma pigrum,[3] and (as Bacon hath said) the arrogance of pusillanimity,[4] which lifts up the idol of a mortal's fancy and commands us to fall down and worship it, as a work of divine wisdom, an ancile or palladium fallen from heaven.[5] By the very same argument the supporters of the

Schrift 254n (*SW* I 389n): "Wir sehen nur dadurch, dass das Licht unsre Augen rührt, u.s.w.—Aber was ist denn das Licht selbst? Wiederum ein Objekt!" ("We see only because the light strikes our eyes etc.—But what then is light? Again an object!") Orsini 204. SC in *BL* (1847) cites Schelling *Ideen Einleitung* 22 (*SW* II 26): "Ihr untersucht wohl sehr scharfsinnig, wie das Licht . . . auf eure Sehnerven wirkt, auch wohl, wie das verkehrte Bild auf der Netzhaut, in eurer Seele doch nicht verkehrt, sondern gerade erscheint? Aber was ist denn dasjenige in euch, was dieses Bild auf der Netzhaut selbst wieder sieht, und untersucht, wie es wohl in die Seele gekommen seyn möge?" ("You curiously inquire how the light . . . works on your optic nerves; also how the image inverted on the *retina,* appears in your soul not inverted but straight. But again, what is that in you which itself sees this image on the *retina,* and inquires how it can have come into the soul.") Tr SC *BL* (1847) I 140n. Cf C's front flyleaf marginal note to Maass (continuing from where quotation of it stopped above, I 131 n 2): "But as the whole is but a choice of incomprehensibles, till the natural doctrine of physical influx, or modification of each by all, have been proved absurd, I shall still prefer it: & not doubt, that the

Pencil of Rays forms pictures on the Retina because I cannot comprehend how this Picture can excite a mental Fac-simile." *CM* (*CC*) III. It seems probable that C made this observation in Maass, who was somewhat of a rationalistic empiricist, before having studied Schelling with care.

[1] The prototype in English of the "accumulative" story; see C's Sonnet III, quoted above, I 27–8, C's n. For the Hindu cosmological legend of the tortoise supporting the world—with which C was familiar from several sources, e.g. Thomas Maurice *The History of Hindostan* (1795) and Locke *An Essay Concerning Human Understanding* bk II ch 13 § 19 and ch 23 § 2—cf *CN* III 3973 and n, *Logic* (*CC*) 169 and n.

[2] "Thus it is pleasing to God".

[3] "Slothful sophism", or, as C tr in *Logic,* "sophistry of indolence". See *Logic* (*CC*) 119 and n.

[4] *Novum Organum* bk I aph 88, which C copied into a notebook in 1801 from *Works* (1740) I 295 and which he quotes below, I 292–3. *CN* I 913 and n. "And what is worst of all, this very littleness of spirit [*pusillanimitas*] comes with a certain air of arrogance and superiority." Bacon *Works* ed J. Spedding, R. L. Ellis, and D. D. Heath (11 vols 1857–68) IV 87. Cf *EOT* (*CC*) III 167 and n.

[5] The safety of Rome was linked with that of the *ancile* ("shield")

Ptolemaic system might have rebuffed the Newtonian, and pointing to the sky with self-complacent * grin have appealed to *common sense*, whether the sun did not move and the earth stand still.[2]

* "And Coxcombs vanquish Berkeley with a grin." *Pope.*[1]

and the *Palladium* (image of Pallas Athene—Minerva—brought by Aeneas from Troy). Ovid *Fasti* 3.365–92, 6.419–24.

[1] Actually John Brown *An Essay on Satire: Occasion'd by the Death of Mr. Pope* (1745) line 224 (var); cf lines 223–4:

> Truth's sacred fort the exploded laugh shall win;

And coxcombs vanquish Berkley by a grin

In *B Poets* x 879. C's error of attribution is probably owing to the fact that Brown's poem was reprinted by Bp Warburton in his edition of Pope's *Works* (1751), before the *Essay on Man*. Cf *CN* III 4397 f 52ᵛ and n.

[2] Cf *AR* (1825) 228, Jacobi *ULS* 123, Kant *KRV* Preface xxii n.

CHAPTER 9

Is philosophy possible as a science, and what are its conditions? [1]— *Giordano Bruno—Literary aristocracy, or the existence of a tacit compact among the learned as a privileged order* [2]—*The author's obligations to the Mystics;—to Immanuel* [a] *Kant—The difference between the letter and the spirit of Kant's writings,* [3] *and a vindication of prudence in the teaching of philosophy—Fichte's attempt to complete the critical system—Its partial success and ultimate failure— Obligations to Schelling; and among English writers to Saumarez*

AFTER I had successively studied in the schools of Locke, Berkeley, Leibnitz, and Hartley, [4] and could find in neither of

a BL (1817): *Emanuel*

[1] Cf Kant *KRV* Einleitung VI (B 20–2): "How is metaphysics, as science, possible?" and "How is pure science possible?" Kant does not specifically ask whether "philosophy" is possible as a science but tends to equate "all pure philosophy" with the kind of *a priori* synthetic judgements found in metaphysics. Cf Kant *Prolegomena zu einer jeden künftigen Metaphysik* (Riga 1783) 4–7, and *Logic* (*CC*) 169. C, having disposed of materialism and (Berkeleyan) subjective idealism in chs 5–8, now embarks on his views of the transcendental or critical philosophy, especially as he encountered it in Kant and Kant's immediate inheritors. It is natural that the first inquiry of ch 9 (including C's question in the opening sentence, "is a system of philosophy . . . possible?") parallels the initial question in *KRV* and the *Prolegomena*.

[2] In this concept we may have the germ of C's "clerisy"; cf *C&S* (*CC*) 46 and n.

[3] The controversy of "letter" vs "spirit" was at the centre of all English theological disputes before

and in C's lifetime. See Rom 7.6 and 2 Cor. 3.6. By the mid-1790s the distinction between the *Geist* and *Buchstaben* of Kant and of the critical philosophy in general was common. Transcendental idealists, notably Fichte, made it a favourite topic: e.g. "Ueber Geist und Buchstab in der Philosophie in einer Reihe von Briefen" (1798: *SW* VIII 270–300), in which at the outset Fichte says that others have made use of this distinction. Schiller (*AE* 86n) and Schelling (*Abhandlungen: Phil Schrift* 275; *SW* I 404–5 and n; *Philosophische Briefe* I: *Phil Schrift* 123–4; *SW* I 288) also rely on the distinction. Kant himself made the distinction in "Erklärung auf Hrn. Schlettweins Herausforderung" *Vermischte Schriften* (1799) III 373. Cf below, I 163. C again separates the letter from the spirit of Kant in his marginalia to Tennemann's *Geschichte der Philosophie* VI (*P Lects* 427–8). The distinction between "letter" and "spirit" represented for C a fundamental approach to all writing, including the Bible.

[4] On the persistence of Hartley's

them an abiding place for my reason, I began to ask myself; is a system of philosophy, as different from mere history and historic classification,[a] possible? If possible, what are its necessary conditions? I was for a while disposed to answer the first question in the negative, and to admit that the sole practicable employment for the human mind was to observe, to collect, and to classify. But I soon felt, that human nature itself fought up against this wilful resignation of intellect; and as soon did I find, that the scheme taken with all its consequences and cleared of all inconsistencies was not less impracticable, than contra-natural. Assume in its full extent the position, *nihil in intellectu quod non prius in sensu,* without Leibnitz's qualifying *præter ipsum intellectum,*[1] and in the same sense, in which it was understood by Hartley and Condilliac: [2] and what Hume had demonstratively deduced from this concession [3] concerning cause and effect,[4] will apply with equal and crush-

[a] *BL* (1817) omits comma

influence on C longer than is commonly thought, at least until 1802, see Richard Haven *JHI* xx (1959) 477–94. Hartley had appealed to C in so many ways (*C Life*—B—12–13) as to have become a part of him; and in continuing to feel the need to answer Hartley, he shows the need to answer his own earlier self. See also above, I 106 n 1. On Berkeley as failing to provide an "abiding place" for his "reason", see a notebook entry of 1804: *CN* I 1842. Cf McFarland 158–9, 300–3.

[1] "There is nothing in the mind that was not before in the senses, except the mind itself". C repeats the remark and comments on it in *P Lects* Lect 13 (1949) 383. Cf also *Logic* (*CC*) 183–4, 226. The position, without Leibniz's qualification, is from Aristotle's *De anima* and was associated closely with Locke's philosophy. For an amusing anecdote on Boyer's translation of this axiom see an annotation on Baxter *Reliquiae*: *CM* (*CC*) I 354. Leibniz's qualification is best expressed in his commentary on Locke, *Nouveaux essais* bk II ch 1 § 8: "Nihil est in intellectu, quod non fuerit in sensu,

excipe: nisi ipse intellectus." *Opera* ed Erdmann I 223. Cf *CL* II 680–1.

[2] Etienne Bonnot de Condillac (1715–80), the French exponent and systematiser of Locke. Principal works include his *Traité des systèmes* (1749), the important *Traité des sensations* (1754), and his posthumous *Logique* (1781). For C on the last work see *P Lects* Lect 12 (1949) 363, 458–9 n 50 and *Logic* (*CC*) 6. See also ch 3, above, I 54 and n 2.

[3] "This concession" does not refer to Leibniz's qualification, but is "the position" as "understood by Hartley and Condilliac", i.e. the first postulate of a thoroughgoing empiricism, the acceptance of which would be a "concession" for C.

[4] What Hume had deduced, once he accepted the rigid empirical premise, is, as Kant explicitly points out in *KRV* Einleitung vi (B 20), that all synthetic *a priori* judgements concerning causes and their effect are impossible, which consequently makes all metaphysics "a mere delusion of pretended reason". C is saying that once a strictly empirical premise is conceded, none of Kant's

ing force to all the* other eleven categorical forms, and the logical functions corresponding to them. How can we make bricks without straw? Or build without cement? We learn all things indeed by *occasion* of experience; but the very facts so learnt force us inward on the antecedents, that must be pre-supposed in order to render experience itself possible. The first book of Locke's Essays (if the supposed error, which it labours to subvert,[2] be not a mere thing of straw, an absurdity, which, no man ever did, or indeed ever could believe) is formed on a σόφισμα Ἑτεροζητήσεως, and involves the old mistake of *cum hoc: ergo, propter hoc.*[3]

The term, Philosophy, defines itself as an affectionate seeking after the truth; but Truth is the correlative of Being.[4] This again

---

* Videlicet; quantity, quality, relation, and mode, each consisting of three subdivisions. Vide Kritik der reinen Vernunft, p. 95, and 106. See too the judicious remarks on [a] Locke and Hume.[1]

[a] *BL* (1817): in

---

categories may be trusted as objective operations of the mind. ("Cause and effect" is Kant's second category of "Relation".)

[1] Pp 95 and 106 of *KRV* contain respectively tables of the "logical function of the understanding in judgements" and of the "categories" corresponding to them. The "judicious remarks" are in *KRV* "Elementarlehre" § 14 (B 127–8), in which Kant asserts that the thorough empiricism of Locke does not admit *a priori* cognitions in forms such as "pure mathematics" and "general natural science", and that, though Hume realised that these sciences ought to have an *a priori* origin, he simply could not explain the unification of synthetic judgements in the understanding necessary for them and thus resorted to experience alone for the basis of all knowledge. In short, says Kant, Locke was too certain of the capabilities of reason and Hume too sceptical.

[2] I.e. the doctrine of innate ideas, *An Essay Concerning Human Understanding* bk I, "Neither Principles nor Ideas Are Innate".

[3] I.e. the fallacy of using an argu-

ment that proves something other than what is claimed to be proved, "the sophism of looking for something else", involving the mistake of "With this, therefore because of this". Cf ". . . Locke's whole Book (as far as it is different from Des Cartes) is one Σόφισμα ἑτεροζητήσεως — = the fallacy, that the Soil, Rain, Air, and Sunshine, *make* the Wheatstalk & it's Ear of Corn, because they are the conditions under which alone the seed can develope itself." To Brabant [? Jun 1815]: *CL* VI 1036. *BL* (1847) I 144n indicates Maass's use of "sophisma heterozeteseos". Maass (366) is criticising Locke, too, and C's sentence in *BL* parallels Maass's: "Sein ganzes System beruhte auf einem Trugschlusse, (einem *sophisma heterozeteseos*). Er verwechselte den Ursprung der Vorstellungen mit ihrer Entwickelung . . .". ("His [Locke's] whole system rested on a fallacy, a *sophisma heterozeteseos*. He confused the origin of representations with their development . . .".)

[4] To say that truth is the correlative of being, especially of a Supreme Being (which C implies

is no way conceivable, but by assuming as a postulate, that both are ab initio, identical and co-inherent; that intelligence and being are reciprocally each other's Substrate.[1] I presumed that this was a possible conception (*i.e.* that it involved no logical inconsonance) from the length of time during which the scholastic definition of the *Supreme Being*, as actus purissimus sine ullâ potentialitate,[2] was

later in the paragraph), and not of matter or of sensuous experience, is common either as a postulate or conclusion of many theological and philosophic system from Plato onwards. Cf e.g. Aquinas *Summa theologica* I qu 16 art 3, qu 87 art 1 on obj 3 and *Quaestiones disputatae de veritate* 1, which begins: "It seems that truth is exactly the same as being". Kant's *KRV* reaches a somewhat similar conclusion, but warns that we can have no accurate idea of exactly what this "Being" is, nor can we "prove" its existence. Kant speaks of "a transcendental substratum in our reason" that is "nothing other than the idea of one total reality". *KRV* "Elementarlehre" (B 603–4). Later (B 706), Kant views the hypothesis of a Supreme Being as "the substratum of the greatest possible unity of experience", an idea that becomes a law to us and from which we deduce the presence of a corresponding archetypal reason responsible for the all-embracing systematic unity of nature (B 722–3). In Kant the idea of being (*Wesen*) is at once based upon "the substratum" of truth (*Erkenntnis*) contained in the unity of our reason and its experience, even while our reason naturally assumes the idea of a higher reason or Supreme Being (*Urwesen* or *Wesen aller Wesen*) as a substratum for unity of human reason and experience. C's position therefore has definite similarities with Kant's in *KRV*. Also cf Jacobi *ULS* 268–77 but esp 402: "The principle of all knowledge is living existence", and 250, in which Jacobi identifies the being of God with

truth. In *Phil Briefe* VI: *Phil Schrift* 152–4n (*SW* I 308–9n) Schelling discusses the issue in relation to the limits of philosophy. See also Thesis I in ch 12, below, I 264.

[1] *OED* cites C (in an annotation on Jeremy Taylor) as the first to use the word "substrate" as a noun for "substratum". C, aside from the possibility of rendering Kant's *das Substratum,* may be anglicising Schelling's use of the noun *Substrat* (e.g. *Abhandlungen: Phil Schrift* 221; *SW* I 364–5). C also uses the word in *CL* IV 770.

[2] C gives a form of a common Scholastic definition of God, originating in Aristotle *Metaphysics* bks XII and XIII, and one on which is based the ontological proof of the existence of a Supreme Being. "The purest act/actuality without any potentiality". Kant in *KRV* denies the ultimate validity of this definition according to the concepts of pure reason, but C suggests (see below, I 154) that Kant did so either out of prudence or from the standpoint of a pure analysis of the speculative intellect alone, which must place "reflection" above the moral sense and conscience. This suggestion of C's is essentially correct. C may have encountered a similar definition of God as an "act" in Leibniz's *Epistola ad Wagnerum:* "God alone is true substance (being) free from any materiality since He is always the pure Act and, unlike matter, is not acted upon". *Opera* ed L. Dutens (6 vols 1768)—C's ed—II 228. C also is recalling the Scholastic split between "active" and "passive" powers: God has no "pas-

received in the schools of Theology, both by the Pontifician and the Reformed divines. The early study of Plato and Plotinus, with the commentaries and the THEOLOGIA PLATONICA, of the illustrious Florentine;[1] of Proclus,[2] and Gemistus[a] Pletho;[3] and at a later period of the "De Immenso et Innumerabili," and

---

[a] *BL* (1817): Gemistius

---

sive" potentiality (C's word *potentialitate* refers to this "passive" potentiality), that is, God acts but is not acted upon. For God as pure act in this sense cf Aquinas *Summa theologica* I q 25 art 1; I q 3 art 1, and I q 3 art 4: "Therefore since in God there is no (passive) potential . . . it follows that there is nothing in His essence [*essentia*] which is not in His existence." Schelling identifies this definition of God as pure act with Descartes and Spinoza and expresses it himself as: "The Highest towards which our ideas can raise themselves is . . . a Being in which all passivity ceases . . . and whose only law is its own Being." *Phil Briefe* VIII: *Phil Schrift* 173 (*SW* I 323); *Über das Wesen: Phil Schrift* 427 (*SW* VII 356), in which Schelling, in contrast to C, takes issue with the sufficiency of defining God as *Actus purissimus*. Cf *CM* (*CC*) I 232 (on Baxter *Catholick Theologie*), 694 (on Böhme *Works*).

[1] Marsilio Ficino (1433–99), president of the Platonic Academy founded in Florence by Cosimo de' Medici. His Latin translation of Plato with commentary (1482), influential in spreading knowledge of Plato, was followed by a Latin translation of Plotinus, published immediately after Ficino's death by Lorenzo de' Medici. His *Platonica theologica de immortalitate animorum* (1482), an erudite work that often confuses strictly Platonic with Neoplatonic doctrines, attempts to lead speculative intellects to God through philosophical discourse. C owned and annotated the 1525 ed

(he inscribed it "Messina, 9 Oct[r] 1805").

[2] Proclus (c 410–85), the greatest of the Athenian Neoplatonists, for whom reality is essentially "ideal" or mental, though this is so in an "objective" way because "universal consciousness" precedes and transcends all individual consciousness. His philosophy is essentially one of emanationism (as distinct from evolutionism involving creation through time), in which the One radiates the Many from itself as a necessary fulfilment of its own potentiality. On C's interest in him, which dates at least from the 1790s, see esp McFarland 356–7. Cf *CN* I 1626, 1727–8, 1740, and nn, II 2447 and n, and the extensive entries under "Proclus" in III. On 3 May 1812 HCR noted "a metaphysical tirade in which Coleridge declared that when many years ago he began to think on philosophy he set out from a passage in Proclus at the point where Schelling appears to be. And here with modifications he, Coleridge, has remained." *CRB* I 70.

[3] Georgius Gemistus Pletho (c 1355–1452), a Byzantine who settled in Mistra, Greece, and known as "the sage of Mistra", in effect introduced Plato to western Europe, thus beginning the overturning of the tyranny of Aristotelianism. At a session in Florence for the union of the Greek and Latin churches, he lectured (1438–9) on Plato and induced Cosimo de' Medici to found the Platonic Academy, of which Ficino was made president.

the "*De la causa, principio et uno,*" of the philosopher of Nola,[1] who could boast of a Sir Philip Sidney, and Fulke Greville among his patrons, and whom the idolaters of Rome burnt as an atheist in the year 1600;[a] had all contributed to prepare my mind for the reception and welcoming of the Cogito quia sum, et sum quia Cogito;[2] a philosophy of seeming hardihood, but cer-

[a] BL (1817): 1660;

[1] Giordano Bruno (c 1548–1600), born in Cicala near Nola, in the course of his peripatetic life spent two years in England (1583–5), during which he made the acquaintance of Sidney and Fulke Greville. Bruno's principal works include *De la causa, principio, ed uno* (1584), *De l'infinito universo e mondi* (1584), *De monade, numero, et figura* (1591), and *De immenso et innumerabilibus* (1591). Interest in Bruno was revived by the enlarged 2nd ed (1789) of Jacobi *ULS*, which includes an extensive excerpt of *De la causa, principio, ed uno* (pp 271–6n). C undoubtedly read this. In Bruno's philosophy, which influenced Schelling (cf esp Schelling's *Bruno* [1802]), the unity that pervades the varied phenomena of the universe is God—at once the "immanent cause" of all things and yet above them, as the universal permits and sustains the particular but is simultaneously distinct from it. See A. D. Snyder's article *MLN* XLII (1927) 426–36. But cf esp *CN* I 927–9, 1369, and nn, and the remarks on Bruno's concept of "polarity" and C's plan to write a life of him, in *Friend* (*CC*) I 94, 117–18. Cf *CN* I 1646. For general discussion of Bruno's place in "the German pantheistic inventory", see McFarland 245–51, who shows C's interest in him "as to some extent reflecting an understandable desire to be fully *au courant*" and adds (381–2) that C's confessed "obligation" to the "polar logic and dynamic philosophy of Giordano Bruno" is "more symbolical than functional". On this latter point, cf also Barfield 179–93. But C may have absorbed some of Bruno through Schelling as well as Jacobi *ULS*. See below, I 161, and ch 12, I 252–4 n 2, 267–8 n 1, 287 n 4.

[2] Prepared him, that is, for the starting-point "I think because I am, and am because I think". C, never sympathetic to the overall approach or system of Descartes, does *not* have in mind Descartes' famous statement, "I think, therefore I am", which he finds "objectionable" (see ch 12, below, I 275, C's n). C likely has in mind the treatment of the "I am" in relation to the "I think" by Kant and Fichte and possibly Schelling, for all of whom these two propositions were initially important and mutually connected. In sections of *KRV* that were by C's own admission of special difficulty and apparently of the greatest importance to him (see below, I 153), Kant states that the "Ich bin" or "*pure original* apperception" (also called the "transcendental unity of self-consciousness") can alone provide to our thought that unified sense of self which is necessary to give our existence an individual wholeness rather than a set of totally disjointed and purely sensuous experiences. Conversely, the "Ich denke" provides the only way in which we can understand, know, and synthetically connect (by an "*empirical apperception*") experiences and things in a self-conscious way that are not themselves derived merely from the self ("das Ich" alone, neither being nor

tainly the most ancient, and therefore presumptively the most natural.[1]

Why need I be afraid? Say rather how dare I be ashamed of the Teutonic theosophist, Jacob Behmen?[2] Many indeed, and gross

thinking). Hence our existence and knowledge depend on the mutual connection between the "Ich bin" and the "Ich denke". Although Kant starts initially from the "Ich bin", which in "an act of spontaneity" intuits the "Ich denke", the "Ich bin" would be totally inert and static without the "Ich denke" that alone makes us permeable by the world and by the manifold of experience. C also significantly states the theorem in its converse form, first "I think because I am", then followed by "I am because I think", an order that parallels Kant's reasoning (see *KRV* "Elementarlehre" §§ 15–18: B 129–40). When C says he was "prepared" for this "philosophy" he seems to mean, at least in part, for the critical philosophy as a whole, especially as founded by Kant. For more on Kant on this topic see Orsini 120–9.

The *Ich* is one of Fichte's two basic assumptions. The other, leaving aside the postulated *Nicht-Ich,* is the *absolutes Ich* or, as it may be interpreted, God. Fichte makes the individual *Ich* depend strictly on the action of itself, which C notes as a refinement of Kant that may go too far (see below, I 158 n 1, 279). Schelling's most characteristic form of expressing the combined propositions of "I am" and "I think" is "the act of self-affirmation" (*Selbstaffirmation*), in which the self affirms its own being through an activity such as thought or through the (artistic) creation of something outside the self—e.g., *STI* 452–72 (*SW* III 611–29). For C's use of this see ch 12, below, I 274–80.

[1] C says "the most ancient" because he considers "the very first revelation" of "the fundamental truth of all philosophy" to be found in God's statement (Exod 3.14), "I am that I am", which C feels ambiguously worded in English and would amend to "I am in that I am" (see ch 12, below, I 275, C's n). C believed Pythagoras to be the first true philosopher because he considered more than material substance and concentrated on "the inner being". *P Lects* Lect 2 (1949) 106–8.

[2] Jakob Böhme (1575–1624), the famous self-taught shoemaker of Görlitz. Beginning with his *Aurora, oder die Morgenröte im Aufgang* (1612), he developed a conception of God as the *Ungrund* (the "undifferentiated Absolute") whose will to self-intuition creates the "eternal generation of the Trinity", in which will is identified with the Father, heart with the Son, and the "moving life" proceeding from them with the Holy Spirit. Refinements, qualifications, and additions appeared in later works, among them his theological treatises *Von der Gnadenwahl* (1623) and his commentary on Genesis, *Mysterium Magnum* (1623). Though evil is sometimes seen as an accidental disruption of the cosmic harmony, Böhme also conceives it at times as an inevitable by-product of the "differentiation" of cosmic creativity, permitting the good to stand out by contrast as darkness is necessary for the conception, again by contrast, of light. McFarland argues persuasively that C became familiar with Böhme before the German Romantics did. *The Works of Jacob Behmen* ed G. Ward and T. Langcake (4 vols 1764–81) was easily available (C owned a copy and annotated it extensively), and C could easily have read in Böhme's *Aurora* while still at school, as he

were his delusions; and such as furnish frequent and ample occasion for the triumph of the learned over the poor ignorant *shoemaker*, who had dared think for himself. But while we remember that these delusions were such, as might be anticipated from his utter want of all intellectual discipline, and from his ignorance of rational psychology, let it not be forgotten that the latter defect he had in common with the most learned theologians of his age. Neither with books, nor with book-learned men was he conversant. A meek and shy quietist, his intellectual powers were never stimulated into fev'rous energy by crowds of proselytes, or by the ambition of proselyting. J A C O B B E H M E N was an enthusiast, in the strictest sense, as not merely distinguished, but as contra-distinguished, from a fanatic.[1] While I in part translate the following observations from a contemporary writer of the Continent,[2] let me be permitted to premise, that I might have transcribed the substance from memoranda of my own, which were written many years before his pamphlet[3] was given to the world; and that I prefer another's words to my own, partly as a tribute due to priority of publication; but still more from the pleasure of sympathy in a case where *coincidence* only was possible.[4]

Whoever[5] is acquainted with the history of philosophy, during

---

told Ludwig Tieck in Jul 1817. *CL* IV 751. Cf C's thought of writing about him in the list of projects both in 1795–6 and in 1803. *CN* I 174, 1646. For full discussion of C and Böhme, see McFarland 249–51, 325–32. Cf also *P Lects* Lect 11 (1949) 327, in which C repeats this passage from *BL* (to "from a fanatic", below).

[1] On "enthusiasm" vs "fanaticism" see above, I 30–1.

[2] Schelling.

[3] *Darlegung des wahren Verhältnisses der Naturphilosophie zu der verbesserten Fichte'schen Lehre* (Tübingen 1806; *SW* VII 1–126).

[4] For the complex relationships of coincidence and debt between C, Schelling, and Böhme as C viewed them, see below, I 161–3 and n 5.

[5] As SC in *BL* (1847) I 146n points out, this paragraph, with the exception of one sentence and several clauses, is taken from Schelling *Darlegung* 154–5 (*SW* VII 119–20): "Wer nur die Geschichte der Wissenschaften in den letzten Jahrhunderten kennt, wird darin einstimmen müssen, dass unter den Gelehrten derselben eine Art von geheimem und stillschweigendem Vertrag stattzufinden schien, über eine gewisse Gränze in der Wissenschaft nicht hinauszugehen [C's first sentence ends here; C renders *Wissenschaft* as "speculative science", natural in this context], und dass die so gerühmte Geistes- und Denkfreiheit jederzeit nur innerhalb dieser Gränze wirklich gegolten hat, kein Schritt ausserhalb derselben aber ungestraft und ungerochen gewagt werden durfte. [C then loosely translates only the second half of Schelling's next sentence] . . . dass selbst die

the two or three last centuries, cannot but admit, that there appears to have existed a sort of secret and tacit compact among the learned, not to pass beyond a certain limit in speculative science. The privilege of free thought, so highly extolled, has at no time been held valid in actual practice, except within this limit; and not a single stride beyond it has ever been ventured without bringing obloquy on the transgressor. The few men of genius among the learned class, who actually did overstep this boundary, anxiously avoided the appearance of having so done. Therefore the true depth of science, and the penetration to the inmost centre, from which all the lines of knowledge diverge to their ever distant circumference, was abandoned to the illiterate and the simple, whom unstilled yearning, and an original ebulliency of spirit, had urged to the investigation of the indwelling and living ground of all things. These then, because their names had never been inrolled in the guilds of the learned, were persecuted by the registered livery-men as interlopers on their rights and priviledges. All with-

---

geistreichsten Männer, die sie [die Grenze] wirklich überschritten, wie Leibnitz [C omits this reference to Leibniz], doch den Schein davon vermieden. Daher blieb denn eben rechte Tiefe der Wissenschaft, und die wirkliche Durchdringung aller Theile der Erkenntniss [literally "of all segments of knowledge", a phrase C omits] mit dem innersten Centrum [C here adds "from which all the lines of knowledge diverge to their ever distant circumference"] derselben, den Ungelehrten und Einfältigen überlassen, welche nichtgestillte Sehnsucht und ursprüngliche Begeisterung zur Erforschung des innwohnenden und lebendigen Grundes aller Dinge hinzog. Diese dann, weil sie nicht gelehrt waren [C renders "because they were not learned" as "because their names had never been inrolled in the guilds of the learned"] und den Neid der so sich nennenden Gelehrten erregten [C changes "and excited the envy of the so-called learned" to "were persecuted by the registered livery-men as interlopers on their rights and priviledges" and there ends his own sentence], wurden von diesen alle ohne Unterschied als

Schwärmer bezeichnet; nicht nur jene, deren wilde und ausschweifende Phantasie wirklich nur abentheuerliche Phantome geboren hatte, und die meist schon ausgeartete Abkömmlinge von ursprünglich Begeisterten waren, sondern auch diese selbst [C renders Schelling's simple pronoun "those themselves" as "the truly inspired likewise, the originals themselves" and there ends his own sentence] und zwar lediglich darum, weil sie Nicht-Gelehrte oder [C omits "or"] Menschen von einfältigem und schlichtem Wandel waren. [C now interpolates the sentence "When . . . unto babes' ".]" C simply paraphrases the rest of Schelling's paragraph, which in Schelling reads literally: "In such a way the arrogance of the learned and of the schools drove them out and put them under a ban in all the marketplaces of science, even banished them from the temples, where meanwhile the sellers and buyers busied themselves and the money-changers opened their tables." C repeats the whole of his own paragraph with slight variations in *P Lects* Lect 11 (1949) 327–8.

out distinction were branded as fanatics and phantasts; not only those, whose wild and exorbitant imaginations had actually engendered only extravagant and grotesque phantasms, and whose productions were, for the most part, poor copies and gross caricatures of genuine inspiration; but the truly inspired likewise, the originals themselves! And this for no other reason, but because they were the *unlearned*, men of humble and obscure occupations. When, and from whom among the literati by profession, have we ever heard the divine doxology repeated, "I thank thee O father! Lord of Heaven and Earth! because thou hast hid these things from the wise and prudent, and hast revealed them unto babes."[1] No! the haughty priests of learning, not only banished from the schools and marts of science all, who had dared draw living waters from the *fountain*,[2] but drove them out of the very temple, which mean time "*the buyers, and sellers, and moneychangers*" were suffered to make "*a den of thieves.*"[3]

And[4] yet it would not be easy to discover any substantial ground for this contemptuous pride in those literati, who have most distinguished themselves by their scorn of Behmen, De Thoyras,[5] George Fox,[6] &c.; unless it be, that *they* could

---

[1] Luke 10.21 (var). Cf C's attitude in ch 12, below, I 232–3. Cf also William Penn's Preface to George Fox's *Journal* (3rd ed 1765) xxvii: ". . . he was an original, being no man's copy. . . . So that I have many times been overcome in myself, and been made to say . . . 'I thank thee, O Father, Lord of heaven and earth, that thou hast hid these things from the wise and the prudent of the world, and revealed them to babes;' for many times hath my soul bowed in an humble thankfulness to the Lord, that he did not choose any of the wise and learned of this world to be the first messenger in our age of his blessed truth to man . . .". For C's reading of the *Journal* see *CN* III 4409 and n.

[2] C echoes Jer 2.13, in which God speaks of Himself as "the fountain of living waters".

[3] Matt 21.12–13 (var).

[4] As SC in *BL* (1847) I 146–7n points out, C in the first sentence of this paragraph continues to draw

from Schelling *Darlegung* 155–6 (*SW* VII 120) but varies it. SC translates Schelling: "So now too may Herr Fichte speak of these enthusiasts with the most heartfelt scholar's pride, although it is not easy to see why he exalts himself so altogether above them, unless it is because *he* can write orthographically, can form periods, and has the fashions of authorship at command; while they, according to their simplicity, just as they found it, so gave it utterance."

[5] De Thoyras—presumably the French historian Paul de Rapin, Sieur de Thoyras (1661–1725)—is almost certainly a slip by C or Morgan as he recorded C's dictation. SC persuasively suggests that C meant to say "Taulerus", referring to the German mystic Johann Tauler of Strassburg (c 1300–61). See *BL* (1847) I 148–9n.

[6] George Fox (1624–91), founder of the "Society of Friends". Cf C's mention of Fox as one of the

write orthographically, make smooth periods, and had the fashions of authorship almost literally *at their fingers ends*, while the latter, in simplicity of soul, made their words immediate echoes of their feelings. Hence the frequency of those phrases among them, which have been mistaken for pretences to immediate inspiration; as for instance, *"it was delivered unto me," "I strove not to speak," "I said, I will be silent," "but the word was in heart as a burning fire," "and I could not forbear."* [1] Hence too the unwillingness to give offence; hence the foresight, and the dread of the clamours, which would be raised against them, so frequently avowed in the writings of these men, and expressed, as was natural, in the words of the only book, with which they were familiar.[2] "Woe is me that I am become a man of strife, and a man of contention,—I love peace: the souls of men are dear unto me: yet because I seek for Light every one of them doth curse me!"[3] O! it requires deeper feeling, and a stronger imagination, than belong to most of those, to whom reasoning and fluent expression have been as a trade learnt in boyhood, to conceive with what *might*, with what inward *strivings* and *commotion*, the perception of a new and vital TRUTH takes possession of an uneducated man of genius. His meditations are almost inevitably employed on the eternal, or the everlasting; for *"the world is not his friend, nor the world's law."* [4] Need we then be surprised, that under an excitement at once so strong and so unusual, the man's body should sympathize with the

"Revolutionary Minds" about whom he hoped to write (1803). *CN* I 1646.

[1] These seem formulaic phrases, found, as C suggests, in several authors. E.g. "and I could not forbear" appears in *The Visions of John Bunyan, Being His Last Remains* (?1720) 8, 112.

[2] *BL* (1847) appends a footnote to this, not in square brackets and therefore presumably from the C-annotated copy with which HNC and SC were working: "An American Indian, with little variety of images, and a still scantier stock of language, is obliged to turn his few words to many purposes, by likenesses so clear and analogies so remote as to give his language the semblance and character of lyric poetry interspersed with the grotesques. Something not unlike this was the case of such men as Behmen and Fox with regard to the Bible. It was their sole armory of expressions, their only organ of thought."

[3] Though untraced, the passage suggests Fox (the use of "Light" and reference to a "man of contention"), whom C may also refer to, below, as one for whom neither the world nor the world's law was a "friend". This would echo comments on the law in Fox's *Journal*. But C implies a group of men like Fox and Böhme, not one man alone.

[4] Shakespeare *Romeo and Juliet* v i 72 (var).

struggles of his mind;[1] or that he should at times be so far deluded, as to mistake the tumultuous sensations of his nerves, and the co-existing spectres of his fancy, as parts or symbols of the truths which were opening on him? It has indeed been plausibly observed,[2] that in order to derive any advantage, or to collect any intelligible meaning, from the writings of these ignorant mystics, the reader must bring with him a spirit and judgement superior to that of the writers themselves:

> And what he brings, what needs he elsewhere seek?
> PARADISE REGAINED.

—A sophism, which I fully agree with Warburton, is unworthy of Milton; how much more so of the awful person, in whose mouth he has placed it?[3] One assertion[4] I will venture to make, as suggested by my own experience, that there exist folios on the human understanding, and the nature of man, which would have a far juster claim to their high rank and celebrity, if in the whole huge volume there could be found as much fulness of heart and intellect, as burst forth in many a simple page of GEORGE FOX, JACOB BEHMEN, and even of Behmen's commentator, the pious and fervid WILLIAM LAW.[5]

---

[1] "What is the Body, but the fixture of the mind?. . . Is Terror in my Soul—my Heart beats against my side—Is Grief? *Tears* form in my eyes. In her homely way the Body tries to interpret all the movements of the Soul." To HCR 12 Mar 1811. ". . . What I keep out of my mind or rather *keep down* in a state of under-consciousness, is sure to act meanwhile with it's whole power of poison on my Body". To Matilda Betham [14 Mar 1811]. *CL* III 305, 310. It is of interest that C coined the term "psychosomatic". *IS* 67, from BM MS Egerton 2800 ff 43–5 (1812?). Cf C's marginal note in Schelling *STI* 260: "Whether from acquired Habit or no, I [can] not, & seem to myself never to have [re]garded my Body as identical with m[y]self . . .". *CM* (*CC*) IV. Cf also *P Lects* Lect 12 (1949) 362–3.

[2] Untraced.

[3] Milton *Paradise Regained* IV

325. C refers to a footnote contributed by William Warburton (1698–1779) to Thomas Newton's ed (1752 and later eds): "The poet makes the old sophister the Devil always busy in his trade. 'Tis pity he should make Jesus (as he does here) use the same arms." *BL* (1975) 83.

[4] As SC in *BL* (1847) I 147n points out, in this last sentence of the paragraph C elaborates Schelling *Darlegung* 156 (*SW* VII 120): ". . . nevertheless Herr Fichte might give his whole rhetoric, if in all his books put together he had shown the spirit and heart-fulness, which often a single page of many so called enthusiasts discovers". Tr SC.

[5] William Law (1686–1761), the great English divine, author of *A Serious Call to a Devout and Holy Life* (1728) and *The Case of Reason* (1732). He became an admirer of Böhme (1734) and conceived

The feeling of gratitude, which I cherish towards these men, has caused me to digress further than I had foreseen or proposed; but to have passed them over in an historical sketch of my literary life and opinions, would have seemed to me like the denial of a debt, the concealment of a boon. For the writings of these mystics acted in no slight degree to prevent my mind from being imprisoned within the outline of any single dogmatic system. They contributed to keep alive the *heart* in the *head*; gave me an indistinct, yet stirring and working presentment, that all the products of the mere *reflective* faculty partook of DEATH, and were as the rattling twigs and sprays in winter, into which a sap was yet to be propelled, from some root to which I had not penetrated, if they were to afford my soul either food or shelter.[1] If they were too often a moving cloud of smoke to me by day, yet they were always a pillar of fire throughout the night,[2] during my wanderings through the wilderness of doubt, and enabled me to skirt, without crossing, the sandy deserts of utter unbelief. That the system is capable of being converted into an irreligious PANTHEISM, I well know. The ETHICS of SPINOZA, may, or may not, be an instance. But at no time could I believe, that *in itself* and *essentially* it is incompatible with religion, natural, or revealed:[3] and now I am most

---

the plan of a collected edition of Böhme's works, carried out by Ward and Langcake, "With figures, illustrating his principles, left by the Reverend William Law" (see above, I 146 n 2). C annotated Law's *Serious Call* (10th ed 1772).

[1] C here appears to echo a favourite topic of Schelling's and may be inventively expanding one of Schelling's metaphors concerning "mere reflection". Cf *Ideen* Einleitung 6 (*SW* II 13): "Die *blosse* Reflexion also ist eine Geistkrankheit des Menschen, noch dazu, wo sie sich in Herrschaft über den ganzen Menschen setzt, diejenige, welche sein höheres Daseyn im Keim, sein geistiges Leben, welches nur aus der Identität hervorgeht, in der Wurzel tödtet." ("*Mere* reflection thus is a spiritual sickness of man and, what is more, in so far as it sets itself in control over the whole man, it is that which kills man's highest existence in its seed and eradicates man's spiritual life, which proceeds solely from his identity.")

[2] Cf Exod 13.21.

[3] The *Ethics* was published posthumously (1677) in the *Opera posthuma*. In 1803 C noted: "If Spinoza had left the doctrine of Miracles untouched . . . his Ethics would never, could never, have brought on him the charge of *Atheism*." *CN* I 1379. Cf C's later marginal note in his copy of Jacobi *ULS* 26: "I do not believe, that Spinoza would have acknowleged the system attributed to him by Jacobi" —i.e. that the system is atheistic. *CM* (*CC*) III. For discussion of these and similar remarks, see McFarland 188–90. C especially feared in Spinozism the possibility of a *material* pantheism, God as the sum of all things rather than as a living spirit

thoroughly persuaded of the contrary. The writings of the illustrious sage of Königsberg, the founder of the Critical Philosophy, more than any other work, at once[1] invigorated and disciplined my understanding. The originality, the depth, and the compression of the thoughts; the novelty and subtlety, yet solidity and importance, of the distinctions; the adamantine chain of the logic; and I will venture to add (paradox as it will appear to those who have taken their notion of I M M A N U E L   K A N T, from Reviewers and Frenchmen) the *clearness* and *evidence*, of the "C R I T I Q U E   O F   T H E   P U R E   R E A S O N ;" of the J U D G M E N T ; of the "M E T A P H I S I C A L   E L E M E N T S   O F   N A T U R A L   P H I L O S O P H Y ," and of his "R E L I G I O N   W I T H I N   T H E   B O U N D S   O F   P U R E   R E A S O N ," took possession of me as with a giant's hand.[2] After fifteen years familiarity with them, I still read these and all his other productions with undiminished delight and increasing admiration. The few passages that remained obscure to me, after due efforts of thought, (as the chapter on *original apperception,*)[3] and the apparent

dwelling in all things (see *CN* I 1561). The latter may be what C meant by pantheism "in the most religious form . . . it could appear". *P Lects* Lect 13 (1949) 384–5, in which C refers to Lessing's comments on Spinoza in Jacobi *ULS,* a book that helped shape C's opinion of Spinoza. Jacobi (*ULS* 223) says that "Spinozism is atheism" but warns he is far from charging all Spinozists with atheism. Cf also *CL* IV 548 and n (10 Mar 1815), in which C calls Spinoza "Righteous and gentle Spirit" but criticises him (avoiding heaviness) for not recognising God as having "the Ground of his own Existence within himself, and . . . in his Will and Word".

[1] Meaning not "immediately" (as Fruman 82 infers) but "at one and the same time invigorated and disciplined . . .". In Dec 1796 C refers to him as "the most unintelligible Emanuel Kant". *CL* I 284n. His serious study of Kant seems to have begun in 1801–2. *CN* I 1517n. For C's early acquaintance with Kant see Wellek 70–2 and Elisabeth Winkelmann *Coleridge und die Kantische*

Philosophie (Leipzig 1933) 38–44. See also *CN* I 1705–10, 1711, 1714, 1715, 1717, 1723, and nn.

[2] *Kritik der reinen Vernunft* (1781; rev 1787, a reprint of which, 1799, C read); *Kritik der Urtheilskraft* (1790); *Metaphysische Anfangsgründe der Naturwissenschaft* (1786; C's ed 1787); *Die Religion innerhalb der Grenzen der blossen Vernunft* (1793; C's ed 1794)—all of which C annotated (*CM—CC—* III). C at one point (1810) is quoted by HCR as considering Kant's *Kritik der Urtheilskraft* "the most astonishing of Kant's works". *CRD* I 305.

[3] *KRV* "Elementarlehre" § 16 (B 131–6); C may also have in mind §§ 15, 17–18 (B 129–31, 136–40). *BL* (1847) I 155–6 and Orsini 185–6, 195 provide extensive discussion at this point. For the importance of these sections to C see above, I 145 n 2. Like Schelling (*STI* 49–50: *SW* III 368), C thinks it important to view Kant's "unity of apperception" as an "act" of the self, hence grounded on a "will". Cf below, I 155 n 3, and ch 12, I 272–81.

contradictions which occur, I soon found were hints and insinuations referring to ideas, which K A N T either did not think it prudent to avow, or which he considered as consistently *left behind* in a pure analysis, not of human nature in toto, but of the speculative intellect alone.[1] Here therefore he was constrained to commence at the point of *reflection,* or natural consciousness: while in his *moral* system he was permitted to assume a higher ground (the autonomy of the will) as a P O S T U L A T E[2] deducible from the unconditional command, or (in the technical language of his school) the categorical imperative, of the conscience. He had been in imminent danger of persecution during the reign of the late king of Prussia, that strange compound of lawless debauchery, and priest-ridden superstition: and it is probable that he had little inclination, in his old age, to act over again the fortunes, and hair-breadth escapes of Wolf.[3] The expulsion of the first among

[1] See above, I 143 n 2.

[2] For C's use of "postulate" see ch 12, below, I 247, in which he cites Schelling. In this context C appears to be borrowing the word from Schelling's use of it in a discussion of Kant similar to C's, *Phil Briefe* I: *Phil Schrift* 123 and n (*SW* I 288 and n). (See below, I 155 n 3.) C's comments parallel remarks in Schelling *Vom Ich* Vorrede: *Phil Schrift* v–vii (*SW* I 152–3) and *Phil Briefe* I, e.g. "that the theoretical reason is too narrow and restricted" to entertain "an absolute cause" such as God. *Phil Schrift* 121–2, cf 123–5; *SW* I 287, cf 288–9. To trust solely in our pure reason gives only the "letter" of the critical philosophy. Like C, Schelling implies that Kant was holding something back. See below, I 155 n 3, I 156 n 2. For the similarity between Schelling's and C's views of Kant see Wellek 95–102, esp 97. Cf *P Lects* Lect 12 (1949) 364. Important here is C's marginal note criticising Schelling's interpretation of Kant in *Phil Briefe* (tipped into his copy of *Phil Schrift* between pp 122 and 123): "By theoretic Reason as opposed to practical, Kant never meant two *Persons* or *Beings;* but only that what we could not *prove* by one train of argument, we might by another—in proportion to the purposes of knowlege—. I cannot theoretically *demonstrate* the existence of God, as a moral Creator and Governor; but I can theoretically adduce a multitude of Inducements so strong as to be all but absolute Demonstration;— and I can demonstrate, that not a word of Sense ever was or ever can be brought against it. In this stage of the argument my Conscience, with its categorical Command, comes in & proves it to be my Duty to *choose to* believe in a God—there being no obstacle to my power so to choose. With what consistency then can Schelling Contend that the same mind having on these grounds fixed its belief in a God, can then make its former speculative infirmities as applied to the Idea of God, a pretext for turning back to disbelieve it?—" *CM* (*CC*) IV.

[3] Christian Wolff was attacked for his liberal religious views by German Pietists at Halle, where he taught. They finally induced Frederick William I to expel him from Prussia (1723), and Wolff went to Marburg. Immediately after the death of the king, he returned to

Kant's disciples, who attempted to complete his system, from the university of Jena, with the confiscation and prohibition of the obnoxious work by the joint efforts of the courts of Saxony and Hanover, supplied experimental proof, that the venerable old man's caution was not groundless.[1] In spite therefore of his own declarations, I could never believe, it was possible for him to have meant no more by his *Noumenon,* or THING IN ITSELF, than his mere words express;[2] or that in his own conception he confined the whole *plastic* power to the forms of the intellect, leaving for the external cause, for the *materiale* of our sensations, a matter without form, which is doubtless inconceivable. I entertained doubts likewise, whether in his own mind, he even laid *all* the stress, which he appears to do on the moral postulates.[3]

Halle at the invitation of Frederick the Great (1740). Kant's trouble with the government was caused by his *Die Religion innerhalb der Grenzen der blossen Vernunft.* When the first part appeared in the *Berlinische Monatsschrift* (1792), he was forbidden to publish the rest. Claiming local privilege, he published the entire work at Königsberg in 1793. Resenting this, the government exacted from him a pledge not to write or lecture on religious subjects. Kant kept the pledge until the death of Frederick William II (1797). C's phrase "lawless debauchery . . ." refers to the loose personal life of Frederick William II (b 1744) and to his handling of foreign affairs (his support of Louis XVI, in opposition to the French Revolution, his rôle in the partition of Poland). When he died, the state was almost bankrupt and the prestige of the monarchy shaken. He had several mistresses and was openly polygamous.

[1] Fichte (see second paragraph below and n) was driven from his professorship at Jena (1798) on charges of atheism. His first work, *Versuch einer Kritik aller Offenbarung* (Königsberg 1792), applied Kantian thought to religion. Kant praised it; it was published anon-

ymously, with the result that many assumed Kant had written it.

[2] The remainder of this sentence paraphrases Schelling *STI* 114 (*SW* III 407) and is taken from one of those pages C had used in ch 8. "Man setze z.B., nur der Stoff gehöre den Dingen an, so muss dieser Stoff, eh er zum Ich gelangt, wenigstens im Uebergange vom Ding zur Vorstellung, formlos seyn, was ohne Zweifel undenkbar ist." ("Let it be supposed, for example, that only the stuff [or material] belongs to things, it follows that this stuff, before it arrives at the I, at least in the transition from the thing to the representation, must be formless, which without doubt is inconceivable.") Tr SC *BL* (1847) I 135n. Schelling, Fichte, J. S. Beck, and others denied any strict conception of the *Ding-an-sich* throughout the 1790s and borrowed from each other. C criticises Kant along similar lines.

[3] Schelling—in the same place he questions how theoretical reason alone can reach the Absolute—also doubts that all of Kant's stress was placed on "moral law" and suggests that a higher (divine) "will" must be behind Kant's thought. *Phil Briefe* I: *Phil Schrift* 119–25, esp 124 (*SW* I 285–90, esp 288): "Should you . . . proceed from the

An IDEA, in the *highest* sense of that word, cannot be conveyed but by a *symbol*;[1] and, except in geometry, all symbols of necessity involve an apparent contradiction.[2] Φώνησε συνετοῖσιν:[3] and

moral law" as a postulate, "your whole system would be so constructed that the moral law comes first and God last". God actually creates the moral law (hence it can be no postulate) by a free act of will. Cf C on this crucial point, ch 12 Thesis VII, below, I 279–80; also part of his marginal note to that passage in *Phil Briefe:* "The proper answer is that God is the originator of the Moral Law; but not per arbitrium, (Willkühr) but because he is essentially wise and holy and good—rather, Wisdom, Holiness, and Love." *Phil Schrift,* leaf tipped in between pp 122 and 123, referring to 123–4. *CM (CC)* IV. C is not far from Schelling's position. Cf Schelling *Über das Wesen: Phil Schrift* 482 (*SW* VII 396): ". . . but God, i.e. the Person of God, is the general law". Wellek 114–16 discusses C's use of Kant's moral position as "a sort of back-door" to admit traditional theology. For C's stress on the moral fabric of religion (reinforced by his reading in Jacobi *ULS*), especially in relation to the will, see also ch 10, below, I 202–3. In 1820 C says about Kant (whether correctly is a matter of opinion) that "In him is contained all that can be *learnt*— & . . . you have a firm faith in God, the responsible Will of Man, and Immortality—& Kant will demonstrate to you, that this Faith is acquiesced in, indeed, nay, confirmed by the Reason & Understanding, but grounded on Postulates authorized & substantiated solely by the *Moral Being*". *CL* v 14. The change from "moral postulates" in *BL* to "Postulates authorized . . . by the *Moral Being*" in C's letter is significant and identifies the crux of the issue.

[1] The idea in the highest sense is "the Universal in the Individual

. . . the Glance and the Exponent of the indwelling Power" (*CN* III 4397 f 53): the universal, in other words, becomes germinal, controlling, formative. As an active process, it is realised, in its concrete implications and fulfilment, by the "imagination"—"that reconciling and mediatory power, which incorporating the Reason in Images of the Sense, and organizing (as it were) the flux of the Senses by the permanence and self-circling energies of the Reason, gives birth to a system of symbols, harmonious in themselves, and consubstantial with the truths, of which they are the *conductors*". *SM (CC)* 29; cf ibid 30, 73, 79; *CN* III 3954 and n; Barfield 116–19; and L. C. Knights *Further Explorations* (1965) 155–68. Cf Schelling *Phil Briefe* IX: *Phil Schrift* 185–8, 186n, 188–9n (*SW* I 332–3 and nn), in which he stresses the intermediary power of the imagination to resolve the problems of the *Ding-an-sich* and the differences between transcendentalism and empiricism.

[2] Cf Schelling *Abhandlungen: Phil Schrift* 276–7 (*SW* I 406): "Diesen übersinnlichen Grund alles Sinnlichen nun *symbolisirte* Kant durch den Ausdruck: *Dinge an sich*—ein Ausdruck, der wie *alle* symbolischen Ausdrücke einen *Widerspruch* in sich schliesst . . ." ("Now this supersensuous ground of all that is sensuous, Kant symbolized by the expression *things in themselves*—which, like all other symbolic expressions, contains in itself a *contradiction* . . ."). Tr SC *BL* (1847) I 158n. But SC omits that later part of Schelling's paragraph specifically connecting this point to the expression of ideas by symbols alone (which in C's own paragraph

for those who could not pierce through this symbolic husk, his writings were not intended. Questions which can not be fully answered without exposing the respondent to personal danger, are not entitled to a fair answer; and yet to say this openly, would in many cases furnish the very advantage, which the adversary is insidiously seeking after. Veracity does not consist in *saying*, but in the intention of *communicating* truth;[1] and the philosopher who can not utter the whole truth without conveying falsehood, and at the same time, perhaps, exciting the most malignant passions, is constrained to express himself either *mythically* or equivocally. When Kant therefore was importuned to settle the disputes of his commentators himself, by declaring what he meant, how could he decline the honours of martyrdom with less offence, than by simply replying, "I meant what I said, and at the age of near four score, I have something else, and more important to do, than to write a commentary on my own works."[2]

FICHTE'S Wissenschaftslehre, or *Lore*[3] of Ultimate Science,

appears as the first sentence): "Solche widersprechende (ungereimte) Ausdrücke aber sind die einzigen, wodurch wir überhaupt *Ideen* darzustellen vermögen." ("But such contradictory [absurd] expressions are the only ones by which we are empowered to represent *ideas* at all.")

[3] Pindar *Olympian Odes* 2.85 (var). Tr: "He spoke to the wise". Cf *LS* (*CC*) 126, *CN* III 4244. See also ch 22, below, in which more of the passage is quoted.

[1] On "veracity" distinguished from "truth" cf *Friend* (*CC*) II 41–3 and *CN* III 3592 f 134v and n.

[2] C is not, as sometimes assumed, fabricating a quotation to dramatise Kant's general attitude. C apparently refers to a particular short piece, "Erklärung in Beziehung auf Fichtes Wissenschaftslehre", in the Intelligence Sheet of the Jena *Allgemeine Literatur-Zeitung* No 109 (28 Aug 1799). Kant himself dated this statement 7 Aug 1799. The occasion was a general controversy over the interpretation of Kant brought to a head by Fichte's *Zweite Einleitung in die Wissenschaftslehre* (1797). Fichte denied that Kant's *Ding-an-sich* caused real sensations or impressions (see Fichte *SW* I 486–8). Kant, anxious because Fichte's system (with which he was perhaps not fully acquainted) had been charged with atheism yet was supposedly built on Kantian principles, defended himself and tried to cool the debate by referring readers back to a strict and literal interpretation of *KRV*. Although Kant does not refer to his age of seventy-five he does say: "Thus with this I explain again that the *Kritik* certainly is to be understood according to its wording, and is to be viewed simply from the standpoint of common understanding refined only by such abstract examinations as are necessary." *Gesammelte Schriften* ed Prussian Academy XII 397. On 29 May 1797 Kant had written an earlier "Erklärung" in which he does mention his age (then seventy-four); C may also have this statement in mind. Cf McFarland 98–9.

[3] C, who had studied Old High German (*lere*), would have been recalling its older meaning, in both

was to add the key-stone of the arch:[1] and by commencing with an *act*, instead of a *thing* or *substance*, Fichte assuredly gave the first mortal blow to Spinozism, as taught by Spinoza himself;[2] and supplied the *idea* of a system truly metaphysical, and of a *metaphysique* truly systematic: (i.e. having its spring and principle within itself.) But this fundamental idea he overbuilt with a heavy mass of mere *notions*, and psychological acts of arbitrary reflection. Thus his theory degenerated into a crude* egoismus, a

---

* The following burlesque on the Fichtean Egoismus[3] may, perhaps, be amusing to the few who have studied the system, and to those who are

English and German: teaching. Cf ". . . our Language has dropt the word 'Lore' at least except in poetry —the lehre of the Germans, the Logos of the Greek". *CN* II 2442.

[1] Johann Gottlieb Fichte (1762–1814), after establishing his reputation by his Kantian *Versuch einer Kritik aller Offenbarung* (see I 155 n 1, above), became professor at Jena at the age of thirty-two (1794) but was forced to leave four years later because of his unorthodox religious views (see I 155, above). He lectured at Erlangen and Königsberg, and then joined the philosophical faculty of the new University of Berlin (1810). Major works of the Jena period include his works on the theory of knowledge, *Ueber den Begriff der Wissenschaftslehre* (1794) and *Grundlage der gesammten Wissenschaftslehre* (1794), and, in practical philosophy, *Grundlage des Naturrechts* (1796) and *System der Sittenlehre* (1798). C was familiar with all of them as well as with Fichte's *Grundriss der Eigenthümlichen der Wissenschaftslehre* (1795), *Bestimmung des Menschen* (1800), *Grundzüge des gegenwärtigen Zeitalters* (1804), and *Anweisung zum seeligen Leben oder auch die Religionslehre* (1806). For his annotations on Fichte see *CM* (*CC*) II. C seems to have been most attracted by the several works on *Wissenschaftslehre*.

Fichte was the first transcendentalist to stress heavily the starting-point of philosophy as an act (*Tathandlung*) of the self or *Ich*. Kant definitely hints at the idea (see above, I 145 n 2), but Fichte unmistakably makes it the foundation of his own system. It is by a (wilful) act that the *Ich* or *Ich bin* becomes the self-conscious *Ich denke*. Fichte *Recension des Aenesidemus* (1792), which C may not have read (*SW* I 8; cf also 431–2, III 22, and I 227, 472, in which Fichte stresses the "act of the imagination" in initiating and unifying all elements of the *Ich*). On Fichte see Orsini 175–91, esp 175–83. Cf C's remark to J. H. Green 13 Dec 1817: "Fichte in his moral system is but a caricature of Kant . . . His metaphysics have gone by; but he has the merit of having prepared the ground for, and laid the first stone of, the *Dynamic* Philosophy by the substitution of Act for Thing, der einfachen Actionen statt der Dinge in sich." *CL* IV 792. Cf *CN* III 3802: "In short, all reasoning commences with a *Postulate* i.e. an *act*."

[2] Fichte denied to Spinozism a material basis, which C implies was taught by Spinoza himself. But for C this would not preclude a spiritual or intelligential pantheism modelled after Spinoza and taught by others who could reconcile it with more orthodox beliefs. Cf above, I 152 n 3.

[3] Cf on Fichte's egoism a letter to DW of 9 Feb 1801: *CL* II 673–4.

boastful and hyperstoic hostility to NATURE, as lifeless, godless, and altogether unholy: while his *religion* consisted in the assump-

---

unacquainted with it, may convey as tolerable a likeness of Fichte's idealism as can be expected from an avowed caricature.

The categorical imperative, or the annunciation of the new Teutonic God, ΄ΕΓΩΕΝΚΑΙΠΑΝ:[1] a dithyrambic Ode, by QUERKOPF VON KLUB-STICK,[2] Grammarian, and Subrector in Gymnasio****.

> Eu! Dei vices gerens, ipse Divus,[3]
> (*Speak English, Friend!*) the God Imperativus,
> Here on this market-cross aloud I cry:
> I, I, I! I itself I![4]
> The form and the substance, the what and the why,
> The when and the where, and the low and the high,
> The inside and outside, the earth and the sky,
> I, you, and he, and he, you and I,
> All souls and all bodies are I itself I!
> > All I itself I!
> > (Fools! a truce with this starting!)
> > All my I! all my I!
> He's a heretic dog who but adds Betty Martin![5]
> Thus cried the God with high imperial tone:
> In robe of stiffest state, that scoff'd at beauty,
> A pronoun-verb imperative he shone—

[1] C's title takes the pantheistic phrase ἐν καὶ πᾶν ("one and all"; see ch 22, below, II 139 and n 2) and prefixes to it the word for "I" (ego). Hence the title could be translated as "I—the [true] One and All". Such a title and yoking together of the "I" with the Spinozistic "one and all" may have been suggested to C by Schelling *Vom Ich: Phil Schrift* 44 (*SW* I 193), which echoes and responds to Fichte. Schelling says "In the *Ich,* philosophy has found its ἐν καὶ πᾶν, which till now it has struggled for as the highest reward of victory." Cf ibid: *Phil Schrift* 45, 13–14 (*SW* I 194, 170–2), in which Schelling relates the *Ich* to Spinoza. C admits his own poem is a "caricature" because he knew that Fichte's *Ich* does not mean personality or individual character and (as the last three lines of his poem show) that the "I" is viewed in relation to an "absolute" or "pure I" more akin to a deity (or at least to an absolute ideal) than to man. C's interest in the "I" was strong and he translated,

with interpolations (not intending and never using it for publication), Schelling's explanation of the *Ich* in *STI* 58–62 (*SW* III 374–6). Orsini 210–11 reprints C's ms, BM MS Egerton 2801 f 103.

[2] With the name "Querkopf [wrong-head] von Klubstick", C also burlesques the odes of F. G. Klopstock (1724–1803). See "Satyrane's Letters", below, II 194.

[3] "Huzzah! God's vicegerent, myself God".

[4] Is C remembering the false prophets in George Fox's *Journal* who cry " 'I, I, I, it is I myself that have been the Ishmael and Esau' "?

[5] In his pun C toys with the proverbial phrase "That's my eye, Betty Martin": "an answer to any one that attempts to impose or humbug". Francis Grose *A Classical Dictionary of the Vulgar Tongue* (1785) 11 (ed Eric Partridge 1931: "*All my Eye* is perhaps the earliest form . . ."). Cf *CN* III 3335 and n; RS *The Doctor* (1848) 311.

tion of a mere ORDO ORDINANS, which we were permitted *exotericé*[2] to call GOD; and his *ethics* in an ascetic, and almost monkish, mortification of the natural passions and desires.[3]

In Schelling's "NATUR-PHILOSOPHIE," and the "SYSTEM DES TRANSCENDENTALEN IDEALISMUS," I first found a genial coincidence with much that I had toiled out for myself, and a powerful assistance in what I had yet to do.[4]

Then substantive and plural-singular grown
He thus spake on! Behold in I alone
(For ethics boast a syntax of their own)
Or if in ye, yet as I doth depute ye,
In O! I, you, the vocative of duty!
I of the world's whole Lexicon the root!
Of the whole universe of touch, sound, sight
The genitive and ablative to boot:
The accusative of wrong, the nom'native of right,
And in all cases the case absolute!
Self-construed, I all other moods decline:
Imperative, from nothing we derive us;
Yet as a super-postulate of mine,
Unconstrued antecedence I assign
To X, Y, Z, the God infinitivus![1]

[1] In the last three lines, the Supreme Being becomes merely a grammatical declension or logical "super-postulate" (in the form: given a, b, c, then x, y, z) curiously dependent on the "I". In a marginal note to Jacobi *ULS* pp xliv–1 (referring to Prop 45–6), C speaks of a God that "*lives* . . . instead of a logical x y z, (which we are compelled by the mechanism of our Reason to postulate, as the ground unconditional of all things, or rather as the one absolute condition of unity of Thought . . . still however ideal and but an ens logicum et hypotheticum)". *CM* (*CC*) III. C later changed his mind about Kant's religious position but apparently maintained his opinion of Fichte's.

[2] "Ordering order . . . popularly".

[3] Aside even from the satiric poem quoted in C's footnote, his judgement of Fichte is harsh and seems primarily based on a knowledge of Fichte's earlier works.

[4] Cf C's remark Dec 1804: "In the Preface of my Metaphys. Works I should say—Once & all read Tetens, Kant, Fichte, &c—& there you will trace or if you are on the hunt, track me. Why then not acknowlege your obligations step by step? Because, I could not do in a multitude of glaring resemblances without a lie/ for they had been mine, formed, & full formed in my own mind, before I had ever heard of these Writers, because to have fixed on the partic. instances in which I have really been indebted to these Writers would have [been] very hard if possible, to me who read for truth & self-satisfaction, not to make a book, & who always rejoiced & was jubilant when I found my own ideas well expressed already by others . . . & lastly, let me say, because (I am proud perhaps but) I seem to know, that much of the matter remains my own, and that the Soul is *mine*." *CN* II 2375.

I have introduced this statement, as appropriate to the narrative nature of this sketch; yet rather in reference to the work which I have announced in a preceding page,[1] than to my present subject. It would be but a mere act of justice to myself, were I to warn my future readers,[2] that an identity of thought, or even similarity of phrase will not be at all times a certain proof that the passage has been borrowed from Schelling, or that the conceptions were originally learnt from him. In this instance, as in the dramatic lectures of Schlegel to which I have before alluded,[3] from the same motive of self-defence against the charge of plagiarism, many of the most striking resemblances, indeed all the main and fundamental ideas, were born and matured in my mind before I had ever seen a single page of the German Philosopher; and I might indeed affirm with truth, before the more important works of Schelling had been written, or at least made public. Nor is this coincidence at all to be wondered at. We had studied in the same school; been disciplined by the same preparatory philosophy, namely, the writings of Kant; we had both equal obligations to the polar logic and dynamic philosophy of Giordano Bruno; and Schelling has lately, and, as of recent acquisition, avowed that same affectionate reverence for the labors of Behmen, and other mystics, which I had formed at a much earlier period.[4] The coincidence of Schelling's system with certain general ideas of Behmen, he declares to have been *mere* coincidence; while *my* obligations have been more direct. *He* needs give to Behmen only feelings of sympathy; while I owe him a debt of gratitude.[5] God forbid! that I

---

[1] His "Logosophia"—see ch 8, above, I 136.

[2] The phrase "future readers" could refer to readers of the "Logosophia", which is "the work I have announced in a preceding page" (see above). Thus C would here be warning about similarities not between *BL* and Schelling but between the planned "Logosophia" and Schelling. Yet C may have *BL* in mind too. See below, I 164.

[3] See above, I 34 and n 3.

[4] In the *Darlegung* (1806) Schelling acknowledged his debts to "enthusiasts", but did not name Böhme. Ludwig Tieck first brought Böhme's writings to Schelling's atten-

tion in 1799. In 1802 Schelling asked Schlegel to buy the quarto ed of Böhme for him; in 1804 received an edition of Böhme from Windischmann, which he gave to Franz Baader, and in 1809 was requesting another edition from a friend. It was not until 1833, in his *History of Modern Philosophy*, that he fully acknowledged his debt to Böhme. James Gutmann *Schelling: Of Human Freedom* (Chicago 1937) Introd xlv–xlvii.

[5] Between himself and Schelling C here generously offers Schelling precedence, but at the same time scolds him for remarking that his ideas were coincidental with

should be suspected of a wish to enter into a rivalry with S C H E L L -
I N G for the honors so unequivocally his right, not only as a great
and original genius, but as the *founder* of the P H I L O S O P H Y O F
N A T U R E, and as the most successful *improver* of the Dynamic *

* It would be an act of high and almost criminal injustice to pass over in
silence the name of Mr. R I C H A R D S A U M A R E Z, a gentleman equally
well known as a medical man and as a philanthropist, but who demands
notice on the present occasion as the author of "a new System of Physiology"
in two volumes octavo, published 1797; and in 1812 of "an Examination of
the natural and artificial Systems of Philosophy which now prevail" in one
volume octavo, entitled, "The Principles of physiological and physical
Science."[1] The latter work is not quite equal to the former in style or
arrangement; and there is a greater necessity of distinguishing the principles
of the author's philosophy from his conjectures concerning colour, the
atmospheric matter, comets, &c. which whether just or erroneous are by no
means necessary consequences of that philosophy. Yet even in this department of this volume, which I regard as comparatively the inferior work, the
reasonings by which Mr. Saumarez invalidates the immanence of an infinite
power in any finite substance are the offspring of no common mind; and
the experiment on the expansibility of the air is at least plausible and highly
ingenious. But the merit, which will secure both to the book and to the writer

Böhme's, whereas C "admits" his
own "debt" to Böhme. This is in
light of C's use of Schelling while
claiming a "coincidence" for his own
in some of those instances. C tries to
explain Schelling's use of Böhme in
a marginal comment on Schelling's
Über das Wesen: Phil Schrift 442:
"How can I explain the strange
Silence [r]especting Jacob Böemen?
. . . the [co]incidence [in] the express[io]ns, illustrations, [& e]ven in
the [m]ystical [ob]scurities, [is] too
glaring [to] be solved [by] a mere
[in]dependent   [co]-incidence   [in]
Thought and [in]tuition. [Pr]obably,
pru[d]ential motives [re]strain Schelling for a while: for [I w]ill not
think, [th]at Pride or [a] dishonest
lurking Desire to appear not only
[a]n original, but *the* Original, can
have influenced [a] man of Genius,
like Schelling." *CM* (*CC*) IV.
  [1] Richard Saumarez (1764–1835),
surgeon, honorary governor of Mag-
dalen Hospital, London. C met him
in Jul 1812 (*CL* III 414, 418, 420).
C probably mentions him here because he wishes to show that some-

thing analogous to the forces and the
organic vitalism (the "Dynamic
System") associated with Schelling
could be arrived at independently by
a man who had obviously never
read Schelling, not to mention Bruno
and Böhme. The theme of Saumarez's *New System of Physiology* (2
vols 1798; 2nd ed 1799; 3rd ed
1813) can be briefly stated: Life is
greater than the sum of its parts.
It is rendered possible by something
that goes beyond mere chemical and
mechanical laws; and when this vital
"power" is lacking, "living matter"
decomposes, separates, and putrefies.
The work, about which there is a
certain home-grown if gifted quality,
is less a philosophical than a descriptive study of physiology in which
vitalism is a premise. In addition to
this work, he wrote *The Principles of
Physiological and Physical Science*
(1812), which contains the discussion of the "expansibility" of air
(257–78) mentioned by C (the subtitle should read "Unnatural and
Artificial . . .", not "natural", as
C has it).

System which, begun by Bruno, was re-introduced (in a more philosophical form, and freed from all its impurities and visionary accompaniments) by KANT; in whom it was the native and necessary growth of his own system. KANT's followers, however, on whom (for the greater part) their master's *cloak* had fallen without, or with a very scanty portion of, his *spirit*, had adopted his dynamic ideas, only as a more refined species of mechanics.[3] With exception of one or two fundamental ideas, which cannot be with-held from FICHTE, to SCHELLING we owe the completion, and the most important victories, of this revolution in philosophy. To me it will be happiness and honor enough, should I succeed in rendering the system itself intelligible to my country-men, and in the application of it to the most awful of subjects for

Bounty !

a high and honorable name with posterity, consists in the masterly force of reasoning, and the copiousness of induction, with which he has assailed, and (in my opinion) subverted the tyranny of the mechanic system in physiology; established not only the existence of final causes, but their necessity and efficiency in every system that merits the name of philosophical; and sub-stituting life and progressive power, for the contradictory *inert force*, has a right to be known and remembered as the first instaurator of the dynamic philosophy in England. The author's views, as far as concerns himself, are unborrowed and compleatly his own, as he neither possessed nor do his writings discover, the least acquaintance with the works of Kant, in which the germs of the philosophy exist; and his volumes were published many years before the full developement of these germs by Schelling. Mr. Saumarez's detection of the Braunonian system was no light or ordinary service at the time: and I scarcely remember in any work on any subject a confutation so thoroughly satisfactory.[1] It is sufficient at this time to have stated the fact; as in the preface to the work, which I have already announced on the Logos, I have exhibited in detail the merits of this writer, and genuine philosopher, who needed only have taken his foundations somewhat deeper and wider to have superseded a considerable part of my labours.[2]

[1] The "Brunonian System", which Saumarez (*New System* I 66–89) attacks because "it makes Life to be an effect instead of a cause", was expounded by Dr John Brown (1735–88), author of *Elementa medicinae* (2 vols 1780) ("Bruno-nian" because first published in Latin; an English version appeared in 1788). The central thesis is that life, in essence, consists in the capacity for "excitability", and the "exciting powers" are the stimuli created by external forces, a mecha-nistic view to which C objected. C became interested in Brown in 1799 and made a detailed digest of a long review of works on the "Brunonian System": "Anzeige verschiedener Schriften das Brownsche System betreffend" *Allgemeine Literatur-Zeitung* (Jena & Leipzig) 11–12 Feb 1799, Nos 48–59. *CN* I 388–9 and nn. Cf his later references in *CN* III 3827 and n, 4269 and n.

[2] On the "Logosophia", see above, I 136 and n 2.

[3] For Kant's "dynamic" see ch 8, above, I 129 n 3.

the most important of purposes.[1] Whether a work is the offspring of a man's own spirit, and the product of original thinking, will be discovered by those who are its sole legitimate judges, by better tests than the mere reference to dates. For readers in general, let whatever shall be found in this or any future work of mine, that resembles, or coincides with, the doctrines of my German predecessor, though contemporary, be wholly attributed to *him*: provided, that the absence of distinct references to his books, which I could not at all times make with truth as designating citations or thoughts actually *derived* from him; and which, I trust, would, after this general acknowledgment be superfluous; be not charged on me as an ungenerous concealment or intentional plagiarism. I have not indeed (eheu! res angusta domi!)[2] been hitherto able to procure more than two of his books, viz. the 1st volume of his collected Tracts, and his System of Transcendental Idealism;[3] to which, however, I must add a small pamphlet against Fichte,[4] the spirit of which was to *my* feelings painfully incongruous with the principles, and which (with the usual allowance afforded to an antithesis) displayed the love of wisdom rather than the wisdom of love. I regard truth as a divine ventriloquist: I care not from whose mouth the sounds are supposed to proceed, if only the words are audible and intelligible.[5] "Albeit, I must confess to be half in doubt, whether I should bring it forth or no, it being so contrary to the eye of the world, and the world so potent in most men's hearts, that I shall endanger either not to be regarded or not to be understood."

MILTON: *Reason of Church Government.*[6]

[1] By this C apparently means religion or a point where philosophy, art, and religion become one.

[2] A common tag. "Alas! the narrow circumstances at home!" Cf Juvenal 3.165, tr "They do not easily rise whose merits are opposed by poverty at home". Paraphrased by Johnson's famous line, "Slow rises worth, by poverty depressed" (*London* line 177).

[3] At the time C wrote this he owned or had read the *Philosophische Schriften* ("his collected Tracts"), *STI, Darlegung,* and *Ideen.* It seems highly likely that he had also read or owned *Ueber die Möglichkeit.* On 31 Aug 1816 C

wrote to the bookseller Thomas Boosey: ". . . I am anxious to have *all* the works of Schelling, with exception of those, I already possess, of which I gave you the List in my last Letter, & to which you have now to add the *Denkmal* . . .". *CL* IV 665. Unfortunately the previous letter containing C's list has not survived.

[4] I.e. *Darlegung;* see previous note and above, I 147 nn 3, 5.

[5] On this favourite image of the ventriloquist cf *EOT* (*CC*) I 120, *Friend* (*CC*) II 127 (I 192), and *SM* (*CC*) 80.

[6] Bk II ch 1: *Works* ed T. Birch (2 vols 1738) I 62. C had copied the

And to conclude the subject of citation, with a cluster of citations, which as taken from books, not in common use, may contribute to the reader's amusement, as a voluntary before a sermon.
"Dolet mihi quidem deliciis literarum inescatos subito jam homines
adeo esse, præsertim qui Christianos se profitentur, ut legere nisi
quod ad delectationem facit, sustineant nihil: unde et disciplinæ
severiores et philosophia ipsa jam fere prorsus etiam a doctis
negliguntur. Quod quidem propositum studiorum, nisi mature
corrigitur, tam magnum rebus incommodum dabit, quám dedit
Barbaries olim. Pertinax res Barbaries est, fateor: sed minus potest
tamen, quám illa mollities et *persuasa prudentia* literarum, quæ si
ratione caret, sapientiæ virtutisque *specie* mortales misere circum-
ducit. Succedet igitur, ut arbitror, haud ita multo post, pro rusticanâ
seculi nostri ruditate captatrix illa *communiloquentia* robur animi
virilis omne, omnem virtutem masculam profligatura, nisi cavetur."
    SIMON GRYNÆUS, candido lectori, prefixed to the Latin
translation of Plato, by Marsilius Ficinus. Lugduni, 1557.[1] A too

passage into a notebook in 1810:
CN III 3678 and n.
    [1] Simon Grynaeus (1493–1541),
German scholar and theologian,
professor first at Heidelberg (1524)
and then Basle (1529), author of
Latin versions of Aristotle, Plutarch,
and Chrysostom. The passage ("to
the candid reader"), prefixed to
Ficino's Latin version of Plato,
Opera omnia (Lyons 1557), was
copied into a notebook (Jul 1810)
with the comment: "An excellent &
all too prophetic Remark, which we
feel in 1810, & our fathers ought to
have felt from 1700—or rather
1680—the birth of our Constitution,
the death of our philosophic mind!"
CN III 3951 and n. With a few
added words and phrases of his own,
the more noticeable of which are
marked with brackets in the tr, C
gives a loose and sprightly translation in the 1818 *Friend* (*CC*) I 23–4:
"In very truth, it grieveth me that
men, those especially who profess
themselves to be Christians, should
be so taken with the *sweet Baits* of
Literature that they can endure to
read nothing but what gives them
immediate gratification, [no matter

how low or sensual it may be].
Consequently, the more austere and
disciplinary branches of philosophy
itself are almost wholly neglected,
even by the learned.—A course of
study [(if such reading, with such a
purpose in view, could deserve that
name)] which, if not corrected in
time, will occasion worse consequences than even barbarism did in
the times of our forefathers. Barbarism is, I own, a wilful headstrong
thing; but with all its blind obstinacy
it has less power of doing harm than
this [self-sufficient, self-satisfied *plain
good common-sense*] sort of writing,
this prudent [saleable popular] style
of composition, if it be deserted by
Reason [and scientific Insight]; piti-
ably decoying the minds of men by
an [imposing] shew of amiableness,
and [practical] Wisdom, [so that the
delighted Reader knowing nothing
knows *all about* almost every thing.]
There will succeed therefore in my
opinion, and that too within no long
time, to the rudeness and rusticity of
our age, that ensnaring meretricious
popularness in Literature, [with all
the tricksy humilities of the am-
bitious candidates for the favorable

prophetic remark, which has been in fulfilment from the year 1680, to the present 1815. N. B. By "persuasa prudentia," Grynæus means self-complacent *common sense* as opposed to science and philosophic reason.

"Est medius ordo et velut equestris Ingeniorum quidem sagacium et rebus humanis commodorum, non tamen in primam magnitudinem patentium. Eorum hominum, ut ita dicam, major annona est. Sedulum esse, nihil temere loqui, assuescere labori, et imagine prudentiæ & modestiæ tegere angustiores partes captûs dum exercitationem et usum, quo isti in civilibus rebus pollent, pro natura et magnitudine ingenii plerique accipiunt."

BARCLAII ARGENIS, p. 71.[1]

"As therefore, physicians are many times forced to leave such methods of curing as themselves know to be fittest, and being over-ruled by the sick man's impatience, are fain to try the best they can: in like sort, considering how the case doth stand with the present age, full of tongue and weak of brain, behold we would (*if our subject permitted it*) yield to the stream thereof. That way we would be contented to prove our thesis, which being the worse in itself, notwithstanding is now by reason of common imbecility the fitter and likelier to be brooked."—HOOKER.[2]

If this fear could be rationally entertained in the controversial age of Hooker, under the then robust discipline of the scholastic

---

suffrages of the judicious Public], which if we do not take good care will break up and scatter before it all robustness and manly vigor of intellect, all masculine fortitude of virtue." The Latin in *BL,* which varies slightly from *The Friend,* is var, with omissions.

[1] John Barclay (1582–1621) *Argenis:* in C's annotated copy (Amsterdam 1659) 71 (var, with omissions). "There is a middle ranke (like that of Knights among the Nobility) of wise men, and useful in affaires, which yet reach not to the first height and greatness . . . Of them there is a more plentiful store. . . . To bee diligent, to speake nothing rashly, to accustome ones selfe to labour, and [by] the shew of wisedome [and modesty] to hide the weaker part of the wits . . .

while custome and use, which in affaires of State make them able, is by the most part taken for nature, and greatnesse of mind." Tr Robert Le Grys (1629) 42–3 (adapted). The words in brackets translate C's text and his variations on it. He has attempted to emend the corrupt text of his edition by omitting the words "parere et" ("to obey and") after "labori". See *CM (CC)* ɪ 219 and n for another attempt at correcting this same passage. C had copied the passage into a notebook in 1809: *CN* ɪɪɪ 3536. On Barclay see also ch 22, below, ɪɪ 121.

[2] Richard Hooker (1554–1600) *Of the Laws of Ecclesiastical Polity* ɪ viii 2 (var, with omissions): *Works* (1682) 80. C had copied the passage into a notebook in 1809. *CN* ɪɪɪ 3574 and n.

logic, pardonably may a writer of the present times anticipate a scanty audience for abstrusest themes, and truths that can neither be communicated or received without effort of thought, as well as patience of attention.[1]

> Che s'io non erro al calcular de' punti,
> Par ch' *Asinina* Stella a noi predomini,
> E'l Somaro e'l castron si sian congiunti.
> Il tempo d'Apuleio piu non si nomini:
> Che se allora un sol Huom sembrava un Asino,
> Mille Asini a' miei dì rassembran Huomini!
> DI SALVATOR ROSA Satir. I. l. 10.[2]

---

[1] Cf a similar remark in the supernumerary essay of *The Friend: CC* II 277 (I 16–17).

[2] Salvator Rosa (1615–73) *La Musica: Satira* I 10–15 (var). C entered the lines in a notebook about the same time he was writing *BL: CN* III 4258 and n. "For if I err not in calculating the points, an asinine star seems to rule us, and the Donkey and the Mule are in conjunction. Let the Time of Apuleius be named no more! For if then one Man alone seemed to be an Ass, a thousand [for Rosa's "many"] Asses in my days resemble Men." Tr *CN*.

CHAPTER 10

A chapter of digression and anecdotes, as an interlude preceding that on the nature and genesis of the imagination or plastic power[1]—On pedantry and pedantic expressions—Advice to young authors respecting publication—Various anecdotes of the author's literary life, and the progress of his opinions in religion and politics

"**E**semplastic. *The word is not in Johnson, nor have I met with it elsewhere.*" Neither have I! I constructed it myself from the Greek words, εἰς ἓν πλάττειν i.e. to shape into one;[2] because,

[1] Ch 10 may have been an abortive or false start on what finally became ch 13, "on the imagination, or esemplastic power". The digressionary nature of ch 10 would then not have been planned deliberately. It is notable that the first word in this chapter that C says he is adopting "from our elder classics" (the word "sensuous") appears conspicuously in the marginal note on Maass in which C experiments with the "sensuous *Einbildungskraft*" as "Eisemplasy". Besides "sensuous", both "intuition" and the pair "objective" and "subjective", words that C discusses in the first two paragraphs of the chapter, could have been activated by his reading of Maass, Kant, Schelling, and other Germans. The German words that he was trying to approximate in English seem to be *empfindlich, Anschauung,* and the *objektiv–subjectiv* pair that occurs so frequently in Germany from 1790 on. All these terms play an important rôle in the discussion of the imagination found in Tetens, Kant, Fichte, and Schelling (see below, I 172–4).

[2] "How excellently the German Einbildungskraft expresses this prime & loftiest Faculty, the power of co-

adunation, the faculty that forms the many into one, *in eins Bildung.*" *CN* III 4176. Shawcross (*BL*—1907 —I 249) assumed that C "misapprehended" the etymology of *Einbildungskraft* (from *ein* = in [not *Eins* = one], *Bildung* = forming, and *Kraft* = power); and his assumption has been followed, though SC long ago pointed out two of the several parallels with Schelling: "Ist das Band die lebendige In-Eins-Bildung des Einen mit dem Vielen" (". . . the bond is the living formation into one of the one and the many"), in the *Darlegung* 61–2 (*SW* VII 60), and the *"In-Eins-Bildung"* of the "real and the ideal", in the *Vorlesungen* (Tübingen 1803) 313 (*SW* V 348). *BL* (1847) I 173n. C had been trying to express the same concept through the analogous "coadunate" (*co-ad-unare,* "to make one with"), as in his description to Sotheby 10 Sept 1802 of the imagination as "the *modifying,* and *co-adunating* Faculty" (*CL* II 866). But the appeal to him of both "plastic" and the German *Bildung* is their stronger suggestions of the process of "shaping", the organic interpenetration of parts, and the formative union of shaping and being shaped. C's

having to convey a new sense, I thought that a new term would
both aid the recollection of my meaning, and prevent its being

coined term "esemplastic" can be traced directly to his front flyleaf note in Maass. C is discussing Maass's definition of form as something *ab intra* and wondering whether the imagination, as a faculty of perception, does not exercise a formative and "external active power" as it experiences the world. C's note reads: "In Maass's introductory Chapters my mind has been perplexed by the division of things into matter (sensatio ab extra) and form (i.e. per- et con-ceptio ab intra.) Now as Time and Space are evidently only the Universals, ⟨or modi communes,⟩ of sensation and sensuous Form, & consequently appertain exclusively to the sensuous Einbildungskraft, (= Eisemplasy, (πλαττειν εις εν) which we call Imagination, Fancy, &c—all poor & inadequate terms, far inferior to the German, Einbildung) the Law of Association derived ab extra from the contempor[an]ëity of the impressions, or indeed any other difference of the characterless Manifold (mannichfaltige) except that of plus and minus of impingence becomes incomprehensible, if not absurd. I see at one instant of Time a Rose and a Lily—Chemistry teaches me that they differ only in form, being both reducible to the same Elements— if then Form be not an external active power, if it be wholly transfused into the Object by the esenoplastic or imaginative faculty of the percipient, or rather Creator, where & wherein shall I find the ground of my perception, that this is the Rose, and that the Lily?" *CM* (*CC*) III. Although Schelling and Maass seem the most likely candidates to act as catalysts in C's mind, causing him to create a word that would provide the psychological and philosophical connotations of *Einbildungskraft,* other German writers had stressed

that *Einbildungskraft* means the power to unify into "one" or into a new whole. In fact, the notion that the imagination forms *ein Ganzes* or *ein Eins* as it blends and actively coalesces associations and perceptions was quite common by the 1790s. In 1804 Jean Paul reiterates this concept. Yet as early as the 1770s Platner, Tetens, Hissmann, and Herder—taking their cue from previous English, German, and even French associationists—all expressed this notion. Kant, Fichte, Schiller, and Schelling add the notion of a dialectic synthesis of opposites into one unity. Finally Schelling splits up the word and rearranges it into *In-Eins-Bildung,* but by this time he is expressing an idea that is at least a generation old in Germany. See above, I lxxxv–lxxxvi, xcix–cii, and McFarland "SI" 235.

The "plasy" or "plastic" part of C's word is partly an attempt to translate the German *Bildung,* which is certainly in C's mind. The word "plastic" or "plastic power" had also been used by Akenside, Gerard, and Tucker in their descriptions of the imagination as a shaping or "plastic power". WW also used it to refer to the imagination in the 1805–6 *Prelude,* perhaps already influenced by C or by the English writers mentioned. See Engell *CI* 45, 49, 84–7, 269, and cf *CN* III 4243–4 and nn. When C speaks of "the usual import of the word, imagination", he means as it pertains exclusively to the creative (as opposed to the perceptive and coalescing) process. Cf C's similar remarks, ch 4, above, I 82–8 ch 7, I 124–5, and below, ch 13, I 304–5, ch 14, II 15–17. German writers, including Schelling and Maass, distinguish between the "common" meaning of imagination as it is applied to art and poetry and its broader and more philosophical (but

confounded with the usual import of the word, imagination. *"But this is pedantry!"* Not necessarily so, I hope. If I am not mis-informed, pedantry consists in the use of words unsuitable to the time, place, and company.[1] The language of the market would be in the schools as *pedantic*, though it might not be reprobated by that name, as the language of the schools in the market. The mere man of the world, who insists that no other terms but such as occur in common conversation should be employed in a scientific disquisition, and with no greater precision, is as truly a *pedant* as the man of letters, who either over-rating the acquirements of his auditors, or misled by his own familiarity with technical or scho-lastic terms, converses at the wine-table with his mind fixed on his musæum or laboratory; even though the latter pedant instead of desiring his wife to *make the tea,* should bid her add to the quant. suff. of thea sinensis the oxyd of hydrogen saturated with caloric.[2] To use the colloquial (and in truth somewhat *vulgar*) metaphor, if

---

less popularised) sense. C views the creative or poetic imagination as the same in kind with the philosophical meaning of imagination, but higher and more intensified in degree. (See ch 13, below, and above, I lxxxix–xcii.) The early meaning of *Einbild-ung,* which Herder points out in ex-plaining his own usage of *Einbildung* and *Einbildungskraft* as forming a unity meant to work into the soul of man, is to unify all perceptions by drawing them into one man's life and total experience. While *ein-* is a preposition with adverbial force there is, in the case of *einbilden,* the additional sense of impressing or imaging things and ideas "into" the soul, thus bringing them together or unifying them there in one whole life, in what Herder calls "ein Seelenmensch" (*Vom Erkennen und Empfinden: SW* VIII 190–2). For this reason, and with the impetus of associationist psychology stressing the coalescing of images into larger wholes (going back to Locke's "complex ideas"), the working (as opposed to the purely grammatical) etymology of *Einbildungskraft* could be said to include, or at least to

imply, the sense of unifying into larger wholes, into one life or one world-view, because the *ein-* in this word refers to the impression of an image in the soul or mind where it will naturally mix with and become part of other images that will aggre-gate, fuse, and be shaped by the active power of the mind into a larger whole or "one" (*Eins*).

[1] This sentence, the rest of the paragraph, and much of the follow-ing paragraph repeat almost ver-batim the opening of Essay III of "On the Principles of Genial Criti-cism", first published in *Felix Farley's Bristol Journal* Aug–Sept 1814. See *BL* (1907) II 228–30.

[2] *Quantum sufficit* of *thea Sinensis:* "As much as suffices of China tea". "Oxyd" is an obsolete term for oxide, and "caloric" in C's time was supposedly an elastic fluid providing or containing heat. The oxide of hydrogen is H_2O. When it is saturated with caloric it is raised to its highest possible temperature. Thus, by "the oxyd of hydrogen saturated with caloric" C means boiling water.

the pedant of the cloyster, and the pedant of the lobby, both *smell equally of the shop*, yet the odour from the Russian binding of good old *authentic-looking* folios and quartos is less annoying than the steams from the tavern or bagnio. Nay, though the pedantry of the scholar should betray a little ostentation, yet a well-conditioned mind would more easily, methinks, tolerate the *fox-brush* of learned vanity, than the *sans culotterie* of a contemptuous ignorance, that assumes a merit from mutilation in the self-consoling sneer at the pompous incumbrance of tails.[1]

The first lesson of philosophic discipline is to wean the student's attention from the DEGREES of things, which alone form the vocabulary of common life, and to direct it to the KIND abstracted from *degree*.[2] Thus the chemical student is taught not to be startled at disquisitions on the heat in ice, or on latent and fixible light. In such discourse the instructor has no other alternative than either to use old words with new meanings (the plan adopted by Darwin in his Zoonomia;) or to introduce new terms, after the example of Linnæus, and the framers of the present chemical nomenclature.[3] The latter mode is evidently preferable, were it only that the former demands a twofold exertion of thought in one and the same act. For the reader (or hearer) is required not only to learn and bear in mind the new definition; but to unlearn, and keep out of his view, the old and habitual meaning; a far more difficult and perplexing task, and for which the mere *semblance* of eschewing pedantry seems to me an inadequate compensation. Where, indeed, it is in our power to recall an appropriate term that had without sufficient reason become obsolete, it is doubtless a less evil to restore than to coin anew. Thus to express in one word, all that

[1] Cf a similar remark in *Friend* (*CC*) II 139, in which David Lloyd's *State-Worthies* is also quoted. Cf *CN* III 3623.

[2] Cf ch 4, above, I 88, and ch 12, below, I 234, 286; *CL* IV 575, *SM* (*CC*) 60–1n, and *TL* (1848) 41.

[3] Erasmus Darwin at the close of his Preface to *Zoönomia, or Laws of Organic Life* (1794) states that he rejected new terms in the belief that "new definitions of words already in use would be less burthensome to the memory of the reader". On the other hand, Linnaeus (Carl von Linné, 1707–78), the great Swedish botanist, starting with his *Genera plantarum* (1737), felt it necessary to create a new nomenclature, which he completed in the 1758 ed of his *Systema naturae*. F. A. Stafleu *Linnaeus and the Linnaeans* (Utrecht 1971) 79–112. The "framers of the present chemical nomenclature" may refer to John Dalton (1766–1844), Antoine Lavoisier (1743–94), and Humphry Davy (1778–1829), preeminently Lavoisier; cf *P Lects* Lect 12 (1949) 342–3.

appertains to the perception considered as passive, and merely recipient, I have adopted from our elder classics the word *sensuous*; because *sensual* is not at present used, except in a bad sense, or at least as a *moral* distinction, while *sensitive* and *sensible* would each convey a different meaning.[1] Thus too I have followed Hooker, Sanderson, Milton, &c. in designating the *immediateness* of any act or object of knowlege by the word *intuition*, used sometimes objectively, even as we use the word, thought; now as *the* thought, or act of thinking, and now as *a* thought, or the object of our reflection; and we do this without confusion or obscurity.[2] The very words, *objective* and *subjective*, of such constant recurrence in the schools of yore, I have ventured to re-introduce, because I could not so briefly, or conveniently by any more familiar terms distinguish the percipere from the percipi.[3] Lastly,

[1] Cf ". . . our language wants terms of comprehensive generality, implying the kind not the degree or species—as in that good and necessary word 'sensuous' which we have likewise dropt, opposed to sensual, sensitive, sensible, &c &c". *CN* II 2442. The word was coined by Milton, used first in *Of Reformation in England* (1641) and then especially in the famous passage in *Of Education* (1644) about poetry as, in comparison with logic, "less subtile and fine, but more simple, sensuous, and passionate". *Works* ed Birch (1738) I 146. Cf *CN* III 3287, notes for a lecture on "the Moderns". In 1755 Johnson records it simply as "not in use". Cf *Friend* (*CC*) I 156; *PGC : BL* (1907) II 230; *Sh C* II 260 (lecture of 28 Oct 1813 in Bristol). "Sensuous" may be C's attempt to find an English word to render the concept of the German *empfindlich*. See above, I 168 n 1. Cf WW *Prelude* (1805–6) XI 169.

[2] C quotes Hooker in *PGC:* "an intuition, that is, a direct and immediate beholding or presentation of an object to the mind through the senses or the imagination". *BL* (1907) II 230. The passage is untraced. In *Logic* C says that Hooker "has expressed the meaning [of "intuition"] by an 'immediate beholding' ". *Logic* (*CC*) 151. C may have in mind a passage on man's desire to know the truth with certainty: "The greatest assurance generally with all men, is that which we have by a plain aspect and intuitive beholding." *Of the Laws of Ecclesiastical Polity* II vii: *Works* (1682) 119. No particular example of the use of "intuition" has been found in the writings of bp Robert Sanderson (1587–1663). But the concept of "immediacy" is commonplace in both seventeenth- and eighteenth-century usage. Cf Johnson's first definition of "intuition": "immediate knowledge". "Intuition" reflects C's attempt to use an English word for the concept expressed by the German *Anschauung* or *intellecktuelle Anschauung*. See above, I 168 n 1.

[3] The terms, which became so important in German thought after Kant, had by now reversed their earlier meaning. When Duns Scotus (c 1265–c 1308) introduced the antithesis into Scholastic thought, *subjectivum* applied to the "subject" of judgements (i.e. the actual object of thought), whereas *objectivum* meant "the thing as constituted through the perceiving mind". See

I have cautiously discriminated the terms, the REASON, and the UNDERSTANDING, encouraged and confirmed by the authority of our genuine divines, and philosophers, before the revolution.[1]

———— both life, and sense,
Fancy, and *understanding*: whence the soul

especially Carl von Prantl *Geschichte der Logik im Abendlande* (Leipzig 1855–70) III 208f. The distinction in this form continued in Descartes and Spinoza and into the later eighteenth century, though in German writing it began to reverse itself and take on its modern implications in C. A. Crusius (1715–75), J. H. Lambert (1728–77), J. N. Tetens (1736–1807), and then Kant. For a brief history see Rudolf Eucken *Geistige Strömungen der Gegenwart* (Leipzig 1904) ch 1. Of less value is the confused history of the terms by C's later enemy, Sir William Hamilton, in his Supplement to *Works of Thomas Reid* (Edinburgh 1863) II 806–8. Historians of thought assume that the reversal of the older antithesis is the product of German Idealism culminating in Kant's premise in which "I think" has transcendental significance and is the *a priori* condition of all knowledge; and that the new distinction was imported into English by C and later Hamilton. But this is true only as far as the specifically Kantian implications are concerned. Like the reversal in the older distinction between "fancy" and "imagination", it first took place in England and reflected the heavy stress on the "subjective" (in the modern sense) by British empirical psychology, with which all the Germans, especially Tetens, were closely acquainted. So by 1725 in his widely used textbook *Logick* (II ii 8) Isaac Watts defines the "objective" as "true in itself" and the "subjective" as our reaction: The one is in things, the other is in our minds" (8th ed 1745 p 150). C was well aware of the switch in meaning of the two terms. In his

marginalia to Heinrich Steffens *Grundzüge der philosophischen Naturwissenschaft* (Berlin 1806) 29, C remarks, "Steffens has needlessly perplexed his reasoning by his strange use of Subjective and Objective—his S=the O of former Philosophers, and his O=their S." *CM* (*CC*) IV. C's note suggests that Steffens's usages were new, or at least noteworthy, for C. Cf *CN* III 4226n and *P Lects* Lect 13 (1949) 371–3.

[1] C has been both castigated and supported for implying that English writers "before the revolution" (1688), including the "Cambridge Platonists", anticipated Kant's distinction between "reason" and "understanding" or at least C's own distinction as he modified that of Kant. Arguments in support can be subsumed by the discussion and quotations in *C 17th C* 108–18. But actually the traditional distinction between a "higher" or "intuitive" and the merely "discursive reason" (whether in Plato, in Scholastic philosophy, or in the sixteenth and seventeenth centuries) has to be considerably stretched in order even to begin to suggest the "reason–understanding" distinction in Kant. C himself admits as much in comments on Henry More and John Smith. McFarland 212–13. Cf Wellek 103–6. What can be argued is that the older distinction, particularly that of the Platonic tradition, did encourage in C a *readiness* for the distinction that he found in Kant and that he then proceeded to modify, raising Kant's conception of *Vernunft* to something like the direct intuitive "reason" (*nous*) of Plato.

> *Reason* receives, and REASON is her *being*,
> DISCURSIVE or INTUITIVE. Discourse *
> Is oftest your's, the latter most is our's,
> Differing but in *degree*, in *kind* the same."
>   PARADISE LOST, *Book V*.[3]

I say, that I was *confirmed* by authority so venerable: for I had previous and higher motives in my own conviction of the importance, nay, of the necessity of the distinction, as both an indis-

---

* But for sundry notes on Shakspeare, &c. which have fallen in my way, I should have deemed it unnecessary to observe, that *discourse* here, or elsewhere does not mean what we *now* call discoursing; but the *discursion* of the *mind*,[1] the processes of generalization and subsumption, of deduction and conclusion. Thus, Philosophy has *hitherto* been DISCURSIVE: while Geometry is *always* and *essentially* INTUITIVE.[2]

[1] Cf "Our Shakespear in agreement both with truth and the philosophy of his age names it '*discourse* of reason', as an instrumental faculty *belonging* to reason . . .". *SM* (*CC*) 69.

[2] The last sentence in C's footnote touches on a point much discussed in German philosophy since Descartes, Spinoza, and Leibniz and especially since Kant's first *Kritik* (1781). By "*hitherto*" discursive, C apparently means to characterise the method of most philosophy up to the introduction of transcendental philosophy in general, which may be said to rely on immediate intellectual intuition or imaginative perception. (E.g. Schelling's "Ohne intellektuelle Anschauung keine Philosophie!") Kant and Schelling discuss the relationship of geometry to philosophy and the similarities of their intuitive "construction". This is particularly true when philosophy escapes purely empirical or "discursive" approaches. For Fichte, philosophy could be said to be purely intuitional, a construct of the imagination or of the spirit of self alone. The words "immediate", "intuition", "sensuous", "subjective" and "objective" occur in Kant's and Schelling's discussions on the intuitive method of philosophy and geometry; so does "discursive", which is associated with pure understanding, whereas "intuitive" is associated with pure reason or the transcendental imagination. C's text and footnote likewise signal a scheme of mental faculties, including the imagination. C's conclusion is very broad but is in basic agreement with transcendental philosophy in general. Yet Leibniz and others, all the way back to Plato, had discussed "intuitive" vs "demonstrative" bases of knowledge and method. C is delighted to find connection between earlier English usage and the present German writers. See e.g. Schelling *Abhandlungen: Phil Schrift* 329–40 (*SW* I 444–52); Jacobi *ULS* 101–2. Also WW *Prelude* (1805–6) XI 123ff and *Excursion* IV 1127ff; and ch 12, below, I 240–1.

[3] Milton *Paradise Lost* V 485–90 (reading "in kind" for "of kind"). Cf *Friend* (*CC*) I 156 and *CN* III 3801 and n. The central distinction is between "discursive" and "intuitive" reason. "Understanding" is being used by Milton not for an inferior faculty of mind but to suggest what Johnson (1755) defines it as in general English speech: "intellectual powers generally" as distinct from the specific act of intellect we call "reason". The lines probably encouraged C in one of his favourite qualifications: differing in degree but not in kind.

pensable condition and a vital part of all sound speculation in metaphysics, ethical or theological. To establish this distinction was one main object of THE FRIEND; if even in a biography of my own literary life I can with propriety refer to a work, which was printed rather than published, or so published that it had been well for the unfortunate author, if it had remained in manuscript![1] I have even at this time bitter cause for remembering that, which a number of my subscribers have but a trifling motive for forgetting. This effusion might have been spared; but I would feign flatter myself, that the reader will be less austere than an oriental professor of the bastinado, who during an attempt to extort per argumentum baculinum[2] a full confession from a culprit, interrupted his outcry of pain by reminding him, that it was "*a mere digression!*" All this noise, Sir! is nothing to the point, and no sort of answer to my QUESTIONS! *Ah! but* (replied the sufferer) *it is the most pertinent reply in nature to your blows.*

An imprudent man of common goodness of heart, cannot but wish to turn even his imprudences to the benefit of others, as far as this is possible. If therefore any one of the readers of this semi-narrative should be preparing or intending a periodical work, I warn him, in the first place, against trusting in the number of names on his subscription list. For he cannot be certain that the names were put down by sufficient authority; or (should that be ascertained) it still remains to be known, whether they were not extorted by some over zealous friend's importunity; whether the subscriber had not yielded his name, merely from want of courage to answer, no! and with the intention of dropping the work as soon as possible. One gentleman procured me nearly a hundred names for THE FRIEND,[3] and not only took frequent opportunity to

---

[1] *The Friend; a Literary, Moral, and Political Weekly Paper, Excluding Personal and Party Politics, and the Events of the Day,* published at Penrith from 1 Jun 1809 to 15 Mar 1810. Only 28 numbers were printed. The irregularity was one reason for the lack of success of *The Friend.* C was often ill and in genuine mental distress. Other reasons include the comparative remoteness for that time of the place of publication, the philosophic and analytic character of the subjects, and the concentrated style in which the work was written. For general background see Introd to *Friend (CC)* by Barbara E. Rooke. For the distinction between "reason" and "understanding" see esp *Friend (CC)* I 154–61 (II 294–7), 177 (II 104), 190 (II 125), 196 (II 129), 199 (II 131); II 77–8, 281, 283, 390, 503–4.

[2] Tr: "by the argument from the stick".

[3] Thomas Clarkson (1760–1846). C discusses the incident in a letter to Lady Beaumont (21 Jan 1810), in

remind me of his success in his canvas, but laboured to impress my mind with the sense of the obligation, I was under to the subscribers; for (as he very pertinently admonished me) *"fifty-two shillings* a year was a large sum to be bestowed on one individual, where there were so many objects of charity with strong claims to the assistance of the benevolent." Of these hundred patrons ninety threw up the publication before the fourth number, without any notice; though it was well known to them, that in consequence of the distance, and the slowness and irregularity of the conveyance, I was compelled to lay in a stock of *stamped* paper for at least eight weeks beforehand; each sheet of which stood me in five pence previous to its arrival at my printer's; though the subscription money was not to be received till the twenty-first week after the commencement of the work; and lastly, though it was in nine cases out of ten impracticable for me to receive the money for two or three numbers without paying an equal sum for the postage.[1]

In confirmation of my first caveat, I will select one fact among *many.* On my list of subscribers, among a considerable number of names equally flattering, was that of an Earl of Cork, with his address.[2] He might as well have been an Earl of Bottle, for aught *I* knew of him, who had been content to reverence the peerage in abstracto, rather than in concretis. Of course THE FRIEND was regularly sent as far, if I remember right, as the eighteenth number: i.e. till a fortnight before the subscription was to be paid. And lo! just at this time I received a letter from his Lordship, reproving me in language far more lordly than courteous for my impudence in directing my pamphlets to him, who knew nothing of me or my work! Seventeen or eighteen numbers of which, however, his Lordship was pleased to retain, probably for the culinary or post-culinary conveniences of his servants.[3]

which Clarkson is said to have procured him "sixty to seventy Names". *CL* III 275–6. In the letter C wrote: "Pity that Mr C. had not added— 'when there are so many other *Objects* of Distress . . .' " etc, which in *BL* C now attributes to him. There were eventually between 630 and 650 subscribers in all. *Friend (CC)* I xlix n and II 407ff.

[1] For the financial problems C is summarising, see *Friend (CC)* I lxiii–lix.

[2] Edmund Boyle, 8th Earl of Cork and Orrery (1767–1856), whose name appeared on a list of subscribers sent to C by George Ward in May 1809. *Friend (CC)* II 422.

[3] The same incident is told in the letter mentioned above (I 175 n 3), but without the embellishments of C's attempts at humour—the word-play with "Cork" and with "post-culinary" (using *The Friend* to wipe dirty pans or using it as toilet

Secondly, I warn all others from the attempt to deviate from the ordinary mode of publishing a work by *the trade*. I thought indeed, that to the purchaser it was indifferent, whether thirty per cent. of the purchase-money went to the booksellers or to the government; and that the convenience of receiving the work by the post at his own door would give the preference to the latter. It is hard, I own, to have been labouring for years, in collecting and arranging the materials; to have spent every shilling that could be spared after the necessaries of life had been furnished, in buying books, or in journies for the purpose of consulting them or of acquiring facts at the fountain head; then to buy the paper, pay for the printing, &c. all at least fifteen per cent. beyond what *the trade* would have paid; and then after all to give thirty per cent. not of the net profits, but of the gross results of the sale, to a man who has merely to give the books shelf or warehouse room, and permit his apprentice to hand them over the counter to those who may ask for them; and this too copy by copy, although if the work be on any philosophical or scientific subject, it may be years before the edition is sold off. All this, I confess, must seem an hardship, and one, to which the products of industry in no other mode of exertion are subject. Yet even this is better, far better, than to attempt in any way to unite the functions of author and publisher. But the most prudent mode is to sell the copy-right, at least of one or more editions, for the most that *the trade* will offer. By few only can a large remuneration be expected; but fifty pounds and ease of mind are of more real advantage to a literary man, than the *chance* of five hundred with the *certainty* of insult and degrading anxieties. I shall have been grievously misunderstood, if this statement should be interpreted as written with the desire of detracting from the character of booksellers or publishers. The individuals did not make the laws and customs of their trade, but as in every other trade take them as they find them. Till the evil can be proved to be removable and without the substitution of an equal or greater inconvenience, it were neither wise or manly even to complain of it. But to use it as a pretext for speaking, or

---

paper). C is fond of referring to the fate of his works in this way. Cf below (I 187), on the servant-girl using a large amount of paper to light a fire, and, checked for her extravagance, replying "it is only WATCHMEN". Or: "I am tempted to add a passage from my own translation" of Schiller's *Wallenstein,* the more since it is extant only by "the kind partiality of trunk-makers". *Friend* (*CC*) I 428n.

even for thinking, or feeling, unkindly or opprobriously of the tradesmen, as *individuals*, would be something worse than unwise or even than unmanly; it would be immoral and calumnious! My motives point in a far different direction and to far other objects, as will be seen in the conclusion of the chapter.

A learned and exemplary old clergyman, who many years ago went to his reward followed by the regrets and blessings of his flock, published at his own expence two volumes octavo, entitled, a new Theory of Redemption. The work was most severely handled in the Monthly or Critical Review, I forget which,[1] and this unprovoked hostility became the good old man's favorite topic of conversation among his friends. Well! (he used to exclaim) in the S E C O N D edition, I shall have an opportunity of exposing both the ignorance and the malignity of the anonymous critic. Two or three years however passed by without any tidings from the bookseller, who had undertaken the printing and publication of the work, and who was perfectly at his ease, as the author was known to be a man of large property. At length the *accounts* were written for; and in the course of a few weeks they were presented by the *rider*[2] for the house, in person. My old friend put on his spectacles, and holding the scroll with no very firm hand, began—*Paper, so much*: O moderate enough—not at all beyond my expectation! *Printing, so much*: well! moderate enough! *Stitching, covers, advertisements, carriage, &c. so much.*—Still nothing amiss. *Selleridge* (for orthography is no necessary part of a bookseller's literary acquirements) £3. 3*s*. Bless me! only three guineas for the what d'ye call it? the *selleridge*? No more, Sir! replied the rider. Nay, but that is *too* moderate! rejoined my old friend. Only three guineas for *selling* a thousand copies of a work in two volumes? O Sir! (cries the young traveller) you have mistaken the word. There have been none of them *sold*; they have been sent back from London long ago; and

---

[1] *A New Theory of Redemption, upon Principles Equally Agreeable to Revelation and Reason* (2 vols 1789, "Printed for the Author"). No author's name appeared on the title-page, but the review in *C Rev* LXIX (Feb 1790) 143–9 noted: "We have been informed that the author of these volumes is the rev. James Newton, vicar of Old Cleve, Somersetshire." Old Cleeve, close to the Bristol Channel and twenty miles west of Bridgwater, is in the west country where C spent the early years of his marriage. The review is not so severe as C claims, though it did suggest that there was no reason for the work's having been written.

[2] A commercial traveller or salesman.

this £3. 3*s.* is for the *cellaridge,* or warehouse-room in our book cellar. The work was in consequence preferred from the ominous cellar of the publisher's, to the author's garret; and on presenting a copy to an acquaintance the old gentleman used to tell the anecdote with great humor and still greater good nature.

With equal lack of worldly knowledge, I was a far more than equal sufferer for it, at the very outset of my authorship.[1] Toward the close of the first year from the time, that in an inauspicious hour I left the friendly cloysters, and the happy grove of quiet, ever honored Jesus College, Cambridge, I was persuaded by sundry Philanthropists and Anti-polemists[2] to set on foot a periodical work, entitled THE WATCHMAN, that (according to the general motto of the work) *all might know the truth, and that the truth might make us free!*[3] In order to exempt it from the stamp-tax, and likewise to contribute as little as possible to the supposed guilt of a war against freedom, it was to be published on every eighth day, thirty-two pages, large octavo, closely printed, and price only FOUR-PENCE. Accordingly with a flaming prospectus, "*Knowledge is Power,*" &c. *to cry the state of the political atmosphere,* and so forth,[4] I set off on a tour to the North, from Bristol to Sheffield, for the purpose of procuring customers, preaching by the way in most of the great towns, as an hireless volunteer, in a blue coat and white waistcoat, that not a rag of the woman of Babylon might be seen on me.[5] For I was at that time and long

[1] Not only in the case of *The Watchman,* as C describes below, but with his translation of Schiller's *Wallenstein* and *Piccolomini* (1800). The majority of the copies in the 1st ed were pulped by the publisher Longman and Rees.

[2] *OED,* defining it "a professed opponent of war" and calling it rare, cites only this example.

[3] C left Cambridge Dec 1794, and began planning *The Watchman* Dec 1795, encouraged by the success of his lectures opposing the war with France. *The Watchman* appeared from 1 Mar to 13 May 1796. The motto (adapted from John 8.32 and appearing in each issue) was: "That all may know the truth; and that the truth may make us free!" The "flaming prospectus" mentioned below (actually Lamb's phrase for the Prospectus of *The Friend*) announced the first number to appear 5 Feb 1796. The "Philanthropists and Anti-polemists" who "persuaded" C to start the periodical were a group of Bristol citizens who met in Dec 1795 at the Rummer Tavern. For background see Introd to *Watchman (CC).*

[4] For the Prospectus see *Watchman (CC)* 3–6; for the quotation, from Bacon "De haeresibus" *Meditationes sacrae,* see 4 and n 2 and cf *SM (CC)* 24.

[5] For the occasion on which C was "overpersuaded" to wear the black priestly gown when preaching see his letter to Wade 2 Feb 1796: *CL* I 180; cf *Watchman (CC)* xxxiv.

after, though a Trinitarian (i.e. ad normam Platonis)[1] in philosophy, yet a zealous Unitarian in Religion; more accurately, I was a *psilanthropist*,[2] one of those who believe our Lord to have been the real son of Joseph, and who lay the main stress on the resurrection rather than on the crucifixion.[3] O! never can I remember those days with either shame or regret. For I was most sincere, most disinterested! My opinions were indeed in many and most important points erroneous; but my heart was single. Wealth, rank, life itself then seemed cheap to me, compared with the interests of (what I believed to be) the truth, and the will of my maker. I cannot even accuse myself of having been actuated by vanity; for in the expansion of my enthusiasm I did not think of *myself* at all.

My campaign commenced at Birmingham;[4] and my first attack was on a rigid Calvinist, a tallow chandler by trade. He was a tall dingy man, in whom length was so predominant over breadth, that he might almost have been borrowed for a foundery poker. O that face! a face κατ᾽ ἔμφασιν![5] I have it before me at this moment. The lank, black, twine-like hair, *pingui-nitescent*,[6] cut in a strait line along the black stubble of his thin gunpowder eye brows, that looked like a scorched *after-math* from a last week's shaving. His coat collar behind in perfect unison, both of colour and lustre with the coarse yet glib cordage, that I suppose he called his hair, and which with a *bend* inward at the nape of the neck (the only approach to flexure in his whole figure) slunk in behind his waistcoat; while the countenance lank, dark, very *hard*, and with strong

---

[1] "Following the pattern of Plato". On C's distinction between his Unitarianism in religion and his philosophic interest in trinitarianism see below, I 204–5.

[2] A believer in Christ's mere humanity; from ψιλός, "mere", and ἄνθρωπος, "man". Cf *LS* (*CC*) 176 and n 4. Cf "psilosophy", below.

[3] C had become essentially a Unitarian by 1794, under the influence of William Frend at Cambridge, and by May 1796 had decided to become a Unitarian minister. *CL* I 210. Especially after 1802 he began to question his position, and a notebook entry of Feb 1805 records his first explicit state-

ment of the trinitarianism toward which he was now moving. *CN* II 2444 and n. See J. Robert Barth *Coleridge and Christian Doctrine* (Cambridge, Mass 1969) 3–13. Cf McFarland 178–81.

[4] Actually at Worcester, several days earlier, where there were too many "aristocrats" for him to make headway with his proposed publication. Letter to Wade 10 Jan 1796: *CL* I 175.

[5] "Emphatically".

[6] A C coinage, meaning "shining with grease" (from *pinguis*, "fat" or "grease", and *nitescere*, "to shine").

perpendicular furrows, gave me a dim notion of some one looking at me through a *used* gridiron, all soot, grease, and iron! But he was one of the *thorough-bred*,[1] a true lover of liberty, and (I was informed) had proved to the satisfaction of many, that Mr. Pitt was one of the horns of the second beast in the Revelations, *that spoke like a dragon.*[2] A person, to whom one of my letters of recommendation had been addressed, was my introducer. It was a new event in my life, my first *stroke* in the new business I had undertaken of an author, yea, and of an author trading on his own account. My companion after some imperfect sentences and a multitude of hums and haas abandoned the cause to his client; and I commenced an harangue of half an hour to Phileleutheros,[3] the tallow-chandler, varying my notes through the whole gamut of eloquence from the ratiocinative to the declamatory, and in the latter from the pathetic to the indignant. I argued, I described, I promised, I prophecied; and beginning with the captivity of nations I ended with the near approach of the millenium, finishing the whole with some of my own verses describing that glorious state out of *the Religious Musings:*

> ——————————— Such delights,
> As float to earth, permitted visitants!
> When in some hour of solemn jubilee
> The massive gates of Paradise are thrown
> Wide open: and forth come in fragments wild
> Sweet echoes of unearthly melodies,
> And odors snatch'd from beds of Amaranth,
> And they that from the chrystal river of life
> Spring up on freshen'd wings, ambrosial gales!
> *Religious Musings,* 1. 356.[4]

My taper man of lights listened with perseverant and praise-worthy patience, though (as I was afterwards told on complaining of certain gales that were not altogether ambrosial) it was a *melting* day with him. And what, Sir! (he said after a short pause) might the cost be? *Only* F O U R - P E N C E (O! how I felt the anti-climax, the abysmal bathos of that *four-pence!*) *only four-pence, Sir, each*

---

[1] As a noun and applied to a person, earlier than any example in *OED.*

[2] Rev 13.11. C, too, at this time, considered Pitt a "Monster" and a "State-Nimrod". *MPL: Lects 1795 (CC)* 3 and n, *Watchman (CC)* 39.

[3] "Lover of Freedom". See *Friend (CC)* I 211 and ch 2, above, I 41, C's n.

[4] Lines 343–51 (var): *PW* (EHC) I 122. (C's line number does not agree with any edition of his poems up to the time of *BL.*)

number, to be published on every eighth day. That comes to a deal of money at the end of a year. And how much did you say there was to be for the money? *Thirty-two pages, Sir! large octavo, closely printed.* Thirty and two pages? Bless me, why except what I does in a family way on the Sabbath, that's more than I ever reads, Sir! all the year round. I am as great a one, as any man in Brummagem,[1] Sir! for liberty and truth and all them sort of things, but as to this (no offence, I hope, Sir!) I must beg to be excused.

So ended my first canvas: from causes that I shall presently mention, I made but one other application in person. This took place at Manchester, to a stately and opulent wholesale dealer in cottons. He took my letter of introduction, and having perused it, measured me from head to foot and again from foot to head, and then asked if I had any bill or invoice of the thing; I presented my prospectus to him; he rapidly skimmed and hummed over the first side, and still more rapidly the second and concluding page; crushed it within his fingers and the palm of his hand; then most deliberately and *significantly* rubbed and smoothed one part against the other; and lastly putting it into his pocket turned his back on me with an *"over-run* with these articles!" and so without another syllable retired into his counting-house. And I can truly say, to my unspeakable amusement.[2]

This I have said, was my second and last attempt. On returning baffled from the first, in which I had vainly essayed to repeat the miracle of Orpheus with the Brummagem patriot,[3] I dined with the tradesman who had introduced me to him. After dinner he importuned me to smoke a pipe with him, and two or three other illuminati of the same rank. I objected, both because I was engaged to spend the evening with a minister and his friends, and because I had never smoked except once or twice in my life time, and then it was herb tobacco mixed with Oronooko.[4] On the assurance

---

[1] The traditional vulgar name for Birmingham.

[2] On 6 Feb 1796, C wrote to Wade: "This morning I called on Mr. ———— with H's letter. Mr. ———— received me as a rider, and treated me with insolence that was really amusing from its novelty. 'Over-stocked with these Articles.' 'People always setting up some new thing or other.' 'I read the Star and another Paper: what can I want with this paper, which is nothing more?' 'Well, well, I'll consider of it.' To these entertaining bon mots, I returned the following repartee,— 'Good morning, Sir.'" *CL* I 184.

[3] Referring to the ability of Orpheus to move beasts, woods, and rocks with his music.

[4] A variety of golden-coloured, strong-scented Virginian tobacco,

however that the tobacco was equally mild, and seeing too that it was of a yellow colour; (not forgetting the lamentable difficulty, I have always experienced, in saying, No! and in abstaining from what the people about me were doing) I took half a pipe, filling the lower half of the bole with salt. I was soon however compelled to resign it, in consequence of a giddiness and distressful feeling in my eyes, which as I had drank but a single glass of ale, must, I knew, have been the effect of the tobacco. Soon after, deeming myself recovered, I sallied forth to my engagement, but the walk and the fresh air brought on all the symptoms again, and I had scarcely entered the minister's drawing-room, and opened a small paquet of letters, which he had received from Bristol for me; ere I sunk back on the sofa in a sort of swoon rather than sleep. Fortunately I had found just time enough to inform him of the confused state of my feelings, and of the occasion. For here and thus I lay, my face like a wall that is white-washing, *deathy*[1] pale and with the cold drops of perspiration running down it from my forehead, while one after another there dropt in the different gentlemen, who had been invited to meet, and spend the evening with me, to the number of from fifteen to twenty. As the poison of tobacco acts but for a short time, I at length awoke from insensibility, and looked round on the party, my eyes dazzled by the candles which had been lighted in the interim. By way of relieving my embarrassment one of the gentlemen began the conversation, with "*Have you seen a paper to day, Mr. Coleridge?*" Sir! (I replied, rubbing my eyes) "I am far from convinced, that a christian is permitted to read either newspapers or any other works of merely political and temporary interest." This remark so ludicrously inapposite to, or rather, incongruous with, the purpose, for which I was known to have visited Birmingham, and to assist me in which they were all then met, produced an involuntary and general burst of laughter; and seldom indeed have I passed so many delightful hours, as I enjoyed in that room from the moment of that laugh to an early hour the next morning. Never, perhaps, in so mixed and numerous a party have I since heard conversation sustained with such animation, enriched with such variety of information and

---

probably not connected with the name of the river Orinoco in South America, which is a Spanish corruption of the Indian "Ibirinoko".

[1] Apparently first used by RS in his ballad *Donica* (1796) line 79 ("Her cheeks were deathy white and wan").

enlivened with such a flow of anecdote. Both then and afterwards they all joined in dissuading me from proceeding with my scheme; assured me in the most friendly and yet most flattering expressions, that the employment was neither fit for me, nor I fit for the employment. Yet if I had determined on persevering in it, they promised to exert themselves to the utmost to procure subscribers, and insisted that I should make no more applications in person, but carry on the canvass by proxy. The same hospitable reception, the same dissuasion, and (that failing) the same kind exertions in my behalf, I met with at Manchester, Derby, Nottingham, Sheffield, indeed, at every place in which I took up my sojourn. I often recall with affectionate pleasure the many respectable men who interested themselves for me, a perfect stranger to them, not a few of whom I can still name among my friends. They will bear witness for me, how opposite even then my principles were to those of jacobinism or even of democracy, and can attest the strict accuracy of the statement which I have left on record in the 10th and 11th numbers of THE FRIEND.[1]

From this rememberable tour I returned with nearly a thousand names on the subscription list of the Watchman; yet more than half convinced, that prudence dictated the abandonment of the scheme. But for this very reason I persevered in it; for I was at that period of my life so compleatly hag-ridden by the fear of being influenced by selfish motives that to know a mode of conduct to be the dictate of *prudence* was a sort of presumptive proof to my feelings, that the contrary was the dictate of *duty*. Accordingly, I commenced the work, which was announced in London by long bills in letters larger than had ever been seen before, and which (I have been informed, for I did not see them myself) eclipsed the glories even of the lottery puffs. But, alas! the publication of the very first number was delayed beyond the day announced for its appearance.[2] In the second number an essay against fast days, with a most censurable application of a text from Isaiah for its motto, lost me near five hundred of my subscribers at one blow.[3] In the

[1] I.e. that he was never himself "at any period of my life, a Convert to the System" of Jacobinism, which he indicated by reprinting his essay "Once a Jacobin Always a Jacobin", which had originally appeared in the *M Post* 21 Oct 1802. See *Friend*

(*CC*) II 144–7; cf *EOT* (*CC*) I 367–73.
[2] Announced for 5 Feb 1796, it appeared 1 Mar.
[3] Using the text "Wherefore my Bowels shall sound like an Harp" (Isa 16.11), C wrote his "Essay on

two following numbers I made enemies of all my Jacobin and Democratic Patrons; for disgusted by their infidelity, and their adoption of French morals with French *psilosophy*;[1] and perhaps thinking, that charity ought to begin nearest home; instead of abusing the Government and the Aristocrats chiefly or entirely, as had been expected of me, I levelled my attacks at *"modern patriotism"*, and even ventured to declare my belief that whatever the motives of ministers might have been for the sedition (or as it was then the fashion to call them, the *gagging*) bills, yet the bills themselves would produce an effect to be desired by all the true friends of freedom, as far as they should contribute to deter men from openly declaiming on subjects, the principles of which they had never bottomed, and from "pleading to the poor and ignorant, instead of pleading *for* them."[2] At the same time I avowed my conviction, that national education and a concurring spread of the gospel were the indispensable condition of any true political amelioration.[3] Thus by the time the seventh number was pub-

---

Fasts" to appear on a special national fast-day (9 Mar 1796). Like most other Dissenters, he was opposed to the setting of special fast-days and viewed it as a formalistic, mediaeval impurity injected into Christianity and as an unthinking insult to the hungry poor. *Watchman* (*CC*) 65–6. It was primarily the satiric tone of the essay that gave offence, though C probably exaggerates the number of subscribers who dropped the paper. Cf his remark eleven days later to the Rev John Edwards: "The Essay on fasting has not promoted my work—indeed altogether I am sorry that I wrote it. What so many men wiser and better than myself think a solemn subject ought not to have been treated ludicrously." *CL* I 191.

[1] A C coinage: *OED*. ". . . from the Greek, psilos slender, and Sophia Wisdom, in opposition to Philosophy, the Love of Wisdom and the Wisdom of Love". To J. H. Bohte 27 Feb 1819: *CL* IV 922n. "A Psilosopher, i.e. a nominal Ph. without

Imagination". *CN* II 3158.

[2] The short satiric essay on "Modern Patriotism" in *Watchman* No 3 is an attack on Godwinism, and in his first essay in No 1 C wrote that though the Two Bills (the Treasonable Practices Bill and the Seditious Meetings Bill, known by the democrats as the "gagging" bills) were "breaches of the Constitution", they "yet will not have been useless if they should render the language of political publications more cool and guarded, or even confine us for a while to the teaching of first principles . . .". *Watchman* (*CC*) 98–100, 13–14. The remark "pleading to the poor and ignorant . . ." is paraphrased from *Friend* No 10 (*CC*) II 137 (I 210): "it is the duty of the enlightened Philanthropist to plead *for* the poor and ignorant, not *to* them". But the position is also in C's first essay in *Watchman* No 1: see *CC* 11–12.

[3] Only twice in *The Watchman* did C write of a need for a national education: in the first essay in No 1

lished, I had the mortification (but why should I say this, when in truth I cared too little for any thing that concerned my worldly interests to be at all mortified about it?) of seeing the preceding numbers exposed in sundry old iron shops for a penny a piece. At the ninth number I dropt the work.[1] But from the London publisher I could not obtain a shilling; he was a ———— and set me at defiance.[2] From other places I procured but little, and after such delays as rendered that little worth nothing: and I should have been inevitably thrown into jail by my Bristol printer, who refused to wait even for a month, for a sum between eighty and ninety pounds,[3] if the money had not been paid for me by a man by no means affluent, a dear friend who attached himself to me from my first arrival at Bristol, who has continued my friend with a fidelity unconquered by time or even by my own apparent neglect; a friend from whom I never received an advice that was not wise, or a remonstrance that was not gentle and affectionate.[4]

---

and in the petition of the "people of Denmark" in the last number: *Watchman* (*CC*) 11, 343–4.

[1] C dropped it not at the ninth but at the tenth number (13 May 1796).

[2] John Parsons of Paternoster Row, who according to Cottle (*E Rec* I 163) refused to pay for any of the copies he sold. The dash substitutes for a word probably no rougher than that C used about him in a letter to J. P. Estlin 6 Jan 1798: "I owe Biggs [the printer] 5£— Parsons, the Bookseller, owes me more than this considerably; but he is a rogue, & will not pay me." *CL* I 368.

[3] The printer was Nathaniel Biggs. C's memory, said Cottle, is "here grievously defective. The fact is Biggs the printer (a worthy man) never threatened or even importuned for his money". He added that he himself "purchased the whole of the paper for the 'Watchman,' allowing Mr. C. to have it at prime cost, and receiving small sums from Mr. C. occasionally in liquidation". Cottle *Rem* 83n; *E Rec* I 162–3. But as Lewis Patton points out, Cottle's

memory could also have been defective, and C is probably thinking of the total loss from *The Watchman*, including the sum owed him by Parsons the publisher. *Watchman* (*CC*) lvii.

[4] Thomas Poole (1765–1837), C's lifelong friend, was perhaps the most widely respected man in his part of Somerset: a tanner endowed with practical knowledge, good sense, interest in the arts and sciences, and remarkable altruism. "A man whom I have seen now in his harvest field, or the market, now in a committee-room . . . now with Wordsworth, Southey, and other friends not unheard of in the republic of letters; now in the drawing-rooms of the rich and the noble, and now presiding at the annual dinner of a Village Benefit Society; and in each seeming to be in the very place he was intended for . . . And yet this is not the most remarkable, not the individualising trait . . . It is almost overlooked in the originality and raciness of his intellect; in the life, freshness and practical value of his remarks and notices, truths plucked as they are growing, and

Conscientiously an opponent of the first revolutionary war, yet with my eyes thoroughly opened to the true character and impotence of the favorers of revolutionary principles in England, principles which I held in abhorrence (for it was part of my political creed, that whoever ceased to act as an *individual* by making himself a member of any *society* not sanctioned by his Government, forfeited the rights of a citizen)—a vehement anti-ministerialist, but after the invasion of Switzerland a more vehement anti-gallican, and still more intensely an anti-jacobin, I retired to a cottage at Stowey, and provided for my scanty maintenance by writing verses for a London Morning Paper.[1] I saw plainly, that literature was not a profession, by which I could expect to live; for I could not disguise from myself, that whatever my talents might or might not be in other respects, yet they were not of the sort that could enable me to become a popular writer; and that whatever my opinions might be in themselves, they were almost equi-distant from all the three prominent parties, the Pittites, the Foxites, and the Democrats. Of the unsaleable nature of my writings I had an amusing memento one morning from our own servant girl. For happening to rise at an earlier hour than usual, I observed her putting an extravagant quantity of paper into the grate in order to light the fire, and mildly checked her for her wastefulness; la, Sir! (replied poor Nanny) why, it is only "WATCHMEN."

I now devoted myself to poetry and to the study of ethics and psychology; and so profound was my admiration at this time of Hartley's Essay on Man, that I gave his name to my first born.[2]

delivered to you with the dew on them, the fair earnings of an observing eye, armed and kept on the watch by thought and meditation; and above all, in the integrity, *i.e. entireness* of his being . . . the steadiness of his attachments, and the activity and persistency of a benevolence, which . . . presses a warm temper into the service of a yet warmer heart . . .". *C&S (CC)* 92–3n.

[1] C was eager to live as near as possible to Poole, who arranged for the cottage at Nether Stowey. C and his family moved into it on 31 Dec 1796. But France first invaded Switzerland in Mar 1798, occasion-

ing C's poem *Recantation: an Ode,* first published in the *M Post* 16 Apr 1798 (rewritten and republished in the *M Post* in Oct 1802 after another invasion of Switzerland). C's first poem in the *M Post* appeared 7 Dec 1797. On his contributions to the *M Post* see below, I 212. Poems included *Lewti, The Recantation [France: an Ode], The Devil's Thoughts, Ode to Tranquillity, Chamouni,* and *Dejection.* Prose pieces included his famous character of William Pitt (19 Mar 1800). See *EOT (CC)* III 285ff, I 219–26.

[2] For Hartley's *Observations,* see above, I 106 n 1. Hartley Coleridge (1796–1849) was born in Clevedon

In addition to the gentleman, my neighbour, whose garden joined on to my little orchard, and the cultivation of whose friendship had been my sole motive in choosing Stowey for my residence, I was so fortunate as to acquire, shortly after my settlement there, an invaluable blessing in the society and neighbourhood of one, to whom I could look up with equal reverence, whether I regarded him as a poet, a philosopher, or a man.[1] His conversation extended to almost all subjects, except physics and politics; with the latter he never troubled himself.[2] Yet neither my retirement nor my utter abstraction from all the disputes of the day could secure me in those jealous times from suspicion and obloquy, which did not stop at me, but extended to my excellent friend, whose perfect innocence was even adduced as a proof of his guilt. One of the many busy *sycophants** of that day (I here use the word sycophant, in its original sense, as a wretch who *flatters* the prevailing party by *informing* against his neighbours, under pretence that they are exporters of prohibited *figs* or fancies! [3] for the moral applica-

---

* Σύκους φαίνειν, to shew or detect figs, the exportation of which from Attica was forbidden by the laws.

---

three months (19 Sept) before C moved to Nether Stowey.

[1] C first met WW in Bristol Aug–Sept 1795 and began corresponding with him the following spring. WW paid a short visit to C in late Mar 1796, and C then paid his own momentous visit to WW at Racedown in Jun 1797, winning the hearts of both WW and his sister. On 1 or 2 Jul he brought them back to Nether Stowey. They discovered that the manor house of Alfoxden, three miles from C's cottage, was to let. With Poole's help the Wordsworths were able to rent Alfoxden for £23 a year, moved in 16 Jul, and stayed until the following Jul. Reed 167–8, 178–9, 195, 198–200.

[2] "I have now known him a year & some months, and my admiration, I might say, my awe of his intellectual powers has increased even to this hour . . . On one subject [politics] we are habitually silent— we found our data dissimilar, & never renewed the subject." To Estlin 18 May 1798: *CL* I 410.

[3] In writing about the "original sense" C is thinking of the sycophants, who are first known from the plays of Aristophanes, which he was evidently reading at this time (see ch 4, above, I 75–6, and ch 15, below, II 25, and a letter of 30 May 1815 to WW: *CL* IV 574). The sycophants made a living as petty informers and prosecutors: see e.g. *Acharnians* 818–28, *Birds* 1410–69. The explanation in C's footnote is given in Plutarch *Lives:* "Solon" 24 as well as by a scholiast on Aristophanes *Plutus* and, later, with other traditional explanations, by John Potter *Archaeologia Graeca* bk I ch 21 (1775) I 122. In modern times the theory of A. B. Cook *Classical Review* XXI (1907) has been favoured (by *OED,* for example), that the meaning developed from the sense of "fig" as an indecent gesture, but see Pierre Chantraine *Dictionnaire étymologique de la langue grecque* vol IV (1977) for another opinion, rejecting this. Cf an annotation on Richard Hooker *Works* (1682) 59: *CM* (*CC*) II.

tion of the term it matters not which)—one of these sycophantic law-mongrels, discoursing on the *politics* of the neighbourhood, uttered the following *deep* remark: "As to *Coleridge*, there is not so much harm in *him*, for he is a whirl-brain that talks whatever comes uppermost; but that ————! he is the *dark* traitor. *You never hear* HIM *say a syllable on the subject."*

Now that the hand of providence has disciplined *all* Europe into sobriety,[1] as men tame wild elephants, by alternate blows and caresses; now that Englishmen of all classes are restored to their old English notions and feelings; it will with difficulty be credited, how great an influence was at that time possessed and exerted by the spirit of secret defamation (the too constant attendant on party-zeal!) during the restless interim from 1793 to the commencement of the Addington administration, or the year before the truce of Amiens.[2] For by the latter period the minds of the partizans, exhausted by excess of stimulation and humbled by mutual disappointment, had become languid.[3] The same causes, that inclined the nation to peace, disposed the individuals to reconciliation. Both parties had found themselves in the wrong. The one had confessedly mistaken the moral character of the revolution, and the other had miscalculated both its moral and its physical resources. The experiment was made at the price of great, almost we may say, of humiliating sacrifices; and wise men foresaw that it would fail, at least in its direct and ostensible object. Yet it was purchased cheaply, and realized an object of equal value, and, if possible, of still more vital importance. For it brought about a national unanimity unexampled in our history since the reign of Elizabeth; and providence, never wanting to a good work when men have done their parts, soon provided a common focus in the cause of Spain,[4] which made us all once more Englishmen by at once gratifying and correcting the predilections of both parties.

[1] Napoleon's defeat at Waterloo (18 Jun 1815) was a recent event.

[2] Henry Addington, Viscount Sidmouth (1757–1844), succeeded Pitt as Prime Minister in Mar 1801. His first achievement was to conclude the popular Treaty of Amiens (25 Mar 1802).

[3] Cf ". . . Hope has died of a dead palsy, occasioned by excess of stimulation". C in *M Post* 27 Feb 1800: *EOT* (*CC*) I 207.

[4] When in 1808 Napoleon replaced the Spanish king with his brother Joseph, there was an insurrection by the Spaniards, an invasion by French troops, and Wellesley landed in Spain to lead the Allied forces in the Peninsular War. Cf C's "Letters on the Spaniards" in the *Courier* 1809–10: *EOT* (*CC*) II 37–100.

The sincere reverers of the throne felt the cause of loyalty ennobled by its alliance with that of freedom; while the *honest* zealots of the people could not but admit, that freedom itself assumed a more winning form, humanized by loyalty and consecrated by religious principle. The youthful enthusiasts who, flattered by the morning rainbow of the French revolution, had made a boast of *expatriating* their hopes and fears,[1] now disciplined by the succeeding storms and sobered by increase of years, had been taught to prize and honor the spirit of nationality as the best safeguard of national independence, and this again as the absolute pre-requisite and necessary basis of popular rights.

If in Spain too disappointment has nipt our too forward expectations, yet all is not destroyed that is checked.[2] The crop was perhaps springing up too rank in the stalk, to *kern*[3] well; and there were, doubtless, symptoms of the Gallican *blight* on it. If superstition and despotism have been suffered to let in their wolvish sheep to trample and eat it down even to the surface, yet the roots remain alive, and the second growth may prove all the stronger and healthier for the temporary interruption. At all events, to *us* heaven has been just and gracious. The *people* of England did their best, and have received their rewards. Long may we continue to deserve it! Causes, which it had been too generally the habit of former statesmen to regard as belonging to another world, are now admitted by all ranks to have been the main agents of our success. *"We fought from heaven; the stars in their courses fought against Sisera."*[4] If then unanimity grounded on moral feelings has been among the least equivocal sources of our national glory, that man deserves the esteem of his countrymen, even as patriots, who devotes his life and the utmost efforts of his intellect to the preservation and continuance of that unanimity by the disclosure and establishment of *principles.* For by these all *opinions* must be ultimately tried; and (as the feelings of men are worthy of regard only as far as they are the representatives of their fixed opinions) on the knowledge of these all unanimity, not accidental and fleeting,

[1] Cf ". . . Each heart proudly expatriated itself, and we heard with transport of the victories of Frenchmen, as the victories of Human Nature". *Watchman* (*CC*) 269–70.

[2] C refers to the restoration of Ferdinand VII (1784–1833) to the Spanish throne in 1814 after the fall of Napoleon. He immediately repudiated the constitution of 1812 and its liberal reforms.

[3] To form seeds. See *CN* I 349 and n.

[4] Judges 5.20 (var).

must be grounded. Let the scholar, who doubts this assertion, refer only to the speeches and writings of EDMUND BURKE at the commencement of the American war, and compare them with his speeches and writings at the commencement of the French revolution. He will find the *principles* exactly the same and the deductions the same; but the practical inferences almost opposite, in the one case,[a] from those drawn in the other; yet in both equally legitimate and in both equally confirmed by the results.[1] Whence gained he this superiority of foresight? Whence arose the striking *difference*, and in most instances even the discrepancy between the grounds assigned by *him*, and by those who voted *with* him, on the same questions? How are we to explain the notorious fact, that the speeches and writings of EDMUND BURKE are more interesting at the present day, than they were found at the time of their first publication; while those of his illustrious confederates are either forgotten, or exist only to furnish proofs, that the same conclusion, which one man had deduced scientifically, *may* be brought out by another in consequence of errors that luckily chanced to neutralize each other. It would be unhandsome as a conjecture, even were it not, as it actually is, false in point of fact, to attribute this difference to deficiency of talent on the part of Burke's friends, or of experience, or of historical knowledge. The satisfactory solution is, that Edmund Burke possessed and had sedulously sharpened that eye, which sees all things, actions, and events, in relation to the *laws* that determine their existence and circumscribe their possibility. He referred habitually to *principles*. He was a *scientific* statesman; and therefore a *seer*.[2] For every *principle* contains in itself the

[a] *BL* (1817) omits comma

[1] ". . . No Man was ever more like himself! From his first published Speech on the American Colonies to his last posthumous Tracts, we see the same Man, the same Doctrines, the same uniform Wisdom of *practical* Councils, the same Reasoning and the same Prejudices against all abstract grounds, against all deduction of Practice from Theory." *Friend* No 9 (*CC*) II 123–4 (I 188). Cf the defence of Burke against "inconsistency" in *CN* III 3609.

[2] In C's discussion of the "Principles of Method" in the 1818

Friend, he uses Burke as the prototype of what "first strikes us, and strikes us at once" in the truly educated and, among the educated, "so instantly distinguishes the man of superior mind . . . It is the unpremeditated and evidently habitual *arrangement* of his words, grounded on the habit of foreseeing, in each integral part, or (more plainly) in every sentence, the whole that he then intends to communicate. However irregular and desultory his talk, there is *method* in the fragments." This C contrasts in detail

germs of a prophecy; and as the prophetic power is the essential privilege of science, so the fulfilment of its oracles supplies the outward and (to men in general) the *only* test of its claim to the title. Wearisome as Burke's refinements appeared to his parliamentary auditors, yet the cultivated classes throughout Europe have reason to be thankful, that

> ———————— he went on refining,
> And thought of convincing, while they thought of dining.[1]

Our very sign boards (said an illustrious friend to me) give evidence, that there has been a Titian in the world.[2] In like manner, not only the debates in parliament, not only our proclamations and state papers, but the essays and leading paragraphs of our journals are so many remembrances of Edmund Burke. Of this the reader may easily convince himself, if either by recollection or reference he will compare the opposition newspapers at the commencement and during the five or six following years of the French revolution with the sentiments, and grounds of argument assumed in the same class of Journals at present, and for some years past.

Whether the spirit of jacobinism, which the writings of Burke exorcised from the higher and from the literary classes, may not like the ghost in Hamlet, be heard moving and mining in the underground chambers[3] with an activity the more dangerous because less noisy, may admit of a question. I have given my opinions on this point, and the ground of them, in my letters to Judge Fletcher occasioned by his charge to the Wexford grand jury, and published in the *Courier*.[4] Be this as it may, the evil

---

with the mind that relates objects and events in the same order as they first occurred to the speaker, in which the accidental and significant are equally mixed, and cites examples from Shakespeare that illustrate both types of mind. *Friend* (*CC*) I 448–53. Cf below, II 48–9, 58–9.

[1] From Oliver Goldsmith's portrait of Burke in *Retaliation* (1774) lines 35–6 (var). Also quoted in *Friend* No 9 (*CC*) II 124 (I 189).

[2] Cf C's Lect 9 of 16 Dec 1811: "He remembered a man equally admirable for his talents and his rank pointing to a sign post observed that had Titian not lived the richness of representation by colour even there could never have existed." *Lects 1808–19* (*CC*) ms. The "illustrious friend" is therefore most likely Sir George Beaumont.

[3] Shakespeare *Hamlet* I v 149–63.

[4] A series of six letters to Judge William Fletcher in the *Courier* from 20 Sept to 10 Dec 1814, signed by an "Irish Protestant", reprinted in *EOT* (*CC*) II 373–414. On "the spirit of Jacobinism" see e.g. II 383–5, 386–9, 392–3.

spirit of jealousy, and with it the cerberean whelps of feud and slander, no longer walk their rounds, in cultivated society.

Far different were the days to which these anecdotes have carried me back. The dark guesses of some zealous Quidnunc[1] met with so congenial a soil in the grave alarm of a titled Dogberry of our neighbourhood, that a SPY was actually sent down from the government *pour surveillance* of myself and friend. There must have been not only abundance, but *variety* of these "honorable men"[2] at the disposal of Ministers: for this proved a very honest fellow. After three weeks' truly Indian perseverance in tracking us (for we were commonly together) during all which time seldom were we out of doors, but he contrived to be within hearing (and all the while utterly unsuspected; how indeed *could* such a suspicion enter our fancies?) he not only rejected Sir Dogberry's request that he would try yet a little longer, but declared to him his belief, that both my friend and myself were as good subjects, for aught he could discover to the contrary, as any in His Majesty's dominions.[3] He had repeatedly hid himself, he said, for

[1] Literally "What now?" Hence an inquisitive, gossipy person generally. By "Dogberry" (the Head Constable of Messina in *Much Ado About Nothing*) C may be referring to the JP Sir Philip Hales, 5th Bt, of Brymore in Somerset (d 1824).

[2] Shakespeare *Julius Caesar* III ii 83.

[3] On 18 Jul 1796 the Wordsworths held a large dinner attended by the radical John Thelwall (1764–1834), whose talk startled Thomas Jones, a local man helping to serve the table. Jones confided to a former Alfoxden employee, Charles Mogg, his belief that the Wordsworths were French emigrants of suspicious background. Mogg also learned that "the French people" had asked neighbours whether the brook was navigable to the sea and, learning it was not, "were afterward seen examining the Brook quite down to the Sea". Mogg immediately passed on his information to a woman who had formerly worked at Alfoxden and now served as cook to Dr Daniel Lysons of Bath. She at once informed Lysons, who then wrote to the Home Secretary, the Duke of Portland, about "a very suspicious business concerning an emigrant family" who "may *possibly* be under Agents to some principal at Bristol". Portland then (11 Aug) sent a government detective, G. Walsh, to investigate. Walsh discovered that the Wordsworths and their friends were not French and concluded they were "a Sett of violent Democrats". The gossip about the Wordsworths soon reached Mrs Lancelot St Albyn, the widowed mother of the infant owner of Alfoxden. Despite Poole's intervention, she did not allow the Wordsworths to stay beyond the following Jul. In short, the main outlines of the story can be substantiated. But C, with his incorrigible love of puns, is probably, as McFarland suggests, inventing the "spynozy" part of the story. C used the pun in another context in 1799. *CN* I 432. McFarland 165n; A. J. Eagleston in *Studies* 73–87; and G. W. Meyer *American Scholar* xx (1950–1) 50–6.

hours together behind a bank at the sea-side (our favorite seat) and overheard our conversation. At first he fancied, that we were aware of our danger; for he often heard me talk of one *Spy Nozy*, which he was inclined to interpret of himself, and of a remarkable feature belonging to him; but he was speedily convinced that it was the name of a man who had made a book and lived long ago. Our talk ran most upon books, and we were perpetually desiring each other to look at *this*, and to listen to *that*; but he could not catch a word about politics. Once he had joined me on the road; (this occurred, as I was returning home alone from my friend's house, which was about three miles from my own cottage) and passing himself off as a traveller, he had entered into conversation with me, and talked of purpose in a *democrat* way in order to draw me out. The result, it appears, not only convinced him that I was no friend of jacobinism; but (he added) I had "plainly made it out to be such a silly as well as wicked thing, that he felt ashamed, though he had only *put it on*." I distinctly remembered the occurrence, and had mentioned it immediately on my return, repeating what the traveller with his Bardolph nose[1] had said, with my own answer; and so little did I suspect the true object of my "tempter ere accuser,"[2] that I expressed with no small pleasure my hope and belief, that the conversation had been of some service to the poor misled malcontent. This incident therefore prevented all doubt as to the truth of the report, which through a friendly medium came to me from the master of the village inn, who had been ordered to entertain the *Government Gentleman* in his best manner, but above all to be silent concerning such a person being in his house. At length, he received Sir Dogberry's commands to accompany his guest at the final interview; and after the absolving suffrage of the *gentleman honored with the confidence of Ministers*[3] answered, as follows, to the following queries? D. Well, landlord! and what do you know of the person in question? L. I see him often pass by with maister ——————, my landlord (*i.e. the owner of the house*) and sometimes with the new-comers at Holford;[4]

---

[1] A nose inflamed by drink, tertiary syphilis, or both. See Bardolph in Shakespeare *1 Henry IV* iii iii 22–5, *2 Henry IV* ii iv 307–12, and *Henry V* ii iii 36–7. Cf Lect 6 of 5 Dec 1811: *Sh C* ii 124.

[2] Milton *Paradise Lost* iv 10, speaking of Satan as "The tempter ere th'accuser of mankind".

[3] On "*Confidence*" as the "corrupt ministerial catch-word" cf *Lects 1795 (CC)* 268 and n 2.

[4] A hamlet in Somerset near Alfoxden.

but I never said a word to him or he to me. D. But do you not know, that he has distributed papers and hand-bills of a seditious nature among the common people! L. No, your honor! I never heard of such a thing. D. Have you not seen this Mr. Coleridge, or heard of, his haranguing and talking to knots and clusters of the inhabitants?—What are you grinning at, Sir! L. Beg your honor's pardon! but I was only thinking, how they'd have stared at him. If what I have heard be true, your honor! they would not have understood a word, he said. When our vicar was here, Dr. L. the master of the great school and canon of Windsor,[1] there was a great dinner party at maister —————'s; and one of the farmers, that was there, told us that he and the Doctor talked real Hebrew Greek at each other for an hour together after dinner. D. Answer the question, Sir! Does he ever harangue the people? L. I hope, your honor an't angry with me. I can say no more than I know. I never saw him talking with any one, but my landlord, and our curate, and the strange gentleman. D. Has he not been seen wandering on the hills towards the Channel, and along the shore, with books and papers in his hand, taking charts and maps of the country? L. Why, as to that, your honor! I own, I have heard; I am sure, I would not wish to say ill of any body; but it is certain, that I have heard—D. Speak out man! don't be afraid, you are doing your duty to your King and Government. What have you heard? L. Why, folks do say, your honor! as how that he is a *Poet*, and that he is going to put Quantock and all about here in print; and as they be so much together, I suppose that the strange gentleman has some *consarn* in the business.—So ended this formidable inquisition, the latter part of which alone requires explanation, and at the same time entitles the anecdote to a place in my literary life. I had considered it as a defect in the admirable poem of the TASK, that the subject, which gives the title to the work, was not, and indeed could not be, carried on beyond the three or four first pages, and that throughout the poem the connections are frequently awkward, and the transitions abrupt and arbitrary.[2] I sought for a subject, that should give equal room and

---

[1] Dr William Langford (1763–1814). For Sydney Smith's review of his soporific *Anniversary Sermon* (1801) see *Ed Rev* I (1802) 113 and *Works* (1854) I 25. The "great school" is Eton.

[2] William Cowper's friend Lady Austen, hoping to divert his mind from melancholy, suggested he write a burlesque poem in Miltonic blank verse on the subject of "the sofa". Cowper started to do so (Oct 1783),

freedom for description, incident, and impassioned reflections on men, nature, and society, yet supply in itself a natural connection to the parts, and unity to the whole. Such a subject I conceived myself to have found in a stream, traced from its source in the hills among the yellow-red moss and conical glass-shaped tufts of bent,*a* to the first break or fall, where its drops became audible, and it begins to form a channel; thence to the peat and turf barn, itself built of the same dark squares as it sheltered; to the sheep-fold; to the first cultivated plot of ground; to the lonely cottage and its bleak garden won from the heath; to the hamlet, the villages, the market-town, the manufactories, and the seaport. My walks therefore were almost daily on the top of Quantock, and among its sloping coombs. With my pencil and memorandum book in my hand, I was *making studies*, as the artists call them, and often moulding my thoughts into verse, with the objects and imagery immediately before my senses. Many circumstances, evil and good, intervened to prevent the completion of the poem, which was to have been entitled "THE BROOK."[1] Had I finished the work, it was my purpose in the heat of the moment to have dedicated it to our then committee of public safety as containing the charts and maps, with which I was to have supplied the French Government

a BL (1817): Bent,

but the potentialities of the subject were quickly exhausted. After about 130 lines he turned to more congenial subjects, wrote another 640 lines or so, made "The Sofa" into the first "Book" of *The Task,* and added five more "Books": "The Time-Piece", "The Garden", "The Winter Evening", "The Winter Morning Walk", and "The Winter Walk at Noon". The completed *Task* was published in 1785. For other remarks on *The Task,* see above, I 25, C's n.

[1] Cf WW's comment on his own sonnet-sequence *The River Duddon* (1820): in writing it over a period of years, he had not at first realised that "I was trespassing upon ground preoccupied, at least as far as intention went, by Mr. Coleridge; who, more than twenty years ago, used to speak of writing a rural Poem, to be entitled 'The Brook,' of which he has given a sketch in a recent publication [*BL,* in the passage above]. But a particular subject, cannot, I think, much interfere with a general one; and I have been further kept from encroaching upon any right Mr. C. may still wish to exercise, by the restriction which the frame of the Sonnet imposed upon me, narrowing unavoidably the range of thought ... May I not venture, then, to hope, that, instead of being a hindrance ... these Sonnets may remind Mr. Coleridge of his own more comprehensive design, and induce him to fulfil it . . . that 'The Brook' will, ere long, murmur in concert with 'The Duddon.'" *WPW* III 503,–4. For verse fragments thought to be studies for *The Brook* see *CN* I 213 and n.

in aid of their plans of invasion. And these too for a tract of coast that from Clevedon to Minehead scarcely permits the approach of a fishing boat!

All my experience from my first entrance into life to the present hour is in favor of the warning maxim, that the man, who opposes in toto the political or religious zealots of his age, is safer from their obloquy than he who differs from them in one or two points or perhaps only in degree. By that transfer of the feelings of private life into the discussion of public questions, which is the *queen bee* in the hive of party fanaticism,[1] the partizan has more sympathy with an intemperate Opposite than with a moderate Friend. We now enjoy an intermission, and long may it continue! In addition to far higher and more important merits, our present bible societies[2] and other numerous associations for national or charitable objects, may serve perhaps to carry off the superfluous activity and fervor of stirring minds in innocent hyperboles and the bustle of management. But the poison-tree is not dead,[3] though the sap may for a season have subsided to its roots. At least let us not be lulled into such a notion of our entire security, as not to keep watch and ward, even on our best feelings. I have seen gross intolerance shewn in support of toleration; sectarian antipathy most obtrusively displayed in the promotion of an undistinguishing comprehension of sects; and acts of cruelty (I had almost said) of treachery, committed in furtherance of an object vitally important to the cause of humanity; and all this by men too of naturally kind dispositions and exemplary conduct.[4]

The magic rod of fanaticism is preserved in the very adyta[5] of human nature; and needs only the re-exciting warmth of a master hand to bud forth afresh and produce the old fruits.[6] The horror of the peasant's war in Germany, and the direful effects of the Anabaptist's tenets (which differed only from those of jacobin-

---

[1] Cf the comparison of fanaticism with the bee-hive in ch 2, above, ɪ 30 and n 4.

[2] On the "bible societies" see *LS* (*CC*) 201 and n and n 1, 165–6n, and 166 n 1.

[3] See above, ɪ 10.

[4] C reprinted this paragraph in *LS*, "from a volume of my own, which has long been printed, for the greater part, and which will, I trust,

now be soon published". *LS* (*CC*) 202n.

[5] On "adyta"—inner sanctuaries, fanes—see ch 6, above, ɪ 107; on fanatics as "those who cluster round the fane" see ch 2, above, ɪ 30 and n 4.

[6] This and the following three sentences, reworked, are reprinted from *Friend* No 7 (*CC*) ɪɪ 106 (ɪ 180).

ism by the substitution of theological for philosophical jargon) struck all Europe for a time with affright. Yet little more than a century was sufficient to obliterate all effective memory of these events. The same principles with similar though less dreadful consequences were again at work from the imprisonment of the first Charles to the restoration of his son. The fanatic maxim of extirpating fanaticism by persecution produced a civil war. The war ended in the victory of the insurgents; but the temper survived, and Milton had abundant grounds for asserting, that "Presbyter was but OLD PRIEST writ large!"[1] One good result, thank heaven! of this zealotry was the re-establishment of the church. And now it might have been hoped, that the mischievous spirit would have been bound for a season, "and a seal set upon him that he might deceive the nation no more."[2] But no! The ball of persecution was taken up with undiminished vigor by the persecuted. The same fanatic principle, that under the solemn oath and covenant had turned cathedrals into stables, destroyed the rarest trophies of art and ancestral piety, and hunted the brightest ornaments of learning and religion into holes and corners, now marched under episcopal banners, and having first crowded the prisons of England emptied its whole vial of wrath on the miserable covenanters of Scotland. (*Laing's* History of Scotland.[3]— *Walter Scott's* bards, ballads, &c.)[4] A merciful providence at length constrained both parties to join against a common enemy. A wise Government followed; and the established church became, and now is, not only the brightest example, but our best and only sure bulwark, of toleration! The true and indispensable bank against a new inundation of persecuting zeal—ESTO PERPETUA![5]

---

[1] *On the New Forcers of Conscience under the Long Parliament* line 14 (var).

[2] Rev 20.3 (var).

[3] *The History of Scotland, from . . . James VI to the . . . Reign of Queen Anne* (2nd ed 4 vols 1804) by Malcolm Laing (1762–1818) III 1–86. (C annotated this ed, calling it an "excellent work written in the true spirit of History". *CM—CC—* III.) Bk VII (IV 1–80) deals with the persecution of the Covenanters after Parliament passed the Episcopacy Act (1662) annulling the authority of presbyteries and repealing the covenants as unlawful.

[4] *Minstrelsy of the Scottish Border: Consisting of Historical and Romantic Ballads . . .* (3 vols 1802–3).

[5] "May it last forever". Paolo Sarpi's last words, of Venice, later often applied to the Church.

A long interval of quiet succeeded; or rather, the exhaustion had produced a cold fit of the ague which was symptomatized by indifference among the many, and a tendency to infidelity or scepticism in the educated classes. At length those feelings of disgust and hatred, which for a brief while the multitude had attached to the crimes and absurdities of sectarian and democratic fanaticism, were transferred to the oppressive privileges of the noblesse, and the luxury, intrigues and favoritism of the continental courts.[1] The same principles dressed in the ostentatious garb of a fashionable philosophy once more rose triumphant and effected the French revolution. And have we not within the last three or four years had reason to apprehend, that the detestable maxims and correspondent measures of the late French despotism had already bedimmed the public recollections of democratic phrensy; had drawn off to other objects the electric force of the feelings which had massed and upheld those recollections; and that a favorable concurrence of occasions was alone wanting to awaken the thunder and precipitate the lightning from the opposite quarter of the political heaven? (See THE FRIEND, p. 110.)

In part from constitutional indolence,[2] which in the very hey-day of hope had kept my enthusiasm in check, but still more from the habits and influences of a classical education and academic pursuits, scarcely had a year elapsed from the commencement of my literary and political adventures before my mind sunk into a state of thorough disgust and despondency, both with regard to the disputes and the parties disputant. With more than *poetic* feeling I exclaimed:

> The sensual and the dark rebel in vain,
> Slaves by their own compulsion! In mad game
> They break their manacles, to wear the *name*
> Of freedom, graven on an heavier chain.
> O liberty! with profitless endeavor
> Have I pursued thee many a weary hour;
> But thou nor swell'st the victor's pomp, nor ever
> Didst breathe thy soul in forms of human power!
> > Alike from all, howe'er they praise thee
> > (Nor prayer nor boastful name delays thee)
> > From superstition's harpy minions

---

[1] From this sentence to the end of the paragraph C is again reprinting, with some revisions, *Friend* No 7 (*CC*) ɪ 106 (ɪ 180).

[2] Cf ch 2, above, ɪ 45 and n 1.

And factious blasphemy's obscener slaves,
Thou speedest on thy cherub pinions,
The guide of homeless winds and playmate of the waves!
                                    FRANCE, *a Palinodia.*[1]

I retired to a cottage in Somersetshire at the foot of Quantock,[2] and devoted my thoughts and studies to the foundations of
religion and morals. Here I found myself all afloat. Doubts rushed
in; broke upon me *"from the fountains of the great deep,"* and
fell *"from the windows of heaven."*[3] The fontal truths of natural
religion and the books of Revelation alike contributed to the
flood; and it was long ere my ark touched on an Ararat, and rested.
The *idea* of the Supreme Being appeared to me to be as necessarily
implied in all particular modes of being as the idea of infinite space
in all the geometrical figures by which space is limited. I was
pleased with the Cartesian opinion, that the idea of God is distinguished from all other ideas by involving its *reality*; but I was not
wholly satisfied.[4] I began then to ask myself, what proof I had
of the outward *existence* of any thing? Of this sheet of paper for
instance, as a thing in itself, separate from the phænomenon or
image in my perception.[5] I saw, that in the nature of things such
proof is impossible; and that of all modes of being, that are not
objects of the senses, the existence is *assumed* by a logical necessity arising from the constitution of the mind itself, by the absence
of all motive to doubt it, not from any absolute contradiction in

[1] Lines 85–98 (substituting
"pomp" for "strain" in line 91,
"From superstition's" for "Alike
from Priestcraft's" in line 95, and
"cherub" for "subtle" in line 97):
PW (EHC) I 247. The poem was
first published in the *M Post* 16 Apr
1798.

[2] The cottage in Nether Stowey
already mentioned above, I 187. The
repetition of "I retired to a cottage"
is another indication that C is
dictating.

[3] Gen 7.11 (var).

[4] In Descartes *De methodo* pt IV:
Opera philosophica (Amsterdam
1685) iii 20–6 (esp 22–5). C refers to
one form of the "ontological proof
of God" first propounded by Anselm
(c 1033–1109): the concept of God
is one than which nothing greater
can be conceived. This involves
existence without beginning or end
since, if either occurred, we could
always conceive of something still
greater (namely that which has such
an existence). Rejected by Aquinas
in favour of the "cosmological"
proof of God (the necessity of a first
cause), Anselm's argument was re-
formulated by Descartes: the attribute of existence is a necessary
predicate of God. Kant's reply to
the argument is that the "predicate"
is not a real one. It is not an
"analytic truth" (involved in the
definition) but a "synthetic" one that
must be tested in other ways.

[5] On the distinction between
"thing in itself" and "the phaenomenon" see Kant *Prolegomena* § 32.
Cf Orsini 72, also ch 9, above, I 155.

the supposition of the contrary.[1] Still the existence of a being, the ground of all existence, was not yet the existence of a moral creator, and governor. "In the position, that all reality is either contained *in* the necessary being as an *attribute*, or exists *through* him, as its *ground*, it remains undecided whether the properties of intelligence and will are to be referred to the Supreme Being in the former or only in the latter sense; as inherent attributes, or only as *consequences* that have existence in other things *through* him. Thus organization, and motion, are regarded as *from* God not *in* God. Were the latter the truth, then notwithstanding all the pre-eminence which must be assigned to the ETERNAL FIRST from the sufficiency, unity, and independence of his being, as the dread ground of the universe, his nature would yet fall far short of that, which we are bound to comprehend in the idea of GOD. For without any knowledge or determining resolve of its own it would only be a blind necessary ground of other things and other spirits; and thus would be distinguished from the FATE of certain ancient philosophers in no respect, but that of being more definitely and intelligibly described." KANT'S *einzig möglicher Beweisgrund: vermischte Schriften, Zweiter Band,* § 102, *and* 103.[2]

For a very long time indeed I could not reconcile personality with infinity; and my head was with Spinoza, though my whole heart remained with Paul and John. Yet there had dawned upon me, even before I had met with the Critique of the Pure Reason, a certain guiding light. If the mere intellect could make no certain discovery of a holy and intelligent first cause, it might yet supply a demonstration, that no legitimate argument could be drawn from the intellect *against* its truth.[3] And what is this more than St.

---

[1] "Assume the existence of God— and then the harmony and fitness of the physical creation may be shown to correspond with and support such an assumption;—but to set about *proving* the existence of a God by such means is a mere circle, a delusion." *TT* 22 Feb 1834. This is of supreme importance for C and helps explain his whole approach in chs 5–9, 12, and 13.

[2] The full title is *Der einzig mögliche Beweisgrund zu einer Demonstration des Daseyns Gottes* (1763). The quotation from Kant

appears in exactly this form, beginning and ending with the same sentences, in Jacobi *ULS* 354–5n. C, who quotes Jacobi in the next paragraph, is doubtless taking the passage directly from *ULS*. But C did check the passage in his copy of Kant *Vermischte Schriften* II 102–3, for Jacobi's reference is "S. 43. und 44.", and in his copy of *ULS* C has written "102–103" alongside Jacobi's page numbers.

[3] Cf Kant's argument in *KRV* "Elementarlehre" (B 699). Orsini 35.

Paul's assertion, that by wisdom (more properly translated by the powers of reasoning) no man ever arrived at the knowledge of God?[1] What more than the sublimest, and probably the oldest, book on earth has taught us,

> Silver and gold man searcheth out:
> Bringeth the ore out of the earth, and darkness into light.
>
> But where findeth he wisdom?
> Where is the place of understanding?
>
> The abyss crieth; it is not in me!
> Ocean echoeth back; not in me!
>
> Whence then cometh wisdom?
> Where dwelleth understanding?
>
> Hidden from the eyes of the living:
> Kept secret from the fowls of heaven!
>
> Hell and death answer;
> We have heard the rumour thereof from afar!
>
> GOD marketh out the road to it;
> GOD knoweth its abiding place!
>
> He beholdeth the ends of the earth;
> He surveyeth what is beneath the heavens!
>
> And as he weighed out the winds, and measured the sea,
> And appointed laws to the rain,
> And a path to the thunder,
> A path to the flashes of the lightning!
>
> Then did he see it,
> And he counted it;
> He searched into the depth thereof,
> And with a line did he compass it round!
>
> But to man he said,
> The fear of the Lord is wisdom for THEE!
> And to avoid evil,
> That is *thy* understanding.
>
> JOB, CHAP. 28th.[2]

I became convinced, that religion, as both the corner-stone and the key-stone of morality, must have a *moral* origin;[3] so far at

---

[1] 1 Cor 1.17–21.

[2] C translates the German verse paraphrase in Jacobi *ULS* 248–9, which gives verses 1–3, 12, 14, 20–8. *BL* (1975) 113n. C uses this because it is consciously written in verse form.

[3] C, as Orsini (35) points out, is here echoing a principal theme of Kant's *Kritik der praktischen Vernunft.*

least, that the evidence of its doctrines could not, like the truths of abstract science, be wholly independent of the will. It were therefore to be expected, that its *fundamental* truth would be such as MIGHT be denied; though only, by the *fool*, and even by the fool from the madness of the *heart* alone! [1]

The question then concerning our faith in the existence of a God, not only as the *ground* of the universe by his essence, but as its maker and judge by his wisdom and holy will, appeared to stand thus. The sciential *reason*, whose objects are purely theoretical, remains neutral, as long as its name and semblance are not usurped by the opponents of the doctrine. But it *then* becomes an effective ally by exposing the false shew of demonstration, or by evincing the equal demonstrability of the contrary from premises equally logical.[2] The *understanding* mean time suggests, the analogy of *experience* facilitates, the belief. Nature excites and recalls it, as by a perpetual revelation. Our feelings almost necessitate it; and the law of conscience peremptorily commands it. The arguments, that at all apply to it, are in its favor; and there is nothing against it, but its own sublimity. It could not be intellectually more evident without becoming morally less effective; without counteracting its own end by sacrificing the *life* of faith to the cold mechanism of a worthless because compulsory assent. The belief of a God and a future state (if a passive acquiescence may be flattered with the name of *belief*) does not indeed always beget a good heart; but a good heart so naturally begets the belief, that the very few exceptions must be regarded as strange anomalies from strange and unfortunate circumstances.

From these premises I proceeded to draw the following conclusions. First, that having once fully admitted the existence of an infinite yet self-conscious Creator, we are not allowed to ground

[1] Cf Ps 14.1.

[2] *BL* (1847) has a note here (I 207n), presumably an annotation by C on a copy of *BL:* "Whether A = B, and A is *not* B, are equally demonstrable, the premise in each undeniable, the induction evident, and the conclusion legitimate—the result must be, either that contraries can both be true, which is absurd, or that the faculty and forms of reasoning employed are inapplicable to the subject—i.e. that there is a μετάβασις εἰς ἄλλο γένος. Thus, the attributes of Space and Time applied to Spirit are heterogeneous—and the proof of this is, that by admitting them *explicite* or *implicite* contraries may be demonstrated true—i.e. that the sense, taken in the same sense, is true and not true.—That the world had a beginning in Time and a bound in Space, and That the world had not a beginning and has no limit;—That a self-originating act is, and is not possible, are instances."

the irrationality of any other article of faith on arguments which would equally prove that to be irrational, which we had allowed to be *real*. Secondly, that whatever is deducible from the admission of a *self-comprehending* and *creative* spirit may be legitimately used in proof of the *possibility* of any further mystery concerning the divine nature. *Possibilitatem* mysteriorum, (Trinitatis, &c.) contra insultus Infidelium et Hereticorum a contradictionibus vindico; haud quidem *veritatem*, quæ revelatione solâ stabiliri possit; says L EIBNITZ in a letter to his Duke. He then adds the following just and important remark. "In vain will tradition or texts of scripture be adduced in support of a doctrine, donec clava impossibilitatis et contradictionis e manibus horum Herculum extorta fuerit. For the heretic will still reply, that texts, the literal sense of which is not so much *above* as directly *against* all reason, must be understood *figuratively*, as Herod is a fox, &c." [1]

These principles I held, *philosophically*, while in respect of revealed religion I remained a zealous Unitarian.[2] I considered the *idea* of the Trinity a fair scholastic inference from the being of God, as a creative intelligence; and that it was therefore entitled to the rank of an *esoteric* doctrine of natural religion. But seeing in the same no practical or moral bearing, I confined it to the schools of philosophy. The admission of the logos, as *hypostasized*[3] (i.e.

---

[1] Loosely quoted from Leibniz's letter of Oct 1671 to Duke Johann Friedrich of Braunschweig-Lüneberg, which appeared in "Zwei ungedruckte Briefe von Leibniz an den Herzog Johann Friedrich von Braunschweig-Lüneberg nebst den Antworten des letztern", article xiv of *Magazin für das Kirchenrecht die Kirchen- und Gelehrten-Geschichte* ed G. W. Böhmer I (Göttingen 1787) 142: "In *Theologia revelata* übernehme ich mich zu demonstriren, nicht zwar veritatem; denn die fleusst a revelatione; sondern *possibilitatem* mysteriorum, contra insultus infidelium et Atheorum, dadurch sie von allen contradictionibus vindicirt werden, nehmlich, *possibilitatem Trinitatis, incarnationis, Eucharistiae* . . . aber es wird alles vergebens seyn, dafern nicht die einige *clava impossibilitatis* et *contradictionis* ex manibus horum

Herculum extorquirt wird. Denn sie bleiben dabey, es sey eine unmügliche, sich selbst contradicirende, alle Vernunfft chagrinirende Sache, die nothwendig *figurate* müste verstanden werden, so wohl, als: *Herodes est vulpes: Agnus est pascha.*" Leibniz's letter is a mixture of German and Latin. Tr of C's quotation: "I am freeing the *possibility* of mysteries (of the Trinity, etc) from contradictions, against the attacks of Unbelievers and Heretics; not, indeed, *the truth*, which can be established only by revelation . . . until the club of impossibility and contradiction has been wrested from the hands of these Herculeses".

[2] See above, I 179–80.

[3] I.e. made into a hypostasis, a self-sufficient substance, or a Person in the theological sense. *OED* cites C as the first to use the word (1809). *Friend* (*CC*) II 75 and n.

neither a mere attribute or a personification) in no respect removed my doubts concerning the incarnation and the redemption by the cross; which I could neither reconcile *in reason* with the impassiveness of the Divine Being, nor in my moral feelings with the sacred distinction between things and persons, the vicarious payment of a debt and the vicarious expiation of guilt. A more thorough revolution in my philosophic principles, and a deeper insight into my own heart, were yet wanting. Nevertheless, I cannot doubt, that the difference of my metaphysical notions from those of Unitarians in general contributed to my final re-conversion to the whole truth in Christ; even as according to his own confession the books of certain Platonic philosophers (*libri quorundam Platonicorum*) commenced the rescue of St. Augustine's faith from the same error aggravated by the far darker accompaniment of the Manichæan heresy.[1]

While my mind was thus perplexed, by a gracious providence for which I can never be sufficiently grateful, the generous and munificent patronage of Mr. JOSIAH, and Mr. THOMAS WEDGWOOD[a] enabled me to finish my education in Germany.[2] Instead of troubling others with my own crude notions and juvenile compositions I was thenceforward better employed in attempting to store my own head with the wisdom of others. I made the

[a] *BL* (1817): WEDGEWOOD

[1] *Confessions* 7.9–21. The words C appears to quote ("books of certain Platonists") are from memory. He is thinking of the passage in 7.9 (cf 8.2): "Thou, God, didst procure for me, through a certain man . . . certain books of the Platonists translated from Greek into Latin" ("Procurasti mihi per quendam hominem . . . quosdam Platonicorum libros et graeca lingua in latinum versos"). For general discussion of the implications of this paragraph, see McFarland (esp 226–8), who shows that C was gradually alienated from Unitarianism by its potentialities for pantheism, though, as McFarland later stresses, the pantheistic writers to whom C was drawn often used a trinitarian schema (362).

[2] Josiah Wedgwood (1769–1843) and his brother Thomas (1771–1805), sons of the famous potter Josiah Wedgwood (1730–95), had heard through Poole that C was being forced to sacrifice his career as a writer. They at first offered C a gift of £100. C refused, saying it would only defer his need for regular employment. The Wedgwoods then wrote (10 Jan 1798) that they wished him to accept a lifetime annuity of £150, "no condition whatsoever being annexed to it". *CL* I 221–2; *C Life* (H) 237–40. Though the annuity permitted C to go to Germany, he afterwards generously handed it over to his wife. When Thomas died (1805), his share was provided for in his will. In 1812 Josiah, who had sustained heavy losses because of the war, informed C of his financial embarrassment, and C at once released him from further obligation. *C Life* (B) 126–7.

best use of my time and means; and there is therefore no period of my life on which I can look back with such unmingled satisfaction. After acquiring a tolerable sufficiency in the German language * at Ratzeburg, which with my voyage and journey thither I have described in THE FRIEND, I proceeded through Hanover to Göttingen.[2]

* To those, who design to acquire the language of a country in the country itself, it may be useful, if I mention the incalculable advantage which I derived from learning all the words, that could possibly be so learnt, with the objects before me, and without the intermediation of the English terms. It was a regular part of my morning studies for the first six weeks of my residence at Ratzeburg, to accompany the good and kind old pastor, with whom I lived, from the cellar to the roof, through gardens, farm yard, &c. and to call every, the minutest, thing by its German name. Advertisements, farces, jest books, and the conversation of children while I was at play with them, contributed their share to a more home-like acquaintance with the language, than I could have acquired from works of polite literature alone, or even from polite society. There is a passage of *hearty* sound sense in Luther's German letter on interpretation, to the translation of which I shall prefix, for the sake of those who read the German, yet are not likely to have dipt often in the massive folios of this heroic reformer, the simple, sinewy, idiomatic words of the original. "Denn man muss nicht die Buchstaben in der Lateinischen Sprache fragen wie man soll Deutsch reden; sondern man muss die Mutter im Hause, die Kinder auf den Gassen, den gemeinen Mann auf dem Markte, darum fragen: und denselbigen auf das Maul sehen wie sie reden, und darnach dolmetschen. So verstehen sie es denn, und merken dass man Deutsch mit ihnen redet."[1]

TRANSLATION.

For one must not ask the letters in the Latin tongue, how one ought to speak German; but one must ask the mother in the house, the children in the lanes and alleys, the common man in the market, concerning this; yea, and look at the *moves* of their mouths while they are talking, and thereafter interpret. They understand you then, and mark that one talks German with them.

[1] Quoted from Luther *Sendbrief vom Dolmetschen der heiligne Schrift* to Wenceslaus Link (1530): *Sämmtliche Schriften* ed J. G. Walch (Halle 1740–50) XXI 318. *BL* (1847) I 212n. C had copied the passage into a notebook in 1799: *CN* I 385 and n. C omits, after "man soll Deutsch reden", Luther's phrase "wie die Esel thun" ("as these asses do", meaning the Catholic translators who preceded Luther). "I can scarcely conceive a more delightful Volume than might be made from Luther's letters . . . if they were translated in the simple, sinewy, idiomatic, *hearty* mother-tongue of the original." *Friend* No 8 (*CC*) II 116n (I 139n). Cf *TT* 25 May 1832. The description in the above note of the way in which C learned German at Ratzeburg, following the pastor about the house and talking with him in German, is exemplified in the list of words he immediately began to jot down for memorising in *CN* I 353–4.

[2] In "Satyrane's Letters" in *Friend* Nos 14, 16, 18, 19 (*CC*) II 187–96, 209–21, 236–47, 256–8. See below, II 160–206.

Here I regularly attended the lectures on physiology in the morning, and on natural history in the evening, under B L U M E N - B A C H , a name as dear to every Englishman who has studied at that university, as it is venerable to men of science throughout Europe![1] Eichhorn's lectures on the New Testament[2] were repeated to me from notes by a student from Ratzeburg, a young man of sound learning and indefatigable industry, who is now, I believe, a professor of the oriental languages at Heidelberg. But my chief efforts were directed towards a grounded knowledge of the German language and literature. From professor T Y C H S E N [3] I received as many lessons in the Gothic of Ulphilas[4] as sufficed to make me acquainted with its grammar, and the radical words

[1] Johann Friedrich Blumenbach (1752–1840), professor at Göttingen from 1776 to his death, ". . . a name so dear to science, as a physiologist and Comparative Anatomist, and not less dear as a man, to all Englishmen who have ever resided at Göttingen in the course of their education". He especially appealed to C as an example of a naturalist opposed to "materialism" and to "the identification of Man with the Brute, in *kind*". *Friend* (*CC*) I 154–6n. He is remembered for his *Institutiones physiologicae* (1787), *Handbuch der Naturgeschichte* (1797), and *Handbuch der vergleichenden Anatomie* (1805), the second of which (the 1799 ed) C at one time intended to translate. *CL* I 590 and *CN* I 1738n. C later annotated Blumenbach's *Über die natürlichen Verschiedenheiten im Menschengeschlechte* (Leipzig 1798). *CM* (*CC*) I 535–41.

[2] Johann Gottfried Eichhorn (1752–1827), appointed professor of philosophy at Göttingen in 1788, lectured on Oriental languages and Biblical exegesis. He was one of the founders of the nineteenth-century "higher criticism" of the OT, arguing that most of the writings had been revised and added to by several hands and that supernatural occurrences could be explained naturally. Of his numerous works C annotated

his *Einleitung ins Alte Testament* (2nd ed 3 vols 1787), his *Einleitung in die apokryphischen Schriften des Alten Testaments* (1795), *Einleitung in das Neue Testament* (3 vols 1804–14), and *Commentarius in Apocalypsin Joannis* (2 vols 1791), as well as the *Allgemeine Bibliothek der biblischen Litteratur* (10 vols 1787–1800), which he edited. See *CM* (*CC*) II.

[3] Thomas Christian Tychsen (1758–1834), professor of theology at Göttingen 1788–1834. Though his special interest was Near Eastern philology, he also taught early German languages. Cf *CL* I 494. C may have studied for a while under Georg Friedrich Benecke (1762–1844), whose *Beyträge zur Kenntniss der altdeutschen Sprache und Litteratur* (1810) became a standard work. In later years Benecke spoke of C at Göttingen as an "idler", who did "not learn the language thoroughly". "Göttingen in 1824" *Putnam's Monthly* VIII (1856) 600.

[4] Ulfilas (c 311–83), bp of Nicomedia, translated the Bible for the Visigoths living along the lower Danube and in the process reputedly created the Gothic alphabet, basing it primarily on the Greek and to some extent the Latin alphabets. Only part of his translation (principally from the New Testament) survives.

of most frequent occurrence; and with the occasional assistance of
the same philosophical linguist, I read through* OTTFRIED'S

* This paraphrase, written about the time of Charlemagne, is by no means
deficient in occasional passages of considerable poetic merit.[1] There is a
flow, and a tender enthusiasm in the following lines (at the conclusion of
Chapter V.) which even in the translation will not, I flatter myself, fail to
interest the reader. Ottfried is describing the circumstances immediately
following the birth of our Lord.

> She gave with joy her virgin breast;
> She hid it not, she bared the breast,
> Which suckled that divinest babe!
> Blessed, blessed were the breasts
> Which the Saviour infant kiss'd;
> And blessed, blessed was the mother
> Who wrapp'd his limbs in swaddling clothes,
> Singing placed him on her lap,
> Hung o'er him with her looks of love,
> And soothed him with a lulling motion.
> Blessed! for she shelter'd him
> From the damp and chilling air;
> Blessed, blessed! for she lay
> With such a babe in one blest bed,
> Close as babes and mothers lie!
> Blessed, blessed evermore,
> With her virgin lips she kiss'd,
> With her arms, and to her breast
> She embraced the babe divine,
> Her babe divine the virgin mother!
> There lives not on this ring of earth
> A mortal, that can sing her praise.
> Mighty mother, virgin pure,
> In the darkness and the night
> For us she *bore* the heavenly Lord![2]

Most interesting is it to consider the effect, when the feelings are wrought
above the natural pitch by the belief of something mysterious, while all the
images are purely natural. Then it is, that religion and poetry strike deepest.

[1] Otfrid (c 800–75) founded a school of literature in the abbey of Weissenburg, Alsace, where he was a monk, and wrote the *Evangelienbuch* (c 870), a poem of 7416 lines paraphrasing the Gospels, the most extensive surviving work in the Franconian dialect of Old High German. "Theotiscan" (from the mediaeval Latin term *lingua theotisca*, "Teutonic tongue"; cf *thiot*, "people") refers to what we call Old High German (c 750–1050).

[2] *Evangelienbuch* ed Johann Kelle (1963) I 43–4. C doubtless made the translation years before, probably in Germany, since he is not now looking at the book. For it is not "at the conclusion of Chapter V", as he says, but in bk I ch 11. The ed he used is that included in Johann Schilter *Thesaurus antiquitatum teutonicarum . . .* (Ulm 1728) I 50–1 (lines 73–108). We cannot be sure how well C actually knew Old High German since, as L. A. Willoughby points out, Schilter parallels the text on each page with a Latin translation. *MLR* XXXI (1936) 181.

metrical paraphrase of the gospel, and the most important remains of the THEOTISCAN, or the transitional state of the Teutonic language from the Gothic to the old German of the Swabian period. Of this period (the polished dialect of which is analogous to that of our Chaucer, and which leaves the philosophic student in doubt, whether the language has not since then lost more in sweetness and flexibility, than it has gained in condensation and copiousness) I read with sedulous accuracy the MINNESINGER (or singers of love, the provençal poets of the Swabian court) and the metrical romances; and then laboured through sufficient specimens of the *master singers*, their degenerate successors;[1] not however without occasional pleasure from the rude, yet interesting strains of HANS SACHS the cobler of Nuremberg. Of this man's genius five folio volumes with double columns are extant in print, and nearly an equal number in manuscript; yet the indefatigable bard takes care to inform his readers, that he never *made a shoe the less*, but had virtuously reared a large family by the labor of his hands.[2]

In Pindar, Chaucer, Dante, Milton, &c. &c. we have instances of the close connection of poetic genius with the love of liberty and of genuine reformation. The *moral* sense at least will not be outraged, if I add to the list the name of this honest shoemaker (a

[1] The Minnesingers (primarily twelfth and thirteenth centuries) wrote songs and poems of courtly love. The work of about 160 survives. They were "provençal" only in the sense that they borrowed many of their elaborate verse forms from the Provençal. In the fourteenth century, with the rise of the burghers and artisans, they were gradually replaced by the Meistersingers, who were grouped together in local guilds of craftsmen and for two centuries and more played an important rôle in the life of German towns. By "degenerate" C refers to their speed of composition, their mechanical use of literary devices, and the prizes they often awarded for mere ingenuity. The first books C borrowed from the Göttingen Library were collections of Swabian poetry: *Proben der alten schwäbischen Poesie des Dreyzehnten Jahrhunderts* (Zür-

ich 1748) and *Sammlung von Minnesingern aus dem schwäbischen Zeitpunkte* (Zürich 1758-9). *CN* I 378n.

[2] Hans Sachs (1494–1576), a master shoemaker and the chief figure among the Meistersingers of Nuremberg, was even more prolific than C implies. The "five folio volumes" were the edition Sachs began in his own lifetime, the last two of which were published posthumously: *Sehr Herrliche Schöne und warhaffte Gedicht* (Nuremberg 1558-79)—the edition in which C first read Sachs at Göttingen in 1799 (though the one he later owned and annotated was that of 1781; *CN* I 453n). The great Stuttgart edition ed A. von Keller and E. Goetze (1870–1908) contains 26 vols and is still incomplete. Sachs claimed to have written 4275 songs, 1700 verse tales, and 208 dramas.

trade by the bye remarkable for the production of philosophers and poets.)[1] His poem intitled the MORNING STAR, was the very first publication that appeared in praise and support of LUTHER; and an excellent hymn of Hans Sachs, which has been deservedly translated into almost all the European languages, was commonly sung in the Protestant churches, whenever the heroic reformer visited them.[2]

In Luther's own German writing, and eminently in his translation of the bible, the *German* language commenced.[3] I mean the language as it is at present *written*; that which is called the HIGH GERMAN, as contra-distinguished from the PLATT-TEUTSCH, the dialect of the flat or northern countries; and from the OBER-TEUTSCH, the language of the middle and Southern Germany. The High German is indeed a *lingua communis*, not actually the native language of any province, but the choice and fragrancy of all the dialects. From this cause it is at once the most copious and the most grammatical of all the European tongues.

Within less than a century after Luther's death the German was inundated with pedantic barbarisms. A few volumes of this period I read through from motives of curiosity; for it is not easy to imagine any thing more fantastic, than the very appearance of their pages. Almost every third word is a Latin word with a Germanized ending, the Latin portion being always printed in Roman letters, while in the last syllable the German character is retained.[4]

---

[1] C often remarked on Böhme's having been a shoemaker, and in an annotation on C. F. Flögel *Geschichte der komischen Litteratur* (4 vols 1784–7) I 262 listed, besides Sachs, three other shoemakers: the Quaker George Fox; Bloomfield, author of *The Farmer's Boy,* and Gifford, editor of *QR. CM (CC)* II. As a boy C had wanted to be a shoemaker, for which he received a flogging from Boyer of Christ's Hospital. *TT* 27 May 1830.

[2] *The Morning Star* ("Wie schön leucht uns der Morgenstern"), on which Bach based a cantata, was actually composed (1597) by Philipp Nicolai (1556–1608). C is confusing it with *Die Wittenbergisch Nachtigall* (1523), which Sachs wrote in praise of Luther. The "excellent hymn" by Sachs is "Warum betrübst du dich, mein Herz?"

[3] In Luther's translation of the Bible (1522–34), which had so much influence in establishing a uniform literary language in Germany, he used the Middle German (with some upper German characteristics) of the chancery of the Saxon Electorate.

[4] "Gothic" type, called "black letter" in England and *Fraktur* in Germany, was first used in Holland c 1445 and introduced to Germany in 1454, where it remained the national typography until World War II. "Roman", first used in 1464, quickly supplanted Gothic outside the German world. The mixed form of which C speaks occurs occasionally in the early seventeenth century.

At length, about the year 1620, OPITZ arose, whose genius more nearly resembled that of Dryden than any other poet, who at present occurs to my recollection. In the opinion of LESSING, the most acute of critics, and of ADELUNG, the first of Lexicographers, Opitz, and the Silesian poets, his followers, not only restored the language, but still remain the models of pure diction.[1] A stranger has no vote on such a question; but after repeated perusal of the work my feelings justified the verdict, and I seemed to have acquired from them a sort of *tact* for what is *genuine* in the style of later writers.

Of the splendid era, which commenced with Gellert, Klopstock, Ramler, Lessing, and their compeers, I need not speak.[2] With the opportunities which I enjoyed, it would have been disgraceful not to have been familiar with their writings; and I have already said as much, as the present biographical sketch requires, concerning the German philosophers, whose works, for the greater part, I became acquainted with at a far later period.

If the root word is Greek, Latin, or French, it is printed in Roman and *Fraktur* used for the German element added: e.g., "chemikaliśch" (chemical), "Konvertierung" (conversion), or "rosenfarbig" (rose-coloured).

[1] Martin Opitz von Boberfeld (1597–1639), the Silesian poet, published his first plea to purify the German language from foreign elements when he was a university student: *Aristarchus, sive De contemptu linguae Teutonicae* (1617). Seven years later his influential *Buch von der deutschen Poeterey* (1624) carried the argument further, laying down strict rules for purity of language and versification that he followed in his own sedate formal verse. The most talented Silesian writers who followed Opitz—the poet Friedrich von Logau (1604–55), whose work C read closely, and the dramatist Andreas Gryphius (1616–64)—were by no means so strict as Opitz. Johann Christoph Adelung (1732–1806), librarian for the Elector of Saxony at Dresden and probably the greatest student of

German philology before Jakob Grimm, is remembered especially for his *Grammatisch-kritisches Wörterbuch der hochdeutschen Mundart* (1774–1806), the 2nd ed of which C owned and studied closely. *CN* I 378n, 1582n; II 2074n, 2354n.

[2] Meaning the first half (c 1740–90) of the so-called "classical period". For C on Klopstock and Lessing, see below, II 109–10, 181–206. Christian Fürchtegott Gellert (1715–69), a member of the *Bremer Beiträger* school of writers at Leipzig (called thus after their journal), was known for the clear, simple style exemplified in his *Fabeln und Erzählungen* (1746–8), modeled on La Fontaine, and his *Geistliche Oden und Lieder* (1747). For C's quotation from Christian Garve's critical work on Gellert, see below, II 90–1. Karl Wilhelm Ramler (1725–98) was noted for his skill in imitating, in German, classical metres and verse forms, especially Anacreontic verse and the Horatian ode. For C's study of Ramler's metrical technique, see *CN* I 373 and n.

Soon after my return from Germany I was solicited to undertake the literary and political department in the Morning Post; and I acceded to the proposal on the condition, that the paper should thenceforwards be conducted on certain fixed and announced principles, and that I should be neither obliged or requested to deviate from them in favor of any party or any event.[1] In consequence, that Journal became and for many years continued *anti-ministerial* indeed, yet with a very qualified approbation of the opposition, and with far greater earnestness and zeal both anti-jacobin and anti-gallican. To this hour I cannot find reason to approve of the first war either in its commencement or its conduct.[2] Nor can I understand, with what reason either Mr. Percival (whom I am singular enough to regard as the best and wisest minister of this reign)[3] or the present administration,[4] can be said to have pursued the plans of Mr. PITT. The love of their country, and perseverant hostility to French principles and French ambition are indeed honourable qualities common to them and to their predecessor. But it appears to me as clear as the evidence of facts can render any question of history, that the successes of the Percival and of the existing ministry have been owing to their having pursued measures the direct contrary to Mr. Pitt's. Such for instance are the concentration of the national force to one object; the abandonment of the *subsidizing* policy, so far at least as neither to goad or bribe the continental courts into war, till the convictions of their subjects had rendered it a war of their own seeking; and

[1] C began writing for the *M Post* in Dec 1797 but had stopped by Jul 1798, well before he left for Germany (Oct), from which he returned in Jul 1799. Though several of his poems were published during the next six months in *M Post,* his first prose contribution seems to have been 7 Dec 1799, when he became in effect its leader-writer. The job proved irksome; he was often ill; he was meanwhile translating Schiller's *Wallenstein;* and though he was offered a proprietary share in *M Post* if he continued (Mar 1800), he declined and then moved north to Keswick. Except for a few poems, he did not resume writing for the *M Post* until 27 Nov 1801. Daniel Stuart the editor denied that C affected the political position of the paper, which had already been established. For authoritative discussion of C's relations with the *M Post* and Stuart see David Erdman in *EOT* (*CC*) I lix–cxxi (on the paper conducted on fixed principles xcii–xciii).

[2] I.e. the war with France ended by the Peace of Amiens (1802).

[3] Spencer Perceval (1762–1812), who succeeded the Duke of Portland as Prime Minister in 1809 and was assassinated in 1812.

[4] That of Lord Liverpool, formed Jun 1812.

above all, in their manly and generous reliance on the good sense of the English people, and on that loyalty which is linked to the very * heart of the nation by the system of credit and the interdependence of property.

* Lord Grenville has lately re-asserted (in the House of Lords) the imminent danger of a revolution in the earlier part of the war against France.[1] I doubt not, that his Lordship is sincere; and it must be flattering to his feelings to believe it. But where are the evidences of the danger, to which a future historian can appeal? Or must he rest on an assertion? Let me be permitted to extract a passage on the subject from THE FRIEND.[2] "I have said that to withstand the arguments of the lawless, the Antijacobins proposed to suspend the law, and by the interposition of a particular statute to eclipse the blessed light of the universal sun, that spies and informers might tyrannize and escape in the ominous darkness. Oh! if these mistaken men intoxicated and bewildered with the panic of property, which they themselves were the chief agents in exciting, had ever lived in a country where there really existed a general disposition to change and rebellion! Had they ever travelled through Sicily; or through France at the first coming on of the revolution; or even alas! through too many of the provinces of a sister island; they could not but have shrunk from their own declarations concerning the state of feeling, and opinion at that time predominant throughout Great Britain. There was a time (heaven grant! that that time may have passed by) when by crossing a narrow strait, they might have learnt the true symptoms of approaching danger, and have secured themselves from mistaking the meetings and idle rant of such sedition, as shrunk appalled from the sight of a constable, for the dire murmuring and strange consternation which precedes the storm or earthquake of national discord. Not only in coffee-houses and public theatres, but even at the tables of the wealthy, they would have heard the advocates of existing Government defend their cause in the language and with the tone of men, who are conscious that they are in a minority. But in England, when the alarm was at its highest, there was not a city, no not a town or village, in which a man suspected of holding democratic principles could move abroad without receiving some unpleasant proof of the hatred, in which his supposed opinions were held by the great majority of the people; and the only instances of popular excess and indignation were in favor of the Government and the Established Church. But why need I appeal to these invidious facts? Turn over the pages of history and seek for a single instance of a revolution having been effected without the concurrence of either the nobles, or the ecclesiastics, or the monied classes, in any country, in which the influences of property had ever been predominant, and where the interests of the proprietors were interlinked! Examine the revolution of the Belgic provinces under Philip 2nd; the civil wars of France in the preceding generation; the history of the American revolution, or the yet more recent events in

[1] William Wyndham Grenville, Baron Grenville (1759–1834), who had briefly served as Prime Minister (1806–7) after the death of Pitt. Cf C's remark in 1823 of Grenville's "assertion of his immense Merits in preventing the imminent danger of a Revolution in England from the immense spread & overwhelming power of Jacobinism". *EOT* (*CC*) III 264–5.

[2] *Friend* No 10 (*CC*) II 142–4 (I 218–20).

Be this as it may, I am persuaded that the Morning Post proved a far more useful ally to the Government in its most important objects, in consequence of its being generally considered as moderately anti-ministerial, than if it had been the avowed eulogist of Mr. Pitt. (The few, whose curiosity or fancy should lead them to turn over the Journals of that date, may find a small proof of this in the frequent charges made by the Morning Chronicle, that such and such essays or leading paragraphs had been sent from the Treasury.) The rapid and unusual increase in the sale of the Morning Post is a sufficient pledge, that genuine impartiality with a respectable portion of literary talent will secure the success of a newspaper without the aid of party or ministerial patronage.[2] But by impartiality I mean an honest and enlightened adherence to a code of intelligible principles previously announced, and faithfully referred to in support of every judgment on men and events; not indiscriminate abuse, not the indulgence of an editor's own malignant passions, and still less, if that be possible, a determination to make money by flattering the envy and cupidity, the vindictive restlessness and self-conceit of the half-witted vulgar;

Sweden and in Spain;[1] and it will be scarcely possible not to perceive, that in England from 1791 to the peace of Amiens there were neither tendencies to confederacy nor actual confederacies, against which the existing laws had not provided sufficient safeguards and an ample punishment. But alas! the panic of property had been struck in the first instance for party purposes; and when it became general, its propagators caught it themselves and ended in believing their own lie; even as our bulls in Borrowdale sometimes run mad with the echo of their own bellowing. The consequences were most injurious. Our attention was concentrated to a monster, which could not survive the convulsions, in which it had been brought forth: even the enlightened Burke himself too often talking and reasoning, as if a perpetual and organized anarchy had been a possible thing! Thus while we were warring against French doctrines, we took little heed, whether the means, by which we attempted to overthrow them, were not likely to aid and augment the far more formidable evil of French ambition. Like children we ran away from the yelping of a cur, and took shelter at the heels of a vicious warhorse."

[1] C refers to the wars of liberation in the Low Countries, especially 1572–83; the struggle in France between the Huguenots and Catholics 1562–98; the deposition of Gustavus IV of Sweden in 1809; and the Spanish insurrection against Napoleon in 1808. *Friend* (*CC*) I 219 nn 2–4.

[2] Stuart said that when he took over the *M Post* (Aug 1795) its circulation was 350; it was 2000 by Dec 1799, when he employed C; it reached 4500 when Stuart sold the *M Post* in Aug 1803. *BL* (1847) II 392, 396. Cf *EOT* (*CC*) I lxix and n 5, civ and nn 1, 2.

a determination almost fiendish, but which, I have been informed, has been boastfully avowed by one man, the most notorious of these *mob-sycophants!*[1] From the commencement of the Addington administration to the present day, whatever I have written in the MORNING POST, or (after that paper was transferred to other proprietors) in the COURIER,[2] has been in defence or furtherance of the measures of Government.

> Things of this nature scarce survive the night
> That gives them birth; they perish in the sight,
> Cast by so far from *after-life*, that there
> Can scarcely aught be said, but that *they were!*
>
> CARTWRIGHT'S *Prol. to the Royal Slave.*[3]

Yet in these labors I employed, and in the belief of partial friends wasted, the prime and manhood of my intellect. Most assuredly, they added nothing to my fortune or my reputation. The industry of the week supplied the necessities of the week. From Government or the friends of Government I not only never received remuneration, or ever expected it; but I was never honoured with a single acknowledgement, or expression of satisfaction.[4] Yet the retrospect is far from painful or matter of regret. I am not indeed silly enough to take, as any thing more than a violent hyperbole of party debate, Mr. FOX's assertion that the *late* war (I trust that the epithet is not prematurely applied) *was a war produced by the* MORNING POST; or I should be proud to have

---

[1] On "mob-sycophants" see *LS* (*CC*) 144, the editor there probably William Cobbett.

[2] C's 140-odd contributions to the *Courier* stretch from Feb 1804 to Mar 1818. For full discussion see *EOT* (*CC*) I cxxii–clxxvii.

[3] Prologue to *The Royall Slave* (1639) lines 7–10: *Comedies, Tragi-Comedies* (1651) I 89, by William Cartwright (1611–43), who had aroused C's interest in 1804 (*CN* II 1914–1949 and nn) and whom he quotes in *Friend* (*CC*) I 272, 482. He had entered the above lines in a notebook in 1809: *CN* III 3521 and n.

[4] Cf "I have too sad an account to settle between my Self that is & has been & my Self that *can* not cease to be, to allow me a single Complaint, that for all my labors in behalf of Truth, against the Jacobins first, then against military Despotism abroad, against Weakness, and Despondency and Faction and factitious *Goodiness* at home—I have never received from those in power even a verbal acknowlegement— tho' by mere reference to dates it might be proved, that no small number of fine Speeches in the House of Commons & elsewhere originated directed or indirectly in my Essays & Conversations. . . . Unthanked and left worse than defenceless by the Friends of the Government and the Establishment . . .". To Stuart 12 Sept 1814: *CL* III 531–2.

the words inscribed on my tomb.[1] As little do I regard the circumstance, that I was a specified object of Buonaparte's resentment during my residence in Italy in consequence of those essays in the Morning Post during the peace of Amiens. (Of this I was warned, *directly*, by Baron VON HUMBOLDT, the Prussian Plenipotentiary, who at that time was the minister of the Prussian court at Rome; and indirectly, through his secretary, by Cardinal Fesch himself.)[2] Nor do I lay any greater weight on the confirming fact, that an order for my arrest was sent from Paris, from which danger I was rescued by the kindness of a noble Benedictine, and the gracious connivance of that good old man, the present Pope.[3] For the late tyrant's vindictive appetite was omnivorous, and preyed equally on a * Duc D'Enghein, and the writer of a

---

* I seldom think of the murder of this illustrious Prince[4] without recollecting the lines of Valerius Flaccus (Argonaut. Lib. I. 30.)

[1] For a history of the remarks by Fox that led C to make this exaggerated attribution, see *EOT* (*CC*) I 401–2.

[2] Karl Wilhelm von Humboldt (1767–1835), elder brother of the more famous Alexander (1769–1859), was appointed Prussian minister to Rome in 1802. Joseph, Cardinal Fesch (1763–1839), abp of Lyons and an uncle of Napoleon, was appointed French ambassador to Rome in 1804. Cottle says that Fesch thought well of C "and sought his company; but that which was more remarkable, Jerome Bonaparte [1784–1860; Napoleon's brother, currently in command of a French squadron in the Mediterranean] was then a resident in Rome, and Mr. C's reputation becoming known to him, he sent for him . . . and thus generously addressed him: 'Sir, I have sent for you to give you a little candid advice. I do not know that you have said, or written anything against my brother Napoleon, but as an Englishman, the supposition is not unreasonable. If you have, my advice is, that you leave Italy as soon as you possibly can.' " C then "soon after quitted Rome, in the suite of Cardinal Fesch". Cottle

Rem (1847) 310–11. Cf *CN* II 2785 and n.

[3] Pius VII (1742–1823), who had become Pope in 1800. According to a note of Jan 1 1806, C also heard of the imminent arrival of the French from a "Mr. Jackson" (presumably Thomas Jackson, British minister to Naples). He then lingered outside Rome for some months, part of the time at the house of the American painter Washington Allston (1779–1843), before definitely leaving Rome in May 1806. *CN* II 2784, 2794, 2796, and nn. From here he went to Florence, then to Leghorn, hoping to get passage. He had left his papers in Rome. But an American captain named Derkheim, captivated by C's conversation, got him a passport by swearing C was an American with whose parents Derkheim was personally acquainted, and then took him to England in his ship the *Gosport*. *CN* II 2836, 2848, 2849, and nn; *C Life* (C) 190–1; *CL* II 1184, 1174–6, 1178. Cf *EOT* (*CC*) I 402.

[4] Louis Antoine Henri de Bourbon-Condé, Duc d'Enghien (1772–1804), son of the Prince de Condé, was arrested by Napoleon on a trumped-up charge as a means of

newspaper paragraph. Like a true* vulture, Napoleon with an eye not less telescopic, and with a taste equally coarse in his ravin, could descend from the most dazzling heights to pounce on the leveret in the brake, or even on the field-mouse amid the grass. But I do derive a gratification from the knowledge, that my essays contributed to introduce the practice of placing the questions and events of the day in a moral point of view; in giving a dignity to particular measures by tracing their policy or impolicy to permanent principles, and an interest to principles by the application of them to individual measures. In Mr. Burke's writings indeed the germs of almost all political truths may be found.[3] But I dare assume to myself the merit of having first explicitly defined and analyzed the nature of Jacobinism; and that in distinguishing the jacobin from the republican, the democrat, and the mere demagogue, I both rescued the word from remaining a mere term of abuse, and put on their guard many honest minds, who even in their heat of zeal against jacobinism, admitted or supported principles from which the worst parts of that system may be legitimately deduced.[4] That these are not necessary *practical* results of such principles, we owe to that fortunate inconsequence of our nature, which permits the heart to rectify the errors of the understanding. The detailed examination of the consular Govern-

---

—————————————— Super ipsius ingens
Instat fama viri, virtusque haud læta Tyranno;
Ergo anteire metus, juvenemque exstinguere pergit.[1]

* Θηρᾷ δὲ καὶ τὸν χῆνα καὶ τὴν Δορκάδα
Καὶ τὸν Λαγωόν, καὶ τὸ τῶν Ταύρων γένος.
PHILE, *de animal. propriet.*[2]

---

intimidating the Bourbons, and then summarily tried and shot. See *EOT* (*CC*) III 84–5.

[1] Valerius Flaccus *Argonautica* 1.29–31. C had been struck by the lines and copied them into a notebook in 1805: *CN* II 2653 and n. Tr LCL: "Moreover, above all, the great renown of the hero himself weighed upon his mind, and prowess never welcome to a tyrant. Wherefore he sought to forestall his fears and to destroy the son."

[2] Manuel Philes (c 1275–1345) of Ephesus, in *De animalium proprietate: De aquilis* lines 12–13. C had copied the lines into a notebook (c 1813–15), from *Poetae graeci veteres* ed P. de la Rovière (Geneva 1614) II 211: *CN* III 4189 and n. Tr: "For he [the eagle] preys even upon the goose, and the antelope, and the hare, and the breed of bulls."

[3] See above, I 191–2.

[4] In his essay "Once a Jacobin Always a Jacobin": see above, I 184 and n 1. Cf also *Friend* No 7 (*CC*) II 105 (I 178–9).

ment and its pretended constitution, and the proof given by me, that it was a consummate despotism in masquerade, extorted a recantation even from the Morning Chronicle, which had previously extolled this constitution as the perfection of a wise and regulated liberty.[1] On every great occurrence I endeavoured to discover in past history the event, that most nearly resembled it. I procured, wherever it was possible, the contemporary historians, memorialists, and pamphleteers. Then fairly substracting the points of difference from those of likeness, as the balance favored the former or the latter, I conjectured that the result would be the same or different. In the series of * essays entitled "a comparison of France under Napoleon with Rome under the first Cæsars," and in those which followed "on the probable final restoration of the Bourbons," I feel myself authorized to affirm, by the effect produced on many intelligent men, that were the dates wanting, it might have been suspected that the essays had been written within the last twelve months.[4] The same plan I pursued at the commencement of the Spanish revolution, and with the same success, taking the war of the United Provinces with Philip 2nd, as the ground work of the comparison.[5] I have mentioned this

---

* A small selection from the numerous articles furnished by me to the Morning Post and Courier, chiefly as they regard the sources and effects of jacobinism and the connection of certain systems of political economy with jacobinical despotism, will form part of "THE FRIEND," which I am now completing, and which will be shortly published, for I can scarcely say republished, with the numbers arranged in Chapters according to their subjects.[2]

> Accipe principium rursus, corpusque *coactum*
> Desere; mutata melior procede figura.[3]

[1] C presumably refers to the series "On the French Constitution" in the *M Post* 7, 26, 27, and 31 Dec 1799. *EOT* (*CC*) I 31–57. By "recantation" on the part of the *M Chron* C may refer to the reservations it expressed about the constitution in its article of 26 Dec 1799.

[2] The revised 3-vol *Friend* did not include this "small selection", though C used bits of his essays without identifying them as such, e.g. Essay IV: *Friend* (*CC*) I 25–6, the opening paragraph of which C took from a *Courier* article of 21 Sept 1811: *EOT* (*CC*) II 305–6.

[3] Claudius Claudianus (c 370–c 404) *Phoenix* lines 53–4 (*Eidyllia* I). C used this as the motto for the 1812 and 1818 eds of *The Friend* (*CC* I 1 and II, II 4). Cf *CN* III 3325 f 14 and n. Tr M. Platnauer: "Receive back thy life, quit the body that must die, and by a change of form come forth more beauteous than ever."

[4] *M Post* 21, 25, and 29 Sept and 2 and 12 Oct 1802. *EOT* (*CC*) I 311–39, 359–66.

[5] Eight "Letters on the Spaniards" in the *Courier* of 7, 8, 9, 15, 20, 21, 22 Dec 1809 and 20 Jan 1810. *EOT* (*CC*) II 37–100.

from no motives of vanity, nor even from motives of self-defence, which would justify a certain degree of egotism, especially if it be considered, how often and grossly I have been attacked for sentiments, which I had exerted my best powers to confute and expose, and how grievously these charges acted to my disadvantage while I was in Malta.[1] Or rather they would have done so, if my own feelings had not precluded the wish of a settled establishment in that island. But I have mentioned it from the full persuasion that, armed with the two-fold knowledge of history and the human mind, a man will scarcely err in his judgement concerning the sum total of any future national event, if he have been able to procure the original documents of the past together with authentic accounts of the present, and if he have a philosophic tact for what is truly important in facts, and in most instances therefore for such facts as the DIGNITY OF HISTORY has excluded from the volumes of our modern compilers, by the courtesy of the age entitled historians.[2]

To have lived in vain must be a painful thought to any man, and especially so to him who has made literature his profession. I should therefore rather condole than be angry with the mind, which could attribute to no worthier feelings, than those of vanity or self-love, the satisfaction which I acknowledge to have enjoyed from the republication of my political essays (either whole or as extracts) not only in many of our own provincial papers, but in the federal journals throughout America.[3] I regarded it as some proof of my not having labored altogether in vain, that from the articles written by me shortly before and at the commencement of the late unhappy war with America,[4] not only the sentiments were adopted, but in some instances the very language, in several of the Massachussets state-papers.

But no one of these motives nor all conjointly would have impelled me to a statement so uncomfortable to my own feelings, had not my character been repeatedly attacked, by an unjustifiable intrusion on private life, as of a man incorrigibly idle, and who intrusted not only with ample talents, but favored with unusual

---

[1] C was in Malta from May 1804 to Aug 1805.

[2] Cf "Letters on the Spaniards" IV: *EOT* (*CC*) II 58–9.

[3] C refers here, and in *LS* (*CC*) 214, to papers that supported the Federalist party generally, not to the now famous *Federalist Papers* (1788), published when he was fifteen.

[4] The War of 1812; see *EOT* (*CC*) II 142, 233–7, 303–5.

opportunities of improving them, had nevertheless suffered them to rust away without any efficient exertion either for his own good or that of his fellow-creatures. Even if the compositions, which I have made public, and that too in a form the most certain of an extensive circulation, though the least flattering to an author's self-love, had been published in *books*, they would have filled a respectable number of volumes, though every passage of merely temporary interest were omitted. My prose writings have been charged with a disproportionate demand on the attention; with an excess of refinement in the mode of arriving at truths; with beating the ground for that which might have been run down by the eye; with the length and laborious construction of my periods; in short with obscurity and the love of paradox. But my severest critics have not pretended to have found in my compositions triviality, or traces of a mind that shrunk from the toil of thinking. No one has charged me with tricking out in other words the thoughts of others, or with hashing up anew the crambe jam decies coctam[1] of English literature or philosophy. Seldom have I written that in a day, the acquisition or investigation of which had not cost me the previous labor of a month.

But are books the only channel through which the stream of intellectual usefulness can flow? Is the diffusion of truth to be estimated by publications; or publications by the truth, which they diffuse or at least contain? I speak it in the excusable warmth of a mind stung by an accusation, which has not only been advanced in reviews of the widest circulation, not only registered in the bulkiest works of periodical literature, but by frequency of repetition has become an admitted fact in private literary circles, and thoughtlessly repeated by too many who call themselves my friends, and whose own recollections ought to have suggested a contrary testimony. Would that the criterion of a scholar's utility were the number and moral value of the truths, which he has been the means of throwing into the general circulation; or the number and value of the minds, whom by his conversation or letters, he has excited into activity, and supplied with the germs of their after-growth! A distinguished rank might not indeed, even then, be awarded to my exertions, but I should dare look forward with

---

[1] "Cabbage already ten times cooked (or warmed over)". The expression *crambe repetita* (warmed-over cabbage) was proverbial. Cf Juvenal 7.154. Cf also *EOT* (*CC*) II 213 and n 9 and a letter to RS 9 Feb 1813: *CL* III 433.

confidence to an honorable acquittal. I should dare appeal to the numerous and respectable audiences, which at different times and in different places honored my lecture-rooms with their attendance, whether the point of view from which the subjects treated of were surveyed, whether the grounds of my reasoning were such, as they had heard or read elsewhere, or have since found in previous publications.[1] I can conscientiously declare, that the complete success of the REMORSE on the first night of its representation[2] did not give me as great or as heart-felt a pleasure, as the observation that the pit and boxes were crowded with faces familiar to me, though of individuals whose names I did not know, and of whom I knew nothing, but that they had attended one or other of my courses of lectures. It is an excellent though perhaps somewhat vulgar proverb, that there are cases where a man may be as well *"in for a pound as for a penny."* To those, who from ignorance of the serious injury I have received from this rumour of having dreamt away my life to no purpose, injuries which I unwillingly remember at all, much less am disposed to record in a sketch of my literary life; or to those, who from their own feelings, or the gratification they derive from thinking contemptuously of others, would like Job's comforters attribute these complaints, extorted from me by the sense of wrong, to self-conceit or presumptuous vanity, I have already furnished such ample materials, that I shall gain nothing by with-holding the remainder. I will not therefore hesitate to ask the consciences of those, who from their long acquaintance with me and with the circumstances are best qualified to decide or be my judges, whether the restitution of the suum cuique[3] would increase or detract from my literary reputation. In this exculpation I hope to be understood as speaking of myself comparatively, and in proportion to the claims, which others are intitled to make on my time or my talents. By what I *have* effected, am I to be judged by my fellow men; what I *could* have done, is a question for my own conscience. On my own account I may perhaps have had sufficient reason to lament my deficiency in self-controul, and the neglect of concentering my powers to the realization of some permanent work. But to verse rather than to prose, if to either, belongs the "voice of mourning" for

---

[1] By this time C had given four courses of lectures, at London, Bristol, and Clifton, 1808, 1811–12, 1812, and 1813–14.

[2] At Drury Lane 23 Jan 1813; it then ran for twenty nights.

[3] Proverbial. "To each his own".

Keen pangs of love awakening as a babe
Turbulent, with an outcry in the heart,
And fears self-will'd that shunn'd the eye of hope,
And hope that scarce would know itself from fear;
Sense of past youth, and manhood come in vain
And genius given and knowledge won in vain,
And all which I had cull'd in wood-walks wild
And all which patient toil had rear'd, and all
Commune with thee had open'd out—but flowers
Strew'd on my corpse, and borne upon my bier
In the same coffin, for the self-same grave!

S. T. C.[1]

These will exist, for the future, I trust only in the poetic strains, which the feelings at the time called forth. In those only, gentle reader,

Affectus animi varios, bellumque sequacis
Perlegis invidiæ; curasque revolvis inanes;
Quas humilis tenero stylus olim effudit in ævo.
Perlegis et lacrymas, et quod pharetratus acutâ
Ille puer puero fecit mihi cuspide vulnus.
OMNIA PAULATIM CONSUMIT LONGIOR ÆTAS
VIVENDOQUE SIMUL MORIMUR, RAPIMURQUE
     MANENDO.
Ipse mihi collatus enim non ille videbor;
Frons alia est, moresque alii, nova mentis imago,
Vox aliudque sonat. Jamque observatio vitæ
Multa dedit:—lugere nihil, ferre omnia; jamque
Paulatim lacrymas rerum experientia tersit.[2]

[1] *To William Wordsworth* lines 65–75, first published in *SL* (1817): *PW* (EHC) I 407. For other passages of self-disparaging comparison with WW see e.g. *CN* II 2086 f 40 and n.

[2] Petrarch *Epistola Barbato Sulmonensi* (the poem from which C quoted in ch 1, above) lines 40–50, 55–7 (var). C patched the end of line 55 to the beginning of line 50, shortening "Vox aliud mutat[a] sonat" to "Vox aliudque sonat" to make his new line scan. C had copied the lines into a notebook in 1813, from Petrarch *Opera* (Basle 1581) III 76: *CN* III 4178 and n. For part of line 39 see ch 14, below, II 16. Tr: "You read of various passions of the mind, of the warfare of persistent malice, you peruse the idle cares that once, in tender youth, my humble pen poured forth. You read too of tears, and of the wound given me, a boy, by that quivered boy with piercing barb. ADVANCING TIME DEVOURS ALL THINGS BY DEGREES, AND AS WE LIVE WE DIE, AND AS WE REST WE ARE HURRIED ONWARD. For, compared to myself, I shall not seem that self; my face is another, my ways are changed, I have a new sort of mind, my voice sounds otherwise. Already the study of life has given me much:—to grieve at nothing, to endure all things; and already experience has little by little wiped away my tears."

CHAPTER 11

An affectionate exhortation to those who in early life feel themselves disposed to become authors

I T W A S a favorite remark of the late Mr. Whitbread's,[1] that no man does any thing from a single motive. The separate motives, or rather moods of mind, which produced the preceding reflections and anecdotes have been laid open to the reader in each separate instance. But an interest in the welfare of those, who at the present time may be in circumstances not dissimilar to my own at my first entrance into life, has been the constant accompaniment, and (as it were) the under-song of all my feelings. W H I T E H E A D exerting the prerogative of his laureatship addressed to youthful poets a poetic C H A R G E, which is perhaps the best, and certainly the most interesting, of his works.[2] With no other privilege than that of sympathy and sincere good wishes, I would address an affectionate exhortation to the youthful literati, grounded on my own experience. It will be but short; for the beginning, middle, and end converge to one charge: N E V E R   P U R S U E   L I T E R A T U R E   A S   A   T R A D E .[3] With the exception of one extraordinary man, I

---

[1] Samuel Whitbread (1758–1815), son of the famous brewer, was a noted political reformer and philanthropist. He chaired the committee for rebuilding and reorganising the Drury Lane Theatre, was distressed at the controversies involved, fell into depression, and committed suicide. Cf *CN* III 3739 and n. In a series of articles in the *Courier* of 2, 4, and 9 Jul 1811, C had attacked Whitbread's speech against tyrannicide, i.e. the attempted assassination of Napoleon. *EOT* (*CC*) II 208–13, 218–21.

[2] William Whitehead (1715–85), who was made poet laureate on the death of Colley Cibber (1757).

C refers to his *Charge to the Poets* (1762) lines 85–6:
> If nature prompts you, or if
>   friends persuade,
> Why write you, but ne'er pursue
>   it as a trade.

In an annotation on Flögel *Geschichte der komischen Litteratur* II 406, C called it "an incomparable Satirical Poem". *CM* (*CC*) II.

[3] Except for the Wedgwood annuity, which he assigned to his wife, C had been supporting himself by "literature", writing or lecturing, for the past twenty years. "O how often do I feel the wisdom of the advice which I have myself given in the eleventh Chapter of my Literary

have never known an individual, least of all an individual of genius, healthy or happy without a *profession*, i.e. some *regular* employment, which does not depend on the will of the moment, and which can be carried on so far *mechanically* that an average quantum only of health, spirits, and intellectual exertion are requisite to its faithful discharge. Three hours of leisure, unannoyed by any alien anxiety, and looked forward to with delight as a change and recreation, will suffice to realize in literature a larger product of what is truly *genial*, than weeks of compulsion. Money, and immediate reputation form only an arbitrary and accidental end of literary labor. The *hope* of increasing them by any given exertion will often prove a stimulant to industry; but the *necessity* of acquiring them will in all works of genius convert the stimulant into a *narcotic*.[1] Motives by excess reverse their very nature, and instead of exciting, stun and stupify the mind. For it is one contradistinction of genius from talent, that its predominant end is always comprized in the means; and this is one of the many points, which establish an analogy between genius and virtue. Now though talents may exist without genius, yet as genius cannot exist, certainly not manifest itself, without talents, I would advise every scholar, who feels the genial power working within him, so far to make a division between the two, as that he should devote his *talents* to the acquirement of competence in some known trade or profession, and his genius to objects of his tranquil and unbiassed choice; while the consciousness of being actuated in both alike by the sincere desire to perform his duty, will alike ennoble both.[2] My dear young friend (I would say) "suppose yourself established in any honourable occupation. From the manufactory or counting-house, from the law-court, or from having visited your last patient, you return at evening,

Life!" To C. A. Tulk 26 Jan 1818: *CL* IV 816. The "extraordinary man" mentioned in the next line is presumably RS.

[1] Cf the remark to HCR 12 Mar 1811: ". . . Moral obligation is to me so very strong a Stimulant, that in 9 cases out of ten it acts as a Narcotic. The Blow that should rouse, *stuns* me." *CL* III 307.

[2] For the distinction between "genius" and "talent" see ch 2, above, I 31. ". . . When a mere Stripling I had formed the opinion, that true Taste, was Virtue—& that bad writing was bad feeling". *CN* II 2728. Cf among his list of "the chief *Subjects* of my own Essays" in the Prospectus to *The Friend* (1809): "The necessary Dependence of Taste on moral Impulses and Habits . . .". *Friend* (*CC*) II 18.

> Dear tranquil time, when the sweet sense of home
> Is sweetest —— 1

to your family, prepared for its social enjoyments, with the very countenances of your wife and children brightened, and their voice of welcome made doubly welcome, by the knowledge that, as far as *they* are concerned, you have satisfied the demands of the day by the labor of the day. Then, when you retire into your study, in the books on your shelves you revisit so many venerable friends with whom you can converse. Your own spirit scarcely less free from personal anxieties than the great minds, that in those books are still living for you! Even your writing desk with its blank paper and all its other implements will appear as a chain of flowers, capable of linking your feelings as well as thoughts to events and characters past or to come; not a chain of iron which binds you down to think of the future and the remote by recalling the claims and feelings of the peremptory present. But why should I say *retire*? The habits of active life and daily intercourse with the stir of the world will tend to give you such self-command, that the presence of your family will be no interruption. Nay, the social silence, or undisturbing voices of a wife or sister will be like a restorative atmosphere, or soft music which moulds a dream without becoming its object. If facts are required to prove the possibility of combining weighty performances in literature with full and independent employment, the works of Cicero and Xenophon among the ancients; of Sir Thomas Moore, Bacon, Baxter, or to refer at once to later and cotemporary instances, DARWIN and ROSCOE, are at once decisive of the question." 2

1 *To William Wordsworth* lines 92–3: *PW* (EHC) I 408.

2 C is no doubt thinking of Cicero as orator and statesman, and Xenophon as military man and sportsman. Sir Thomas More (1478–1535), after two brief periods of asceticism and retirement, led an extremely active life in law and politics. Both he and Bacon had been lord chancellor. Richard Baxter (1615–91), the Puritan divine, though ill much of his life, led a strenuous career of preaching, public disputation, and ecclesiastical business. Erasmus Darwin (see above, ch 1, I 19 n 3) had a busy practice as a physician in Lichfield. William Roscoe (1753–1831), the historian, while working as an attorney and afterwards a banker, wrote poetry, two biographies, *The Life of Lorenzo de' Medici* (1796) and *The Life and Pontificate of Leo X* (1805), as well as works concerned with the slave-trade, jurisprudence, and even botany. C had met Darwin at Derby, on his tour to gain subscribers to *The Watchman,* and Roscoe, who had subscribed to both *Watchman* and *Friend,* admired C's compositions and in 1796 had suggested that C settle in Liverpool. See *Watchman* (*CC*) xxxiv, 351 and n 5, *CL* I 230.

But all men may not dare promise themselves a sufficiency of self-controul for the imitation of those examples; though strict scrutiny should always be made, whether indolence, restlessness, or a vanity impatient for immediate gratification, have not tampered with the judgement and assumed the vizard of humility for the purposes of self-delusion. Still the church presents to every man of learning and genius a profession, in which he may cherish a rational hope of being able to unite the widest schemes of literary utility with the strictest performance of professional duties.[1] Among the numerous blessings of christianity, the introduction of an established church makes an especial claim on the gratitude of scholars and philosophers; in England, at least, where the principles of Protestantism have conspired with the freedom of the government to double all its salutary powers by the removal of its abuses.

That not only the maxims, but the grounds of a pure morality, the mere fragments of which

> —— the lofty grave tragedians taught
> In chorus or iambic, teachers best
> Of moral prudence, with delight received
> In brief sententious precepts;
>   PARADISE REGAINED[2]

and that the sublime truths of the divine unity and attributes, which a Plato found most hard to learn and deemed it still more difficult to reveal; that these should have become the almost hereditary property of childhood and poverty, of the hovel and the workshop; that even to the unlettered they sound as *common place*, is a phenomenon, which must withhold all but minds of the most vulgar cast from undervaluing the services even of the pulpit and the reading desk. Yet those, who confine the efficiency of an estab-

---

[1] The remainder of this paragraph and the larger part of the next (to "withhold five") were reprinted (with changes and with the Milton passage omitted) in *C&S* (*CC*) 75–6. Their central position suggests that ch 11 is not just a warning against literature as a trade but a heart-felt exhortation to the ministry, to which C as a Unitarian had early felt a pull, preaching as a layman especially 1795–6, and to which he continued to be attracted later in life as a trinitarian. C seems to have believed that a settled life as a member of the clergy would have solved many of the personal problems he had experienced and was still facing. It is revealing that the quotation closing this chapter C takes from Herder's *Letters Concerning the Study of Theology*. Cf the end of a letter of 14 Apr 1816: *CL* IV 633.

[2] Milton *Paradise Regained* IV 261–4.

lished church to its *public* offices, can hardly be placed in a much higher rank of intellect. That to every parish throughout the kingdom there is transplanted a germ of civilization; that in the remotest villages there is a nucleus, round which the capabilities of the place may crystallize and brighten; a model sufficiently superior to excite, yet sufficiently near to encourage and facilitate, imitation; *this,* the inobtrusive, continuous agency of a protestant church establishment, *this* it is, which the patriot, and the philanthropist, who would fain unite the love of peace with the faith in the progressive amelioration of mankind, cannot estimate at too high a price. "It cannot be valued with the gold of Ophir, with the precious onyx, or the sapphire. No mention shall be made of coral or of pearls; for the price of wisdom is above rubies."[1] The clergyman is with his parishioners and among them; he is neither in the cloistered cell, or in the wilderness, but a neighbour and a family-man, whose education and rank admit him to the mansion of the rich landholder, while his duties make him the frequent visitor of the farm-house and the cottage. He is, or he may become, connected with the families of his parish or its vicinity by marriage. And among the instances of the blindness, or at best of the shortsightedness, which it is the nature of cupidity to inflict, I know few more striking, than the clamors of the farmers against church property. Whatever was not paid to the clergyman would inevitably at the next lease be paid to the landholder,[2] while, as the case at present stands, the revenues of the church are in some sort the reversionary property of every family, that may have a member educated for the church, or a daughter that may marry a clergyman. Instead of being *foreclosed* and immovable, it is in fact the only species of landed property, that is essentially moving and circulative. That there exist no inconveniences, who will pretend to assert? But I have yet to expect the proof, that the inconveniences are greater in this than in any other species; or that either the farmers or the clergy would be benefited by forcing the latter to become either *Trullibers,*[3] or salaried *placemen.* Nay, I do not hesitate to declare my firm persuasion, that whatever *reason* of discontent the farmers may assign, the true *cause* is this; that they may cheat the *parson,* but cannot cheat the steward; and they are

---

[1] Job 28.16, 18.
[2] On tithing see also *LS* (*CC*) 167.

[3] Parson Trulliber, the loud, boorish farmer-parson in Fielding *Joseph Andrews* (1742) II xiv.

disappointed, if they should have been able to withhold only two pounds less than the legal claim, having expected to withhold five. At all events, considered relatively to the encouragement of learning and genius, the establishment presents a patronage at once so effective and unburthensome, that it would be impossible to afford the like or equal in any but a christian and protestant country. There is scarce a department of human knowledge without some bearing on the various critical, historical, philosophical, and moral truths, in which the scholar must be interested as a clergyman; no one pursuit worthy of a man of genius, which may not be followed without incongruity. To give the history of the bible as a *book*, would be little less than to relate the origin or first excitement of all the literature and science, that we now possess. The very decorum, which the profession imposes, is favorable to the best purposes of genius, and tends to counteract its most frequent defects. Finally, that man must be deficient in sensibility, who would not find an incentive to emulation in the great and burning lights, which in a long series have illustrated the church of England; who would not hear from within an echo to the voice from their sacred shrines,

Et Pater Æneas et avunculus excitat Hector.[1]

But whatever be the profession or trade chosen, the advantages are many and important, compared with the state of a *mere* literary man, who in any degree depends on the sale of his works for the necessaries and comforts of life. In the former a man lives in sympathy with the world, in which he lives. At least he acquires a better and quicker tact for the knowledge of that, with which men in general can sympathize. He learns to manage his genius more prudently and efficaciously. His powers and acquirements gain him likewise more real admiration; for they surpass the legitimate expectations of others. He is something besides an author, and is not therefore considered merely as an author. The hearts of men are open to him, as to one of their own class; and whether he exerts himself or not in the conversational circles of his acquaintance, his silence is not attributed to pride, nor his communicativeness to vanity. To these advantages I will venture to add a superior

[1] Virgil *Aeneid* 3.343. Tr: "His father, Aeneas, and his uncle, Hector, inspire him".

chance of happiness in domestic life, were it only that it is as natural for the man to be out of the circle of his household during the day, as it is meritorious for the woman to remain for the most part within it. But this subject involves points of consideration so numerous and so delicate, and would not only permit, but require such ample documents from the biography of literary men, that I now merely allude to it *in transitu*. When the same circumstance has occurred at very different times to very different persons, all of whom have some one thing in common; there is reason to suppose that such circumstance is not merely attributable to the *persons* concerned, but is in some measure occasioned by the one point in common to them all. Instead of the vehement and almost slanderous dehortation from marriage, which the *Misogyne*, Boccaccio (*Vita e Costumi* di Dante, p. 12, 16) addresses to literary men,[1] I would substitute the simple advice: be not *merely* a man of letters! Let literature be an honourable *augmentation* to your arms; but not constitute the coat, or fill the escutchion!

To objections from conscience I can of course answer in no other way, than by requesting the youthful objector (as I have already done on a former occasion) to ascertain with strict self-examination, whether other influences may not be at work; whether spirits, *"not of health,"* and with whispers *"not from heaven,"* may

[1] In C's annotated ed of Boccaccio *Opera* (6 vols Florence 1723–4) IV iii 12–16, the famous attack on marriage in "Origine, vita, studi e costumi del chiarissimo Dante Alighieri", which describes Dante's relatives finding him a wife and ends with the injunction to philosophers not to marry. Cf e.g. "Accustomed to devote himself by night to his sacred studies as often as was pleasing to him, he conversed with emperors, kings, and other most exalted princes of the earth, and found pleasure in the most delightful poets, calming his own sorrows by listening to theirs. Now he is with them only as much as is pleasing to his bride, and such time as she wills to withdraw him from such high company, he must spend in listening to womanish conversation. . . . Accustomed . . . to speculate . . . what are the causes of things; or brood on rare conceits; or compose verses . . . he is now . . . deprived of all this sweet contemplation at the whim of his bride. . . . Oh, weariness not to be reckoned, that of having to live, converse, and finally to grow old, and die with such a suspicious animal! . . . Let no one believe that . . . I would conclude that men should not marry. On the contrary, I recommend marriage, but not to all. Let philosophers leave it to the rich and foolish, to nobles and to peasants, and let them take their delight with philosophy, a much better bride than any." Tr G. R. Carpenter (NY 1900) 52–6. We may note the relevance of the passage to Mrs C and C's unfortunate marriage. In Sept 1814 C proposed to John Murray to translate Boccaccio's prose works. *CL* III 529.

not be walking in the *twilight* of his consciousness.[1] Let him catalogue his scruples, and reduce them to a distinct intelligible form; let him be certain, that he has read with a docile mind and favorable dispositions the best and most fundamental works on the subject; that he has had both mind and heart opened to the great and illustrious qualities of the many renowned characters, who had doubted like himself, and whose researches had ended in the clear conviction, that their doubts had been groundless, or at least in no proportion to the counter-weight. Happy will it be for such a man, if among his contemporaries elder than himself he should meet with one, who with similar powers, and feelings as acute as his own, had entertained the same scruples; had acted upon them; and who by after-research (when the step was, alas! irretrievable, but for that very reason his research undeniably disinterested) had discovered himself to have quarrelled with received opinions only to embrace errors, to have left the direction tracked out for him on the high road of honorable exertion, only to deviate into a labyrinth, where when he had wandered, till his head was giddy, his best good fortune was finally to have found his way out again, too late for prudence though not too late for conscience or for truth! Time spent in such delay is time won; for manhood in the mean time is advancing, and with it increase of knowledge, strength of judgement, and above all, temperance of feelings. And even if these should effect no change, yet the delay will at least prevent the final approval of the decision from being alloyed by the inward censure of the rashness and vanity, by which it had been precipitated. It would be a sort of irreligion, and scarcely less than a libel on human nature to believe, that there is any established and reputable profession or employment, in which a man may not continue to act with honesty and honor; and doubtless there is likewise none, which may not at times present temptations to the contrary. But woefully will that man find himself mistaken, who imagines that the profession of literature, or (to speak more plainly) the *trade* of authorship, besets its members with fewer or with less insidious temptations, than the church, the law, or the different branches of commerce. But I have treated sufficiently on this unpleasant subject in an early chapter of this volume.[2] I will

[1] Shakespeare *Hamlet* I iv 40–1: "Be thou a spirit of health or goblin damn'd, | Bring with thee airs from heaven or blasts from hell . . .".

[2] Ch 2, "Supposed irritability of men of Genius", above, I 30.

conclude the present therefore with a short extract from HERDER, whose name I might have added to the illustrious list of those, who have combined the successful pursuit of the muses, not only with the faithful discharge, but with the highest honors and honorable emoluments, of an established profession.[1] The translation the reader will find in a note below.* "Am sorgfältigsten, meiden sie die Autorschaft. Zu früh oder unmässig gebraucht, macht sie den Kopf wüste und das Herz leer; wenn sie auch sonst keine üble Folgen gäbe. Ein Mensch, der nur lieset um zu drucken, lieset wahrscheinlich übel; und wer jeden Gedanken, der ihm aufstösst, durch Feder und Presse versendet, hat sie in kurzer Zeit alle versandt, und wird bald ein blosser Diener der Druckerey, ein Buchstabensetzer werden.

HERDER.[2]

*TRANSLATION.

"With the greatest possible solicitude avoid authorship. Too early or immoderately employed, it makes the head *waste* and the heart empty; even were there no other worse consequences. A person, who reads only to print, in all probability reads amiss; and he, who sends away through the pen and the press every thought, the moment it occurs to him, will in a short time have sent all away, and will become a mere journeyman of the printing-office, a *compositor*."

To which I may add from myself, that what medical physiologists affirm of certain secretions, applies equally to our thoughts; they too must be taken up again into the circulation, and be again and again re-secreted in order to ensure a healthful vigor, both to the mind and to its intellectual offspring.

[1] Johann Gottfried Herder (1744–1803), after studying theology, worked in Riga first as assistant master at the Cathedral school and then assistant pastor (1764–9), having been ordained in the Lutheran Church. After an interlude as tutor to the prince of Eutin-Holstein, he was appointed court preacher at Bückeburg (1771) and, through Goethe's influence, held the demanding position of superintendent of educational and religious affairs at Weimar from 1776 till his death.

[2] *Briefe, das Studium der Theologie betreffend* No 23 (Frankfurt & Leipzig 1790) I 371 (var: in particular omitting "die Bibel" before "nur lieset"), a passage C had copied into a notebook: *CN* III 4192 and n. The translation in C's note is his own. For C's annotations on the *Briefe* see *CM (CC)* II.

CHAPTER 12

A Chapter of requests and premonitions concerning the perusal or omission of the chapter that follows

IN THE perusal of philosophical works I have been greatly benefited by a resolve, which, in the antithetic form and with the allowed quaintness of an adage or maxim, I have been accustomed to word thus: *"until you understand a writer's ignorance, presume yourself ignorant of his understanding."* 1 This *golden rule* of mine does, I own, resemble those of Pythagoras in its obscurity rather than in its depth. If however the reader will permit me to be my own Hierocles,2 I trust, that he will find its meaning fully explained by the following instances. I have now before me a treatise of a religious fanatic, full of dreams and supernatural *experiences*.3 I see clearly the writer's grounds, and their hollowness. I have a complete insight into the causes, which

1 A favourite maxim of C's, first expressed in 1801. *CN* I 928 f 27; cf a letter to Lady Beaumont 21 Jan 1810: *CL* III 278. C's first two paragraphs amount to a genial but indirect warning to readers about judging the content of his planned ch 13 on the imagination and perhaps of ch 12 as well. In the next four paragraphs the warning and C's plea for fairness become more direct.

2 The Neoplatonist Hierocles of Alexandria (fl A.D. 430), whose principal extant work is a commentary on the neo-Pythagorean *Carmina aurea*, or "golden verses", on which see *EOT* (*CC*) I 92.

3 C may refer to Böhme: in the letter to Lady Beaumont he ties the maxim to Böhme. But the "treatise" here described sounds more like a work of Emanuel Swedenborg, possibly *De coelo et ejus mirabilibus*

et de inferno, ex auditis et visis (1758), which, among other works, C read and annotated. Cf his remarks about Swedenborg's "memorable Experiences", which "arose out of a voluntary power of so bedimming or interrupting the impressions from the outward Senses as to produce the same transition of thoughts into things, as ordinarily takes place on passing into Sleep". *CN* III 3474; cf III 3847 f 126. In his annotations on *De coelo* C states several times that he does not suspect him "of any intentional falsehood" (e.g. that he does not suspect Swedenborg's "veracity", annotations on pp 29, 126). Cf also an annotation on Samuel Noble *Appeal in Behalf of the Views of the Eternal World* (1829), on Swedenborg's "assertion . . . of a supernatural Illumination". *CM* (*CC*) IV, III.

through the medium of his body had acted on his mind; and by application of received and ascertained laws I can satisfactorily explain to my own reason all the strange incidents, which the writer records of himself. And this I can do without suspecting him of any intentional falsehood. As when in broad day-light a man tracks the steps of a traveller, who had lost his way in a fog or by treacherous moonshine, even so, and with the same tranquil sense of certainty, can I follow the traces of this bewildered visionary. I UNDERSTAND HIS IGNORANCE.

On the other hand, I have been re-perusing with the best energies of my mind the Timæus of P L A T O. Whatever I comprehend, impresses me with a reverential sense of the author's genius; but there is a considerable portion of the work, to which I can attach no consistent meaning. In other treatises of the same philosopher intended for the average comprehensions of men, I have been delighted with the masterly good sense, with the perspicuity of the language, and the aptness of the inductions. I recollect likewise, that numerous passages in this author, which I thoroughly comprehend, were formerly no less unintelligible to me, than the passages now in question. It would, I am aware, be quite *fashionable* to dismiss them at once as Platonic Jargon. But this I cannot do with satisfaction to my own mind, because I have sought in vain for causes adequate to the solution of the assumed inconsistency. I have no insight into the possibility of a man so eminently wise, using words with such half-meanings to himself, as must perforce pass into no-meaning to his readers. When in addition to the motives thus suggested by my own reason, I bring into distinct remembrance the number and the series of great men, who after long and zealous study of these works had joined in honoring the name of P L A T O with epithets, that almost transcend humanity, I feel, that a contemptuous verdict on my part might argue want of modesty, but would hardly be received by the judicious, as evidence of superior penetration. Therefore, utterly baffled in all my attempts to understand the ignorance of Plato, I CONCLUDE MYSELF IGNORANT OF HIS UNDERSTANDING.

In lieu of the various requests which the anxiety of authorship addresses to the unknown reader, I advance but this one; that he will either pass over the following chapter altogether, or read the whole connectedly.[1] The fairest part of the most beautiful body will appear deformed and monstrous, if dissevered from its place in the organic Whole. Nay, on delicate subjects, where a seemingly trifling difference of more or less may constitute a difference in *kind*,[2] even a *faithful* display of the main and supporting ideas, if yet they are separated from the forms by which they are at once cloathed and modified, may perchance present a skeleton indeed; but a skeleton to alarm and deter. Though I might find numerous precedents, I shall not desire the reader to strip his mind of all prejudices, or to keep all prior systems out of view during his examination of the present. For in truth, such requests appear to me not much unlike the advice given to hypochondriacal patients in Dr. Buchan's domestic medicine; videlicet, to preserve themselves uniformly tranquil and in good spirits.[3] Till I had discovered the art of destroying the memory *a parte post*,[4] without injury to its future operations, and without detriment to the judgement, I should suppress the request as premature; and therefore, however much I may *wish* to be read with an unprejudiced mind, I do not presume to state it as a necessary condition.

The extent of my daring is to suggest one criterion, by which it may be rationally conjectured before-hand, whether or no a reader would lose his time, and perhaps his temper, in the perusal of this, or any other treatise constructed on similar principles. But it would be cruelly misinterpreted, as implying the least disrespect either for the moral or intellectual qualities of the individuals thereby precluded. The criterion is this: if a man receives as fundamental facts, and therefore of course indemonstrable and incapable of further analysis, the general notions of matter, spirit, soul, body, action, passiveness, time, space, cause and effect, consciousness, perception, memory and habit; if he feels his mind completely at rest concerning all these, and is satisfied, if only he can analyse all other notions into some one or more of these supposed elements with plausible subordination and apt arrange-

---

[1] In light of C's headnote to ch 12, "the following chapter" seems to refer to ch 13. But if C were dictating rapidly, he might not have foreseen how ch 12 would grow to such length and complexity.

[2] On the distinction between "kind" and "degree" see above, I 88, 171.

[3] Dr William Buchan (1729–1805), whose *Domestic Medicine; or the Family Physician* (1769) had sold widely for decades. Ch 43 ("Of Nervous Diseases") contains the advice: "Cheerfulness and serenity of mind are by all means to be cultivated." *CN* III 4268 and n.

[4] A slip for *a parte prius*?

ment: to such a mind I would as courteously as possible convey the hint, that for him the chapter was not written.[1]

Vir bonus es, doctus, prudens; ast *haud tibi spiro.*[2]

For these terms do in truth *include* all the difficulties, which the human mind can propose for solution. Taking them therefore in mass, and unexamined, it requires only a decent apprenticeship in logic, to draw forth their contents in all forms and colours, as the professors of legerdemain at our village fairs pull out ribbon after ribbon from their mouths. And not more difficult is it to reduce them back again to their different genera. But though this analysis is highly useful in rendering our knowledge more distinct, it does not really add to it. It does not increase, though it gives us a greater mastery over, the wealth which we before possessed. For forensic purposes, for all the established professions of society, this is sufficient. But for philosophy in its highest sense, as the science of ultimate truths, and therefore scientia scientiarum,[3] this mere analysis of terms is preparative only, though as a preparative discipline indispensable.

Still less dare a favorable perusal be anticipated from the proselytes of that compendious philosophy, which talking of mind but thinking of brick and mortar, or other images equally abstracted from body, contrives a theory of spirit by nicknaming matter, and in a few hours can qualify its dullest disciples to explain the omne scibile[4] by reducing all things to impressions, ideas, and sensations.[5]

But it is time to tell the truth; though it requires some courage to avow it in an age and country, in which disquisitions on all

---

[1] C had observed in 1807: "Time, Space, Duration, Action, Active, Passion, Passive . . . Reason, Causation, Affinity—here assemble all the Mysteries—known, all is known —unknown, say rather, merely known, all is unintelligible/ and yet Locke & the stupid adorers of that *Fetisch* Earth-Clod, take all these for granted . . .". *CN* II 3156; cf 3156n.

[2] "You are a good man, learned, prudent; but *I do not blow for you.*" The second clause, "haud tibi spiro", is a variant of the motto on the emblem of the pig and sweet-marjoram in Joachim Camerarius *Symbolarum et emblematum ex re herbaria desumtorum centuria* No 93 (1590 etc). In *Friend* No 3 C had quoted the motto with "Sus, apage!" as part of it, but here in *BL* C says that he is being "courteous" and so substitutes the good and learned man for the pig. See *Friend (CC)* II 41n, I 41n and n 1.

[3] "The science of sciences".

[4] "Everything knowable". Cf *CN* III 4134 f 167v and n, and below, I 303.

[5] C refers to the "mechanical" philosophy.

Chapter 12

subjects, not privileged to adopt technical terms or scientific symbols, must be addressed to the P U B L I C .[1] I say then, that it is neither possible or necessary for all men, or for many, to be P H I L O S O P H E R S . There is a *philosophic* (and inasmuch as it is actualized by an effort of freedom, an *artificial*) *consciousness*,[2] which lies beneath or (as it were) *behind* the spontaneous consciousness natural to all reflecting beings.[3] As the elder Romans distinguished their northern provinces into Cis-Alpine and Trans-Alpine, so may we divide all the objects of human knowledge into those on this side, and those on the other side of the spontaneous consciousness; citra et trans conscientiam communem.[4]

[1] The attitude that the practice and understanding of philosophy is restricted to a small number of people appeared often in German discussions of the critical philosophy, especially with repeated frequence in Fichte and Schelling. E.g. Fichte *Grundlage* 278 (*SW* I 284): Solely on the power of the creative imagination "it depends whether one philosophises with or without spirit . . . in that the whole work of man's spirit proceeds from his imagination, but an imagination none other than that which can be grasped through imagination". Cf also Schelling *Abhandlungen: Phil Schrift* 290, 291 (*SW* I 416, 417), and esp *Vorlesungen* 19 (*SW* V 219): "But knowledge, especially of a philosophic kind, is not every man's possession and—without other attributes—is even with the best intention not at all obtainable". Cf ibid 117–18 (*SW* V 265). This and other similarities (above, ch 10, I 168 n 2, and below, I 287) suggest that C might have read the *Vorlesungen*, which, next to *STI*, is considered Schelling's clearest and most synoptic work published before 1815. However, the concept of a philosophical élite was far from new. For C's contempt of the reading "public", see above, ch 3, I 59, and *SM* (*CC*) 36–8n.

[2] C's use of "artificial" consciousness is paralleled several times by Schelling, who enthusiastically describes the whole approach of transcendental philosophy as "in no way a natural, but an artificial [*künstliche*] one". *STI* 10 (*SW* III 345).

[3] Cf Schelling *Abhandlungen: Phil Schrift* 324–7 (*SW* I 440–2), from that section of Essay IV, part of which C translates below (I 243 n 1). Schelling discusses "transcendental freedom" and a "transcendental faculty" as beyond the merely sensuous and consequently open only to some; also *Phil Schrift* 292 (*SW* I 417): "Now if philosophy is knowledge, which in order to be understood demands a certain measure of spiritual freedom, then it cannot be everybody's possession. . . ." Cf *Vorlesungen* 7, 19 (*SW* V 213, 218–19), in which Schelling again connects the idea of a special degree of conscious and wilful freedom with the ability to be philosophic; cf also *STI* 48–51 (*SW* III 368–9) and below, I 240 n 1.

[4] Cf C's extended metaphor here and to the end of the paragraph with Abraham Tucker *The Light of Nature Pursued* (2 vols in 5 pts 1768) Introd I i xxxiii: "Thus the land of philosophy contains partly an open champain country, passable by every common understanding, and partly a range of woods traversable only by the speculative. . . ." Cf *CN* III 4088 (from Jean Paul) and n and also Schelling *Vom Ich*

The latter is exclusively the domain of PURE philosophy, which is therefore properly entitled *transcendental*, in order to discriminate it at once, both from mere reflection and *re*-presentation on the one hand,[1] and on the other from those flights of lawless speculation which abandoned by *all* distinct consciousness, because transgressing the bounds and purposes of our intellectual faculties, are justly condemned, as * *transcendent*. The first range of hills,

* This distinction between transcendental and transcendent is observed by our elder divines and philosophers, whenever they express themselves *scholastically*.[2] Dr. Johnson indeed has confounded the two words;[3] but his own authorities do not bear him out. Of this celebrated dictionary I will venture to remark once for all, that I should suspect the man of a morose disposition who should speak of it without respect and gratitude as a most instructive and entertaining *book*, and hitherto, unfortunately, an indispensable book; but I confess, that I should be surprized at hearing from a philosophic and thorough scholar any but very qualified praises of it, as a

Vorrede: *Phil Schrift* xix (*SW* I 159), which contains a metaphor of mountains, fog, and sun similar to C's.

[1] C's stress on "*re*-presentation" may be an attempt to convey the meaning expressed by the German *Wiedervorstellung*, the repetition in the mind of an original impression or perception and usually used in reference to objects of the senses and always distinguished from *Idee*, *Anschauung*, and *Vorstellung* itself, which can denote a synthesising or productive act of mind. On presentation vs representation cf *CN* III 3602, 3605 ff 118v, 117v.

[2] As C explains it, the distinction between transcendental and transcendent is basically Kantian. Cf *KRV* Einleitung § VII (B 24–7), and esp "Elementarlehre" (B 352–3), in which Kant specifically discriminates between the terms, using words like "border", "demarcation", and "boundary stakes". The transcendental supposes a reality beyond our senses and our empirical awareness yet necessarily views this transcendental reality in reference to our senses, our experience, and our empirical consciousness. But the transcendent goes beyond "all

bounds of experience" and has no use for consciousness understood in an empirical way. Reading Kant, C would have become aware of the distinction as used in the critical philosophy. But what probably suggested to C the importance of stressing it is in Schelling *Abhandlungen: Phil Schrift* 326–7 (*SW* I 442). C's view is paralleled there by Schelling's discussion and quotations of what Kant and Reinhold mean by the transcendental and the transcendent. It is several lines further on this same page of Schelling (327) that C will later begin an extensive borrowing in *BL* (see below, I 243 n 1). Cf *Abhandlungen: Phil Schrift* 239 (*SW* I 378–9). There is little evidence to support C's claim that "elder divines and philosophers" distinguished between the terms. At least they do not do so in a way foreshadowing Kant's usage, which is what C's own description follows.

[3] Johnson defines "transcendent" as "Excellent; supremely excellent; passing others". His first definition of "Transcendental" is "General; pervading many particulars". Only the second definition equates it with "transcendent" ("Supereminent; passing others").

that encircles the scanty vale of human life, is the horizon for the majority of its inhabitants. On *its* ridges the common sun is born

---

dictionary. I am not now alluding to the number of genuine words omitted; for this is (and perhaps to a greater extent) true, as Mr. Wakefield has noticed, of our best Greek Lexicons,[1] and this too after the successive labors of so many giants in learning. I refer at present both to omissions and commissions of a more important nature. What these are, me saltem judice,[2] will be stated at full in THE FRIEND, re-published and completed.[3]

I had never heard of the correspondence between Wakefield and Fox till I saw the account of it this morning (16th September 1815) in the Monthly Review.[4] I was not a little gratified at finding, that Mr. Wakefield had proposed to himself nearly the same plan for a Greek and English Dictionary, which I had formed, and began to execute, now ten years ago.[5] But far, far more grieved am I, that he did not live to compleat it. I cannot but think it a subject of most serious regret, that the same heavy expenditure, which is now employing in the *republication* of STEPHANUS augmented,[6] had not been applied to a new Lexicon on a more philosophical

[1] Gilbert Wakefield (1756–1801), noted for his ed of Lucretius (1796–7). In 1800 Wakefield circulated a "Plan" for his *Greek and English Lexicon* (he was then in prison for a libel), noting that he would add between 15,000 to 20,000 words, from his reading over the years. *Memoirs of the Life of Gilbert Wakefield* (2 vols 1804) II 210–12. Cf *CN* III 3780 and n.

[2] "At least in my opinion".

[3] C neglected to do this in the revised *Friend*.

[4] The book to which C refers is *Correspondence of the Late Gilbert Wakefield, B.A., with the Late Right Honourable Charles James Fox . . . Chiefly on Subjects of Classical Literature* (1813), which was reviewed in *M Rev* LXXVII (Aug 1815) 381–91. The date of this note (16 Sept 1815) is interesting. On 19 Sept C dispatched the ms of *BL* to John Gutch. See Introd above, I liv–lvii. Unless he inserted this note after completing the section of *BL* he presumably wrote last (chs 5–13), he finished chs 12 and 13 in three days.

[5] There was as yet no Greek

lexicon that gave definitions in English, and only one with definitions in German. Wakefield's would give all definitions in English, not Latin. The sense of every word was to be given in chronological order, from the oldest to the latest authors. There would be greater simplicity in stating primary and derivative meanings of words. C's "Greek and English Lexicon" was to be "on philosophical Principles in which the one sole meaning, or original sensuous Image, of each word, will be first given, and then the different applications of this one meaning developed and explained". *CN* III 4210 (dated Jun 1814). In Dec 1808 C had written to his brother George that he would publish his Greek lexicon in the spring. *CL* III 133.

[6] The *Thesaurus graecae linguae* (5 vols 1572) by Henri Estienne or Henricus Stephanus (1531–98), the most comprehensive Greek lexicon. Abraham John Valpy (1787–1854), who had started the *Classical Journal,* reissued the *Thesaurus,* edited by himself and E. H. Barker, in 12 vols, published from 1816 to 1828.

and departs. From *them* the stars rise, and touching *them* they vanish. By the many, even this range, the natural limit and bulwark of the vale, is but imperfectly known. Its higher ascents are too often hidden by mists and clouds from uncultivated swamps, which few have courage or curiosity to penetrate. To the multitude below these vapors appear, now as the dark haunts of terrific agents, on which none may intrude with impunity; and now all *a-glow*, with colors not their own, they are gazed at, as the splendid palaces of happiness and power. But in all ages there have been a few, who measuring and sounding the rivers of the vale at the feet of their furthest inaccessible falls have learnt, that the sources must be far higher and far inward; a few, who even in the level streams have detected elements, which neither the vale itself or the surrounding mountains contained or could supply.[1] How and whence to these thoughts, these strong probabilities, the ascertaining vision, the intuitive knowledge, may finally supervene, can be learnt only

plan, with the English, German, and French Synonimes as well as the Latin. In almost every instance the precise *individual* meaning might be given in an English or German word; whereas in Latin we must too often be contented with a mere general and *inclusive* term. How indeed can it be otherwise, when we attempt to render the most copious language of the world, the most admirable for the fineness of its distinctions, into one of the poorest and most vague languages? Especially, when we reflect on the comparative number of the works, still extant, written, while the Greek and Latin were living languages. Were I asked, what I deemed the greatest and most unmixt benefit, which a wealthy individual, or an association of wealthy individuals could bestow on their country and on mankind, I should not hesitate to answer, "a philosophical English dictionary; with the Greek, Latin, German, French, Spanish and Italian synonimes, and with correspondent indexes." That the learned languages might thereby be acquired, better, in half the time, is but a part, and not the most important part, of the advantages which would accrue from such a work. O! if it should be permitted by providence, that without detriment to freedom and independence our government might be enabled to become more than a committee for war and revenue! There was a time, when every thing was to be done by government. Have we not flown off to the contrary extreme?

[1] *BL* (1847) prints a note here, apparently from a C-annotated copy of *BL*: "April, 1825. If I did not see it with my own eyes, I should not believe that I had been guilty of so many hydrostatic *Bulls* as bellow in this unhappy allegory or string of metaphors! How a river was to travel *up* hill from a vale far *inward*, over the intervening mountains, Morpheus, the Dream-weaver, can alone unriddle. I am ashamed and humbled. S. T. Coleridge."

by the fact.[1] I might oppose to the question the words with which *
Plotinus supposes N A T U R E to answer a similar difficulty. "Should

* *Ennead*, iii. 1. 8. c. 3.[2] The force of the Greek συνιέναι is imperfectly
expressed by "understand;" our own idiomatic phrase *"to go along with me"*
comes nearest to it. The passage, that follows, full of profound sense, appears
to me evidently corrupt; and in fact no writer more wants, better deserves,
or is less likely to obtain, a new and more correct edition[3]—τί οὖν συνιέναι;
φιλοθεάμονα ὑπάρχει. (*mallem*, καί μοι ἡ γενομένη ἐκ θεωρίας αὐτῆς ὠδίς) "what
φύσει γενόμενον θεώρημα, καί μοι γενομένη ἐκ θεωρίας τῆς ὠδὶ τὴν φύσιν ἔχειν
φιλοθεάμονα ὑπάρχει. (*mallem*, καί μοι ἡ γενομένη ἐκ θεωρίας αὐτῆς ὠδίς) "what
then are we to understand? That whatever is produced is an intuition, I silent;
and that, which is thus generated, is by its nature a theorem, or form of
contemplation; and the birth, which results to me from this contemplation,
attains to have a contemplative nature."[4] So Synesius: 'Ωδὶς ἱερά, 'Αρρητε
γονά.[5] The after comparison of the process of the natura naturans[6] with
that of the geometrician is drawn from the very heart of philosophy.[7]

[1] "Vision" and "intuitive knowledge". See below, C's translation
and his own note on Kant's use of
"intuition", I 288–9. C's position is at
first confusing. In his note on Kant,
below, C says Kant "rightly" denies
"intellectual intuitions" (i.e. those
not based on sensuous experience),
but C then says he sees "no adequate
reason for this" and will indeed use
"intuition" in its broadest sense
(which Kant would consider transcendent). It is this "wider signification" C apparently means here, and
C uses Plotinus as one source to
explain such "intuition". By "the
fact" C apparently means the belief
in or the actual experience of what
can only be called "vision" or intellectual "intuition" and of the
truths or "strong probabilities" that
such intuitions present us. The connection between intellectual intuition
and "an effort of freedom" implied
by C in this paragraph (see also
above, I 236 n 3) is made specifically by Schelling in several
places, e.g. *STI* 48–51 (*SW* III 368-
9), in a passage that C draws from
below.

[2] In modern eds this is *Ennead*
3.8.4. C translates the beginning of
the chapter in the text, continues
without a break in Greek and in
English in the footnote, and continues again, below, I 251.

[3] C owned a copy of the only
edition (Basle 1580), with M.
Ficino's Latin translation; see ch 6,
above, I 115 n 1. This was reprinted
(1615), but the first new edition was
that of F. Creuzer (Oxford 1835).

[4] C introduces two emendations
of the Greek with "mallem" ("I
should prefer"). The first of these
is substantially accepted by modern
editors, and C is cited for it by A. H.
Armstrong in LCL. The second
shows a confusion partly owing to
his edition (γενομένη for γενομένη)
and partly perhaps to his confusing
ὠδί ("thus") with ὠδίς ("childbirth").
Modern editors keep the old reading,
which translates (LCL) as "and that
I, originating from this sort of contemplation, have a contemplative
nature".

[5] Hymn III lines 226–7 (var).
From *Poetae graeci veteres* ed P. de
la Rovière II 169. Tr: "Sacred Tra-
vail, ineffable Generation".

[6] "Naturing nature" (active or
creative nature) as contrasted with
natura naturata (the world of
phenomena acted upon by the creative spirit). Cf the crucial passage in
CN III 4397 f 50ᵛ, the entry on which
is based *PA: BL* (1907) II 257. The
terms, which go back to mediaeval
Scholasticism, originated with Averroes (1126–98), in his commentary
on Aristotle *De coelo* 1.1. Bruno,

any one interrogate her, how she works, if graciously she vouchsafe to listen and speak, she will reply, it behoves thee not to disquiet me with interrogatories, but to understand in silence, even as I am silent, and work without words." [1]

Likewise in the fifth book of the fifth Ennead, speaking of the highest and intuitive knowledge as distinguished from the discursive,[2] or in the language of Wordsworth,

The vision and the faculty divine;[3]

he says: "it is not lawful to enquire from whence it sprang, as if it were a thing subject to place and motion, for it neither approached hither, nor again departs from hence to some other place; but it either appears to us or it does not appear. So that we ought not to pursue it with a view of detecting its secret source, but to watch in quiet till it suddenly shines upon us; preparing ourselves for the blessed spectacle as the eye waits patiently for the rising sun." [4] They and they only can acquire the philosophic imagination,[5] the sacred power of self-intuition,[6] who within themselves can inter-

---

Bacon, Spinoza, and Schelling all used the distinction. Cf Spinoza *Ethics* pt I props 29, 31. For Schelling see e.g. *Ideen* Einleitung 79 (*SW* II 67); *Phil und Rel* 44 (*SW* VI 44); *Jahrbücher der Medicin* I i (1805) 50 (*SW* VII 173) and esp I ii (1806) 10–18, 27–30, II ii 126 (*SW* VII 202–8, 214–16, 223). See also *P Lects* Lect 13 (1949) 370.

[7] C refers to those lines of *Ennead* 3.8.4 quoted below, I 251.

[1] *Ennead* 3.8.4.

[2] For "intuitive" and "discursive" cf above, I 174, and below, I 295. For C there is a connection between intuitive knowledge ("intellectual intuition"), "the very heart of philosophy", and the process of geometrical reasoning that involves postulates (see below, I 247–51).

[3] WW *Excursion* I 79.

[4] For this favourite passage from *Ennead* 5.5.8, cf *CN* I 209, 1678 and nn.

[5] For Fichte's similar stress on the special and exclusive nature of

a philosophic imagination see above, I 236 n 1.

[6] "Self-intuition", or *Selbstanschauung*, is a pivotal postulate in Schelling's *STI*, first explained on the page (11; *SW* III 345) immediately following those from which C translates below (I 259–60): "In common actions, the *action* itself becomes forgotten due to the object of the action; the philosophic process is also an *action*, yet not an action only, but at the same time a constant *self-intuition* in this action." Cf also *Abhandlungen: Phil Schrift* 223, 241 (*SW* I 366, 380) and *Vom Ich* § 16: *Phil Schrift* 82 (*SW* I 219). Fichte stresses *"SelbstAnschauung"*; cf *Versuch einer neuen Darstellung der Wissenschaftslehre* (*SW* I 529, 530): "The intelligence intuits itself . . . as pure intelligence and even in this self-intuition consists its being." Fichte distinguishes self-intuition from both sensuous and intellectual intuitions. Cf *KRV* "Elementarlehre" (B 68–9), in which Kant denies that

pret and understand the symbol, that the wings of the air-sylph are
forming within the skin of the caterpillar; those only, who feel in
their own spirits the same instinct, which impels the chrysalis of the
horned fly to leave room in its involucrum for antennæ yet to come.
They know and feel, that the *potential* works *in* them, even as the
actual works on them! In short, all the organs of sense are framed
for a corresponding world of sense; and we have it. All the organs
of spirit are framed for a correspondent world of spirit; tho' the
latter organs are not developed in all alike. But they exist in all,
and their first appearance discloses itself in the *moral* being. How
else could it be, that even worldlings, not wholly debased, will
contemplate the man of simple and disinterested goodness with
contradictory feelings of pity and respect? "Poor man! he is not
made for *this* world." Oh! herein they utter a prophecy of universal
fulfilment; for man *must* either rise or sink.[1]

It is the essential mark of the true philosopher to rest satisfied
with no imperfect light, as long as the impossibility of attaining a
fuller knowledge has not been demonstrated. That the common
consciousness itself will furnish proofs by its own direction, that
it is connected with master-currents below the surface, I shall
merely assume as a postulate pro tempore. This having been
granted, though but in expectation of the argument, I can safely
deduce from it the equal truth of my former assertion, that philos-

self-intuition ("eine Anschauung
seiner selbst") represents the self as
it is; rather it represents only the
self as it *appears* to itself ("wie es
sich erscheint"). Cf also в 131–2,
157–8 and n.

[1] Throughout the latter part of
this paragraph C repeats almost verbatim sections of an 1811 notebook
entry: "And what is Faith?—it is
to the Spirit of Man the same
Instinct, which impels the chrysalis
of the horned fly to build its involucrum as long again as itself to make
room for the Antennae, which are
to come, tho' they never yet have
been—O the *Potential* works *in* us
even as the Present mood works *on*
us!—. . . In short, all the organs of
Sense are framed for a corresponding World of Sense: and we have it.

All the organs of Spirit are framed
for a correspondent World of Spirit:
& we cannot but believe it. The
Infidel proves only that the latter
organs are not yet developed in
him—. . . . How comes it that even
Worldlings, who are not wholly
Worldlings in their thoughts, as well
as conduct, will contemplate the man
of simple goodness & disinterested-
ness with the contradictory feeling of
Pity and of Respect—'He is not
made for this World'—O therein
he utters a prophecy for himself. . . ."
In those sentences about "the organs
of Spirit" C has considerably softened the charge of who is an
"Infidel". *CN* III 4088. On the caterpillar and the horned fly see *CN* I
1378.

ophy cannot be intelligible to all, even of the most learned and
cultivated classes. A system,[1] the first principle of which it is to
render the mind intuitive of the *spiritual* in man (i.e. of that which
lies *on the other side* of our natural consciousness) must needs
have a great obscurity for those, who have never disciplined and
strengthened this ulterior consciousness. It must in truth be a land ✳
of darkness, a perfect *Anti-Goshen*,[2] for men to whom the
noblest treasures of their own being are reported only through the
imperfect translation of lifeless and sightless *notions*. Perhaps, in
great part, through words which are but the shadows of notions;
even as the notional understanding itself is but the shadowy abstraction of living and actual truth. On the IMMEDIATE, which
dwells in every man, and on the original intuition, or absolute
affirmation of it, (which is likewise in every man, but does not in
every man rise into consciousness) all the *certainty* of our knowledge depends; and this becomes intelligible to no man by the

---

[1] For the rest of this paragraph
C has used Schelling *Abhandlungen:
Phil Schrift* 327–8 (*SW* I 442–3).
As SC's tr, *BL* (1847) I 251–2n, does
not differ greatly from C's own
prose, the German is given here, with
brackets noting the important
changes and interpolations C makes.
"Eine Philosophie, deren erstes
Princip das *Geistige* im Menschen,
d. h. dasjenige, was *jenseits* des
Bewusstseyns liegt, zum *Bewusstseyn*
hervorrufen will [C's "to render the
mind intuitive"], muss nothwendig
eine grosse Unverständlichkeit haben
für diejenigen, welche dieses geistige
[C's "ulterior"] Bewusstseyn nicht
geübt und gestärkt haben [C ends his
sentence here and then paraphrases
and greatly expands the end of
Schelling's:], oder denen auch das
Herrlichste, was sie in sich tragen,
nur durch todte, anschauungslose
Begriffe zu erscheinen pflegt. [C now
returns to a more literal translation]
Das Unmittelbare, das in jedem ist,
und an dessen ursprünglichem
Anschauen (das gleichfalls in jedem
ist, aber nicht in jedem zum Bewusstseyn kommt) alle Gewissheit
unsrer Erkenntniss hängt, wird

keinem durch Worte, die von aussen
in ihn dringen, verständlich. Das
Medium, wodurch *Geister* sich
verstehen, ist nicht die umgebende
Luft, sondern: die gemeinschaftliche
Freyheit [C adds "as the common
ethereal element of their being"],
deren Erschütterungen bis ins Inn-
erste der Seele sich fortpflanzen. Wo
der Geist eines Menschen nicht vom
Bewusstseyn der Freyheit *erfüllt* ist
[C here adds his parenthesis], ist alle
geistige Verbindung unterbrochen,
nicht nur mit Andern, sondern sogar
mit *ihm selbst* [C ends his own
sentence here]; kein Wunder, dass er
sich selbst eben so gut als Andern
unverständlich bleibt, und in seiner
fürchterlichen Einöde nur mit eiteln
Worten sich ermüdet, denen kein
freundlicher Wiederhall (aus eigner
oder fremder Brust) Antwortet [C
adds the lines from "or bewilders" to
"stagnant understanding!" and then
names Schelling while paraphrasing
the next sentence from him:] Einem
solchen unverständlich zu bleiben,
ist Ruhm und Ehre vor Gott und
Menschen."

[2] Cf *EOT* (*CC*) I 120 and n 2.

ministery of mere words from without. The medium, by which
spirits understand each other, is not the surrounding air; but the
freedom which they possess in common, as the common ethereal
element of their being, the tremulous reciprocations of which
propagate themselves even to the inmost of the soul. Where the
spirit of a man is not *filled* with the consciousness of freedom
(were it only from its restlessness, as of one still struggling in
bondage) all spiritual intercourse is interrupted, not only with
others, but even with himself. No wonder then, that he remains
incomprehensible to himself as well as to others. No wonder, that
in the fearful desert of his consciousness, he wearies himself out
with empty words, to which no friendly echo answers, either from
his own heart, or the heart of a fellow being; or bewilders himself
in the pursuit of *notional* phantoms, the mere refractions from
unseen and distant truths through the distorting medium of his
own unenlivened and stagnant understanding! To remain unintelligible to such a mind, exclaims Schelling on a like occasion, is
honor and a good name before God and man.

The history of philosophy (the same writer observes)[1] contains
instances of systems, which for successive generations have remained enigmatic. Such he deems the system of Leibnitz, whom
another writer (rashly I think, and invidiously) extols as the *only*
philosopher, who was himself deeply convinced of his own
doctrines. As hitherto interpreted, however, they have not produced
the effect, which Leibnitz himself, in a most instructive passage,
describes as the criterion of a true philosophy; namely, that it
would at once explain and collect the fragments of truth scattered
through systems apparently the most incongruous. The truth,[2]

[1] C's first sentence in this paragraph continues to draw from the
same place in Schelling (*Phil Schrift*
328; *SW* I 443): "Die Geschichte
der Philosophie enthält Beyspiele
von Systemen, die mehrere Zeitalter
hindurch räthselhaft geblieben sind."
C then freely alters and adds to
Schelling's next sentence: "Ein
Philosoph, dessen Principien alle
diese Räthsel auflösen werden, ur-
theilt noch neuerdings von *Leibnitz,*
er sey wahrscheinlich der einzige
Ueberzeugte in der Geschichte der
Philosophie, der Einzige also, der im

Grunde recht hatte." "A philosopher
whose principles are to solve all
these riddles, declares lately of
Leibnitz, that he is probably the
only man, in the history of philosophy, who has attained conviction,
the only man therefore who is right
at bottom." Tr SC *BL* (1847) I
252n.

[2] It is of extreme interest that
from this sentence until the end of
this paragraph ("qu'elles nient") C
is, with exception of his footnote,
translating from Jacobi (*ULS* 395,
396–7, and 1), who in turn is

says he, is diffused more widely than is commonly believed; but it is often painted, yet oftener masked, and is sometimes mutilated and

quoting three passages from Leibniz's French and translating two of them into German (395–7), leaving in French the one sentence (*ULS* 1) that C likewise gives in French. Jacobi for his translations uses quotation marks and gives sources from a collection of Leibniz. In view of C's specific wording, which throughout is closer to Jacobi's translation than to Leibniz's original (down to the interpolated "says he" in the first sentence), but more importantly because of the proximity of the same passages in *ULS* 395–7 (which occur in two different works of Leibniz), C clearly is not using an edition of Leibniz but in fact translates directly from Jacobi's translations. Therefore for the first two passages Jacobi's German rather than the French original is given. The first passage: " 'Die Wahrheit,' sagt er, 'ist allgemeiner verbreitet, als man glaubt; aber oft ist sie geschminkt, noch öfter verhüllt, zuweilen gar geschwächt, verstümmelt, und durch Zusätze verdorben.' " *ULS* 395. This is C's sentence ending "mischievous errors". Jacobi's reference to Leibniz is "Recueil de div. Pieces par des Maizeaux, Tom. *II.* p. 145"; this is the *Trois Lettres à M. Remond de Montmort* (*Opera* ed Erdmann II 704). On the next page (*ULS* 396) Jacobi quotes and translates from a different place in Leibniz (Jacobi's reference: "Recueil de div. Pieces par des Maizeaux, Tom. *II* p. 417. Opp Omn. T. *II. P. 1*, p. 79"; this is Leibniz's *Éclaircissement de difficultés que M. Bayle a trouvées . . .* [*Opera* I 153–4], which Jacobi identifies as "seine Antwort an Bayle"). Jacobi's German, which C then follows in his own next four sentences from "The deeper" to "conceptions of others" is this (*ULS* 396–7): " '. . . je tiefer man in den Grund

der Dinge eindringt, desto mehr Wahrheit in den Lehren der meisten philosophischen Secten sich entdecken lasse. Der Mangel an substanzieller Wirklichkeit in den sinnlichen Gegenständen, nach der Behauptung der Skeptiker; die Harmonieen, oder Zahlen, Urbilder und Begriffe, worauf die Pythagoräer und Platoniker alles zurückführten; das Eins und Alles des Parmenides und Plotin, ohne Spinozismus; die Verknüpfung der Dinge nach den Stoikern, vereinbar mit der Spontaneität der andern Schulen; die Vital-Philosophie der Cabalisten und Hermetisten, welche überall Empfindung annehmen; die Formen und Entelechieen des Aristoteles und der Scholastiker, nebst der mechanischen Erklärung aller besonderen Erscheinungen nach dem Demokrit und den Neuern—alles dieses findet man in einem perspectivischen Mittelpunkte vereinigt, der in eben dem Gegenstande, welcher aus jedem andern Gesichtspunkte verworren erscheint, Regelmässigkeit, und die Uebereinstimmung aller seiner Theile zeiget. Sectengeist ist bisher der Fehler gewesen. Man hat sich selbst eingeschränkt, indem man verworfen hat, was andere lehrten.' " The quotation with which C then ends his own paragraph is in Leibniz's own French (*Trois Lettres: Opera* II 702, the work from which the first passage from Leibniz also came), but it too appears in *ULS* (1) as the epigraph to the book. And Jacobi, like C, leaves this sentence in French (Jacobi gives no specific reference but only Leibniz's name). In short, C strings together three passages from Leibniz, the first two of which he found on three consecutive pages of *ULS* and the last of which is the epigraph to *ULS*. Cf *CL* IV 567. C's quotations from Leibniz should probably not be taken as support for

sometimes, alas! in close alliance with mischievous errors. The deeper, however, we penetrate into the ground of things, the more truth we discover in the doctrines of the greater number of the philosophical sects. The want of *substantial* reality in the objects of the senses, according to the sceptics; the harmonies or numbers, the prototypes and ideas, to which the Pythagoreans and Platonists reduced all things; the ONE and ALL of Parmenides and Plotinus, without * Spinozism; the necessary connection of things according

---

* This is happily effected in three lines by SYNESIUS, in his Fourth Hymn:

> ῾Εν καὶ Πάντα—(taken by itself) is *Spinosism*.
> ῾Εν δ᾽ ᾽Απάντων—a mere *anima Mundi*.
> ῾Εν τε πρὸ πάντων—is mechanical Theism.[1]

But unite all three, and the result is the Theism of Saint Paul and Christianity.

Synesius was censured for his doctrine of the Pre-existence of the Soul; but never, that I can find, arraigned or deemed heretical for his Pantheism,[2] tho' neither Giordano Bruno, or Jacob Behmen ever avowed it more broadly.

> Μύστας δὲ Νόος,
> Τά τε καὶ τὰ λέγει,
> Βυθὸν ἄρρητον
> ᾽Αμφιχορεύων.
> Σὺ τὸ τίκτον ἔφυς,
> Σὺ τὸ τικτόμενον·
> Σὺ τὸ φώτιζον,
> Σὺ τὸ λαμπόμενον·
> Σὺ τὸ φαινόμενον,
> Σὺ τὸ κρυπτόμενον
> ᾽Ιδίαις αὐγαῖς.
> ῾Εν καὶ πάντα,
> ῾Εν καθ᾽ ἑαυτό,
> Καὶ διὰ πάντων.[3]

---

a simple "Eclectic Philosophy" or "Syncretism".

[1] Hymn III 180–2. From *Poetae graeci veteres* II 168. "One and all"; "one of all"; "one before all". Here and throughout the rest of the note, except for the concluding paragraph, C is transcribing, with slight changes, an entry in a notebook: *CN* III 4189. On the "one and all" of Parmenides see ch 22, below, II 139 and n 2. Plotinus often discusses the problem of "the one and the many": e.g. *Ennead* 6.4.5, and, on the eternity of τὸ πᾶν ("the all") *Ennead* 3.7.4.

[2] The hymns of Synesius (c 370–c 414), bp of Ptolemais, were written at various times, some dating from his pre-Christian period.

[3] Hymn III 187–200. From *Poetae graeci veteres* II 168. "The mind initiated in the mysteries says such and such things, moving in harmony the while around Thy awful abysm. Thou art the Generator, Thou the Generated; Thou the Light that shineth, Thou the Illumined; Thou what is revealed, Thou that which is hidden in thine own beams; The One and All, The One Self-contained and dispersed through all things." Tr Augustine Fitzgerald.

to the Stoics, reconcileable with the spontaneity of the other schools; the vital-philosophy of the Cabalists and Hermetists, who assumed the universality of sensation; the substantial forms and entelechies of Aristotle and the schoolmen, together with the mechanical solution of all particular phenomena according to Democritus and the recent philosophers—all these we shall find united in one perspective central point, which shows regularity and a coincidence of all the parts in the very object, which from every other point of view must appear confused and distorted. The spirit of sectarianism has been hitherto our fault, and the cause of our failures. We have imprisoned our own conceptions by the lines, which we have drawn, in order to exclude the conceptions of others. J'ai trouvé que la plupart des sectes ont raison dans une bonne partie de ce qu'elles avancent, mais non pas tant en ce qu'elles nient.[3]

A system, which aims to deduce the memory with all the other functions of intelligence, must of course place its first position from beyond the memory, and anterior to it, otherwise the principle of solution would be itself a part of the problem to be solved. Such a position therefore must, in the first instance be demanded, and the first question will be, by what right is it demanded? On this account I think it expedient to make some preliminary remarks on the introduction of POSTULATES in philosophy.[4] The word

---

Pantheism is therefore not necessarily irreligious or heretical; tho' it may be taught atheistically. Thus Spinoza would agree with Synesius in calling God Φύσις ἐν Νοεροῖς,[1] the *Nature* in Intelligences; but he could not subscribe to the preceding Νοῦς καὶ Νοερός, i.e. Himself Intelligence and intelligent.

In this biographical sketch of my literary life I may be excused, if I mention here, that I had translated the eight Hymns[a] of Synesius from the Greek into English Anacreontics before my 15th year.[2]

[1] This and the next Greek phrase are from Hymn III 185, 177. From *Poetae graeci veteres* II 168. In each case the English phrase immediately following is C's tr.

[2] Though it is not positive proof that C had not made these translations, which could understandably seem inadequate to him later, we should note that C at twenty-three told his brother George (26 Mar 1794) that he had sold some of his books when he enlisted in the Dragoons and would like to buy them back, among them editions of Casimir and Synesius, both of which "I mean to translate". *CL* I 76–7.

[3] "I have found that most [philosophical] sects are right in a good deal of what they affirm, but not so much in what they deny."

[4] For discussion concerning C's use of "postulates" against the background of Kant and especially of the

postulate is borrowed from the science of mathematics. (See Schell.
abhandl. zur Erläuter. des id. der Wissenschaftslehre).[1] In geom-

ensuing passage C translates from Schelling (below, this page), see Elinor S. Shaffer *Comparative Literature Studies* VII (1970) 297–313. C attempts to blend the intellectual intuition of "constructive philosophy", exercised only in some individuals, with "the organs of spirit" present—though not fully developed—in the "*moral* being" of all (see above, I 242).

[1] C, beginning with the previous sentence, freely adapts Schelling *Abhandlungen: Phil Schrift* 329–32 (*SW* I 444–6). This follows what C has taken earlier (see above, I 244 n 1), so that he has in effect omitted four sentences from just over three consecutive pages in Schelling. Schelling's numerous italics are not indicated, and C's significant changes are given in brackets: "Der Ausdruck Postulat ist von der Mathematik entlehnt. In der Geometrie wird die ursprünglichste Construktion nicht demonstrirt, sondern postulirt.—Diese ursprünglichste (einfachste) Construktion im Raume ist der bewegte Punkt, oder die Linie.—Ob der Punkt nach Einer und derselben Richtung bewegt wird, oder seine Richtung continuirlich ändert, ist damit noch nicht bestimmt. Ist die Richtung des Punkts bestimmt, so ist sie es entweder durch einen Punkt ausser ihm, und dann entsteht die gerade Linie, (die keinen Raum einschliesst), oder die Richtung des Punkts ist nicht bestimmt durch einen Punkt ausser ihm, so muss er in sich selbst zurückfliessen, d. h. es entsteht eine Kreislinie, (die einen Raum einschliesst).—Nimmt man die gerade Linie als positiv an, so ist die Kreislinie die Negation der geraden, d. h. eine Linie, die in keinem Punkt zur geraden ausschlägt, sondern continuirlich ihre Richtung ändert. Nimmt man aber die ursprüngliche Linie als unbegränzt an, die gerade als schlechthin begränzt, so wird die Kreislinie das dritte aus beyden seyn [C ends his own sentence here], sie ist unbegränzt und begränzt zugleich: unbegränzt durch einen Punkt ausser ihr, begränzt durch sich selbst.

"Die Mathematik [C uses "Geometry"] gibt also der Philosophie das Beyspiel einer ursprünglichen Anschauung, von der jede Wissenschaft ausgehen muss, welche auf Evidenz Anspruch machen will. Sie [C's "mathematician"] fängt nicht von einem Grundsatz an, der demonstrirbar ist; sondern von dem Undemonstrirbaren, ursprünglich Anzuschauenden. [C renders this "with an intuition, a practical idea" and then begins a new paragraph.] Hier thut sich aber sogleich ein bedeutender Unterschied hervor. Die Philosophie hat mit Gegenständen des innern Sinns zu thun, und kann nicht wie die Mathematik ["geometry"] jeder Construktion eine ihr entsprechende äussere Anschauung beygesellen. Nun muss aber die Philosophie, wenn sie evident werden soll, von der ursprünglichsten Construktion ausgehen; es fragt sich also, was die ursprünglichste Construktion [C adds "or first productive act"] für den innern Sinn sey?

"Die Beantwortung dieser Frage hängt von der Richtung ab, die dem innern Sinne gegeben wird. In der Philosophie aber kann dem innern Sinn seine Richtung gar nicht durch einen äussern Gegenstand bestimmt werden. Die Linie ursprünglich zu construiren, kann ich genöthigt werden durch die Linie, die man auf Papier, oder auf einer Tafel zieht [C: "drawn before me on the slate or on sand"]. Dieser gezogne Strich ist freylich nicht die Linie selbst, sondern nur das Bild derselben [C ends his sentence here]; wir lernen

etry the primary construction is not demonstrated, but postulated. This first and most simple construction in space is the point in

die Linie nicht dadurch erst kennen, sondern umgekehrt wir halten diese auf der Tafel gezogene [C omits this adjectival phrase] Linie an die ursprüngliche Linie (in der Einbildungskraft) [C: "generated by the act of the imagination"], sonst würden wir bey derselben nicht von aller Breite, Dicke u. s. w. abstrahiren. Aber dieser Linie ist doch das sinnliche Bild der ursprünglichen Linie, und ein Mittel, diese ursprüngliche Anschauung in jedem [C: *every* imagination"] zu erregen.

"Es fragt sich also, ob es in der Philosophie irgend ein Mittel gebe, die Richtung des innern Sinns eben so zu bestimmen, wie sie in der Mathematik durch äussere Darstellung [C adds or "specific image"] bestimmt werden kann? Dem innern Sinn wird seine Richtung grösstentheils nur durch Freyheit bestimmt [C changes "freedom" to "an act of freedom"; cf Schelling *STI* 49 (*SW* III 368–9)]. Das Bewusstseyn des Einen erstreckt sich nur auf die angenehmen oder unangenehmen Empfindungen, die äussere Eindrücke in ihm verursachen; der andre erweitert seinen innern Sinn bis zum Bewusstseyn der Anschauung [C alters "consciousness of intuition" to "consciousness of forms and quantity"]; ein dritter wird sich ausser der Anschauung auch des Begriffs bewusst; ein vierter hat noch den Begriff des Begriffs [C adds "—he reflects on his own reflections"], und so kann man mit Recht sagen, dass er Eine mehr oder weniger innern Sinn habe, als der Andere. Dieses Mehr oder Weniger verräth schon, dass die Philosophie in ihren ersten Principien schon eine praktische [C, significantly, adds "or moral, as well as a theoretical or speculative side"] Seite haben müsse. Ein solches Mehr oder Weniger gibt es in der Mathematik nicht. Sokrates (bey Plato) zeigt, dass man auch

einen [C adds "ignorant"] Sklaven bis zu verwickelten geometrischen Demonstrationen bringen kann. Sokrates zeichnet ihm die Figuren in Sand. [Schelling here refers to Plato's Meno.] Die Kantianer [C: "The disciples of the critical philosophy"] könnten zwar auch, wie weiland einige Cartesianer [C elaborates this in his parenthesis], den Ursprung der Vorstellungen nach ihrem System in Kupfer stechen lassen, doch hat es noch keiner versucht, und es würde zu nichts helfen. Einem Esquimo oder Feuerländer [C changes this from native of Tierra del Fuego ("Land of Fire") to "New Zealander"] müsste auch unsre allerpopulärste Philosophie ganz unverständlich seyn. Er hat nicht einmal dafür Sinn [C elaborates: "the inward organ, for it"]. So fehlt Manchem, der unter uns sich Philosoph zu seyn dünkt, ganz und gar das philosophische Organ . . .". From here until he cites Plotinus, C freely adapts Schelling (the German is given, with a literal translation): ". . . die Philosophie ist ihm ein Luftgebäude, etwa so wie dem Taubgeborenen die trefflichste Theorie der Musik, wenn er nicht wüsste oder nicht glaubte, dass andre Menschen einen Sinn mehr haben, als Er, als ein eitles Spiel mit Begriffen vorkommen müsste, das in sich selbst zwar Zusammenhang haben mag, aber im Grunde ganz und gar keine Realität hat." ("Philosophy is to him a fabric of air, even as to one born deaf the most excellent theory of music if he knew not, or did not believe, that other men have a sense more than he, must seem a vain play with conceptions, which may have connection in itself indeed, but at bottom has absolutely no reality." Tr SC *BL*—1847—I 255n.) Contrast Kant's position in *KRV* "Elementarlehre" §§ 22–5 (B 146–59).

motion, or the line. Whether the point is moved in one and the same direction, or whether its direction is continually changed, remains as yet undetermined. But if the direction of the point have been determined, it is either by a point without it, and then there arises the strait line which incloses no space; or the direction of the point is not determined by a point without it, and then it must flow back again on itself, that is, there arises a cyclical line, which does inclose a space. If the strait line be assumed as the positive, the cyclical is then the negation of the strait. It is a line, which at no point strikes out into the strait, but changes its direction continuously. But if the primary line be conceived as undetermined, and the strait line as determined throughout, then the cyclical is the third compounded of both. It is at once undetermined and determined; undetermined through any point without, and determined through itself. Geometry therefore supplies philosophy with the example of a primary intuition, from which every science that lays claim to *evidence* must take its commencement. The mathematician does not begin with a demonstrable proposition, but with an intuition, a practical idea.

But here an important distinction presents itself. Philosophy is employed on objects of the INNER SENSE, and cannot, like geometry, appropriate to every construction a correspondent *outward* intuition. Nevertheless philosophy, if it is to arrive at evidence, must proceed from the most original construction, and the question then is, what is the most original construction or first productive act for the INNER SENSE. The answer to this question depends on the direction which is given to the INNER SENSE. But in philosophy the INNER SENSE cannot have its direction determined by any outward object. To the original construction of the line, I can be compelled by a line drawn before me on the slate or on sand. The stroke thus drawn is indeed not the line itself, but only the image or picture of the line. It is not from it, that we first learn to know the line; but, on the contrary, we bring this stroke to the original line generated by the act of the imagination; otherwise we could not define it as without breadth or thickness. Still however this stroke is the sensuous image of the original or ideal line, and an efficient mean to excite *every* imagination to the intuition of it.

It is demanded then, whether there be found any means in philosophy to determine the direction of the INNER SENSE, as in mathematics it is determinable by its specific image or outward picture. Now the inner sense has its direction determined for the greater part only by an act of freedom. One man's consciousness extends only to the pleasant or unpleasant sensations caused in him by external impressions; another enlarges his inner sense to a consciousness of forms and quantity; a third in addition to the image is conscious of the conception or notion of the thing; a fourth attains to a notion of his notions—he reflects on his own reflections; and thus we may say without impropriety, that the one possesses more or less inner sense, than the other. This more or less betrays already, that philosophy in its first principles must have a practical or moral, as well as a theoretical or speculative side. This difference in degree does not exist in the mathematics. Socrates in Plato shows, that an ignorant slave may be brought to understand and of himself to solve the most difficult geometrical problem. Socrates drew the figures for the slave in the sand. The disciples of the critical philosophy could likewise (as was indeed actually done by La Forge[1] and some other followers of Des Cartes) represent the origin of our representations in copperplates; but no one has yet attempted it, and it would be utterly useless. To an Esquimaux or New Zealander our most popular philosophy would be wholly unintelligible. The sense, the inward organ, for it is not yet born in him. So is there many a one among us, yes, and some who think themselves philosophers too, to whom the philosophic organ is entirely wanting. To such a man, philosophy is a mere play of words and notions, like a theory of music to the deaf, or like the geometry of light to the blind. The connection of the parts and their logical dependencies may be seen and remembered; but the whole is groundless and hollow, unsustained by living contact, unaccompanied with any realizing intuition which exists by and in the act that affirms its existence, which is known, because it is, and is, because it is known. The words of Plotinus, in the assumed person of nature, hold true of the philosophic energy. Τὸ θεωροῦν μου θεώρημα ποιεῖ, ὥσπερ οἱ γεωμέτραι θεωροῦντες γράφουσιν· ἀλλ᾽ ἐμοῦ μὴ γραφούσης, θεωρούσης δέ, ὑφίστανται αἱ τῶν σωμάτων γραμμαί.[2] With me the act of contemplation makes the

---

[1] See above, I 93 and n 4.

[2] *Ennead* 3.8.4. The following two sentences are C's translation of the passage. This is the continuation of the passage C quotes above, I 240n.

In *Logic* (*CC*) 74 C writes of "the exceeding velocity of motion" of ephemerae as "a symbol of what Plotinus meant when, speaking of the geometricians and then of Nature

thing contemplated, as the geometricians contemplating describe lines correspondent; but I not describing lines, but simply contemplating, the representative forms of things rise up into existence.

The postulate of philosophy and at the same time the test of philosophic capacity, is no other than the heaven-descended K N O W T H Y S E L F! (*E cælo descendit, Γνῶθι σεαυτόν*).[1] And this at once practically and speculatively. For as philosophy is neither a science of the reason or understanding only, nor merely a science of morals, but the science of B E I N G altogether, its primary ground can be neither merely speculative or merely practical, but both in one.[2] All knowledge rests on the coincidence of an object with a subject.[3] (My readers have been warned in a former chapter that

as acting geometrically, he says . . . her contemplative act is creative and is one with the product of contemplation".

[1] Juvenal 11.27. "It descended from heaven, *Know thyself*." The words "Know thyself" were inscribed over the temple at Delphi. Cf below, I 291, and C's poem *Self-knowledge* (1832), which takes Juvenal's line as its motto. *PW* (EHC) I 487. Cf also *Logic* (*CC*) 116, 143, 205. In C's present context the motto implies more than a moral warning not to overstep man's bounds. C says it concerns "BEING altogether". Since the self *is* being and by its intuitions, speculation, moral will, feeling, and knowledge can contain much of the universe, and since these intuitions etc may actually be constitutive with the laws of nature and eternal mind (as in the example of mathematical postulates) and thus with nature's creator, God, "Know thyself" may be interpreted as "Know all this that is within the self, the laws of nature and the sense of a creating intelligence, and know also even how the self knows and reflects on this knowledge in its consciousness of self". This makes "Know thyself" both "the postulate of philosophy and . . . the test of philosophic capacity". See below, II 240, C's n.
[2] Cf Schelling *Abhandlungen:*

Phil Schrift 332 (*SW* I 446; this follows—with an intervening paragraph, which C omits—the passage he draws from in the above paragraph): "So zeigt sich hier abermals . . . dass das erste Princip der Philosophie *theoretisch und praktisch zugleich* . . . seyn müsse." ("Again it here thus appears . . . that the first principle of philosophy must be *at once theoretical and practical*.")
[3] From this sentence until the clause ending "intelligence and self-consciousness" four paragraphs below (and not, as SC states, until "heavenly motions"), C draws from the opening of *STI* 1–5 (*SW* III 339–41). As *BL* (1847) I 258n notes, C adds a few expressions and alters and arranges differently some sentences. Schelling's German is given here, with C's more important changes noted in brackets: "Alles Wissen beruht auf der Uebereinstimmung eines Objectiven mit einem Subjectiven. [C here adds his parenthesis referring to I 172, above; "quicquid objicitur menti": whatever is thrown before, hence presented to the mind]—Denn man *weiss* nur das Wahre; die Wahrheit aber wird allgemein in die Uebereinstimmung der Vorstellungen mit ihren Gegenständen gesetzt [C · uses singular nouns and adds "of the thought with the thing"].

for their convenience as well as the writer's, the term, subject,[a] is
used by me in its scholastic sense as equivalent to mind or sentient

[a] *BL* (1817) omits comma

"Wir können den Inbegriff alles blos *Objectiven* in unserm Wissen *Natur* nennen [C adds "confining . . . the other hand"]; der Inbegriff alles *Subjectiven* dagegen heisse das *Ich,* oder die *Intelligenz.* Beide Begriffe sind sich entgegengesetzt [C stresses the antithesis is "necessary"]. Die Intelligenz wird ursprünglich gedacht als das blos Vorstellende, die Natur als das blos Vorstellbare, jene als das Bewusste, diese als das Bewusstlose. Nun ist aber in jedem [C adds "positive"] *Wissen* ein wechselseitiges Zusammentreffen beider (des Bewussten und des an sich Bewusstlosen) nothwendig; die Aufgabe ist: dieses Zusammentreffen zu erklären [C stresses: "its possibility and its necessity"].

"Im Wissen selbst—*indem* ich weiss [C omits this, implying it by "act of"]—ist Objectives und Subjectives so [C adds "instantly"] vereinigt, dass man nicht sagen kann, welchem von beiden die Priorität zukomme. Es ist hier kein Erstes und kein Zweites, beide sind gleichzeitig und Eins.—Indem ich diese Identität *erklären will,* muss ich sie schon *aufgehoben* haben. Um sie zu erklären, muss ich, da mir ausser jenen beiden Factoren des Wissens (als Erklärungs-Princip) sonst nichts gegeben ist, nothwendig den Einen dem andern *vorsetzen,* von dem Einen *ausgehen,* um von ihm auf den andern zu kommen; von *welchem* von beiden ich ausgehe, ist durch die Aufgabe nicht bestimmt [C has divided Schelling's sentence into two, rearranged clauses, and added clarifying appositions].

"Es sind also nur zwei Fälle möglich.

"*Entweder wird das Objective zum Ersten gemacht, und gefragt: wie ein Subjectives zu ihm hinzukomme, das mit ihm übereinstimmt?*

"Der Begriff des Subjectiven ist nicht *enthalten* im Begriff des Objectiven, vielmehr schliessen sich beide gegenseitig aus. Das Subjective muss also zum Objectiven *hinzukommen.*—Im Begriff *der Natur* liegt es nicht [C cautions "apparently"], dass auch ein Intelligentes sey, was sie vorstellt [C adds the important phrase "making an ideal duplicate of it". C then gives the specific example of the desk where Schelling gives a general statement that "Nature, so it appears, would exist, even if there were nothing that represented her". C's next sentence, "This then", is inserted from Schelling's next paragraph:] Sie ist also ohne Zweifel Aufgabe der *Naturwissenschaft* . . . Die Aufgabe kann also auch so ausgedrückt werden [C adds "It assumes . . . as the first"]: Wie kommt zu der Natur das Intelligente hinzu, oder wie kommt die Natur dazu, vorgestellt zu werden? [C puts the second half of this question in more clearly antithetical form. The next sentence in C beginning "If it should" very loosely paraphrases Schelling's next paragraph, which reads literally: "The problem takes nature or the *objective* as the *first* factor. . . . That natural philosophy—and without realizing it—at least actually approaches to the solution of this problem can here be indicated only briefly."]

"Wenn alles *Wissen* gleichsam zwei Pole hat, die sich wechselseitig voraussetzen, und fordern [C now condenses three clauses of Schelling into one: "all sciences . . . on the other":], so müssen sie in allen Wissenschaften sich suchen; es muss daher nothwendig *zwei* Grundwissenschaften geben, und es muss unmöglich seyn, von dem Einen Pol auszugehen, ohne auf den andern

being, and as the necessary correlative of object or *quicquid objicitur menti.*) For we can *know* that only which is true: and the truth is universally placed in the coincidence of the thought with the thing, of the representation with the object represented.

Now the sum of all that is merely O B J E C T I V E , we will henceforth call N A T U R E , confining the term to its passive and material sense, as comprising all the phænomena by which its existence is

getrieben zu werden [C adds: "as far as . . . identical", a notion possibly suggested by Heinrich Steffens; cf *CN* III 4226, 4333 and nn]. Die nothwendige Tendenz aller *Naturwissenschaft* ist also, von der Natur auf's Intelligente zu kommen. Diess, und nichts anders liegt dem Bestreben zu Grunde, in die Naturerscheinungen *Theorie* zu bringen.— Die höchste Vervollkommung der Naturwissenschaft wäre die vollkommene Vergeistigung aller Naturgesetze zu Gesetzen des Anschauens und des Denkens. Die Phänomene (das Materielle) müssen völlig verschwinden, und nur die Gesetze (das Formelle) bleiben. Daher kommt es, dass je mehr in der Natur selbst das Gesetzmässige hervorbricht, desto mehr die Hülle verschwindet, die Phänomene selbst geistiger werden, und zuletzt völlig aufhören [C adds "in our consciousness", a bit in anticipation since Schelling has not yet assumed an intelligence present in nature]. Die optischen Phänomene sind nichts anders, als eine Geometrie, deren Linien durch das Licht gezogen werden, und dieses Licht selbst ist schon von zweideutiger Materialität. In den Erscheinungen des Magnetismus verschwindet schon alle materielle Spur, und von den Phänomenen der Gravitation, welche selbst Naturforscher [C's "not a few among the most illustrious Newtonians"] nur als unmittelbar geistige Einwirkung begreifen zu können glaubten, bleibt nichts zurück, als ihr Gesetz, dessen Ausführung im Grossen der Mechanismus der Himmelsbewegungen ist. [The first half of C's next sentence, from "The theory" to "self-consciousness", is then a conflation of the beginning of Schelling's next sentence plus, skipping down over a half dozen lines, the last two lines of Schelling's paragraph:] Die vollendete Theorie der Natur würde diejenige seyn, kraft welcher die ganze Natur . . . identisch ist mit dem, was in uns als Intelligentes und Bewusstes [C's "self-consciousness"] erkannt wird." In this sentence the lines C skips in Schelling are as follows: "The dead and unconscious products of Nature are only abortive attempts of Nature to reflect herself; but the so named *dead* nature in general is an unripe intelligence; thence through her *phaenomena*, even while yet unconscious, the intelligent character discovers itself. [To which C objects in a marginal note on *STI* 4–6: "*True* or *false,* this Assertion was too early. Nothing precedent [has explained, much less proved,] it *true.*" *CM (CC)* IV.] The highest aim, to become completely an object to self, Nature first attains through the highest and last reflection, which is no other than man, or that which we commonly call reason, through which Nature first returns completely into herself, and whereby it becomes evident . . . [the rest of the sentence C has used; see this n, above]". Tr SC *BL* (1847) I 261n. The scheme of objective taken first vs subjective taken first was not uncommon. Cf Jacobi *ULS* 261–306, which follows Bruno; also Fichte *Grundlage* 52–60 (*SW* I 125–31).

made known to us. On the other hand the sum of all that is SUBJECTIVE, we may comprehend in the name of the SELF or INTELLIGENCE. Both conceptions are in necessary antithesis. Intelligence is conceived of as exclusively representative, nature as exclusively represented; the one as conscious, the other as without consciousness. Now in all acts of positive knowledge there is required a reciprocal concurrence of both, namely of the conscious being, and of that which is in itself unconscious. Our problem is to explain this concurrence, its possibility and its necessity.

During the act of knowledge itself, the objective and subjective are so instantly united, that we cannot determine to which of the two the priority belongs. There is here no first, and no second; both are coinstantaneous and one. While I am attempting to explain this intimate coalition, I must suppose it dissolved. I must necessarily set out from the one, to which therefore I give hypothetical antecedence, in order to arrive at the other. But as there are but two factors or elements in the problem, subject and object, and as it is left indeterminate from which of them I should commence, there are two cases equally possible.

1. EITHER THE OBJECTIVE IS TAKEN AS THE FIRST, AND THEN WE HAVE TO ACCOUNT FOR THE SUPERVENTION OF THE SUBJECTIVE, WHICH COALESCES WITH IT.

The notion of the subjective is not contained in the notion of the objective. On the contrary they mutually exclude each other. The subjective therefore must supervene to the objective. The conception of nature does not apparently involve the co-presence of an intelligence making an ideal duplicate of it, i.e. representing it. This desk for instance would (according to our natural notions) be, though there should exist no sentient being to look at it. This then is the problem of natural philosophy. It assumes the objective or unconscious nature as the first, and has therefore to explain how intelligence can supervene to it, or how itself can grow into intelligence. If it should appear, that all enlightened naturalists without having distinctly proposed the problem to themselves have yet constantly moved in the line of its solution, it must afford a strong presumption that the problem itself is founded in nature. For if all knowledge has as it were two poles reciprocally required and presupposed, all sciences must proceed from the one or the other, and must tend toward the opposite as far as the equatorial point in which both are reconciled and become identical. The

necessary tendence therefore of all natural philosophy is from nature to intelligence; and this, and no other,[a] is the true ground and occasion of the instinctive striving to introduce theory into our views of natural phænomena. The highest perfection of natural philosophy would consist in the perfect spiritualization of all the laws of nature into laws of intuition and intellect. The phænomena (*the material*) must wholly disappear, and the laws alone (*the formal*) must remain. Thence it comes, that in nature itself the more the principle of law breaks forth, the more does the *husk* drop off, the phænomena themselves become more spiritual and at length cease altogether in our consciousness. The optical phænomena are but a geometry, the lines of which are drawn by light, and the materiality of this light itself has already become matter of doubt. In the appearances of magnetism all trace of matter is lost, and of the phænomena of gravitation, which not a few among the most illustrious Newtonians have declared no otherwise comprehensible than as an immediate spiritual influence, there remains nothing but its law, the execution of which on a vast scale is the mechanism of the heavenly motions. The theory of natural philosophy would then be completed, when all nature was demonstrated to be identical in essence with that, which in its highest known power exists in man as intelligence and self-consciousness; when the heavens and the earth shall declare not only the power of their maker, but the glory and the presence of their God, even as he appeared to the great prophet during the vision of the mount in the skirts of his divinity.[1]

This may suffice to show,[2] that even natural science, which commences with the material phænomenon as the reality and substance of things existing, does yet by the necessity of theorising

---

[a] *BL* (1817) omits comma

[1] Cf Ps 19.1; Exod 24.12–18.

[2] The framework of this paragraph follows the next paragraph in Schelling *STI* 5 (*SW* III 341); C's interpolations are noted in brackets: "Diess mag hinreichend seyn, zu beweisen, dass die Naturwissenschaft ["which commences . . . of things existing"] die nothwendige Tendenz hat ["of theorising . . . instinctively"], die Natur intelligent zu machen; eben durch diese Tendenz wird sie zur *Natur-Philosophie,* welche die Eine nothwendige Grund-

wissenschaft der Philosophie ist." Schelling does not mean that natural philosophy is the one and *only* "ground-knowledge of philosophy", as SC's tr implies (*BL*—1847—I 262n), but one of the two ground-knowledges; for Schelling in *STI* 6–7 (*SW* III 342) identifies transcendental philosophy as *"die andere nothwendige Grundwissenschaft der Philosophie".* C understood this perfectly, as the conclusion to his own paragraph shows.

unconsciously, and as it were instinctively, end in nature as an intelligence; and by this tendency the science of nature becomes finally natural philosophy, the one of the two poles of fundamental science.

2. OR THE SUBJECTIVE IS TAKEN AS THE FIRST,[1] AND THE PROBLEM THEN IS, HOW THERE SUPERVENES TO IT A COINCIDENT OBJECTIVE.

In the pursuit of these sciences, our success in each, depends on an austere and faithful adherence to its own principles with a careful separation and exclusion of those, which appertain to the opposite science.[2] As the natural philosopher, who directs his views to the objective, avoids above all things the intermixture of

---

[1] C continues to draw from Schelling *STI* 5 (*SW* III 341): *"Oder das Subjective wird zum Ersten gemacht, und die Aufgabe ist die: wie ein Objectives hinzukomme, das mit ihm übereinstimmt?"*

[2] As *BL* (1847) I 262n points out, the remainder of this paragraph C takes from *STI* 8 (*SW* III 343). Schelling's relevant German is given here, with C's numerous additions and deletions briefly noted, followed by SC's tr of the whole of Schelling's paragraph for comparison because C varies *STI* so extensively: "Wie der nur aufs Objective gerichtete Natur-Philosoph nichts so sehr zu verhindern sucht, als Einmischung des Subjectiven in sein Wissen [C adds: "as for instance . . . efficient causes"], so umgekehrt der Transcendental-Philosoph nichts so sehr, als Einmischung des Objectiven in das rein subjective Princip des Wissens [C adds "as for instance . . . of explanation"; for this example cf above, I 137 and n 6].—Das Ausscheidungsmittel ist der absolute Skepticismus . . . der durchgreifende Skepticismus [C adds "to which . . . future certainty" and also the next sentence containing the quotation from Descartes]. . . . Denn ausser der künstlichen in den Menschen hineingebrachten Vorurtheilen, giebt es weit ursprünglichere, nicht durch Unterricht oder Kunst, sondern durch die Natur selbst in ihn gelegte, die, ausser dem Philosophen, allen übrigen statt der Principien alles Wissens, und dem blossen Selbstdenker sogar als Probierstein aller Wahrheit gelten." C has shortened and paraphrased this last sentence to conclude his own paragraph. SC tr Schelling: "As the natural philosopher, whose attention is directed solely to the objective, seeks to prevent nothing so much as the blending of the subjective in his knowledge, so, conversely, the Transcendental philosopher (objects to nothing so much) as any admixture of the objective in the pure subjective principle of knowledge. The means of separation is absolute scepticism—not the half sort, directed only against the common prejudices of men, which yet never sees into the ground; but the comprehensive scepticism, which is aimed not against single prejudices, but against the fundamental prejudice, with which all others must fall of themselves. For beside the artificial prejudices, introduced into man, there are others, far more original, planted in him not by instruction or art, but by Nature herself; which with all but the philosopher, stand for the principles of all knowledge, and by the mere self-thinker are even considered the touchstone of all truth." *BL* (1847) I 262n.

the subjective in his knowledge, as for instance, arbitrary supposi-
tions or rather suffictions, occult qualities, spiritual agents, and
the substitution of final for efficient causes; so on the other
hand, the transcendental or intelligential philosopher is equally
anxious to preclude all interpolation of the objective into the
subjective principles of his science, as for instance the assumption of impresses or configurations in the brain, correspondent
to miniature pictures on the retina painted by rays of light
from supposed originals, which are not the immediate and real
objects of vision, but deductions from it for the purposes of
explanation. This purification of the mind is effected by an absolute
and scientific scepticism to which the mind voluntarily[a] determines
itself for the specific purpose of future certainty. Des Cartes who
(in his meditations) himself first, at least of the moderns, gave a
beautiful example of this voluntary doubt, this self-determined
indetermination, happily expresses its utter difference from the
scepticism of vanity or irreligion: Nec tamen in eo scepticos
imitabar, qui dubitant tantum ut dubitent, et preter incertitudinem
ipsam nihil quærunt. Nam contra totus in eo eram ut aliquid certi
reperirem. DES CARTES, *de Methodo*.[1] Nor is it less distinct
in its motives and final aim, than in its proper objects, which are
not as in ordinary scepticism the prejudices of education and
circumstance, but those original and innate prejudices which
nature herself has planted in all men, and which to all but the
philosopher are the first principles of knowledge, and the final
test of truth.

Now[2] these essential prejudices are all reducible to the one

[1] *De methodo* III: *Opera philosophica* (Amsterdam 1685) iii 18.
"Nor yet did I in this imitate the
sceptics, who doubt only for doubt-
ing's sake and seek nothing but a
distinction [by] uncertainty, for on
the contrary my whole soul was
engaged in this, the hope of discovering something certain." Tr *P
Lects* Lect 12 (1949) 344. Cited
in C's letter to Josiah Wedgwood (24
Feb 1801: *CL* II 688) and a notebook entry of the same month (*CN*
I 914 and n). C repeats (var)
several parts of this paragraph, both

his own examples and material being
drawn from *STI*, in *P Lects* Lect 12
(1949) 344.

[2] As *BL* (1847) I 264n notes,
this paragraph—with the exception
of C's parenthesis beginning "in
other words"—corresponds to the
next paragraph in *STI* 8–9 (*SW* III
343–4): "Das Eine Grundvorurtheil,
auf welches alle andre sich redu-
cieren, ist kein andres, als *dass es
Dinge ausser uns gebe;* ein Fürwahr-
halten, das, weil es nicht auf
Gründen noch auf Schlüssen beruht
(denn es giebt keinen einzigen

fundamental presumption, THAT THERE EXIST THINGS WITH-OUT US. As this on the one hand originates, neither in grounds or arguments, and yet on the other hand remains proof against all attempts to remove it by grounds or arguments (*naturam furca expellas tamen usque redibit;*) on the one hand lays claim to IMMEDIATE certainty as a position at once indemonstrable and irresistible, and yet on the other hand, inasmuch as it refers to something essentially different from ourselves, nay even in opposition to ourselves, leaves it inconceivable how it could possibly become a part of our immediate consciousness; (in other words how that, which ex hypothesi is and continues to be extrinsic and alien to our being, should become a modification of our being) the philosopher therefore compels himself to treat this faith as nothing more than a prejudice, innate indeed and connatural, but still a prejudice.

The other position,[1] which not only claims but necessitates the

---

probehaltigen Beweis dafür), und doch durch keinen entgegengesetzten Beweis sich ausrotten lässt (*naturam furca expellas, tamen usque redibit* [Horace *Epistles* 1.10.24 (var): "You may drive nature out with a pitchfork but she will return"; *BL* (1975) 147n], Ansprüche macht auf *unmittelbare* Gewissheit, da es sich doch auf etwas von uns ganz Verschiedenes, ja uns Entgegengesetztes bezieht, von dem man gar nicht einsieht, wie es in das unmittelbare Bewusstseyn komme [C here adds his parenthesis and then begins his final clause with "the philosopher therefore compels himself"],—für nichts mehr, als für ein Vorurtheil—zwar für ein angebohrnes und ursprüngliches [C's "connatural"]—aber desswegen nicht minder für Vorurtheil geachtet werden kann."

[1] This entire paragraph C has freely mixed, condensed, and conflated from the next two paragraphs in *STI* 9–10 (*SW* III 344): "Den Widerspruch, dass ein Satz, der seiner Natur nach nicht unmittelbar gewiss seyn kann, doch eben so blindlings, und ohne Gründe, wie ein

solcher angenommen wird, weiss der Transcendental-Philosoph nicht zu lösen, als durch die Voraussetzung, dass jener Satz versteckterweise und ohne dass man es bis jetz einsieht—nicht zusammenhange, sondern identisch, und Eins und dasselbe sey, mit einem unmittelbar Gewissen, *und diese Identität aufzuzeigen, wird* eigentlich das Geschäft der Transcendental-Philosophie seyn.

"Nun giebt es aber selbst für den gemeinen Vernunftgebrauch nichts unmittelbar Gewisses ausser dem Satz: *Ich bin;* der, weil er *ausserhalb* des unmittelbaren Bewusstseyns selbst die Bedeutung verliert, die individuellste aller Wahrheiten, und das *absolute Vorurtheil* ist, das zuerst angenommen werden muss, wenn irgend etwas anderes gewiss seyn soll.—Der Satz: *Es giebt Dinge ausser uns,* wird also für den Transcendental-Philosophen auch nur gewiss seyn durch seine Identität mit dem Satze: *Ich bin,* und seine Gewissheit wird auch nur *gleich* seyn der Gewissheit des Satzes, von welchem er die seinige entlehnt."

"The contradiction, that a position, which, by its own nature,

admission of its immediate certainty, equally for the scientific reason of the philosopher as for the common sense of mankind at large, namely, I A M, cannot so properly be intitled a prejudice. It is groundless indeed; but then in the very idea it precludes all ground, and separated from the immediate consciousness loses its whole sense and import. It is groundless; but only because it is itself the ground of all other certainty. Now the apparent contradiction, that the former position, namely, the existence of things without us, which from its nature cannot be immediately certain should be received as blindly and as independently of all grounds as the existence of our own being, the transcendental philosopher can solve only by the supposition, that the former is unconsciously involved in the latter; that it is not only coherent but identical, and one and the same thing with our own immediate self-consciousness. To demonstrate this identity is the office and object of his philosophy.

If it be said,[1] that this is Idealism, let it be remembered that it

cannot be immediately certain, is nevertheless so blindly, and groundlessly received as such, the Transcendental philosopher can only solve by presuming that the aforesaid position, hiddenly and hitherto unperceivedly, does not (merely) cohere, but is identical—one and the same—with an immediate consciousness; and to demonstrate this identity will be the peculiar business of Transcendental philosophy.

"Now for the common use of reason there is nothing immediately certain but the position *I am,* which, because out of immediate consciousness it even loses its meaning, is the most individual of all truths, and the absolute prejudice, which must be assumed in the first place if anything else is to have certainty. Consequently the position, *There are things without us,* for the Transcendental philosopher will only be certain through its identity with the position *I am,* and its certainty will only be equal to the certainty of the position from which it borrows its own." Tr SC *BL* (1847) I 264–5n.

In brief, the proposition that there exist things outside the self, which seems a fundamental principle of natural or objective philosophy, actually must first assume that there already exists a self (the "I am"); thus the assumption of "I am" belonging to the transcendental or subjective philosopher must take precedence and in fact becomes "identical" with the proposition that there exist things outside the self.

[1] As *BL* (1847) I 265–6n notes, this paragraph, as far as the sentence ending "mechanical philosophy", is paraphrased from *Abhandlungen: Phil Schrift* 273–4 (*SW* I 403) and has similarities with *STI* 147–9 (*SW* III 427–8). The German from the *Abhandlungen* is given here, with C's two substantive additions in brackets and also a translation, since C himself alters phases and changes the tone and form of address. " 'Er ist ein Idealist, sein System ist ein idealistisches', so sprechen Manche. . . . Lieben Freunde, wenn Ihr wüsstet, dass er nur *insofern* Idealist ist, als er *zugleich* und *eben*

is only so far idealism, as it is at the same time, and on that very account, the truest and most binding realism. For wherein does the realism of mankind properly consist? In the assertion that there exists a something without them, what, or how, or where they know not, which occasions the objects of their perception? Oh no! This is neither connatural or universal. It is what a few have taught and learnt in the schools, and which the many repeat without asking themselves concerning their own meaning. The realism common to all mankind is far elder and lies infinitely deeper than this hypothetical explanation of the origin of our perceptions, an explanation skimmed from the mere surface of mechanical philosophy. It is the table itself, which the man of common sense believes himself to see, not the phantom of a table, from which he may

---

desswegen der strengste und bündigste Realist ist, würdet Ihr anders reden.—Was ist denn *Euer* Realismus? worin besteht er eigentlich?—In der Behauptung: dass Etwas ausser Euch—ihr wisst nicht was, noch wie, noch wo—Eure Vorstellungen veranlasse?—Mit Erlaubniss gesagt, diess ist falsch. [C adds: "This is neither connatural nor universal."] Ihr habt das nicht aus Euch selbst geschöpft, ihr habt es in irgend einer Schule gehört und sprecht es nach, ohne euch selbst zu verstehen. Euer Realismus ist weit älter, als jene Behauptung, auch liegt er unendlich tiefer als jene von der obersten Oberfläche abgeschöpfte Erklärung des Ursprungs Eurer Vorstellungen [C adds mention of the "mechanical philosophy"]." "Thus many say, 'He is an idealist, his system is an idealistic one'. . . . Dear Friends, if only you knew that he is an idealist only in so far as he is *at the same time* and *even on that account* the most strict and precise realist, you would say something else. What, then, is *your* realism? in what does it actually consist?—In the assertion: that something outside yourselves—you know not what, nor how, nor where—occasions your perceptions? with permission granted, this is false.

You have heard it in one of the schools and repeat it without understanding it yourselves. Your realism is far older than such an assertion, it lies infinitely deeper than such an explanation of the origin of your perceptions skimmed from the shallowest superficiality."

SC tr the similar relevant passage of *STI* 147–9 (*SW* III 427–8) in *BL* (1847) I 266n: "Thence the improper Idealism . . . which converts all knowledge into mere appearance, must be that which takes away all immediateness in our perceptions by placing originals out of us independent of our representations; whereas a system, which seeks the origin of things in the activity of the spirit, even because it is the most perfect Idealism, must at the same time be the most perfect Realism. . . . If the most perfect Realism is that which knows the things in themselves and immediately, this is possible only in a Nature, which beholds in the things her own, through her own activity limited, Reality. For such a Nature, as the indwelling soul of the things, would penetrate them as her own immediate organism: and, even as the artificer most perfectly knows his own work, would look through their inner mechanism."

argumentatively deduce the reality of a table, which he does not see. If to destroy the reality of all, that we actually behold, be idealism, what can be more egregiously so, than the system of modern metaphysics, which banishes us to a land of shadows, surrounds us with apparitions, and distinguishes truth from illusion only by the majority of those who dream the same dream?[1] "*I* asserted that the world was mad," exclaimed poor Lee, "and the world said, that I was mad, and confound them, they outvoted me."[2]

It is to the true and original realism, that I would direct the attention.[3] This believes and requires neither more nor less, than

[1] Nothing in Schelling appears to parallel the wording of this sentence, but the thought is expressed in similar terms in *Abhandlungen: Phil Schrift* 217–18, 212–13, 206–7 (*SW* I 362, 358, 353).

[2] Nathaniel Lee (c 1653–92), Restoration dramatist, confined to Bedlam 1684–9, received many visitors, to whom he made epigrammatic remarks that found their way into a number of books. This one has not been traced. His most famous remark, his answer to a poet who told him it was easy to write like a madman, was reported in a letter of Dryden to John Dennis: "*No*, said he, '*tis very difficult to write like a Madman, but 'tis a very easie matter to write like a Fool.*" *Letters upon Several Occasions* (1696) 56. Cf the title of a Wycherley poem: "To Nath. Lee in Bethlem, (who was at once Poet and Actor) complaining, in His Intervals, of the Sense of His Condition; and that He ought no more to be in Bethlem for Want of Sense than other Mad Libertines and Poets abroad, or any Sober Fools Whatever". *Miscellany Poems* (1704) 300–6. Cf C's remark at the end of an annotation on a back leaf of Kant *KRV*: "The man in the fever is only *outvoted* by his attendants— He does not see their Dream, and they do not see his.—" *CM* (*CC*) III. C had wanted his poem *Limbo*

to be published with a "conjectural Note of it's having been written by Lee while in Bedlam". *CL* v 779; cf *CN* III 4073n.

[3] As *BL* (1847) I 267n notes, C takes this paragraph from *Abhandlungen: Phil Schrift* 274 (*SW* I 403–4), thus returning to the same place where he left off in the preceeding paragraph. C's changes are given in brackets: "An diesen [C adds "true and"] *ursprünglichen* Realismus verweisen wir euch. Dieser glaubt und will nichts anders, als dass der Gegenstand, den ihr [C adds "beholds or"] vorstellt, zugleich auch der wirkliche sey . . . und so sehr ihr Euch dagegen sträuben mögt, seyd ihr [C's "we"] doch alle zusammen *geborne Idealisten* [C adds "and therefore . . . realists"].

"Vom *diesem* Realismus [C clarifies the meaning by omitting this usage of "realism" here] wissen Eure [C's "the"] Schulphilosophen nur desswegen nichts [C adds "or despise . . . ignorant vulgar"], weil ihnen die menschliche Natur unter einem eiteln Spiel mit Begriffen längst verschwunden ist [C elaborates this slightly, adds the command ending "your own hearts", then returns to paraphrase Schelling:] *Ihr* sollt fühlen, dass ihr einer bessern Philosophie werth seyd. Lasst die Todten ihre Todten begraben, ihr aber bewahrt Eure

that the object which it beholds or presents to itself, is the real and very object. In this sense, however much we may strive against it, we are all collectively born idealists, and therefore and only therefore are we at the same time realists. But of this the philosophers of the schools know nothing, or despise the faith as the prejudice of the ignorant vulgar, because they live and move in a crowd of phrases and notions from which human nature has long ago vanished. Oh, ye that reverence yourselves, and walk humbly with the divinity in your own hearts,[1] ye are worthy of a better philosophy! Let the dead bury the dead,[2] but do you preserve your human nature, the depth of which was never yet fathomed by a philosophy made up of notions and mere logical entities.

In the third treatise of my *Logosophia*, announced at the end of this volume,[3] I shall give (deo volente) the demonstrations and constructions of the Dynamic Philosophy scientifically arranged. It is, according to my conviction, no other than the system of Pythagoras and of Plato revived and purified from impure mixtures. Doctrina per tot manus tradita tandem in VAPPAM desiit.[4] The science of arithmetic furnishes instances, that a rule may be useful in practical application, and for the particular purpose may be sufficiently authenticated by the result, before it has itself been fully demonstrated. It is enough, if only it be rendered intelligible.[5]

Menschennatur, deren Tiefe noch keine Philosophie aus Begriffen [C adds "and mere logical entities"] ergründet hat. Cf *CN* III 4153, 4088, and nn.

[1] Micah 6.8: ". . . what doth the Lord require of thee, but to do justly, and to love mercy, and to walk humbly with thy God?"

[2] Matt 8.12 (var), Luke 9.60 (var).

[3] The announcement was not printed. For possible notes for the "third treatise", written c Sept 1814–Oct 1815 and based on Heinrich Steffens *Grundzüge der philosophischen Naturwissenschaft* (Berlin 1806), see *CN* III 4226 and n. A letter of 27 Sept 1815 describes the treatise: "The III. (Logos Architectonicus) on the Dynamic or Constructive Philosophy—preparatory to the IV. or a detailed Commentary on

the Gospel of St John". *CL* IV 589. By 7 Oct 1815 it had become "The third, the Science of Premises, or transcendental Philosophy—i.e. the examination of the Premises, which in ordinary & practical reasoning are taken for granted. (As the whole proceeds on actual Constructions in the mind, I might call it, *intellectual Geometry*.)" *CL* IV 592.

[4] A doctrine passed through so many hands ends up as *flat wine*." The quotation, as SC notes, is applied to Leibniz by Schelling in *Abhandlungen: Phil Schrift* 212 (*SW* I 358). *BL* (1847) I 268n. The source is untraced.

[5] Cf above, I 250. *CN* III 4265, presumably written at this time (Sept 1815), contains a rough draft of this paragraph as well as of the following theses. It is of interest that the *close* (ff 26, 26v, 27) of this

This will, I trust, have been effected in the following Theses for those of my readers, who are willing to accompany me through the following Chapter, in which the results will be applied to the deduction of the imagination, and with it the principles of production and of genial criticism in the fine arts.[1]

THESIS I.

Truth is correlative to being. Knowledge without a correspondent reality is no knowledge; if we know, there must be somewhat known by us. To know is in its very essence a verb active.[2]

long entry contains the draft of this paragraph, which in *BL* precedes the theses. C may originally have written the theses with the "Logosophia" in mind. But after writing a rough draft of them he may have suddenly thought of an immediate use in *BL,* and then written an introductory paragraph for them, stating that "The Demonstrations, the actual Constructions as they beget & necessitate each the following, will be given, Deo volente, in the third Treatise of the Logosophia", and also referring to "the following Chapter" and "a preceding Chapter" in the *BL* (two references the first of which appears in his paragraph introductory to the theses and the second of which appears recast as "a preceding page", below, I 286, after the theses are presented).

[1] It is worth note that the whole of *STI* climaxes not simply with the deduction of the imagination in general, but specifically with the aesthetic or artistic imagination of genius in the fine arts, which alone reconciles real and ideal, subjective and objective, and all such seeming "contradictions". See esp *STI* 18–20, 358, 451–70, 475–86 (*SW* III 349–51, 554, 611–24, 628–34).

[2] This thesis has close affinities with Schelling *Vom Ich* § 1: *Phil Schrift* 1–3 (*SW* I 162–3), condensing from: "Wer etwas wissen will, will zugleich, dass sein Wissen Realität habe. Ein Wissen ohne

Realität ist kein Wissen." ". . . Das Princip seines Seyns und das Princip seines Erkennens muss zusammenfallen, muss Eines seyn, denn nur, weil es *selbst,* nicht weil irgend etwas anders ist, kann es gedacht werden. Es muss also gedacht werden, nur weil es ist, und es muss seyn, nicht weil irgend etwas anders, sondern weil es selbst gedacht wird: sein Bejahen muss in seinem Denken enthalten seyn . . .". "Der letzte Grund aller Realität nämlich ist ein Etwas . . . *bey dem das Princip des Seyns und des Denkens zusammenfällt.*" ("Who would know something would know at the same time that his knowledge had reality. A knowledge without reality is no knowledge." ". . . The principle of its being and the principle of its knowing must coincide, must be one, since it [this first and ungrounded principle] can be thought only because it itself exists, not because something else exists. It must therefore be thought only because it exists, and it must exist, not because something else is thought, but because it itself is thought [as the first ground and highest principle]: its affirmation must be contained in its being thought . . .". "The ultimate ground of all reality specifically is a something . . . *by which the Principle of being and of thinking* [knowing] *coincide.*") This may be partially paraphrased: the mind affirms its own being by the same act in which

THESIS II.

All truth is either mediate, that is, derived from some other truth or truths; or immediate and original. The latter is absolute, and its formula A. A.; the former is of dependent or conditional certainty, and represented in the formula B. A. The certainty, which inheres in A, is attributable to B.[1]

---

it affirms its decision of what to consider as the first ground of its knowledge. This implies that the mind must decide by an act of will (see Theses VII and IX, below) to consider its own self-consciousness (the "I am") as this ground (see Thesis VI, below). Shedd (*CW* III 342) notes C's indebtedness to "the first part of the *Vom Ich*" for Theses I–VI. This and the following nn discuss parallels in detail.

Cf *Abhandlungen: Phil Schrift* 222 (*SW* I 365): "The problem may also be stated: to explain the absolute correspondence of the object and of the representation, of being and knowing." Cf *STI* 1 (*SW* III 339), quoted above (I 252 n 3) and Jacobi *ULS* 402. Thesis I is given rearranged but otherwise almost verbatim from *CN* III 4265 (§ I). C was probably dictating at this point from N 61. Cf above, ch 9, in which C anticipates this thesis.

[1] C appears to have taken the basis of this paragraph, along with its connection to the other theses, from several places. *STI* 37–57 (*SW* III 361–73) presents the concept of mediate and immediate truths in terms of the subjective and objective and their union in the self-conscious *Ich* or *Ich bin* (cf Theses VI–X, below). E.g. *STI* 38–40: "Denn in dem Urtheil A = A wird ganz von dem Inhalt des Subjects A abstrahirt. . . . Das Wissen in diesem Satz ist also blos *durch mein Denken* (das Subjective) bedingt, d. h. nach der Erklärung, es ist *unbedingt.* . . . Nun sind aber synthethische Sätze nicht *unbedingt* . . . (und diess geschieht in jedem synthetischen Urtheil

A = B. . . .)." ("Thus in the judgment A = A, A is completely abstracted [derived or drawn] from the inherent property of the subject. . . . The knowledge in this proposition is thus conditional only *on my thinking* (the subjective), i.e. according to the explanation, it is *unconditional.* . . . Now synthetical propositions are, however, not *unconditional* . . . and this occurs in each synthetical judgement A = B. . . .") Schelling (p 41) speaks of identical (A = A) propositions as immediate ("unmittelbar"). *CN* III 4265n (§ v) gives equally similar points of contact in *STI* 24–37 (*SW* III 353–61) concerning "mediate" and "immediate" truths.

Schelling *Vom Ich* § 16: *Phil Schrift* 78–91 (*SW* I 216–25) gives a complex discussion of material C summarises here. Again Schelling writes in the context of the *Ich* as the ultimate condition of knowing and being. The passage is quoted at length (*Phil Schrift* 81–2; *SW* I 218–19) to show how C streamlines and clarifies: "Eine einzelne Art thetischer Sätze, sind *identische* Sätze, dergleichen A = A als besondrer Satz betrachtet ist. . . . Identische Sätze sind nothwendig thetische, weil in ihnen A schlechthin als solches, und, *weil* es A ist, gesetzt wird. Aber thetische Sätze sind nicht nothwendig identisch, denn thetische Sätze sind alle, deren Gesetzseyn nicht durch ein anders Gesetzseyn bedingt ist. So kann A = B ein thetischer, obwohl kein identischer Satz seyn, wenn nemlich durch das *blosse* Setzen von A, B, aber nicht umgekehrt durch das blosse Setzen

SCHOLIUM. A chain without a staple, from which all the links derived their stability, or a series without a first, has been not inaptly allegorized, as a string of blind men, each holding the skirt of the man before him, reaching far out of sight, but all moving without the least deviation in one strait line. It would be naturally taken for granted, that there was a guide at the head of the file: what if it were answered, No! Sir, the men are without number, and infinite blindness supplies the place of sight?[1]

von B, A gesetzt ist. . . . Wenn ich urtheile, A = B, so urtheile ich nicht von A, insofern es durch irgend etwas *ausser* sich, sondern insofern es blos durch sich selbst, durch Einheit seines Gesetzseyns im Ich, nicht als bestimmtes *Objekt,* sondern als Realität überhaupt, als im Ich überhaupt setzbar bestimmt ist. Ich urtheile also . . . A, *als* solches, insofern es A ist, durch eben die Bestimmung, durch die es A, d. h. sich selbst gleich ist = B." ("*Identical* propositions are a unique class of self-evident propositions, of which A = A is considered as a special case. . . . Identical propositions are necessarily self-evident, because in them A is proposed simply as such, and for no other reason than it is A. But self-evident propositions are not necessarily identical, since self-evident ones are all those whose authenticity is not conditional upon the authenticity of another [different proposition]. Thus A = B can be a self-evident, though not an identical proposition, namely if from the *mere* proposition of A the element of B can be supposed, but not conversely, from the mere proposition of B can the element of A be supposed. . . . If I judge A = B, then I judge not about A, since it is not determined by something *outside* itself, but insofar as it is simply determined by its own self and through the unity of its supposition in the Ego, not as a conditional *object* but as reality in general, as ultimately attributed to the supposition of the Ego. I judge thus . . . A *as* such—insofar that

it is A through the very attribution that is A, i.e. similar [only] to itself—is equal to B.")

Cf Fichte *Grundlage* 8–13 (*SW* I 95–6, 98). This anticipates both Schelling and C in ideas and notation. C, by delaying the principle of the *Ich bin* to Thesis VI, has tended to clarify and break down Schelling's reasoning into more orderly steps. But it could be objected that C's "being" in Thesis I already slips in the notion of "I am". Only part of Thesis II in rough and shortened form appears in *CN* III 4265 (§ II).

[1] The image of "a chain without a staple", that of a line of reasoning held logically together but ungrounded in an acceptable first principle, is a favourite of C's. E.g. his comment on Spinoza's philosophy: "that iron Chain of Logic . . . which falls of itself by dissolving the rock of Ice, to which it is stapled". *CL* IV 548. The "string of blind men" had been "allegorized" by C himself: see his "Allegoric Vision" in LRR I: *Lects 1795 (CC)* 92–3; in *EOT (CC)* II 269 (31 Aug 1811); and a third version appeared the same year as *BL,* in *LS (CC)* 137.

For this paragraph and Thesis II generally cf *Vom Ich* § 2: *Phil Schrift* 3 (*SW* I 163–4): "Ein Wissen, zu dem ich nur durch ein anders Wissen gelangen kann, heisse ich ein *bedingtes* Wissen. Die Kette unsers Wissens geht von einem Bedingten zum andern: entweder muss nun das Ganze keine Haltung

Equally *inconceivable* is a cycle of equal truths without a common and central principle, which prescribes to each its proper sphere in the system of science. That the absurdity does not so immediately strike us, that it does not seem equally *unimaginable*, is owing to a surreptitious act of the imagination, which, instinctively and without our noticing the same, not only fills out[a] the intervening spaces, and contemplates the *cycle* (of B. C. D. E. F. &c.) as a continuous *circle* (A.) giving to all collectively the unity of their common orbit; but likewise supplies by a sort of *subintelligitur* the one central power, which renders the movement harmonious and cyclical.[1]

[a] *BL* (1817): at

haben, oder man muss glauben können, dass es so ins Unendliche fortgehe, oder es muss irgend einen letzten Punkt geben, an dem das Ganze hängt, der aber eben desswegen allem, was noch in die Sphäre des Bedingten fällt, in Rücksicht auf das Princip seines Seyns geradezu *entgegengesetzt,* d. h. nicht nur unbedingt, sondern schlechthin *unbedingtbar* seyn muss." ("Something known, at which I can arrive only through something else that is known, I call *conditional* knowledge. The chain of our knowing proceeds from one condition to another: either the whole must have no directing tendency, or one must be able to believe that it thus proceeds infinitely, or there must be some one ultimate point on which the whole depends, a point that, however, in consideration of the principle of its being, is therefore directly contrasted to all [of those other points] that fall within the sphere of the conditional. That is, this one ultimate point is not only *unconditional* [lit: "unconditioned"] but simply must be *unconditionable*.") Cf below, I 283–5.

[1] *CN* III 4265n (§ II) tentatively suggests Schelling *STI* 34–5 (*SW* III 359) as an indirect source. Fichte *Ueber den Begriff der Wissenschaftslehre* (1793) 38–9 (*SW* I 61–2)

contains an image of a circle used in a way similar to C's. This may be an original source. C's whole paragraph apparently refers to self-consciousness as it unifies or synthesises the manifold of experience through itself or through imagination. C's position is general, almost abstract, and Kant is also one of several possibilities he has in mind. Cf *KRV* "Elementarlehre" § 10 (B 103): "By *synthesis,* in its most general sense, I understand the act of putting different representations together, and of grasping what is manifold in them in one [act of] knowledge. . . . Synthesis is that which gathers the elements for knowledge, and unites them to [form] a certain content. It is to synthesis, therefore, that we must direct our attention, if we would determine the first origin of our knowledge.

"Synthesis in general . . . is the mere result of the power of imagination, a blind but indispensable function of the soul, without which we should have no knowledge whatsoever, but of which we are scarcely ever conscious." Tr Norman Kemp Smith. Cf also B 151–2, 179–81, A 103.

C may be thinking of "the one central power" in even more universal terms. Cf *ULS* 305–6, in

THESIS III.

We are to seek therefore for some absolute truth capable of communicating to other positions a certainty, which it has not itself borrowed; a truth self-grounded, unconditional and known by its own light. In short, we have to find a somewhat which *is*, simply because it *is*.[1] In order to be such, it must be one which is its own predicate, so far at least that all other nominal predicates must be modes and repetitions of itself. Its existence too must be such, as to preclude the possibility of requiring a cause or antecedent without an absurdity.[2]

which Jacobi gives Bruno's one principle of knowledge and being that unites the multiple variations and sensations we experience and leads to deep secrets of art and religion.

Finally, it is of interest that Thesis II and Theses I, III, VI, VII, IX, and X have definite, though not strictly verbal, parallels with Jacobi *ULS* 398–434, esp 415–34, sections that also influenced Schelling. Jacobi discusses the possibility of one central, unconditional cause—the "being of all being"—and concludes it is God (427; cf Thesis VI Scholium, below). Thus C's religious stance, interwoven with the points contained in his theses, is paralleled—with similar points—by Jacobi. For Thesis II cf esp *ULS* 406–8 and the following: "All that is dependent depends *on something*" (416); "I take the whole man, without splitting him up, and find that his consciousness comes from two original conceptions; that of the *conditional* and that of the *unconditional* are placed together" (423); "Thus the unconditional . . . must itself become the conditions [of everything else]. . . . And further: that all which lies outside the order of the conditional [C's B. C. D. E. F. etc] also lies outside the sphere of our distinct knowledge, and cannot be understood by concepts [but] can . . . [only] be given us; namely, *as fact— It is!*" (426–7). This is similar to C's "surreptitious act of the imagina-

tion", which we do not notice but which must exist to provide the harmony and unity of all. C used a revised version of Thesis II in *Logic* (*CC*) 85–6.

[1] Besides the affinity of Thesis III with Jacobi *ULS* 426–7, which assumes such an absolute truth *"as fact—It is!"*, cf also *ULS* 286–7, which concludes that such a truth is not in the sphere of usual knowledge and that "we have no eyes . . . for the magnitude of this light"; and Schelling *Vom Ich* § 3: *Phil Schrift* 9 (*SW* I 168): ". . . *denn es ist gar nicht denkbar, als insofern es sich selbst denkt*, d. h. *insofern es ist*" (". . . *because it is not at all conceivable except in so far as it conceives of itself, i.e. insofar as it is*").

[2] For Thesis III cf Schelling *Vom Ich* § 1: *Phil Schrift* 1–3 (*SW* I 162–3) and Vorrede: *Phil Schrift* xii (*SW* I 155): "Wenn wir freilich das, was das letzte in unserm Wissen ist, nur als ein stummes Gemählde ausser uns (nach Spinoza's Vergleichung) betrachten müssten, so würden wir neimals wissen, *dass* wir wissen: wenn dieses aber selbst Bedingung alles Wissens, ja Bedingung seiner eigenen Erkenntniss, also das einzige Unmittelbare in unserm Wissen ist, so wissen wir eben dadurch, *dass* wir wissen, wir haben das Princip gefunden, von dem Spinoza sagen konnte, es sey das Licht, das sich selbst und die Finsterniss erhelle." ("If, to be sure,

THESIS IV.

That there can be but one such principle, may be proved a priori; for were there two or more, each must refer to some other, by which its equality is affirmed; consequently neither would be self-established, as the hypothesis demands. And a posteriori, it will be proved by the principle itself when it is discovered, as involving universal antecedents in its very conception.[1]

SCHOLIUM. If we affirm of a board that it is blue, the predicate (blue) is accidental, and not implied in the subject, board. If we affirm of a circle that it is equi-radial, the predicate indeed is

we were obliged to view that which is the ultimate in our knowledge only, according to Spinoza's simile, as a dumb picture outside ourselves, then we would never know that we *do* know: but if this [ultimate] is itself the condition of all knowledge—yes, even the condition of its own knowledge—then it is the unique, immediate element in our knowledge; and so we know by this that we *do* know, we have found the principle of which Spinoza could say, it is the light that illuminates the darkness and itself.") Schelling *Vorlesungen* 48 (*SW* v 234) also speaks of knowledge as it is constructed out of itself and presented by an inner, living intuition. Cf *STI* 25 (*SW* III 353): "*There must consequently be some generally mediating factor in our knowledge, which is the sole ground of knowing*", a position also bearing on C's second thesis.

Thesis III alters *CN* III 4265 (§ III) to a more orderly proposition that clarifies the progression of the theses.

[1] Though not exact in its parallel, cf Schelling *Vom Ich* § 2: *Phil Schrift* 3–4 (*SW* I 164), a passage immediately following the one C apparently draws upon in Thesis II, above: "Alle mögliche Theorien des Unbedingten müssen sich, wenn die Einzig-richtige einmal gefunden ist, a priori bestimmen lassen; so lange diese selbst noch nicht aufgestellt ist, muss man dem empirischen Fortgang der Philosophie folgen; ob in diesem alle mögliche Theorien liegen, muss sich am Ende erst ergeben." ("If once the uniquely proper hypothesis [lit: theory] of the unconditional is found, all possible hypotheses must *a priori* be determined; as long as this [proper hypothesis] itself is not yet presented, one must follow the empirical procedure of philosophy; but whether all possible hypotheses do lie within this [empirical procedure] must, after all, be conceded in the first place.")

Cf *STI* 25–6 (*SW* III 354), parts of which C also appears to use: "*Dieses Princip kann nur Eines seyn. Denn alle Wahrheit ist sich absolut gleich. . . . Dass aber die Wahrheit aller Sätze des Wissens eine absolut gleiche sey, ist unmöglich, wenn sie ihre Wahrheit von verschiedenen Principien (Vermittlungsgliedern) entlehnen, es muss also nur Ein (vermittelndes) Princip in allem Wissen seyn.*" ("Because all truth is strictly *identical* with itself, *there can be only one such principle. . . .* But that the truth of all propositions of knowledge be strictly identical is impossible if they derive their truth from differing principles or mediating agencies, there must therefore be only one mediating principle in the whole of knowledge.") Thesis IV does not appear in *CN* III 4265. A considerably revised version of Thesis IV reappears in *Logic* (*CC*) 86–7.

implied in the definition of the subject; but the existence of the subject itself is contingent, and supposes both a cause and a percipient.[1] The same reasoning will apply to the indefinite number of supposed indemonstrable truths exempted from the prophane approach of philosophic investigation by the amiable Beattie,[2] and other less eloquent and not more profound inaugurators of common sense on the throne of philosophy; a fruitless attempt, were it only that it is the two-fold function of philosophy to reconcile reason with common sense, and to elevate common sense into reason.

THESIS V.

Such a principle cannot be any THING or OBJECT. Each thing is what it is in consequence of some other thing.[3] An infinite,

[1] That is, even the *a priori* truths of geometry and mathematics (as C understood them) are not simply "given" to our common sense such that they appear irrefutable yet underived; they must first be perceived or conceived by something or—according to C's point of view—by some being. And therefore some act, apparently willed by this being, *causes* such truths to exist and to be thought of (see Thesis VII, below). Cf "But the Circumference of a Circle does not (except by accident) mean a limit of vision: but has its essential character *objectively,* as the necessary product of the omni-radiancy of the central point: as we may see daily in the concentric lines on a pond, from a drop of Rain or a leaping minow". *CN* III 4266 ff 69v–70.

[2] James Beattie (1735–1803), Scottish poet and philosopher, remembered now especially for his poem *The Minstrel* (1771–4). C here refers to his *Essay on the Nature and Immutability of Truth* (1770), an attack on Hume and philosophical scepticism based on an appeal to "moral sentiment". For C's lack of respect for him, see *Friend* (*CC*) I 28 and n, and *L&L* 124. C uses "prophane" ironically. Yet see also *P Lects* Lect 6 (1949) 202–3.

[3] For Thesis V and his own footnote, C draws and condenses from one or more of several Schelling works. Cf *Vom Ich* § 3: *Phil Schrift* 7–9 (*SW* I 166–7) and § 2: *Phil Schrift* 4 (*SW* I 164): "Das Unbedingte im *Objekt,* im *Ding* suchen, kann nicht heissen es im *Gattungsbegriff* von Ding suchen. . . . Allein, was Ding ist, ist zugleich selbst *Objekt* des Erkennens, ist also selbst ein Glied in der Kette unsers Wissens, fällt selbst in die Sphäre der Erkennbarkeit, und kann also nicht den Realgrund *alles* Wissens und Erkennens enthalten." ("To search for the unconditional in an *object* or in a *thing* cannot mean to look for it in the *generic notion* of thing. . . . Simply put, whatever is a thing is itself at the same time the *object* of perception, and thus itself is a link in the chain of our knowledge, falls itself within the sphere of perceptibility, and therefore cannot embody the actual ground of *all* knowledge and perception.") Orsini 207 also points out *Abhandlungen: Phil Schrift* 224 (*SW* I 367) and *STI* 49 (*SW* III 368): "Ebendesswegen kann dieses Unbedingte

3. Notebook 61 ff 21v–22 (actual size),
containing a draft of the theses in
Chapter 12. See p 271
Victoria College Library, University of
Toronto

reproduced by kind permission

independent * *thing*, is no less a contradiction, than an infinite circle or a sideless triangle. Besides a thing is that, which is capable of being an object of which itself is not the sole percipient. But an object is inconceivable without a subject as its antithesis. Omne perceptum percipientem supponit.[2]

But neither can the principle be found in a subject as a subject, contra-distinguished from an object: for unicuique percipienti aliquid objicitur perceptum.[3] It is to be found therefore neither in object or subject taken separately, and consequently, as no other third is conceivable, it must be found in that which is neither subject nor object exclusively, but which is the identity of both.[4]

---

* The impossibility of an absolute thing (substantia unica) as neither genus, species, nor individuum; as well as its utter unfitness for the fundamental position of a philosophic system will be demonstrated in the critique on Spinozism in the fifth treatise of my Logosophia.[1]

---

nicht in irgend einem Ding gesucht werden, denn was Object ist, ist auch ursprünglich Object des Wissens, austatt dass das, was *Princip* alles Wissens ist, gar nicht ursprünglich, oder an sich, sondern nur *durch einen besondern Act der Freiheit* Object des Wissens werden kann." ("And for this reason, this unconditional element cannot be looked for in any given thing, because whatever is an object is also originally an object of knowing instead of that which, as the *principle* of all knowledge, cannot originally or in itself be an object of knowing, but *only* become so *through a specific act of freedom*.") This passage from *STI* also bears directly on the last two sentences of Thesis VII, below. *CN* III 4265 (§ IV) also points out other passages in *STI* 47–9 (*SW* III 367–8) that oppose the *Ich* or "I am" (see Thesis VI) to either a thing or an object.

[1] The point of C's footnote appears in Schelling *Vom Ich* § 2: *Phil Schrift* 4 (*SW* I 164), in the two sentences omitted from the quotation in n above. C in part takes directly from Schelling: "Denn dass ein Gattungsbegriff nichts unbe-

dingtes seyn könne, springt in die Augen. Mithin muss es *so* viel heissen, als das Unbedingte in einem *absoluten* Objekt suchen, das weder Gattung, noch Art, noch Individuum ist—" ("For it is plain to see that a generic notion cannot be unconditional. Consequently, it must be tantamount to meaning, to look for the unconditional in an *absolute* object that is neither genus, nor species, nor individual—").

According to a letter of 27 Sept 1815, the fifth treatise of the "Logosophia" would deal with "the Pantheists and Mystics; with the Lives and Systems of Giordano Bruno, Jacob Behmen, George Fox, and Benedict Spinoza". *CL* IV 589–90; cf 592.

[2] "Everything perceived supposes a perceiver".

[3] "For every perceiver there is an object perceived".

[4] C's position that "such a principle" is neither subject nor object but "the identity of both" has several parallels in Schelling. Most important are in *Vom Ich* § 2: *Phil Schrift* 3–7 (*SW* I 164–6), *STI* 28–30, 42–3 (*SW* III 356, 364–5). These long passages in the two works make

Thesis VI.

This principle, and so characterised manifests itself in the Sum or I am;[1] which I shall hereafter indiscriminately express by the

the same point that C here condenses and incorporates. Sections that are equivalent, or nearly so, to C's condensation are quoted. *Vom Ich: Phil Schrift* 5–6 (*SW* I 165): ". . . Es ist nur *insofern Objekt*, als ihm seine Realität durch etwas anders bestimmt ist: ja insofern es Objekt ist, setzt es nothwendig etwas voraus, in Bezug auf welches es *Objekt* ist, d. h. ein Subjekt." ". . . So ist der nächste Gedanke, das Unbedingte in dem durch's Subjekt bestimmten, nur in Bezug auf dieses denkbaren Objekt . . . zu suchen". "Ebendesswegen, weil das Subjekt nur in Bezug auf ein Objekt, das Objekt nur in Bezug auf ein Subjekt denkbar ist . . . denn beyde sind wechselseitig durch einander bedingt, beyde einander gleich gesetzt." ("It is only an *object in so far as* its reality is determined by something else: indeed, in so far as it is an object it necessarily presupposes something in reference to which it is an *object,* i.e. a subject." ". . . Thus the resulting thought, the determination of the unconditional through a subject is to be sought only in reference to this conceivable object. . . ." "And even for this reason, because the subject is conceivable only in reference to the object, and the object only in reference to the subject . . . for both are mutually conditional through each other, both likewise suppose the other.")

STI 29 (*SW* III 356): ". . . Wir müssen die Reihe willkürlich abbrechen, dadurch, dass wir ein Absolutes, das *von sich selbst* die Ursache und die Wirkung—Subject und Object—ist . . . setzen" ("We must interrupt the series arbitrarily by something we fix as an absolute, which is *its own* cause and effect—subject and object"); and 42–3 ". . . *Einen Punct finden, in welchem das Object und sein Begriff, der Gegen-*

stand und seine Vorstellung ursprünglich, schlechthin und *ohne alle Vermittlung* Eins sind. . . . Den Punct zu finden, wo *Subject* und *Object* unvermittelt Eines sind." ("*. . . To find a point in which the object and the conception, the thing and its representation are originally, simply* and *without any mediation* one. . . . *To find the point where subject and object* are *suddenly* one.*")

CN III 4265n (§ VI) cites *STI* 56 (*SW* III 372–3). This concludes with the idea of self-consciousness and thus seems especially appropriate as a source for the end of Thesis V, which stands just before the naming of the principle of self-consciousness in Thesis VI. In *STI* 56: "Ein solcher Begriff ist der eines Objects, das zugleich sich selbst entgegengesetzt, und sich selbst gleich ist. Aber ein solches ist nur ein Object, *was von sich selbst zugleich die Ursache und die Wirkung,* Producirendes und Product, *Subject* und *Object* ist.— Der Begriff einer ursprünglichen Identität in der Duplicität, und umgekehrt, ist also nur der Begriff eines Subject–Objects, und ein solches kommt ursprünglich nur im Selbstbewusstseyn vor." ("Such a concept is that of an object that is at once equal to itself and opposed to itself. Such can only be an object *that is at once its own cause and its effect,* producing agent and product, *subject* and *object.*—The concept of an original identity in duplicity, and vice versa, is thus simply the concept of subject–object, and such occurs in origin only in self-consciousness." Tr *CN* III 4265n). A draft of Thesis V is contained in all but the last sentence of *CN* III 4265 (§ IV). A revised and expanded version of Thesis V appears in *Logic (CC)* 83–4.

[1] For Thesis VI see also ch 9,

words spirit, self, and self-consciousness.[1] In this, and in this alone, object and subject, being and knowing, are identical, each involving and supposing the other. In other words, it is a subject which becomes a subject by the act of constructing itself objectively to itself; but which never is an object except for itself, and only so far as by the very same act it becomes a subject. It may be described therefore as a perpetual self-duplication of one and the same power into object and subject, which presuppose each other, and can exist only as antitheses.[2]

above, I 142–3. The "I am" or *Ich bin* appears so frequently and in so many contexts throughout numerous works C read that in dealing with Thesis VI only those likely uppermost in C's mind are listed. Kant *KRV* "Elementarlehre" §§ 15–18 (B 129–40) is a good starting-point. Cf Fichte *Grundlage* 9–13 (*SW* I 96–8), which identifies the *Ich* as the first and completely ungrounded principle of knowledge. Schelling *Vom Ich* § 3: *Phil Schrift* 7–9 (*SW* I 166–7), influenced by Fichte, is in C's thought, as were parts of it in Theses I–IV (see above, I 264 n 2, 268 n 1). Cf also *STI* 12–19 (*SW* III 365–8). Both Fichte (*Grundlage* 3–13: *SW* I 91–8) and Schelling (*Vom Ich* §§ 1–3: *Phil Schrift* 1–9; *SW* I 162–7) have followed similar paths. The closer parallels in C's theses tend to be with Schelling, though not exclusively. Cf C's quotation from Fichte *Ueber den Begriff der Wissenschaftslehre* in *CL* II 674; cf also Orsini 183.

[1] In Kant, Fichte, and Schelling—in German transcendentalism as a whole—the words *Geist, Ich,* and *Selbstbewusstsein* are often used as equivalents for the *Ich bin* or for the general approach developed by accepting the *Ich bin* as the first principle. E.g. for "self-consciousness" see Kant *KRV* B 132, 139–40; Schelling *STI* 42–7 (*SW* III 365–7); for "spirit" see Fichte *Grundlage* 168, 278 (*SW* I 208, 284). Cf also *ULS* 423, in which Jacobi clusters "Geist", "den ganzen Menschen" and "sein

Bewusstseyn" together in a discussion that ends (427) with all of these affirmed in God, a conclusion parallel to the next paragraph (C's scholium) in this thesis.

[2] Most immediately parallel to C's conclusion here are Schelling *Vom Ich* §§ 3, 16: *Phil Schrift* 9–12, 81–2 (*SW* I 167–70, 218–19) and *STI* 43–8 (*SW* III 364–8). In *Vom Ich:* ". . . The self alone is nothing, is not itself conceivable, without at the same time having its being established, *since it is not at all conceivable, except insofar as it conceives of itself,* i.e. insofar as it is" (*Phil Schrift* 9). ". . . The concepts of subject and object are themselves guarantors towards the absolute, unconditionable self" (12). "The self exists simply in that it is, i.e. that it is like itself and is so through the pure *unity of its own intuition*" (82). Schelling here speaks of "the pure identity of the self". *BL* (1847) I 271n notes esp *STI* 43–7 *SW* III 364–7). Discussion centres on the fact "That in self-consciousness the subject and object of thought are one. . . . Self-consciousness is the act whereby the conceiver [the subjective self or simply the subject] immediately becomes the object" (44). C appears in part to be paraphrasing *STI* 48 (III 367): "Das Ich ist allerdings Object, aber nur *für sich selbst,* es ist also nicht *ursprünglich* in der Welt der Objecte, es *wird* erst zum Object, dadurch dass es sich selbst zum Object macht, und es wird

SCHOLIUM. If a man be asked how he *knows* that he is? he can only answer, sum quia sum.[1] But if (the absoluteness of this certainty having been admitted) he be again asked, how he, the individual person, came to be, then in relation to the ground of his *existence*, not to the ground of his *knowledge* of that existence, he might reply, sum quia deus est, or still more philosophically, sum quia in deo sum.[2]

Object nicht für etwas äusseres, sondern immer nur für sich selbst." ("The I is certainly an object, but only *for itself;* it is not therefore *originally* in the world of objects. It first *becomes* an object by making itself an object, and it becomes an object not for something without, but ever for itself alone." Tr *BL*—1847—ɪ 271n.) Through Schelling or directly, C may also be recalling Fichte *Grundlage* 11 (*SW* ɪ 96–7).

[1] "I am because I am". Cf Schelling *Vom Ich* § 3: *Phil Schrift* 8, 9 (*SW* ɪ 167, 168): "Ich bin, weil Ich bin." ("I am because I am.") Since C has in part been using the *Vom Ich* this seems the closest parallel and occurs in Schelling in a place corresponding to C's use of the *Vom Ich* in Theses ɪ–vɪ. Cf Fichte *Grundlage* 12 (*SW* ɪ 98), which Schelling himself followed: *"Ich bin schlechthin, weil ich bin."* (*"I simply am because I am."*)

[2] "I am because God is". "I am because I exist in God". In this paragraph C intentionally affirms and expands a position that Schelling fully explains but sets aside as untenable "in theoretical philosophy", in *Vom Ich* §§ 2–3: *Phil Schrift* 5, 10n (*SW* ɪ 164–5, 168–9n), near lines that C has been using in Theses ɪ–vɪ. Schelling states that theoretical philosophy cannot, given its own criteria, successfully assert that God is the ground of our *knowledge* (5), nor can it identify God with the *Ich;* God is an object determined by the *Ich,* an object whose *existence* cannot be proved ontologically (10n). This position is similar to Kant's in *KRV*. C's whole intention is to include but also to proceed directly beyond such a "theoretical philosophy" into theology and religious beliefs (which C realised Kant and Schelling themselves treated in other of their works—e.g. Schelling's *Fernere Darstellungen*). C is not disagreeing with Schelling but rather accepting points about God and the "I" that Schelling himself outlines yet does not include in a rigorous and purely theoretical system. Cf also Orsini 207–8.

C's marginal note on the last page of *STI* (486, actually referring to p 118—*SW* ɪɪɪ 410) shows a similar reaction to and concern with the relationship between "I am" and "God is" as Schelling expresses it: ". . . In short, the Attributes of the Absolute Synthesis, the I AM in that I am are falsely transferred to the I AM in that God is.—Aye (replies Schelling) this would be secundum Principium Essendi; but I suspect only secundum Principium Essendi; but I speak only secundum Principium Sciendi—. True (I rejoin)—but you assert that the two principles are *one* . . . What is this but to admit that the I itself even in its absolute Synthesis supposes an already perfected Intelligence, as the ground of the possibility of its existing as it does exist?" *CM* (*CC*) ɪv. (For *principium essendi* and *sciendi* see Thesis ɪx, below.) C feels that Schelling's position concerning the *Ich* or self-consciousness must necessarily lead to "an already perfected Intelligence", or God.

In *Grundlage* 15–17 (*SW* ɪ 100–1)

But if we elevate our conception to the absolute self, the great eternal I A M, then the principle of being, and of knowledge, of idea, and of reality; the ground of existence, and the ground of the knowledge of existence, are absolutely identical, Sum quia sum;* I am, because I affirm myself to be; I affirm myself to be, because I am.[3]

* It is most worthy of notice, that in the first revelation of himself, not confined to individuals; indeed in the very first revelation of his absolute being, Jehovah at the same time revealed the fundamental truth of all philosophy, which must either commence with the absolute, or have no fixed commencement; i.e. cease to be philosophy. I cannot but express my regret, that in the equivocal use of the word *that,* for *in that,* or *because,* our admirable version[1] has rendered the passage susceptible of a degraded interpretation in the mind of common readers or hearers, as if it were a mere reproof to an impertinent question, I am what I am, which might be equally affirmed of himself by any existent being.[2]

Fichte introduces the idea of divinity in discussing Spinoza's position. Spinoza, says Fichte, separates the pure from the empirical consciousness; the former he places in God, the latter in the particular modifications of divinity. Fichte says we cannot know that this is so, but that it *should* be. "I only remark that if one goes beyond the (empirical) *I am,* one must necessarily arrive at Spinozism!" The idea would both attract and disturb C. It is interesting that throughout the Theses, where C's German counterparts discuss Spinozism, C avoids the issue, at least by name. Jacobi *ULS* 172n quotes Spinoza *Ethics* pt I prop 28 scholium: "At omnia, quae sunt, in Deo sunt, & a Deo ita dependent, ut sine ipso nec esse, nec concipi possunt." ("But all that is exists in God and is so dependent upon God, that without Him it can neither exist nor be conceived.") The position is close to C's own scholium. See also C's footnote and nn, below, I 275–8.

[1] Exod 3.14: "And God said unto Moses, I AM THAT I AM: and he said, Thus shalt thou say unto the children of Israel, I AM hath sent me unto you."

[2] Cf C's ms note in RS's copy of *Omniana* I 58 on the words "I am that I am" and on RS's comment "*I am he who am,* is better": "No! the sense of *that* is = because, or in that—[I a]m, in [tha]t I am! [meani]ng I [affi]rm myself [and], affir[min]g myself to be, I am. Causa Sui. My own [ac]t is the ground of my own existence." *CM* (*CC*) IV. Cf *TT* 1 Nov 1833: ". . . None but one—God—can say 'I am I,' or 'That I am'."

[3] Cf ch 9, above, I 145–6, 158–60 and nn. C applies the "I am" directly to God as a self-affirming being. Schelling's *Vom Ich* and *STI,* while not following this path, suggest it and both could have prompted C to this conclusion. E.g. C's marginal note to *STI* 78 (*SW* III 386), in which Schelling discusses the becoming and being of the *Ich:* "The 'To Be' whose act of Being is the self-affirming, that it *is,* is a spirit or Intelligence." *CM* (*CC*) IV. Jacobi *ULS* (203, esp 426–8) may have encouraged C to pursue this. Schelling's *Über das Wesen* could also have had a similar effect; e.g. *Phil Schrift* 429–32 (*SW* VII 357–9) discusses the self-substantiating

THESIS VII.

If then I know myself only through myself, it is contradictory to require any other predicate of self, but that of self-conscious-

The Cartesian Cogito, ergo sum is objectionable,[1] because either the Cogito is used extra Gradum, and then it is involved in the sum and is tautological, or it is taken as a particular mode or dignity, and then it is subordinated to the sum as the species to the genus, or rather as a particular modification to the subject modified; and not pre-ordinated as the arguments seem to require.[2] For Cogito is Sum Cogitans. This is clear by the inevidence

ground of God's existence contained within God himself. "Self-affirmation" (*Selbstaffirmation*) is stressed by Schelling in its divine and humanly creative aspects, e.g. *Vorlesungen* 263 (*SW* v 327).

Finally, Schelling—like C—at times identifies the absolute identity of subject and object as originating not in an ideal "I am" but, on another level, in God Himself. *Vorlesungen* (*SW* v 324–5), *Fernere Darstellungen* (*SW* IV 417 and n), and *Phil und Rel* 13–14 (*SW* VI 24–5). Schelling in several places speaks of "Subjekt-Objektivirung" (e.g. *Phil und Rel* 30: *SW* VI 35), the concept C mentions in the first paragraph of this thesis, "the subject which becomes a subject by the act of constructing itself objectively to itself".

The whole of Thesis VI thus draws inspiration from several authors, especially from various of Schelling's works and from an interwoven complex of Schelling's ideas, many of which were themselves derivative. *CN* III 4265 (§ IV) contains a draft of Thesis VI. A revised version of Thesis VI appears in *Logic* (*CC*) 84–5.

[1] The Latin here and in the rest of this footnote may be tr: "I think, therefore I am". (C means this is objectionable as the starting-point or as the absolute and fundamental truth of philosophy.) "I think is *I am* thinking"; "He [or "it"] thinks, therefore he is"; "Whatever is in the genus is also in the species. He is (thinking), therefore he is"; "But he

is, therefore he thinks is illogical: for what is in the species is not by *necessity* in the genus"; "Whatever truly is, exists through the true affirmation of itself".

[2] C's argument in the second paragraph of his footnote has several parallels and possible sources. Of general but definite importance here, and for all of Thesis VI, is Kant *KRV* "Elementarlehre" (B 399–432, esp 403–11, 423n; cf also B 131–40). Fichte *Grundlage* 9–17 (*SW* I 96–101) discusses the relationship of the individual's self-consciousness to the "absolute subject" and, more importantly, on 14–16 (99–100) criticises Descartes' "I think, therefore I am" in terms and reasoning quite similar to C's: "Vor ihm [Kant] hat *Kartes* einen ähnlichen angegeben: cogito, ergo sum, welches nicht eben der Untersaz, und die Schlussfolge eines Syllogism seyn muss, dessen Obersaz hiesse: quodcunque cogitat, est: sondern welches er auch sehr wohl als unmittelbare Thatsache des Bewusstseyns betrachtet haben kann. Dann hiesse es soviel, als cogitans sum, ergo sum (wie wir sagen würden, sum, ergo sum). Aber dann ist der Zusaz cogitans völlig überflussig; man denkt nicht nothwendig, wenn man ist, aber man ist nothwendig, wenn man denkt. Das Denken ist gar nicht das Wesen, sondern nur eine besondre Bestimmung des Seyns; und es giebt ausser jener noch manche andere Bestimmungen unsers Seyns." "Before Kant, Descartes stated something similar: I think, therefore I

of the converse. Cogitat ergo est is true, because it is a mere application of the logical rule: Quicquid in genere est, est et in specie. Est (cogitans) ergo est. It is a cherry tree; therefore it is a tree. But, est ergo cogitat, is illogical: for quod est in specie, non *necessario* in genere est. It may be true. I hold it to be true, that quicquid vere est, est per veram sui affirmationem; but it is a derivative, not an immediate truth. Here then we have, by anticipation the distinction between the conditional finite I (which as known in distinct consciousness by occasion of experience is called by Kant's followers the empirical I) and the absolute I AM, and likewise the dependence or rather the inherence of the former in the latter: in whom "we live, and move, and have our being," as St. Paul divinely asserts,[1] differing widely from the

am, which must not only be the minor proposition and the conclusion of a syllogism the major proposition of which states: whatever thinks, is: but which he could also have well enough viewed as the immediate fact of consciousness. Then it would mean as much as: I am thinking, therefore I am (as we would say, I am, therefore I am). But then the proposition "thinking" is completely superfluous; if one is, one does not necessarily think, but one necessarily *is*, if one thinks. The thinking is not at all the being, but only a special determination of being; and there are besides it many other determinations of our being." C, having used Schelling's *Vom Ich* already (a work heavily influenced by Fichte), was also likely guided by its discussions of the "I am" and the "I think" (*Phil Schrift* 8–12, 20–2; *SW* I 167–70, 176–7). But here there is no specific mention of Descartes. *CN* III 4265n points out also the relevant passage *STI* 47 (*SW* III 367) and tr: "It is this 'I think' that accompanies all ideas and maintains the continuity of the consciousness amongst them.—But if one frees oneself of all ideas, in order to become conscious of oneself at origin, then what arises is not the proposition *I think*, but the proposition 'I am', which is without doubt a higher proposition. The proposition 'I think' already includes a determination or modification of the I; on the other hand, the proposition *I am* is an infinite proposition, because it is a

proposition that has no *real* predicate, but is for that reason the position of an infinity of *possible* predicates."

Especially for C's religious position, cf also Schelling in *Jahrbücher der Medicin als Wissenschaft* I i (1805) 15: (*SW* VII 148): "Das *Ich* denke, *Ich* bin, ist, seit Cartesius, der Grundirrthum in aller Erkenntniss; das Denken ist nicht mein Denken, und das Seyn nicht mein Seyn, denn alles ist nur Gottes oder des Alls." ("The *I* think, *I* am, has been, since Descartes, the basic error in all knowledge; the thinking is not my thinking, and the being is not my being, because all is God's alone, or all in All.") This bears on the whole of Thesis VI, including C's footnote, and also the end of Thesis IX. Cf also Leibniz *Nouveaux essais* bk IV ch vii 7. C is trying to condense and unify into the theses what Schelling and others each developed by stages in over a decade of their own work: a union of natural, theoretical, practical, and religious philosophy. In his copy of Platner *Philosophische Aphorismen* (2 vols Leipzig 1793–1800) C wrote an annotation on the flyleaves similar to his footnote here to Thesis VI. *CM* (*CC*) IV.

1 Acts 17.28: "For in him we live, and move, and have our being . . .". Schelling *Über das Wesen: Phil Schrift* 404 (*SW* VII 340) paraphrases this text. Orsini 208 (but reading 340 for 349). Cf *CL* IV 768–70, and for Thesis VI generally 548 and nn, 805, 807, 849–50.

ness.[2] Only in the self-consciousness of a spirit is there the required identity of object and of representation; for herein consists the essence of a spirit, that it is self-representative.[3] If therefore this be the one only immediate truth, in the certainty of which the reality of our collective knowledge is grounded, it must follow that the spirit in all the objects which it views, views only itself. If this could be proved, the immediate reality of all intuitive knowledge would be assured. It has been shown, that a spirit is that, which is its own object, yet not originally an object, but an absolute subject

---

Theists of the mechanic school (as Sir I.[a] Newton, Locke, &c.) who must say from *whom* we *had* our being, and with it life and the powers of life.[1]

[a] *BL* (1817): J.

[1] The individual must depend upon or adhere in a higher being, which for C is God. Cf *CL* iv 770. C believed this since youth, in one form or another, sometimes with pantheistic overtones. That this is an "anticipation" of the difference Fichte and then Schelling saw between the "empirical" and the "absolute I" is true to some degree, though C's particular stance in Thesis vi as a whole, including his footnote, is itself partly derived from "Kant's followers" (see nn above). For "empirical" and "absolute I" see e.g. Fichte *Grundlage* 43 (*SW* i 119) and Schelling *Abhandlungen: Phil Schrift* 321 (*SW* i 442) and *STI* 59–60 (*SW* iii 374–5). Cf Orsini 122–3, 207–8. C drafted his footnote in *CN* iii 4265 (§ iv Scholium). A revised version of this paragraph of the footnote appears in *Logic* (*CC*) 85n.

[2] C now begins to draw more from *Abhandlungen* and *STI* than from *Vom Ich*. As *BL* (1847) i 273n indicates, *Abhandlungen: Phil Schrift* 223–6 (*SW* i 366–8) appears to be the primary source for the first six sentences of Thesis vii. The first sentence C takes from 223: "Da ich mich nicht anders kenne, als *durch mich selbst,* so ist es widersinnig, vom *Ich* noch ein anderes Prädikat, als das des *Selbstbewusstseyns* zu verlangen."

[3] In this and the next two sentences, ending with "be assured", C continues to take from *Abhandlungen: Phil Schrift* 223 (*SW* i 366); he paraphrases and rearranges slightly: "Eben darin besteht das Wesen eines Geistes, dass er für sich kein anderes Prädikat hat, *als* sich selbst.

"Nur in der Selbstanschauung eines Geistes also ist Identität von Vorstellung und Gegenstand. Also müsste sich, um jene absolute Uebereinstimmung von Vorstellung und Gegenstand, worauf die Realität unsers *ganzen* Wissens beruht, darthun zu können, *erweisen* lassen, dass der Geist, indem er *überhaupt* Objekte anschaut, nur *sich selbst* anschaut. Lässt sich dies erweisen, so ist die Realität unsres Wissens gesichert." ("Even therein consists the essence of a spirit, that for itself it has no other predicate than its own self. Thus only in the self-intuition of a spirit is there identity of representation and object. In order to be able to show each coinciding of representation and object, on which the reality of our *whole* knowledge rests, it must therefore be possible to prove that the spirit, in that it views *all* objects, views only *itself*. If this be proved, then the reality of our knowledge is assured.")

for which all, itself included, may become an object.[1] It must therefore be an A C T ; for every object is, as an *object*, dead, fixed, incapable in itself of any action, and necessarily finite. Again, the spirit (originally the identity of object and subject)[2] must in some sense dissolve this identity, in order to be conscious of it:[3] fit alter et idem.[4] But this implies an act,[5] and it follows therefore

[1] This and the next sentence (ending "necessarily finite") C has paraphrased and condensed from *Abhandlungen: Phil Schrift* 223–4 (*SW* I 366–7): "*Geist* heisse ich, was nur *sein eignes* Objekt ist. Der Geist soll Objekt seyn *für sich selbst,* der doch insofern nicht *ursprünglich* Objekt ist, sondern absolutes *Subjekt,* für welches *Alles* (auch Er selbst) *Objekt* ist. . . . Was Objekt ist, ist Etwas *Todtes,* Ruhendes, das keiner Handlung *selbstfähig,* nur *Gegenstand* des Handelns ist." ("I call *spirit* what alone is *its own* object. The spirit should be an object *for itself,* which yet is not insofar an *original* object, but an absolute *subject,* for which *all*—even itself—is an *object.* . . . What is an object is something *dead,* resting, that is *incapable* of any action and exists only as an *object* of action.") For C's "necessarily finite", see Thesis VIII, below.

[2] The phrase "identity of object and subject" appears in *Abhandlungen: Phil Schrift* 223 (*SW* I 366) ("Identität des Subjekts und des Objekts"). *BL* (1847) I 273n.

[3] Schelling makes the same point in *Abhandlungen: Phil Schrift* 226–9 (*SW* I 368–70). He uses the notion of free activity. The spirit, says Schelling, is the object of its own act of intuition and cannot, as such, be separated from itself. But we know, as one of our starting-points, that we *can* differentiate between object and representation. Therefore we can look at self-intuition in this manner and, by an act of original freedom, abstract ourselves from our intuition of self. This means that in the deduction of theoretical philos-

ophy we exercise a very practical step, a free act—as it were—of abstracting the self from our intuition of self. This is one reason C (above, I 252) says "Know thyself" is the postulate and test of philosophic capacity "at once practically and speculatively". Schelling says (*Phil Schrift* 228): "auch dass theoretische und praktische Philosophie ursprünglich gar nicht getrennt sind" ("and that theoretical and practical philosophy are originally not at all separated"). Cf *CN* I 921: "Now (let me) think of *myself*—of the thinking Being—the Idea becomes dim whatever it be—so dim that I know not what it is—but the Feeling is deep & steady—and this I call *I*—identifying the Percipient & the Perceived—." See *CN* I 921n, also Orsini 178–83.

[4] "It is made another and the same". See also C's "Deus alter et idem" that he attributes to Philo: e.g. *SM* (*CC*) 95 and n 3, *C&S* (*CC*) 84n.

[5] Cf ch 9, above, I 158. Besides *Abhandlungen: Phil Schrift* 225–31 (*SW* I 367–72), C may have encountered this notion of an act of the self in Schelling *Ueber die Möglichkeit einer Form der Philosophie überhaupt* (1794): *SW* I 100 and n, and *STI* 68, 44–9 (*SW* III 380, 365–8), e.g. 45: "The concept of the 'I' is established through the act of self-consciousness, and therefore *outside* of this act the 'I' does not exist; its whole reality rests only on this act and *is itself nothing but this act.*" Kant said that the *Ich denke* is, as a representation of the *Ich bin,* "an act of spontaneity" producing the original apperception

that intelligence or self-consciousness is impossible, except by and in a will.[1] The self-conscious spirit therefore is a will; and freedom must be assumed as a *ground* of philosophy, and can never be deduced from it.[2]

THESIS VIII.

Whatever in its origin is objective, is likewise as such necessarily finite. Therefore, since the spirit is not originally an object, and as the subject exists in antithesis to an object, the spirit cannot originally be finite. But neither can it be a subject without becoming an object, and as it is originally the identity of both, it can be conceived neither as infinite or finite exclusively, but as the most original union of both.[3] In the existence, in the reconciling, and

or transcendental unity of self-consciousness. *KRV* "Elementarlehre" § 16 (B 131–2; cf also B 157–8 and n). Cf Fichte *Grundlage* 9–10 (*SW* I 95–6) and esp *Grundlage des Naturrechts* (1796): *SW* III 22, in which Fichte identifies the "I" as "*acting;* it is what it does, and if it does nothing then it is nothing". Cf also Jacobi *ULS* 417.

[1] Cf Schelling *Abhandlungen: Phil Schrift* 262 (*SW* I 395): "Each self-determination of the spirit is called *will*. The spirit *wills,* and it is *free*. For that it *wills* permits no further ground to serve. And even on this account, because this act *simply* happens, is it a *willing.*" ". . . The act of *willing* is in general the *highest condition of self-consciousness*". 270: "The origin of self-consciousness is the *will*." Cf also ibid 280, 324–5 (*SW* I 408, 440–1). Cf also *STI* 322–40 (*SW* III 533–43). E.g. 324: "Each self-determination of the intelligence is called *will* in the most general sense of the word." Cf Jacobi *ULS* 418; Orsini 195, 208.

[2] Cf Schelling *Abhandlungen: Phil Schrift* 230 (*SW* I 371): "No *consciousness of the object without consciousness of freedom, no consciousness of freedom without consciousness of the object*." Since

in *self*-consciousness the "I" is its own object, the "consciousness of freedom" must be present at this starting point. Cf also ibid 280 (*SW* I 408): "In the *practical* philosophy [of Kant] appears all at once, as the principle of our *acting*— the *autonomy* of the *will,* and, as the sole supersensuous quality of which we have certainty, the *freedom* in us." Cf also *Vom Ich* § 6: *Phil Schrift* 22 (*SW* I 177): "Der Anfang und das Ende aller Philosophie ist— *Freiheit!*" ("The beginning and end of all philosophy is—*freedom!*") Cf also § 8: *Phil Schrift* 25 (*SW* I 179). In addition, *STI* 62 (*SW* III 376) repeats "that the beginning and end of this philosophy is *freedom,* the absolute indemonstrable, which evidences itself only through itself". Cf *Vorlesungen* 19 (*SW* V 218–19). Schelling discusses freedom and the will in *Über das Wesen: Phil Schrift* 419–22 (*SW* VII 350–2), especially in relation to Spinoza. There are religious and moral considerations. Schelling identifies the will as the last and highest instance of "being" in Spinoza's scheme. Cf *CN* III 4265 §§ VI–VII and nn for a draft of Thesis VII.

[3] As *BL* (1847) I 273n indicates, Thesis VIII is to this point taken from Schelling *Abhandlungen: Phil Schrift*

the recurrence of this contradiction consists the process and mystery of production and life.[1]

THESIS IX.

This principium commune essendi et cognoscendi,[2] as subsisting in a WILL, or primary ACT of self-duplication, is the mediate or indirect principle of every science; but it is the immediate and direct principle of the ultimate science alone, i.e. of transcendental philosophy alone.[3] For it must be remembered,

---

224–5 (*SW* I 367). C is actually condensing and paraphrasing: "Was nun Objekt ist (ursprünglich), ist *als* solches nothwendig auch ein *Endliches*. Weil also der Geist nicht ursprünglich Objekt ist, kann er nicht ursprünglich seiner Natur nach endlich seyn.—Also unendlich? Aber er ist nur insofern *Geist,* als er *für sich selbst Objekt,* d. h. insofern er *endlich* wird. Also ist er weder unendlich ohne endlich zu werden, noch kann er endlich werden, (für sich selbst) ohne unendlich zu seyn. Er ist also keines von beyden, weder unendlich noch endlich, allein, sondern in ihm ist die ursprüngliche *Vereinigung von Unendlichkeit und Endlichkeit* (eine neue Bestimmung des geistigen Charakters)." ("Whatever is originally objective is, *as* such, necessarily also *something finite.* Yet because the spirit is not originally an object, it cannot of its own nature be originally finite.—Therefore infinite? But it is *spirit* only insofar as it becomes *an object for itself,* i.e. insofar as it becomes *finite.* Therefore it is neither infinite without becoming finite, nor can it become finite for itself—without being infinite. It is thus neither of these two, neither infinite nor finite alone; but in it is the original *union of the infinite and the finite,* a new condition of the character of spirit.")

[1] Cf Schelling *Abhandlungen: Phil Schrift* 225 (*SW* I 368), from the section C has been using: "Endlichkeit und Unendlichkeit aber

ist nur im *Seyn* einer geistigen Natur *ursprünglich vereinigt.* In dieser absoluten *Gleichzeitigkeit* des Unendlichen und des Endlichen liegt das *Wesen* einer *individuellen* Natur, (der Ichheit)." ("But only in the *being* of a spiritual nature are the finite and infinite *originally unified.* In this ultimate *simultaneous co-existence* of infinite and finite lies the *essence* of an *individual* nature—the 'selfness'.")

The idea of life as a multiple and constant inner dialectic is in Fichte; cf *Grundlage* 195 (*SW* I 227): "The possibility of our consciousness, our life, our being for ourselves, i.e. our being as selves ["als Ich"] grounds itself on each act of the imagination." C, in a front flyleaf note on his copy of this work, expands the idea: ". . . The *Ich* does but *one* thing at a time, & all things successively—now what if it did a 1000 things simultaneously—? = *Leben.*" *CM* (*CC*) II. Cf *CN* I 1561.

[2] "Common principle of being and of knowing". Cf Schelling *STI* 48 (*SW* III 368): "Was höchstes Princip des Wissens ist . . . muss also auch für uns sein *principium essendi* und *cognoscendi* Eins seyn und in Eins zusammenfallen." ("What is the highest principle of knowledge . . . must therefore for us be one and coincide as one in its principle of being and of knowing.")

[3] From "is the mediate" until the end of his sentence here, C employs *STI* 26 (*SW* III 354):

that all these Theses refer solely to one of the two Polar Sciences, namely, to that which commences with and rigidly confines itself within the subjective, leaving the objective (as far as it is exclusively objective) to natural philosophy, which is its opposite pole.[1] In its very idea therefore as a systematic knowledge of our collective KNOWING, (scientia scientiæ) it involves the necessity of some one highest principle of knowing, as at once the source and the accompanying form in all particular acts of intellect and perception.[2] This, it has been shown, can be found only in the act and evolution of self-consciousness.[3] We are not investigating an absolute principium essendi; for then, I admit, many valid objections might be started against our theory; but an absolute principium cognoscendi.[4] The result of both the sciences, or their equatorial point,[5] would be the principle of a total and undivided philosophy, as for prudential reasons, I have chosen to anticipate

"Dieses Princip ist mittelbar oder indirect Princip jeder Wissenschaft, aber unmittelbar und direct nur Princip *der Wissenschaft alles Wissens,* oder der Transcendental-Philosophie." C has substituted "ultimate science" for "Wissenschaft alles Wissens", a phrase C gives below as "scientia scientiae".

[1] See above, I 254–60.

[2] For this cf *STI* 25 (*SW* III 354): ". . . wenn es ein System des Wissens giebt, das Princip desselben *innerhalb des Wissens selbst liegen.*" ("If there is a system of knowledge the principle of the same must *lie within the knowing itself.*" Tr SC *BL*—1847—I 275n.) Cf also *STI* 25–6 (*SW* III 354): *"This principle can be the only one."* Cf Thesis IV, above.

C may also be thinking of Kant *KRV* "Elementarlehre" § 16 (B 131–2, as noted above, an especially crucial section for C). Kant says: "It must be possible for the 'I think' to accompany all my representations; for otherwise something would be represented in me which could not be thought at all, and that is equivalent to saying that the representa-

tion would be impossible, or at least would be nothing to me." Tr Kemp Smith.

[3] C apparently refers to a process Schelling outlines in *STI* 80–321 (*SW* III 388–531). Cf *CN* III 4265n (§ VII). E.g. Schelling (95) says that each original act of self-consciousness ("jener ursprüngliche Act des Selbstbewusstseyns") by its free activity connects the whole series of the individual's perceptions into a progression or evolution ("Evolution"). Philosophy is that process "in which the one act of self-consciousness evolves itself". Cf also C's comments above, I 241–2.

[4] C paraphrases *STI* 27 (*SW* III 354): "Es ist gar nicht die Rede von einem absoluten Princip des *Seyns,* denn gegen ein solches gelten alle jene Einwürfe, sondern von einem absoluten Princip des *Wissens.*" ("This is not speaking of an absolute principle of *being,* for against such a one all the objections are valid, but of an absolute principle of *knowing.*")

[5] A favourite image of C's to describe the union of polarities or opposites.

in the Scholium to Thesis VI. and the note subjoined.[1] In other words, philosophy would pass into religion, and religion become inclusive of philosophy.[2] We begin with the I KNOW MYSELF, in order to end with the absolute I AM. We proceed from the SELF, in order to lose and find all self in GOD.

THESIS X.[3]

The transcendental philosopher does not enquire, what ultimate ground of our knowledge there may lie out of our knowing, but

[1] Cf above, I 274–8 and nn.

[2] For this and C's two concluding sentences to Thesis IX see Thesis VI and nn, above. C's reference to "I know myself" leading to God provides another way to grasp the importance of "Know thyself" for him. Schelling, Kant, Fichte, Jacobi, and others likewise carried philosophy into religion and vice versa (e.g. Schelling *Ideen* Einleitung 87–8: *SW* II 73), as did their predecessors Leibniz, Spinoza, and Bacon. C is not stepping outside the mainstream of transcendental philosophy taken *as a whole;* and he is within a great philosophic tradition centuries long. See also above, I 275 n 3, and Introd, I lxxviii. Cf C's similar remarks in *Friend (CC)* I 463; *P Lects* Lect 8 (1949) 247.

[3] As *BL* (1847) I 276n notes, Thesis X is, until the last two sentences of the second paragraph beginning "In this sense", taken from Schelling *STI* 27–8 (*SW* III 355–6). As far as the sentence in the second paragraph that ends "exists for *us*" C is translating closely: "Der Transcendental-Philosoph fragt nicht, welcher letzte Grund unsers Wissens mag *ausser* demselben liegen, sondern, was ist das Letzte *in unserem Wissen selbst,* über das wir nicht hinauskönnen?—Er [C changes the subject to "It"] sucht das Princip des Wissens *innerhalb des Wissens;* (es ist also selbst etwas, das gewusst werden kann). [C makes this parenthesis a separate sentence and then, unlike Schelling, does not begin a new paragraph but skips one of Schelling's own and then continues to translate fairly closely from midway in the first sentence of this new paragraph.] ". . . so behauptet er auch nur, dass es subjectiv [C's "act of self-consciousness"] . . . dass es *für uns* irgend ein *erstes Wissen* gebe [C writes "the source and principle of all *our* possible knowledge" and ends his sentence here]: ob es abstrahirt von uns, jenseits dieses *ersten* Wissens noch überhaupt etwas gebe, kümmert ihn vorerst gar nicht, und darüber muss die Folge entscheiden."

C now skips to midway in Schelling's next paragraph. "Dass das Selbstbewusstseyn der feste Punkt sey, an den *für uns* alles geknüpft ist, bedarf keines Beweises. —Dass nun aber dieses Selbstbewusstseyn nur die Modification eines höhern Seyns — (vielleicht eines höhern Bewusstseyns, und dieses eines noch höhern, und so ins unendliche fort seyn könnte)—mit Einem Wort, dass auch das Selbstbewusstseyn noch etwas überhaupt *Erklärbares* seyn möge, erklärbar aus etwas, von dem wir nichts wissen *können,* weil eben durch das Selbstbewusstseyn die ganze Synthesis unsers Wissens erst gemacht wird— geht uns als Transcendental-Philosophen nichts an; denn das Selbstbewusstseyn ist uns nicht eine

what is the last in our knowing itself, beyond which *we* cannot pass. The principle of our knowing is sought within the sphere of our knowing. It must be something therefore, which can itself be known. It is asserted only, that the act of self-consciousness is for *us* the source and principle of all *our* possible knowledge. Whether abstracted from us there exists any thing higher and beyond this primary self-knowing, which is for us the form of all our knowing, must be decided by the result.

That the self-consciousness is the fixt point, to which for *us* all is morticed and annexed, needs no further proof. But that the self-consciousness may be the modification of a higher form of being, perhaps of a higher consciousness, and this again of a yet higher, and so on in an infinite regressus; in short, that self-consciousness may be itself something explicable into something, which must lie beyond the possibility of our knowledge, because

---

Art des *Seyns,* sondern eine Art des *Wissens,* und zwar die höchste und äusserste, die es überhaupt für uns giebt."

Now C turns to a freer borrowing. This begins Schelling's next paragraph (*STI* 29): "Es lässt sich sogar, um noch weiter zu gehen, beweisen, und ist zum Theil schon oben (Einl §.1.) bewiesen worden, dass selbst, wenn das *Objective* willkührlich als das Erste gesetzt wird, wir doch nie *über* das Selbstbewusstseyn hinauskommen. Wir werden alsdann in unsern Erklärungen entweder in's Unendliche zurückgetrieben, vom Begründeten zum Grund, oder wir müssen die Reihe willkührlich abbrechen, dadurch, dass wir ein Absolutes, das *von sich selbst* die Ursache und die Wirkung —Subject und Object—ist, und da diess ursprünglich nur durch Selbstbewusstseyn möglich ist,—dadurch, dass wir wieder ein *Selbstbewusstseyn* als Erstes setzen; diess geschieht in der Naturwissenschaft, für welche das Seyn eben so wenig ursprünglich ist, wie für die Transcendental-Philosophie . . . und welche das einzig Reelle in ein Absolutes setzt, das von sich selbst Ursache und Wirkung ist—in die absolute Identität des Subjectiven und Objectiven, die wir Natur nennen, und die in der höchsten Potenz wieder nichts anders als Selbstbewusstseyn ist."

("To go yet further, it may be shown, and has already been shown in part [Introd. § 1.] that even when the objective is arbitrarily placed as the first, still we never go beyond self-consciousness. We are then in our explanations either driven back into the infinite, from the grounded to the ground; or we must arbitrarily break off the series by setting up an Absolute, which of itself is cause and effect—subject and object; and since this originally is possible only through self-consciousness—by again putting a self-consciousness as a First; this takes place in natural philosophy, for which Being is not more original than it is for Transcendental philosophy, and which places the Reality in an Absolute, which is of itself cause and effect— in the absolute identity of the subjective and objective which we name Nature, and which again in its highest power is no other than self-consciousness." Tr SC *BL*—1847—I 276n.)

the whole synthesis of our intelligence is first formed in and through the self-consciousness, does not at all concern us as transcendental philosophers. For to us the self-consciousness is not a kind of *being*, but a kind of *knowing*, and that too the highest and farthest that exists for *us*. It may however be shown, and has in part already been shown in pages 256–8 that even when the Objective is assumed as the first, we yet can never pass beyond the principle of self-consciousness. Should we attempt it, we must be driven back from ground to ground, each of which would cease to be a Ground the moment we pressed on it. We must be whirl'd down the gulph of an infinite series. But this would make our reason baffle the end and purpose of all reason, namely, unity and system. Or we must break off the series arbitrarily, and affirm an absolute something that is in and of itself at once cause and effect (*causa sui*),[1] subject and object, or rather the absolute identity of both. But as this is inconceivable, except in a self-consciousness, it follows, that even as natural philosophers we must arrive at the same principle from which as transcendental philosophers we set out; that is, in a self-consciousness in which the principium essendi does not stand to the principium cognoscendi in the relation of cause to effect, but both the one and the other are co-inherent and identical. Thus the true system of natural philosophy places the sole reality of things in an ABSOLUTE, which is at once causa sui et effectus, πατὴρ αὐτοπάτωρ, υἱὸς ἑαυτοῦ[2]—in the absolute identity of subject and object, which it calls nature, and which in its highest power is nothing else but self-conscious will or intelligence. In this sense the position of Malbranche, that we see all things in God,[3] is a strict philosophical truth; and equally true is the

[1] Besides paraphrasing Schelling (see n directly above), C here may have in mind Jacobi *ULS* 416–17 and nn. Cf also two sentences below, C's "causa sui et effectus", which repeats Jacobi's point (416–17n).

[2] Synesius Hymn III lines 146, 148 (var). From *Poetae graeci veteres* II 168. Cf *CN* III 4189 and n. "Father of himself, son of himself". Tr Augustine Fitzgerald (Oxford 1930). C has personalised—or deified—the idea expressed in *STI*. The context of C's Greek is religious and its implications parallel Jacobi's

discussion *ULS* 411–28, which concludes that the "causa sui et effectus" ("cause and effect of self") is God. Schelling's later works also tend to arrive at this conclusion.

[3] *De la recherche de la vérité* (1674) III ii 6 ("Que nous voyons toutes choses en Dieu"). *BL* (1847) I 278n, 364–6n. Cf *CN* III 3592 f 134 and n, 3974 and n. Kant quoted this sentence from Malebranche in Latin in *De mundi sensibilis atque intelligibilis forma et principiis* IV scholion: *Vermischte Schriften* II 474. For this dissertation see I 288 and n 2, below.

assertion of Hobbes, of Hartley, and of their masters in ancient Greece, that all real knowledge supposes a prior sensation. For sensation itself is but vision nascent, not the cause of intelligence, but intelligence itself revealed as an earlier power in the process of self-construction.

Μάκαρ, ἵλαθί μοι!
Πάτερ, ἵλαθί μοι
Εἰ παρὰ κόσμον,
Εἰ παρὰ μοῖραν
Τῶν σῶν ἔθιγον! [1]

Bearing then this in mind, that intelligence is a self-developement, not a quality supervening to a substance, we may abstract from all *degree*, and for the purpose of philosophic construction reduce it to *kind*,[2] under the idea of an indestructible power with two opposite and counteracting forces, which, by a metaphor borrowed from astronomy, we may call the centrifugal and centripetal forces.[3] The intelligence in the one tends to *objectize* itself, and in the other to *know* itself in the object. It will be hereafter my business to construct by a series of intuitions the progressive schemes, that must follow from such a power with such forces, till I arrive at the fulness of the *human* intelligence.[4] For my present purpose, I *assume* such a power[5] as my principle, in order to deduce from it a faculty, the generation, agency, and application of which form the contents of the ensuing chapter.

In a preceding page I have justified the use of technical terms in

[1] Synesius Hymn III lines 113–17. From *Poetae graeci veteres* II 167. "Be full of goodness unto me, Blessed One, be full of goodness unto me, Father, if beyond what is ordered, beyond what is destined, I touch upon that which is thine." Tr Augustine Fitzgerald. Cf above, I 246 n 3.

[2] On "degree" as distinct from "kind", see above, I 171.

[3] C more immediately borrows the metaphor of these forces from Schelling. *CN* III 4265 and n (§ VIII); also e.g. Schelling *Phil und Rel* 64 (*SW* VI 57). Cf also *STI* 97 (*SW* III 398), in which Schelling describes the *Ich* as a struggle of two opposite forces ("*entgegengesetzter Thätig-*

keiten"), and 155 (432), in which he refers to the "Expansion und Contraction" of the process. For C's use of this concept and its relation to Schelling's idea of "Subjekt-Objektivirung" see Thesis VI, above, I 273 and n 2. But cf also Fichte *Grundlage* 262–4 (*SW* I 273–4), which preceded *STI*.

[4] Orsini 209 points out that this is a major part of the design of *STI*. Cf above, I 282 and n 3.

[5] C's concept of "power" here is allied to Schelling's *Potenz*. See below, I 287 n 4. Among other places, *Potenz* appears in the passage (*STI* 29: *SW* III 356) C uses earlier in Thesis X (see above, I 283–4 n 3).

philosophy,[1] whenever they tend to preclude confusion of thought, and when they assist the memory by the exclusive singleness of their meaning more than they may, for a short time, bewilder the attention by their strangeness. I trust, that I have not extended this privilege beyond the grounds on which I have claimed it; namely, the conveniency of the scholastic phrase to distinguish the kind from all degrees, or rather to express the kind with the abstraction of degree,[2] as for instance multeity[3] instead of multitude; or secondly, for the sake of correspondence in sound in interdependent or antithetical terms, as subject and object; or lastly, to avoid the wearying recurrence of circumlocutions and definitions. Thus I shall venture to use potence,[4] in order to express a specific degree of a power, in imitation of the Algebraists. I have even hazarded the new verb potenziate with its derivatives in order to express the combination or transfer of powers. It is with new or unusual terms, as with privileges in courts of justice or legislature; there can be no legitimate *privilege*, where there already exists a positive law adequate to the purpose; and when there is no law in existence, the privilege is to be justified by its accordance with the end, or final cause, of all law.[5] Unusual and new coined words are doubtless an evil; but vagueness, confusion, and imperfect conveyance of our thoughts, are a far greater. Every system, which is under the necessity of using terms

[1] See above, I 171.

[2] Kant used Scholastic and Latin terms generally for similar reasons. C particularly worries that English lacks an accepted, clearly understood body of philosophic terms and concepts.

[3] Cf C's justification of the term in *PGC* and *TL*, in *BL* (1907) II 230, 310. C may have had several things in mind: Kant's "manifold" (Orsini 171), the "many" of the "one and many" presented in Jacobi *ULS* and also by Schelling, or as a way to render what he read in German as *Mannigfaltigkeit*. Cf *CN* III 4352, 4449 f 25ᵛ, 4450. "Multeity" is one of a group of words, e.g. omneity, aureity, based on Scholastic terms, that C found useful. See *CN* III 4352n.

[4] *OED* credits *BL* with the first English use of the word. Doubtless suggested by Schelling's *Potenz*, which he in turn took from Bruno via Jacobi. McFarland xxxiii. Cf "potenziation" in *CN* III 4418 f 13ᵛ. For references see e.g. Jacobi *ULS* 277, 283, 286 and Schelling *STI* 29 (*SW* III 356); also *Ideen* 78 (*SW* II 66), *Darstellung meines Systems der Philosophie: SW* IV 134, and *Fernere Darstellungen: SW* IV 468–75. Schelling uses the verb *potenzieren* (C's "potenziate"); cf esp *Vorlesungen* 121 (*SW* V 268): "*potenziiren*". Orsini 234 and nn.

[5] Cf C's plan to "extract the eloquent defence of technical new words, & old words used in a new sense" from the Preface to Paracelsus' works (*Opera omnia* Geneva 1658). *CN* III 3660 and n.

not familiarized by the metaphysicks in fashion, will be described as written in an unintelligible style, and the author must expect the charge of having substituted learned jargon for clear conception; while, according to the creed of our modern philosophers, nothing is deemed a clear conception, but what is representable by a distinct image.[1] Thus the *conceivable* is reduced within the bounds of the *picturable*. Hinc patet, quî fiat ut, *cum irrepræsentabile* et *impossibile* vulgo ejusdem significatûs habeantur, conceptus tam *Continui*, quam *infiniti*, a plurimis rejiciantur, quippe quorum, *secundum leges cognitionis intuitivæ*, repræsentatio est impossibilis. Quanquam autem harum e non paucis scholis explosarum notionum, præsertim prioris, causam hic non gero, maximi tamen momenti erit monuisse: gravissimo illos errore labi, qui tam perversâ argumentandi ratione utuntur. Quicquid enim *repugnat* legibus intellectûs et rationis, utique est impossibile; quod autem, cum rationis puræ sit objectum, legibus cognitionis intuitivæ tantummodo *non subest*, non item. Nam hic dissensus inter facultatem *sensitivam* et *intellectualem*, (quarum indolem mox exponam) nihil indigitat, nisi, *quas mens ab intellectu acceptas fert ideas abstractas, illas in concreto exsequi, et in Intuitus commutare sæpenumero non posse*. Hæc autem reluctantia *subjectiva* mentitur, ut plurimum, repugnantiam aliquam *objectivam*, et incautos facile fallit, limitibus, quibus *mens humana* circumscribitur, pro iis habitis, quibus *ipsa rerum essentia* continetur.[2] *—Kant de Mundi Sensibilis atque Intelligibilis forma et principiis,* 1770.

> *TRANSLATION.
>
> "Hence it is clear, from what cause many reject the notion of the continuous and the infinite. They take, namely, the words irrepresentable and

[1] Cf an 1811 notebook entry: "The image-forming or rather re-forming power, the imagination in its passive sense, which I would rather call Fancy . . . the Fetisch & Talisman of all modern Philosophers (the Germans excepted) . . .". *CN* III 4066.

[2] Kant *De mundi sensibilis . . .* I § 1: *Vermischte Schriften* II 439–40. In one of his annotated copies of the *Schriften* (on a front flyleaf) C called the work "that Masterwork of profundity and precision, that model of steady investigation, clear conceptions, and . . . *elegant* Dem-

onstration". *CM* (*CC*) III. In reusing the passage in *Logic* (*CC*) 243–4 C gave the background of Kant's dissertation, "delivered . . . 20th August, 1770, on taking his degree as professor ordinarius of logic and metaphysic, the (afterwards justly celebrated) physician and physiologist Marcus Herz, the friend and townsman of Moses Mendelssohn, being the respondent", and added: "I cannot too earnestly recommend the student by careful and repeated perusal to impress the contents both on his memory and his understanding".

impossible in one and the same meaning; and, according to the forms of sensuous evidence, the notion of the continuous and the infinite is doubtless impossible. I am not now pleading the cause of these laws, which not a few schools have thought proper to explode, especially the former (the law of continuity). But it is of the highest importance to admonish the reader, that those, who adopt so perverted a mode of reasoning, are under a grievous error. Whatever opposes the formal principles of the understanding and the reason is confessedly impossible; but not therefore that, which is therefore not amenable to the forms of *sensuous* evidence, because it is exclusively an object of pure intellect. For this non-coincidence of the sensuous and the intellectual (the nature of which I shall presently lay open) proves nothing more, but that the mind cannot always adequately represent in the concrete, and transform into distinct images, abstract notions derived from the pure intellect. But this contradiction, which is in itself merely subjective (i.e. an incapacity in the nature of man) too often passes for an incongruity or impossibility in the object (i.e. the notions themselves) and seduces *a* the incautious to mistake the limitations of the human faculties for the limits of things, as they really exist."

I take this occasion to observe, that here and elsewhere Kant uses the terms intuition, and the verb active (Intueri, *germanice* Anschauen) for which we have unfortunately no correspondent word, exclusively for that which can be represented in space and time. He therefore consistently and rightly denies the possibility of intellectual intuitions. But as I see no adequate reason for this exclusive sense of the term, I have reverted to its wider signification authorized by our elder theologians and metaphysicians, according to whom the term comprehends all truths known to us without a medium.[1]

a BL (1817): seduce

[1] Cf above, I 172 n 2. C's general usage of "intuition" extends beyond Kant's (as C notes) and follows one established English usage. Unlike the instance of the transcendent–transcendental distinction, above, I 237, there is ample evidence in English for C's claim about the "wider signification" of intuition to include "intellectual intuition", e.g. the passage from *Paradise Lost* C quotes in chs 10 and 13 or Hooker's "intuitive intellectual judgement" (*Of the Laws of Ecclesiastical Polity* bk I ch 8). Yet C is also approximating the idea of "intellectual intuition" expressed by Fichte (cf *Grundlage* 191–3: *SW* I 225) and especially by Schelling, for whom "die intellektuelle Anschauung" is vital. E.g. *STI* 51 (*SW* III 369); also *Abhandlungen: Phil Schrift* 208, 329–32 (*SW* I 355, 444–6), which C has translated above, I 248–52, and *Vorlesungen* 153, 97 (*SW* v 280, 255). Cf Wellek 87–8, 90–101 and Orsini 202. Kant denies intellectual intuition in *KRV* "Elementarlehre" (B 307, 68–72). Confusion may arise since Kant (B 131–2) says that the *Ich bin* represents to itself the intuition (*Anschauung*) of the *Ich denke* in "an act of spontaneity" (see ch 9, above, I 145–6 n 2, 158 n 1). This particular intuition Kant insists is thus *not* sensuous. Yet it is not "intellectual" either, but a unique intuition of "pure apperception" and "self-consciousness". Cf *CN* III 3801, 4259, and nn; *P Lects* Introd, Lect 13 (1949) 61–3, 388–91, 464–5, and ch 10, above, I 172. Cf Kant *Kritik der Urtheilskraft* Introd, in which imagination is discussed "as the faculty of intuitions *a priori*". This may bear also on C's note below, I 293n.

Critics,[1] who are most ready to bring this charge of pedantry and unintelligibility, are the most apt to overlook the important fact, that besides the language of words, there is a language of spirits (sermo interior) and that the former is only the vehicle of the latter. Consequently their assurance, that they do not understand the philosophic writer, instead of proving any thing against the philosophy, may furnish an equal and (cæteris paribus) even a stronger presumption against their own philosophic talent.

Great indeed are the obstacles which an English metaphysician has to encounter. Amongst his most respectable and intelligent judges,[2] there will be many who have devoted their attention exclusively to the concerns and interests of human life, and who bring with them to the perusal of a philosophic system an habitual aversion to all speculations, the utility and application of which are not evident and immediate. To these I would in the first instance merely oppose an authority, which they themselves hold venerable, that of Lord Bacon: non inutiles scientiæ existimandæ sunt, quarum in se nullus est usus, si ingenia acuant et ordinent.[3]

[1] *BL* (1847) i 282n notes that C's paragraph is slightly altered from Schelling *Abhandlungen: Phil Schrift* 203 (*SW* i 346–7). Schelling refers to critics who have charged Kant with an unintelligible idiom: "Sie bedachten nicht, dass es, ausser der *Wortsprache,* auch eine *Sprache der Geister* giebt, dass jene nur das Vehikel von dieser ist, dass also ihre Versicherung, anstatt gegen jene *Philosophie,* eben so leicht und in dubio noch leichter, gegen ihr *philosophisches Talent* beweisen konnte." ("They do not consider that besides the *language of words* there is a *language of spirits;* that the first is simply the vehicle of the latter; and therefore that their assurance, instead of being able to prove against this *philosophy,* just as easily—doubtless more easily—proves against their own *philosophic talent.*")

[2] As *BL* (1847) i 282n notes, C loosely paraphrases this sentence from Schelling *Abhandlungen: Phil Schrift* 204 (*SW* i 347–8): "Einige jener Philosophen trugen diesen Namen als Männer, die, von spekulativen Untersuchungen weit entfernt, ihre ganze Aufmerksamkeit dem *menschlichen Leben* gewidmet hatten, und die jetzt, durch einen ungünstigen Zufall, zur Prüfung jener Philosophie, ihre ganze Abneigung gegen alle—nicht unmittelbar ins Leben eingreifenden— Untersuchungen . . . mitbrachten." ("Some of these philosophers bore this title [Anti-Kantians] as men who, far removed from speculative researches, had devoted their whole attention to *human life,* and who now, through an unfavourable coincidence, have, in their examination of this philosophy [Kant's], brought with them their total aversion to all researches not immediately influencing life.")

[3] *De augmentis scientiarum* (1623) iv 3. *BL* (1847) i 282n. C had copied the remark into a notebook in 1811. *CN* iii 4117 and n. "Those sciences ought not to be thought useless that are in themselves useless, if they sharpen and order the wits."

There are others, whose prejudices are still more formidable, inasmuch as they are grounded in their moral feelings and religious principles, which had been alarmed and shocked by the impious and pernicious tenets defended by Hume, Priestley, and the French fatalists or necessitarians; some of whom had perverted metaphysical reasonings to the denial of the mysteries and indeed of all the peculiar doctrines of christianity; and others even to the subversion of all distinction between right and wrong. I would request such men to consider what an eminent and successful defender of the christian faith has observed,[1] that true metaphysics are nothing else but true divinity, and that in fact the writers, who have given them such just offence, were sophists, who had taken advantage of the general neglect into which the science of logic has unhappily fallen, rather than metaphysicians, a name indeed which those writers were the first to explode as unmeaning. Secondly, I would remind them, that as long as there are men in the world to whom the Γνῶθι σεαυτόν[2] is an instinct and a command from their own nature, so long will there be metaphysicians and metaphysical speculations; that false metaphysics can be effectually counteracted by true metaphysics alone; and that if the reasoning be clear, solid and pertinent, the truth deduced can never be the less valuable on account of the depth from which it may have been drawn.

A third class profess themselves friendly to metaphysics, and believe that they are themselves metaphysicians. They have no objection to system or terminology, provided it be the method and the nomenclature to which they have been familiarized in the writings of Locke, Hume, Hartley, Condilliac, or perhaps Dr. Reid, and Professor Stewart.[3] To objections from this cause,[4]

---

[1] The "defender" has not been identified. Cf an annotation on Edward Stillingfleet *Origines sacrae* (1675) 329–31: "And why is Philosophy for ever to be set up as the Rival rather than as the Friend & natural companion of Christianity? What is Xtianity but divine & preeminent Philosophy? . . ." *CM* (*CC*) IV. Cf *Friend* (*CC*) I 440–1, 447.

[2] "Know thyself"; see above, I 252 and n 1.

[3] Thomas Reid (1710–96), virtual founder of the "Scottish Common-Sense School" and lifelong opponent of Hume's scepticism. Principal works are his early *Inquiry into the Human Mind on the Principles of Common Sense* (1764) and his *Essays on the Intellectual Powers of Man* (1795). Dugald Stewart (1753–1828), professor at Edinburgh (1775–1820), further developed Reid's premises. In vol I of his widely read *Elements of the Philosophy of the Human Mind* (1792–1827) he anticipates some aspects of C's distinction between "fancy" and "imagination". See above, I 86.

[4] For this sentence and especially

it is a sufficient answer, that one main object of my attempt was to demonstrate the vagueness or insufficiency of the terms used in the metaphysical schools of France and Great Britain since the revolution, and that the errors which I propose to attack cannot subsist, except as they are concealed behind the mask of a plausible and indefinite nomenclature.

But the worst and widest impediment still remains.[1] It is the predominance of a popular philosophy, at once the counterfeit and the mortal enemy of all true and manly metaphysical research. It is that corruption, introduced by certain immethodical aphorisming Eclectics, who, dismissing not only all system, but all logical connection, pick and choose whatever is most plausible and showy; who select, whatever words can have some semblance of sense attached to them without the least expenditure of thought, in short whatever may enable men to talk of what they do not understand, with a careful avoidance of every thing that might awaken them to a moment's suspicion of their ignorance. This alas! is an irremediable disease, for it brings with it, not so much an indisposition to any particular system, but an utter loss of taste and faculty for all system and for all philosophy. Like echoes that beget each other amongst the mountains, the praise or blame of such men

---

the one preceeding, *BL* (1847) I 283–4n points out C's use of Schelling *Abhandlungen: Phil Schrift* 204 (*SW* I 348–9): "Andere waren nicht gegen Nomenklatur, Terminologie, Systemgeist überhaupt, sondern nur gegen *diese* Nomenklatur etc. eingenommen; grossentheils an Leibnitzens Vortrag . . . längst gewöhnt, oder gar in der Wolfischen Schulsprache und Methode steif geworden." ("Others were not prejudiced against nomenclature, terminology,—the spirit of system in general,—but only against *this* nomenclature [Kant's] etc.; for the most part because of their having long been accustomed to the statements of Leibniz, or to their having *grown stiff* in the school-language and method of Wolf." Tr SC in *BL*—1847—I 283–4n.)

[1] C continues to draw from Schelling *Abhandlungen: Phil Schrift*
204 (*SW* I 349) and in the first four sentences of this paragraph partially renders and expands Schelling's observations: "Endlich die letzten unter allen hatten durch die kraftlose Scheinphilosophie einiger wässrigten Schriftsteller, oder die Pandekten-weisheit aphoristischer Eklektiker allen Sinn und Geschmack—nicht etwa für ein bestimmtes System—sondern für *Philosophie überhaupt* verloren, ehe Kant einen Buchstaben von seiner Philosophie bekannt gemacht hatte." ("Finally, the last of all, through the impotent sham philosophy of some waterish authors, or the pandect wisdom of aphoristic eclectics, had lost all sense and taste, not perhaps for a determined system, but for philosophy in general, before Kant had published a syllable of his philosophy." Tr SC *BL*—1847—I 284n.) Cf *P Lects* Lect 13 (1949) 388–9.

rolls in vollies long after the report from the original blunderbuss. Sequacitas est potius et coitio quam consensus: et tamen (quod pessimum est) pusillanimitas ista non sine arrogantiâ et fastidio se offert. *Novum Organum.*[1]

I shall now proceed to the nature and genesis of the imagination; but I must first take leave to notice, that after a more accurate perusal of Mr. Wordsworth's remarks on the imagination in his preface to the new edition of his poems, I find that my conclusions are not so consentient with his, as I confess, I had taken for granted.[2] In an article contributed by me to Mr. Southey's *Omniana*, on the soul and its organs of sense, are the following sentences. "These (the human faculties) I would arrange under the different senses and powers; as the eye, the ear, the touch, &c.; the imitative power, voluntary and automatic; the imagination, or shaping and modifying power; the fancy, or the aggregative and associative power; the understanding, or the regulative, substantiating and realizing power; the speculative reason—vis theoretica et scientifica, or the power by which we produce, or aim to produce unity, necessity, and universality in all our knowledge by means of principles* a priori; the will, or practical reason; the faculty of choice (*Germanice,* Willkühr) and (distinct both from the moral will and the choice) the *sensation* of volition, which I have found reason to include under the head of single and double touch."[4]

---

* This phrase, *a priori,* is in common most grossly misunderstood, and an absurdity burthened on it, which it does not deserve! By knowledge, *a priori,* we do not mean, that we can know any thing previously to experience, which would be a contradiction in terms; but that having once known it by occasion of experience (i.e. something acting upon us from without) we then know, that it must have pre-existed, or the experience itself would have been impossible. By experience only I know, that I have eyes; but then my reason convinces me, that I must have had eyes in order to the experience.[3]

---

[1] Bacon *Novum Organum* I Aphorisms 77 and 88 (var). C had copied these and other aphorisms from Bacon's *Works* ed David Mallet (1740) in 1801. *CN* I 913 and n. "It is a following and going along together rather than a consent; and, what is worst of all, this very littleness of spirit comes with a certain air of arrogance and superiority." Tr J. Spedding, R. L. Ellis, and D. D. Heath.

[2] See above, ch 4, I 82–8.

[3] Cf "We may illustrate the sense of this so frequent and so frequently misused term '*a priori*' by likening it to the stains in the old cathedral glass which predetermine the character of the rays which it transmits and which it reflects." *Logic (CC)* 76. For C's concept of *a priori* see Orsini 76–8. Cf also Schelling *Vom Ich: Phil Schrift* 20–1n (*SW* I 176n).

[4] *Omniana* II 13–14 (No 174), which also contains the footnote C

To this, as far as it relates to the subject in question, namely the words (*the aggregative and associative power*) Mr. Wordsworth's "only objection is that the definition is too general. To aggregate and to associate, to evoke and combine, belong as well to the imagination as the fancy."[1] I reply, that if by the power of evoking and combining, Mr. W. means the same as, and no more than, I meant by the aggregative and associative, I continue to deny, that it belongs at all to the imagination; and I am disposed to conjecture, that he has mistaken the co-presence of fancy with imagination for the operation of the latter singly. A man may work with two very different tools at the same moment; each has its share in the work, but the work effected by each is distinct and different. But it will probably appear in the next Chapter, that deeming it necessary to go back much further than Mr. Wordsworth's subject required or permitted, I have attached a meaning to both fancy and imagination, which he had not in view, at least while he was writing that preface. He will judge. Would to heaven, I might meet with many such readers. I will conclude with the words of Bishop Jeremy Taylor: he to whom all things are one, who draweth all things to one, and seeth all things in one, may enjoy true peace and rest of spirit. (*J. Taylor's* Via Pacis.)[2]

---

reproduces here. Cf ". . . double Touch—the generation of the Sense of Reality & Life out of us, from the Impersonation effected by a certain phantasm of double Touch . . . and thence my Hope of making out a radical distinction between this Volition & Free Will or Arbitrement, & the detection of the Sophistry of the Necessitarians/ as having arisen from confounding the two". *CN* I 1827; see esp 1827n, also II 2399, III 4046. On "single and double touch" cf Keats's list of the topics C discussed as they walked together across Hampstead Heath (11 Apr 1819):

"Nightingales, Poetry—on Poetical sensation — Metaphysics — Different genera and species of Dreams—Nightmare—a dream accompanied by a sense of touch—single and double touch . . .". *Letters* ed H. E. Rollins (Cambridge, Mass 1958) II 88–9.

[1] Preface to *Poems* (1815): *W Prose* III 36. See above, ch 4, I 87–8.

[2] *The Golden Grove: a Choice Manual* . . . (1655): Sunday Decad I § 8 (e.g. 11th and 15th eds 1677 and 1685 p 62). C had copied the remark into a notebook in Dec 1800. *CN* I 867 and n.

CHAPTER 13

On the imagination, or esemplastic power [1]

O Adam! one Almighty is, from whom
All things proceed, and up to him return
If not depraved from good: created all
Such to perfection, one first nature all
Indued with various forms, various degrees
Of substance, and in things that live, of life;
But more refin'd, more spiritous and pure,
As nearer to him plac'd or nearer tending,
Each in their several active spheres assign'd,
Till body up to spirit work, in bounds
Proportion'd to each kind. So from the root
Springs lighter the green stalk: from thence the leaves
More airy: last, the bright consummate flower
Spirits odorous breathes. Flowers and their fruit,
Man's nourishment, by gradual scale sublim'd,
To *vital* spirits aspire: to *animal*:
To *intellectual!*—give both life and sense,
Fancy and understanding: whence the soul
REASON receives. And reason is her *being,*
Discursive or intuitive.

PAR. LOST, b. v.[2]

"Sane si res corporales nil nisi materiale continerent, verissime dicerentur in fluxu consistere neque habere substantiale quicquam, quemadmodum et Platonici olim recte agnovêre.—Hinc igitur, præter purè mathematica et phantasiæ subjecta, collegi quædam metaphysica solâque mente perceptibilia, esse admittenda: et massæ materiali *principium* quoddam superius et, ut sic dicam, *formale* addendum: quandoquidem omnes veritates rerum corporearum ex solis axiomatibus logisticis et geometricis, nempe de magno et parvo, toto et parte, figurâ et situ, colligi non possint; sed alia de causâ et effectu, *actioneque* et *passione*, accedere debeant, quibus ordinis rerum rationes salventur. Id principium rerum, an ἐντελέχειαν an vim appellemus, non refert,

[1] See ch 10, above, I 168.
[2] Milton *Paradise Lost* v 469–88 (var); quoted in part above, ch 10,

I 173–4. Cf *P Lects* Lect 12 (1949) 349.

modó meminerimus, per solam *Virium* notionem intelligibiliter explicari."

LEIBNITZ: Op. T. II. P. II. *p.* 53.—T. III. *p.* 321.[1]

Σέβομαι Νοερῶν
Κρυφίαν τάξιν
Χωρεῖ ΤΙ Μ′ΕΣΟΝ
Οὐ καταχυθέν·

SYNESII, *Hymn III. l.* 231.[2]

DES CARTES, speaking as a naturalist,[3] and in imitation of Archimedes, said, give me matter and motion and I will

---

[1] The first sentence, ending "recte agnovere", is from *De ipsa natura* § 8: *Opera omnia* ed Louis Dutens (6 vols Geneva 1768) II ii 53. The remaining two sentences, in which C substitutes *phantasiae* for *imaginationi* and *rerum* for *formam,* are from *Specimen dynamicum* in *Opera omnia* ed Dutens III 321.

Although *BL* (1847) I 288n says C quoted from Dutens, it is of special interest that C is here almost surely taking his Leibniz quotations *and* their references not from Dutens directly but from Jacobi *ULS* 365n, 369–70n. Jacobi reproduces the two quotations from Leibniz along with their references to Dutens. It seems certain, in light of C's earlier use of *ULS* for quoting Leibniz, Lessing, and Kant (see above, ch 12, I 244 n 2, and ch 10, I 202 n 2), that this epigraph and its references are similarly drawn from Leibniz as quoted and cited in *ULS,* the first and remaining two sentences of C's epigraph there being only four pages apart, whereas they are in two different volumes of Dutens.

Tr: "If indeed corporeal things contained nothing but matter they might truly be said to consist in flux and to have no substance, as the Platonists once rightly recognized. . . . And so, apart from the purely mathematical and what is subject to the fancy, I have come

to the conclusion that certain metaphysical elements perceptible by the mind alone should be admitted, and that some higher and, so to speak, *formal principle* should be added to the material mass, since all the truths about corporeal things cannot be collected from logistic and geometrical axioms alone, i.e. those concerning great and small, whole and part, shape and position, but others must enter into it, i.e. cause and effect, *action* and *passion*, by which the reasons for the order of things are maintained. It does not matter whether we call this principle of things [Leibniz: "a form" for C's "of things"] an entelechy or a power so long as we remember that it is intelligibly to be explained only by the idea of *powers.*" For C on "entelechie" and its religious importance see *P Lects* Lect 5 (1949) 187–8, 415 n 21.

[2] Synesius Hymn III lines 231–4. From *Poetae graeci veteres* II 169. "I venerate the hidden ordering of intellectual things, but there is some medial element that may not be distributed." Tr A. Fitzgerald. Cf *CN* III 4189 and n, and ch 12, above, I 246 and nn. For the significance of the "middle ground" or "mean" in C's religious and philosophical thought and his German readings see Engell *CI* 221–3, 363.

[3] As *BL* (1847) I 289n notes, this

construct you the universe. We must of course understand him to have meant; I will render the construction of the universe intelligible. In the same sense the transcendental philosopher says; grant me a nature having two contrary forces, the one of which tends to expand infinitely, while the other strives to apprehend or *find* itself in this infinity, and I will cause the world of intelligences with the whole system of their representations to rise up before you. Every other science pre-supposes intelligence as already existing and complete: the philosopher contemplates it in its growth, and as it were represents its history to the mind from its birth to its maturity.

The venerable Sage of Koenigsberg has preceded the march of this master-thought as an effective pioneer in his essay on the introduction of negative quantities into philosophy, published 1763.[1] In this he has shown, that instead of assailing the science of mathematics by metaphysics, as Berkley did in his Analyst,[2] or of sophisticating it, as Wolff did by the vain attempt of deducing the first principles of geometry from supposed deeper grounds of ontology,[3] it behoved the metaphysician rather to examine whether the only province of knowledge, which man has succeeded in

---

first paragraph is—with the exception of the second sentence—taken from Schelling *STI* 147 (*SW* III 427): "*Cartesius* sagte als Physiker [C adds "and in imitation of Archimedes"]: gebt mir Materie und Bewegung, und ich werde euch das Universum daraus zimmern. Der Transcendental-Philosoph sagt: gebt mir eine Natur von entgegengesetzten Thätigkeiten, deren eine in's Unendliche geht, die andere in dieser Unendlichkeit sich anzuschauen strebt, und ich lasse euch daraus die Intelligenz [C makes this plural] mit dem ganzen System ihrer Vorstellungen entstehen. Jede andere Wissenschaft setzt die Intelligenz schon als fertig voraus, der Philosoph betrachtet sie im Werden, und lässt sie vor seinen Augen gleichsam entstehen [C's last clause departs from this and stresses the evolutionary nature of intelligence]." Cf Orsini 212–13. C's allusion is to Archimedes' "Give me somewhere to stand and I

will move the earth". Jacobi used the Greek of the first clause of this on the title-page of *ULS*. See also *CN* I 1166, III 3592, and nn.

[1] C refers to Kant's *Versuch den Begriff der negativen Grössen in die Weltweisheit einzuführen* (1763): *Vermischte Schriften* I 611–76.

[2] *The Analyst; or, a Discourse Addressed to an Infidel Mathematician: wherein it is examined whether the object, principles, and inferences, of the modern Analysis are more distinctly conceived, than more evidently deduced, than religious mysteries and points of faith* (1734). Cf *BL* (1847) I 289–90n.

[3] C has Wolff's whole philosophical approach in mind and is likely thinking specifically of Wolff's *Philosophia prima sive ontologia* (Frankfort & Leipzig 1730), a work that proclaims a scientific method in which the principles of all human thought, especially mathematics and geometry, are contained.

erecting into a pure science, might not furnish materials or at least hints for establishing and pacifying the unsettled, warring, and embroiled domain of philosophy. An imitation of the mathematical *method* had indeed been attempted with no better success than attended the essay of David to wear the armour of Saul.[1] Another use however is possible and of far greater promise, namely, the actual application of the positions which had so wonderfully enlarged the discoveries of geometry, mutatis mutandis,[2] to philosophical subjects.[3] Kant having briefly illustrated the utility of such an attempt in the questions of space, motion, and infinitely small quantities, as employed by the mathematician, proceeds to the idea of negative quantities[4] and the transfer of them to metaphysical investigation. Opposites, he well observes, are of two kinds, either logical, i.e. such as are absolutely incompatible; or real without being contradictory. The former he denominates Nihil negativum irrepræsentabile,[5] the connexion of which produces nonsense. A body in motion is something—Aliquid cogitabile;[6] but a body, at one and the same time in motion and not in motion, is nothing, or at most, air articulated into nonsense. But a motory force of a body in one direction, and an equal force of the same body in an opposite direction is not incompatible, and the result, namely rest, is real and representable. For the purposes of mathematical calculus it is indifferent which force we term negative, and which positive, and consequently we appropriate the latter to that, which happens to be the principal object in our thoughts. Thus if a man's capital be ten and his debts eight, the subtraction will be the same, whether we call the capital negative debt, or the debt negative capital. But in as much as the latter stands practically

---

[1] 1 Sam 18.38–9.

[2] "Changing the things that must be changed".

[3] *BL* (1847) I 291n refers to the Preface of Kant's *Versuch,* the first sentence of which SC translates: "The use which may be made of mathematics in philosophy consists either in an imitation of the method or in the real application of their positions to the objects of philosophy." *Vermischte Schriften* I 613.

[4] Beginning with this sentence and ending with the example of "10 − 8", C summarises Kant's *Versuch,* the Preface and the first few pages of the Erster Abschnitt "Erläuterung des Begriffs von den negativen Grössen überhapt": *Vermischte Schriften* I 613–26. C borrows a few terms and examples but is basically just giving a *précis.*

[5] "Nothing in a negative sense, not representable" (the logical opposite)—i.e. the state of a body both at rest and in motion, as C goes on to explain, following Kant. *Vermischte Schriften* I 620.

[6] "Something conceivable". Ibid I 620–1.

in reference to the former, we of course represent the sum as
10 − 8. It is equally clear that two equal forces acting in opposite
directions, both being finite and each distinguished from the other
by its direction only, must neutralize or reduce each other to
inaction. Now the transcendental philosophy demands;[1] first, that
two forces should be conceived which counteract each other by
their essential nature; not only not in consequence of the accidental
direction of each, but as prior to all direction, nay, as the primary
forces from which the conditions of all possible directions are
derivative and deducible: secondly, that these forces should be
assumed to be both alike infinite, both alike indestructible. The
problem will then be to discover the result or product of two such
forces, as distinguished from the result of those forces which are
finite, and derive their difference solely from the circumstance of
their direction. When we have formed a scheme or outline of these
two different kinds of force, and of their different results by the
process of discursive reasoning, it will then remain for us to elevate
the Thesis from notional to actual, by contemplating intuitively
this one power with its two inherent indestructible yet counteracting forces, and the results or generations to which their interpenetration gives existence, in the living principle and in the
process of our own self-consciousness. By what instrument this is
possible the solution itself will discover, at the same time that it
will reveal, to and for whom it is possible. Non omnia possumus
omnes.[2] There is a philosophic, no less than a poetic genius,

[1] From here until the end of the
next paragraph (see below, I 300,
and ch 12, above, I 286) C summarises an outline or schema of a
definition of the imagination that has
clear similarities to long deductions
and definitions of the imagination
in Fichte and Schelling. Two forces
or concepts in dynamic tension both
find themselves in the imagination,
which reconciles and unifies them:
the self or mind ("I am") with
nature or the cosmos, the subjective
with the objective. Briefly, in Fichte
the imagination unifies the *Ich* and
the *Nicht-Ich*. It hovers as a single
power between them ("Schweben
der Einbildungskraft"). In Schelling

the imagination performs similarly
but there is more stress on nature
and on the self as it develops its
unifying capacity. The imagination
finally resolves all contradictions of
real and ideal, nature and mind. The
imagination is, sparely put, an act of
ultimate synthesis in the dialectic of
mind and nature. In Fichte see e.g.
Grundlage 52–195, esp 178–95 (*SW*
I 125–227, esp 215–27); Schelling
STI 87–91, 156–92, 472–3 (*SW* III
392–4, 432–54, 626). Many other
references could be cited; cf Engell
CI 132, 227, 234, 301–6, 329–42.

[2] Virgil *Eclogues* 8.63. Tr: "We
are not all capable of everything."

which is differenced from the highest perfection of talent, not by degree but by kind.[1]

The counteraction then of the two assumed forces does not depend on their meeting from opposite directions; the power which acts in them is indestructible; it is therefore inexhaustibly re-ebullient; and as something must be the result of these two forces, both alike infinite, and both alike indestructible; and as rest or neutralization cannot be this result; no other conception is possible, but that the product must be a tertium aliquid, or finite generation. Consequently this conception is necessary. Now this tertium aliquid can be no other than an inter-penetration of the counteracting powers, partaking of both.[2]

* * * * * * * * * * * * * *

Thus far had the work been transcribed for the press, when I received the following letter from a friend, whose practical judgement I have had ample reason to estimate and revere, and whose taste and sensibility preclude all the excuses which my self-love might possibly have prompted me to set up in plea against the decision of advisers of equal good sense, but with less tact and feeling.[3]

"*Dear C.*

"*You ask my opinion concerning your Chapter on the Imagination, both as to the impressions it made on myself, and as to those which I think it will make on the* PUBLIC, *i.e. that*

---

[1] On the distinction between "genius" and "talent" see ch 2, above, I 31 and n 5. For C's view on the select company of philosophy see ch 12, above, I 236.

[2] Cf above, I 44, C's n. C continues to outline a deduction of the imagination. Cf Schelling *STI* 92–147, esp 100–3; 156–69, esp 168–9 (*SW* III 395–427, esp 399–401; 432–40, esp 439–40); also *Ideen* 77–8 (*SW* II 65–8); Fichte *Grundlage* 55–195, esp 163–7 (*SW* I 127–227, esp 205–6) and, most significantly, *Grundriss der Eigenthümlichen der Wissenschaftslehre* (1795) 81 (*SW* I 391): ". . . i.e. the straightforward meeting together of the force of the Ich and that of the Nicht-Ich *in a*

third, which neither is at all, nor can be, anything but that in which they join together . . .". Kant, in discussing the unifying act of synthesis, speaks of the *tertium medium* of schemata used by the imagination. Cf also C's letter to Wedgwood 24 Feb 1801: *CL* II 688.

[3] The following letter C actually wrote himself. See Introd above, I lvii. Cf his remark to Thomas Curtis (29 Apr 1817): ". . . that letter addressed to myself as from a friend, at the close of the first volume of the Literary Life, which was written without taking my pen off the paper except to dip it in the inkstand". *CL* IV 728.

part of the public, who from the title of the work and from its forming a sort of introduction to a volume of poems, are likely to constitute the great majority of your readers.

"As to myself, and stating in the first place the effect on my understanding, your opinions and method of argument were not only so new to me, but so directly the reverse of all I had ever been accustomed to consider as truth, that even if I had comprehended your premises sufficiently to have admitted them, and had seen the necessity of your conclusions, I should still have been in that state of mind, which in your note, p. 72, 73, you have so ingeniously evolved, as the antithesis to that in which a man is, when he makes a bull. In your own words, I should have felt as if I had been standing on my head.

"The effect on my feelings, on the other hand, I cannot better represent, than by supposing myself to have known only our light airy modern chapels of ease, and then for the first time to have been placed, and left alone, in one of our largest Gothic cathedrals in a gusty moonlight night of autumn. 'Now in glimmer, and now in gloom;'[1] often in palpable darkness not without a chilly sensation of terror; then suddenly emerging into broad yet visionary lights with coloured shadows, of fantastic shapes yet all decked with holy insignia and mystic symbols; and ever and anon coming out full upon pictures and stone-work images of great men, with whose names I was familiar, but which looked upon me with countenances and an expression, the most dissimilar to all I had been in the habit of connecting with those names. Those whom I had been taught to venerate as almost super-human in magnitude of intellect, I found perched in little fret-work niches, as grotesque dwarfs; while the grotesques, in my hitherto belief, stood guarding the high altar with all the characters of Apotheosis. In short, what I had supposed substances were thinned away into shadows, while every where shadows were deepened into substances:

If substance may be call'd what shadow seem'd,
For each seem'd either!

MILTON.[2]

[1] *Christabel* line 169: *PW* (EHC) I 221. For this paragraph cf WW *Prelude* (1805) v 619–29.
[2] *Paradise Lost* v 669–70 (var). Significantly, when C quotes these lines in Lect 7 of 9 Dec 1811, he says: ". . . there is an effort in the mind when it would describe what it cannot satisfy itself with the description of, to reconcile opposites and to leave a middle state of mind more strictly appropriate to the

"Yet after all, I could not but repeat the lines which you had quoted from a MS. poem of your own in the FRIEND, *and applied to a work of Mr. Wordsworth's though with a few of the words altered:*

——————— An orphic tale indeed,
A tale *obscure* of high and passionate thoughts
To *a strange* music chaunted! 1

"Be assured, however, that I look forward anxiously to your great book on the CONSTRUCTIVE PHILOSOPHY, *which you have promised and announced:* 2 *and that I will do my best to understand it. Only I will not promise to descend into the dark cave of Trophonius* 3 *with you, there to rub my own eyes, in order to* make *the sparks and figured flashes, which I am required to* see.

"So much for myself. But as for the PUBLIC, *I do not hesitate a moment in advising and urging you to withdraw the Chapter from the present work, and to reserve it for your announced treatises on the Logos or communicative intellect in Man and Deity.* 4 *First, because imperfectly as I understand the present Chapter, I see clearly that you have done too much, and yet not enough. You have been obliged to omit so many links, from the necessity of compression, that what remains, looks (if I may recur to my former*

imagination than any other when it is hovering between two images: as soon as it is fixed on one it becomes understanding and when it is wav[er]ing between them attaching itself to neither it is imagination". *Lects 1808–19 (CC)* ms. C's letter, in its effort to characterise the imagination, "would describe what it cannot satisfy itself with the description of".

1 *To William Wordsworth* lines 45–7 (var): *PW* (EHC) I 406. See *Friend (CC)* II 258 (I 138).

2 C may be referring not to the "Logosophia" but to a more systematic, unified approach—something begun in his "Logic" and "Opus Maximum". He conceives of a constructive philosophy on the analogy of mathematics, especially geometry, and may have Kant in mind (see

above, I 297–8), and probably Schelling too, for whom *Konstruktion* was a key idea in developing a philosophical system, e.g. *Ueber die Construktion in der Philosophie* (1803). See also ch 12, above, I 248–50. The idea of a "constructive philosophy" was not uncommon.

3 Architect in Greek legend who with his brother Agamedes built the temple of Apollo at Delphi. After his death, where the earth swallowed him up an oracle was sacred to him in a cave in the grove of Lebadeia. Those consulting the oracle were dragged to the bottom of the cave and subjected to unearthly noises and lurid lights and sudden glares before receiving their revelation. Cf *P Lects* Lect 11 (1949) 269.

4 See above, I 263.

illustration) like the fragments of the winding steps of an old ruined tower. Secondly, a still stronger argument (at least one that I am sure will be more forcible with you) is, that your readers will have both right and reason to complain of you. This Chapter, which cannot, when it is printed, amount to so little as an hundred pages, will of necessity greatly increase the expense of the work; and every reader who, like myself, is neither prepared or perhaps calculated for the study of so abstruse a subject so abstrusely treated, will, as I have before hinted, be almost entitled to accuse you of a sort of imposition on him. For who, he might truly observe, could from your title-page, viz. "𝔐𝔶 𝔏𝔦𝔱𝔢𝔯𝔞𝔯𝔶 𝔏𝔦𝔣𝔢 𝔞𝔫𝔡 𝔒𝔭𝔦𝔫𝔦𝔬𝔫𝔰," published too as introductory to a volume of miscellaneous poems, have anticipated, or even conjectured, a long treatise on ideal Realism,[1] which holds the same relation in abstruseness to Plotinus, as Plotinus does to Plato. It will be well, if already you have not too much of metaphysical disquisition in your work, though as the larger part of the disquisition is historical, it will doubtless be both interesting and instructive to many to whose unprepared *minds your speculations on the esemplastic power would be utterly unintelligible. Be assured, if you do publish this Chapter in the present work, you will be reminded of Bishop Berkley's Siris, announced as an Essay on Tar-water, which beginning with Tar ends with the Trinity,[2] the omne scibile[3] forming the interspace. I say in the* present *work. In that greater work to which you have devoted so many years, and study so intense and various, it will be in its proper place. Your prospectus[4] will have described and announced both its contents and their*

---

[1] For "ideal Realism", a concept reinforced by C's reading especially in Schelling, see ch 12, above, I 260–2.

[2] Berkeley's *Siris: a Chain of Philosophical Reflexions and Inquiries Concerning the Virtues of Tar Water, and Divers Other Subjects . . . Arising One from One Another* (Dublin 1744), a copy of which C annotated. It starts with the medicinal uses of tar mixed with water (used both as an expectorant in bronchitis and as a lotion for skin diseases, including smallpox), and then turns to a vision of the charm of being, through evolution and ascent, from the humblest aspect of creation to the Trinity. In an annotation on a front flyleaf C wrote: "This great man needed only an entire instead of partial emancipation from the fetters of the mechanic philosophy to have enunciated all that is true and important in modern Chemistry . . .". *CM* (*CC*) I 410. For extracts from *Siris* quoted by C, see *SM* (*CC*) 27–8, *LS* (*CC*) 192–4.

[3] See ch 12, above, I 235.

[4] For the "prospectus" see below, I 304 and n 2.

nature; and if any persons purchase it, who feel no interest in the subjects of which it treats, they will have themselves only to blame.

"*I could add to these arguments one derived from pecuniary motives, and particularly from the probable effects on the* sale *of your present publication; but they would weigh little with you compared with the preceding. Besides, I have long observed, that arguments drawn from your own personal interests more often act on you as narcotics than as stimulants,*[1] *and that in money concerns you have some small portion of pig-nature in your moral idiosyncracy, and like these amiable creatures, must occasionally be pulled backward from the boat in order to make you enter it. All success attend you, for if hard thinking and hard reading are merits, you have deserved it.*

Your affectionate, &c."

In consequence of this very judicious letter, which produced complete conviction on my mind, I shall content myself for the present with stating the main result of the Chapter, which I have reserved for that future publication, a detailed prospectus of which the reader will find at the close of the second volume.[2]

The IMAGINATION then I consider either as primary, or secondary. The primary IMAGINATION I hold to be the living Power and prime Agent of all human Perception, and as a repetition in the finite mind of the eternal act of creation in the infinite I AM.[3] The secondary I consider as an echo of the former, co-existing with the conscious will, yet still as identical with the primary in the *kind* of its agency, and differing only in *degree*, and in the *mode* of its operation. It dissolves, diffuses, dissipates, in order to re-create; or where this process is rendered impossible, yet still at all events it struggles to idealize and to unify. It is essentially *vital*, even as all objects (*as* objects) are essentially fixed and dead.[4]

[1] See above, ch 11, I 224.

[2] The prospectus does not appear in the 1817 ed and apparently was never written.

[3] According to SC, the final clause of the sentence ("and as a repetition . . . I AM") was "stroked out" in a copy of *BL* containing a few marginal notes by C. *BL* (1847) I 297n. On the phrase "I AM" see above, I 272–5, 275–7 (C's n) and nn.

[4] On the complex distinction between "primary" and "secondary" imagination and on its precedents and earlier parallels in English and German writers, see Introd, above, I lxxxv–xciii; also McFarland "SI" 195–246, esp 205–223; McFarland 249, 309, 327–32; and Engell *CI* 121, 124–6, 220, 267, 271–2, 306–9, 343–6. Directly or indirectly C is drawing on similar distinctions be-

FANCY, on the contrary, has no other counters to play with, but fixities and definites. The Fancy is indeed no other than a mode of Memory emancipated from the order of time and space; and blended with, and modified by that empirical phenomenon of the will, which we express by the word CHOICE. But equally with the ordinary memory it must receive all its materials ready made from the law of association.[1]

tween various levels of the creating or imaginative power formulated by (among many) Vives (see ch 5, above, I 99), Locke (*Essay Concerning Human Understanding* bk I ch 12), Wolff (esp *Psychologia empirica* chs 3–4), Akenside, Alexander Gerard, who greatly influenced Nicolaus Tetens's own distinction in *Philosophische Versuche über die menschliche Natur und ihre Entwickelung* (1777), a book that in turn strongly coloured Kant's several distinctions (esp *KRV* and *Anthropologie in pragmatischer Hinsicht*); also Ernst Platner (*Anthropologie*), Maass, Herder, Schiller (*AE*), and Schelling in several of his works.

Only the more containable references and selected verbal similarities are given here, including C's possible earlier versions of this distinction. Cf C's phrase "the original unific Consciousness, the primary Perception . . ." (*CN* III 3295; also III 3744, and above, I 124–5) for a link between imagination, imitation, and repetition ("Imaginatio = imitatio vel repetitio *Imaginis*"); and *CN* III 4066, in which C speaks of "The image-forming or rather re-forming power, the imagination in its passive sense" in contrast to "poetic Imagination . . . the fusing power, that fixing unfixes & while it melts & bedims the Image, still leaves in the Soul its living meaning—". (Cf also *CN* III nn to 3295, 3744, 4066.) For C's "Agent" cf WW *Prelude* (1805) II 245–76 (271–3: ". . . his mind | Even as an agent of the one great mind, | Creates, creator and receiver both"). For C's "eternal act

of creation" cf Schelling's "in dem ewigen Akt der Subjekt-Objektivirung" (*Vorlesungen* 254: *SW* v 324), a concept intimately associated with the creative acts of the self (see ch 12, above, I 278–80, and *CN* III 4066). Cf also Schelling *Vorlesungen* 158 (*SW* v 282). For "repetition", "echo", and "*degree*" cf esp *STI* 473 (*SW* III 626) ("Es ist das Dichtungsvermögen . . . und zusammenzufassen, — die Einbildungskraft"). For "fixed and dead" objects cf ch 8, above, I 135, and ch 12, I 279.

[1] See above, ch 4, I 84 n 2. For the history and multiple, interrelated sources—English and German—of the distinction between fancy and imagination see also Introd, above, I xcvii–civ, McFarland "SI", and Engell *CI* 172–83. C is working from a long line of various distinctions (at once tangled and yet progressing to a relatively settled agreement of terms) to which Leibniz, Wolff, Platner, Tetens, Johann Sulzer, Michael Hissmann, Maass, Kant, Schiller, Fichte, and Schelling all contributed. In England Hester Piozzi, James Beattie, William Duff, Dugald Stewart, and Robert Scott all make the distinction, in one form or another, before 1805. These and more are discussed in detail in the references given above in this note.

Significantly the phrase "mode of Memory" applied to fancy and the imagination as it simply represents images is in WW's 1815 Preface (*W Prose* III 30). For "choice" vs the will in general see ch 12, above, I 293. Cf *CN* III 4066, 4176, and nn.

Whatever more than this, I shall think it fit to declare concerning the powers and privileges of the imagination in the present work, will be found in the critical essay on the uses of the Supernatural in poetry and the principles that regulate its introduction: which the reader will find prefixed to the poem of 𝕿𝖍𝖊 𝕬𝖓𝖈𝖎𝖊𝖓𝖙 𝕸𝖆𝖗𝖎𝖓𝖊𝖗.[1]

END OF VOLUME FIRST

---

[1] The essay, if written, has not survived. In a letter to Byron Easter Week 1815 C described the preface as "on the employment of the Super- natural in Poetry and the Laws which regulate it—in answer to a note of Sir W. Scott's in the Lady of the Lake". *CL* IV 561.